The Liberation of Tolstoy

The Liberation of Tolstoy

Ivan Bunin

A TALE OF TWO WRITERS

Edited, translated from the Russian, and with an introduction and notes by
Thomas Gaiton Marullo and Vladimir T. Khmelkov

NORTHWESTERN UNIVERSITY PRESS / EVANSTON, ILLINOIS

Northwestern University Press
Evanston, Illinois 60208-4210

Printed in the United States of America
10 9 8 7 6 5 4 3 2 1

ISBN 0-8101-1752-5

Library of Congress Cataloging-in-Publication Data

Bunin, Ivan Alekseevich, 1870–1953.
  [Osvobozhdenie Tolstogo. English]
  The liberation of Tolstoy : a tale of two writers / Ivan Bunin ; edited, translated from the Russian, and with an introduction and notes by Thomas Gaiton Marullo and Vladimir T. Khmelkov.
      p. cm. — (Studies in Russian literature and theory)
  Includes bibliographical references (p.) and index.
  ISBN 0-8101-1752-5 (alk. paper)
  1. Tolstoy, Leo, graf, 1828–1910. 2. Tolstoy, Leo, graf, 1828–1910—Religion. 3. Tolstoy, Leo, graf, 1828–1910—Philosophy. 4. Bunin, Ivan Alekseevich, 1870–1953. I. Marullo, Thomas Gaiton. II. Khmelkov, Vladimir T. III. Title. IV. Series.
  PG3410.B813 2001
  891.73'3—dc21
                                                              00-011025

For Helen Sullivan, colleague and friend

Contents

Preface

> An effort at reflection during my illness showed
> that a biography [about me written in the style
> that] biographies usually are, passing in silence
> over all the viciousness and guilt of my life,
> would be false, and that if a biography [about
> me] is to be written, the whole truth must be
> told. Only a biography of this kind—however
> ashamed one may be to write it—can be of any
> genuine benefit to its readers.
> —Leo Tolstoy, from the introduction to his
> *Recollections*

Leo Tolstoy, in his 1895 *Last Will and Testament,* wrote: "There is one more request [that I wish to make], and it is the most important [of all]. I ask that [after my death] relatives and strangers do not praise me. . . . [I also ask that] if people are going to occupy themselves with my writings, let them dwell on those passages in which the Divine Power has spoken through me, and let them use these passages in their lives."[1]

Tolstoy, of course, fully realized that no one would heed his request. He was all too familiar with how people were using his writing for their own ends. Tolstoy would have been aghast, though, to discover how, in the twenty-five years or so after his death, Soviet, émigré, and Western readers and reviewers were distorting his work in such a severe and shameless way. Such individuals cared little for the "Divine Power" that had spoken through Tolstoy. Rather, the author of *War and Peace* and *Anna Karenina* was important to them only as a justification of their own secular (read: sociopolitical) beliefs. What Anton Chekhov had feared for Tolstoy's posthumous fate had come true. "After Tolstoy's death," he had warned Maxim Gorky, "people will bestir themselves, write reminiscences, and lie."[2]

For instance, in the quarter century after Tolstoy's death in 1910, the Soviets saw Tolstoy as a "man of the people" who had endorsed a "dictatorship of the proletariat" against autocrats, aristocrats, and priests. Émigrés, though, downplayed Tolstoy's "revolutionary" bent by casting him in multiple poses—the writer was variously a staunch aristocrat opposed to revolution, war, and totalitarian states; a pagan hedonist concerned only with earthly and fleshly delights; and a Christian "apostle of love" who espoused nonviolence to solve the world's ills. Westerners regarded Tolstoy as a "noble savage" who lived in a backward and barbaric land but who unmasked "civilization" and defended preindustrial life.

Tolstoy would have been gratified to see that at least one individual was reflecting upon his life and writing with sensitivity and aplomb. Indeed, he would have relished the efforts of his fellow writer Ivan Bunin, who, in his 1937 work *The Liberation of Tolstoy (Osvobozhdenie Tolstogo)*, sought to dismiss long-standing appraisals of the writer as "mere verbiage"[3] and to champion Tolstoy as a religious figure who wrestled with soul and self to reveal the path to salvation and truth.

Although *The Liberation of Tolstoy* is one of the least studied of Bunin's works, it is important for several reasons. First and foremost, *The Liberation of Tolstoy* is a "tale of two writers"; that is, it is a Bakhtinian-type "dialogue" in which Bunin engaged Tolstoy on the *proklyatye voprosy*, or "damned questions," of life. If in *The Liberation of Tolstoy* Bunin showed a "meeting of minds" between himself and the subject of his study, it is because he believed that, metaphysically, he and Tolstoy led remarkably similar lives. Both men were taken with intellectual and spiritual "enlightenment," particularly Buddhism. Both also engaged in a titanic battle with self. On the one hand, Bunin and Tolstoy were egomaniacs: greedy, grasping, and all too fond of the pleasures of this world. On the other hand, both Bunin and Tolstoy were consumed by what psychologists today call "sacred anxiety"; that is, they sought "liberation" from earthly bonds by disavowing their bodies, escaping time and space, and discerning their proper place in the universe. It was one of Bunin's singular joys in life to assert that he and Tolstoy were often successful in their quest. At various moments in their lives, both men encountered a harmonic world and a personal, loving God. They made peace with their past, lived for the present, and hoped for the future. They triumphed over sickness, old age, and death by championing multiple existences and other forms of life beyond the grave. Above all, Bunin and Tolstoy asserted that life was worth living and that it was filled with beauty, order, and peace.

In the "tale-dialogue" of *The Liberation of Tolstoy,* though, Bunin also dramatized the "dark night of the soul"—the heart-wrenching suffering, doubt, and angst—that Tolstoy, as the quintessential seeker, often encountered in his spiritual search. Thus, a second reason why *The Liberation of Tolstoy* is important is Bunin's wish to peek under the Olympic pedestal on which sociopolitically minded scholars, critics, and readers had placed Russia's famed writer and to present him, clay feet and all, as a mortal stumbling through life's dilemmas. Again, Bunin saw Tolstoy's confusion and doubt as resonating with his own. In family life, both men knew more sadness than joy. They saw their vocations as artists threatened by material cares and concerns; they fretted over earthly success, spiritual exile, and physical decline; they did not "remain silent" about the political and social conflicts that ultimately destroyed "gentry" Russia. With interest bordering on grotesque fascination, Bunin focused *The Liberation of Tolstoy* on the darkest days of Tolstoy's life, for example, his excommunication by the Russian Orthodox Church; his difficulties with his wife, Sofya; and, most searingly, his escape from Yasnaya Polyana in his last days on this earth. Indeed, Bunin believed that if he and Tolstoy periodically experienced "liberation" in life, it was only after a prolonged "agony in the garden" and an equally harrowing crucifixion at the hands of people whom, as part of their "emancipatory" struggle, they begged their heavenly Father to forgive.

A third reason why *The Liberation of Tolstoy* is important is that Bunin made his case for a spiritually free Tolstoy by expanding his "dialogue" with the writer to include excerpts from Tolstoy's personal, political, and literary writings; the memoirs of Tolstoy's wife, family, and friends; citations from Western and Eastern philosophers and religious figures; and, finally, recollections of Tolstoy and interpretive commentary by Bunin himself. In so doing, Bunin orchestrated his work as a human chorus which lifts its often disparate "voices" to question, critique, and crown Tolstoy as a true religious seeker who, following the lead of the Buddha, Mohammed, and Christ, spurned earthly comforts to find everlasting life.

In publishing this first English translation of *The Liberation of Tolstoy*, I wish to present Bunin not only as an sensitive critic of Tolstoy's life and work but also as an engaging philosopher with his own perceptive views on existence. I also hope that readers will take up Bunin's fictional works and accord him the respect and admiration he so richly deserves. It is my further desire that my audience will return to—or perhaps read for the first time—works from the rich and complex corpus of Tolstoy's writings, so that they, too, may join the writer in his spiritual quest and find answers to their own "damned questions" about life.

For their invaluable assistance in the preparation of this book. I wish to thank my wife, Gloria Gibbs Marullo, and Sister Mary Colleen Dillon, S.N.D., of the Sisters of Notre Dame, Covington, Kentucky, who read the manuscript innumerable times and, in truth, learned more about Ivan Bunin and Leo Tolstoy than they really cared to; my colleagues Andrew Wachtel, Ruth Rischin, and Gary Hamburg for their valuable suggestions and advice; my research assistant, Matthew Anderson, and the staffs of the Departments of Reference and Interlibrary Loan of the Theodore M. Hesburgh Library at the University of Notre Dame for obtaining needed materials and researching notes; my typist, Nancy McMahon, for her superb preparation of the manuscript; my editor, Susan Harris of Northwestern University Press, who believed in this project from the beginning and who, with graciousness and aplomb, guided it (and me) through its various stages; and, finally, my cats, Gonzaga ("Gonzo"), Bernadette Marie, Monica Anne, and Margaret Mary, who provided affection and support, and who kept things in perspective—that they, not Bunin or Tolstoy, were the center of the universe.

I also wish to cite my co-editor on this project, Vladimir Tikhonovich Khmelkov, for reviewing my translation of *The Liberation of Tolstoy,* for answering questions on Bunin and Tolstoy that often defied responses, and for keeping me physically and spiritually whole throughout the process. To my mind, Vladimir represents the very best of the *l'âme russe,* and it is to Russians like himself and his wife, Lina, that I look for the rebirth of their homeland.

Finally, it is with special warmth and affection that I acknowledge Helen Sullivan, manager of the Slavic Reference Service at the University of Illinois, for her generous and expert assistance not only in the preparation of this study but also with my other works on Bunin. For over two decades, Helen has been a vital force in my growth as a scholar, and it is to her that I dedicate this work as a token of my heartfelt affection and esteem.

T.G.M.
Notre Dame, Indiana
Feast of Saint Thomas the Apostle
July 3, 1999

Editors' Introduction

Every great philosophy is a confession, an involuntary memoir.
—Friedrich Nietzsche

I

On June 12, 1890, a twenty-year-old Ivan Bunin wrote to Leo Tolstoy: "I am one of many who have followed your every word with great interest and respect, and who dare trouble you with my own doubts and thoughts about my own life. I know you are probably tired of listening to the same trite and monotonous questions. Thus it is doubly awkward for me to ask if I can sometime come and visit you, and talk with you if only for a few minutes. . . . Your thoughts have affected me so deeply."[1]

Shortly thereafter, Bunin resolved to take a bold step: He would meet Tolstoy personally at the writer's home at Yasnaya Polyana. So, on a bright summer day, Bunin saddled his horse and raced across the Russian steppe. About a hundred miles from his destination, though, Bunin lost his nerve. Tolstoy, it seemed, loomed too large in the young man's imagination for him to see the writer in person. Bunin returned home, angry at his cowardice but relieved that he had not gone through with his plan.[2]

Throughout his years in Russia and as an exile abroad, Bunin faced many hurdles and challenges. Politically, he witnessed the demise of "patriarchal" Russia and the rise of the new Soviet state. Socially, he was a child of the "cherry orchard," that is, the landed gentry who surrendered first to the petty bourgeois and then to the workers and peasants. Aesthetically, he watched how the color of Russian literature changed from "golden" to "silver." Bunin, though, never retreated from confrontation or change. In fact, he welcomed controversy even when it threatened his well-being. With Tolstoy, though, Bunin felt overwhelmed and outclassed. Indeed, with the writer of *War and Peace* and *Anna Karenina,* he always seemed to follow the "one step forward, two steps back" that marked his first attempt to meet his literary hero.

It was a full three years before Bunin summoned sufficient courage to reconnect with Tolstoy. As before, however, his efforts were tragicomic. For instance, when in February 1893 Bunin heard that Tolstoy needed help with his everyday affairs, he volunteered his services, but only for a short period of time: his vacation from work.[3] Tolstoy politely declined the offer.[4]

Five months later, Bunin again wrote to Tolstoy, but this time he boldly included a pamphlet of his verse. His fear and awe of the writer continued unabated, though. "Perhaps you will find my work completely useless and boring," Bunin apologized to Tolstoy, "but I am sending it to you nonetheless . . . because your every word is dear to me, and because your work rouses my soul and awakens in me a passionate desire to write (if I dare use this word about myself)."[5]

Despite such reticence, Bunin demanded that Tolstoy take him seriously. Indeed, it was both a supreme act of courage and an audacious belief in self for Bunin, in this letter to Tolstoy, to set himself apart from glory-seekers who wished to hobnob with the writer. Bunin saw himself not only as an artist and a student of life but also as one who had taken Tolstoy's ideals for his own. "I have wanted to write to you many times about many things, to come and see you," Bunin boldly confessed to Tolstoy. "But I was afraid that you would have counted me among those who besiege you from motives of vulgar impetuosity and the like. Please do not take [what I am saying] for impudence or insincerity."[6] This time, Tolstoy did not answer Bunin's letter.[7]

It was only after several harrowing months as a member of a Tolstoyan community in Poltava that in January 1894 in Moscow Bunin finally realized his dream to meet Tolstoy. If Bunin's encounter with Tolstoy had been long on expectations, it was decidedly short on results. No sooner had Bunin exchanged pleasantries with his literary idol than Tolstoy was called away by his wife, Sofya, to meet with other guests. Bunin left, bitterly disappointed at the turn of events. A fellow Tolstoyan, Nikolai Leontiev, remarked to Tolstoy on January 30, 1894: "Bunin was very upset because he had spent so little time with you. . . . He loves you very much. . . . He cannot talk about you calmly, without agitation."[8]

Bunin articulated similar sentiments when two weeks later he himself wrote to Tolstoy, saying: "Although out conversation was brief, and our meeting was unsuccessful, your works made a clear and kind impression on me. Something bright and lively shone from them."[9]

Tolstoy was quite moved by the young man's candor and admission of love. In the only other letter that Tolstoy wrote to Bunin, he imparted to his young colleague a lesson that had taken Tolstoy himself a lifetime to learn. "Do not expect anything from existence," Tolstoy counseled. "The best is what you have right now. The most important and serious moment in life is the one you are living. . . . It alone is genuine and under your control. Do not think about another, more attractive existence; one is the same as the other. The best in life demands intense spiritual effort. . . . Continue to move forward in Christian perfection and in service to God."[10]

Bunin met Tolstoy two other times in the famed writer's life: once again at Tolstoy's home in Moscow; the other time was a chance 1901 encounter in the famed Arbat district in that city. Both meetings proved unsatisfactory because Bunin was still uneasy in Tolstoy's presence,[11] and because Tolstoy was showing the symptoms of sickness and old age—features that Bunin did not wish to see in the writer. In fact, Bunin, almost neurotically uncomfortable with corpses and other aspects of human suffering, declined to pay his respects to Tolstoy's remains at Yasnaya Polyana when the writer died in 1910.

II

Even the most casual observer can see vast differences in the lives of Bunin and Tolstoy. Simply put, if Tolstoy was "patriarchal" man, Bunin was a more "modern" if diminished variant. For instance, Tolstoy, forty-two years older than Bunin, had been born to a position of privilege and power in the heyday of estate Russia. He had known a close-knit clan, idyllic friendship, and advanced education. He had been a societal lion, an officer in the Caucasus, and a proprietor of myriad estates. His marriage, though troubled, had endured for almost fifty years; he had sired thirteen (legitimate) children. To his very last days, the robust Tolstoy lived life to the fullest. He wrestled Bashkirs, hunted bears, and dominated everyone and everything. In a word, he was as engaging and expansive as the country he called home.

By contrast, Bunin knew no such stability or largesse. Indeed, as much as life kept unfolding for Tolstoy, it seemed to shrink and die for Bunin. Having entered the world almost a decade after the Emancipation, Bunin knew only "faded gentlemen's nests." His family was not like Tolstoy's Rostovs and Bolkonskys; rather, it recalled Mikhail Saltykov-Shchedrin's Golovlyovs: unstable, perverse, and ill equipped to handle change. One great-aunt, Olga Dmitrievna, was the antithesis of Tolstoy's pious mother, Maria Volkonskaya. Olga, a religious fanatic with a vow of virginity, would run about at night, screaming that the "snake of Adam" had entered her and was driving her to frenzy. While Tolstoy's fictional characters projected a wholesome "roundness," Bunin's aunt, Varvara Nikolaevna Bunina, seemed a web of lines, angles, and arcs; that is, she was Baba-Yaga, Russia's mythic witch, come to life. Varvara was "hunchbacked, with a waxen oval face, a hooked nose, and a sharp chin . . . like the bill of a bird," and "when she played the piano and tried to sing with her toothless mouth, she was somehow not normal."[12]

While Tolstoy knew power and wealth, Bunin waged a desperate and even Darwinian struggle for survival. For instance, at age twenty-six, he saw himself as a "hanged man."[13] Fourteen years later, he declared to his brother, Yuly, that his life was a "joke"[14] and that existence meant only sickness, sadness, and pain. The "patriarchal" Tolstoy grabbed lustily at life, but the "modern" Bunin hoped that an early death (or suicide) would solve his problems. Poverty was a constant companion, and his own attempt at family life was a disaster: A first marriage failed in eighteen months; his only son, Kolya, died at the age of five.[15] In further contrast to Tolstoy, Bunin bitterly regretted that he never had a group or place to call his own. Years later as an émigré, he recalled: "I grew up a solitary soul. Everyone else was preparing for something, and at a well-appointed time each stepped forth and took his place in the general enterprise. But where was I heading? I grew up without people my own age. . . . Everyone was studying somewhere; each had his own circle. . . . But I did not study anywhere. I had no circle."[16] Both as a youth and later in life, Bunin "lived *internally* . . . looking at everybody and everything from the sidelines."[17]

Whereas Tolstoy spent most of his life in the comfort of his estate of Yasnaya Polyana, Bunin tramped about Russia, searching for his place in life. "I am sick to death of the road," Bunin wrote to Gorky in 1913. "I am literally crazy with the doggedness of a drunkard. I keep looking for a place where I could find some warmth but find only hellish weather instead."[18] Worse, sociopolitical events—the revolution of 1917 and the ensuing civil war—compelled Bunin to seek haven in France as a permanent exile from his homeland. "What if I will not be buried next to my loved ones?"[19] Bunin asked prophetically in Odessa in May 1919, less than a year before he left Russia forever. Tolstoy had long sensed the dark night enveloping his land, but he remained tied to its soul and soil. It was Bunin's lot to live through Tolstoy's premonition, to endure the nightmare that destroyed gentry Russia.

Not surprisingly, Bunin and Tolstoy often had radically different views of Russia and life. Through *War and Peace* and *Anna Karenina,* Tolstoy celebrated Russia; in *The Village* and *Dry Valley,* Bunin cursed it. If the "patriarchal" Tolstoy saw the present as sweet and the future as bright, Bunin viewed both periods as harsh and bitter. Indeed, it was more an acknowledgment of mental distress than creative fervor when Bunin told Galina Kuznetsova that he was more "insane" than Tolstoy.[20]

Despite their radically different backgrounds and careers, Bunin never focused on the dissimilarities between himself and Tolstoy. Rather, he always vaunted the confluences of literature, life, and worldview that he believed he shared with his elder colleague.[21] Indeed, whenever Bunin told the story of Tolstoy's life, he believed that he was also telling his own. Bunin was "modern," but he desperately wished to be "patriarchal." For instance, he delighted in the fact that both he and Tolstoy traced their roots to the region near Tula and Oryol, the famed *chernozyom,* or "black-earth" heartland, that had nurtured almost all of Russia's great writers. Bunin also rejoiced that he and Tolstoy were *dvoriane,* or "gentrymen," whose families had contributed to the rise of imperial Russia[22] and who lived by the principles of droit du seigneur and noblesse oblige; that is, they had full right to the joys and pleasures of this world, but with a corresponding commitment to care for others, particularly the "humiliated and oppressed" of their land. As a result, both Bunin and Tolstoy engaged in a Manichaean struggle; they were torn between the "darkness" of their physical desires and the "light" of their spiritual yearnings and ideals. In one moment, Bunin and Tolstoy were sybarites and cynics, voluptuaries and roués; in the next, they were penitents and mystics, ascetics and saints. They vacillated between orgasmic self-excitement and morbid self-reproach, between corporal pleasures that were easily satisfied and spiritual quests that were always out of reach.

At times, both Bunin and Tolstoy saw the world as their oyster, a heady mix of wine, women, and song. Their "patrician" stance toward the world often led them to be arrogant and mercurial, self-absorbed and self-possessed. Indeed, nothing fascinated Bunin and Tolstoy so much as themselves. Both men saw themselves as centers of the universe, as God's gifts to humankind, and even as one-of-a-kind works in progress with unique, if exclusive, views of literature and life.

They were very close temperamentally. Both Bunin and Tolstoy often appeared to be manic-depressives. Wallowings in self-pity could be immediately, if inexplicably, juxtaposed with rushes of joy. They also could scarcely tolerate fools. Particularly in their early years, Bunin and Tolstoy skewered opponents with raised eyebrows, lingering smirks, and looks of boredom and contempt. Young turk modernists,[23] carping intellectuals, political and church officials, family and friends, even humankind at large, all felt the sting of Bunin's and Tolstoy's tongues.

At other times, Bunin and Tolstoy fulfilled their civic duty with bravery and heroism. They often preferred rags to riches. Tolstoy labored with peasants in the fields and battled famine in the villages and destitution in the cities. Bunin loved the "hardworking and ascetic way of life"[24] and exposed the plight of Jews in pogrom-ridden Odessa.[25] Both men set aside the prejudices of race and nationality, gender and class, to style themselves as citizens of the universe and as "eternal pilgrims, the happiest of all men, who see everything, know everything, and will know everything."[26]

"Gentry" images and ideals were also the stuff of Bunin's and Tolstoy's writing. On the one hand, both Bunin and Tolstoy extolled the beauty of existence, for example, the cycle of the seasons on Russia's rivers, mountains, and steppes. Both men approached life with an animal-like, even Dionysiac, sensuousness. They strode through the world with eyes that were penetrating, ears that were pricked, and nostrils that were flared. The rustle of leaves, the smell of plowed earth, and the taste of an apple set every sense on fire. Bunin and Tolstoy had no difficulty in imagining what the world was like to a lord, a peasant, a woman, a child, or a horse. For them, the "cold" present was always warmed by the "radiant" past. Conscious memory and childhood recollections moved from self-record to self-transformation, projection, and myth; "patriarchal" estates became paradises found and even mythic cosmologies for Adamic dwellers to "reclaim their senses" and to "restore purity and innocence" to the soul.[27]

On the other hand, the noblesse oblige that Bunin and Tolstoy felt in life they also brought to their works. As writers, Bunin and Tolstoy routinely rose to the challenge of *pravedniki,* or "righteous men," who, like Old Testament prophets, thundered against political and social ills, urged their nation to recovery and renewal, and even sought martyrdom for their beliefs. It was also with unabashed pride that Bunin saw himself as standing side by side with Tolstoy in safeguarding "classical" Realism from what they considered to be the aesthetic evils of the day, that is, the "monologic" civic trend of *intelligenty* and proletarians, and the tradition-shattering experiments of Decadents, Symbolists, and the like.[28]

The pride and protection that Bunin felt toward "classical" Realism gained new momentum with Tolstoy's death and the rise of the new Soviet state. Bunin publicly bemoaned but privately relished the fact that he was the "last of the Mohicans"[29] in the gentry tradition of Russian literature. Indeed, he saw it as his mission in life to keep alive the legacy that had begun with *Eugene Onegin* and had passed through *Fathers and Sons* but that had attained near perfection in *War and Peace* and *Anna Karenina.*

From this vantage point, Bunin often looked to Tolstoy not only as a kindred spirit but also as a student, son, and disciple at the feet of a teacher, father, and guide. For instance, in the last letter that Bunin wrote to Tolstoy, he confessed to the writer on March 21, 1896: "I feel like kissing your hand passionately, as if you were my father!"[30] Forty years later, he admitted to a friend: "Tolstoy is very close to me not only as an artist . . . but also as a religious soul."[31]

Metaphorically, if Tolstoy was akin to Dostoevsky's Father Zosima, Bunin was like Alyosha, who learned about life by drinking in his elder's wisdom, knowledge, and strength. At times, Tolstoy served as a sounding board for Bunin's angst with existence. Indeed, the great writer must have smiled ruefully when he learned that Bunin's adolescent yearnings and anguish were so hauntingly like his own. For instance, in the same 1896 letter, Bunin complained to his spiritual elder that he was a "vagabond" whose "incredibly fragmented life . . . tormented [him] to the point of psychosis." Like the youthful Tolstoy, Bunin knew only "shattered sympathies, false friendships, and moments of love"; his education was also "most rudimentary . . . the most pitiful bits and pieces of things"; and his wish was to have "friendship and youth, to understand everything, to have bright and quiet days . . . [and] to know something: its very beginnings, its very essence!"[32]

Also as was the case with Tolstoy in both his early and later years, Bunin sought to deny death, ponder God, and situate his "small world amidst countless other worlds." He likewise drove himself to frenzy with endless musings, tautologies, and syllogisms. "Let us suppose that the world . . . is something like a sphere," Bunin continued to Tolstoy. "But then what surrounds this sphere? Nothing? What precisely is this 'nothing'? Where is the end to this 'nothing'? What is there behind this 'nothing'? When did everything begin? And what was there before the beginning? That's quite enough to think about!"[33]

At other times, Tolstoy was for Bunin the Way, the Truth, and the Life, a life-affirming counterbalance against youthful cynicism, indifference, and despair. "I have become rather indifferent to everything," Bunin confessed to his brother, Yuly, on July 22, 1890. "But I am reading *War and Peace;* and, in several places, I have gone into complete rapture. What mastery! I simply adore Tolstoy!"[34]

More than two decades later, Bunin's enthusiasm for Tolstoy had only intensified. Memoirists recall that as soon as Bunin heard Tolstoy's name, "his soul caught fire, and he wanted to write because he had faith in literature."[35] Only Tolstoy, Bunin insisted, was "a teacher in everything."[36] Scenes from *Anna Karenina* left him "shaking" and caused him to see Tolstoy as a "god."[37] In *War and Peace,* Tolstoy's description of Napoleon was "beyond words"; and the famed "piti-piti" that Prince Andrei hears moments before his death was "simple, powerful, and profound," the "height of genius," and "an entire symphony of human suffering and love."[38]

Other pieces of Tolstoy's also earned Bunin's affection and respect. *Family Happiness* enthralled him, and *The Cossacks* was "something superhuman." *The Death of Ivan Ilyich* was "unforgettable"; *Father Sergius* was "sensational"; and *Hadji-Murad* led him to exclaim: "How can anyone write like that?! . . . After Tolstoy, everyone should quit writing." Even the tendentious *Resurrection* had features Bunin found "simply supernatural."[39] In fact, Bunin so admired Tolstoy that he often imitated the writer's stance and dress. For instance, Valentin Kataev recalls how Bunin often wore a peaked linen hat and tucked his hands behind in his belt "in the manner of Tolstoy."[40] Georgy Ivanov relished what he saw as Bunin's "Tolstoy exit"; that is, whenever the writer tired of conversation, he "got up quietly, picked up the long folds of his robe, with a light, old man's gait, made for the door in silence, without offering any explanations, excuses, or requests."[41]

Four aspects of Tolstoy's fiction evoked particular praise from Bunin. The first was Tolstoy's portrayal of social types. "How splendidly does Tolstoy describe . . . both plebeians and patricians," Bunin remarked to a friend. "In this he is a genius, an individual with a gigantic, grandiose mind."[42] The second was the economical simplicity of Tolstoy's writing. For instance, having read Tolstoy's "Father Vasily," Bunin told his nephew, Nikolai Pusheshnikov:

This is a piece in which nothing is written or said, but something only barely touched upon. Two words about a peasant, two words about a priest, and no more than two or three words about the landscape—but the result is an absolutely singular work of art. For this one piece, one could give away all of contemporary writing . . . with its Andreevs, Artsybashevs, and the like, and literature would be the winner. There would not be the lies and nonsense, the vulgarity and tastelessness [that we have now]. . . . [Because of such economy,] I do not understand how literary historians and critics can, in one heap, put Tolstoy together with, say, Turgenev or Dostoevsky! . . . What a savage mistake![43]

The third feature of Tolstoy's writing to draw Bunin's applause was what he saw as the absolute truth of his art. Because of this truth, he posited, "the nightingale, the moon, and the female buffalo as it lies down in a pasture are accessible to Tolstoy as they are to no one else in the world."[44] Finally, the fourth aspect of Tolstoy's writing that so thrilled Bunin was that his fiction was always strikingly fresh and new, that it appealed to readers of all ages, and, most important, that it acted as a mentor and a guide in their own passage through life. "I would find life impossible without Tolstoy," Bunin told Irina Odoevtseva.

How many times have I read his writing, but each time I pick up one of his works, it always seems that I am doing so for the first time. Have you ever noticed that the works of a writer like Tolstoy . . . "age" with readers? Young people think that Tolstoy's stories have been written exclusively for them. Middle-aged readers, though, find in his writing a maturity and experience that correspond to their time in life; and an elderly man like myself discovers in them the enlightened wisdom of old age, something that he, too, has learned and internalized. Such is the exclusive characteristic of a genius.[45]

To be sure, Bunin periodically rebelled against his mentor. Sometimes the argument concerned content. For instance, Bunin had little use for the idealized "masters" that sprang from the pages of *War and Peace* and *Anna Karenina*. In 1911, he told an interviewer from *Moscow News* (*Moskovskie vedomosti*): "One cannot judge the mass of Russian gentry from the gentry of . . . Tolstoy . . . since he portrayed the upper strata: rare oases of culture. The life of most of the gentry in Russia was much more typically Russian than Tolstoy depicted. This life has not yet been captured in fiction about noblemen."[46]

Bunin also cared little for Tolstoy's "men." For instance, in *The Village*, he has the peasant, Balashkin, identify the folk ideal not with Tolstoy's Platon Karataev in *War and Peace* but with the scoundrel-villains of Russian literature. "Why Karataev," he asks, "and not Karamazov and Oblomov, not Khlestakov and Nozdryov? The lice have eaten your Karataev. I see no ideal here."[47]

Other times, Bunin's quarrels with Tolstoy revolved around form. For instance, Bunin believed that there was so much "raw, superfluous stuff" in Tolstoy's writing that he planned someday to rewrite *Anna Karenina.* He told Kataev: "I would like to make a clean copy of *Anna Karenina,* removing all the long passages . . . making the sentences more precise and graceful, but, of course, not adding a word of my own, leaving everything of Tolstoy's absolutely intact." Even more audaciously, perhaps, Bunin continued: "I am deeply convinced that Tolstoy, edited like that—not by some Strakhov, but by a genuine great artist—would be read with more pleasure and would gain those readers who cannot abide Tolstoy's novels because of their stylistic flaws."[48] In fact, Bunin was so annoyed by what he saw as Tolstoy's infelicities of style that, even on his deathbed, he angrily censured the writer for the "many unnecessary and unartistic pages" in *Resurrection.* "How could Tolstoy do such a thing?" Bunin lamented to Alexander Bakhrakh.[49]

Such deficiencies, though, paled in the glow of Bunin's ongoing admiration for Tolstoy.[50] Indeed, it was one of Bunin's greatest joys to defend Tolstoy against detractors, political, social, and aesthetic. For instance, in Russia in 1919, he sought to rescue Tolstoy from conservatives who believed that the writer had single-handedly brought down the tsarist government as well as from liberals and revolutionaries who, Bunin charged, were using Tolstoy's ideas for their own ends. Rather, Bunin posited that Tolstoy was like "Christ, the Buddha . . . and all other great teachers of humankind . . . in that they spoke for all time, not a specific moment in history."[51]

Later, as an exile, Bunin took on émigré writers and critics who believed that Tolstoy's philosophy interfered with his art or that he cared little for literary form.[52] Also, given Bunin's wish to preserve the "memory" of both Tolstoy and the national literary tradition, it is not surprising that he "spoke about Tolstoy constantly"[53] and that he often scolded his colleagues-in-exile for what he considered as their lackadaisical attitude toward both. For instance, Bunin berated Adamovich for his (unfounded) belief that Tolstoy was "old-fashioned" and a writer "whom enlightened youths had cast aside in their rush to move forward."[54] He "turned black with rage" and "let loose a string of four-letter words" when, in 1927, Vladimir Nabokov confessed to him that he had never read *The Sevastopol Tales* and thus had no opinion about the work.[55] Even more telling, perhaps, Bunin (playfully) threatened André Gide with a knife when the French writer said that *War and Peace* was *un monstre d'ennui.*[56]

It also thrilled Bunin when readers, scholars, and critics posited a tie between himself and his mentor-guide. Although Bunin rejected the influence of any and all writers on his fiction, he welcomed claims as to Tolstoy's influence on his art. "Tolstoy should be imitated in the most shameless, unrestrained way," he told an interviewer.

If I were reproached for imitating Tolstoy, I would only be too glad [for such a rebuke]. What the critics cite as his weaknesses, are his greatest strengths. . . . All his so-called primitive, roughly hewn phrases are exclusively singular examples of a literary mastery that no one has attained before him. . . . This was something that that "cantankerous old man" [*parshivyi starichishka*] knew and understood quite well. . . . All writers should imitate Tolstoy. They could only gain from such a move . . . for they would give up telling lies in art.[57]

Not surprisingly, Bunin would smile when fellow émigrés said that, in both literature and life, he was Andrei Bolkonsky come to life or that he "walked hand in hand with Tolstoy through the galleries of flesh-and-blood ancestors."[58] Bunin's characters, they said, resonated with the same "metallic rumble"[59] as those of Tolstoy. His *Mitya's Love* continued Tolstoy's *The Devil (D'iavol)*.[60] It was, however, Zinaida Gippius who paid the highest compliment to Bunin when, in a 1926 article, she wrote: "When one thinks of . . . 'art mirroring life' à la Leo Tolstoy . . . Bunin immediately springs to mind."[61]

Such sentiments were not confined to Bunin's countrymen. "Has Russia a new Tolstoy?" a critic asked apropos of Bunin's *Gentleman from San Francisco* in August 1916.[62] More than thirty years later, Western Europeans still saw Bunin as being in sync with Tolstoy. "Eighty years! Not many Russian writers reach that age," a reviewer from *Le Monde* wrote on October 24, 1950. "But Ivan Bunin, still full of creative energy, is following in the steps of Leo Tolstoy."[63] In fact, several émigré and Western critics became so carried away with their admiration for Bunin that they insisted he had even outstripped his older associate. One Bunin fan wrote: "Bunin is more demanding, and therefore more metaphysically truthful, than Tolstoy." Another sniffed decisively: "As for Bunin being the legitimate heir to the mantle of Tolstoy, the question can be safely dismissed. Tolstoy never received the Nobel Prize."[64]

III

The concurrences in literature and life that Bunin believed he shared with Tolstoy moved him to posit what he considered to be the ultimate affinity in their lives: Privately and publicly, both men engaged in titanic struggles to discern the meaning of existence.[65] At times, both Bunin and Tolstoy reflected upon life on earth with gusto. More often, though, they attacked it with a vengeance. On bad days, Bunin and Tolstoy were philosophical wanderers, beset by the chaos and agony of life. They brooded over ego and self, the threat of impending chaos and change, and, most dramatically, the loss associated with sickness, old age, and death.[66] They were particularly bitter that they had only one life, after which they and their accomplishments would be lost to oblivion.

For instance, Tolstoy wrote about Levin in *Anna Karenina:* "Death . . . confronted him for the first time with irresistible force. . . . It was within himself too, he felt it. . . . Death would come and end everything; so it was useless to begin anything. . . . Yes, it was terrible but true."[67] Bunin similarly railed: "How can it be? Everything will be as before. The sun will set, the peasants will return from the fields with their plows. . . . And I will not see any of this because I will no longer exist! And though a thousand years will pass by, I will never again appear on this earth; I will never come and sit on this hill! Just where will I be?"[68]

On good days, Bunin and Tolstoy were philosophical pilgrims who, filled with faith and hope, relished the sweep and cycle of history. They transcended temporal, spatial, and biological confines and saw their world as one of many in the course of humankind. Their goal was to live in "joyous union with the eternal and temporal, with the near and the far, with all times and countries, with all the past and present."[69]

Both Bunin and Tolstoy appealed to the wisdom of the ages for answers to the questions that bedeviled them. Almost instinctively, they rejected secular, sociopolitical, and scientific philosophies of progress and life for views that were cosmic, organic, and mystical, for example, the insights of German idealism and the writings of Mohammed, Confucius, and, most important, Gautama Siddartha, the Buddha or the "Enlightened One."

In truth, both Bunin and Tolstoy came to Buddhism indirectly. Well in advance of their encounter with Gautama, they had intuited that they were victims of craving and self and that their unhappiness was affecting their physical and spiritual states in a negative, "regressive" way. Both men saw the fallacy of "I want, therefore I am." For instance, on Easter in 1858, Tolstoy confessed to a friend: "When I look at myself, I see that I am still the same: a day-dreaming egoist, *incapable* of becoming anything else. How is one to look out for others and practice self-sacrifice when there is nothing in one's soul but self-love and pride!" Thirteen years later, Tolstoy was still indicting himself as the proudest of men. He wrote to another colleague: "It is very sad that the world is made up entirely of egoists, of whom I am the first."[70] Bunin also understood the harm caused by self. For instance, to brother Yuly he confessed that he was a victim of a *"mania grandiosa"* that was shallow and false;[71] and to Tolstoy himself he divulged that he was a "great egoist" who would do well to "be rid of such a burden."[72]

At times, both the pre-Buddhistic Bunin and Tolstoy responded to their ego-fed shortcomings with self-flagellation and doubt. In more reasoned moments, though, they concluded that "indifference" was a key to happiness and peace. For instance, as a young soldier in the Caucasus, Tolstoy wrote: "There is something fine and noble in manifesting indifference to life; I delight in this feeling."[73] In similar fashion, Bunin came to see that one should reflect on the world with inner simplicity and let creation yield its secrets to those who smell, watch, and listen. "What a great joy merely to exist!" he exclaimed to Nikolai Pusheshnikov. "If I had no arms and legs, I would be content only to sit . . . and to look at the setting sun. This would not prevent me from being happy, for only one thing is necessary: to sit and to breathe."[74]

Having learned, by trial and error, the workings of craving, self, and inner peace, both Bunin and Tolstoy were well disposed toward accepting all that the Buddha had said about desire, regression, and rebirth.[75] The ways in which the two encountered and understood Gautama, though, show revealing differences in the personalities and worldviews of both men. Simply put, if Tolstoy chose an intellectual and scholarly path to Buddhism, Bunin preferred a more emotive and experiential one.

Andrew D. White once remarked that it was Tolstoy's chief defect to have lived most of his life in provincial Russia and to have developed opinions and outlooks that remained unmodified by rational exchange with other individuals. "Under such circumstances," White affirmed, "any person, no matter how noble and gifted, gives birth to striking ideas, but he cuddles and pets them until they become full-grown spoiled children of his brain."[76]

Tolstoy's in-depth understanding of Buddhism shows how incorrect White was in his view. For instance, Tolstoy's personal and publicistic writings are rife with references to the Buddha as well as to his images and ideals.[77] Tolstoy encountered Siddartha somewhat late in life. For instance, in September 1884, at age fifty-six, he wrote in his diary: "Read about Buddhism and its teaching. It is wonderful."[78] In January 1886, he wrote to Vladimir Chertkov: "I have taken up study of the Buddha"; four months later, he reiterated to his wife, Sofya: "I am busying myself with the Buddha. He engages me very much."[79] Evidently, Tolstoy was quickly taken with the great teacher, for no sooner had he informed Sofya and Chertkov of the object of his study than he planned to include the teachings of Siddartha in a series of books that he intended to write on key religious systems. "I really would like to do such a thing," he confessed to Chertkov in an early July letter written that same year, "and to present [Buddhism] in the simplest, most accessible form."[80]

Chertkov, together with the Russian critic Nikolai Strakhov, gladly assisted Tolstoy in his project, sending the writer materials that greatly influenced him in his study, for example, Edward Arnold's *Light of Asia* (1879), Samuel Beal's *Outline of Buddhism: From Chinese Sources* (1870), and Eugene Burnouf's *Lotus de la bonne loi, traduit du Sanscrit, accompagné d'un commentaire et de vingt et un memoires, relatifs au Buddhism* (1852). Later, Tolstoy also became familiar with such scholarly tomes as David Rhys's *Buddhism* (1878), Herman Oldenberg's *Buddha, sein Leben, seine Lehre, seine Gemeinde* (1881), Philippe Edouard Foucaux's *Lalita Vistara* (1884–92),[81] Subhadra Bhikschu's *Buddhistischer Katechismus* (1908), and, finally, the writings of the philosopher Arthur Schopenhauer on Gautama's life and thought.

Unfortunately, Tolstoy's grand plans to write a book about Buddhism never materialized; instead, they transmuted into periodic references and short pieces about Siddartha's life and teachings. Tolstoy first mentions Gautama and his worldview in such pieces as his *Confession* (*Ispoved'*, 1879–80), *What I Believe* (*V chem moia vera*, 1883), and *What Then Should We Do?* (*Tak chto nam delat'?* 1886). In these works, Tolstoy cites Gautama along with other religious and philosophical figures who had come into his scholarly purview: The Buddha takes his place with Moses, David, Isaiah, and Solomon on the one hand; and with Socrates, Zoroaster, Confucius, Christ, Mohammed, and Lao-tzu on the other.[82]

Gradually, though, the Buddha assumes a greater focus in Tolstoy's writing. For instance, in 1889, Tolstoy wrote a short piece entitled "Siddartha, Called 'the Buddha' or 'the Holy One.' His Life and Teachings" ("Siddarta, prozvannyi 'Buddoi,' t.e., 'Sviatym.' Zhizn' i uchenie ego") in which he summarized the high points of the great teacher's instruction and time on earth.[83] Also, in 1905, Tolstoy authored an article entitled "The Buddha" for his famed anthology *The Circle of Reading* (*Krug chteniia*);[84] and in 1909–10 he edited Pavel Boulanger's scholarly study, *The Life and Teachings of Siddartha Gotama, Called the Buddha or the Most Perfect One* (*Zhizn' i uchenie Siddarty Gotamy, prozvannogo Buddoi [sovershenneishim]*), which was published by Tolstoy's publishing house, The Intermediary (Posrednik), a year later.[85] The most interesting of Tolstoy's forays into Buddhism, though, was his reworking and translation of a tale entitled "Karma," which had been written by the American writer Paul Carus in 1894 and published in the *Open Court,* a journal that focused on religious and philosophical questions. (Tolstoy's adaptation of the piece appeared in the journal *Russian Herald* [*Russkii vestnik*] that same year.)

Despite the relative paucity of Tolstoy's actual writing on Buddhism, he was well aware of its key concepts and beliefs. References to *karma* and *samsara* (rebirth) take their place with allusions to craving, desire, and the like. For instance, with his relentless penchant for categorization, Tolstoy believed that Gautama focused on eleven sins: "Three [were] related to the body; four to the tongue; and three to the mind. The first group embraced murder, theft (the appropriation of property), and lust (fornication). The second took in double-talk, equivocation, slander, flattery, and lying; and the third included envy, anger, and deception (delusion)."[86]

Like Gautama, Tolstoy upheld the notion that people incurred their own redemption or ruin. "The doer of evil cannot avoid the consequences of his actions," a monk tells the brigand Kandata in "Karma." "Do not despair, though, for anyone can find liberation by destroying the deceptions of the self."[87] At first, Kandata heeds the monk's advice. Having been "reborn" as a devil in hell, he cries out to Gautama, who has appeared before him: "O Holy Buddha, take pity on me for I am suffering terribly! Although I did evil [in my former life], I now wish to follow the path of righteousness. But I cannot free myself from the net of grief. Help me! . . . The law of *karma* is such that evil deeds lead to destruction."[88]

The Buddha pities Kandata and holds out a spiderweb to pull him from his torment. Kandata grabs hold and begins to emerge from hell; but in a manner hauntingly like Grushenka's story of the sinner and the onion in *The Brothers Karamazov,* countless other sinners attach themselves to Kandata to escape relief from their torment. The unfortunate man, fearing—wrongly—that the web will break under the strain, cries out to his fellow sufferers: "Let go, for the web is *mine!*"[89] The web breaks, and Kandata falls back into hell. "The delusion of self still lived in Kandata," the monk in the work pronounces summarily. "As soon as there arose in his heart the thought that the spiderweb was *his,* and that the joys of righteousness belonged to *him* alone . . . the web broke and he returned to his previous state. The individual self is a curse, but the merging [of one with the universe] is a blessing. What is hell? Hell is none other than self-love, but Nirvana is the union of all life."[90]

In his own writings, Tolstoy often sounded like the Buddha himself. For instance, he was particularly intrigued with the workings of ego and self. "In moments of passion," he wrote, "the only means of self-conquest is to destroy the illusion that it is the self who suffers and desires."[91] Furthermore, in the Sturm und Drang of his life, Tolstoy relished moments of what he perceived as a Nirvana-like state. "Old as I am," he wrote in 1897, "I have discovered a new state of consciousness, that of Eternal Goodness. . . . Just as one experiences heat and cold, so does one [in this state] feel the passing from confusion and suffering to clarity and calm."[92]

In fact, it was such Buddhistic concepts as Nirvana and *samsara* that helped Tolstoy to explain (and endure) what he considered to be the most traumatic moment of human existence: the imminent approach of one's end. For instance, in an 1876 letter to Afanasy Fet, Tolstoy wrote: "When death draws near, intercourse with men who look beyond the bounds of life is precious and comforting. You and other rare genuine individuals . . . look first at Nirvana—the illimitable, the unknown—and now at *samsara,* and that sight of Nirvana strengthens their vision."[93] Thirty years later, he continued: "Nirvana is not destruction, but that new, unknown, and incomprehensible life in which self-renunciation is no longer necessary."[94]

Tolstoy's interest in Buddhism continued to the very last days of his life. Indeed, he rejoiced not only over the growing popularity of Buddhism in the West but also over the fact that, in its most pristine form, Gautama's beliefs accorded so well with his own. For instance, on March 10, 1910, he wrote to a friend:

In recent times Buddhism has become more and more free of the refuse that has covered it. The Christian world is getting to know its true essence more and more; and people who have moved from Christianity to Buddhism are becoming more and more numerous in both Europe and America.

[I find] particularly attractive . . . the moral efficacy of . . . Buddhism's five commandments: (1) Do not kill any living creature; (2) do not appropriate to yourself another's property; (3) do not give way to sexual lust; (4) do not lie; and (5) do not stupefy yourself with smoking or alcohol.

One cannot help thinking what an enormous change would take place in life if people knew of these commandments and considered them as binding as they do the fulfillment of external rituals.[95]

Although Bunin was not the scholar of the Buddha that Tolstoy was, he, too, had an enduring history with Buddhism. Bunin knew at least two books on Buddhism. The first one was a travelogue entitled *A Record of Buddhistic Kingdoms: The Account by the Chinese Monk Fa-Hein of His Travels in India and Ceylon (A.D. 399–414) in Search of the Buddhist Books of Discipline.* The second and more important was the *Sutta-Nipata,* an anthology of Buddha's discourses, thought to have been compiled in the third century before Christ and including verse-style stories, dialogues, lyrics, proverbs, and ballads.[96]

Bunin became more intimate with Buddhism, though, through his travels abroad. Visits to Buddhistic churches and shrines in India and Ceylon in 1907 and in Ceylon again in 1911 so intrigued Bunin that he became a lifelong disciple of Gautama. Years later as an émigré, he told Irina Odoevtseva: "In India I thoroughly mastered [*osnovatel'no izuchil*] Buddhism. I was very attracted to its system of beliefs . . . its religious patience . . . and its great love for every living thing. . . . There were even times . . . when I very much wanted to become a Buddhist."[97]

Like Tolstoy, Bunin internalized key Buddhistic truths and images, and he, even more than his older colleague, filled his personal and artistic writings with references, implicit or direct, to Buddhistic doctrine, mythology, and beliefs.[98] (He even wanted to write a play about the "tragedy of the Buddha's life.")[99] Unlike Tolstoy, though, Bunin had a far more pronounced, almost palpable sense of such concepts as *karma* and rebirth. For instance, he wrote in "The Book of My Life" ("Kniga moei zhizni," 1924): "Each in his own life must and will feel that which I also feel: that . . . *karma* is not a philosophy but a physiognomy."[100]

Bunin was particularly obsessed with the *paticca-samuppada,* or the "chain of causation," a cause-and-effect process in which "links" of human ignorance, desire, and craving shackle humankind in continuous rounds of births, deaths, and rebirths and of misery, suffering, and pain. For instance, in *Liberation,* Bunin wrote of the "Chain": "There are two classes of people. The first, a large group, features people focused in the present moment, preoccupied with everyday building and deeds, people who are almost with-out a past or without ancestors, veritable links of the Chain about which the wisdom of India speaks. What do people in this first group care that they slip so terribly into infinity, into both the beginning and end of this Chain?" Bunin contrasted these "men of action" with another group: "nonbuilders and nondoers . . . and genuine destroyers who know the vanity of action and building. These are the people of the dream, of contemplation, of wonder at themselves and the world. . . . They are people who have secretly an-swered the ancient call—'Leave the Chain!'—they long to disappear, to dis-solve into the All-One."

Bunin's "philosophers" included such historical figures as the Buddha, King Solomon, Francis of Assisi, Mohammed, and Bunin's saint for modern times, Leo Tolstoy. It was Bunin's personal and philosophical closeness to his longtime mentor and guide, though, that led him to attempt with Tol-stoy something that he did not do with the other hero-thinkers in his pan-theon. Specifically, Bunin sought to write a life of Tolstoy from the vantage point of self and regression, liberation and rebirth, that is, from all that he had learned from the Buddha about the workings of humankind and life.

IV

Bunin wrote *The Liberation of Tolstoy* in 1937, though for over a decade he had been writing articles on Tolstoy in such émigré journals and newspa-pers as *Contemporary Notes* (*Sovremennye zapiski*), *Russian Notes* (*Russkie zapiski*), *Latest News* (*Poslednie novosti*), and *Renaissance* (*Vozrozhde-nie*).[101] In truth, the reasons why Bunin chose this period in his life to write a large work about Tolstoy had as much to do with himself as it did with the subject of his study.[102] Four years previously, Bunin had been awarded the Nobel Prize in literature, the first Russian writer and also the first writer in exile ever to be accorded this honor. Bunin had "yearned" (in the Buddhistic sense of this word) for the prize ever since he had been nominated by the French writer Romain Rolland in 1922.[103] Needless to say, Bunin was greatly pleased with being named as a Nobel laureate, but he was ill-prepared for the harsher, if more glaring, aspects of the literary limelight. For instance, exactly one year after Bunin received his award, his wife, Vera Muromtseva-Bunina, wrote: "We have yet to have a moment's peace. Everything has been turned upside down . . . and has gotten confused, tangled, and inter-twined. . . . Fame, money, congratulations, screams of joy, envy, requests, insults, happiness . . . anguish, disenchantment, powerlessness, flattery. . . . [Such things] have kept us from concentrating and working, not to mention bringing us to endless grief."[104]

In a manner not unlike Stavrogin and his disciples in Dostoevsky's *Possessed,* Bunin was now seen by Russian exiles as an idol or a god who would breathe life into their dying hopes and dreams. As they saw it, anything that Bunin said, thought, or wrote should advance the émigré cause, denigrate the Soviet state, and continue the work of the gentry masters, with Tolstoy at their head. With a persistence that was both irksome and poignant, Russian exiles advised Bunin on what to say, how to dress, where to live, and even how to arrange the furniture in his home.

For instance, an irritated Mark Aldanov wrote to Bunin on May 5, 1934: "What's the point of your being awarded the Nobel Prize if you are going to rot in that hole, Grasse! You should travel around France and Europe!"[105] Less than a year later, Aldanov continued to Muromtseva-Bunina: "I have not been to your apartment, but just as well; for I am sure that it would annoy me greatly. . . . In my opinion, you should rent an apartment that is somewhat nicer . . . and buy some furniture that is more fashionable so that you can receive French people and foreigners. . . . After all, Ivan Alexeevich is the only person whom we can call our cultural 'ambassador' to Europe."[106]

Russian émigrés also kept a strict eye on Bunin's fictional activities, chiding him whenever the quantity or quality of his work did not measure up to their expectations. For instance, fifteen months after Bunin was honored with the Nobel Prize, Aldanov wrote to him: "The rumor is that you have not written a line since your award. . . . Your friends are angry with you, not to mention the public at large."[107] Even more stringent, Russian exiles took every measure to see that their Nobel laureate was not appropriated by the new Soviet state. "Rumors are flying around Moscow that you have decided to return [to Russia]!!" a disconcerted Aldanov wrote to Bunin on June 22, 1935. "What the hell have you been up to?!"[108]

Whatever stress Bunin endured outside his home, he also suffered within it. Bunin himself was shocked to see how quickly his life had lost its momentary luster and was resuming its tedious and trifling course. For instance, in May 1934, less than five months after Bunin had been feted in Sweden, Muromtseva-Bunina wrote: "All of us . . . are disenchanted [for] we are living the same way as before."[109] Speaking specifically of "Ian," her name for her husband, she elaborated: "Ian is very disturbed. He looks terrible and sad. The problem is that he does not know what he wants. He lives for excitement, but he suffers whenever he encounters it."[110] Bunin concurred, writing in his diary on September 17, 1934: "Days flash by in sadness, trifles, in petty concerns and frivolous correspondence."[111] A year later, he added: "Time is terrible, burdensome, and drags on without end."[112]

Bunin was particularly distressed at the fleeting nature of his fame. Indeed, he saw that no sooner was he out of sight than he was also out of mind. "I am surprised by England's lack of attention toward me," Bunin wrote to Pyotr Struve on May 29, 1934. "No one there is publishing anything of mine. And my agents are not doing anything to get even the least little something to an editor or journal there."[113] Over the next two years, he was overwhelmed not only by inner rage but also by the fear that he was finished as a writer. "I suffer from feelings of injury, of total insult—as well as of shame for the way that I have been acting," Bunin lamented. "Truly . . . I am spiritually sick . . . [a condition] that I fear is permanent. . . . I am clearly horrified by how low I have fallen. . . . full-blown inertia, lack of will, and a monstrous lack of talent!"[114]

Such disaffection was exacerbated by constant worries over money, as well as by the equally enduring threats of sickness, old age, and death. For instance, when Bunin wrote *The Liberation of Tolstoy*, he was sixty-seven years old. Always a hypochondriac, he believed not only that he was at death's door but also that people and events were conspiring to shove him across the threshold. "For the first time in my life, I had a fainting fit," Bunin wrote in the summer of 1934. "I suddenly *disappeared*. . . . I was no more. . . . Sudden death must be like that."[115] Eleven years later, he wrote to Boris Zaitsev: "I keep thinking about Tolstoy's Ivan Ilyich. Remember that his illness begins with something trifling—a bad taste in his mouth and something aching somewhere besides. . . . God grant that there is nothing seriously wrong with me."[116]

Thus, although Bunin was deeply gratified to be named as a Nobel laureate, his fame was beginning to leave something more than sourness in his mouth. Bile and gall welled from within. Indeed, Bunin began to wonder if such a distinction was a cross, not a crown, and if it was worth all the torment and suffering both of his present and his past.

V

Bunin's disaffection with his Nobel status is a key reason why, in *The Liberation of Tolstoy*, he appears as an individual who—tentative, probing, and brooding—explores the causes of Tolstoy's angst as well as his own. His narrative approach to the work is a case in point. Sometimes Bunin is an investigative reporter who penetrates a maze of oral and written testimony to understand Tolstoy and his work.[117] Other times, though, Bunin is a poignant memoirist who relives his youth by recalling his time as a Tolstoyan and his meetings with the writer. Still other times, Bunin is a *raisonneur*, or a even a one-man Greek chorus, who comments insightfully on the triumphs and tragedies of his hero.

More satisfying, if trenchant, are those moments in *Liberation* where Bunin adopts the tone of his religious and philosophical fiction. That is, he boldly steps forward as a homilist who updates medieval Russian *slova*, or "sermon-parables of solemn narration," to instruct individuals who, he hopes, are as earnest in their spiritual search as he and the subject of his study.[118]

With his *slovo,* Bunin accomplishes several goals. He can discourse about Tolstoy using a plethora of oral and written genres. In *Liberation,* threads of philosophical speculation bind a narrative fabric made up of folktales, saints' lives, confession, biography, autobiography, literary criticism, and religious and secular myth. Also as Russian homilists did in their *slova,* Bunin can direct *Liberation* to extol virtue and condemn vice, dazzling his audience with his insights and erudition and urging them to seek God and the higher things in life. Most important, perhaps, Bunin as sermon-giver can instill in his readers a desire to read "sacred scripture," for example, the testaments of the Buddha, along with selections from his own and Tolstoy's writings, so that they can be guided to inner contentment and peace as well as be alerted to the temptations and pitfalls that can distract them from their search.

Throughout *Liberation,* Bunin sees the spiritual path as strewn with more obstacles than opportunities. For instance, the gnawing disaffection that Bunin experienced with fortune and fame he saw also in Tolstoy. Initially in *Liberation,*[119] Bunin sees the object of his study as a giant, a genius, and a god. Strong in body and sound in mind and soul, Bunin's Tolstoy is a larger-than-life, almost mythical figure with a seemingly flawless mastery of life. A key metaphor of *Liberation* is that, initially, Bunin's Tolstoy travels the Road of Egression—that is, he turns his back on Universal Life to focus solely both on the present: bodily pleasures and personal gain. Indeed, earthly joys seem to be Tolstoy's for the taking. In each "decade" or "phase" of his life, he advances as a husband, a father, a landowner, a writer, and a seer. Fear and failure do not darken Tolstoy's path; pedigree, privilege, and power light his way. Women are at his beck and call; works of publicism and art multiply as rapidly as children, property, and wealth. So empowered, Bunin's Tolstoy "takes" not only for himself but also for his "family, tribe, and people."

Bunin posits, though, that Tolstoy's victories brought him only fleeting happiness in life. No amount of fortune and fame, it seemed, could satisfy the great writer. In fact, such largesse only seemed to whet his appetite for more. As Bunin sees it, therefore, Tolstoy's lust for life was often a tragedy, not a triumph, a curse, not a blessing. Bunin's Tolstoy obsessed over possessions and power; he focused on things he did not have rather on than those he did. Whatever he acquired, he immediately cast aside for something he thought was bigger, better, and brimming with contentment and peace. He failed miserably in his quest. Indeed, Tolstoy was like a primordial hunter who ran his spear into everything—real and imagined—only to find that his "catch" was ephemeral, illusory, or too burdensome for him to bear.

To his increasing dismay, Bunin's Tolstoy found that whatever gains he scored in the physical realm were nullified by his losses in the philosophical one. It was Tolstoy's most ardent desire to explain the unexplainable; for example, he wished to make God in his own self-image and likeness, according to his own wishes and ideas. It was also his equally fervid wish to channel the flow of existence (his own and that of humankind) into "symmetrical" intervals so as to show the triumph of (his) reason over the random chaos and agony of life.

Even worse, perhaps, were those instances when Bunin's Tolstoy sought to translate such ideas into reality. A "materialist" Christ, he rushed to impose the Kingdom of God on this earth. He rescued prostitutes and peasants; campaigned against illiteracy, hunger, and war; rewrote the Gospels; and railed against science, society, the government, and the church. He was hardest of all on himself. Metaphorically speaking, he sought "perfection" by wearing sackcloth and ashes, by disciplining the flesh, and by ordering his life with scads of (unrealizable) rules, commandments, and goals. For his idea of brotherhood, Bunin's Tolstoy was willing to carry his cross and to suffer, die, and even rise from the dead. "If anyone wants to be heard," Tolstoy wrote in 1900, "one must speak out from the top of Golgotha and affirm the truth by suffering and, better yet, by death."[120]

As with his quest for fame and fortune, though, Tolstoy's appeal to reason came to a dead end. Sometimes, he lacked direction or a focus. Stances as a philosopher, moralist, and teacher melded with poses as an infidel, anarchist, and rebel. Brutal skepticism and endless analysis hurled him into space without a safety net to break his fall upon reentry. Other times, Bunin's Tolstoy succumbed to the "subjugation" of cruel life forces: the advance of sickness, old age, and death; the inertia and hostility of people and institutions; alienation from his wife, family, and friends; horror at his pride, ambition, and debauchery; remorse over sins of commission and omission; and bitter wrangles with competing factions over his ideas, works, wills, property, and literary heritage. Still other times, he so succumbed to passionate sensibilities—the addictions of sex, gambling, and the like—that he abandoned reason altogether. Bunin's Tolstoy loved to pound his head against the wall if only because it felt so good when he stopped. Like an inner clock, questions such as "who are you?" and "what are you?" ticked away at him with brutal persistence. Indeed, the only thing that Bunin's Tolstoy "knew" for certain was the folly of his existence and that God, contentment, and peace were nowhere within his reach.

Tolstoy's yearnings to conquer earthly and cerebral realms drove him to frenzy and exhaustion, to physical and spiritual breakdown, to near insanity, dissolution, and ruin. Indeed, for the Buddhist-minded Bunin, the formerly larger-than-life Tolstoy had become so whittled away by the daily "grind" of his urges and desires that he seemed to have lost all human semblance and even to have "regressed" to a lower physical form. "Atavistic" craving and desire had reduced Tolstoy to a caveman as well as to various types of animals. Bunin's Tolstoy is alternately a "bulldog," a "hedgehog," and a "wolf." His ears are large and high; his teeth are clenched. His hair bristles and his jaw protrudes. Most often, though, Bunin's Tolstoy appears as a "gorilla," with massive shoulders, hands, and arms, as well as with a shaggy face graced with arched eyebrows, small, piercing eyes, and a pensive, somber gaze. Bunin's Tolstoy cups his fingers, lumbers through rooms, eats quickly and greedily, and frightens family and friends with his piercing cries and yawns.[121]

Gradually, Bunin's Tolstoy sees the errors of his ways; but, like many of his fictional characters, he repeats his mistakes again and again before he acts positively on his self-knowledge. In his mind and heart, Bunin's Tolstoy knows that all that glitters is not gold; but, self-deceptively, he wishes to be an alchemist, giving luster and shine to things that are dull and gray. He raises pedigree sheep, builds a distillery, and plants groves of trees. He grows "an almost absurd quantity of cabbage"; tills fields with a "passion that bordered on the ridiculous"; and convinces himself that "he could not be happy" unless he owns Japanese piglets. Moreover, Bunin's Tolstoy fills his day with meaningless activity. He hauls water, lights samovars, and makes boots. He almost ruins his health with self-consuming interests in pedagogy, Hebrew, and Greek. To astonished onlookers, he seeks to prove that sun revolves around the earth. He continues to acquire and think and rush about, but he gains only in unhappiness and discontent.

It was only when Bunin's Tolstoy is at a physical and philosophical nadir, when his body and soul cries out for release, that he hears "the voice of a Higher I" and seeks radical change in life. At times, Tolstoy pursues physical escape from his problems, for example, his flight from Yasnaya Polyana. Although Bunin describes Tolstoy's desertion of home and hearth no less than three times in *Liberation,* he portrays his subject's "liberation" in the final hours of his life as being unsatisfactory. However riveting and dramatic, Tolstoy's departure from Yasnaya Polyana reeks of desperation, not dispassion; of suicide, not salvation; of cowardice and surrender, not understanding and peace. In flight, Bunin's Tolstoy is not a aging Hindu seeking solitude in a forest; rather, he recalls Shakespeare's King Lear, a figure he detested. Bunin's Tolstoy-Lear is trembling, fearful, and weak; he is also consumed with anger, bitterness, and guilt. Like a thief, he leaves his home, donning old clothes, stumbling into doors, and buffeted by wind, darkness, and cold. Fearful that his wife will find him, he hops from village to village, train to train. Surrounded by foulness and filth, he finds only fleeting respite in hermitages and convents. In letters, he begs his family for forgiveness and understanding but justifies his desire for escape.

Furthermore, although Bunin posits that Tolstoy's death at Astapovo is the culminating "liberation" of the great writer's life, precisely the opposite seems to be the case. Speaking in conventional Christian terms, Bunin's Tolstoy does not have a "happy death." He does not depart this world joyous, peaceful, or confident that he will see God. In his end, he brings to mind not Andrei Bolkonsky in *War and Peace* but Serpukhovskoy in "Kholstomer" or the unfortunate woman in "Three Deaths." "Vaulted" heavens and wellings of eternal love—physical and spiritual liberation—are not in the purview of Bunin's Tolstoy. Rather, in his final moments, Bunin's subject seems not only to be eaten away by the malignant cancer of self but also to be crushed by the very time, space, and causality that he has spent a lifetime trying to transcend. Simply put, Bunin's Tolstoy is broken in body and soul. His lips, nose, and hands are blue; his face is contracted and thin. His convulsing body is alternately feverish and cold; his mind is delirious. Even more revealing, perhaps, is that in his final moments Bunin's Tolstoy does not favor the world with wisdom, kindness, or strength. He does not bid farewell to family members. He is also silent on the meaning and nature of life, death, and other realities which he had hoped would reveal themselves to him at his end. Rather, beyond "scattered, unintelligible words," Bunin's Tolstoy tells his attendants only to "keep searching"; that is, the answers to the *proklyatye voprosy*, or "damned questions of life," are open-ended or, worse, beyond the ken of those who pose them. Instead of encountering liberation in his final hours, Tolstoy seems to forge yet another link in the torments and suffering of life within the Chain.[122]

More satisfactory in *Liberation* are those passages where Bunin's Tolstoy seeks Buddhist-style "enlightenment" in his mind and heart.[123] Again using the language in *Liberation,* Bunin follows Tolstoy moves from the Road of Egression to the Road of Return. That is, Bunin's Tolstoy denies his personal and social self; "gives back" what he has taken from nature, people, and the world; and seeks Nirvana and God. In a word, he begins a genuine spiritual life.

As seen by Bunin, Tolstoy's inner liberation embraces three facets. First, Bunin's Tolstoy understands that he is not alone in his quest, but that in seeking enduring truths, he enters into spiritual union with such individuals as Mohammed, Francis of Assisi, and, of course, the Buddha himself. All have been "noble youths" who renounced power and glory to discern the true meaning of life. Formerly "masters" and "sires," they are now "men" and *startsy:* monks, pilgrims, and God's fools who resist Mara, Maya, and Satan and who seek the Deity in poverty and wandering. With almost obsessive focus, Bunin's Tolstoy ponders and internalizes the "thoughts of wise people" to learn that ego, with its notions of body, wealth, and power, is illusory; and that God is the ultimate source of peace, contentment, and love.

A second characteristic of Tolstoy's spiritual freedom was that, unlike his Romantic or Modernist confreres, he rejects the need for hallucination, madness, sex, or drugs to enter into other realms. Rather, he again appeals to reason, but with a different focus than previously. That is, whereas Tolstoy used his mental faculties to control life, he now employs them to move peacefully with life's flow; a meld of faith, awareness, emotion, and intuition enable him to see existence as wonderment and rhythm, not riddle and wrath. "Reason is the child of life," the "liberated" Tolstoy wrote in his diary, "and being the child of life, reason cannot deny life."[124]

Free of the desires and cravings of self, Bunin's Tolstoy rises to the point where he "can see himself" from both without and within. Having found a measure of fulfillment and peace, he can free himself from the darkness and doubt of his soul, as well as from the coldness and closure of life, from the stranglehold that his times seemed to have on him. Also, Bunin's "liberated" Tolstoy can find a suprapersonal meaning to life, searching for values and ideals and delighting in all he had found and learned.

Indeed, the very things that Bunin's Tolstoy denied or feared previously, he now embraces as the foundation of his existence For instance, Bunin's Tolstoy posits not only the existence of an incomprehensible loving God but also the need to know, love, and serve this God and to accept—gratefully—His holy will. He also understands that he is the Deity's partner, not his pawn; that is, he harbors "a particle of the One Godhood" within him, with the potential to be fully one with his Creator.

Having moved from "existence to the eternal," Bunin's "liberated" Tolstoy also sees sickness, old age, and death not as signaling the end of a short and brutish life but rather as heralding life's beginning: a gateway to new, countless, infinite, and more authentic levels of reality. Tolstoy wrote in *The Death of Ivan Ilyich:* "Where is death? What death? [Ivan Ilyich] was not afraid anymore because there was no more death. Instead of death, there was life."[125]

Finally, in loving awe of God and His world, Bunin's Tolstoy is no longer a conqueror of nature but its child.[126] He delights in flowers and mushrooms and rejoices that he is like the "mosquito and the deer." He chooses a final resting place in a grove of trees, content that the "only thing that will remain of [him] is the grass on [his] grave." Seeking to proceed quietly through life, he is thankful for its momentary favors, content to sit quietly, absorb, and even shed tears at the beauty of the world. Time, space, and causality no longer have any meaning for the "liberated" Tolstoy, for he knows that, psychically, he can slow, stop, and reverse the course of history. He can even reenter Eden itself.[127] Even more amazing, perhaps, Bunin's Tolstoy knows he can appeal to memory to merge with his ancestors and to infuse both his present and future with the warmth and wisdom of multiple pasts. With full confidence, Bunin's Tolstoy can reject his earlier penchant for building "materialist" Edens on abstract knowledge, social causes, or material well-being. Rather, knowing that life is indeed worth living, he can proclaim a more genuine Kingdom of God and appeal to his world with faith, hope, and love. Simply put, the "liberated" Tolstoy is like a lily in the

Russian field. He neither cares nor spins nor toils, for he knows that his Heavenly Father cares for him.

The final aspect of Tolstoy's "liberation," though, contains this sobering truth: Whatever peace and contentment he experiences from his spiritual breakthrough is not destined to last. Bunin's Tolstoy encounters only glimpses of God and moments of Nirvana before Mara, Maya, and the Devil recapture him in their nets. To his horror, Bunin's "liberated" Tolstoy sees that he is again a victim of self—that is, he is consumed by pride, ambition, and lust; terrified by sickness, old age, and death; and threatened by rebirth and Chain. Having experienced genuine "liberation," though, Bunin's Tolstoy knows that, at will, he can embrace joy and light over darkness and sorrow. His heart, mind, and soul tell him that, at any time, he can still craving and desire and cherish God, Nirvana, and the glories of existence. They also show him the way to happiness, contentment, and peace.

In Tolstoy's 1856 story "A Landowner's Morning" ("Utro pomeshchnika"), the young Prince Nekhlyudov writes to his aunt: "Do not form ambitious plans about me, but accustom yourself to the idea that I am going on an absolutely peculiar path, but one that is good and which I think will bring me happiness."[128] For Bunin, the story of Tolstoy's "path," his enduring struggle between Egression to self and Return to God, is both as old as history itself and as new as the present day. Therein lies the timelessness of the human struggle to make sense of life; therein also lies the timelessness of Bunin's message in *The Liberation of Tolstoy*.

The Liberation of Tolstoy

Chapter One

"HE WHO HAS ATTAINED perfection, my dear brothers, does not live in contentment. He who has attained perfection, O brothers, is the saintly and Most Very Exalted Buddha. Open your ears, for liberation from death has been found."

Here is what Tolstoy says about "liberation":

"It is not enough that time and space and reason are forms of thought, and that the essence of life lies outside these forms. More and more all of our existence first submits itself to time and space and causality, and then finds release from them."

No one has ever noticed these words of Tolstoy's, but they hold the key to understanding what was essential to him. Despite all the great power of Tolstoy's "submission" [to time, space, and reason], it was at Astapovo[1] that he achieved the culminating "liberation" of his life.

––––––

I recall the great delight with which Tolstoy once cited the words of Pythagoras of Samos: "You, man, have nothing but your soul!"[2] and the thoughts of Marcus Aurelius: "Our highest purpose is to prepare ourselves for death. . . . One constantly prepares oneself for death. One learns how to die in a little better way."

"I am [Marcus] Antonius [Aurelius], but I am also a man. For Antonius the Emperor, the city and country are Rome; but for Antonius the man, the city and country are the world."[3]

During the years of Tolstoy's greatest wisdom, however, he had neither the city nor country nor even the world; there remained only one thing: God. The principal dynamic for Tolstoy was "liberation," that is, withdrawal, return to God, and dissolution—but positive dissolution of self—in God.

––––––

[In *War and Peace*] Prince Andrei, listening to Natasha as she sang,

3

"[sensed] a terrible dichotomy between something that was endlessly great, indefinite, and within him and something that was narrow, corporeal, but also part of him and even her—and this dichotomy both tormented and gladdened him as she sang."

This "dichotomy" tormented Tolstoy from his birth to his last breath.

———

How did Prince Andrei experience death?

"After he had been wounded, in those hours of painful solitude and delirium, the more he kept thinking about the new principle of eternal love which had been revealed to him, the more unconsciously he kept renouncing earthly life. *To love everyone and everything, always to sacrifice oneself for love, meant never to love anyone, never to have lived an earthly life.*"[4]

———

"Open your ears, O brothers: liberation from death has been found. I will teach you, I will preach to you the Law.[5] If you will live according to its teachings, you will attain the highest fulfillment of sacred striving for which well-born youth leave their countries for other lands. Still in this life, you will know truth, you will see it with your very own eyes."

Christ also called men "to leave their country for other lands": "A man's enemies are those who live under his roof. . . . He who will not leave both his mother and father for my sake cannot be my follower."[6]

There were many of them, these "noble youths who abandoned their country for other lands." For example, there were Prince Gautama, Alexis, the Man of God, Julian the Hospitaller,[7] and Francis of Assisi. To these must be added the *starets*[8] Leo from Yasnaya Polyana.[9]

Chapter Two

"I WAS BORN and spent my early childhood in the village of Yasnaya Polyana."

With these words, Tolstoy began his *First Memories*,[1] which he never completed, but which he began for his friend and follower, Biryukov,[2] who had undertaken to write his biography.[3] At that time, Tolstoy divided his life into seven-year periods, saying that "just as certain physiologists acknowledge seven-year periods in a person's physical existence, so can one establish similar time spans for the development of the spiritual life." There were approximately twelve of these seven-year periods in Tolstoy's life.

The first one covered his childhood: his birth and life at Yasnaya Polyana. He was born to Count Nikolai Ilyich Tolstoy and Countess Maria Nikolaevna Tolstaya, née Princess Volkonskaya, on August 28, 1828.[4] His mother died at age thirty-nine,[5] when Tolstoy was only two years old. He began his studies at home with a German tutor (whom he later portrayed as Karl Ivanovich in *Childhood*).[6]

The second seven-year period took in his adolescence.

Tolstoy lived with his family and continued to study in Moscow. There, when he was eight years old, his father died of a sudden heart attack at the age of forty-two.[7]

The third interval was his youth.

He moved to live with his paternal grandmother[8] and to study at University of Kazan.[9] Because he had so few successes in school,[10] and because he was fully convinced that "everything he was being taught was useless,"[11] he left school and returned to Yasnaya Polyana, where he devoted himself to farming and to the needs of his peasants. But after he became disenchanted with such things also,[12] he went first to Moscow and then to Petersburg, where he intended to work in civil service.

The fourth stage was from ages twenty-one to twenty-eight:

In Petersburg, Tolstoy once more became disillusioned, this time with his dreams of working for the state.[13] He served with the army in the Caucasus[14] and in the siege of Sevastopol,[15] and it was at this time that he began writing. In seven years he wrote *Childhood, Adolescence, Youth, The Sevas-*

topol Tales, "The Storm," "Two Hussars," and "A Landowner's Morning."
He also began *The Cossacks*.[16]

The fifth stretch was from ages twenty-eight to thirty-five:

He left military service, traveled abroad to become familiar with European systems of education,[17] took up teaching[18] and judicial activities[19] in Yasnaya Polyana—and married Sofya Andreevna.[20] He completed *The Cossacks* and began *War and Peace*.[21] Also during this time, his brother Dmitri died, and then another brother, Nikolai.[22]

The sixth interval was from ages thirty-five to forty-two:

He spent time with his family (he and Sofya already had four children),[23] and he pursued farming, writing, and the publishing of *War and Peace*.

The seventh stage was from ages forty-two to forty-nine:

He sought to be cured of illness by mare's milk in the region of Samara[24] and also campaigned against hunger there. He wrote *Anna Karenina*[25] and sired four more children (two other boys died).[26]

The eighth period was from ages forty-nine to fifty-six:

He wrote his *Confession*[27] and moved to Moscow to educate his children. He became acquainted with Chertkov.[28] He wrote *What People Live By*, *What I Believe*, and *What Then Should We Do?*[29] He became the father of one more son and one more daughter, Alexandra.[30]

The ninth interval was from ages fifty-six to sixty-three:

He lived in Moscow and wrote stories for the people,[31] along with *The Death of Ivan Ilyich, The Power of Darkness, The Fruits of Enlightenment,* and *The Kreutzer Sonata*.[32] He began writing *Resurrection*[33] and welcomed the arrival of another son, Vanechka.[34]

The tenth period was from ages sixty-three to seventy:

He began a new campaign against hunger in the Tula region,[35] and he surrendered his authorial rights to everything he had written after 1881.[36] He wrote *The Kingdom of God Is within You, Master and Man,* and *About Art*[37] and endured the death of his son Vanechka.[38]

The eleventh span was from ages seventy to seventy-seven:

He became seriously ill for the first time. He published *Resurrection* and was excommunicated by the [Russian Orthodox] church.[39] He moved his entire family to Yasnaya Polyana. He spent the winter in the Crimea, where he survived both pneumonia and typhoid fever.[40] He began to assemble *The Circle of Reading*,[41] and he wrote letters and appeals to spiritual friends and followers, to members of the government, to soldiers, to church officials, and to political and social figures.

Finally, he entered the twelfth and final period of his life, ages seventy-seven to eighty-three.

He suffered the loss of his most beloved daughter, Masha, who, of all his children, was closest to him in heart and soul.[42] He secretly wrote his last will and testament in which he gave all the rights to his writing to his daughter Alexandra L'vovna, but which he sought to have executed by Chertkov.[43] He fled from Yasnaya Polyana on the night of October 27, 1910; he became ill along the way and died at the railway station at Astapovo on November 7.

This death was his final "liberation."

Tolstoy had tried to leave [Yasnaya Polyana], to escape from there for a very long time.[44] As early as 1884 he had written in his diary:

"Things are unbearably difficult now. I should have left a long time ago. . . . I have to leave sometime."[45]

In 1897 he had again been on the verge of leaving. He had even written a farewell letter to Sofya Andreevna, but, as before, he did not go through with his plans. After all, the wish to abandon his family, he believed, would mean only to think about himself.[46] What would happen to his family if they suffered such a blow! He wrote at the time:

"Like those Hindus who leave for the forest when they are approaching sixty years old, or like any religious person who, in the last years of his life, wishes to give up jokes, puns, gossip, and tennis, and devote himself to God,[47] so it is also the case with me that, having come upon my seventieth year, I want, with all the strength of my soul, to have this peace, this solitude, even if I am not fully in accord or even have glaring discrepancies with my conscience and beliefs."[48]

He wrote the same thing on the night he fled from his home:

"I am doing what is usual for people of my age to do, that is, to leave this worldly existence to live in solitude and silence for the rest of their lives."

Right up until the time he left, people were urging him to flee. A month before his flight from home, he wrote:

"I have just received a letter from Chertkov filled with denunciation and reproach"[49]—all because Tolstoy continued to live as he had been living. "They are tearing me to pieces. *I sometimes feel like running away from everyone.*"[50]

Chertkov later tried to justify himself, saying that he never insisted that Tolstoy leave home. Indeed, he was very unsure of such a course of action. For example, Chertkov wrote to Dosev, a Tolstoyan from Bulgaria:[51]

"Even if Tolstoy had left home for good, he would not have survived simply because his advanced years[52] and attendant illnesses would have prevented him from doing any physical labor. He simply could not go out into the world, staff in hand, to die somewhere on a highway, or live as a wandering pilgrim in some stranger's hut.[53] . . . Furthermore, he would not have done such a thing because of his unadorned love for cherished individuals, his daughters and friends, who were close to his soul and heart. He would not have been that cruel to them."[54]

7

No matter what his motives, though, Tolstoy finally decided to leave home, fully aware of the possibility that he "would die somewhere on the highway" and maybe even "be cruel to his family." On October 28, he was already in Optina Hermitage.[55] He wrote:

"October 28, 1910. Optina Hermitage. Yesterday while I was still at home, I went to bed at 11:30 and slept until three. I woke up and again, like on previous nights, I heard someone stepping about and opening doors. Previously, I had not looked through my door, but this time I did. I saw that someone had turned on the light in my study and was poking around in there. It was Sofya Andreevna. She was looking for something, and probably reading things as she was going along.[56]

"The night before, she had asked and even demanded that I not lock the doors to my study. Both of her doors are always open so that she can hear the slightest sound. Day and night she must know and control everything that I say and do. So again I heard her steps, the way she carefully opened the door and passed through. I did not know why her actions called forth such unrestrained repulsion and indignation within me.[57] I wanted to go back to sleep, but I could not. I tossed and turned for about an hour, then I lit a candle and sat up.

"The door opened and in came Sofya Andreevna, asking me about 'my health' and expressing surprise that my light was on. I could feel my repulsion and indignation growing. I gasped for breath and counted my pulse: it was ninety-seven. I could not lie down, but suddenly made a final decision to leave.[58]

"I woke up Dushan and [Tolstoy's daughter] Sasha[59] to help me pack. I shuddered at the thought that Sofya would hear what was going on and come out, and that there would be a scene, hysterics. After all, there would be no way that I could leave without a scene.[60]

"At 6 o'clock, things had been thrown together. I went to the stable to have a carriage harnessed. Dushan, Sasha, and Varya[61] were finishing packing. It was still dark out, and I could not see a thing. I lost my way, heading toward the guesthouse and winding up in a thicket. I first fell into a bush covered with thorns; then I bumped into a tree, fell, and lost my hat. I could not find the thing, but, with difficulty, I got out of where I was. I headed for home and got another hat and also a lantern. I again made my way to the stable and ordered that a carriage be harnessed. Sasha, Dushan, and Varya came out to meet me. I was shaking, all the time expecting that someone would come after us. But we finally took off.

"We waited in the village of Shchyokino[62] for an hour, where I expected Sofya to appear at any moment. We spent some anxious moments in the train car, but then my fear gave way not only to pity for her, but also to confidence that I had done what I had to do. Perhaps I am wrong in trying to justify myself, but it also seems that I was saving myself—not Lev Nikolaevich, but something that, from time to time, is in me.

"We reached Optina safe and sound, but I scarcely slept or ate along the way. Leaving Gorbachyovo,[63] I found it good and very instructive to travel in a third-class coach filled with working people,[64] though I did not have a clear idea of what was going on around me. It is now 8 o'clock, and we are in Optina."[65]

Tolstoy had only a vague idea of where he would go after he fled from Yasnaya Polyana. "Somewhere abroad . . . ," he wrote, "perhaps to Bulgaria . . . or to Novocherkassk[66] and beyond . . . or somewhere in the Caucasus." At the last minute, he chose as his first destination a monastery in the village of Shamardino,[67] where his extremely elderly sister, the nun Mother Maria, was living out her days.[68]

"You will stay here, Sasha," Tolstoy told his daughter on the night of his escape. "I will call for you in a couple of days, when I finally decide where I will go. In all probability, I will go to Mashenka's in Shamardino."

"To Mashenka's" meant to go to the one person left on this earth who had come from that endlessly far-off time when life had only just begun. It was that time when, as Tolstoy wrote, "I was five, Mitenka was six, and Seryozha was seven"; and when "Nikolen'ka (who was eleven) told us that he had a secret, which, when people would discover it, would make everyone happy and end all sickness and unpleasantries. No one would be angry at anyone else; everyone would love each other, become 'Ant Brothers.' Of course, everyone in the family knew precisely who these 'Ant Brothers' were.

"Most likely," Tolstoy continued, "what Nikolen'ka had read or heard was about some 'Moravian,' not 'Ant,' Brothers.[69] But I remember that we liked the word 'ant' very much, since it reminded us of the little creatures that we had seen in anthills. We even played at being 'Ant Brothers.' We would get under chairs, surround them with boxes, decorate them with kerchiefs, and then sit in the darkness, pressing close to each other. I remember that I enjoyed this game very much, and that I came away with a special feeling of love and tenderness every time I played it.[70]

"We knew what 'Ant Brothers' were. But we were less certain regarding Nikolen'ka's secret as to how to shield people from all kinds of unhappiness, how to keep them from quarreling and being angry, and how to insure that they would always be happy. Such a secret, Nikolen'ka told us, was written on a green stick that was buried near the road at the very edge of the ravine at old Zakaz.[71] It was in that very same place where I, thinking that my corpse had to be buried somewhere, had asked that it be placed there, in memory of Nikolen'ka."[72]

The last years of Tolstoy's life were ineffably splendid and touching. It was during this time that he once went riding with Alexandra L'vovna and passed by "Nikolen'ka's" place.

"Father and I were returning home," she wrote. "We came across a small glade where forget-me-nots covered the hilly area like a blue field in

spring; and where, in summer, the mushrooms were large, edible, and velvet-looking, with rose-colored stems and brown linings. Father called out to me:
"'Sasha!'

"When I, having spurred my horse, approached him, he said to me:

"'There, between these two oaks . . .' He first pulled on the reins with his whip, making his horse jerk nervously; then he pointed out the place to me. 'When I die,' he said, 'bury me here.'"[73]

Now, on the very last night in the home where he had spent almost all his life, he was even giving up his dream to lie in a grave amidst his native oak trees, the place which was linked to Nikolen'ka's memory. "I sometimes feel like running away from everyone." He could have added: from everything.

Why did Tolstoy run away? Because, as the Buddha used to say, "home was too confining, a place of uncleanliness." He also left because he no longer had the strength to endure the constant strife between himself and Sofya Andreevna over Chertkov or over property[74]—a struggle that had gone on for many years. Toward the end, Sofya Andreevna had become sick intellectually and spiritually; and she had become genuinely horrible in the way she persecuted her husband.[75] Also, he had become extremely ashamed to live amidst such chaotic strife, as well as in that "luxury" in which his entire family seemed to him to be living and in which he himself had been forced to live.[76] But were these the only reasons that prompted him to leave?

"I find it very burdensome to live in this madhouse," he wrote in his diary.

But Tolstoy also wrote things that were far more important, for instance:

"I like J. P. Richter's tale about the father who had raised his children underground. They had to die to enter the world. And they wished terribly for death."[77]

"There is no more widespread falsehood that there is something authentic about the individual and body."

"I have thought long and hard *about the senselessness of personal life—not only of my personal life, but also of all temporal life, in general.*"

"Who am I? Why do I exist?"

"*It is time to awake, that is, to die.*"

"*Substance and space, time and movement separate me and all living things from everything that is God.*"

"Less and less do I understand the material world. And more and more am I conscious of what *one cannot understand, but can only be aware of.*"

"What is this thing called the human race? I do not know. I only know that one need not submit to the law of copulation."[78]

"To rise to that point from which one can see oneself. This is everything."

"My spirit lives and will continue to live. But people tell me: 'But this will not be your own personal spirit.' I answer: '*But such a thing is good because what will live after me, will not be tied to my personality,* for the personality is everything that prevents the union of my soul with Everything.'"

"The body? What is it for? What is the purpose of time, space, and causality?"

Tolstoy escaped to "somewhere," but he could not but know that with all his years, physical weaknesses, and the fits of fainting that he fell into even when he was only slightly fatigued, only death awaited him along the way. "But this was also good," he said. He sought to die not like a person but like an animal, according to the most ancient law of nature, that is, that sacred mystery in which any free animal, any free bird, dies "somewhere," for no man ever comes across a free animal or bird that is dead in the city, or in the village, or even in an open field.

When he lay dying, externally incoherent but internally completely sound, Tolstoy cited a Hindu saying that fully corresponded to everything he had said earlier:

"All that is I . . . all that is appearance . . . enough of such things."

Tolstoy's secretary, Bulgakov, stunned everyone when he wrote in his book:[79] "Four months before he died, Lev Nikolaevich told me: 'I no longer love the Gospels.'"[80]

But such words are not surprising if one recalls what Tolstoy said about his life when he divided it into "three parts." First, he sorted out his life into seven-year intervals. He wrote to Biryukov:

"When I first thought to write the entire genuine truth about myself, without hiding anything bad about my life, I was horrified by the impression that such a biography would make. . . .

"On January 6, 1903, I wrote the following in my diary: 'At this moment I am experiencing the very torments of hell, for I am recalling all the vileness of my earlier years, as well as the fact that these memories have remained with me and have poisoned my existence.'"

Later, he divided his life into "periods," pronouncing a more merciful judgment on himself:

"Recalling my life, that is, looking back upon all my good and evil, I saw that my entire long life embraced four stages. The first was the period from my childhood until I was fourteen years old; and, compared to what would follow, it was a time that was marvelous and innocent, joyous and poetic. The second stage lasted twenty terrible years. It was an interval of coarse debauchery and of service to vainglory, ambition, and, most of all, lust.[81]

"The third span continued for eighteen years, beginning with my marriage and ending in my spiritual birth. From a worldly point of view, these years could be called my moral period, since, during this time, I lived a regular and honest family life. I did not fall victim to any of the vices that society had condemned. All my interests centered about egoistical concerns

11

for my family, about augmenting my well-being, and about attaining literary success and all kinds of pleasures.

"Finally, there is the fourth period, one that has also lasted for twenty years and is now the one which I am currently living and hope to die in. From this time span, I see the entire meaning of my past. I do not wish to change a thing, other than the evil habits of earlier years."

In his last years, Tolstoy kept organizing his life into "phases."

"The individual undergoes three phases," he wrote, "and I am currently experiencing the last of them. In the first phase, the individual lives only to satisfy his passions: he eats, drinks, hunts, chases after women, seeks vainglory, and sates his pride.[82] His life is full. That was my existence until I reached age thirty-four. Then I became interested in the welfare of people, of all people, of humanity.[83] (I was suddenly became very involved with education, though this concern had already entered my personal life.)

"In the first period of my family life, my interest in humanity was on the verge of dying out; but it rose again with new and terrible force, once I became aware of the vanity of personal existence. My entire religious consciousness was centered on insuring the welfare of people, on realizing the kingdom of God on this earth. And this striving was as strong, passionate, and consuming as my search for my own well-being.

"At present, I feel that my interest in humanity is weakening. It does not fill my entire life, nor does it hold an immediate attraction for me. I must decide whether my activities in this area are good, that is, my attempts to help people materially, to wage war on alcoholism, and to battle the superstitions of both the government and the church.

"I feel that something is rising up within me, that a new foundation of life is breaking free from the chains, and that it includes the striving for both social and personal good. This foundation is service to God, the fulfillment of the Almighty's will as regards the divine essence within me.

"This is not self-perfection, no, not at all. Self-perfection is something that happens earlier, for self-perfection involves a great deal of love for the personality. What is happening now is something different—it is a striving for divine purity, one that is beginning to take hold of me more and more. I see how it engrosses my entire being, how it replaces my former endeavors, and how it makes my life so very full. . . .

"When I lost my interest for personal life, and when I saw that my religious proclivities had still not taken root, I was horrified, for I felt that I had nothing to live for. But then when there arose in me *a religious feeling to strive for the well-being of humankind,* I found full satisfaction in seeking my own welfare as well.

"It is the same way even now. As my earlier passion for the welfare of all people is losing force, I again feel somewhat ill at ease, even empty. But little by little, I feel that my striving and preparing myself for another life is taking the place of everything that has gone before. It is emerging from my youthful years in much the same way that my search for my personal well-being had become more effective and fulfilling than my earlier seeking of the common good.

"Indeed, as I prepare myself solely for that other life, I believe that I am working to better both humankind and myself more effectively and genuinely than I did when I had set social or personal concerns as my exclusive goals. *Indeed, tending as I am now to God, to the divine purity within me,* to that life for which this purity reveals itself on this earth, I believe that I am simultaneously perfecting my own well-being as well as that of humankind in ways that are not only more authentic and exact, but also somehow joyous, peaceful, and assured."

Ancient Hindu wisdom says that the individual must pass through two roads in life: the Road of Egression and the Road of Return. When the individual travels the Road of Egression, he initially feels only his own "form"; his own temporary, bodily existence; his isolation from the All. He lives only within his own personal boundaries; he breathes only part of Universal Life; he focuses only on personal gain.

But this sense of well-being soon widens. The individual lives not only for himself but also for the life of his family, his tribe, his people. His conscience also grows, that is, he feels shame for living for personal profit, though he continues to be driven by a thirst for "seizure," "to take" for himself, for his family, for his tribe, and for his people.

"But on the Road to Return, the individual loses the boundaries of his personal and social 'I.' His thirst for taking comes to an end; and, more and more, he surrenders to a yearning 'to give back' those things which he has taken from nature, people, and the world. Thus the consciousness and the life of the individual merges with the One Life, the One 'I'; and his spiritual existence begins.

"The individual undergoes three phases."

AS MAKOVITSKY RECORDED with remarkable accuracy—he kept daily notes on Tolstoy for many years[1]—Tolstoy left Yasnaya Polyana between the hours of four and five in the morning. The old coachman, Adrian, took him away in an old carriage drawn by two horses. The stableman, Filip, accompanied him on horseback, lighting the way with a torch. The group first went to the train station at Shchyokino on the Moscow-Kursk[2] railway (about three miles from Yasnaya Polyana). It was cold on the way there, and Makovitsky put a second hat on Tolstoy's head.

At Shchyokino station, they boarded a commercial passenger train that was going from Tula to Oryol.[3] At the junction station at Gorbachyovo (seventy miles from the town of Kozel'sk in the Kaluga region),[4] they got on another train. At 4:50 P.M. they arrived at Kozel'sk, about three miles from the ancient monastery, the "Optina Presentation Hermitage," and an additional nine miles from the large village of Shamardino and the convent where Tolstoy's sister, Maria Nikolaevna, had long ago become a nun.[5]

When Tolstoy and company arrived at Kozel'sk, it was completely dark. From the station, they went to the monastery in a coachman's cart along the river lowlands that separated Kozel'sk from the hermitage. In his notes, Makovitsky says that the way there was filthy and foul. It was quite dark. A moon shone from behind the clouds. The horses went along at a trot.

Makovitsky continues: "All the time that Tolstoy was on the train to Kozel'sk, and now when he was riding in the coach to the hermitage, he kept asking the driver for the names of the elders at 'Optina Presentation'; and he also said that he would like to see them."

Not far from the monastery, Tolstoy and his group crossed the river by ferry. When they got to the hermitage, they stopped at the guesthouse where the host monk, Father Mikhail, lived. Father Mikhail was a gracious individual with a rust-colored, almost red beard and hair. He led them into a spacious room with two beds and a wide couch. Their things were carried in. Lev Nikolaevich said: "How good it is to be here!" And he immediately sat down to write. He wrote a rather long letter and telegram to Alexandra

L'vovna.[6] He then drank some tea with honey but did not eat anything solid. He also asked for an apple to have in the morning and a glass for his fountain pen for the night. He next began writing in his diary, asking what the date was. At 10 o'clock, he went to bed. . . . He had written more hurriedly than usual.[7]

When Tolstoy was preparing to sleep, Makovitsky wanted to help him take off his shoes, but Tolstoy got angry with him.

"I want to do it myself!" he said.

Even now no one knows: Did Tolstoy want to stay at the Optina Hermitage or in Shamardino? And how could he have stayed at the monastery, since he had been excommunicated from the church and had refused to become reconciled with it?

Several people have suggested that, perhaps, Tolstoy wanted to make his peace with the church; and there exists some evidence for such a view.

My deceased friend Lopatina, the sister of the well-known philosopher Lev Lopatin, told me:

"Once, I was in Shamardino after Tolstoy had died. Monks in white cassocks and skullcaps transported me across the wide river to the monastery. These same monks also worked in the fields. It was a hot summer day, and everything about the surroundings was joyous: serene, beautiful, and peaceful. The room in the guesthouse where I stayed was clean, bright, cozy, and sparsely furnished. There was a small, strange, wooden bed, which, perhaps, dated back to the time of Boris Godunov.

"Over tea and unblessed communion bread, one of the monks spoke for a long time about Tolstoy's last visit to the monastery:

"'He arrived, knocked on the door, and asked: "May I come in?"'

"'The monk at the guesthouse said: "By all means, please come in."'

"'"But I am Tolstoy. Perhaps you won't take me in?"'

"'"We accept everyone," the monk said. "Anyone who wants to come in."'

"'So Tolstoy and his friends stayed with us. First they went to see the superior. Next they traveled to Shamardino, to his sister, the nun. . . . Then they came to get them. . . .'

"The monk also said that Tolstoy stood before the superior's house in the cold and slush with his hat in his hands. As before, he did not wish to enter right away; and he again asked the lay brother to inform the superior:

"'Tell him that I am Leo Tolstoy, and that, perhaps, I may not come in?'

"The superior himself went out to him, opening his arms in an embrace, and saying: 'My brother!' Lev Nikolaevich rushed toward him, threw himself on his chest, and broke out into sobs. . . .

"When Tolstoy arrived at Shamardino to visit his sister, Maria Nikolaevna, he joyously told her: 'Mashenka, I am staying here!'[8] She was so surprised at his arrival that she could not immediately believe her happiness at seeing him. She told him: 'Think about what you are doing, rest awhile. . . .'

"Sister and brother agreed that he would return in the morning, but when he did so, he was not alone. The people who had accompanied him to Shamardino were also there. Confused and depressed, he would not look at his sister. Makovitsky and the others told her that they were continuing on to the Dukhobors.[9]

"'Lyovochka, why are you doing this?' she exclaimed.

"He looked at her with eyes full of tears.

"Alexandra L'vovna told Maria: 'Aunt Masha, you always see the darkest side in everything and you are only upsetting Papa. Everything will be fine, you'll see. . . .'[10]

"And so they set out with him for the last leg of his journey. . . ."[11]

If all the evidence matched Lopatina's story, one could dismiss it for this reason. Lopatina and others like her were devout Christians; they could easily have succumbed to temptation and invented a story that Tolstoy had, in fact, sought to become reconciled with the church. But there is further evidence for such a view.

It could not be by accident that Tolstoy went to Shamardino. Did he stop there on the way to somewhere else? But where was this "somewhere"? Why did he stop there? Merely to see his sister? What for? Simply to visit a relative? Perhaps there was something else on his mind?

The fact of the matter is that he went to Shamardino by way of Optina Hermitage and that, when he got to Kozel'sk, he first asked the driver about the monks; then he spent the night and the entire next day in the monastery guesthouse. Why? Everyone knows that Tolstoy spoke for a long time with Father Mikhail. He again asked about those monks who were seeking salvation in a smaller community on the monastery grounds, and he expressed a desire to meet them. "Tolstoy then went out, walked around where they lived, and twice went up to the place where Father Varsonofy lived. He stood by the door, but did not enter."

This last quotation is from the well-known journalist Ksyunin, who, having visited Shamardino immediately after Tolstoy's death, supports what Lopatina says. He notes many other things in his book, *The Departure of Tolstoy,*[12] that is, stories that his mother, Maria, told him, including, incidentally, the following:

When Tolstoy arrived at his sister's—he had also stopped at the monastery guesthouse at Shamardino—everyone else was locked out of her room, and sister and brother talked for a long time. They came out only toward dinnertime. While they were eating, Tolstoy said:

"Sister, I was at Optina, how good it was there! I would so love to live there, doing the most menial and difficult tasks. The only thing I would ask from the monks there is that I do not have to go to church."

"That would be splendid," Maria answered. "But the monks would insist that you not teach or preach while you are there."

Tolstoy became lost in thought, lowered his head, and remained like that for a rather long time, until his sister reminded him that he had not as yet finished his dinner.

"Did you talk to the monks at Optina?" his sister asked.

He answered:

"No. . . . But do you really think that they would take me in? You forget, the church has excommunicated me."

How would all this have ended? Perhaps he would have met with the monks at Optina, and perhaps they would have helped him to return to the bosom of the church.[13]

But the following day, Alexandra L'vovna came to Shamardino with terrible news: Sofya Andreevna, having learned about her husband's flight on the morning of October 28, had twice attempted suicide by trying to drown herself in a pond.[14] She had sobbed all day long. She had beaten herself on the chest first with a heavy paperweight, then with a hammer. She had stabbed herself with knives and scissors. She ran to throw herself out the window,[15] all the time crying:

"I'll find him. I'll leave the house and run to the train station! Oh, if I could only find out where he is! I will never let him out of my sight. I'll keep guard over him day and night. I'll sleep by the very door to his room!"

Sofya's letter to him, which Alexandra L'vovna brought along with her, was utterly appalling in its despair. Indeed, so shaken was Tolstoy by Sofya's missive[16] (as well as by everything else that had happened since he had fled Yasnaya Polyana), and so seized was he with horror that all Sofya Andreevna had to do was look around to find out where he was and come after him, that he hurriedly pressed on further.

"I cannot return, I will not return," he kept repeating on the day that Alexandra L'vovna arrived. "I wanted to stay here; I was even going to rent a hut as a place to live."[17]

But now it was impossible for him to remain there. He spent the day of September 30 anxiously writing a new letter to Sofya Andreevna.[18] He sat in a sweltering room under an open *fortochka*,[19] which he would not allow anyone to close. He then went to bed, anxious, sad, and torn between his pity for Sofya Andreevna[20] and the impossibility of returning home.

It was 4 A.M. and still dark out when he again jumped out of bed. Alexandra L'vovna writes: "At 4 A.M., he woke up Dushan Petrovich and sent for the drivers. Remembering the promise that I had made to Aunt Masha that we would see her without fail in case we decided to go on further, I immediately sent for her. It was still completely dark out. By the light of a candle, I hurriedly collected our things and tied up the trunks. Dushan Petrovich arrived. The drivers from Kozel'sk had gotten hold of some horses. . . . Father was very upset, but he finally decided to go, without waiting to see Aunt Masha and Obolenskaya.[21] He wrote them the following letter:

"'4 A.M., October 31, 1910. Shamardino Monastery. Dear friends, Mashen'ka and Lizan'ka. Do not be surprised, or judge us, me especially, that we are leaving without bidding proper farewells to you. To both of you, and especially to you, Mashen'ka, I cannot express my gratitude for your love and concern for what I am going through now. Although I have always loved you, Mashen'ka, I cannot recall any such tenderness toward you as the one that I have been feeling for you during these past few days—and especially now that I am going away. We are leaving so unexpectedly because I am afraid that Sofya Andreevna will find me here; and the only train out of here departs at 8 A.M. I kiss you both, dear friends, and I love you so very much. L.T.'"

Where would he run off to now? It was decided, for the time being, to go to Novocherkassk. But it was his fellow travelers who made the decision. He himself, crushed and reeling from exhaustion and the distress of the past few days, only hastened to escape: "I don't care where we go . . . only not to any colony of Tolstoyans,[22] but to a simple peasant's hut."[23]

When Tolstoy and his group reached the station at Kozel'sk, they barely managed to get on the train that was heading south. They jumped in the train car without tickets. At the station at Volovo,[24] they purchased tickets to go as far as Rostov-on-the-Don.[25] This was on the morning of October 31; but, the following day, Alexandra L'vovna telegraphed Chertkov:

"Yesterday we got off at Astapovo. He had a high fever and was delirious. This morning, his temperature was normal, but now he is shivering again. There is no way that we can continue our journey."

She also said that, that morning, her father had dictated the following thoughts for her to put in his notebook:

"God is the boundless All; the individual is only a limited manifestation of God."

She wrote this down and waited for him to dictate something else, but he said:

"I have nothing else to say."

He lay for awhile in silence; then he called for her again:

"Take my notebook and pen, and write this down:

"It is better to put it this way: God is that boundless All of which the individual feels himself only to be a limited part. Truly, only God exists. The individual is the manifestation of God in mass, time, and space. The more the manifestation of God in the individual (life) is united to the manifestation (in the lives) of other entities, the more the individual exists. The union of one's life with the lives of other entities is accomplished through love.

"God is not love. But the more that one loves, the more one gives witness to God, the more one truly exists.

"We know God only by being conscious of the divine presence in us. Anything that arises from this consciousness, including the living of one's life, should, always and completely, satisfy the individual's yearning to know the Deity, and to live his life with this knowledge."

After some time, he again called for his daughter.

"I now want to write to Tanya and Seryozha."[26]

Periodically he had to stop dictating his letter because of the sobs that welled up in his throat, and there were moments when Alexandra could barely hear his voice.

"My dear children, Tanya and Seryozha!

"I hope and am confident that you will not reproach me for not calling for you before I left. But to do so without seeing Mama would have been a great sorrow not only to her but also to your brothers. I am sure that you both will understand that I called for Chertkov because of his special relationship with me. He has dedicated his life to serve the same things which I have served during the last forty years of my existence. Not only are these things dear to me, but I also acknowledge their importance for everyone including yourselves, be I right or wrong in doing so.

"I thank you for your good relationship with me. I do not know if this is the time to say farewell or not, but I felt the necessity of saying everything I said.

"I wanted to give you some additional advice, Seryozha,[27] as to how to think about your life, about *who you are*, about *what you are,* about the purpose of human existence, and about how any intelligent individual should conduct his affairs. The ideas that you have adopted as your own—Darwinism, evolution, and the struggle for existence[28]—will not impart any sense to your life, nor will they tell you how to think and act; and to live life without any explanation as to its significance and sense is a pitiful way of going about things. Think about it. On the eve of my death, I say all of this to you with love.

"Farewell. Try to calm your mother, for whom I have the most sincere feeling of compassion and love. You loving father, Lev Tolstoy."

"Give this letter to them after I die," he told Alexandra L'vovna, and with that, he again burst into tears.[29]

On the morning of November 2, Chertkov arrived; and so agitated was Tolstoy by his friend's arrival that he again burst into tears.[30] His condition was getting more and more serious. Periodically he spit up blood, his fever got worse, and his heartbeat became weak and irregular. Someone gave him some champagne to drink. Several times in the afternoon, he himself took his temperature. But by evening his condition had deteriorated further. He would groan loudly, and his breathing became short and labored. He again asked for a thermometer, and when he took it from his mouth and saw that it had registered 39.2 degrees,[31] he said loudly:

"Please, Mother, don't be upset with me!"

Sergei L'vovich[32] arrived at 8 P.M., and Tolstoy again became very disturbed when he saw him. After Sergei had left the room, Tolstoy called for Alexandra L'vovna and said:

"Seryozha's a dear, dear boy!"

"What do you mean, Papa?"

Sobbing all the time, he said with difficulty: "How was he able to find me! I am so glad, I like him a lot. . . . He even kissed my hand."

On the third of November, Chertkov read to him from the newspapers as well as from four letters which had come addressed to Tolstoy. Tolstoy listened attentively, just as if he were at home; he then asked that the envelopes be marked so that people would know what to do with them later on.

The night of November 3 was one of the most difficult times for him.[33] In the evening when people were making up his bed, he said:

"But the peasants, look at how the peasants die!" And again he burst out crying.

At approximately eleven o'clock, he began raving. He again asked that someone take notes for him, but he uttered only scattered, unintelligible words. When he asked that his notes be read back to him, the people there became flustered and did not know what to say. But he kept asking:

"Read them to me; read to me, I say!"

The morning of November 4 was also a very alarming time. There now appeared a new, sinister sign. He would keep taking the blanket into his hands, running his fingers down one of its edges over to the other and then back again. Also, he would sometimes try to prove something, to express some kind of obsessive idea.

"Try not to think," Alexandra L'vovna told him.

"Ah! But how can I not think!" he replied. "I have to think, I simply have to!"

All day long he tried to say something; he tossed and suffered. By evening, he was again delirious, and he kept begging for someone to help him, to understand what he was trying to say.

"Sasha, come here, come and *see how it will all end,*" he said.

She tried to distract him.

"Perhaps you'd like something to drink?"

"Oh no, no. . . . How can one not understand. . . . It's all so simple!"

And again he would rave on:

"Come here. What are you afraid of? Don't you want to help me? I'm begging all of you. . . . *Keep searching, always keep searching. . . .*"

Varvara Mikhailovna [Feokritova] came into the room. He rose up momentarily in bed, stretched out his hands, and, looking straight at her, cried out to her in a loud and joyous voice (he had mistaken her for his dead daughter):

20

"Masha, Masha!"

All night long Alexandra L'vovna did not leave his side. He kept toss-ing about and moaning. Again he asked for someone to take notes. Al-though he gave her nothing to write down, he kept asking her:

"Read me what you wrote! Why are you silent? What did you write?"

Throughout the ordeal, people sought to attend to him in pairs; but there was one time when Alexandra L'vovna was there with him alone. He had apparently fallen asleep; but, with a powerful movement, he suddenly rose up and began sticking his legs out from the bed. She went up to him quickly, saying,

"What's the matter, Papasha?"

"Let me go! Let me go!" he said.

He then lunged forward with all his might.

"Let me go, let me go! Don't you dare hold me back! Let me go!"

At 10 A.M. on November 6, doctors came from Moscow.[34]

When he saw them, he said:

"I remember them. . . ."

On the same day, he seemed to bid farewell to everyone. He looked at Dushan Petrovich with tenderness and said with deep affection:

"My dear Dushan, my dear Dushan!"

"When they changed his sheets, I supported him from behind," Alexandra L'vovna writes. "And I felt that his hand was searching for mine. I thought that he wanted to lean on me, but he firmly pressed my hand, first one time, then another. Trying to hold back my tears, I squeezed his hand and brought it to my lips. On that day Father told us things that forced us to realize that life had been given to us for a reason; that no matter what the circumstances, we were obliged to continue this life; and that, however weak we might be, we must try to serve the One who had sent us as well as others.

"His bed stood in the middle of the room. We sat close by. Suddenly, Father raised himself up with a powerful motion and almost sat up straight. I went up to him and said:

"'Should I fix your pillows?'

"'No, no,' he replied, clearly and firmly enunciating each word. 'I wish to advise you only of this, that there are many people in this world be-sides Leo Tolstoy, but that you are looking only at me.'

"His heart was very weak; he hardly had a pulse; and his lips, nose, and hands had turned bluish. Somehow his face had become thin, as if it had shrunk or contracted. His breathing was barely audible. . . .

"In the evening, after everyone had gone to bed, I also fell asleep. I was awakened at ten o'clock. Father had gotten worse. He began to gasp for breath. We raised him a little on his pillow; and, with our support, he sat up, his legs hanging from the bed.

21

" 'It's hard for me to breathe,' he said with difficulty and in a hoarse voice.

"Everyone was aroused from their beds. The doctors kept giving him oxygen to help him breathe. After an injection of camphor, he seemed to be better.[35] He summoned his brother:

" 'Seryozha!'

"And when Seryozha approached him, he said:

" 'Truth. . . . I love so many things . . . like they. . . .'

"These were his final words."[36]

According to Sergei L'vovich, he had also said something else in his ravings on November 6, something that I have already noted:

"Everything that is I . . . all these illusions . . . enough of such things . . . that is all. . . ."

On that day, Father Varsonofy, the elder from Optina Hermitage, arrived at Astapovo. People later said that he had come on "some order of [people] in Petersburg." But this was not true. When he got there, Father Varsonofy asked to be admitted to see the dying man; but he was refused. He then wrote this letter to Alexandra L'vovna:

"I respectfully thank your Highness for your letter in which you write that as far as you and your entire family are concerned, the wishes of your parent take precedence over everything else. But as you know, Countess, your father told your aunt, the nun Mother Maria, that he wished to see us and talk with us."

The claim of "an order from Petersburg" is thus fiction, not fact. If Tolstoy had not expressed to his sister a wish to see the elders, Father Varsonofy would not have referred to her.[37]

But what would have happened if Alexandra L'vovna had allowed him to see her father? One might propose that there would have been a reconciliation of the dying man with the church. But would such a move have negated the essence of Tolstoy's ravings, the words that Sergei L'vovich had heard?

Indeed, what Tolstoy had said was great beyond measure; for as he himself once wrote in his diary: "The words of a dying man are especially important."

Chapter Four

EVEN NOW, I REMEMBER the day when the large print of the telegramlike newspaper hit me in the eyes.

"Astapovo, November 7. At 6:05 A.M. Lev Nikolaevich Tolstoy quietly passed from this life."[1]

The page had a black border around it. In the middle was a darkened portrait known to the entire world: an old peasant in a baggy blouse, with woefully gloomy eyes and a huge tapering beard.[2] I remember that when I read this news it was eleven o'clock on a wet and warm morning in Petersburg. As I looked at his portrait, I kept recalling Tolstoy's story *The Cossacks*, envisioning a bright and hot day in the Caucasus, the forest around the Terek,[3] and a thin, sunburned cadet making his way through the woods and wearing a "small white Caucasian fur cap with a drooping, yellowed tassel, a dirty, white Circassian coat with wide folds," and a rifle in his hand.

"The next day Olenin went alone to that place where he and the old man had earlier scared off the deer. . . . The day was absolutely clear, quiet, and hot. The morning freshness had already withered away in the forest, and swarms of mosquitoes were literally clinging to his face, back, and hands. . . . These swarms well suited the wild, unbelievably lush vegetation, the great multitude of beasts and the nests of birds that filled the forest, the dark verdure, the warm, fragrant air, and the ditches of murky water which oozed from the Terek and which gurgled from under the hanging leaves. . . .

"Going around the place where he had come across the animal the day before, and not having encountered anything along the way, Olenin suddenly wanted to rest. . . . He followed the tracks that the deer had made yesterday; and stealthily he made his way under the bush into the thicket, to the very place where yesterday the deer had been lying, having settled in its lair. . . .

"Suddenly Olenin was seized by such a strange feeling of pointless happiness, as well as love for everything in the world that he, as had been his custom as a child, began to cross himself and to express his gratitude to someone. It suddenly became very clear to him that he, Dmitri Olenin, was a special entity apart from everyone else, and that he was now lying alone,

God knows where, in the same place where a deer had once lived, a deer that was old, handsome, and, perhaps, had never seen a human being. . . .

"'Around me,' Olenin thought, 'the mosquitoes buzz and fly through the leaves, like islands floating in the air. One, two, three, four, a hundred, a thousand, a million mosquitoes, and each one of them is as special as I myself, Dmitri Olenin.' . . .

"And it became clear to him that in no way was he a Russian noble-man, a member of Moscow society, the friend and relative of so-and-so and such and such, but that he was simply like the mosquito and deer, both of which now lived near him. 'Just like them, just like Uncle Eroshka, I will live and die,' Olenin continued to think. 'And it is true when he says that the only thing to remain of me is the grass on my grave.'[4]

"'So what if grass is the only thing that remains?' Olenin asked him-self. 'All the same one must live, one must be happy. . . . It is all the same who or what I am: whether I am an animal or like everything upon which grass grows and nothing more than that; or if I am a frame which contains a particle of the One Godhood. Nonetheless, I must live in the best way I can. But how can one live happily? And why have I not been happier earlier?'

"Then Olenin began to recall his past life, and he was filled with shame for the way he had conducted his affairs. . . . But suddenly he seem-ingly discovered a new ray of light. 'Happiness,' he told himself, 'happiness results when we live for others. . . . Humankind has an innate need to be happy; indeed, such a need is legitimate. When one seeks to satisfy egotis-tical desires, that is, when he searches for riches, fame, or the comforts of life and love, it may happen that even when he realizes such things, he still finds it impossible to satisfy this need to be happy. Consequently, such de-sires are illegitimate; but the desire for happiness is not.'

"'But which are the desires that can always be stilled, regardless of ex-ternal circumstances? Which ones? Love and the renunciation of self!'

"And when Olenin discovered what seemed to him to be a new truth, he became so excited and happy that he jumped for joy and impatiently be-gan to search for someone for whom he could immediately sacrifice himself, someone to whom he could be kind and whom he would love right away."[5]

Sofya Andreevna would say:

"I lived with Lev Nikolaevich for forty-eight years, but I still did not know what kind of person he was!"[6]

The many facets of this man always surprised the world. But the im-age which I recalled on that November 7 a quarter of a century ago was that of a cadet in the Caucasus with thoughts and feelings amidst the "wild, un-believably lush vegetation" on the Terek, the "vast multitude of beasts" and birds flying over it, and the countless mosquitoes in the air, each one "so very distinct from the rest," just as the lieutenant was "distinct from every-one around him." Is this not a key image [in Tolstoy]?[7]

And this cadet, thinking about his "specialness," was detaching himself from the emotions that this "specialness" aroused. "And it became clear to him that in no way was he a Russian nobleman, a member of Moscow society, the friend and relative of so-and-so and such and such, but that he was simply like the mosquito and deer, both of which now lived near him. 'Just like them, just like Uncle Eroshka, I will live and die,' Olenin continued to think. 'And it is true when he says that the only thing to remain of me is the grass on my grave.'"

The attempt to lose one's "distinctiveness," together with the secret joy of having lost this "distinctiveness"—this was a key Tolstoyan trait. "The words of the dying are especially noteworthy," he noted. And, as he lay dying, he, one of the greatest of the great, said: "There are many Leos in this world, but you are thinking only of this Leo!" Was this not, surely, the same thing that the young cadet thought and said to himself about "distinctiveness"? In similar fashion, it later delighted Tolstoy to take Napoleon, Pierre, and Prince Andrei and to divest them of the imaginary heights of their situations and self-appraisals.[8] It delighted Tolstoy to deprive them of their "distinctiveness," to use them as examples to show that the essence of life lay outside of temporal and spatial forms, and to move them among mosquitoes and deer. And it also delighted Tolstoy to do the same for himself.[9]

Not one deer, not a single Uncle Eroshka, ever upheld his "distinctiveness" with the same passion or force as Tolstoy did. One only needs to recall how rabidly jealous he could be when he was in love. But at the same time, he sought to destroy this "distinctiveness" throughout his life, and the older he became, the more passionately, the more powerfully, he sought to defeat what separated him from others.

But how could it be otherwise? How could Tolstoy not destroy this "distinctiveness"? After all, it was not destined for this cadet in the Caucasus throughout his extremely long life to journey to that sacred, animal-like stage where he could "live a bit and die" and where "nothing would remain of him but the grass on his grave." How could he not destroy such "distinctiveness" if he often saw it as "repulsive for himself" and if he believed that "happiness was living for others"?

"And when Olenin discovered what seemed to him to be a new truth, he became so excited and happy that he jumped for joy and impatiently began to search for someone whom he could immediately sacrifice himself. . . ."

How many times in his life did Tolstoy discover "what seemed to him to be a new truth," which was, for him, however, a fatal one? With it one could be neither a deer nor an Uncle Eroshka. "It is all the same who or what I am: whether I am an animal like everyone else, or a frame which contains a particle of the One Godhood." But herein lies the problem. It is not all the same who or what I am, once I understand myself to be a "frame." The deer and Uncle Eroshka are also "frames," but do either of them think

25

about such things?! The deer and Uncle Eroshkas, each in their own "distinctiveness," their own "selfness," do not at all seek to find "someone whom they should quickly sacrifice themselves for."[10] That is why the particularly fatal path of life is mandated for one who is born as a deer and as Uncle Eroshka and, at the same time, as a Dmitri Olenin, who in no way could die so that the grass on his grave would be the only thing that would remain of him. "Some people live without noticing their existence." No, not just a few, but as many as there are mosquitoes and deer on this planet. But how many people exist who take note of existence?

Tolstoy was one of those individuals who took much too great a note of existence. There is no way that he could have died like a deer. Either he had to die like Ivan Ilyich or like Prince Serpukhovskoy in "Kholstomer,"[11] or, in the best case scenario, like Kholstomer himself. Or he had to die with an unquestioning belief in the words of Christ: "My kingdom is not of this world. He who believes in me will never die";[12] or in the teaching of Hindu sages: "Open your ears, for liberation from death has been found! Liberation is the release of the spirit from its material garb, the union of the temporal 'I' with the eternal one."

But this trust was acquired at a terrible cost. For at Astapovo station, at 6:05 on the morning of November 7, 1910, there came to an end not only the life of one of the most unusual people who had ever lived on this earth, but also of a certain human achievement that was unusually forceful, sustained, and heroic. That is, there came to an end the struggle for that which is "liberation," for that which, as the Hindus say, is the passage from "Existence to the Eternal," and for that which, in the words of the Gospels, is the path to "life." This "liberation" also coincided markedly with the anthology, entitled *Thoughts of Wise People for Each and Every Day*, which he assembled in the last years of his life. For instance, on the page for the seventh day of November, one reads: "Enter by the narrow gates; for wide are the gates and vast the path that lead to destruction and that are the lot of many. But narrow are the gates and small the path that lead to life and that are the lot of few."[13]

In this anthology, Tolstoy included the ideas that touched him the most and that answered the questions of his mind and heart most satisfactorily. These "thoughts of wise people" included the reflections of various countries, peoples, and times, as well as several musings of his own. He wrote in the preface: "From time immemorial, the best, that is, the most genuine, people thought about these things." By "these things" he meant ideas that he himself had contemplated throughout his life, even when he was preoccupied with other things, for example, "How it will all end?" and his own imperative that one had to "search, always keep searching." Always remarkable in everything, he was also exceptional in the persistence with which he had begun to speak about "these things" from his very earliest years on. Indeed, he seemed obsessed by what he was saying, a phenomenon that one sees in the lives of the saints or in the case histories of the insane. There is a legend that Saint John, the favorite disciple of Christ, lived out his old age by saying the same thing: "Children, love one another." The way Tolstoy constantly talked about "these things" can also be found in his last letters and notes and recalls the repetition innate to the ancient sacred books of India, the writings of the Jewish prophets, the exhortations of the Buddha, and the lessons of the Koran.[14]

"Existence is for me something that is most incomprehensible," Tolstoy would often repeat in various ways.

"Who am I? *Reason cannot explain the questions of the heart. Only some emotion in the depths of consciousness can answer these queries.* Since the beginning of time, people *have answered these questions not with words, that is, an instrument of reason,* a part of the phenomenon of existence, but with all life of itself."

"God forbid that one lives only for this world. For existence to have meaning, *it is necessary that the goal of life go beyond the limits perceived by the human mind.*"[15]

"Joyous and cherished are encounters with those people who see beyond the limits of this life."

"For me, God is the One to Whom I am striving—the One to Whom this striving makes up my entire life. Thus, God has to be for me an entity that I cannot understand or name."[16]

"I went riding on the top of a horse-tram and kept looking at the houses, signs, storefronts, cabbies, and people who were walking or riding about. And suddenly it became clear to me that the entire world, and my life in it, is only one of countless possibilities of other worlds and other lives. I also understood that, for me, this world is also one of countless stages which I am passing though (as it seems to me, through time)."

"Are not our constant strivings toward the future a sign that life is the expansion of consciousness? One gradually discerns that there is no such thing as the material or the spiritual, but only one's passage across the boundaries of that which is eternal and endless, a place where Everything and Nothing merge (Nirvana)."[17]

"My 'I' seeks to expand and, in the attempt, comes into conflict with its limits in space. . . . Besides one's consciousness of limits in space, there is also the consciousness of self—that is, that being which discerns these limits. What is this consciousness? And if this consciousness senses boundaries, this means that, by its very nature, it constantly seeks to go beyond these limits."

"The life which I am aware of is the passage of a spiritual and unbounded (divine) essence through matter which is defined by limits."

"The life of the individual expresses itself in the relationship of the finite to the infinite."

"The infinite, of which the individual discerns that he is a part, is God."

"If one can sometimes forget about people, he experiences some ecstasy of freedom."

"If I were alone, I would be a God's fool, that is, I would not value anything in life."

"One should also be a God's fool in writing."

Not long before his flight from Yasnaya Polyana, Tolstoy loved to talk to his older daughter, Tatyana L'vovna, telling her that he dreamed of settling in her village, where no one would know him.[18] "There I could go about and beg for alms under people's windows," he would say. Such words are infinitely important—they reveal his dreams of becoming a God's fool who values nothing in life and is despised by everyone; his vision of being unknown to anyone, a beggar who, with a sack on his shoulders, humbly begs for a piece of bread under the windows of peasants' homes.

Indeed, is it possible to think, as people think even now, that Tolstoy had long sought to flee Yasnaya Polyana only because he had wished to be rid of arguments with his wife and children? After all, even as a cadet he would experience "ecstasies of freedom," that is, happiness to imagine that in no way was he a Russian nobleman, a member of Muscovite society, a friend and relative of so-and-so and such and such, but simply an "entity like a mosquito or a deer." With enthusiasm, Cadet Olenin sought to lose his "distinctiveness"; nevertheless, just as enthusiastically, he dreamed of celebrating this "distinctiveness" throughout the entire world. But how did all this end?

"There once was a man in the land of Uz, and his name was Job. . . . He had seven sons and three daughters. He also had seven thousand sheep and goats, three thousand camels, five hundred pairs of oxen, five hundred female asses, and innumerable servants. And he was more noble than all the sons of the East."

But this man was brought to "ruin," losing everything he had. "A great wind rose up from the desert and seized the four corners of his home; and the home fell on his children, and they died."[19]

Over the course of entire decades, Tolstoy gradually sought his own ruin; and finally he ruined himself in full—down to his very being. The destruction of his entire "home" was also something biblical. Indeed, it was as if "a great wind had risen up from the desert, and had seized the four corners of his home, and his home had fallen on his sons."

And where are they now, these "children" who have been scattered all around the world? One, Ilya L'vovich, recently died in America, having perished not only from illness but also in abject poverty![20] Tolstoy himself kept calling for this "great wind" to come upon his "house"; and he finally succeeded in bringing it about, if only because submissiveness became his alpha and omega.

"Hold out your hand to your servant, Job, and touch everything that he has.

"And the Lord held out His hand and touched—'everything except Job's soul.'

"And Job got up. He tore his outer garments, shaved his head, fell on the earth, bowed, and said: 'Naked I left my mother's womb, and naked I will return there.'"[21]

Naked also was he who "died quietly" under someone else's roof, at some railway station then unknown to anyone.

When one thinks about Tolstoy's very long life, one remarkable for all that he said and did, one immediately sees that the highest point of that life, one that explains everything, was his flight from Yasnaya Polyana and his death at that train station. Also reflecting on the long years of great suffering that others before him had experienced, one has no choice but to think about the life paths of Job, Buddha, and even the Son of Man himself.

"By and by the devil took Him to an extremely tall mountain and showed him all the kingdoms of this world and all their glory. And he said to Him: 'I will give all this to you, if you fall down on your feet, and worship me.' But Jesus said to him: 'Be gone from me, Satan.'"[22]

Who else was so tempted like Tolstoy, who else so loved "the kingdoms of this world and all their glory"?

"Good God," Prince Andrei thought on the night before the Battle of Austerlitz,[23] "what am I to do if I love nothing but glory and the love of other people? My father, sister, wife, and all the people who are the dearest to me—I would surrender them all for a minute of glory, of triumph over others, for the love of people toward me, people whom I don't even know!"

The "gates leading to destruction" were open extremely wide to Tolstoy. He achieved the greatest "triumph over others." "But so what? What next?"[24] And having achieved what he wanted, he "got up, took a piece of tile to scrape himself, and sat in the ashes *outside the settlement.*"[25]

Like Job, like the writer of Ecclesiastes,[26] and like the Buddha, Tolstoy was destined for "ruin" from his very birth. The entire lives of such people are lived under the shadow of this destiny: All their "actions and labor," all their riches and glory, all their "vanity of vanities" end with a scraping tile, ashes, and their living "outside the settlement" in the groves of Uruvela,[27] Astapovo.

The greater the "ruin," the "dissolution," of these people is destined to be, the more "the One who keeps creating according to his own design" gives to them. The more devastating the curses on all their earthly labors and acquisitions, the more the One forces them to labor and acquire with passion. One man has seven sons, three daughters, hundreds of male and female slaves, thousands of cattle, and the primary place among all the sons of the East. Another is high born, physically and spiritually strong, with kingly blood in his veins and a "palace for every season of the year." Still another is a son of David, a king of Israel, and a great "doer of deeds," who says: "I have undertaken a great many things. I have built homes for myself, planted vineyards, gardens, and groves, constructed reservoirs, and garnered gold, silver, and treasures from kings and countries of the world."[28]

But they all met a common end. "What benefit does the individual gain for all his labors, all that he has worked for under the sun?"[29] asks one who had toiled so hard under this sun. "Naked did I leave my mother's womb, and naked I shall return to it," says another. "The kingdom of this world and the kingdom of death are one; it is all the deceiver, Mara,[30] for Mara, too, is death," says a third. And a fourth, recalling his life, writes: "I am enduring the torments of hell: I recall all the vileness of my former life."[31]

What was Tolstoy's "vileness"? What mortal sins had he committed? They were *only the failings that people call "the sins of the saints"*; yet such people always considered themselves to the greatest of sinners. But all the same, for how many years and with what self-recrimination did he, with a piece of tile, scrape away the leprosy of his sins and tremble like Job. [Tolstoy confessed:] "There was not a single terrible crime that I would not have committed."

[Job said:] "The sufferings and deprivations that brought me horror have overtaken me, and that which I was afraid of has come to me."[32]

Tolstoy expressed almost the same sentiment.

"I keep going down the slope of death. But I do not want to die, I want and love immortality. I love my life—my family, my farming, my art."[33]

"How can I save myself? I feel that I am perishing. I love life, but I am dying. How can I save myself?"

"Levin was a noted healthy, happy family man; but even he was occasionally so close to suicide that he would hide the rope so as not to hang himself, and he feared traveling with a rifle lest he shoot himself."

Levin was also perishing. "But Levin did not hang himself, nor did he shoot himself, but continued to live." Why did he continue to live? Because that was the will of the Master which Levin constantly discerned as strongly as did his worker, Fyodor. This will (this striving) toward earthly and temporal life took place within the body, even though Levin often hated the body—his own or that of others—with a passion. It was because of this hatred that he was tempted to hang or shoot himself; but, at the same time, he felt that there would be no salvation for him if he did so. He kept hearing within himself "the voice of a Higher I." Why did Levin have to continue living? Because this voice told him that he had to "save himself" in life. And what did this salvation consist of? Not in the murder of the body, or in "being ready" to exit it, but in triumphing over it and in losing "everything but the soul."[34]

AFTER TOLSTOY'S FUNERAL, Yasnaya Polyana quickly became deserted. Some relatives and close friends lingered, but they were leaving one by one. Sofya Andreevna told Ksyunin about the soon-to-be-deserted home which she had entered as a young girl and in which she had spent the next forty-eight years:[1]

"In three days my home will be completely dead. . . . Everyone will have left."[2] At that time, the one with whom she had entered this home was at the full flowering of his matchless powers; and he had so loved her that he would say: "Mine is the happiness of one in a million." He wrote in his diary:

"I love her. Be it morning or night, I wake up and see that she is looking at me with love in her eyes. . . . I love it when she sits close to me, when we know that we love each other as much as possible, and when she asks: 'Lyovochka!' and pauses. 'Why are the pipes in the fireplace straight?' Or 'Why don't horses take a long time to die?'

"I love when we are alone for a long periods of time and I ask, 'What shall we do? Sonya, what shall we do?'—and she laughs in reply. I love when she gets cross with me and suddenly thinks or says something rather sharp—'Leave me alone! It's boring to be with you!'—but then almost right away smiles shyly at me. I love when she acts like a little girl, wearing a yellow dress and sticking out her tongue and jaw; I love when her head is tilted back, and her face is serious, frightened, childlike, and passionate."

He wrote in letters to friends:

"I am writing this, listening to my wife's voice upstairs. I love her more than anything else in the world. I lived my first thirty-four years without knowing that one could love someone so much and be so happy."[3]

Sofya Andreevna, recalling the time when he began writing *War and Peace,* said:

"He once came to me all excited and happy, and said: 'I'm coming up with the most splendid type of diplomat [for *War and Peace*]!' And I asked him: 'Lyovochka, what's a "diplomat?"' After all, I was only twenty years old."

"'I never loved anyone but you,' Lev Nikolaevich told me throughout his life. But after all, it was not easy to make Tolstoy happy! I remember that once our friend, the poet Fet, said about me: 'Sofya Andreevna walks a sharp line.' But I have walked a sharp line throughout my entire life."

Tolstoy was happy like "one in a million." But then why, soon after he had married and experienced the first thrill of farming, did he write in his diary:

"It is terrible! I am a gambler and a drunkard. I am also getting carried away by farming. I have wasted nine months—time which will never return and which I have turned into almost the worst period of my life . . . for in these nine months I have been the most insignificant, weak, senseless, and vulgar person."

Tolstoy kept a huge apiary and would sit out there for hours on end, observing and studying the life of bees. He raised pedigree sheep and had even convinced himself that he "could not be happy in life" until he got hold of some Japanese piglets. He planted an orchard and groves of fir trees.[4] He raised a huge, almost absurd quantity of cabbage, built a distillery, tilled the fields with a passion that bordered on the ridiculous, and spent every free moment indulging his love of hunting. He once broke his arm in a frenzied chase after a hare and wrote to his wife from Moscow where he was receiving medical treatment:

"You say that I will forget you. Not for a minute, especially when I am with other people. I am oblivious only when I am hunting, for then I think only about snipe. But when I am with people, whenever I talk with them or come into conflict with them, I think about you. . . . I love you so very much, with all kinds of love."[5]

He wrote to his friend Alexandra Andreevna Tolstaya:[6] "I have never felt as I do now my intellectual and even my entire moral prowess to be so free and so inclined to work. And I do have work to do. A novel from the time of the 1810s and 1820s, a time that has engaged me fully. . . . I am now a writer, with all the developed force of my soul, and I write and think about things in a way that I have never written or thought about them before. I am a happy and serene husband and father, who has no wishes or secrets from anyone other than everything continues as before."

This novel—*War and Peace*—also sings the praises of family happiness, of family virtues, and of simple, healthy human foundations and supports. But is it really true that during this time, he did not keep "secrets from anyone"? At this time, in his diaries, he wrote something that was very secret:

"It is terrible, awful, and absurd to tie one's happiness to material things—to a wife, children, health, farming, riches."[7]

"Where is that 'I,' that former 'I' whom I myself loved and knew, and who sometimes now emerges to meet me face-to-face, and both gladdens and frightens me? I am a small and insignificant person. And I have become such a being ever since my marriage to a woman whom I love."

This "secret" sometimes burst through in life, however. Sofya Andreevna's sister[8] writes in her memoirs about one event involving this happy husband and master:

"Sonya was sitting upstairs in her room on the floor alongside an open chest of drawers and going through some bundles of old clothes. (She was with child.) Lev Nikolaevich entered the room and said:

"'Why are you sitting on the floor? Get up!'

"'Right away, I'm just putting everything away.'

"'I said, get up now!' he shouted loudly and went off to his study.

"Sonya did not understand why he was so angry. His actions had offended her, and so she went off to his study. From my room, I heard their angry voices, but though I listened intently, I learned nothing. Suddenly I heard something falling, the crash of broken glass, and a cry:

"'Get out of here, get out of here at once, I say!'

"I opened the door, but Sonya was not there. On the floor lay a broken dish and a thermometer which had been hanging on the wall. Lev Nikolaevich was standing in the middle of the room, pale, with trembling lips. His eyes were fixed on one spot. . . . I ran off to Sonya. She looked pitiful. Just like someone who has lost her mind, she kept repeating: 'What was that all about? What's the matter with him?' Later on, she told me what had happened:

"'I went to his study and asked him: "Lyovochka, what's the matter with you?"

"'"Get out, get out of here!" he cried out hatefully.

"'I went up to him, fearful and perplexed, but he waved me off with his hand, grabbed hold of a tray with coffee and a cup, and hurled it to the floor. . . .'

"Neither Sonya nor I had the slightest inkling what had brought him to such a frenzy."[9]

"Sonya, what are we to do now?" [Tolstoy would say.] This meant: We get along way too well, we are almost too happy for comfort! But forty-eight years later, "Sonya" was living in a train car[10] on the rails alongside the station at Astapovo,[11] and she had not been allowed to see the one whom she had once asked about fireplaces and horses.[12] Leaning on the hand of one of her sons, she would walk under the covered windows behind which he lay dying and press herself up to them, trying to see even the least little bit behind the curtains. Then she would walk back to her train car, sitting there and crying over herself and "Lyovochka."[13] Later on, she would say:

"I was allowed to see him only when he was barely breathing, lying still on his back, his eyes closed. I quietly went up to his ear and tenderly told him that I hoped that he could still hear me, that I had been here at

Astapovo the entire time, and that I loved him to the very end. . . . I do not remember what else I said to him, but two deep sighs, as if called forth with terrible effort, answered my words, and then everything went still."[14]

Now the long years of married life at Yasnaya Polyana were entering their final days.

"In three days my home will be completely dead," Sofya Andreevna said. "Everyone will have left."

Ksyunin writes that this white house with its glassed-in porch and low roof had already begun to resemble a museum, and that in these now empty rooms Tolstoy's eyes still looked out and penetrated the soul. He also writes that in the study and bedroom, everything stood as frozen and untouched as the night when Tolstoy had left—a candlestick with a burned-out candle, a candle ring filled with oil, two apples, a pillow on the sofa where he would rest, a chair near the desk on which Sofya Andreevna loved to sit, a chess game, three photos of him taken at different periods in his life, and a copy of *The Circle of Reading,* which was open to November 7 (the day he died) and read: " 'Death is the beginning of another life.' Montaigne."[15]

[Ksyunin continues:] On the bed in his bedroom was his favorite cushion, which had been sewn by the nun Maria. Next, on a small table, was a bell, an ancient round clock, a candle, matches, and several boxes with medicine in them. Over the bed was a portrait of Tatyana L'vovna. One corner of the room had a sink; in the other was a small round table with a carafe of water and a saddle on the floor. On the wall were portraits—his father in a military uniform, his deceased daughter Maria, and two portraits of Sofya Andreevna. One of them showed her as quite young and remarkably good-looking. Between the windows was a mirror, and from the windows one could see a wide alley that opened out onto a garden; to the right, barely visible in the glade, was a fir tree.

This room, Ksyunin notes, had a particularly funereal look, for in it, near the bed, was a huge laurel wreath with red ribbons and an inscription that read:

"I fill the desert of life with this cry: 'I cannot remain silent.' "[16]

In the small living room alongside the study there lay open still another book—*Thoughts of Wise People for Each and Every Day:* "November 7. 'Enter by the narrow gates; for wide are the gates and vast the path that are the lot of many and lead to destruction. But narrow are the gates and small the path that are the lot of a few and lead to life.' Matthew, Chapter Seven."

In the last years of her life, Sofya Andreevna seemed tall, but she had become thin, somewhat hunchbacked, quiet, and weak. Every day she would walk the mile or so to the grave where there lay "Lyovochka," who was sleeping the sleep of the dead in a park at the edge of a ravine, under old spreading trees. Every day during the summer and fall, she would carry fresh flowers to the site, sit on the bench there for long periods of time, and perhaps remember [her husband saying,] "Sonya, what are we to do?"[17]

One of the people who visited her at that time recalled: "Sofya Andreevna met me with a tired air, but also with quiet dignity. When she spoke, she did not smile or raise her voice. And it was then that she said:

"'I lived with Lev Nikolaevich for forty-eight years, but I still did not know what kind of person he was!'"[18]

Now, when an entire quarter of a century has passed since his death, a great number of new inquiries as to "what kind of person he was" can be added to the countless testimonies about him and judgments of him—questions as to why Sofya Andreevna "walked a fine line" her entire life and what forced Tolstoy to flee his home seem completely resolved. But it only seems this way.

[Tolstoy wrote:] "I find it both terrible and strange to think that from the day I was born to the time when I turned three years old—a period when I suckled at the breast and was weaned away from it, when I first started to crawl, walk, and talk—no matter how much I search my memory, I cannot recall a single impression [of the period]. . . .

"When did I first take hold? When did I first begin to live? Why is it that in the past, I, like many people, was frightened by my impending death, but that now in the present, I experience joy whenever I imagine myself entering that condition of death which negates all those memories that can be expressed in words?

"After all, wasn't I alive then, when I learned to see, hear, understand, and speak, and when I slept, suckled, and kissed my mother's breast, and laughed and made my mother glad? Yes, I lived then, and in a very blissful way. Was it not then, at that time, that I was acquiring everything by which I now live, and was achieving everything so quickly and in such quantity that for the rest of my life I would never acquire even one percent of what I had gotten then?

"The interval from five years old to my present age is only a step; but the interval between being newly born and being five years old is a terrible expanse. The time from conception to birth is an abyss; and from nonexistence to conception is not only an abyss but something that is inscrutable.[19]

"It is not enough that space, and time, and causality are forms of thought, and that the essence of life lies outside these forms. One must also know that our life is, initially, an ever greater submission of self to these forms, and then a liberation from them."[20]

These lines are from Tolstoy's *First Memories*.[21]

Why no one, over the course of the twenty-five or so years since his death, has paid attention to these remarkable lines from *First Memories* is impossible to understand.

No one has noticed these lines from *First Memories* either:

"When I was carried downstairs to [my tutor] Fyodor Ivanovich and the other boys, I experienced for the first time, and thus more forcefully than later on, that feeling which is often called 'duty,' a cross which every person is called upon to carry. I found it sad to abandon that which was familiar (*familiar from eternity*). I also found it sad, poetically sad, to part not so much with people—my sister, my nurse, and my aunt—as with my little bed, canopy, and pillow. Terrible was that new life into which I was ushered. I tried to find something happy in the new existence that stood before me. I tried to believe in the tender speeches with which Fyodor Ivanovich tried to win me over to his side; and I tried not to see the suspicious looks with which the other boys regarded me, the youngest of them all.

"I tried to think that it was shameful for a big boy to live with girls and that there was nothing good about my life with my nurse upstairs. But my soul was terribly sad, and I knew that I had lost my innocence and joy forever. Indeed, my one support, my one feeling of worth, was the consciousness that I was doing my duty.[22]

"Later on in life, I often had to endure such moments, times when I was at a crossroads and had to step out onto new paths. Each time I would experience the quiet grief of something that had been lost forever. But even at that moment, when I was brought downstairs to Fyodor Ivanovich, I did not believe that what confronted me would be my future. . . .

"I remember the robe that they put on me had suspenders sewn in the back and that it cut me off from everything upstairs. And for the first time, I noticed not all the people with whom I had lived upstairs, but the face of a key individual whom I had also spent time with but had not known earlier. This was Aunt Tatyana Alexandrovna.[23] I remember her as ample, diminutive, black-haired, tender, and compassionate. She had been the one who had dressed me in a robe and put a belt about me, hugging and kissing me as she did so. I understood that she was feeling the same things as I, things that were necessary, but also things that she very, very much regretted. For the first time in my life, I felt that existence was not a game but a rather difficult affair. Indeed, my feelings about life were not unlike what I would later feel when I would die and leave this world, that is, I would understand that death and future life are not games but difficult affairs."

Nothing in world literature can compare to these lines.

"Submission and again liberation."

What precisely distinguishes one life from another? Is it not, in one degree or another, the extent of one's "submission" and "liberation"? An individual enters this world, and throughout his entire life he recalls the pain, pity, and sadness that he experiences on the very threshold of this "submission," his movement "downstairs" [as a child], and, in general, his passage to that certain something that lies beyond the average human memory:

"Here are my first recollections (which I cannot put in order, since I do not know which comes earlier or later, or whether some of these happened in a dream on in real life). But here they are. Someone has tied me up.[24] I want to free my hands, but I cannot. I am screaming and crying. And even though I find the sounds of my distress very unpleasant, I cannot stop. Someone is bending over me, and everything is in half-darkness. I remember that there are two such figures and that my crying worries them; but they do not do what I want and untie me, and so I cry even more loudly. The two think that I have to be tied up, but I disagree and want to show them how I am feeling. So I let out another yell, one that repulses even me, though I cannot help it. I experience the cruelty and injustice of fate, not a sense of the people who take pity on me. I also feel sorry for myself.

"I do not know and will never find out why they have done such a thing. Were they swaddling me because I was a toddler flaying my hands or because I was more than a year old and wanted to scratch my ringworm? I am not sure if I have gathered many impressions into one recollection, as often happens in a dream. But the one thing I know for sure is that being tied up was the first and most powerful impression of my life. I recall not my crying or suffering, but the complexity and contradiction of that feeling. I wanted freedom, a freedom that would not hinder anyone else. I who needed strength was weak, but they were strong. . . ."

"Someone has tied me up." The result was that he would seek to "untie himself" more and more, to rush back "from eternity to that which he had been accustomed."

"Another impression of mine is more cheerful. I was sitting in a tub and surrounded by the new and not unpleasant smell of some essence that someone was rubbing into my little body. Most likely, it was the bran that was in the water and the tub, but the novelty of this impression of bran awakened something in me. For the first time, I noticed and loved my dark smooth tub, my little body with its prominent ribs, the arms of my nurse with her rolled-up sleeves, the warm, steamy, and somewhat menacing water, its very sound, and especially the feeling of smoothness of the tub's wet edges when I passed my little hands over it. . . ."[25]

What is this all about? When people read these lines, they are surprised. "What an extraordinary memory this man had!" they say. But in no way do these terrible lines speak about memory in the usual sense of this word. If we speak about memory in the way that people usually do, there is no memory here. Indeed, no one in the world has such a memory of things, nor can he have. What is it then? Something that only people who are ultimately "regressing" are born with: "I remember that myriads of years ago I was a baby goat"; the Buddha uttered these absolutely terrible words. And what does it mean for someone to possess such a "memory"?

Soon after Tolstoy's death, I visited the tropics in India.[26] When I returned to Russia, I spent the summer on the steppelike shores of the Black Sea. And having thought and experienced several things in these Indian tropics as well as on these shores with their summer nights resonant with the vibrant sounds of steppe cicadas, I wrote:

"A certain group of people have the ability to feel strongly not only their own time, but also another, earlier time, not only their own country and their own tribe, but also other countries and tribes as well; not only themselves, but also individuals who are close to them. That is, to put it pleasantly, they have the 'ability to reincarnate themselves' through an especially lively and especially graphic (sensual) 'memory.'[27]

"To be among these individuals, one has to journey down the chain of one's ancestors, that long path of many, many existences; and suddenly realize within oneself a complete sense of one's savage ancestor with his immense consciousness, freshness of sensations, and vividness of thought; and, together with this ancestor, to return [to the present] immeasurably empowered to follow one's own long path with great consciousness.[28]

"Is such a person a great martyr or an extremely fortunate individual? Both. He encounters both the joys and the sorrows of being the harborer of an extremely powerful 'I,' which yearns to affirm itself, but which, by virtue of the rich experiences this 'I' has acquired in the great chain of existences, also has a sharpened awareness of Existence and the folly of this yearning.

"Such is the lot of poets, artists, saints, sages, the Buddha, Solomon, and Tolstoy.

"Gorillas are extremely spontaneous both in their youth and in their adult stages. Indeed, they are terrifying in their great physical strength, their immense sensitivity to the world, and the mercilessness with which they satisfy the many desires of the flesh.[29] In their old age, however, gorillas become pensive, indecisive, mournful, solemn, and sad.[30]

"How many individuals in the royal tribe of geniuses and saints are like gorillas even in their appearance! Everyone knows Tolstoy's arched eyebrows, Buddha's gigantic height and the swelling of his skull, and Mohammed's epilepsy,[31] that is, those attacks he suffered when, against a lightning-filled sky, angels revealed to him 'mysteries and unearthly abysses' and, 'in the twinkling of an eye' (that is, beyond all the laws of time and space) transported him from Medina to Jerusalem, to Mount Moriah,[32] which 'constantly swung between heaven and earth,' as if joining the two and merging the momentary and the eternal.[33]

"Such individuals receive the world first with great greediness, but later curse its temptations with equal passion. All of them are first great sinners, then great enemies of sin; they are first great acquisitors, then great spenders. They are all insatiable slaves of Maya[34]—yet, with the years, they all penetrate the meaning of Existence and of their own inevitable disappearance into it.

"There are two classes of people. The first, a large group, features people focused in the present moment, preoccupied with everyday building and deeds, people who are almost without a past or without ancestors, veritable links of the Chain about which the wisdom of India speaks. What do people in this first group care that they slip so terribly into infinity, into both the beginning and end of this Chain?

"A second, smaller group embraces not only nonbuilders and nondoers but genuine destroyers who know the vanity of action and building. These are the people of the dream, of contemplation, of wonder at themselves and the world. These are the people of that 'wisdom' which Ecclesiastes speaks about;[35] they are people who have secretly answered the ancient call—'Leave the Chain!'—they long to disappear, to dissolve into the All-One, but they still suffer fiercely and yearn for all the faces, all the incarnations with whom they have spent time, and especially for each moment of their present.

"These are people endowed with a great wealth of perception which they received from their countless ancestors, people who sense the endless distant links of the Chain, beings who (not for the last time?) reincarnate in their person all the strength and freshness of their Edenic forefather, his bodily essence.[36] Hence their great dilemma: the torture and horror of leaving the familiarity of the Chain and of coming to understand its vanity warring with their deep fascination with its folly. Each of these people can, fully and rightfully, repeat the age-old complaint: 'Eternal and All-Embracing One! You have never known Desire and Want![37] You lived in peace, but then you yourself destroyed this peace. You conceived and wove an endless Chain of transformations in which each person must forever seek to quit his body and move more closely to the Divine Beginning. Now your call to me resounds ever more loudly: Escape the Chain! Escape it without a trace, without a legacy, without an heir! Return to me!' "[38]

The Buddha was a prince in this world; not for nothing did he descend "from that clan whose pride has become legendary."[39] When it was time for the Buddha to get married, all the best and most beautiful marriageable young women were summoned from all ends of the kingdom. He wanted to choose "the best" and to be "the first" in contests of strength and skill with other men to win her hand; and he was successful in his wish. He triumphed over everyone and everything. To show his prowess, he once shot an arrow seven thousand miles. And he knew great happiness in that marriage and in his son,[40] the most splendid child in the world.

But then three visits to the city and three encounters there darkened all his joys, for he saw things in this world that he had not known before: illness, old age, and death.[41] And in his heart, he decided to leave his wife and son, to free himself from the "silk nets"[42] of the earth, and to escape his home and the world. "Domestic life is confining," he said to himself. "Home is a place of filth, and freedom lies outside of it! I will not return to the world, for I never knew it before!"

On a stormy night, after he had reached a great river and crossed into complete isolation from the world, the prince got down from his horse, took off his wealthy clothes, and cut his long hair—a mark of his nobleman's status. Having given his horse to the stableboy who had accompanied him to the river, he set out to seek "sacred salvation." He encountered many teachings which turned out to be false, and he endured many self-inflicted trials which did not lead to knowledge. When he reached the end of these tribulations, however, he became enlightened in the groves of Uruvela. There he came upon a sudden and splendid insight; that is, he grasped the nature of genuine liberation, of deliverance from the sufferings of this world, and of salvation from mortal perdition. And his teachings sounded forth "like a silver bell, hung from the vault of heaven."

"Listen with open ears: Liberation (salvation, deliverance) from death has been found!"

He proclaimed the good news, adhering closely to sacred ancient wisdom that says:

"The kingdom of this world and the kingdom of death are one and the same; for the Tempter, Mara, is also death."

"Liberation is the spirit's casting off of its physical covering."

"Liberation is self-renunciation."

"Liberation is the penetration of the spirit into the one, truthful existence. It is also Brahma-Atman, the basis of all life and the true essence of the human spirit. Brahma is the genuine 'I' in all humans; it is the Atman, the One, the Whole, and the Eternal that exists in the darkness of the flesh."

"Liberation is the striving for Atman, for that condition which is like sleep, but without dream or desires."

"The human 'I' is the earthly incarnation of Atman, its manifestation in the world."

"Liberated and saved are those who know Atman to the end, and who return to it, without any wish for posterity."

Chapter Six

I BEGAN TO DREAM about the good fortune of meeting Tolstoy at a very early age.

Even as a boy, I already had some notion of who he was—not from his books, but from the conversations in our home. I remember how my father would laugh whenever he would tell us about how our gentry neighbors would read *War and Peace*. One would read only *War;* the other, only *Peace.* The one who read only the "war" parts would skip over anything having to do with peace; the one who read only about "peace" would skip over the parts on war. Even at that time, though, my feelings for Tolstoy were not simple. My father, who like Tolstoy took part in the defense of Sevastopol, told me: "I knew him somewhat. I met him during the Sevastopol campaign."[1] When I heard this, I looked at him with wide-open eyes: My father had seen Tolstoy in person!

During my adolescent years, I was completely in love with Tolstoy, with an image that I had conjured up in my mind and that tormented me with the desire to see him in the flesh.[2] My dream was persistent, but how was I going to make it come true? Should I go to Yasnaya Polyana? And what would be my reason? I could just imagine the people there asking, "And what can I do for you, young man?" And what would I give as an answer?

But one time I could not restrain myself any longer. On a beautiful summer day, I suddenly ordered my "Kirghiz" to be saddled, and off I went to Efremov,[3] a provincial city in the Tula province, no more than a hundred miles from Yasnaya Polyana. When I reached Efremov, however, I was seized with fright and decided to think a bit more seriously about what I was doing. So I spent the night there; but, instead of going to sleep, I kept changing my mind—should I go to Yasnaya Polyana or not? I wandered through the city the entire night, and I got so tired that when I entered the municipal garden at dawn, I fell asleep on the first bench that I came to. When I woke up, my mind had become completely clear. I thought about things a bit more and rode back home.[4]

Later on, I passionately dreamed about a life that was fresh, clean, healthy, and "good," a life amidst nature, and I was dressed in simple clothes that I had made with my own hands. I had fallen in love with Tolstoy as an artist, so I became one of his followers, a Tolstoyan. I did this, of course, with the secret hope that such an action would give me a pretext to see him and even, perhaps, to enter into the circle of those who were closest to him. So began my Tolstoyan "obedience."

At that time I was living in Poltava,[5] where, for some reason, there were a number of Tolstoyans to whom I quickly drew close. It was here that I learned what most of Tolstoy's followers were really like. With some exceptions, the Tolstoyans in Poltava were an absolutely unbearable lot.

I met Chertkov, "his very self." He was a tall, large-built, noble-looking individual with a small, very proud head; a cold, arrogant face; a tiny, hawk-like, well-shaped nose; and similarly predatory-looking eyes.

[Tolstoy's wife, Sofya Andreevna, also did not care for Tolstoyans, in part because] she was artistically talented, her giftedness being either inborn or drawn from her association with Tolstoy, with whom she had spent three-quarters of her life. Sofya Andreevna often spoke with keen powers of observation. She once said about a revolutionary who had visited Yasnaya Polyana: "He came, sat down, and remained seated. He was stubbornly silent, with a lifeless face, very black hair, blue glasses, and a skewed eye."[6] She used to refer to Chertkov as a "graven image." I saw him only once or twice, but I could never figure out precisely what kind of man he was. But the impression he made was indeed that of a "graven image."[7] The following recollection of Alexandra L'vovna supports this view:

"How happy Father looked whenever he left his study after a day of successful writing! His walk was cheerful and light, his face was happy, and his eyes had a merry air.[8] Sometimes, he would turn around on the heel of his shoe, or quickly and lightly bend his leg over the back of a chair. In my view, any self-respecting Tolstoyan would have been horrified by his teacher's behavior. But Father did not get away with such playfulness. For instance, one time we were eating supper on the porch. The 'chairman's place,' as we used to call it, was occupied by Mama. Father was to her right, and Chertkov was sitting next to him. It was hot, and the mosquitoes were not giving us any peace. They were flying in the air, buzzing in a loud and obnoxious way, and stinging our faces, arms, and legs.

"Father was talking to Chertkov, and the rest of us were listening. The atmosphere was animated, joyful, and filled with witticisms and laughter. Suddenly, Father looked at Chertkov's face and hit him with a quick, skillful movement right on his bald spot. A bloody spot appeared—the remains of a fat mosquito. Everyone burst out laughing, including Father. But suddenly the laughter stopped. Chertkov, his handsome brows gloomily knit, looked at Father with reproach:

"'What have you done?' he mumbled. 'What have you done, Lev Nikolaevich! You have deprived a living creature of life! How can you not be ashamed of yourself!'[9]

"Father was embarrassed. Everyone else felt awkward."

The first person whom I got to know in Poltava was an individual by the name of Klopsky.[10] At that time, Klopsky was rather well known among Tolstoy's followers, so much so that he was a model for the hero in Karonin's story "The Teacher of Life,"[11] which created quite a stir at the time. Klopsky was a tall, slender man who had a broad, gray face and turquoise eyes, and who wore tall boots and a blouse.[12] He was a cunning scoundrel and rogue. He was also a tireless chatterbox who sought to teach and admonish anyone who fell in his path, and who loved to impress people with his bold antics and insolence. Not surprisingly, such behavior allowed him to roam from city to city in a rather merry and fruitful way.

The Poltava doctor, Alexander Alexandrovich Volkenshtein, was also a Tolstoyan. By breeding and background, he was a *barin* in the grand style, somewhat like Stiva Oblonsky in *Anna Karenina*.[13] When Klopsky came to Poltava, the first thing he did was to look up Volkenshtein, and, through him, he very quickly gained access to Poltava's salons, where Volkenshtein introduced him as a preacher for "ideological" reasons and, for simple amusement, as a curiosity item. For instance, Klopsky would say things like:

"Yes, yes, I see how you live. You lie, you gorge yourself on candy, and you worship idols in churches that should have been blown up a long time ago! Oh, when will all these absurdities cease? Who will put an end to this sea of abominations that are engulfing the world? For instance, I was on my way here from Kharkov. Well, here comes this guy who for some reason is called conductor and who says to me:

"'Your ticket.'

"I answered him: 'Ticket? What ticket? Just precisely what do you mean by the word "ticket"?'

"He replied: 'You know, the thing that lets you travel on this train.'

"But I responded: 'Allow me to state that I am traveling on this train not because of a ticket but because of the rails of this track.'

"'Does that mean that you're saying you do not have a ticket?'

"'That's what I have been trying to tell you. Of course, I don't have one.'

"'Well, in that case, we'll have to let you out at the next station.'

"'Fine,' I told him, 'that's your business, but it's my business to keep on traveling.'

"We got to the station, and he told me: 'Please get off.'

"'But why should I get off?' I said. 'I'm doing just fine as I am.'

"'Then we'll have to take you off.'

"'Take me off? But I'm going nowhere.'

"'Then we'll drag you off, we'll carry you out, if we have to.'

"'Well, carry me out then. That's your business.'

"And that's what they did. They really did drag me out. To the surprise of the entire honored public, I was carried out by two grown peasant-idlers who could have spent their time more profitably by plowing the land."

That was Klopsky. The others were different, but also just as good. There were the brothers D.,[14] who farmed land around Poltava. Although they looked humble, they were, in fact, very boring, dumb, and insecure. There was also a certain Leontiev, a small and puny young individual, who exhibited a rare, if sickly, type of beauty. Leontiev had been a former court page who tormented himself by doing peasant labor and by lying to himself and others that he was happy doing such work.[15]

There was also a huge Jew, who looked like the classic Russian peasant and who later became well known as the journalist Teneremo. Teneremo always treated simple mortals with unusual arrogance and condescension. He was an unbearable rhetorician and a sophist who earned a living as a cooper. It was Teneremo to whom I first turned as a Tolstoyan. He was my teacher both in "religious instruction" and in the ways of manual labor. I was his apprentice, and from him I learned how to bind a barrel with hoops. Why did I need those hoops? Again because they somehow joined me to Tolstoy and gave me the secret hope that I might see him someday and come into close contact with him.[16]

To my great delight, this hope came true quite unexpectedly. Soon after I had joined the Tolstoyans, all the "brethren" regarded me as one of their own; and Volkenshtein—all this happened at the very end of 1893— suddenly invited me to go with him first to stop in at the "brothers" of the Kharkov province,[17] to the peasants of the village of Khilkovo, which belonged to the well-known Tolstoyan Prince Khilkov,[18] and then on to Moscow, to visit Tolstoy himself.

The journey was difficult. We went third class[19] and had to change trains, always trying to get seats that were designated for the "common people." We ate things that "had not been killed," that is, God-knows-what, although Volkenshtein sometimes could not resist temptation and would suddenly run off to the buffet, where he would greedily gulp down two or three shots of vodka and snack on meat pies, which were so hot they burned his hands. He would then tell me in an extremely serious way:

"I have again succumbed to my cravings and am suffering greatly for my weakness. But, just the same, I continue to struggle with myself, for I know that the meat pies do not control me, but I control them. I am not their slave, and I eat them or do not eat them, as I want to."

The most difficult thing about my journey, though, was that while I burned with impatience and the desire to get to Moscow as soon as possible, we had to take slow-moving trains, not quick, express ones. We also had to live for awhile with the "brothers" at Khilkovo and to enter into a personal relationship with them so as to "strengthen" both ourselves and them to continue on the road of the "good" life. And this is just what we did. I think that we stayed with peasants from Khilkovo for three or four days; during that time, I began to hate all those rich, pious, and externally handsome louts with every fiber of my being. I hated sleeping in their houses, their potato pies, their singing of the psalms, their stories about their fierce and constant struggle with "bosses and priests," and their pedantic arguments about the Bible.[20]

Finally, on January 1, we moved on. I remember that I woke up in such a state of delight that I forgot where I was and said: "Happy New Year, Alexander Alexandrovich!" For that indiscretion, Alexander Alexandrovich gave me a severe scolding. "What does 'Happy New Year' mean?" he asked me. "Did you not understand what nonsense you were repeating?" But I was too preoccupied with other things. I kept listening and thinking: "All right, all right, this is all nonsense, but tomorrow evening we will be in Moscow, and the day after that I will see Tolstoy." And that is indeed what happened.

But Volkenshtein hurt me deeply. He went to see Tolstoy the very minute after we got to our hotel in Moscow, but he did not take me with him. "You cannot come now, you cannot come now," he told me. "I have to notify Lev Nikolaevich. I have to tell him about you. I have to tell him that you have come." And he left immediately. He returned home late that night and told me nothing about his visit other than to say to me hurriedly: "It is as if I have drunk my fill of living water!" But from the smell that was coming from him, I had no doubt that, after having drunk some "living water," he also had partaken of some Chambertin—probably to show that he was not Chambertin's slave but just the reverse. The only good thing about his return was that he had, in fact, informed Tolstoy that I was here, even though I had no great hope that anything would come of this. After all, Volkenshtein was a very flighty fellow who was also slightly womanish, an ample, handsome brunette. But I was wrong. That following evening, beside myself with excitement, I finally rushed over to Khamovniki.[21]

How should I tell you what happened next?

It was a frosty, moonlit night. I ran all the way; but once I got there, I stood for a moment, barely catching my breath. All around was backwoods and quiet, an empty moonlit alley. In front of me were the gates, an open carriage, and a snowy yard. In the distance, to the left, was a wooden home, with several windows lighted with a reddish color. Still further to the left, behind the house, was a garden, and above it were charming, fairy-tale-like winter stars with varicolored rays that played lightly in the night. Truly, everything about the place was like a fairy tale. What a special garden, what an unusual home! How mysterious and pregnant with meaning were these lighted windows. After all, behind them was—He!

It was so quiet that I could hear only my heart beating both from joy and from a paralyzing thought: Would it not be better for me to take a quick look at this house and then to run away to where I had come from!

In anguish, I finally headed for the courtyard, to the porch of the house, and rang the bell. All of a sudden, the door opened, and I saw a servant in a shabby-looking tailcoat framed against a lighted hallway, which was warm and comfortable, where various kinds of fur coats were hanging on a coatrack. Among these there was an old, knee-length sheepskin coat that stood out sharply from the rest. Immediately before me was a circular staircase covered with red cloth. Underneath it, on the right, was a locked door behind which one could hear the sounds of guitars and merry young voices, which seemed markedly heedless of the fact that they were making so much racket in such an absolutely unusual home.

"Whom should I say is calling?" the servant asked.

"Bunin."

"How's that again, sir?"

"Bunin."

"I will inform the master, sir."

The servant ran upstairs, and, to my surprise, he immediately came running back down, skipping sideways, his hand constantly grabbing the handrail.

"Please wait upstairs, in the hall."

When I got to the hall, I was even more surprised. I did not have to wait at all. Indeed, I had barely entered when immediately in the distance, over to the left, a small door opened, and out stepped a man who walked with a clumsy gait, huge, with a gray beard, and slightly bowlegged. He was wearing blunt-nosed shoes, a wide, baggy blouse made from gray fustian, and trousers made from the same material but fashioned somewhat like harem pants.[22] He was quick, deft, piercing, and sharp eyed, with knitted eyebrows.[23] He immediately headed my way, and I noticed immediately that the way he walked and his entire bearing were somehow like that of my father. He came up to me quickly and, bowing a bit, extended—more accurately, thrust out—his big hand with the palm up. He then took my hand into his, shook it gently, and suddenly smiled a charming smile, tender but also slightly sad. I saw that his small gray-blue eyes were not at all terrible or sharp, but that they were bright, like those of an animal. The thin, light hair that remained on his head was gray and slightly curled at the ends and parted straight in the middle, peasant-style. His very large ears were unusually high on his head, and the arches of his eyebrows hung down low over his eyes. His beard was dry, thin, uneven, and transparent, allowing one to see his slightly protruding jaw.

"So you are Bunin?" he said. "Was it your father whom I ran across in the Crimea? Are you planning to stay in Moscow for a long time? Why have you come here? To visit me? So, you're a young writer? Write, write, but only if you really want to. Just remember that such a thing can in no way be the purpose of your life. . . . Sit down, please, and tell me about yourself."

He began speaking, as hurriedly as he had moved when he entered, but he immediately pretended not to notice my confusion, and he hastened to distract me and put me at ease.

What else did he say?

He kept asking:

"Are you single? Married? You can live with a woman only if she is your wife, and you must never leave her.[24] . . . Do you want to live a simple, hardworking life? That is good, only do not force yourself to do so. Do not make a dress uniform out of it, for one can be a good person in any walk of life."

We were sitting next to a small table. A rather tall ancient stoneware lamp burned softly under a rose-colored lampshade. The lamp hid his face, and in the light shadow I saw only the soft gray fabric of his blouse and his large hand, which I wanted to hold with all the enthusiastic tenderness of a devoted son. I also heard his elderly, slightly deep voice, which seemed to come from his somewhat protruding jaw.

Suddenly I heard the rustling sounds of silk. I looked up in surprise, shuddered, and stood up. From the dining room there seemingly floated by a large and elegant lady with black hair and lively, completely dark eyes, wearing a glistening black silk dress.[25]

"Leon," she said. "You've forgotten that people are waiting for you."

He also stood up and, excusing himself with what seemed to be a guilty smile, looked straight at me with his small eyes, which still seemed somewhat dark and sad. He again took my hand into his and said:

"Well, good-bye, good-bye. God grant that you come and see me again the next time you are in Moscow. . . . Do not expect much from life, for there is no better time in life than the one you are living now. . . . There is no happiness in life, only flashes of happiness—value them, live for them."[26]

I left. I ran back to where I had been staying and there spent an absolutely insane night, constantly seeing him in a dream, first with striking clarity and then in some confused muddle.

When I returned to Poltava, I wrote to him and received several kind letters in reply. In one of them, he informed me that it was not worth my while to be a Tolstoyan, but I continued on just the same. I quit making hoops and began selling books published by Mediator, Tolstoy's publishing house in Moscow,[27] and even opened up a branch of it in Poltava.[28] Yes, no matter how strange it sounds, I once used to sell books. I had this small shop in Poltava, which smelled wonderfully of new wooden shelves and of equally new books and brochures. I even had a sign over the entrance that said "Bunin's Bookstore." At that time, I also worked as a librarian for the Poltava *zemstvo*,[29] sitting in a vaulted basement hall with deep windows, from which I would look out onto an old garden that belonged to the local government there. There, alone in the silence, I would read, write poems, and, for a time, work on a compilation of essays which the statistical bureau had ordered me to write (on ways to harvest wheat and grain and to battle harmful insects). Incidentally, I wrote so many of these essays while I was at the *zemstvo* that, if they were to be collected now and added to editions of my works, three or four more volumes would suddenly appear.

That was how I spent my time before lunch. After lunch, I would go off to my bookstore and wait for customers who thirsted for Tolstoy's enlightenment. But no one came. So I sought to spread this enlightenment by giving out several of Mediator's free brochures to the *zemstvo* doorkeepers. When nothing came of this either—for example, after I had given one doorkeeper a brochure on the perils of smoking, he told me that he had immediately used it to wrap around shag and make cigarettes—I decided on a bolder course of action. Taking advantage of the freedom which my job afforded me, I began to travel throughout the province to sell publications by Mediator at fairs and markets. One time, though, I was detained by a police officer and charged with "violating the law, i.e, selling books without permission," which resulted in a court hearing. The verdict was quite severe: I was sentenced to three months in jail. I was happy finally to "suffer" for my beliefs, but even here I failed: I did not go to jail, since an amnesty had been declared with the ascension of a new emperor to the throne.[30] I was thus spared any suffering.

I gave up my store. Despite the small number of sales, I had so messed up my accounts that I often thought about committing suicide from helplessness and shame. Instead, I moved to Moscow. But even there I tried to assure myself that I was a colleague and sympathizer of the leaders of Mediator as well as of those people who constantly hung around its premises and regularly instructed each other in the "virtuous life."[31]

It was in Moscow, though, that I saw Tolstoy several times more. He would sometimes go to the headquarters of Mediator—more accurately, he would run there (for he was agile and quick). Without taking off his sheepskin coat, he would sit for an hour or two, surrounded on all sides by "brothers," who tended to ask him questions like these:

"Lev Nikolaevich, if a tiger attacked me, what should I do? Would I have to kill it?"

In such cases, he would smile in a confused way.

"A tiger? What tiger? Where would it come from? I've never seen a single tiger in my entire life."[32]

At that time, I did not know nor had I met any of Tolstoy's sons. But I did meet his daughters. One evening, I found him at Mediator with all three of his daughters: Tanya [Tatyana], who was the eldest; Masha [Maria], the middle one; and Sasha [Alexandra], the youngest. He was sitting along-side a large wooden table which took up the middle of the room and which was lit from above by a hanging lamp. Shivering from the cold, he had drawn his hands up into the sleeves of his old, worn sheepskin coat, placing them on the table. He had a slight frown on his face, as he listened to the members of Mediator surrounding him.

Two stood out amidst the crowd. One was a somewhat small individual with broad shoulders and wide cheekbones who looked like a country schoolteacher. He was dressed in felt boots and a gray blouse, and he had a sharp, insane look behind his glasses. The other was a tall, handsome, well-built, but passionately morose-looking type with blue-black hair and an ab-solutely wild, ecstatic expression on his thin, swarthy face.

Tolstoy's daughters were sitting on a couch in the corner of the room and watching attentively with shining young eyes. When I sat down at the table, they began looking at me with curiosity, whispering something to each other and laughing. They fixed their eyes on me in a lively and amused way, each mumbling something to the other and bursting out with laughter. I did not understand: What was going on? What did they find that was so funny about me?

I started to blush, pretending that I had not noticed them, when Tol-stoy suddenly looked at me, smiled a merry smile, and, without turning his head, shouted to his daughters in feigned, severe way:

"Quit laughing!"[33]

I also remember that I once tried to say something pleasant and even slightly flattering by telling him:

"Sobriety societies[34] are popping up everywhere nowadays."

He frowned:

"What kind of societies?"

"Sobriety societies."

"Do you mean to tell me that people come together not to drink vodka? This is nonsense. If people cannot drink, there is no reason for them to come together. And if they do gather, they have to drink. Everything is nonsense, lies, no action. People only appear to do things."[35]

I visited Tolstoy's home only once more after that. I was shown the way first into the room where I had first sat with him alongside that dear rose-colored lamp and then through a single little door, up some stairs, and finally through a narrow corridor, where I shyly knocked on a door to the right.

"Come in," answered a deep elderly voice.

I entered and saw a low, small room that was sunk in darkness. A metal shield hung over two candles in an ancient candlestick that stood on a table. Alongside the table was a leather sofa where Tolstoy himself sat with a book in his hands. Seeing me enter the room, he got up quickly and awkwardly—or so it seemed to me—and with a confused air threw the book in the corner of the couch. But my eyes were sharp, and I saw that he had been reading, or more accurately rereading (and apparently not for the first time, as we writers, sinful people that we are, are wont to do), one of his recently published works, *Master and Man*.[36] In my excitement, I tactlessly cried out with delight, but he turned red and waved his hands, saying: "Oh, let's not talk about this! It's a horrible thing; it's so worthless that I am ashamed even to go out on the street!"

On that evening his face was thin, dark, and severe. His seven-year-old Kolya had died only a short time before;[37] so, after disavowing *Master and Man*, he began to talk about his son.

"Yes, yes, he was a dear, charming boy. But what does it mean that he is dead? There is no death. As long as we continue to love him, to live for him, he has not died!"

We soon left the house and went off to Mediator. It was a dark March night, and a spring wind was blowing and making the streetlights brighter. We ran through the snow-covered Maiden's Field.[38] I could hardly keep up with the way he was jumping over the ditches. Again he said abruptly, severely, and sharply:

"There is no death, there is no death!"

Several years later, I saw him once again. On a terribly cold evening in Moscow, I was walking along the Arbat,[39] illumined by the lights coming from the frosted, shining windows of the stores. I bumped into him suddenly, for he, with his springing gait, happened to be heading right for me. I stopped and took off my hat. He recognized me immediately:

"Oh, so it is you! Hello, hello. Put your hat back on, please. . . . Well, so how are you, what have you been doing, where have you been, and what are you up to now?"

His old face was so frost-nipped and blue that it looked absolutely pathetic.[40] Something like an old lady's hat made from blue fox fur was perched on his head, and his huge hand, which he took out of his fox glove, was completely frozen. Having spoken to me for awhile, he shook my hand firmly but kindly. He looked sadly into my eyes, and with raised brows he said:

"Well, Christ be with you. Christ be with you. Good-bye."[41]

Chapter Seven

I DO NOT RECALL PRECISELY what year it was when I saw Tolstoy on the Arbat in Moscow on that winter evening.[1] I also do not remember what we talked about. I recall only that, during our short conversation, he asked me if I was writing anything. I answered:

"No, Lev Nikolaevich. I am hardly writing at all. And everything that I have written now seems so bad that it would be better not even to think about it."

He suddenly became alive and said:

"Oh, yes, yes. How well I know that feeling!"

"And, besides, there is nothing to write," I added.

He looked at me somewhat indecisively; then, as if remembering something, he said:

"How can there be nothing to write about? If there is nothing to write about, then write that you have nothing to write about and describe why. Think precisely about the why and write about it. Yes, yes, try to do that," he said firmly.[2]

That was the last time I saw him. I often told myself that I had to see him again without fail, but I knew that he was not long for this world. I kept putting off trying to arrange a meeting with him, thinking, "What am I to him?" I was in Saint Petersburg when the news arrived that he had died. I immediately thought, "Should I go and see him one last time, even if he is in a coffin?" But an inexplicable feeling kept me from doing so. I felt that it was something that I should not do.

I returned quickly to Moscow, where Tolstoy was the only topic of conversation. The people who had been at his funeral kept saying: "What a grand, wonderful, tremendous sight it was, an event that truly belonged to the people, despite all the efforts of the government to prevent it from happening."[3] They talked about how his remains were taken from the station at Astapovo to Kozlova Zaseka[4] and how a huge crowd carried and accompanied the coffin through the fields to Yasnaya Polyana. I was happy that I had been spared seeing how he had been buried by "grateful peasants," "student youth," and "all the Russian progressive intelligentsia"—societal figures, lawyers, doctors, and journalists.[5] These people were alien to him; they admired him only for his opposition to the government and to the church. At his funeral, they even experienced happiness in the depths of their souls. That is, they experienced that theatrical ecstasy which seizes the "progressive" crowd at all "civic" funerals, a euphoria generated by a certain revolutionary allure and accompanied by a joyous consciousness that, for the moment, the police are powerless to do anything and that the more of them who enter into the "huge social surge" the better.[6]

During those days, we received precise information from Tolstoy's eldest son, Sergei L'vovich, who, though a permanent resident in Moscow, had just returned from Yasnaya Polyana. He told us clearly why "Lev Niko-laevich's cup of patience had overflowed," and he described how his father had escaped from his home. Later accounts of the last days of Tolstoy's life corresponded to what Sergei L'vovich repeated from Alexandra L'vovna. Listening to Sergei, I let my imagination relive every minute of that recent night of October 27, since Tolstoy had died only two weeks earlier.

At that time, people said what is common knowledge now: Tolstoy had run away because, during the last year of his life, he had been especially tormented by his wife and several of his sons, who believed rumors that he had written a last will and testament in which he had refused all authorial rights to his works. The consensus was that Sofya Andreevna, with maniacal persistence, had been trying to find out whether such a will actually existed. For a long time, she had felt that something secret was going on around her and that Lev Nikolaevich and Alexandra L'vovna had been carrying on some clandestine business. Specifically, she feared that her husband and daughter had entered into written and oral negotiations with Chertkov and his assistants, and had been concealing from her several papers and new diaries of Lev Nikolaevich's. It had become an obsession, therefore, for her to watch him and to search the house for these papers and diaries.

On the night of October 27, Sergei L'vovich told me, Alexandra L'vovna was awakened by Tolstoy's light knocking at the door. She heard his hesitant voice: "Sasha, I am leaving now." He was standing there in his gray shirt, a candle in his hand. His face ("rose-colored") was "bright, splendid, and full of determination." Sergei L'vovich added that his father was shaking all over but, with the help of Alexandra L'vovna, was packing for the road in a haphazard way. "Take only things that are the most essential, Sasha, pens and pencils, and no medicine!" His hands kept jerking as he tightened the belt about his suitcase. Then he ran to the stable to wake up the hired hands and to order that horses be harnessed. The night was cold, damp, and impenetrable, however; so he lost his way in the dark, ran into some bushes, lost his hat, and almost poked his eyes out. He came back into the house, put on another hat, and headed again for the stable; but this time he lighted the way with an electric light. He tried to help harness the horses; but, trembling more and more from the fear that Sofya Andreevna might wake up at any moment, he could barely put the bridle on the horse. He felt very weak. He gave up helping the hired hands and went to a corner in the carriage barn that was dimly lit by the light of a candle end. Here, completely exhausted, he sat down in the half-darkness. On that night he wore an old knit hat—perhaps it was the very same one that I saw him wearing on the Arbat—along with an old tight-fitting blue coat, old knit gloves, and old rubber boots. But on his deathbed on November 7, he was wearing a gray flannel shirt, gray pants, gray woolen stockings, and bedroom slippers.

At that time, I found it horrible to read the newspaper stories with their vulgar solemnity:

"At 10 o'clock on November 7, anyone who wanted to say good-bye to Tolstoy was allowed into the room where the body of the great old man was lying.[7] Railway workers placed juniper branches about his coffin, and laid the first wreath with this touching inscription: 'To the Apostle of Love.'[8] Then peasants from the neighboring districts and the village schoolchildren came. Many parents brought their children with them so that they could see and remember forever the face of the great defender of workers and the downtrodden."

"The first civil service was organized at noon. The crowd sang 'Eternal Memory.'"[9]

"On the following day, the coffin was put on a cargo car, decorated with pine branches and straw wreaths. The train, crowded with relatives, close friends and admirers, and representatives of the press and of social organizations, slowly moved forward."

Of this event, the poet Bryusov wrote in the newspaper *Russian News:*[10] "The journalist Popov and I arrived at Yasnaya Polyana on the day of the funeral, and we went to the estate on foot. . . . Here was the fruit orchard which Tolstoy had planted; there was the covered alley where he liked to sit and rest; and still further on was the grove where a grave had been dug for him. . . . Off in the distance was the typical estate of a country nobleman, a simple two-story building. . . . In the yard were crowds of people, university students, high-school girls, and photographers. . . . Police constables and Cossacks on horseback were stationed in the park. . . . Somewhere off in the distance one could hear the choral singing of the approaching procession:

"'They are bringing him!'

"The procession came closer. In the front were peasants, carrying a banner which was held up by sticks and which read: 'Lev Nikolaevich, to the memory of the many kindnesses that you rendered us and which we will never forget. Your orphaned peasants at Yasnaya Polyana.' Behind them was carried the open coffin of simple oak. Further on were three carts laden with wreaths."

Of the events later that day, Bryusov wrote: "The doors of the house were again opened at dusk. The coffin was carried out, slowly and quietly; his sons were carrying him.[11]

"Someone began singing 'Eternal Memory,' and the entire crowd joined in, even those who had never sung in their lives. In that moment, this chorus was Russia itself.

"'On your knees!' someone said.

"And everyone who was on the way to the grave kneeled down."

This Popov whom Bryusov referred to in his account was an acquaintance of mine; and when he returned to Moscow, he told me more about this "grand spectacle." An individual named Myortvago, who also had traveled to Yasnaya Polyana, told me still more. For instance, the evening after the funeral, Myortvago sat down with some peasants from Yasnaya Polyana, who asked:

"'Well, now here we carried that very banner. What do you think? Will we get some kind of reward from our boss or from the countess? We tried so hard—all day long on our feet! And we spent money on a wreath, too.'

Popov was very deeply disturbed by the way the peasants had acted. [He thought:] Just think how the deceased treated his peasants throughout his entire life, how many good things he did on their behalf! Had they already forgotten that, some sixty years ago and before the government had liberated peasants from serfdom, the young Count Tolstoy had offered them their freedom and that they had not trusted that his motive could be disinterested?[12]

Nothing had changed since then. But Myortvago, an old landlord who knew the peasants well, merely chuckled. He described how one peasant from Yasnaya Polyana spoke about Tolstoy in such a bilious way:

"'Yes, the deceased was a good landlord, all right! "Everything," he would say, "is no longer mine, because I have already given it all to my wife and children. After all, I do not need it, I love the working people." . . . And if anyone would be out at dawn, he'd be rushing up and down through the dew, to the very edge of his forest. With his eyes darting about, he would ask: "Do you know where any trees are being cut?"'

"I tried shaming the peasant," Myortvago said, "trying to convince him that Tolstoy walked through the forest in the early morning for his health. But it was no use. The peasant held his ground. 'We know what kind of health he had! No, his landowner's eyes were sharp!'"[13]

Tolstoy's flight from Yasnaya Polyana, his death at a remote railway station, and his "civil" funeral reinstated him with "progressive" Russian society and elicited endless opinions about him.

54

When I was very young, people spoke a great deal about Tolstoy, but differently from the way they do now. Then everyone was struck by the fact that he was a count, an aristocrat, a rich man, and a famous novelist who had suddenly put on peasant clothing and had begun to plow, make stoves and shoes, and attend to his own needs. They were struck, however, by *The Kreutzer Sonata* and especially by the "Afterword,"[14] in which a man who had fathered thirteen children rose up against conjugal love[15] and even against the continuation of the human race itself. They said that *The Kreutzer Sonata* could best be explained by the fact that Tolstoy was old and that he "hated his wife."[16]

Teneremo told me what Tolstoy had supposedly said to him:

"I hate Sofya Andreevna and all women! When I die, they will put me in a coffin and close the lid; but I will get up, throw it off, and shout at Sofya Andreevna, 'I hate you!'"

An individual named Lazursky, who later became a professor at Novorossisk University,[17] lived for a time with the Tolstoy family as a tutor to the children.[18] He told me how once Sofya Andreevna was talking to him about *The Kreutzer Sonata*, when Tolstoy suddenly walked into the room.

"What were you talking about?" he asked. "About love, about marriage? Marriage is death. A man walks alone for awhile, lightly, freely; but then he ties his leg to that of a woman."[19]

Sofya Andreevna asked:

"Then why did you get married?"

"I was stupid. I thought differently then."

"But it's always like that with you. Today you think one thing; tomorrow, another. You always keep changing your beliefs."[20]

"Every person has to change his beliefs to keep finding better ones. People come together in marriage only to annoy each other. Two strangers meet and remain strangers to each other throughout their entire life. People say that a husband and wife go down parallel lines. Nonsense. These lines intersect; but as soon as they do, they go off in different directions."

In their discussions about Tolstoy, people carried on endless, heated conversations about his sermons on "passivity" and "nonactive resistance to evil."[21] Those who opposed all existing governmental systems in Russia, and who argued for political and social struggles for "the good of the people" as well as for a new type of government, saw Tolstoy as a dangerous enemy because of the influence his name had. In their view, it was untimely for "his excellency" to preach nonactivity and nonresistance, and to "withdraw to his cell under the pine tree" to save sinful souls from all types of worldly deeds and temptations! Moreover, he pontificated on saintly poverty and "nonactivity" while wearing *lapty*,[22] living in a luxurious house, and eating from the hands of a white-gloved servant! Such activist critics were on Tolstoy's side only when he was "indicting" someone or something.

Others hated him when he did speak out. They criticized his struggle with the clergy and his "mocking" of the church's time-honored understanding of Christianity. Everyone told the same stories about his "eccentricities," harshness, absurd and crude opinions and beliefs, passionate temper which he seemed unable to keep under control, and the weaknesses and contradictions that were inherent in his nature.[23] They would say:

"Who else, more than he, could condemn over and over again the arrogant, the proud, the ambitious, the high-strung, the self-assured, and the self-confident? Why, he had more of these faults than anyone else around. He gorged himself and indulged in all kinds of vices and passions, in his devil-like pride!"[24]

"I heard a great deal about him in my youth," Lopatina told me. "I well remember the gray wooden home with its big old garden alongside Maiden's Field, the residence of Count Lev Nikolaeivch Tolstoy on Khamovnichesky Lane, dubbed Khamovniki. People would talk a great deal about this house and its owner, and about what Lev Nikolaevich called its 'dark people,' local disciples who would show up there in blouses and shoes— more accurately slippers, since they did not wear the 'skin of slaughtered animals.' These 'people' would sit quietly in the corners of the room, looking at guests of Tolstoy with an air of challenge and condemnation. They were gloomy, unsociable, and terrible to behold, if only because of their shaggy beards and hair. (People called them 'fir trees.')[25]

"At that time, there was not a household in Moscow which did not discuss Tolstoy's sermons and quarrel over their meaning. They took note, too, of how he, in his winter coat, with his gray beard, hard and intelligent eyes, and bushy eyebrows, would first run here, then there, along the streets and alleys of Moscow, sometimes pulling a barrel of water on a sledge covered with ice. . . .[26]

"I always recall his relationship with Vladimir Solovyov.

"Everyone knew that Lev Nikolaevich did not like Solovyov and that Solovyov did not show Tolstoy any special deference, either. When people in Moscow were reading Tolstoy's manuscript *What I Believe,* Solovyev wrote to Professor Kareev:

"'Lev Tolstoy is trying to publish his new book, entitled *What I Believe.* One of my friends read the proofs for it and told me that he had never read a more impudent and stupid thing in his life. Essentially, the book is a bitter diatribe against the church, the government, and the social order. It also attacks the immortality of the soul—all in the name of the Gospel. For instance, the Apostle Paul is called a "half-crazy slavedriver, who completely distorted Christianity." Of course, publication will be forbidden. Such an action will not prevent it from being circulated among the public, though; but its prohibition will preclude the possibility of it being denounced in the press.'[27]

"Solovyov also took exception with N. N. Strakhov: 'I totally disagree with what you write about Dostoevsky and Tolstoy.[28] You speak fluently about the peculiarities of Dostoevsky's writing—its artificiality and circuitousness. But these features are only superficial; Dostoevsky could dispense with these, and there would appear much that was genuine and good. The artificiality and circuitousness in Tolstoy are much more profound, but I do not wish to talk about this at length, first, because of your feelings for him; second, because it is Lent; and third, because I continue to understand the commandment 'Do not judge' not in a legal sense but in a moral one. . . .

[Solovyov continued:] "'Today at Fet's, I saw Tolstoy himself. He was citing the ideas of some German and his own formulations, trying to prove that the earth does not revolve around the sun, that it stands still, that it is the single "solid" form known to us, and that the sun and other stars are essentially pieces of light flying over the earth because light is weightless. . . .'

[Lopatina added:] "I can just hear Solovyov's typically unrestrained laughter. . . .

"Solovyov used to visit Khamovniki, and Lev Nikolaevich would return his visits. Solovyov once wrote to Strakhov that he had become completely reconciled with Tolstoy. 'Tolstoy visited me to explain some of his strange behavior, and I also went to his place for a pleasurable evening. If he is always going to be so nice, I will continue visiting him.'

"Solovyov then told me the basic issue over which he disagreed with Tolstoy: the resurrection of Christ. But how many other disagreements and differences existed between them!

"I remember that the entranceway, the staircase, the hall of the house in Khamovniki, and the garden that was attached to it were always astir with the noise and laughter of the young Tolstoys. I remember Tolstoy himself in his blouse with a leather belt, under which he would tuck his hands. I also recall his gloomy face with its unforgettable eyes and the endless conversations about whether one should eat meat or drink coffee, or whether one could morally assist people with money. There was also a big tea table which was carefully tended by a young servant who called everyone 'your Highness.'

"I also remember Solovyov and his homeless wanderings in and out of hotel rooms and of friends' homes: his tall figure in a long frock coat and scarf, his exaggerated pose as an intellectual, his hair down to his shoulders, his chronic illnesses, his regularity in taking communion, and his absolute fearlessness toward death. . . .

"Everything was so different between Tolstoy and Solovyov. Tolstoy insisted that Solovyov's religious system and his faith were purely cerebral. And Solovyov, comparing Tolstoy to Dostoevsky, would speak of Tolstoy's circuitousness, his insincerity."[29]

Later on, I often met and became friends with Ilya L'vovich [Tolstoy].[30] He was a happy, cheerful individual: talented but dissolute. He liked to talk about his father and told me many stories about him. One of these was remarkable. Ilya happened to discover his father's nurse, a woman of almost one hundred years old, who had lived with Tolstoy both in his youth and as a family man, and who had become the prototype of Agaf'ya Mikhailovna, Levin's nurse and friend in *Anna Karenina*.[31] She lived out her last years at the home in Yasnaya Polyana, completely alone in a closetlike room.

"You cannot even imagine what kind of woman she was," Ilya L'vovich told me. "She would say, 'Day and night I lie in my closet all alone. The only thing I hear is the clock ticking on the wall. And it keeps asking and asking: *"Who are you?" "What are you?"* and *"Who are you?"* and *"What are you?"*' I lie there, listening, and keep thinking: "Who are you really, and what are you in this world?"'

"Father would be absolutely delighted whenever he would hear such a thing. 'Yes, yes,' he would repeat, 'that's the entire essence of life: Who are you? What are you?'"

But Ilya L'vovich would also often reiterate things that everyone knew.

During the Great War, he told me: "You might be surprised to hear what I am going to say, but I still think that if Father were alive today, he would be a true patriot to the depths of his soul. The minute the war broke out, he would wish for our victory over the Germans. He would curse the conflict, but he would also follow its course passionately.[32] You really should not be surprised. After all, he was constantly changing his mind, and no one could get a hold on him right up until the end."

"So you want to say, as others do, that he was unstable, fickle?" I asked.

"No, this is not what I want to say. I want to say that he is still not understood as he should be. After all, he is part Natasha Rostova and Eroshka, part Prince Andrei and Pierre, part old man Bolkonsky and Karataev, part Princess Mary and Kholstomer. Do you know what Turgenev told Tolstoy after he had read 'Kholstomer'? 'Lev Nikolaevich, I am absolutely convinced that you were once a horse!'[33] In a word, Tolstoy always had to be understood in some kind of very complex way. . . .

"He loved me," Ilya L'vovich continued. "And he forgave me a great deal. One time a group of young people and I left to go hunting in a distant field. While we were out there, we got so drunk that we decided to eat some frozen plants with our vodka and to walk about on all fours as if we were wolves. . . . You cannot imagine how Father screamed with laughter when I later told him what we had done!"

I also remember a similar story that was once told to me by someone named Sulerzhitsky,[34] a frequent guest in the Tolstoys' home:

"Yes, Lev Nikolaevich could be baffling! For instance, he was an enemy of anything that had to do with the military! But then, one freezing winter day, he returned home from a walk through Moscow, and from the hallway shouted out at me with his old man's voice: 'Listen to me! I just saw two of the most wonderful-looking cadets on Kuznetsky Bridge! Good God, what fine fellows they were! What fine figures they cut! What fine clothes they were wearing—overcoats that came down almost to the floor, with a slit in the back that went up to the very waist! What height, what freshness, what power! How rare for even a young stallion to exhibit such beauty!

"'Then, all of a sudden, as if on purpose, a general came out to meet them. . . . You should have seen how they stamped their feet and jingled [their] spurs and immediately stood erect, how they saluted and opened their eyes wide! Oh, what charm, what splendor!'"[35]

LOPATINA WAS A REMARKABLE woman in some respects, but she also could be very biased in her opinions. Here, however, I am rendering everything exactly as she told it to me about Tolstoy, his family and friends, and about the Moscow circles to which he belonged and in which she also had grown up.

"Like you, I learned of Tolstoy very early in life, when I was still a little girl," Lopatina continued. "In our living room with its piano, with its chairs along the walls, and under hanging 'mournful lamps'"—this is exactly the way she expressed it—"my father would read to my mother this new novel, *Anna Karenina,* that was being published in the *Russian Herald.*[1] Several of its phrases whizzed by my ears, and I marveled at how strangely good they were!

"At that time, everyone in our house talked about Anna Karenina for days on end. Finally, Misha Solovyov, Vladimir's brother, brought [my brother] Lev some news: 'Did you read that Anna Karenina threw herself under a train?' And we would talk and talk and argue about her, as if she were someone we had known personally.

"Then one sunny winter day, I found a tattered book with a blue cover on the floor in front of the bookshelves in my father's study. I picked it up, and as I read it, I could readily see a picture of a dirty, dug-up road and of a soldier in a gray coat, running from a bastion with two rifles on his shoulders. . . .

"It was Tolstoy's *Sevastopol Tales!* I could not even hear this title with indifference. When I visited the Crimea for the very first time, Sevastopol seemed to be such a romantic, poetic place! It was still all in ruins. On the streets and squares were the skeletons of homes, and it still seemed that a soldier was leading the horses of a troika by their bridles; that the officer, Mikhailov, was putting on a white glove and climbing up a hill; and that the rose-colored sea at sunset was host to the sounds of a Strauss waltz which an orchestra had been playing on the boulevard. My heart ached from the sounds of the ship bells, and I found it sad that the night showed only huge stars, and not grenades, flying slowly and shining in the dark sky. . . .

"Even when the Tolstoys were living at Yasnaya Polyana, everyone talked about them, especially women of high society in Moscow.

"I would sit and listen to my parents' conversation with some woman guest who would talk about the sufferings and difficulties of Sofya Andreevna. They would go on about 'poor Sonya' and about how the lives of her children had to conform to the latest views of her husband. First they had foreign governesses[2] and a strictly English upbringing.[3] Later, they suddenly had to wear Russian shirts, even *lapty;* they kept company with peasant children and were allowed to do exactly as they pleased. Still later, everything was as before: Tolstoy's children were surrounded by English governesses and wore short pants and bows in their hair. . . .

"At that time, there lived in Moscow the extremely interesting and even remarkable family of Count Olsufiev. The Olsufiev family, by virtue of its origins and social position (the count had been a general in the tsar's entourage), belonged both to the court and to the highest strata of the Petersburg aristocracy. As a result of the various personal circumstances of the countess, Anna Mikhailovna, and her changing political views and intellectual interests, the family had become one of the centers in Moscow for the educated and professorial elite. There one could meet scholar-positivists,[4] artists, and writers. Tolstoy was also among the guests, and the countess loved him very much. He was not like the others, for he came to her both as a friend and as one who was close to her upbringing and position.

"I saw Tolstoy for the first time on Myortvyi Lane,[5] in an enormous mansion that had been rented by the Olsufievs for the winter so that they could come back and forth from their country house near that city.

"The huge hall featured a long table covered with a blindingly white tablecloth. There were two servants, an old one and a young one, both of whom wore tails and who, hurried and anxious, were setting the table with silver and plates filled with cookies and cakes. In the living room was a small group of people playing cards. Suddenly Tolstoy entered with a light, young gait. He was wearing soft, soundless boots and a gray blouse with a thin leather belt. His face, with its huge beard, was sharply irregular and defied description, but it would be etched in my memory forever. His eyes were penetrating, sharp, and intelligent; but to me, they at once appeared harsh and cruel—'wolflike,' as my father used to say about them.[6] (I would see Tolstoy's eyes like that for the rest of my life.) Later on, whenever Tolstoy suddenly entered a room, he always made me feel awkward and frightened, as if someone had opened the door to a dark basement on a bright sunny day.

"I was introduced to him very simply: 'This is so-and-so's daughter. . . .' 'I know,' he said, shaking my hand. I could not believe that I was actually in his presence—the very one who could describe the sky over Austerlitz, the Battle of Borodino,[7] the mother in *Childhood,* and Anna [Karenina's] meeting with her son.

"Having said hello to the countess and all the others who were there, he immediately began talking to a professor of natural sciences by the name of Usov.

"'I have been wanting to ask you, Sergei Alexeevich,' he said. 'Is it true that when a mad dog bites someone, the victim will most likely die within six weeks?'

"Usov answered:

"'Some may die in six weeks; others after several months or a year; still others—so they say—after many years. But it is also possible that one may not die at all. Not all people who have been bitten by a dog die.'

"'Oh, what a pity,' Tolstoy said with perverse liveliness. 'I very much liked the idea that people die when they are bitten. I think that it is just great. A dog bites a person, and the person knows that he will die within six weeks. In the meantime, he can do what he wants; he can hit someone with truth right between the eyes! . . . But do you know for sure that a person who has been bitten might actually go on living?' he stubbornly repeated.

"How many times I was to hear that persistent tone in his discussions and arguments and to note the way he would talk more quickly than his companion! And how many times would I study his eyes as he did so!

"It was just that very summer that Olsufiev's home was in an uproar. A mad dog was running around nearby, and no one could catch it. Everyone calmed down only after a police officer finally appeared and, having saluted, reported: 'Your excellency, I have the honor to report to you that the dog has gone off to Podsolnechnaya Station.'[8] Before the officer arrived, Olsufiev's peasants did not even think about catching and killing the dog.

"'They acted splendidly!' Tolstoy said.

"And suddenly he began talking—simply, quietly, but vividly—about how, when he had lived in the Caucasus, his puppy, Bul'ka, had gone mad and would lick and bite his boots with his teeth. . . .[9]

"The people in our circle constantly discussed not only Tolstoy but his entire family. For example, Tanya's entry into society, her first ball at the Shcherbatovs' home, I think, was discussed in our family, even between my brothers and me, though I did not know her at the time. The people who had been at the affair talked about her simple white dress, her enchanting smile, and her distinctive, if somewhat abrupt, mannerisms, which did not conceal her endearing shyness.[10] . . . I recall that it was the only ball that she attended, for soon after that Lev Nikolaevich would not let her attend any such occasions. Later on, when the Beklemishevs had such a gathering, she was there only at the very beginning, in a simple dress and only to observe what was going on. The rooms were still cold, but brightly lit and perfumed by the many fresh flowers. As the rooms gradually filled with a great number of Muscovite maidens in the latest hairstyles and wearing flowers, airy dresses, and fur capes on their bare shoulders . . . Tanya looked at them all with curiosity.

"'How funny you all look!' she finally said in a Tolstoy-like manner. 'Naked but with flowers!'[11]

"I met Tanya for the first time at the Olsufievs'. From their mansion on Myortvyi Lane, we drove together in an elegant carriage to Pokrovskoe-Glebovo,[12] where a greenhouse had been arranged for tea and music was provided for dances. Again Lev Nikolaevich appeared quite suddenly, wearing his winter coat and carrying a walking stick, his eyes penetratingly cruel under his bushy brows. He had come to see everyone off and to check on Tanya: with whom she was sitting and how she was behaving herself. Everyone was touched by his concern—'just like an ordinary person,' they said.

"We had a wonderful day during that spring. . . . I still remember that it was the feast of Saint Nicholas.[13] The dust and dry spring heat had been followed by a powerful thunderstorm, the first of the season. People put jars under their drainpipes to collect water for washing. After that, the sun began to shine blindingly in our little garden with its ruined summerhouse. The windows in our house were open, the small tips on the buds were turning green, the puddles began to glisten, and our old nurse said with delight as she wiped the windowsill: 'Saint Nicholas is bringing us such fine weather for the cattle.'

"At the time, I was in the throes of my first love, and life seemed to me to be an unusual discovery that I myself had made. On that day, I could have cared less about how the people in my home were busy bustling about, preparing for a visit by Lev Nikolaevich.

"That evening, he, wearing his blouse, sat in our formal living room. He and several other guests talked about art and about what he was writing at the time. I am ashamed to confess that I quickly became bored and went into the garden. The night was wet and fresh, there was a sharp smell of young poplars, and the sky was clear and green. There was no way that I could I leave the garden because everything that I felt there seemed to me more interesting than the brilliant writings of Tolstoy.

"But how modest, serious, and courteous he was that evening!

"At dinner, one could feel that the conversation that had broken off earlier had been long and intense and that everyone was reserved and sad, as if a bit offended by something. Apparently, right before dinner, the group had been trying to convince Lev Nikolaevich to write something artistic. When I arrived, one guest was saying to Tolstoy in a nervous but quiet way:

"'Good God! Your very images . . . are truth and beauty themselves! They show more truth than any discussions or proofs. . . .'

"Tolstoy's answer was extremely modest. He said:

"'I humbly thank you. . . . It is pleasant to hear such a thing! . . . But everybody says things like that. After all, Nemirovich-Danchenko thinks that he is saving the world with his novels. . . .'[14]

"I was also on friendly terms with Verochka Tolstaya, the daughter of Count Sergei Nikolaevich. It was she who was with me when I went to Tolstoy's house at Khamovniki for the first time.

"Tolstoy's house was so enticing that one felt almost overwhelmed just to be there. But, at that time, there was also something burdensome about the place that countered my enthusiasm for it. All, or almost all, of the Tolstoys were talented, original, and witty. But they never forgot for a minute that they were Tolstoys. I never heard the young Tolstoys going into raptures over any literary works other than their father's. They belittled everyone and everything else, saying that no one would read Turgenev and Gogol in the future and that Tolstoy was the only great writer around. But one time, when they started to discuss *The Sevastopol Tales*, Tanya suddenly said:

"'To tell you the truth, I haven't read them. . . .'

"In the spring, the huge garden at the Tolstoys' home in Khamovniki resounded with laughter, guitars, and Gypsy songs. The Tolstoys were all very musical. Love was the key interest of the young people there, the main topic of their conversations. They spoke about it freely, and sometimes even crudely, with the usual Tolstoyan daring. Also, anyone who happened to be in their company might not feel comfortable. The guest could not relax because at any moment he could be asked an unpleasant question. For example, if an individual with a crooked nose—but forgetful of that shortcoming—showed up, the young Tolstoys would remind him of his shortcoming at that very moment when he would feel most uncomfortable.

"I would forgive Tanya more than the others for such antics because she was captivating with her talent and charm. For example, she was a master at imitating monkeys. One time she truly frightened me by the way she suddenly grabbed me by the hair. But she also clicked her front teeth and blinked her brown eyes in such a funny way that one could not get angry at her.

"Sofya Andreevna talked in a simple, lively, and openly sincere way about things which no one else would discuss. Once we talked about marriage. She said: 'Marriage, of course, is only sin and degradation; children are its only redemption.'[15] One time she asked about one of our mutual acquaintances, whom I praised lavishly. Suddenly Sofya Andreevna interrupted: 'Yes, yes, I just knew it! She's a wonderful woman! But all of Russia sees me as a dolt.[16] But if that is so, then tell me, who runs this home? Who has raised all these children?' She did not conceal the fact that she was writing a novel, something to refute *The Kreutzer Sonata*.[17] But Tanya, who had no respect for her mother,[18] remarked in her presence: 'So long as we are alive, nothing that Mother writes will be published.'[19]

"One time, when the two younger Tolstoys were leaving to retake an examination, Lev Nikolaevich came out and said to them: 'Please know that you would give me the greatest pleasure if you both failed the test.'[20] They did not disappoint him. But Sofya Andreevna said with irritation: 'Good God, take a look around. The most ordinary people have clever and talented children who are good students. But just look at what my genius has produced!'[21]

"I liked Sofya Andreevna because of her tall, erect figure, her smoothly combed, shiny black hair, her lively attractive face; her expressive, well-shaped mouth, her smile, and even the way she examined things closely, squinting her big black eyes as she did so. She was a genuine woman and mother, caring, energetic, protective of the family interests, a real mother hen![22] The children told me that when she went to the empress (to ask that the ban against *The Kreuzer Sonata* be removed),[23] the entire conversation focused on children, each one telling about her own. . . .

"Speaking about the children, the last of Sofya Andreevna's sons was Vanechka, whose death she would later mourn so deeply. He was a charming, lively boy, with intelligent Tolstoyan eyes and with the typical Tolstoyan face and tender laughter. I saw him for the first time at a gathering where Tanya and a mutual acquaintance were amusing themselves by throwing back and forth a huge doll that belonged to Vanechka. It was a rather strange sight. It was as if a person were flying through the air with his hands extended, and everyone was only looking on and laughing at what was going on. Vanechka waited for the right moment and grabbed hold of the doll. 'I'm not giving it back!' he announced with a decisive air, together with a stubborn and lively smile. 'Not for anything in the world!' And he looked at everyone with the eyes of a wolf cub. . . .[24]

"The generation of Tolstoy's siblings was very interesting. Both Lev Nikolaevich's brother, Count Sergei Nikolaevich,[25] and their sister, Countess Maria Nikolaevna, had a distinct Tolstoyan appearance. One could never forget them even after meeting them only once; in fact, he would constantly see their faces before his eyes.

"The family of Sergei Nikolaevich—Volodya in *Childhood, Adolescence,* and *Youth*—was very close to me. Judging from a daguerreotype of him in a circular frame, he was at one time strikingly handsome. He was enchanting and well-built, wearing the uniform of an archer of the royal family. Even when I came to know him, he was still slim and well-formed with regular features and big dark eyes. Maria Nikolaevna also had the same sharp Tolstoyan features, a distinct mouth with a prominent jaw, big eyes that were passionate, intelligent, cruel, and which her eyeglasses made look even terrible. In those eyes and lively face, one could see a strong spirituality . . . and an absolutely hellish temper.

"Sergei Nikolaevich married a Gypsy woman from a chorus or, maybe, from a Gypsy camp itself. She was a small, fat woman, taciturn, even cowed. She never said a word against her husband and even smiled quietly at his cruel jokes. She was also religious and kind, and always had a cigarette in her hands.[26]

"Sergei Nikolaevich had three daughters, all of whom were disciples of their uncle. They were of the Gypsy type, resolute in their behavior and views, spirited and mocking. I had a long friendship with the eldest daughter, Verochka.

"Sergei Nikolaevich's estate was located in the village of Pirogovo,[27] located on the bank of a river and strewn with huts over a vast expanse. It stood alongside an old house and a densely shadowed park of linden trees with dark alleys. In this park was a tiny, clay-walled cottage which had been built by Tolstoy's followers to realize one of Lev Nikolaevich's ideas; nearby they grew beans on several acres of land. On this estate, I met some very strange people, healthy types but also quite awkward. They used to hide from Sergei Nikolaevich and read books published by Mediator. They were like *raisonneurs* who rambled on in such a boring, persistent, and contradictory way that I always wanted to get away from them as soon as possible.

"Pirogovo was also the locale of Maria Nikolaevna's estate. We would sometimes visit her to talk and to drink tea and have gooseberries on her balcony. I loved Maria for her intelligence and wit, and because we shared a common religious faith. She later became a nun. She would often tell me about her brothers and herself. She owned a bit of wasteland with the awkward name of 'Portochki.'[28] She reminisced that, when she was young, and when guests were present, her brothers, in a straight-faced way, would ask her:

"'Now, what's the name of that wasteland that belongs to you? What do you call it?'

"Sergei Nikolaevich, who was well aware of my religious convictions, would sometimes say in my presence:

"'It is wonderful, absolutely wonderful that Lyovochka proclaims to the peasants that hymns like "Who Are the Cherubim?"[29] are nonsense and that they should ignore the priests. But I also have always told my brother that it is criminal the way he rouses the peasants against the gentry, telling them that they should be given all the land. No one can run an estate that way, and today's folk are depraved enough without his putting any ideas into their heads.'

"The way Sergei Nikolaevich treated Verochka reminded me of the relationship between old Prince Bolkonsky and Princess Mary in *War and Peace*. There was the same love, the same near adoration of his daughter, but also the same merciless torment. Sergei Nikolaevich and Verochka always spoke English to each other.

"Lev Nikolaevich dearly loved Maria Nikolaevna. But they argued and fought all the time. Usually when she visited him, the noise and shouting began right away. I can well imagine the faces they made, the terrible look in their Tolstoyan eyes. Such confrontations usually ended with Maria Nikolaevna's jumping up and running away. Tolstoy would follow her, crying:

"'Mashen'ka, forgive me, for God's sake!'[30]

"At other times, with her or with other people, however, something else would happen: How simply, softly, and seriously did he sometimes speak and argue, completely trying to adopt his opponent's point of view!

"One time Verochka and I started discussing love and happiness, life and morality. Tolstoy, wearing felt boots and an unbuttoned sheepskin coat, entered and asked us what we had been talking about. Blushing, I started to explain:

"'I was saying that no amount of preaching makes any difference in life. Only what people experience, feel, and suffer can influence them. . . .'

"He looked and searched around, as if taking stock and trying to express something.

"'Yes, that is the main thing,' he said at last. 'One should influence through example.'

"Another time, amidst a crowd of people at Khamovniki, he came up to me and suddenly asked:

"'Do you go to confession and take communion?'

"Knowing that everyone was listening, I became even more disconcerted.

"'Yes, Lev Nikolaevich, I go to confession and take communion.'

"'And what about Mikhail Nikolaevich?' he asked about my father. 'Is he also a believer?'

"'Yes, Lev Nikolaevich.'

"'And does he go to church?'

"'Yes.'

"'And does he go to confession and take communion?'

"'Every year.'

"He suddenly became thoughtful, but said nothing.

"Once I actually had the courage to get into an argument with Tolstoy. Whatever the issue, he disagreed with me, on purpose, perhaps; but this time, for some reason, he also became angry. I continued to argue with him, but I began to feel that I was getting confused and that I was doing something stupid. I turned pale, as I suddenly saw those familiar angry eyes and heard his absolutely impassioned voice. At last, to stop the argument, I said:

"'No, I don't agree with you.'

"He suddenly became silent and looked at me in an unfriendly way.

"'You are so terribly like Grand Duke Vladimir Alexandrovich,' he said suddenly. 'Yes, you really are. One time at a meeting of the Academy of Arts,[31] people were trying to prove to him something that everybody knows, something as indisputable as "two plus two equals four." He heard them all out, but he took the bell and said: "I still don't agree with you. The meeting is closed." Then he rang the thing.'

"After the argument had ended, I hastened to leave. When I was on the landing of the staircase, he suddenly appeared before me.

"'Forgive me, for God's sake,' he said, bowing. . . .

"Tolstoy's excommunication from the church caused a storm of indignation both among the people nearest him and those who were otherwise indifferent to religious questions but who saw Tolstoy as justification for their own revolutionary bent.

"People have told me that during that time, the entire home in Khamovniki was filled with presents and expressions of sympathy for Tolstoy's plight,[32] and that Tolstoy himself would allegedly 'sit all decked out in flowers and blaspheme so uncontrollably that one's hair stood on end.' But is it correct to say that this event did not at all affect him spiritually? Everything that I found out later indicates precisely the opposite. For instance, about the blasphemous passages in *Resurrection*,[33] he later said with great dismay and pain, 'Yes, what I did was not right, not right at all. . . . I should never have done what I did.' When Sergei Nikolaevich was dying of cancer of the cheek,[34] Tolstoy was the first one to ask his brother if communion would not console him. And he himself went to the priest to ask him to visit his brother.[35] In fact, people say that he would never sit down to write something new without first crossing himself. . . .

"The time of Tolstoy's departure from his estate and his death coincided with the passing of my mother. We followed the news coming from Astapovo as well as reports of the deep sufferings of the unhappy and ailing Sofya Andreevna.

"One psychiatrist told me that Tolstoy's departure was motivated by the beginnings of pneumonia,[36] and that old people afflicted with this illness often have a strong desire to move, to go somewhere. But when I repeated what the doctor had said, my listeners—'liberals,' of course—were terribly offended:

"'What you are saying is unforgivable, for it debases the majesty of his genius. He quit life not because of an old man's illness, but because existence ran counter to his beliefs!'"

Chapter Nine

"TOLSTOY MERGED SIMPLICITY with royal bearing, inner grace, and outward sophistication. He was a *grand seigneur* in everything, for example, the way he shook hands, the manner in which he asked a guest to be seated, the way he listened to people. . . . I have had a close-up view of that crowned dandy, the extremely outwardly elegant Edward VII of England; the charmingly ingratiating Abdul-Hamid II; and the iron Bismarck, who knew how to captivate. . . . Each in his own way made a strong impression. But in their manners and in the way they related to people, I could feel something superficial and calculating. But Tolstoy's actions and attitudes as a *grand seigneur* were integral to his being; and if someone were to ask me who was the most cosmopolitan person that I had ever met, I would say 'Tolstoy.' He was dignified in the course of a normal conversation. But as soon as the topic touched upon something that was even slightly serious, this *grand seigneur* would vent his volcanic soul. His eyes, which otherwise lacked a definite color, would suddenly become blue, black, gray, brown. They shone with all the colors of the rainbow."

Such is the opinion of one extremely "enlightened" individual about him. But, throughout his entire life, Tolstoy would say about himself (either in real life or through the characters of his fiction) that he was awkward, tactless, shameful, puffed up "to the gills"; that he was "bitterly shy, lazy, irritable, and weak"; and that he always deeply hated someone or something.

"Levin stared at Grinevich's hands with hatred, despising [his adversary's] long white fingers with their long yellow nails bent at the end."

The circle that Tolstoy depicted so cruelly in his fiction—the one to which he belonged from birth—was the group that was also the closest to him in life. When I met him for the first time, I noticed how he suddenly changed when he began to recall my father. Tolstoy had met him in Sevastopol during the siege of the city, as part of "his own" circle. I also recall the lively way in which he began to question me: "Well, so then you must also be related to so-and-so? And the others who were there—are they also your relatives?"

His secretary, Bulgakov, said that "even as an old man, Lev Nikolae-vich exhibited the prejudices of his class. . . . When his daughters were in-volved in 'love affairs' (innocent ones, of course) with people 'not of our' circle, he would get very displeased and angry, for he feared that they would marry beneath themselves."

According to Bulgakov also, Tolstoy, in his final years, would mention Chertkov "in either a restrained or negative way."[1] Was perhaps one of the reasons why Tolstoy was attracted to Chertkov that, among the Tolstoyans, it was only Chertkov who was really one of "us," of "our" circle?[2]

In this circle also there were some who hated Tolstoy with such a pas-sion that even his own son Andrei L'vovich once cried out: "If I were not his son, I would hang him myself!"[3] But this group still thought of him as one of "its own." Later on I met people in Moscow from this circle and saw that many were still calling attention to the fact that "in essence, he was and still is a *barin*." They also said with pride:

"Oh, to the people who knew him, he was nothing but a former soci-ety lion! But even now, despite his whims, when he is with people, he is charming—a gentleman from head to toe."

Lopatina always used to enumerate his many "whims":

"When I recall my youth," she would say, "I often recall him. One time, I was walking along one of our alleyways alongside Starokonyushen-nyi Lane[4] and ran into him—he was walking his setter dog. He came up to me, said 'hello,' and immediately began talking about his son Ilyusha: 'He is entering the Sumskoy Regiment[5] as a volunteer, but I told him: "Join the infantry first of all, if you want to try the soldier's life. You will get a more accurate idea there of what it is like." But then with his name, they would carry him around in their arms.'

"Imagine how strange it was for me to hear such words from him! As I see it, it was all the result of his borderline psychological illness. Our coachman once said it well. One winter day, when he and I were riding along in a carriage, we came across Tolstoy, hauling an ice-covered barrel of water on a sleigh.[6] Our coachman, a rather severe type of individual who was always drunk, remarked: 'Only the devil knows what kind of count he is! He's off his rocker!' What he said was true. For example, how often Tolstoy would vent his madness in his passion for seizing on all the horrible and re-pulsive things in life!

"Remember the spot of light which Ivan Ilyich [in *The Death of Ivan Ilyich*] saw somewhere in front of him as he lay dying and thinking that he was being shoved into some kind of black sack? This impression was some-thing that Tolstoy took from life. One of our mutual acquaintances had a brother who died; and, according to the story, right before the brother passed from this life, the raving man kept insisting that he was being shoved into a black sack. It is a wonderful thing, of course, that Ivan Ilyich nonetheless saw a bright spot that was 'getting bigger and bigger'; but did Tolstoy himself actually believe in such a spot? In my opinion, he believed only in the black sack.

"'Lyovochka is an unhappy man," his brother Sergei Nikolaevich would often say about him. 'How well he used to write! I think that, at one time, he was the best writer around; but then he went crazy. Not for nothing do I, from my childhood on, remember him as being somewhat strange. . . .'

"Maria Nikolaevna, with great compassion, would say the same thing: 'What kind of person is Lyovochka? An absolutely remarkable one. What interesting things he has written! Yet now that he has started interpreting the Gospels,[7] he has no energy for anything else. Truly, there has always been a devil in him.'

"She would always say such a thing with confidence and, of course, was completely correct. I, for one, never doubted this for a moment. For example, I remember this one event. At someone's wedding in Moscow, a certain well-known associate professor, the son of an educated theologian and priest, and also a mutual acquaintance of Tolstoy's and mine, got drunk before the ceremony. Serving as a witness, he signed the marriage certificate; but he then entered the sanctuary and placed the document on the altar. When he was told that one does not do such things—this was the altar, after all—he answered with such blasphemy that everyone's hair stood on end. When the story was repeated to Tolstoy, he was not only went into hysterics, but he wanted everyone else to do so, too. 'Hey you, come here!' he would say. 'Did you hear what happened to the professor at the wedding . . . ?' He then would roll over with laughter, slapping his thighs as he did so. 'Now there's a splendid answer for you!' Yes, I have no doubt that a devil always had him in his grip!

"He liked my now deceased brother, Volodya, very much," Lopatina continued. "I remember that one time at a Christmas party at the Tolstoys' home in Khamovniki, the place was filled with a great many people in costumes, and that Tolstoy himself stood at the top of the staircase, greeting everyone with a smile, his hand tucked under the belt of his blouse. Everyone there bowed low to him, but guess what happened then? Imagine everyone's surprise when they saw a different Tolstoy, the real one, suddenly make his appearance and when they learned that Volodya had been made up to look just like the great writer himself! Lev Nikolaevich was the most delighted of everyone there. He kept repeating: 'But this is remarkable! Vladimir Mikhailovich, you really do look like me, even though I am almost three times your age. You simply must be very talented to pull off something like this!'[8]

"Another time in Yasnaya Polyana, some of Tolstoy's admirers had volunteered to stage *The Fruits of Enlightenment*. Volodya played the 'third peasant,' and, at the rehearsals, Lev Nikolaevich again received him with the most unrestrained praise. 'What a talent you have!' he said. 'And how you have explained this peasant to me. It is only now that I understand him as I should!' And he kept adding new sections to the manuscript of the play.[9]

"You knew Volodya. He truly was very talented. It was not an accident that, in his old age, he found himself at the Moscow Art Theater,[10] but he was also a very intelligent and incisive individual. He would always tell me: 'How is it that no one can see how Tolstoy has suffered and continues to suffer a terrible tragedy; that is, he is really a hundred completely different people, except one: the individual who can believe in God. He was a genius who wanted to believe in God but could not.' You may laugh at such words, but they are the absolute truth. . . .

"In their early years, Tolstoy's children went to church, but they quickly and blithely (or so it seemed on the surface) gave up their faith and chose to believe in other things. This was especially true with Masha. She used to have this rule—every Saturday to visit friends and to spend the night at their place so that they could all go to services on the following morning. Her older siblings would laugh at her, but she stubbornly kept to her routine. She gave it all up abruptly, however, once she took it into her head to marry a key Tolstoyan. Her actions, though, were completely in keeping with her father's influence over her. To poke fun at priests and to call Shakespeare a talentless hack were everyday occurrences in the Tolstoy household; but a clarification is needed. Tolstoy once said about Shakespeare: 'My children do not understand all the wonderful things in Shakespeare, nor can they do so; for they have picked up only on all my abuse of him.'[11]

"One can see the same inconsistencies in Tolstoy's stance toward religion.[12] One time Tatyana L'vovna and I were visiting the Olsufievs. We were staying upstairs, in what looked like a hotel, a long corridor with rooms on either side. One night I was about to fall asleep when, for some reason, I suddenly asked her: 'Tanya, do you believe in life after death?' Boldly, without thinking, she replied: 'Of course not. Who believes in such nonsense?' But then Lev Nikolaevich began saying something different: that without a doubt there was life after death, but that one had to deserve it, to have it awarded like a 'Cross of Saint George.'[13] After that, all the young Tolstoys began to repeat these new words.

"I also remember one time when Sonya Samarina, whom people called the most enchanting girl in Moscow, told me indignantly: 'One of the strangest things that Tolstoy ever did was this. After he had written *The Kreutzer Sonata*, he kept complaining, for everyone to hear, that Tanya and Masha were still not married. He would say: "Are they worse than anyone else? Why will no one take them?"[14] He was an absolutely insane individual. He would always keep changing his mind about things.'[15]

"One time Verochka (the daughter of Sergei Nikolaevich) and I arrived unexpectedly at Yasnaya Polyana. As usual, a great many people were sitting at the table, having lunch on the porch. In front of everyone, Lev Nikolaevich began asking Verochka: 'Well, how are things at your house? How is your father?' Verochka, who was shy, sweet, and honest to the point of seeming simple, murmured in a confused way: 'Everything is fine. . . . Except Papa is very upset. . . . The priest's pigs got into our garden and destroyed all our apple trees.' The entire table began to roar with laughter, including all the Tolstoys who were there—all those Tolstoyan eyes, jaws, and teeth. But Lev Nikolaevich did not laugh. He became serious and said sadly, with irritation: 'Yes, yes, this may all seem amusing to you, but to tell you the truth, there is nothing funny about it at all; for this is life, and everything that interferes with life, is very bad!'"

"All those Tolstoyan eyes, jaws, and teeth." What absolutely marvelous words.

Chapter Ten

IT IS NOT CORRECT to say that Tolstoy had "wolflike eyes," though such a description conveys the sharp impression that his eyes made on people. His eyes were like his smile in that their special qualities affected everyone who knew him throughout his life—from his youth to his old age. On second thought, there was, at times, something wolflike about his eyes, since he could look at people from under his brows with a sullen and distrustful air.

Only in Tolstoy's final portraits does there begin to appear gentleness, resignation, goodwill, and sometimes even a smile and tender merriness. All his other pictures, beginning almost with his adolescence, strike one with his power, seriousness, severity, and distrust, his cold and provocative contempt; his malevolence and dissatisfaction, his sadness. What somber, keenly inquisitive eyes, what firmly clenched teeth![1]

"Pervasive malice," he once said for some reason about something or somebody. But such a description did not apply to him. He justly said of himself: "I have never been evil. I confess to two or three sins which, when I committed them, tormented me greatly; but I was never cruel."

Nonetheless, looking at the many portraits of both his young and adult years, one unwittingly recalls this phrase: "pervasive malice." At one time, people used to describe Tolstoy with words from Pushkin. "The spirit of negation, the ghost of doubt,"[2] they said, "the destroyer of commonly accepted truths." For such designations, he did give his accusers countless grounds.

On the table before me is his diary for his 1857 visit to Switzerland.[3] Everywhere he was true to himself. "It is a strange thing!" he wrote. "*Whether because my spirit is one of opposition or because my tastes conflict with those of the majority,* I have never liked a single thing that was famous for its beauty."

Depending on his mood or his surroundings or his spiritual state, which—as everyone knows—could change radically and often, he was first one thing, then another. Indeed, how he was feeling could also influence his entire demeanor. He said of himself: "What impact do society and books

have in life? With good people, I am one thing; with bad people, I am someone quite different."

Just the same, in the pictures of his youth, adulthood, and the first
years of his old age, there is something overwhelming, which, in any case,
cannot be called kindness.

Before me is a portrait from when he was a student in Kazan.[4] He is
a rather well-built youth. His hair is cut like a hedgehog's; his face is serious and dissatisfied, resembling that of a bulldog.[5] Here is also a portrait
of him as an officer. His hair still resembles a hedgehog's, only more pointed
and full. His face looks a bit longer, flanked with side whiskers, with a
glance that is haughty and cold. Thrown about his shoulders and covering
his uniform is a dandyish coat with an upraised beaver collar from the time
of Nicholas I.[6] Another portrait of him as an officer, though, stands in complete contrast to the first two; and, in my opinion, it is one of his most remarkable pictures. This one was taken when he came to Petersburg from
Sevastopol and entered the literary circles there.[7] At this time, he was not
yet thirty, massive, thin, and wearing the very simple uniform of someone
from the artillery. The picture shows him only from his waist up; but one
can easily guess that he is tall, agile, and strong. His face, with its handsome
features and soldierly simplicity, is also thin. His somewhat prominent
cheekbones are balanced by a sparse mustache bent around the corners of
his mouth and by the small, intelligent eyes which, the way his head is bent,
look upward with a sad and somber gaze.[8]

After Tolstoy retired from the military,[9] he lived as a dandy in Petersburg and Moscow, indulging in societal life: balls, theaters, nightly carousing. He again resumed the lifestyle of his early youth, when he had thought
that the mark of a distinguished person was to be *comme il faut*.[10] I have not
seen any portraits of him from this time, and I think that none exists. But
there is a picture from the period that follows, that is, the time of his first
trip abroad, his visit to Paris and Switzerland.[11] There is also another portrait of him as a handsome man (no matter how strange this epithet to describe him). Here he is still thin, with a young face, but by this time his face
is framed with a small beard. His lower lip is still pleasant and youthful, if
somewhat protruding. His eyes look out calmly, but with a somewhat questioning air, as if expectantly, but also distrustfully. There is a certain sadness
in them.

After seeing such a portrait, one is surprised by his Swiss diary, one of
the most captivating of his works. How many things in this diary are so fresh,
bold, joyful, and poetically charming. His relative Alexandra Andreevna
Tolstaya lived on Lake Geneva[12] during the spring of that year, and after his
visit there, he maintained a friendship with her that would last many years.
A sizable group of Russian high society regarded Tolstoy as "charming everyone there with his childlike gaiety and endless amusing escapades." After

taking leave of the Russians there, he embarked on a two-week journey, by foot, across the mountains to Fribourg.[13]

"Nature here has had a remarkably calm, harmonic, and Christianizing influence on me," he wrote on the day he began his journey. "Today the weather was clear. Lake Leman[14] shone before my eyes, its pulsing light and dark blues studded with the white and black dots of boats and sailboats. Around Geneva, in the distance over the glistening lake, the hot air shimmered and became hazy. On the opposite shore, the green Savoy mountains[15] rose sharply. Small white houses stood at the bottom; the fissures of a cliff looked like a huge white woman in an ancient costume.

"On the left, one could clearly see close up the village of Montreux[16] and its grandiose church perched over red grape arbors and the dark green thickets of fruit gardens. One could also make out the city of Villeneuve[17] standing on the very shore, the iron roofs of its homes blazing brightly in the midday sun. The mysterious canyon in the Vallais Alps[18] was surrounded by mountains seemingly piled one on top of another. The white, cold village of Chillon[19] stood out above the very water, and a small island, long the subject of poems and songs, protruded fancifully but splendidly across from Villeneuve. The lake was covered with ripples, the sun stroked its dark blue surface from above, and it seemed that the sails scattered over the lake stood motionless in the distance.[20]

"It is a remarkable thing. During my two-month stay in Clarens,[21] anytime in the morning and especially before evening, after dinner, when I opened the shutters of the shadowed window and looked out onto the lake, the verdure, and further on, the blue mountains that were reflected in it, the beauty of the scene blinded me and immediately made such an unexpected and powerful impression on me that I was seized by a feeling of love. I even felt a love for my very self rising in me; and I mourned my past and hopes for my future. I began to live in a joyous way. I wanted to live for a very long time, and the thought of death filled me with a poetic and childlike horror. . . . A physical impression, like beauty before me, shot through my eyes and entered my soul. . . .[22]

"I cannot talk to loved ones immediately before bidding them farewell.[23] I am ashamed to say that I love them. Why didn't I ever tell them such a thing earlier? And I also find it difficult to talk about trifles. . . . Our dear little group[24] had broken up, probably, forever. . . . Suddenly I felt lonely, and so very sad as we were parting for the very first time."

In this diary, where are his "wolflike eyes"? And why even here is there "the thought of death"?

Tolstoy introduced literary words into the fiction of that time: "Suddenly we were struck by an unusual *joyous, white* spring smell"; or: "It was black all around. The moon shone on the wide open field, the streams hummed evenly in the depths of the ravine, and the white heady smell of narcissus spilled out into the air."

Later portraits of Tolstoy show a seemingly different person. Having become a husband, a family man, a village mediator, and a tireless and a prudent master who transformed the landowning nobility into a cult, Tolstoy came to take on the gentry look of his time. He was at the height of his powers, living the practical and self-contented life that came with his privileged position, his increasing income, and his inherited traditions. In these portraits, he is again very well dressed. One picture even depicts him wearing a top hat. His poses are proud, handsome, and relaxed; his eyes show a gentrylike abhorrence of things; he holds a cigarette with careless ease.[25]

Looking at these pictures, one cannot but marvel that during these years he was writing *War and Peace* and depicting Natasha and Petya Rostov, Pierre, the death of the "little princess," Natasha's last meeting with Prince Andrei, their love, his death. One marvels at something else, too— that Tolstoy, always easily prone to tears, could still, even in these "gentry" years, suddenly burst out crying in a compassionate and tender way. Tenderness, compassion—such words sound strange when applied to him. But he once wrote to Sofya Andreevna: "I love you so very much! I carry myself back to the past—Pokrovskoe,[26] a lilac dress, a feeling of tenderness—and my heart begins to beat."

His inquisitiveness, mistrust, and severity—where do these come from?

"To be accepted as one of my chosen readers, I ask very little, only that you be sensitive . . . and devout so that, when reading my works, you will look for places that will touch your heart. . . . One can sing from either the throat or the chest. The voice that issues from the throat is more supple than the one that comes from the chest, but, on the other hand, it does not influence the soul. . . . But even with the most shallow melody, when I catch hold of a note that is sung with a full chest, my eyes invariably well up with tears.

"The same thing can also be said about literature: One can write from the head or from the heart. . . . I always stopped myself when I began writing with my head and tried to write only with my heart."[27]

Goethe[28] said: "Nature does not permit jokes. It is always serious and severe. It is always truth."

Like nature, Tolstoy was also staunchly "serious" and immensely "truthful."

"The hero of my story is Truth, which I love with all my soul, which I have tried to show in all its beauty, and which was, is, and will always be splendid."[29]

Tolstoy made this statement almost at the very beginning of his career, and he would often repeat it later on. He believed that "the only thing needed in both art and life is not to lie," and he applied this principle to all his writings, as well as to his entire spiritual life. Here one sees the legacy of his mother, from whom, generally speaking, he inherited a great deal.[30] He wrote about her: "There is a still another characteristic that distinguished my mother from her circle—the truthful and simple tone of her correspondence . . . for at that time, people especially loved to exaggerate emotions in their letters."

Goethe said: "People want nothing to do with ideas and thoughts. They are satisfied with words. Even my Mephistopheles knew such a thing." He then cited from his character:

> Should one have an urge for thought
> One can replace it with words. . . .[31]

Schopenhauer[32] believed that most people pass off words as thoughts and that most writers think only to write. Such a thing can be said even about many great writers, but never about Tolstoy.

The language of Tolstoy's writings is marvelous and truthful. It distinguishes itself from all of Russian literature by its complete lack of belletristic decorations, of trite devices and conventions. It strikes one with the boldness, necessity, and the precise resourcefulness of every word. The same thing can also be said about his letters: invariably genuine and straightforward, like the simple and precise manner of his speech.[33]

Incidentally, a well-known Russian musician, Goldenweiser, who was a frequent guest at Tolstoy's home for fifteen years, kept notes on his host during that time and has given us a list of some of the peculiarities of Tolstoy's speech.[34] For instance, Tolstoy pronounced "g" in an aspirated, peasantlike way, almost like a "h." He preferred old-fashioned variants for many words, for example, "Shtockholm." He used many local words from the Tula region; he loved to express himself in proverbs; he talked with the peasants in their language, addressing them informally but without being condescending.[35]

Goldenweiser was correct in what he said. But I, who come from the same region as did Tolstoy and hail from the same gentry-village milieu as he did, feel compelled to note: All our fathers and grandfathers spoke this way.[36] I also take exception to Goldenweiser's statement that Tolstoy never used "coarse" or "vulgar" words. He most certainly did use them, and quite freely. In fact, his sons and even daughters also used such words, just like the folk do from habit, without paying attention to the meaning or consequences of what they are saying.

Many people who were close to Tolstoy support my assertion. One said: "When Tolstoy's secretary, Gusev, wrote his biography of the writer,[37] he quoted Doctor Makovitsky as saying that 'generally speaking, Tolstoy could not swear.'" But from Lev Nikolaevich's diaries, we know that as a youth he would get so angry that he would beat his serfs.[38] But could he have done such a thing in silence or use polite words? Such silence or politeness would have shown not his short temper but a cruelty that was not typical of him.

Generally speaking, Tolstoy cannot be included among people whose tongues cannot utter vulgar words.[39] Even when, as a very old man, he would tell an anecdote in the presence of ladies, he could let loose words that were normally not said aloud. When Gorky first met Tolstoy, he was offended by Tolstoy's obscenity, since he believed that the great writer was using such language only because Gorky was from the proletariat.[40] But Gorky had little reason to take offense. For example, whenever Tolstoy quoted peasant speech, he did not refrain from using the most vulgar expressions in front of his guests.

Returning to the subject of Tolstoy's appearance, I repeat what I said earlier, about the first time that we met:

"I had hardly entered the hall, when I noticed that somewhere at the far end, over to the left, a small door immediately opened and out stepped a huge old man with a great beard, walking with a gait that was seemed both agile and awkward. He was light-footed and lively, but also terrible and sharp-eyed, with knitted brows. . . . He quickly headed my way, and as he approached me, he bowed slightly, held out his hand palm side up, and totally wrapped my hand in his."

About the last fact, I wanted to say that such a gesture was somehow animalistic.

I continue: "He then took my hand into his, shook it gently, and suddenly smiled a charming smile, tender but also slightly sad. I saw that his small gray-blue eyes were not at all terrible or sharp, but that they were bright, like those of an animal. The thin, light hair that remained on his head was gray and slightly curled at the ends and parted straight in the middle, peasant-style. His very large ears were unusually high on his head, and the arches of his eyebrows hung down low over his eyes. His beard was dry, thin, uneven, and transparent, allowing one to see his slightly protruding jaw."[41]

I must repeat: In my opinion, there was something sad and pitiful in his eyes and slightly protruding jaw.

Goldenweiser also made a list of Tolstoy's physical peculiarities. For instance, he noted a certain defect in the writer's speech: "Lev Nikolaevich had a lisp. . . . But I do not know if it was because he was an old man who was missing several teeth or whether he always spoke like that."

I asked Ilya L'vovich:

"Perhaps the reason why Lev Nikolaevich spoke the way he did was because of his slightly protruding jaw?"[42]

"Most likely," his son answered. "I and especially my older brother, Sergei, have the same type of jaw. As I see it, we are the two who look most like our father. Sergei's jaw is particularly prominent. And, as regards the way we walk, you are right when you say that father had something of the gorilla in him; but with my brother and me, that animal resemblance is even more pronounced. I am exactly like father. I walk quickly, almost at a run and as if walking on springs, but Sergei crouches down and bounces about just like a gorilla would."

Goldenweiser writes: "Lev Nikolaevich would take small, quick steps. When he walked, he would spread his toes and go down initially on his heels. Tolstoy's mother used to walk the same way. (So did Princess Mary in *War and Peace:* 'She walked into room with a heavy gait, stepping on her heels as she did.') Such a walk was a notable trait of almost all the Tolstoys."

When I saw him for the last time, on the Arbat in Moscow, he looked like an old man: shrunken and small. But formerly he had been quite tall. I well remember that when I first met him, I looked upward when he was shaking my hand, and I am average in height.

He was broad-shouldered and big-boned. Goldenweiser writes that Tolstoy was, in fact, unusually broad-shouldered: "Once I happened to be sleeping in his nightgown, and the shoulders of the thing hung down on me almost to my elbows." But Goldenweiser was short and small.

Tolstoy was shortsighted, but right up to his death he read and wrote without glasses.

For the most part, he talked in a very quiet manner, but when he called out for someone, the resonance of his voice was surprising.

As a youth, he was very strong.[43] And he remained so well into his old age. "One time," Goldenweiser writes, "we were all sitting at the table and arm wrestling. He beat everyone there." And that was only a year before his death.

His hands were big and could have belonged either to a lord or a peasant; and, as Goldenweiser accurately noted, Tolstoy's fingers had "firm, well-shaped nails."

Tolstoy would eat hurriedly, and sometimes even greedily. He usually did not eat much, but when there was something that he liked, he ate so excessively that he became sick afterward.[44] He did not care for fish or milk and did not eat meat either, even before he became a vegetarian.[45]

Whenever he was sick, he yawned loudly and so regularly that he could be heard throughout the house.

Alexandra L'vovna used to say about Sergei Nikolaevich: "When Uncle Sergei did not feel completely well, or when he would remember something unpleasant, he would start shouting in his study: 'Aaaaaa!'"

She would say the same thing about her father:

"One could suddenly hear father's terrible noises: 'Oookh, oookh, ookh!'

"People who were unaccustomed to such goings-on would ask fearfully: 'What's happening? Who's crying like that? Is it Lev Nikolaevich? Is he sick?'

"'No,' we would say with laughter. "Lev Nikolaevich is just yawning.'"

Everyone knows that he loved all kinds of physical exercise. He loved to go swimming, and he did so until the end of his life. Goldenveiser writes: "I remember that the first time I went swimming with him, I paid attention to a very big birthmark on the right side of his body. He swam somewhat like a frog, and also like a peasant—slowly, seriously, and purposefully."

Tolstoy was extremely courageous and brave. "I cannot imagine him being afraid,"[46] Goldenweiser writes. "Once on a winter day we were riding in a small sleigh. He was driving. A snowstorm came up and became so strong that we lost our way. We saw a house in the forest, so we set out for it to ask the forester who lived there how to get back onto the road. When we approached the house, three or four huge sheepdogs came running out, barking madly and surrounding our horse and sleigh. Tolstoy gave me the reins with a decisive air. Then he stood up, stepped out of the sleigh, whistled loudly, and, with nothing but his bare hands, headed straight for the dogs. The threatening dogs quieted down. As if acknowledging his power over them, they backed off and let him go his way. He passed among them quietly and entered the hut, his gray beard flying in the wind."

During the Caucasian "affair" and the siege of Sevastopol, he had conducted himself in a courageous—even dauntless—way; but he was terrified of rats. One time he was sitting in one of the trenches at Sevastopol, when he suddenly jumped out and ran to the fort, even though it was being severely bombarded by the enemy. He had seen a rat.[47]

Everyone knows that he was a passionate hunter[48] and that he loved horses and dogs.[49] Hunting he gave up only as an old man,[50] but his passion for riding horses continued until his death. He was a remarkable horseman. When he got on a horse, he was completely transformed: younger, stronger, and more hale and hearty. He truly knew horses; and as genuine connoisseur of these animals, he would rarely praise them without some criticism.[51] As for dogs, he could not stand their barking. Whenever a dog barked close by, he truly suffered. It was one of his stranger traits. Goethe was the same way. Indeed, he regarded the barking of a dog as something mystical.[52]

"Horses and horseback riding played a great role in our lives," Alexandra L'vovna wrote.

"If you were ever out riding with Father, you had to pay attention to what you were doing! He would ride through ravines, swamps, dense forests, and narrow paths, without considering the obstacles involved. . . .

"If Father saw a stream in front of him, he would not think about it for long, but would kick his horse, Délire; and the animal would fly like a bird to the other side. . . .

"Sometimes he would jump over a stream and head up a hill at full gallop. Everywhere were bushes and trees, and you had to watch out, if you did not want to crash into a trunk or have a branch poke out your eye.

"'Well?' he would shout, turning around.

"'I'm fine. I'm still here.'

"'Hold on tightly! Here we go!' . . .

"One time we were riding along the Zaseka,[53] and Father stopped in the forest and began talking with some woodcutters. Flies and gadflies kept biting the horses. My horse, a slow, lazy animal, was trying to shoo them off with its legs, head, and tail, when all of a sudden it bent its legs and lay down on the ground. Father started shouting loudly. By some miracle, I had just managed to jump off the animal and had not even gotten steady on my feet, when Father, as if he were a young man, hit the horse with such a powerful blow that it immediately jumped back up. . . .

"I was fifteen years old when he taught me to ride.

"'Hey, Sasha, don't use the stirrup. Just try riding at a gallop!' . . .

"One time he fell together with his horse. The animal, a hot-tempered brute from the steppe, became frightened by something. It jumped to the side and fell. Father, with lightning quickness and still holding on to the reins, freed his leg from the stirrup and was up on his feet before the horse got up on its legs."

Still another noticeable peculiarity about Tolstoy was the way he held his pen. He did not extend his fingers forward but cupped them together. He would also move the pen quickly, in circular fashion, almost without taking it from the paper or putting any pressure on it whatsoever. Again there is something from the animal world in movements such as these.

Can one tie all these characteristics to his unusual penchant for tears? Many people who knew him have commented on this trait. Throughout his life, Tolstoy cried easily, most often not from grief, but when he was telling a story or when he heard or read something that touched him.[54] For instance, he cried whenever he listened to music.

"He was musical by nature," Alexandra L'vovna writes. "From his youth on, he loved playing the piano.[55] In no way was he a musician, but he had an outstanding sensitivity for music. He sometimes did not like or was indifferent to something that I thought was wonderful—for example, the music of Wagner.[56] But what he approved of was always truly good.[57] When there was something that he especially disliked, the music of Mussorgsky, for example, he would say: 'It's shameful to listen to such a thing!' On the other hand, he was extremely fond of Russian folk songs, cheerful ones more than sad ones.[58] He rarely laughed; but, when he did, it was always to the point of tears."[59]

One can keep adding to this list of Tolstoy's personal characteristics. But I have cited enough of them to show how primitive he was, physically and spiritually; but for all this primitiveness,[60] he harbored such a wonderful fullness—a convergence of the finest and richest development of everything that humanity had acquired in the journey of its spirit throughout its history.

Zola once accurately expressed the essence of European opinion about Tolstoy,[61] a view that was typically Western—ignorant and self-assured. Simply put, Europeans believed that Tolstoy was, in truth, a major talent, but that he was also quite barbaric and a genuine child of his extremely emotional people. He was an individual whose thoughts were naive, who kept reinventing the wheel, and who kept getting confused by things that had been explained a long time ago.

In fact, there was a great deal of "naïveté" in Tolstoy. It is equally true that he kept reinventing the wheel, since he had little confidence in the discoveries of others. It is also beyond question that he was extremely emotional and that he had long been confused by things that were clear to people like Zola. Again speaking about music, he would say: "If all of civilization went to the devil, I would not regret anything except for the loss of music. . . . I love Pushkin and Goldenweiser, but if I were dying, the only art I would find it painful to part with is music."[62]

Music could move him almost to the point of pain. Bers, the brother of Sofya Andreevna, wrote in his memoirs:[63] "The sensations that music aroused in Tolstoy made him turn pale and grimace as if in horror."

Chapter Eleven

"TO BE ACCEPTED as one of my chosen readers, I ask that you be sensitive . . . and devout. . . ."

"There was a time when I reveled in my intelligence, in the name that I had made for myself; but now I know that if there is something good inside of me, it is a kind heart, one that is sensitive and able to love."

"I had grown fond of my dog, Dorka, because it is not an egoist. How can one learn to live like that, always to rejoice in the good fortune of others?"

With the years, he became more and more "sensitive," and by the end of his life, he had become so to an extreme.

"Approaching Ovsyannikovo,[1] I watched a splendid sunset. A shaft of light penetrated though the accumulating clouds, and the sun looked like a red burning coal. Below was a forest and a field of rye. How happy I was. And I thought: 'No, this world is not a joke or a valley of tears in passage to a better, eternal place; no, it is one of many eternal worlds, an abode which is joyous and splendid, and which we can—and must—make even more splendid for those who live with us and after us.'"

"I was passing through Turgenev's forest[2] at sunset. There were fresh grass, stars in the sky, the smells of flowering willows and of dying birch leaves, the sounds of nightingales, the hum of insects and a cuckoo bird. Here it was—a cuckoo bird, solitude, the pleasant, brisk movement of the horse under me, and a sense of physical and spiritual well-being. But as I always do, I also thought about death. And it became so very clear to me that on the other side of death, I would feel this good, no, even better, but in a different type of way. *As before, I tried to doubt that other life, and, also as before, I could not; and I became convinced of its existence.*"

"It seemed to me," Alexandra L'vovna recalled, "that it was typical of Father to enjoy life, flowers, trees, children, everything that surrounded him. In fact, his relish for such things grew stronger after his illnesses in the Crimea. Even now I can see him walking out of the forest, his collarbones protruding, and dressed in a white blouse that was too big for his gaunt body and with a collar that was too large for his neck. He is walking without a hat, the thin hair on his head is all ruffled.

84

"'Look what I have,' he said, smiling happily.

"I looked into his hat and saw some mushrooms arranged neatly on a burdock leaf.

"'Take a whiff. See how pleasant they smell!'

"Little by little, he grew stronger. . . . I remember the first time he rode a horse after his illness. With difficulty, Father put his left leg into the stirrup and, with even greater effort, swung his body atop the animal. The horse reared up and dashed off with Father along the 'prispekt' [prospect]. Needless to say, I was sick with worry. It seemed to me that Father would not be able to manage such a young, hot-tempered creature—I had purchased the animal only recently—and I impatiently waited his return.

"'I was in Kozlovka!' he shouted happily to me, as he came up to the house.

"As soon as I saw him, I knew that I had worried in vain. Délire was walking with a regular, peaceful step. . . .

"Father loved flowers, always picking them without their leaves, and pressing them tightly together. Whenever I would make bouquets for him, adding leaves and spreading out the petals, he did not like what I had done:

"'That's not the way you should do it.' he said. 'It should be simpler. . . .'

"Father was the first to bring home barely budding violets, forget-me-nots, and lilies of the valley. He enjoyed them all and gave them to everyone to smell. He especially liked forget-me-nots and clinging vines, and he would get upset that these vines did not stand up in water because their stems were too short.

"'Take a whiff. How finely they smell, like bitter almond. Don't you think so? And look at their colors and hues. Just look!'"

I repeat: Now that an entire quarter of a century has passed since his death, and as the result of all kinds of new evidence and testimony about him, people have greatly reexamined Tolstoy's image. Now everyone seems to think that this image has been scrutinized so precisely, objectively, and completely that we now know not only his main features but also his very essence. But this is not the case. Several new characteristics have finally been noticed, accepted, and understood; but they not have succeeded in altering previous ideas about him. People still call attention to his "wolfish eyes"; they still see him as a "great sinner." He continues to be the "apostle of love"—even though such a designation came into being only as a bit of eloquence that marked the solemn days after his passing.

But even such a label as "apostle of love" does not save Tolstoy from his critics.

For example, in a very recent article, Amfiteatrov, one of our oldest and most educated Russian writers says, "Tolstoy is hailed by all the countries and the peoples of the world. And in all the languages that have an alphabet, he has been the subject of voluminous tracts."

Yes, a great deal has been written about him and continues to be written about him, but what and how? Amfiteatrov waxes enthusiastically about a "great and superb piece of work" on Tolstoy, written by the Italian belletrist and poet Chinelli on the occasion of the twenty-fifth anniversary of the writer's death. According to Chinelli, who precisely is this Tolstoy? Indeed, what he thinks about Tolstoy corresponds completely well with what most enlightened people "in all the countries of the world" think about him.

[Chinelli writes:] "Tolstoy is neither a prophet nor a saint. Everything about him is human, healthy, and normal.[3]

"When one thinks about the paths that Tolstoy has taken in life, his Golgotha, one wants to compare him with the happiest and most saintly of people—Saint Francis of Assisi."

If Chinelli thinks that everything about Tolstoy is seemingly "human, healthy, and normal," why does he speak about the man's Golgotha? Do "healthy and normal" people pass through Golgotha? And if Tolstoy is "neither a prophet nor a saint," why does Chinelli draw parallels between Tolstoy and a saint? Such an allegation is even more incomprehensible because no one has yet canonized Tolstoy. And even if he were to be canonized, why should he invariably have to be like Saint Francis? After all, a great many saints do not resemble Saint Francis. But one thing is clear: Chinelli uses Saint Francis to criticize Tolstoy.

Chinelli begins by saying that Saint Francis, while still a youth and without any hesitation or doubt, turned his back on his home, his family, and all earthly temptations and delights; but that Tolstoy "sought simplicity" only in his old age—that is, it was right before his death that he abandoned the luxurious lifestyle in which he had lived his long life. Yes, let us begin with this.

Everyone in the world still believes that, despite all of Tolstoy's "simplicities" and his rejection of every kind of gentry lordliness and largesse, he still enjoyed a luxurious and affluent lifestyle. But it is also noteworthy that it was Tolstoy himself who was responsible for the myth about his gentry lavishness and wealth, just as he was guilty of the tall tales about his great sinfulness. What Tolstoy would not do to malign himself![4] No one remembers these modest words: "I have never been angry. At one time, two or three things tormented my conscience, but I have never been cruel." But can anyone forgo all the terrible stories that he told about his youth and middle age?

"I cannot recall those years without horror, loathing, and heartfelt pain. . . . I slayed people in war, I challenged people to duels to kill them, I lost money at cards. I lived off the labor of peasants, I deceived them, committed adultery with them, and put them to death. Lies, thievery, all kinds of adultery, violence, and murder. . . . There is not a single crime that I have not committed."[5]

He also talked about his weakness for "luxury" when he wrote: "I was completely under the sway of earthly temptations and sought to live lavishly." How many times did he write such things? One cannot keep count.[6] But is there even one truthful word in this confession? It is not true, for instance, that he fell "completely under the sway of earthly temptations," for "living in luxury" tormented him terribly throughout his life. Indeed, for entire decades on end, he desired to part with such luxury, but he did not do so only because, in his own words, he did not have sufficient cruelty to treat his family in such an egotistical and inhumane way. The reference to his "earthly temptations" is also false. Indeed, anyone who was the least bit familiar with Tolstoy's life would simply laugh at the word "temptation."

"All my life I lived in wealth. . . ." But the Tolstoys were never rich. As Tolstoy wrote in his memoirs, his paternal grandmother[7] was the daughter of "blind prince Gorchakov, who had accumulated a great deal of property"; but Ilya Andreevich Tolstoy, her husband and his grandfather, squandered both his own fortune and hers. Her husband was "not only lavish, but stupid, wasteful and most of all, naive. . . . His estate was the site of endless parties, theaters, dinners, and balls. Such affairs, coupled with Ilya's passion for card games, which he had no talent for, as well as with his willingness to lend money to anyone who asked even though most never paid him back, resulted in his wife's huge estate being irreversibly in debt. The couple had no money to live on, and he had to obtain a position as the governor of Kazan."[8]

Tolstoy's grandfather on his mother's side (Nikolai Sergeevich Volkonsky) was quite rich; but he used a good part of the money that had come from his wife, Maria Nikolaevna, to cover Ilya Andreevich's debts. From Nikolai Ilyich's estate, there remained only Yasnaya Polyana, but Nikolai inherited this property from his wife, not his father. Simply put, the supposedly rich Leo Tolsoy was born into and grew up in poverty, suffering great need as a youth.[9] Later on, when he considered himself to be rather secure financially, he would despair over the least little extraneous expense. Indeed, he was just like Levin, who had to pay an "entire" seven rubles, wining and dining with Oblonsky in a restaurant.

Furthermore, whatever "luxury" surrounded him in his old age can be seen, for example, from the notes of his friend Boulanger, who, in 1901, accompanied the sick Tolstoy for a cure in the Crimea where he had been invited to stay with Countess Panina.[10] "Lev Nikolaevich looked at her home almost in horror," Boulanger wrote, "for he was accustomed to the simple, modest, if not absolutely poor surroundings of Yasnaya Polyana, where the floors in many of the rooms were unpainted, and the windows had rotten frames with chipped paint."[11]

Alexandra L'vovna, who also had accompanied Tolstoy to the Crimea, had the same feeling about Panina's house as her father: "I was stunned by the luxury of the palace. I had never lived in such a place. I felt uncomfortable and ill at ease: the marble windowsills, the carved doors, the heavy expensive furniture, the large rooms with their high ceilings."[12]

One should also correct misconceptions as regards Tolstoy's simple taste in clothes. For some reason, people have unjustly fixated on Tolstoy's manner of dress, a preoccupation that continues to the present day. Even before he purposely simplified his attire, Tolstoy was like all country landlords in that, in the winter, he wore the same half-length, sheepskin coat that he became famous for later on. (Sometimes he wore this same coat even when he was in the city.) He also wore a blouse, long boots, and felt shoes. He sometimes would even plow the soil and mow the grass.

But then people began to marvel at such things. Why? Of course, they would probably be surprised if Anatole France wore a half-length coat, or Marcel Proust held a scythe in his hands, or Baudelaire dug up the earth with a wooden plow. But Tolstoy? (Incidentally, I understand that Merezhkovsky, in his book *Tolstoy and Dostoevsky*,[13] has devoted a great many uninformed pages to Tolstoy's sheepskin coat (together with the scythe and saw that hung in his workroom). It would be difficult to find even among contemporary Russian writers a more urban dweller than Merezhkovsky, who, perhaps from birth, has never laid eyes on a scythe or saw, and once called a saw a "file."[14]

"Saint Francis of Assisi," Chinelli writes further, "was a cheerful person. He sang and taught joy in life. But Lev. . . ."

What about "Lev"? Already an old man, "Lev" once wrote: "Having listened to political discussions and arguments, I went into another room where people were singing and playing a guitar, and I clearly felt a sacred happiness."

Chinelli continues: "Lev suffered mortal torment in his intellectual struggles with beauty and nature. . . . He received from God the gift to understand nature, and he enjoyed it thoroughly. But for him, such a gift was not enough. In his human pride, he could not accept such enjoyment in a spontaneous way. He wanted to scrutinize it, to know it thoroughly. . . . Both men, Francis and Lev, loved animals; but how differently! Leo, a hunter from his youth, had to pledge not to kill animals. But Francis. . . ."

Again one has to remind Chinelli that many saints have wanted to "scrutinize and come to know something thoroughly." As for hunting, Saint Estafy differed from Saint Francis in that he, too, was a "great hunter" but "also pledged not to kill animals."[15] But Estafy was not alone. Consider Julian the Hospitaller, for example.

Chinelli repeats, word for word, the malicious and persistent opinions about Tolstoy, views that contradict the reality of the writer and that gave rise to the enmity and even hatred that a great many people have for Tolstoy.

"My genuine 'I' is despised by those around me," Tolstoy noted bitterly when, as an old man, he was writing about his "deeds and days" in Yasnaya Polyana. This "I" was despised not only by several of the people who surrounded him there but also by thousands upon thousands of people who surrounded him in Russia, Europe, and America. His "I" is being despised even now. I did not select Chinelli to critique on purpose. I learned of his "great and splendid work" accidentally, from Amfiteatrov, but I immediately saw how typical and mundane Chinelli's ideas on Tolstoy were. Consider how a young Italian writer and an old Russian one could share a hatred for Tolstoy. The Russian writer would have to know and understand Tolstoy a hundred times better than any foreign writer would. But Amfiteatrov agrees fully with Chinelli—so much so that the more one reads Amfiteatrov's article, the less one understands who is writing: Amfiteatrov or Chinelli.

Amfiteatrov writes:

"Everything in Tolstoy is about loving a woman and about rebelling against this love. Tolstoy loved so much that he overflowed with this emotion. But how did he love? No one loved more humanly and less spiritually than Tolstoy did. And, as soon he entered upon physical decline, he became angry that he was losing the bodily strength that linked him to mother earth. For an entire thirty years, he vented his rage, crudely cursing and protesting his condition as an old man would. One only has to remember the dark lust of Father Sergius, while his creator preached absolute chastity."[16]

Chinelli says the same thing:

"For Tolstoy, sermons on purity and chastity were discourses of imperious force, accusatory polemic, and the most profane and indecent mockery of nature and life."

It would not be worth citing this slander had it occurred by chance or had it been uttered only by some Chinelli. But is Chinelli the only one who forgets all of Tolstoy's passionate and heartfelt strivings precisely for this purity and chastity, strivings that were innate to him from his very early youth on? Is Chinelli the only one who ignores Tolstoy's horror, his almost mystical fear of sin, which he expressed whenever he wrote about the loss of his youthful innocence?

Tolstoy wrote about this youthful loss in "How Love Will Die."[17] In middle age, he wrote about it again; for example, how Nikolai Rostov, who had yet to be with a woman, went with Denisov to visit a Greek girl. "He went as if to commit one of the most horrible and irrevocable of crimes," Tolstoy wrote. "He felt that the decisive moment had come, one which he had thought about and wavered over a thousand times. . . . He shuddered from fear, angry with himself, and feeling that he was taking an irrevocable step in life, and that something criminal and terrible would happen at this very minute."

About Rostov after his fall Tolstoy wrote in a still more heartrending way: "He woke and kept crying from shame and regret about his fall, which, he believed, separated him from Sonya forever"—or more accurately, from the woman whom he saw as his ideal of love which could never be defined. [Rostov thought:] "Whether it was because of my dreams of first love or a recollection of my mother's gentleness, I do not know [why I did what I did]. I did not know who this woman was; but she had everything that one loved, and—sweetly, painfully—an irresistible power attracted me to her."[18]

These lines occur in excerpts that Tolstoy did not include in *War and Peace,* since their overtly lyrical style was not in keeping with the overall tone of the novel. But the sentiments expressed in these lines continued in Tolstoy's soul, even when he was an old man.

He wrote: "Even today I still think about the charm—precisely the charm of a newborn love. It is like the sudden smell of a freshly flowering linden tree, or a moonlit shade when it begins to fall."

After these lines, what is one who reads Chinelli to think: "On Tolstoy's lips, sermons on innocence and chastity are only imperative acts of force, the stuff of accusatory polemics."

But can one judge all these Chinellis harshly? Did not Tolstoy himself proclaim repeatedly that almost throughout his life he committed "all kinds of adultery"! Also, some of Tolstoy's friends and acquaintances were quite eager to indict him for his sins. The deceased Boborykin told me:

"Nekrasov—whom Tolstoy considered to be one of the most intelligent people that he had ever met[19]—called Tolstoy a great voluptuary, and I would often remind Tolstoy of what Nekrasov had said. As soon as Tolstoy would start reproaching me for the coarse way we all lived, and how little we thought about our souls, I would immediately say to him: 'You, Lev Nikolaevich, you're the one who needs salvation from all your great sins, but what do I have to worry about? The people in heaven will take me with open arms. They'll tell me: "Come right in, dear Pyotr Nikolaevich, you have lived your entire life without ever having drunk that extra glass of wine, not like that Leo Tolstoy!"[20] Unlike you and the Buddha, I did not renounce my kingdom or my wife; and I hope that I do not die like the Buddha did. That one reached all kinds of holiness when he was eighty years old; but, while visiting the home of a tanner friend of his, he ate too much pork and then could not resist yet another temptation: He went swimming in a river and, on that very same evening, gave up his soul to God.'"[21]

"A great voluptuary" and because of "all [his] great sins. . . ." What is the basis for such assertions? That Tolstoy had a great passionate nature is without question, and even greater was his attraction to all the carnal delights of this world. But should one understand the word "voluptuousness" in its usual sense? And where in Tolstoy's life can we find factual evidence for instances of this "great voluptuousness"? Even now everyone unanimously asserts that Tolstoy had a "very stormy youth."[22] But what was so unusual about such a youth? And what precisely were these storms?

Regarding his early years, Tolstoy wrote: "I solemnly revered the ideal of virtue, as well as the conviction that one must constantly improve himself. . . . I made it a rule to read an hour from the Gospels daily, to give one-tenth of all my money to the poor, to seek them out and assist them. . . . I also made it a daily habit to clean my own room, to keep it in perfect condition, and not to force my servant to do anything on my behalf, for he was like myself. . . . I also made it a rule to go to the university on foot . . . and in general to live a life that was moral, meaningful, and sinless."[23]

Did this "solemn reverence for virtue" disappear in his later years? Sometimes he played a reckless game of cards, sometimes he visited Gypsy women. He had two relationships with women before he was married. He was in love first with Molostvova,[24] then Arsenieva.[25] But are these really "storms"?!

Boborykin would offer evidence for Tolstoy's "great passion for the flesh" by saying:

"There is a great deal of evidence for Tolstoy's sinful nature. First of all, there are his own confessions about his youth; for example, those awful diaries which he, cruelly and basely, handed over to that poor girl, Sofya Andreevna, for her to read on the night before their marriage."[26]

Confessions, diaries. . . . But one must know how to read such things. "Lies, thievery, all kinds of adultery, violence, murder. . . . There is not a single crime that I have not committed." A legendary scoundrel!

Chapter Twelve

TOLSTOY'S LAST SECRETARY, Bulgakov,[1] empha-
sizes in one of his jottings that Tolstoy passionately yearned to learn the secrets of the soul. This yearning, Bulgakov continues, was something that
everyone knew about, but hardly anyone knows that Lev Nikolaevich could
also be found eavesdropping at doors.

Bulgakov also emphasizes Tolstoy's rapt attention to his "strict observation of all the phenomena" in the love between a man and a woman. He
writes that Tolstoy was for complete chastity between a couple and saw
physical relations, even in marriage, as dirty and debasing.[2]

Bulgakov continues: "I once read in a letter that Tolstoy had just written
to a certain Petrovskaya: 'There is no other sin that I believe to be more vile
and blameworthy than the sin against chastity, and that is probably why, rightly
or wrongly, I consider this evil to be one of the most destructive for life.'"

Bulgakov recalled yet another letter of Tolstoy's: "You say that the human being draws from both a physical and spiritual beginning. Such a view
is completely just; but unjust is your statement that these physical and spiritual beginnings are equally destined for good. . . . Good is natural only to
the spiritual side, since good is the ongoing liberation of the spirit from a
body that is doomed to evil and singularly impedes the soul from attaining
this spiritual good."

People in general believe that Tolstoy took such a view of this "physical beginning" only in old age. I repeat what one hears from just about anyone: "Tolstoy's notion of 'physical beginnings' was drawn from the stormy
sensuality of his youth, the rare male passion by which he sired thirteen
children, and the sheer power with which he always talked about everything
that had to do with the body."[3]

As for offspring, Tolstoy did not have thirteen children but fourteen.
In the summer of 1909 he wrote:

"Looking at the bare feet of some women, I recalled Aksinya—that
she was alive, and that people said that Ermil was our son."[4]

Generally speaking, this Aksinya can be seen as a trump ace in the
hands of those who believe that Tolstoy was a great "sinner." It was this same

Aksinya, after all, who inspired him in his old age to write *The Devil,* as well as several lines in other works of that period that were matchless in their explicit descriptions of the physical feelings of love.[5] In that same year, Sofya Andreevna, while recopying his new story, "Who Are the Murderers?"[6] noted:

"The story is about revolutionaries, executions, and the origins of such things. It could have been an interesting piece. But he is using the same devices as before. He is still describing peasant life. He is still delighting in the *strength* of a young woman's body, in her sunburned legs, in things that so powerfully had seduced him at another time. He is still talking about that very Aksinya with her shining eyes; and at eighty years old, he is doing so almost unconsciously, drawing anew from the depths of his memories and the sensations of previous years. Aksinya was a woman from Yasnaya Polyana, the last of Lev Nikolaevich's mistresses before he got married."

About this Aksinya, Sofya Andreevna also wrote at the very beginning of their married life, only a few months after their wedding. Aksinya, together with another peasant woman from Yasnaya Polyana, would wash the floors in the Tolstoys' home. Sofya Andreevna wrote: "[He writes] that 'he is in love as never before!'[7] And with a peasant woman, a fat, pallid peasant woman. It is awful to behold. With what interest do I look at the dagger, at the rifles. . . ."[8]

Aksinya was "the last of Lev Nikolaevich's mistresses before he got married." That means there were others. About such liaisons, he himself would say: "When I was young, I led a very bad life, but there are two events which particularly torment me even now. . . . The first one was my affair with a peasant woman from our village—there is a hint of it in my story *The Devil.* The second was my wrongdoing with a maid named Glasha who lived in my aunt's home. She was naive, and I seduced her. She was chased out of the house and perished."

Such was the case of Katyusha Maslova in *Resurrection.* Here anyone can ask me: What more proof of Tolstoy's sensual nature do you need if he could write that at the time of his affair with Aksinya, he had the "feeling of a stag-deer" toward her?

Tolstoy wrote to Chertkov about still another woman, that is, the cook Domna, who aroused in him a passion which "made him suffer terribly as he experienced but struggled with his weakness."[9] And notice, Tolstoy's detractors will tell me, how vividly he could remember his feelings over the course of entire decades, right up to advanced old age, how well he could preserve within himself a freshness that could only be attributed to "devilish appeal," and which he captured in the first stages of love between Nekhlyudov and Katyusha in *The Devil.* [Readers should] recall, these same people continue, that all his earlier, most astounding descriptions were of fleshly and material realities.

[Readers should also] recall the "infinity" of animals, birds, and insects in the steamy woods over the Terek. Remember [in *The Cossacks*] Uncle Eroshka, Maryanka, Lukashka who killed an Abrek[10] . . . Recall the "dead body of Prince Serpukhovskoy that traveled around the world" in "Kholstomer," or [in *Anna Karenina*] the way Stiva Oblonsky shifted his well-groomed body on the couch as he was waking up, or the greasy body of Vasen'ka Veslovsky, . . . or the bodies of Anna and Vronsky and their terrible carnal fall ("as an executioner looks upon the body of his victim, so Vronsky looked upon Anna after their tryst"). What about the body of Hélène [in *War and Peace*]? And the "white leg" of her wounded, howling brother as he was undergoing the amputation? What about Trukhachevsky in *The Kreutzer Sonata,* who so greedily and lustfully tore into the lamb chop with his red lips?

The body, the body, always the body.[11] Prince Andrei, mortally wounded at Borodino, is brought to the emergency hospital, and once again one reads: "Everything that he saw about him merged in one impression, that is, a human body, naked, covered with blood, a body that seemed to take up the entire low tent, just as several weeks earlier, on that hot August day, another body took up the dirty pond on the road to Smolensk.[12] Yes, it was the same body, that same *chair à canon,*[13] the sight of which, as if to predict what was happening now, had so horrified him then."

How can anyone object to such proof?

People still say: "Tolstoy, of course, exaggerated his passions, his sinfulness in his repentant confessions. But how can one deny and explain his rapt attention to all kinds of earthly flesh and, in particular, to the human body—and most of all the feminine form?"

I do not deny such a thing, and I am even ready to quote again from his notes:

"I passed by some sheds. I remember the nights that I spent there, the youth and beauty of Dunyasha (I never had a tryst with her), her strong womanly body. Where is that body now?"

Here it is again: That "strong womanly body." But what deep sorrow emerges from this "Where is it now"! What can compare with the poetic charm and sadness of these lines? Perhaps no one else in world literature could feel the various types of earthly flesh with such sharpness, if only because no one else had yet another gift, that is, such a piercing feeling of doom, of the decay of all worldly flesh, felt with an intensity that was innate and that filled his entire life. He was well aware of *chair à canon,* the "meat" that was destined for the cannons during war and, in all times and centuries, for death.

To the dying Prince Andrei, death was something that had become "already close, something that was could almost be understood and touched.

It was threatening, eternal, distant and unknown, an entity whose presence he had always felt throughout his life." Tolstoy felt it, too.

"You are cold, death, but I was your master," Hadji-Murad would sing his favorite song. "The earth will take my body, the heavens will accept my soul."

Tolstoy was not a "master" of death. Indeed, all his life he was horrified by death; he would not accept it. "It is coming! Here it is! But it's not supposed to be here!" He experienced envious joy before the wild savagery of Hadji-Murad and Eroshka. They were wondrously strong, innocent, and carefree. Unconsciously, they brought their bodies to realize the "will to live," almost like the one whom Tolstoy likened to Hadji-Murad as he fought for his life in a field of thistle.[14]

Tolstoy always hated this bestial human flesh, this "meat" that was destined for an unclean death. He thought differently about the flesh of an animal, a "stag-deer," for example, or the flesh of "a strong woman's body." But the "stag-deer" within him also made him shudder. After all, he had not been born a deer, a Hadji-Murad, or an Eroshka. Already in his mother's womb he had been marked with a terrible sign; that is, he would sense "the threatening, the eternal, and the unknown" throughout his life. He reviled his body from youth on; and the older he got, the more often and strongly he did so, to the point that in the last years of his life he constantly prayed to God: "Father, deliver me from this life! Father, vanquish, expel, and destroy my loathsome flesh! Help me, Father!"

In other words, he was saying: "Give me the power totally to survive my material being, to defeat the death that rules my flesh, 'to be liberated' and to merge with you! For it is the 'devil,' in the personage of Mara and Death, that is tempting me with the charms of this fleshly world, and with its new conceptions and births—help me father in my struggle with him!"

Once he asked Professor Usov in a demanding way:

"I have been wanting to ask you, Sergei Alexeevich, is it true that when a mad dog bites someone, the victim will most likely die within six weeks? . . . I very much liked the idea that people die when they are bitten. I think that it is just great. A dog bites a person, and the person knows that he will die within six weeks. In the meantime, he can do what he wants; he can hit someone with truth right between the eyes!"

Yes, it was not for nothing that Tolstoy pestered Usov. He loved to "cut people to pieces." He saw the world about him with brilliant clarity and wisdom. In this he was like Anna [Karenina], who, on the threshold of death, awoke from her dream of life and regained insight. He could be as merciless as Anna as she traveled from station to station.

"I again understand everything," Anna said to herself, as soon as the carriage began to move. . . . "Yet, what was the last thing that I thought about so clearly?" She tried to remember. "Yes, it was Yashvin who told me: 'The struggle for existence and the emotion of hatred are the only things that unite people.'" "No, you are traveling in vain," she mentally addressed the other people in the four-horse carriage who appeared to be on the way for a holiday in the country. "And the dog that you are taking along will not help you. For you cannot run away from yourself." Having thrown a quick look in the direction where Pyotr was turning his head, she saw a drunken, half-dead factory worker swinging his head as he was being led somewhere by a policeman. . . . [Anna thought:] "'Count Vronsky and I also did not find this pleasure, although we expected a lot from it.' And for the first time, Anna now turned to that bright light in which she saw everything, her relationship with him."

At the station, "sitting on a star-shaped sofa waiting for the train, she looked with disgust at the people who were coming and leaving. . . . The bell had sounded, and some young men passed by, ugly, impudent, scurrying off somewhere, and but also very cognizant of the impression that they were making. Pyotr with his livery, laced-up boots, and dumb animal-like face, also made his way through the hall to escort her to the train car. The noisy young men quieted down when she passed by them on the platform, but one turned to another and seemed to whisper something repulsive. She climbed the tall steps and, having entered the compartment, sat by herself on a spring sofa, which was now dirty, although it once had been white. . . . Pyotr, with a foolish smile on his lips, passed by the window and raised his lace-decorated hat as a sign of farewell, but the impudent conductor slammed the door shut and latched it. An ugly lady with a bustle (Anna mentally undressed the woman and shuddered at her ugliness), along with some girls laughing in an unnatural way, ran below. . . .

"A dirty, deformed peasant with disheveled hair sticking out from his hat went by the window and bent down to the wheels of the car. . . . The conductor opened the door, letting in a man with his wife. . . . The couple sat facing her, looking attentively but furtively at her dress. . . . The pair were repulsive to Anna. She saw clearly how tired of each other they were, how they hated each other. And could anyone not hate such poor freaks. . . .

"'Now where did I leave off? [Anna continued to think.] That I cannot think of a situation in life that would not be a torture, that we are created only to suffer, that we all know such things, and that we constantly come up with the means to deceive ourselves. And when we see the truth, what do we do? We get rid of it. Why don't we merely extinguish the candle when there is nothing more to look at, when everything that we see is repulsive? Why are those young people shouting in the next car? Why are they laughing? Everything is falsehood and lies, everything is deception, everything is evil!'

"When the train approached the platform, Anna left with the other passengers but shunned them as if they were lepers."

Later on one reads: "The candle by which she had been reading a book that was full of worries, deception, sadness, and grief suddenly burst forth with a light that was brighter than before. It lit for her everything that formerly had been in the darkness. It crackled, began to flicker, and went out forever."

Chapter Thirteen

SOFYA ANDREEVNA ALWAYS INSISTED:
"No one knows Lyovochka but me. I am the only one who knows him. He is a sick and abnormal person."

Tolstoy died at the age of eighty-three. Such longevity means he must be counted among the most select group of people who enjoy good physical health. (As the Bible says: "We live to our seventies, and those with better health, to eighty.")[1] Furthermore, his death happened by chance. If he had not left his home, and if he had not lived his life under the pressures of constant work, in a state of such "abnormal" sensitivity, and in such terrible physical and spiritual tension, he would have most likely lived to be a hundred. But individuals who reach a hundred are a rare breed. People have long insisted that Tolstoy enjoyed very good health; but he justly said about himself: "I have always had poor health, despite my strong physical makeup." From his childhood on, he was subject to various illnesses. Even as a youth, he wrote:

"My health is not good, my soul is at its darkest, I am extremely weak, and when I become the least bit tired, I feel attacks of fever coming on."[2]

As a result, he often had deep fits of fainting followed by such convulsions that it is still unknown whether one Moscow professor was right when he alleged that Tolstoy suffered from a form of epilepsy.[3] More important, he had the beginnings of tuberculosis (which, as everyone knows, gives its victims a special spiritual frame of mind).[4]

His family, also, was not "normal."

His mother died at the age of thirty-nine; his father, at forty-two. All that is known about his father was that he was very "sensitive"[5] and that he had a tic (his head would twitch).[6] Also as everyone knows, his mother, Maria Nikolaevna Volkonskaya,[7] was a model for Princess Mary in *War and Peace,* because of Maria's exalted spirit, religious fervor, and passion for talking with all kinds of "God's people": men and women pilgrims, God's fools,[8] and saintly types.[9] His paternal aunt[10] was particularly religious. "Her favorite activities were to read from the lives of the saints, to talk with pilgrims, God's fools, monks, and nuns. (Some would visit her, others always lived in her house.) . . . She not only observed the fasts, prayed a great deal, and kept in contact with religious people, but she also genuinely lived the Christian life, seeking to avoid all kinds of luxury and conveniences. She tried to serve others as much as she could and never had any money because she gave everything she had to the poor. In matters of food and dress, she was so simple and nondemanding that it defied the imagination.

"This is unpleasant for me to say," Tolstoy wrote, "but from childhood on, I remember my aunt's sour smell, most likely the result of her slovenliness. But she was also a graceful, poetic Hélène, with splendid blue eyes, who loved to read and copy French poems, played the harp, and was the center of attention at the balls! She died in a monastery, at Optina Pustyn." (Tolstoy's sister, Maria Nikolaevna, also died there.)

Tolstoy's brothers, Dmitri and Nikolai, died of tuberculosis in their youth. Dmitri was also mentally ill. In him were merged extreme irritability with extreme kindness, extreme selfishness and great pride with morbid humility and self-abasement, and ascetic proclivities with bouts of sensuality, drinking, and debauchery. I cite from [Biryukov's] first recollections:[11]

"Miten'ka was a year younger than I. He had big black, severe-looking eyes . . . and was very willful as a child. . . . For instance, he would get angry and burst out crying whenever his nurse did not look at him. . . . Mother had a lot of difficulty with him. . . . When I was a student in Kazan, I took after my brother Seryozha, following down his corrupt path. . . . I tried to appear sophisticated, *comme il faut*. But there was not a trace of such things in Miten'ka. . . . He was always serious, thoughtful, and chaste. He was also decisive, hot-tempered, and did everything to the best of his abilities. . . .

"Miten'ka had a servant named Vanyusha. He treated this individual badly and, it seems, even beat him. . . . I remember Miten'ka once standing before Vanyusha, confessing his wrongs and begging for the servant's forgiveness in an abject way. . . . Miten'ka grew up a loner, and, except for moments of anger, was always serious and quiet, with huge dark eyes that were thoughtful and severe. He was tall, quite thin, with big, long arms, and a hunched back. . . . From his very first year at the university, he became extremely religious; and, as with everything he did, he was like that to the end. He observed the fasts and went to all the church services. . . . He did not dance, avoided society, and always wore the same student uniform with a narrow tie. From a very early age, he had a tic: He kept twitching his head, as if he were trying to free himself from a tie that was too tight. . . .

"Of all the friends that Miten'ka could have had, he chose a poor, pitiful student and was close only with him. . . . Out of pity, our family had taken in a very strange and mournful-looking being, a girl, one Lyubov' Sergeevna. . . . She was not only pathetic, but also repulsive. . . . Her face was all swollen. . . . Her eyes were like little cracks between two distended, glossy, browless pillows. Her cheeks, nose, lips, and mouth were similarly swollen, glossy, and yellow. She talked with difficulty, as if there were a boil in her mouth. In summer, flies landed on her face, but she did not notice them. . . . Her hair was still black, but thin and failed to hide her bare scalp. . . . She always gave off a foul odor. . . . But this very Lyubov' Sergeevna became Miten'ka's friend. . . .[12]

"After he left the university, Miten'ka lived the same strict, subdued life as before, without wine, tobacco, or women until he reached the age of twenty-six. . . . He hung around monks and pilgrims. . . .[13]

"But then he changed suddenly. He immediately started to drink, smoke, spend money, and visit women. . . . The first woman whom he met, a prostitute by the name of Masha, he purchased and took for himself. . . . As I see it, it was not his immoral, unhealthy lifestyle that killed Miten'ka's strong organism so much as it was his internal struggle, his pangs of conscience. He fell ill with consumption. . . . He looked awful. His huge hand seemed glued to the two bones of his arm. His face featured only eyes that were still serious and splendid, but now with an inquisitive look about them. . . . He did not want to die; he did not want to believe that he was dying. Masha, the pockmarked prostitute that he had purchased for himself, was with him, dressed in a shawl. . . . He asked that a miracle-working icon be brought to him. I still remember the expression on his face when he prayed to it."[14]

Tolstoy's family has lived in Russia for almost six hundred years. It traces its beginning to a "a nobleman named Indris"[15] who came to Russia "from the lands of Caesar, from the 'Germans'" (the word which Russians in ancient times used to call all foreigners). Within some three hundred years, the family became famous in Russian history: It occupied an honored position of service under the Russian tsars,[16] having received the title of "count" and increasing their blood ties with well-known Russian families.[17] Tolstoy's great-grandfather married Princess Shchetinina, his grandfather (Ilya Andreevich) married Princess Gorchakova, and his father (Nikolai Ilyich) married Princess Volkonskaya, who was a direct descendant of the Ryurikovichians themselves, the progeny of the first tsarist dynasty in Russia.[18] Volkonskaya's mother was a Trubetskaya, but her father traced his lineage to those Volkonskys[19] whose direct ancestor was a Ryurikovichian: Saint Michael, the sovereign prince of Chernigov.[20]

Everyone knows how robust were the members of these ancient clans, this physical and spiritual aristocracy. Such a select group, strong not only in body but also in soul, can also be found among the simple common folk of any nationality. Among Russian peasants, for instance, there have been and continue to be "pedigrees" who distinguish themselves from the crowd externally and internally.[21] Quite a few of them live a long life; but, for the most part, they are atavistic types, akin to cavemen and gorillas, savage, passionate, speaking a language filled with rich and powerful images. Such atavism is also the lot of most Russian noblemen: tall, big-boned, with strong arms and legs, and faces that are huge, like those of the folk. Their language is expressive, rich, and filled with images and emotions. Tolstoy belonged to this group. Like them, he was very "strong" physically. But is this type always "normal"?

Leibniz labeled the "eternal part of our moral nature" as a "monad."[22] Goethe called it "entelechy"[23] and added that geniuses had two periods of youth, whereas others had only one. "If this 'entelechy' is weak, it yields to the primacy of the body during its physical decline (in earthly life). When the body grows old, 'entelechy' can do nothing to stop the aging process. But if this 'entelechy' is strong, from the time of its entry into the body, it not only strengthens and ennobles the organism, but it also invests the body with an eternal youth which this 'entelechy' itself possesses. That is why especially gifted people have two periods of personal productivity. They become young again, they enter into a second youth." How strong must Tolstoy's "entelechy" have been!

Alexandra L'vovna writes in her memoirs that in the summer of 1901 her father became dangerously ill. He had begun to experience fever and angina pectoris and was taken to the Crimea. But there he again fell much more seriously ill than previously: first pleurisy, next creeping pneumonia, and then typhoid fever. He spent four months in bed. She records her impression: "That an old man in his eighties, with heart problems and debilitating angina, could overcome pneumonia and the typhoid fever that almost immediately followed was the greatest of miracles."[24]

Another miracle was to happen later. After all these illnesses, he would live on for nine more years, not in a state of decline but in constant work, and at times with such great physical verve that no one among the young could compare with him in energy and vigor (and in that spiritual joy which continued to enlighten him).[25]

Such was the way he lived even during part of the very last year of his life. More than once during that time, his loved ones noted: "Papasha is very busy, healthy, hale, and hearty"; and: "Lev Nikolaevich is very young, robust, and well. He is so remarkably active that we can hardly keep up with him."

These two excerpts were written in early spring 1910; and it was no mere coincidence that he had entered into a prespring "youth," for he always had an accurate sense of the rise and fall of forces in nature. He himself would say: "I always work best during the end of winter and the beginning of spring."

"And the body will return to earth, just as the soul will return to God. . . ."

Who loved and felt the earth more than he did? He would talk about Homer whom, after having learned Greek in two months,[26] he could begin

101

to read in the original. "What earthly excitement, what earthly power!" he would say.

"Reading Homer is like drinking water from a spring. It hurts the teeth with coldness, it glistens and shines, even its specks of dirt make it seem cleaner and sweeter."[27]

In June 1878, he wrote:

"At midday, it is quiet and hot. The fragrance of clover and of Saint-John's-wort is overwhelming, intoxicating, and sweet. The grass is even higher over by the woods in the dell, but with the same intoxicating smell. The forest paths are breathless, like a hothouse. . . . Bees on a wood stump take their turn, going from flower bed to flower bed, filled with yellow blossoms. . . . It is hot on the road, and the dust and tar exude a fiery smell."

Such a description is extremely striking for its strength, its praise of earthly charms—all the more so since these years were the most devastating in his life. They were filled with the horror of that "body" which was doomed to return to the earth, and which he would soon write about in his *Confession*. Such a passage is still more unusual when one considers that, several years before it was written, people took every opportunity to assert that he was "crazy."

Chapter Fourteen

AKSAKOV WOULD SAY about Gogol:

"Perhaps, Gogol's nerves were a hundred times more sensitive than ours. They were attuned to things that ours are not, they shuddered from things that we do not know. . . . Most likely, his entire organism was built differently than ours."[1]

Tolstoy's body was also built "differently."

"Tolstoy?" one famous Russian writer[2] said about him jokingly. "What did Jules Verne once write? *Twenty Thousand Leagues under the Sea*?[3] One could say something similar about Tolstoy: He, too, traveled twenty thousand leagues in search of himself."

People constantly repeated this phrase. But neither this Russian writer nor the people who repeated the witticism could ever imagine that they were poking fun at one of Tolstoy's most profound attributes.

"Who are you? What are you?" Not for nothing did such questions excite him, as they were precisely what his old nurse had heard even in the ticking of the clock that marked the passage of her wretched life in this world. She could have heard just "tick-tock, tick-tock. . . ." But she heard something else, something particular to herself: "Who are you? What are you?" And Tolstoy heard these same internal questions throughout his life—from childhood to the very last minute of his existence.

"My penchant for reflection," he wrote in *Adolescence*, "was destined to cause me a great deal of harm in life. . . . I loved that minute when, ascending higher and higher into the realm of thought, I suddenly sensed its lack of boundaries."[4]

His "reflection" also had this remarkable feature. He always tried to look at himself from the outside in.

"During the year in which I led a solitary, moral, and focused existence, I pondered all the abstract questions about the meaning of the individual, about future life, and about the immortality of the soul."[5]

"Why is symmetry pleasant to the eye? Symmetry is an inborn feeling,[6] I said to myself. But what is this feeling based on? Is everything in life symmetrical? Just the opposite. Here is life: I draw an oval on the board. After death, the soul goes to eternity. Here is eternity: I draw a line from one end of the oval to the very edge of the board. But why doesn't the other side of the oval have such a line? In reality, how can one have eternity existing only on one side? *Truly, we existed before this life, although we have lost the consciousness of this existence.* . . . Not a single philosophy engaged me more than skepticism; at one point of life, however, it led me almost to the brink of madness. I thought that, other than myself, there did not exist anyone or anything in this world and that objects were not objects. I also thought that images came into being only when I focused attention on them and that they would immediately disappear as soon as I stopped thinking about them."

"Often, whenever I would begin thinking about the least little thing, I would fall into a hopeless circle as I analyzed my thoughts. . . . I would ask myself: 'What am I thinking about?' And I would answer: 'I am thinking about what I am thinking about.' But now what am I thinking about? 'I am thinking about what I am thinking about two times over.' I could go out of mind thinking like that."[7]

"So don't think," Alexandra L'vovna told him as he lay dying.

"But how can one not think? One has to think, one simply has to!" he answered.

With Tolstoy *everything* was so "singular," so remarkable, that there was seemingly nothing that could evoke surprise. But one nonetheless is surprised. Again and again one tells oneself: How great was the "activity" to which Tolstoy had devoted his entire life, this very person who preached "nondoing"! How much did he "give of this legacy to the Savior"! How tirelessly did he work to acquire an "estate" (which he would later reject in all its forms)! And then there was his constant need to "tell all," to "confess." There exist entire volumes of confessions and diaries! He began keeping a diary already as a youth, and he continued to write in it almost every day throughout his life. Even more remarkable, he continued keeping it right up until his very end and even on his deathbed, using every moment whether he was delirious or not.

"One has to think, one simply has to!" He often repeated such things, even moments before he died.

"As if I were a teenager, I keep wanting to understand things that cannot be understood."

"Not normal" was the quantity of notes in which he jotted down his daily thoughts, feelings, and deeds; also "not normal" was their quality: their frankness and veracity. Merezhkovsky was correct when he said: "In the literatures of all peoples and times one can hardly find another writer who so bared his soul as did Tolstoy."

Sofya Andreevna agreed: "I do not understand how, in his diaries, he could write the things he did! In them he wrote such things about himself that I do not understand how he could do so!"

Was this almost obsessive writing atavistic self-exposure? Or the self-accusation so characteristic of the saints?

"Not normal" was also the fact that from childhood to his very death-bed he sought to "become better, to attain perfection." Not for nothing did the mother of Dmitri Nekhyudov tell Kolen'ka Irteniev [in *Childhood*]:

"*C'est vous qui etes un petite monstre de perfection.*"

Sofya Andrevna often wrote and said [about her husband]:

"Such mental faculties are being wasted in cutting wood, lighting samovars, and making boots!"[8]

"If a happy man suddenly sees life as Lyovochka does, if he sees only the bad and closes his eyes to the good, it is because he is sick."[9]

And she would turn to him directly and add:

"You need medical help."

Yes, he really was "a victim of an illness." God gave him a matchless talent and extraordinary mental faculties, and this he very well knew about himself. So what did he seem to need? The main labor of his life, his goal, should have been to use his intelligence and talent to benefit his loved ones. But here he wasted his gifts by cutting wood and building stoves. Sometimes, for entire years on end, he would interrupt his artistic work for pedagogy.[10] On the threshold of old age, he suddenly began studying ancient Greek, then ancient Hebrew.[11] He learned both languages with incredible speed, but also with such pervasive stress that he had to go to Bashkiria[12] and drink fermented mare's milk to ward off fatal exhaustion and the threatening symptoms of consumption, consumptive coughing and sweat.[13] He then compiled a primer[14] and authored an arithmetic book as well as several elementary readers for use inside and outside of school. He also studied astronomy and drama—Shakespeare, Goethe, Molière, Sophocles, and Euripides. He would say: "I think only of teaching and formation. So I am now all involved in pedagogy, as I was fourteen years ago."

From the vantage point of common sense, Sofya Andreevna was completely correct [in her judgments about her husband]. "I despise these primers, these arithmetic and grammar books," she wrote. "He should be writing novels."[15]

But he studied and taught his entire life. Was this simply a passion peculiar to him, or was it akin to the passion (or the duty) that seized biblical prophets, the Buddha, and the Brahmans?

"The highest caste, the caste of the Brahmans, the teachers of the people, demands that the individual be indifferent to earthly delights and that his higher nature triumph over the lower one. It was believed that a person who belonged to this caste had passed through all the lower levels of existence and had acquired moral wisdom and strength as the result of obedience, the absolute fulfillment his duty, and his efforts to fight for good. The fact that he had passed through all his previous incarnations gave him the right and obligation to teach. The ideal and goal of all Brahmans was wisdom, purity, inner freedom, mercy for everyone, love for all living things, and union and with the Original Source of life."

People say about Tolstoy that "he was the conscience of the world." His conscience was also not normal, being way out of proportion to the rest of his intellectual and spiritual faculties. Once, on a cold winter day, he saw a village beggar woman. Good Lord, what pangs of heartfelt pain, shame, and disgust with himself he felt. The woman was hungry and cold, but, [he writes,] "I was in a warm fur coat and was coming home to gorge on eggs."

Once, at night on a Moscow street, he saw the police taking a fifteen-year-old prostitute to the police station. Again he felt horror and shame. "She was being taken away to the police station, and I was on my way to a nice clean room to sleep, read books, and eat figs in water. What was happening here?"[16]

Yes, precisely what was happening here? Millions of ordinary people say that much empathy is "normal," but "one cannot cry over everyone who lies in a churchyard! That would be simple madness." He would agree: "I myself know that I am crazy!"

During the famine of 1865, he wrote with a force that could only be his: "Our table had rose-colored radishes, golden butter, fresh crusty bread wrapped in a clean towel, and vegetables from the garden. Our young ladies, dressed in muslin dresses, were happy that it was warm and that they were in the shade. But hunger turned the fields into weeds. It made the dry land crack, flaying the calloused heels of the peasant and cracking the hooves of cattle."[17]

Yes, such a famine was indeed horrible. But, after all, people live through such things. Why couldn't he? Why did he have to cry over everyone who lay in a churchyard? "He traveled twenty thousand leagues in search of himself." And the whole world besides. Could anyone have the conscience, the great physical and spiritual strength, the immense life experience, and the truly "sensitive heart" that he had in his early youth and middle age? A man of absolutely "abnormal" contradictions!

I repeat, throughout Tolstoy's youth, maturity, and old age, [one marvels at] the great abundance of earthly and animal-like forces he possessed! How he wished to pursue them! How he felt and appreciated them!

After all, it was he who, in his youth, created such characters as Eroshka and Lukashka—people who were indeed quite "shameless"—as if they were his own body and soul. He witnessed inestimable suffering and death in the Caucasus and at Sevastopol. And as a mature man—not only in life but also at his desk, working many years on *War and Peace*—he displayed such a knowledge of human life and all its cruel and immutable laws that it seemed as if he did not have to shed tears over a beggar woman or curse himself for eating an egg. But he did so just the same.

"He embodied the gnawings of social conscience," Merezhkovsky proclaimed at the centennial celebration of Tolstoy's birth.[18] "Social!" Merezhkovsky said. But Aldanov may have put it more accurately when he wrote: "Throughout his life, Tolstoy tried to escape his social obligations (though he could not always do so). One could even say that he was an *antisocial* activist."

In old age, Tolstoy strove to renounce all types of activity, all types of "doing." He could not have done otherwise. After all, as Plotinus said: "The doer is always limited, the essence of all activity is self-limiting. And he who cannot think, acts." And only he who "races from existence to nonexistence" can begin to ask: "But, perhaps, life is death, and death is life?"[19]

Regarding such a question, the philosopher Shestov[20] notes: "From the usual point of view, to merge life with death and death with life is madness." In other words, it is not normal. Tolstoy's sufferings in his conscience were so great for so many reasons; but principally because he came from a highborn family and because, as he himself would say, his imagination was "more developed than others."

Generally speaking, one has to remember this about Tolstoy's life: The clans that were closest to him, to his character, were sharply delineated, physically and spiritually. Moreover, they were quite different from each other—even opposites. The Tolstoy counts, together with the Gorchakov and Trubetskoy princes, all hailed from ancient families who played an active role in the history of our land.[21] They all had large, well-defined features. Hence all the sharp contrasts, all the energy, all the peculiarities in Tolstoy's personal character.

Even more important, one of the countless sins which burdened him throughout his life and of which he convinced humankind was that he belonged to the "princes of this world." Of course, he was innocent of that sin, but that did not matter to him. "Our fathers ate the grapes," he wrote, "but we have the sourness."

Most of all, Tolstoy's extreme pangs of conscience were rooted in his feeling for the "Unity of Life" (again drawing on the words of Indian wisdom). The Buddha could not help but know that the world contained sickness, suffering, old age, and death; so why was he so shocked when he saw such things during his famous visits to the city?[22] Because he saw them with the eyes of an Adam and because the endless chain of previous existences suddenly formed a circle, the last link joined to the first, causing Gautama's particular feeling for the "Unity of Life." From this insight also came his finely developed conscience, which, in Indian wisdom, testifies to the highest development of human consciousness.

Once, when Tolstoy was sitting and reading, a cutting knife made of bone slipped from his knees as "if it were something completely alive." He "shuddered at this impression of genuine life in this knife." So how can one be surprised at his tears, his shame, his horror at a village beggar woman!

TOLSTOY WAS A PHILOSOPHER, a moralist, and a religious teacher. But for the majority of people, he remains primarily a rebel, an anarchist, a nonbeliever. They see his philosophy as ambiguous and unintelligible, his religious pronouncements as an unwieldy confusion of atheism and blasphemy, and his moral teachings as arousing a smile ("splendid but impractical nonsense") or anger ("a rebel for whom nothing was sacred").

The views that contemporaries in Russia had on Tolstoy continue to this day but in a different form. In his majority, only the "left" acclaim him as an enlightened humanist and revolutionary, a champion of the people and an enemy of the rich and powerful. From them derive his titles as "conscience of the world"[1] and the "apostle of truth and love."

"Politics," Goethe said, "can never be the stuff of poetry."

Could the great poet Tolstoy ever be a politician? From childhood on, his soul strove for what was "most important" in life; it rejected the transience and vanity of all earthly things. He wrote: "There is nothing truthful in life, except for the insignificance of everything that I understand, and the majesty of all that is most important and incomprehensible."

People say: "He denounced everybody and everything." But Christ also denounced things. After all, he said: "My kingdom is not of this world."[2] The same can be said about the Buddha, who warned: "Woe to you, all ruling princes, rich and sated as you are!"

"Such mental faculties are being wasted in cutting wood, lighting samovars, and making boots!"

"If a happy man suddenly sees life as Lyovochka does, if he sees only the bad and closes his eyes to the good, it is because he is sick."

"You need medical help."

But in no way were his intellectual powers wasted on making boots. For did he really seek to champion "social" improvements, to end "class inequalities"?

He was a "happy" man, yet he saw only the bad in life. But what life are we talking about? Russian, European, or his own domestic situation? All these lives are like drops in the sea; and these lives are terrible, intolerable. To him even more horrible is any form of human life that "lacks sense and salvation from death." Furthermore, one cannot run away from life's difficulties; one cannot run away either from Yasnaya Polyana or from Russia, Europe, and, generally speaking, earthly and human life.

"You are sick. You need treatment." But how can one talk about "health" and cures for the Buddha and Tolstoy!

"The conscience of the world, of civilized society." But what he said and what the world said were purely coincidental.

He would say:

"We Christians often deceive ourselves when, having encountered revolutionaries, we think that we stand side by side with them. It seems to be one and the same thing, but there is a great difference between them and us; there are no people who are further from us than revolutionaries."

He would ask:

"Machines, to do what? Telegraphs, to send what?[3] Schools, universities, academies to teach what? Meetings to discuss what? Books and newspapers, to spread information about what? Railroads, to take whom where? To gather millions of people together and to have them submit to a single authority, what for?"[4]

Polner, in his biography on Tolstoy, explains this remarkable excerpt in a simplistic way: "Given the circumstances of social inequality, Tolstoy could not find satisfactory answers to these questions." But what if there were no social inequality? Furthermore, Polner ignores the last of Tolstoy's questions:

"Hospitals, doctors, drugstores to continue life, but *why should we continue to live?*"

It is strange to explain all this, but one has to. I recall the words of one of our most brilliant Russians, the famous lawyer and political figure Maklakov, who for many years was one of the Tolstoys' closest friends. In a lecture he delivered in Prague,[5] Maklakov tried to explain Tolstoy's questions, saying:

"It is worth noting in these days of celebration[6] that the world understands Tolstoy only as an artist and a political figure and that it is silent about his religious and philosophical thought. As an artist, of course, Tolstoy's greatness is beyond doubt. What else cannot be disputed? His political activities. Political figures—some with sorrow, others with praise—point out Tolstoy's struggle with the government, with violence of every kind, with privilege, with the powerful and the rich. Some despise him for these activities, seeing him as an ideologue of revolution. Others applaud him, deploring only his didacticism about nonresistance to evil and his 'inability to think things out,' which, they claim, arose doubly from his unfamiliarity with the teachings of Marx and his ignorance of even the most elementary notions of government.

"But can one say that Tolstoy was a politician, even though he wrote 'For Shame'[7] and 'I Cannot Remain Silent,' discussed politics even in *Resurrection,* and asked the powers in the State Duma to implement the ideas of Henry George?[8]

"Despite these sorties, Tolstoy was not a politician, and he saw politics as evil. In his book *Christian Teaching,*[9] he asked himself why the world did not follow Christ, and his answer was that worldly 'temptations,' which bore a likeness to good, caught people in a trap. In fact, he thought that political statutes were the most dangerous of these 'temptations,' because by means of them governments seek to justify their sins by claiming that they were doing good for the majority of people, for nations, and humankind.

"Yes, Tolstoy talked a great deal about the failings of the human community, just as we politicians and people of the world are also wont to do. But does that justify our counting him—even superficially—among our ranks? For Tolstoy, human failings were not a priority. He thought very little about the things which we who live unconsciously—by instinct, as it were—think about in the hustle and bustle of our daily existence. Specifically, he thought about the meaning of life and the inevitability of death.

"He himself said in his *Confession* that what led to his 'inner crisis'[10] were thoughts about death. It began to seem to him that if everything we live for—all those earthly joys, all the pleasures of life, all riches, glory, honors, and power—can be taken away from us by death, these pleasures have no meaning at all. If life has an end, it is simply absurd; and if it is not at all worth living, then one should escape it as soon as possible in suicide. Such is the sudden and joyless conclusion that Tolstoy's thoughts of death led him to."

I do not understand why Maklakov used the word "sudden." But he is again correct when he says: "The problem of meaning in life is not the province of any one epoch, any one nation, or any one form of government. . . . One should compare Tolstoy not with us, or with politicians, or with those who worry about ways to increase wealth and how to distribute it justly in society. Rather, one should compare Tolstoy with teachers of religion. . . . Tolstoy was *the son of a positivist century, and he himself is a positivist;* but as regards questions of the soul, his views were primarily religious in scope."

All of what Maklakov said is true (except for calling Tolstoy a "positivist"). He could have cited many other sources of proof for his assertions. Tolstoy himself said something similar:

"People who hate the existing structure and government imagine another order of things; and even those who cannot imagine a new order seek to destroy the old one through all kinds of godless and inhuman means, through arson, robbery, and murder. . . . But a change in government will accomplish nothing. Will life truly be better if Petrunkevich takes the place of Nicholas II as head of state?"[11]

Alexandra L'vovna writes that Tolstoy expected a revolution after the [Russo-]Japanese War. He sensed the mood of the workers, soldiers, and peasants not only from his conversations with them but also from endless letters which came to him from all parts of Russia. For him several things were clear: Revolution would not improve the position of the people; and since every type of government is founded on violence, government is bad in itself. He said: "A new government will arise from violence the same as the old one. As Cromwell and Murat did to their opponents, so will the liberals in a new government do to the conservatives."

He wrote in "[An Appeal] to the Government, Revolutionaries, and the People":[12]

"To improve the condition of people, people themselves have to become better.[13] It is a truism that to heat a jar of water all the drops must be heated. For people to become better, they must pay more and more attention to themselves, to their inner life. External social activity—particularly social struggle—always distracts the attention of people from their inner life, invariably corrupting them and lowering the level of social morality. Because the most immoral people rise to prominence, they bring to the fore a similarly immoral public opinion which allows and even approves of wrongdoing. A vicious circle comes into play. In any type of social struggle, the worst elements of society readily indulge in social activities that correspond to their own level of moral development. Similarly, these social activities attract the worst people of society."

Maklakov, in his speech, also said that "the most important element in Tolstoy's worldview was his religious beliefs."

I have purposely chosen this part of Maklakov's speech because the judgments of individuals like himself cannot but attract the special attention of people, if only because of Maklakov's exceptional knowledge of Tolstoy's life. So what did Maklakov have to say about Tolstoy as a religious teacher?

Here is the substance of his argument.

Tolstoy insisted not only in writing but also in numerous conversations with Maklakov that he was not creating his own personal Christian philosophy; he was seeking only to reinstate the genuine Christ who had been misrepresented by the world and the church.[14] Tolstoy revered Christ but did not see him as God. He often told Maklakov that if he saw Christ as God, Christ would lose all charm for him. Such is the *typical view* of a nonbeliever.[15]

For Maklakov, Tolstoy was a modern person, a positivist. He was an extremely intelligent person who could not understand the limits of reason;

but, even while Tolstoy acknowledged these limits, he could not accept that the mind could know absolute truth through revelation and faith.

Also according to Maklakov, Tolstoy loved to use such words as "God," "religion," and "immortality." But, for Tolstoy, God was an incomprehensible, primordial power; and the immortality of the soul meant that because spiritual life had an obscure beginning, it will also have an obscure end.[16] As regards faith, Tolstoy loved to quote Ivan Kireevsky, who said that faith was not so much a knowledge of the truth as a devotion to it. Of course, such assertions are very far from the teachings of the church, and Tolstoy's worldview marks him as a genuine positivist, a son of our time.

Maklakov finds it remarkable, though, that Tolstoy did not say, as did the positivists, that the teachings of Christ contradict human nature or that they should be seen only as an ideal that cannot be achieved on this earth. He believed, rather, that Christ's teaching must be and should be realized in life. That is why he taught people to live according to God's commandments.

"Why live according to God's commandments?" he asked. "Because otherwise a life that ends in death is nonsense."

Maklakov quotes what Jesus said in his parable about the rich man who collected great wealth in his granaries and who wanted to share his largesse with his friends.[17] But would this madman have truly thought of doing such a thing if he had known that, on that night, he would have been called by the Savior Himself?

Tolstoy believed that people who do not think about death behave like this madman. In the presence of death, he continued, one should freely quit this life or change it, finding a purpose in it—one that death cannot destroy.

Maklakov notes that people still seek to prove the absurdity of Tolstoy's idea of nonresistance to evil, thinking that if such an idea were put into effect our life, culture, and government would perish and that we would be victimized by aggressors. But Tolstoy would see that argument as absurd; for what would be the point of our life and all its pleasures if everything could be swallowed up by death? The more things one fears that he will lose when he dies, the more pronounced his fear of death. So what does one need? A life in which death is not horrifying. But what kind of life is this? The question, Tolstoy believed, could be answered only by religion, Christianity, the religion of "the poor, the humble, those who do not philosophize."

But it was just such a conclusion, Maklakov goes on to say, that led to Tolstoy's struggle with the church.[18] First of all, the mysticism of religion and the church ran counter to Tolstoy's positivism; but this disagreement was not what caused him to withdraw from the church. Rather, it was the way the church looked upon earthly life: It did not reject what Christ had condemned. For instance, regarding the worldly struggle for earthly goods, the church did not say as Christ did: Give away our possessions; do not counter evil with violence; turn the left cheek when someone strikes you on the right; do not judge; do not put people to death.

No. The church accepted, confirmed, and even blessed all secular notions and institutions, together with all their sins and crimes; it even taught obedience to these institutions. Moreover, the church showed, through its representatives, that it, too, valued earthly possessions. To Tolstoy's question—why live if we are going to die?—the mysticism of the church answers: We are immortal. After physical death, we have an eternal, heavenly existence and either reward or punishment for the temporal existence we have lived here on earth. Such mysticism resigned the individual to the meaninglessness and absurdity of his or her life.

Yes, there will be punishment for sins, the church says; but it endorsed the mundanely absurd life of man on earth. By teaching life after death, the church affirmed people's taste for earthly goods, joys, sins, temptations. It also upheld the right of the individual to excuse his behavior on human weaknesses. God's church had forgotten Christ, Tolstoy said, and begun to teach Christianity without God.

Maklakov posits that already as a youth, Tolstoy said that man must not see himself as something opposed to the world, but as one small part of a world that is huge and eternally living. This is exactly what Jesus says: "Love your neighbor as yourself."[19] Furthermore, there is but one happiness for the person—to live for others. Sacrificing oneself for others, one becomes more powerful than death. It is because of such tenets that God's commandments revealed to Tolstoy the meaning of earthly life, as well as destroyed his earlier fear of death.

As Maklakov sees it, both positivism and the church could object to much in Tolstoy's teaching. Positivism would argue: Why does one need some meaning to existence when there exists a life instinct and all its joys? And the church would say: If Christ were only a man, that would deny his resurrection, and thus debase Christianity to a moral system that is dead, boring, and inaccessible to human powers. But can rational theories that take in all worldly life, and that seemingly destroy the fear of death, displace a faith in God's mercy and love, in the care of Divine Providence for people and in the joy of final union with God after death?

Tolstoy went against the world and the church, and the world and the church rose up against Tolstoy.

This is how Maklakov explains Tolstoy. And it is amazing how many of Maklakov's insightful judgments on the writer alternated with those that are simply beyond comprehension.

"Tolstoy is the son of a positivist century, and he himself is a positivist," Maklakov says.

It is extremely strange to call someone "the son of a positivist century" when this person constantly wrote and said: "There is no greater supersti-

tion than the belief that a person with his body is something that is real. . . .
Matter and distance, time and movement, separate me and all living things
from God. . . . Less and less do I understand the world of matter, and more
and more do I realize that which I cannot understand but only discern. . . .
Matter is for me the most incomprehensible thing. . . . What am I? My reason does not answer these questions of the heart. . . .

"From the time that people have walked this earth, they have answered these questions not with words, that is, the tool of reason, but rather
with all of life itself. . . . For life to have meaning, it should go beyond the
limits of what the human mind can comprehend."

The church teaches that we are immortal. But Tolstoy also talked constantly about immortality. "I am always thinking about death," he wrote.
"And it has became very clear to me that when I am on the other side of
death, I will also be all right, but in a different way. . . . I will also be all
right—no, even better. As before, I tried to doubt that other life, and also
as before, I could not; but I became convinced of its existence."

"I am more and more certain that a fire which has died out here will
reappear in a new form, *but not here*—this very same fire."

"Yesterday I had a very interesting conversation with Konshin, an enlightened materialist. I could not convince him of the existence of God, or
of future life, but I convinced myself even more."

Tolstoy did not see God in Christ. But is this the "typical stance of a
nonbeliever"? After all, there are millions of non-Christians who do not accept Christ as God, but who are, nevertheless, believers.

Chapter Sixteen

THE PHILOSOPHER SHESTOV says an ancient book of wisdom has this saying: "He who wants to know what will be, what is under the earth and over the sky, would better not to have been born into this world at all. The angel of death that comes to man to take away his soul from his body is completely covered with eyes. If this angel comes for a man's soul too early, before it is his time to quit this earth, this celestial being will withdraw from this person but not without marking him with a special sign. The angel will take two eyes from his own countless ones and give them to this person along with his human ones. Henceforth this person will not be like others. With his native eyes, he will see everything that all other people see, but with those eyes given to him by the angel, he will see things that other mortals cannot. He will see with the eyes not of people but of 'beings from other worlds.' And so different will one view be from the other that there *will arise a struggle within the person, a struggle between his two different visions.*"

Shestov uses this quotation in his article about Dostoevsky.[1] He attributes two pairs of eyes to the author of *Notes from the Underground.*[2] But reading this article, one thinks of Tolstoy, for if there ever was a person with double vision, with another pair of eyes, given to him by the *angel of death* who flew down to him while he was still in his cradle, it was Tolstoy. The angel erred about the actual date of Tolstoy's passing, but he left the writer with new eyes just the same. As a result, everything that Tolstoy would see over the course of his very long life, he would reevaluate under the sign of death, the greatest reevaluator of all values. He would do exactly what Prince Andrei did at Austerlitz, and Anna, immediately before her suicide.

Shestov, in his article, recalls the words of Plato: "*Anyone who has given himself over to philosophy has done nothing else other than to prepare for death and dying.*" Shestov also cites Euripides, who said what many people would later repeat: "*Who knows? Perhaps life is death, and death is life.*" Again one thinks of Tolstoy. Euripides is not convinced of this idea. He says: "Who knows? . . . Perhaps . . . ." *But Tolstoy, more than once and more and more uncompromisingly and dogmatically, affirmed: "Life is death."*

"The terrible thing which I feared has gotten ahold of me."

This "terrible thing" got ahold of him early in life. The older he got, however, the more frequent and powerful its force, so much so that finally one day this "terrible thing" horrified him to the "point of madness." On that day Tolstoy understood beyond the shadow of a doubt that he was "crazy." Over a long period, he periodically had thought: "No, something strange is happening. The life that I am living on this earth is not like that of others. I see, feel, and think differently than they do. . . . One thing, though, is clear: either they are crazy or I am. And as there are millions of them and only one of me, it is obvious who the crazy person is—it is I. And the day has come when it is completely clear—yes, I am insane!"[3]

In a letter to Sofya Andreevna, he wrote about this day in a restrained way: *"Something unusual has happened to me."* Everyone knows what really happened to him: In August 1869, when he was only forty-one years old, he, driven by his "love for his family, for farming," went to the Penza[4] province with a very modest goal; that is, he wanted to look at and perhaps buy an estate which, rumor had it, was being sold at a very reasonable price. On the way there, he spent the night in the city of Arzamas,[5] and it was there that an event occurred which he would tell Sofya Andreevna about in his letter:

"How are you and the children? Has anything happened while I have been gone? I have been in a state of distress for two days now. The other day I spent the night at Arzamas, and something unusual happened to me there. It was 2 A.M., and I was terribly tired, though I felt fine. I wanted to get some sleep, but suddenly I was seized by angst, fear, and horror, the likes of which I have never encountered before. The details of my distress I will tell you later, but God forbid that anyone ever suffer the torment that gripped me so severely.

"I got up and ordered that the horses be readied. While they were being prepared, I fell asleep and woke up feeling fine. But yesterday while I was riding around, I again fell victim to this distress. This time, however, I was ready for such disquiet and did not surrender to it, all the more so since this angst was not as strong as it had been earlier. Today I feel happy and healthy, as much as I can be without my family. . . . *I can be alone only if I am constantly busy, but as soon as I have nothing to do, I am firm in my resolve that I must not be alone."*

The last phrase is particularly important. Tolstoy could be alone only when he was constantly doing something, when he was engaged in activity. But without such things to distract and engulf him, his mind and soul were host to "angst, fear, and horror, such things that, God forbid, anyone would have to suffer!" He could not but have noted such anguish earlier—perhaps that is why he sought to numb himself with his passion for activity? At Arzamas, he understood these feelings clearly, to the point of horror. But after Arzamas, did they disappear in new activities at home and with his family?

One can show that this anguish remained with Tolstoy in his story "Notes of a Madman,"[6] which he wrote a full fifteen years after Arzamas. In essence, this story recounts exactly everything that he had written in his letter to Sofya Andreevna, but with new details elaborating upon what he had experienced. The main character in the work also goes to look at an estate that he is planning to buy. Together with his servant, Andrei, he also goes to the Penza province and spends the night at Arzamas. There he stays in a hotel and goes to bed. He tries to sleep, but cannot.

"I felt that there was no way that I could fall asleep. Why did I come here? Where am I going? Why and what am I running away from? I am running away from something horrible, but I cannot do so. I am always with myself, always torturing myself. And here I am, my entire being. Neither the estate in Penza nor any other estate anywhere can add or detract anything from me. *I am bored, unbearable, and tormented.* I want to sleep, to lose consciousness, but I cannot. I cannot run away from myself.

"I went out into the hallway. [Andrei] was sleeping on a narrow bench, his arm hanging limp. He was sleeping deeply, as was the night watchman. I stepped out into the hallway, thinking to run away from everything that was tormenting me. But *it* came out after me and darkened everything around me. I became even more terrified than before. 'What is this nonsense?' I said to myself. 'Why am I so anxious, what am I afraid of?'

"'*You are afraid of me,' the voice of death answered inaudibly.* 'I am here.' My skin crawled. Yes, it was the voice of death. It would come—here it was now, *but it was not supposed to be here.* If death were truly standing before me, I could not have felt all that I was feeling now. I truly would have been afraid. Now I was not afraid, even though I saw and felt that death was coming. But, *at the same time, I felt that it was not supposed to be here.* With my entire being, I felt the need, the right to live a life; but, simultaneously, I felt that death was happening. This inner conflict was terrible. I tried to ward off this horror. I found a copper candlestick with a burned-out candle and lit the candle. The red light coming from it, together with its size—the flame was a bit smaller than the candlestick—kept saying the same thing. '*There is nothing in life, but death, and it should not be here.*'

"I tried to think about something that interested me, about my upcoming purchase, my wife. But there was nothing comforting in such things, for they meant nothing. Fear for my perishing life clouded everything else. I had to get some sleep. I was about to lie down, but as soon as I did so, I jumped up in horror. Distress upon distress—the very same type of inner anguish one gets right before vomiting, but this was an intense spiritual nausea. I was panic-stricken, beside myself. It seems that death is terrifying, but when one starts remembering and thinking about existence, a life that is dying is also frightening. Life and death were somehow becoming one. Something was tearing my soul to pieces but could not do so. Once more I went out to look at the people who were sleeping. Once more I tried to fall asleep, but there was still that same horror—red, white, and square-like.[7] Something was straining, tearing itself apart, but remained whole. It was tormenting, and terrifyingly evil and arid. I did not feel the least bit of kindness inside myself. I felt only a steady, quiet *malice for myself and for what had happened to me.*"[8]

In the end, this person who sees that something—"red, white, and squarelike"—insists on his "madness," even with a type of joy.

"Today I was taken for a psychiatric examination in the local hospital, but the doctors had various opinions about me. They argued and decided that I was not crazy. . . . They regarded me as being under some kind of influence, but also as being of sound mind and body. They can think what they want, but I know that I am crazy!"

Thus, there happened what was destined to happen—that which had been written "from birth." The man tried, with all his might, to overcome the preeminent, genuine self that he had been born as. He tried to live life "like everyone else," "practically, positively," as a family man, a father, and a master. He tried to suppress that something—"red, white, and squarelike"— with unlimited "activities." So as not to be "alone," he surrounded himself with family, children and grandchildren, and a house full of people. . . . But no, he did not succeed in his ruse. As a youth, he experimented, chaotically, with how he could best find a place in the big, wide world. He knew that this place must not harbor the "unusual things" that happened at Arzamas, but he also was uncertain about where this place should be: Yasnaya Polyana, civil or military service. As a youth, he wrote to his brother:

"Seryozha, I am writing to you from Petersburg, where I intend to stay forever. . . . I am now fully aware that one cannot live by philosophy and speculation, but that one should live positively, practically."

During his mature years, he seemed calmer, living so "positively" that he once wrote:

"There is a certain Baron Shening here in Moscow who owns these Japanese pigs. I saw such pigs at Shatilov's, and I feel that I cannot be happy in life until I get some of my own."

But everyone knows that, at the very same time, he also wrote things that were quite different: "I cannot live without knowing who I am and why I am here. And, as this is something that I cannot know, it follows that I cannot live."

"The other day I read something that I had not read earlier but that I continue to read and show with joy: the Wisdom of Solomon, Ecclesiastes, and the Book of Wisdom of Jesus, son of Sirach."[9]

118

It is easy to guess which book made him "shout" with joy:

"I decided in my heart to have my reason study and experience everything that was going on under the sun. This was a burdensome task, but one that God had given to his human sons so that they could torment themselves."

In these words of Ecclesiastes,[10] one finds all of Tolstoy. Indeed, this "burdensome task" became the main undertaking of his entire life. Everything, everything "that was going on under the sun," he studied and experienced, thought about and felt with utmost urgency and skepticism.

"I developed and gained more knowledge than all those who went before me to Jerusalem, and my heart was filled with great wisdom and learning. But I realized how useless it was for my heart to focus on what was wisdom and what was madness and stupidity. For he who has great wisdom also has great fits of anger; and he who increases his knowledge also increases his sorrow."

"I said to my heart: Enjoy the good things in life, but know that they are vanity."

For how many years did Tolstoy enjoy the "good things in life," only finally (in the "third phase" of his life) to renounce them all!

"I did great things. I built myself homes, I planted grape arbors. . . . I acquired servants and sired a family. . . . I accumulated silver and gold and treasures from countries and kings. . . . But all these are vanity, triflings, and worthless under the sun. . . . And my lot will be that of a fool. . . . Alas, the wise man dies like an ignoramus. . . . *And I came to hate life, as I hated everything done under the sun. . . . And I hated all my labors, everything I had toiled for under the sun.*"

"I saw all kinds of oppression that were also going on under the sun. I saw the tears of the oppressed, and that there was no one to comfort them. I saw the violence at the hands of the oppressors, and that there was no relief in sight. *And I thought that the dead who had died long ago were happier than the living.*"

Was it only because of people's oppressions that he considered the dead to be happier than the living?! But both the oppressors and the oppressed are the same vanity of vanities. All are idle ventures before that which awaits both the former and the latter at that hour when "those who watch the house will shudder, and the heights will become terrible, and not on the road will terrible things happen. . . . when a person goes to his eternal home and people will follow him along the street, crying. . . ."

Among the many myths that hound Tolstoy's image even to this day is that he was supposedly an ignoramus despite his education. I repeat, almost all of these legends were something that he himself gave evidence for, as a result of his harsh self-assessments. He himself started rumors regarding his ignorance. "I am almost a complete ignoramus. Anything that I know I learned somehow, by myself, in bits and pieces, unsystematically, with no logic and very little sense." But who among those who wrote about him screened out these pretenses to ignorance? I cannot think of a single person except Aldanov, who justly wrote in his book *The Riddle of Tolstoy*:[11]

"Tolstoy was one of the most broadly educated people of our time. . . . As regards his main 'craft,' literature, he knew all types of writing—ancient, contemporary, and the most recent. He knew a great many cultured languages, even Greek and Hebrew. At various times in his life, he concentrated his abilities passionately on philosophy, natural sciences, theology, theories of art, and pedagogy. In his own words, he was busy 'from morning to night' with studying the Greek classics in original, or being carried away with astronomy, or trying to prove the Pythagorean theorem to anyone who visited him. People who came to Yasnaya Polyana encountered his 'ignorance' firsthand when they saw the fourteen thousand volumes in his library, filled with his comments and notes! Indeed, his far-reaching, anarchical frame of mind questioned the sovereignty of science, just as it had questioned the sovereignty of the state."

Aldanov adds: "Even Chekhov, who most likely had not read one-tenth of all the books that Tolstoy did, liked to joke about Tolstoy's ignorance."

Aldanov is right here. Chekhov indeed liked "to joke about" Tolstoy; but Tolstoy had a great influence on Chekhov and not only as an artist. Chekhov often told me about that winter which the sick Tolstoy spent in the Crimea.[12]

"Tolstoy will die soon, and everything will go to hell!"

"You mean literature?"

"Everything. Literature, too."[13]

Chekhov would say:[14]

"I am afraid of him. Just think. After all, it was he who wrote what Anna [Karenina] herself saw and felt how her eyes shone in the darkness!

"Seriously, I am afraid of him," he would say laughing, as if he truly rejoiced in his fear.[15] Another time, Chekhov said:

"What I most admire about him is his contempt for all us other writers. Actually, it is not so much contempt as it is the fact that he sees all of us as nonentities. He sometimes praises Maupassant and me.[16] . . . But why does he do so? Because he regards us as children. Our stories, tales, and novels are for him children's plays. But he sees Shakespeare differently. He looks upon Shakespeare as an adult; that is why he is miffed that Shakespeare does not write in the Tolstoyan manner."[17]

But sometimes Chekhov would say something different:

"Only why does he speak about things which he does not understand at all? Medicine, for example? He sometimes disturbs me. For instance, he writes this absolutely wonderful piece, 'How Much Land Does a Person Need?'[18] And he writes it in a way that no one will match in a thousand years.

But what does he say? That a person needs only six feet of land. That is nonsense. A person does not need six feet of land but the entire earth. Only a dead person needs six feet. But the living need not think about death and dying."

Yes, yes:

"You shouldn't think!" [his daughter told him, as he lay dying.]

But such a request was in vain.

"Oh, but how can one not think!" he replied. "One has to think. One simply has to!"

As he himself would say, he was, from childhood on, "extremely sensitive and prone to analysis." His main interests were to observe and think in solitude. In adolescence, these proclivities and traits had become so pronounced in him that he wrote in *Youth:*

"One can hardly believe what the constant and favorite objects of my reflections were, for they were not in keeping with my age and position in life. But as I see it, the incongruity between one's position and moral awareness is a most reliable sign of that person's truth."

(Anyone who thinks about Tolstoy's life should keep in mind the previous remarkable lines.)

"During the year in which I led a solitary, moral life, I focused on myself. All the abstract questions about one's purpose in life, about life after death, and about the immortality of the soul, came under scrutiny; and my weak, childish mind, with all the passion of inexperience, tried to clarify these questions that can be posed only by the highest levels [of thought] to which the human mind could rise. *But the human mind cannot solve these questions.*"

"The thoughts that came to my mind were so clear and direct that I even tried to realize them in life, for I imagined that I was the *first* to discover such great and useful truths."

"Once I came up with the idea that happiness does not depend on external causes but on our attitude toward it, and that man, who is used to suffering, cannot be unhappy. I would try to teach myself to be impervious by holding Tatishchev's lexicons[19] in my outstretched hands for five minutes at time, trying not to notice the pain. Or I would go into the closet and beat my bare back with a rope, causing myself such pain that tears would suddenly appear in my eyes."

"Another time, I suddenly recalled that death was waiting for me every hour, ever minute. So I decided that a person could be happy only if he lived in the present and did not think about the future. But, like many people even now, I did not understand this idea. Yet, I quit my lessons for three days and lay in bed, enjoying myself by reading a novel and eating cookies."

[I repeat a cited passage from Tolstoy:] "Once, when I was standing at a blackboard and drawing various figures with a piece of chalk, I suddenly wondered: Why is symmetry pleasing to the eye? Exactly what is symmetry? Symmetry is an inborn sense, I told myself. But what is this symmetry based on? Is everything in life symmetrical? Quite the opposite. Here is life, and I drew an oval on the blackboard. After life the soul goes off to eternity. And here is eternity. I drew a line from one side of the oval to the very edge of the blackboard. But why is it that the other side of the oval does not have the same line? In reality, how can eternity only be on one side of the board? Most likely, we existed in a previous life but have lost all recollections of it."

(Incidentally, one should remember that he used to be roused to great depths of feeling whenever his mother played the piano. "In my imagination, there rose some kind of light, bright, translucent memories. She had begun to play Beethoven's *Pathetique*,[20] and I recalled something that was gloomy, burdensome, and sad. . . . Such a feeling was not unlike my memories. But memories of what? It seems as though I was trying to recall something that never had been.")

What were these "reflections," as he used to call them?

We recall again.

[Tolstoy said:] "Not a single philosophy engaged me more than skepticism; indeed, at one point of life, it led me almost to the brink of madness. I thought that, other than myself, there did not exist anyone or anything in this world and that objects were not objects, but images that came into being only when I focused attention on them, that they would immediately disappear as soon as I stopped thinking about them."

[I repeat another cited passage from Tolstoy:] "My penchant for abstract thinking dominated my consciousness in such an unnatural way that often whenever I would begin thinking about the least little thing, I would fall into a hopeless circle as I analyzed my thoughts. . . . I would ask myself: 'What am I thinking about?' I would answer: 'I am thinking about what I am thinking about.' But now what am I thinking about? 'I am thinking about what I am thinking about what I am thinking about two times over.' . . . *I would be at my wit's end.*"

"The living must not think about death and dying." But it is futile to preach such a thing to "madmen" who see the world not as others do but rather as "beings from other worlds," as people "who have given themselves over to philosophy." What did Prince Andrei experience when he heard Natasha sing? And about another hero who heard someone sing, Chekhov would write:

"As she sang, he felt as though he were eating a ripe, tasty melon."

In *Childhood,* there is a passage about how Volodya, who, as he grows older, begins to "show off." For instance, on a hike with some children in the forest, he lets them know that he considers all children's games to be nonsense. Such words sadden Nikolen'ka. He replies: "I know that one cannot really shoot or kill a bird with a stick; pretending to do so is just a game. And if one keeps thinking it, one cannot really go riding around on chairs either. But if one looks at everything the way it really is, there will be no games at all. And if there are no games, what will be left?"

But Nikolen'ka also grows up. Less and less does he believe that one can make believe about riding around on chairs, and more and more he looks rationally at all the "games" going on in the world. "But what is going on here? Are they crazy?"

But he continues to take part in the games adults play and does what he finds hateful. Perhaps, he exclaims in the words of Paul the Apostle, "I do not understand what I am doing, for I am not doing what I want but am doing what I hate!"[21]

But how could he not play such games? "Good God, what am I to do if I love nothing but glory and the love of other people? My father, sister, wife, and all the people who are the dearest to me—I would surrender them all for a minute of glory, of triumph over others, for the love of people toward me, people whom I don't even know!"

Nikolen'ka-Lyovochka also thinks: "All these games are madness, terrible and absurd! But what am I to do? If there are no games, what would be left?"

When he was thirty-five, Tolstoy wrote in fear, even distress: "I am rolling, rolling down the mountain of death. I do not want death. . . . I do not want to die, I love immortality. . . . I love my life—my family, my farming, my art."

As the years passed by, he "rolled" but "did not want to roll." He did to want to believe that he was rolling, so he sought to numb himself with the achievements of fame, with the love of people, and with dreams of "perfecting pig farming."[22] He sought to buy, at bargain prices, as many estates as possible, to purchase, for pennies, six thousand acres of land in the Samara province,[23] and to acquire three hundred horses. But then there was that night at Arzamas, and the heady deception which he had long felt to be false—that intoxicating fog into which he had entered and out of which he had departed—dissipated into thin air.

"Why did I come here? Where am I going? Why am I running off somewhere? Should I fall asleep? But there is no way I can sleep! But one thing is clear: It is I who am crazy, not the world. The world about me does not feel any anguish, any horror or fear. It does not see this 'red, white, and squarelike' something. It continues to 'play' and will do so until the end of time. But I? I am crazy!"

"They can think what they want, but I know that I am crazy!"

TOLSTOY WAS ONLY TWENTY-TWO when he began writing *Childhood.* Here, he described the way he felt about death when he saw a dead body for the first time. (By the way, just when is "first"? I am referring to the chapter in *Childhood,* entitled "Grief," which deals with the death of Nikolen'ka's mother, that is, of Lyovochka Tolstoy's own mother. But Lyovochka's mother died when he was only two years old.[1] Why does the theme of death appear in his very first work?)

"The next day, late at night, I wanted to look at her one more time (at my mother in the coffin). Having overcome an instinctive fear of death, I quietly opened the door and tiptoed into the room. The coffin was on a table in the middle of the room, surrounded by snuffed-out candles in tall silver candleholders. In the far corner was a sexton who was reading the psalter in a quiet, monotonous voice.

"I stopped by the door and looked, but my eyes were so swollen from tears and my nerves were so on edge that I could not see anything. Everything had somehow merged together: the light, the brocade, the velvet, the tall candleholders, the rose-colored lace pillow, the *venchik,*[2] the bonnet with ribbons, and *something of a transparent waxen color.* I got up on a chair to see her face better, but where that face was supposed to be, I now saw a *transparent whitish-yellowish object.* I could not believe that this was my mother's face. I began to look at it more attentively, and little by little I started to recognize her dear, familiar features. I shuddered from horror when I realized that this was Mother. Why were her closed eyes so shrunken? Why was her skin so terribly white? Why did one cheek have this black spot under her transparent skin? Why were her lips so pale, but also so splendid, solemn, and telling of such a heavenly peace that a cold shiver ran down my spine when I looked at them?

"I looked and felt that *some incomprehensible, overwhelming force was drawing my eyes to this lifeless face.* I kept looking at her, and my imagination conjured up pictures, full of life and happiness. I kept forgetting that the dead body which lay before me and which I was looking at so mindlessly, as if at an object which had nothing in common with my memories, was her. I imagined her in different situations: alive, happy, and smiling. But then my eyes seized upon some striking feature on her pale face, and I recalled the terrible reality about me. I shuddered, but I could not stop looking at her. Again reality gave way to dreams, and again the consciousness of this reality destroyed my dreams. Finally, my imagination grew tired and stopped deceiving me. The awareness of reality, of life, also disappeared, and I fainted dead away. . . . *For awhile I lost the consciousness of my existence and experienced something that was lofty, inexplicably pleasant, and filled with sad delight.*"

This scene is absolutely extraordinary in both its external and internal details. At first, the power of the external details seems to predominate. "The light, the brocade, the velvet, . . . the rose-colored lace pillow, . . . the bonnet with ribbons, and something of a transparent waxen color." But these externals give way to genuine inner horror: How much is said by this "something"!

[Tolstoy continues:] "One of the last people to bid farewell to the deceased was a peasant woman, carrying a very pretty five-year-old girl in her arms. God knows why the woman brought the child with her. At that very moment, I accidentally dropped my wet handkerchief and wanted to pick it up. But as soon as I bent down, I heard an awful, penetrating shriek that was filled with a horror I will never forget as long as I live. I raised my head. Alongside the coffin stood the same peasant woman, barely able to hold the little girl in her arms. The girl was crying in a terrible, unnatural voice. She had thrown back her frightened little face and was waving her hands as she fixed her eyes on the face of the deceased."

Nikolenka-Lyovochka, looking at this transparent "something" of waxen color, this transparent whitish-yellowish object, "loses the consciousness of his existence and experiences something that was lofty, inexplicably pleasant, and filled with sad delight." Such emotions were the genuine beginnings for a whole range of feelings which would later inform Tolstoy's perception of death and lead him to something "lofty."

But now these emotions were only just beginning. In this scene, horror predominates. "A cold shiver ran down my spine as I looked at her." And the peasant child, after only a single momentary glimpse at this "something," lets loose with a "terrible, unnatural" cry.

Seven years later, Tolstoy followed these early pages on death with a story entitled "Three Deaths."[3] In this piece, a rich young woman is dying of consumption. She is filled with false hopes, clutching at life, and angry at everyone and everything. There is also a poor worker, a driver, who, like a weakened animal, is dying a resigned but meaningless death. Finally, there is a tree which is passing from this life in sacred and splendid unconsciousness. Only the rich young woman is guilty before God in her disobedience of His exalted, solemn, and inscrutable will, in her childish and stubborn ignorance of His laws and plans. "My ways are higher than your ways, my thoughts are higher than your thoughts."[4]

Tolstoy utters his own words about death with both majesty and reproach:

"On that evening the sick young woman had become a body, and that body lay in the coffin in the room of a large house. . . . The bright waxen light that poured forth from the tall silver candleholders fell on the dead woman's pale forehead, on her heavy waxen arms, on the stonelike folds of the pall which looked strange as it rose up around her knees and toes."

"'If You cover Your face, O Lord, the people will become confused,' the psalter said, 'and if You take away their soul, they will die and return to ashes. But if You send them Your spirit, they will come into being and renew the face of the earth. Let us praise God now and always.'"[5]

"The face of the dead woman was solemn and strict. Nothing moved on her clear, cold forehead or on her firmly pursed lips. She was all attention. But did she understand these great words?"

When he wrote "Three Deaths," Tolstoy himself "did not understand" these words. A year later, in 1860, his brother Nikolai was dying of consumption; and for the great writer, the ashes of death covered his entire world. "What's the point of anything," he wrote, "when tomorrow there will begin the torments of death with all its repulsive lies and self-deceit, and with its conclusion in nothingness, null!"[6]

Another year later, he started "Kholstomer,"[7] "the story of a horse," which could have been titled "Two Lives and Two Deaths." The story features the life of a skewbald by the pedigree name of Muzhik I, but which was called Kholstomer on the street because its "long and gangly walk was without equal in Russia." The story also features the life of one of Kholstomer's masters, the great *barin*, the Hussar Prince Serpukhovskoy.

If one wants to talk about Tolstoy's mercilessness as a writer of worldly "histories," it is here, in "Kholstomer," where he is the most merciless of all. The gelding,[8] a former celebrity, is now lonely and miserable, living out his final days in a herd of other horses in the master's compound. "Old age can be splendid, but it can also be pitiful and repulsive." The old age of this skewbald gelding was exactly like this. There was something grand in its figure but also something terrible. Together with his splendor, Kholstomer showed the repugnant features of old age, exacerbated by the piebald color of his coat and the various expressions and ways that the animal showed consciousness of his former beauty and force, his self-assurance and calm. Kholstomer was a "living ruin," one which the young horses tormented with their cruel amusements and jokes. "He was old; they were young. He was thin; they were stocky. He was bored; they were happy. He was the complete stranger, the outsider, an absolutely different creature than they; hence he could not evoke pity. *Horses pity only themselves and sometimes only those that they can easily imagine themselves to be."*

At night, Kholstomer regales the young horses with the story of his past life and his long service to people. He tells them how his owners called him "my horse"—which at first seemed to him to be as strange as the words "my land, my air, my water"—and how his career ended when his Hussar owner rode him almost to death. Serpukhovskoy "never loved anyone or anything"; but the gelding liked him "precisely because the master was handsome, happy, rich, and thus did not love anyone else." The gelding would say about the Hussar: "His coldness and my dependence on him strengthened my love for him. 'Kill me, ride me to death,' I would think to myself during all our happy times together, 'for I will be all the happier if you do so.'"

And Serpukhovskoy did just that—he rode Kholstomer almost to death.

"'The master's mistress was beautiful, he was handsome, even his coachman was good-looking.'"

When Serpukhovskoy's lover ran away from him, he pursued her and rode the gelding almost to death. But he did the same thing to himself. When, some fifteen years later, Serpukovskoy visited that *barin* who happened to be Kholstomer's last owner, he had also become a "living ruin":

"The visitor, Nikita Serpukhovskoy, was over forty-years old, tall, stout, bald, with a huge mustache and sidewhiskers. [As a youth] he must have been quite handsome. But now he had let himself go, physically, morally, and financially."

"He was dressed in a military tunic and blue trousers. His tunic and pants were things that only the rich could afford. His underwear was also of quality. His watch was made in England. His shoes had special soles, as thick as a finger."

"Nikita Serpukhovskoy had squandered his fortune of two million rubles and owed 120,000 rubles more. But his way of life granted him access to credit and the opportunity to live luxuriously for another ten years."

"But these ten years were coming to an end, his lavish way of life was almost over, and Nikita's life was growing sad."

But his host, the *barin,* was young, strong. and rich. He was "one of those whose name is legion, and who drives around in sable furs, throws expensive bouquets at actresses, drinks the most expensive wine, the very latest brands, lives in the most expensive hotel, and keeps the most expensive mistress."

The host bragged to Serpukhovskoy of his happiness and wealth. He bade his guest to help himself to more of his expensive cigars, making Serpukhovskoy feel awkward and insulted. As if equals, they talked the entire evening about horses, about women, about "who had what—a Gypsy woman, a dancer, a French woman." But they got bored listening to each other. Each one wanted to talk only about himself. It was late at night when they finally parted.

The host lay in bed with his mistress: "He is impossible. He got drunk and kept lying nonstop."

"He also flirted with me."

"I'm afraid that he will ask me for money."

Serpukhovskoy also lay on the bed, still dressed and breathing heavily.

"It seems that I lied a lot," he thought. "But never mind! The wine was good and he's a pig. There's something of the merchant in him. And I'm a big pig, too!" he said to himself and burst out laughing.

"He sat up and somehow got his tunic off, along with his vest and pants. But he could not take off his boots, since his soft belly got in the way. Finally, he got one boot off, then pulled the other off halfway. But he struggled so hard that he got tired and was gasping for breath. So, with one foot still inside his boot, he fell asleep and started snoring, filling the room with the smell of tobacco, wine, and rotten old age."

Old Kholstomer, covered with scabs, was slaughtered in a ravine behind a brick barn outside the estate. A tanner flayed his old hide.

"The herd was climbing up a hill, and those on the left saw something red below, around which dogs were busily roaming and crows and hawks were flying overhead."

This horrible "story of a horse" ends with these solemn, rhythmic lines:

"At sunset, in the ravine of an old forest, in the bottom of an overgrown grade, wolf cubs with large heads were howling with great joy. There were five of them. Four were roughly the same size; the fifth was smaller with a head that was bigger than its body. A lean she-wolf, its fur shedding and its belly with its hanging nipples almost touching the ground, came out of the bushes and sat down across from her cubs. The cubs formed a semicircle in front of her. She approached the smallest one, kneeling on her paw and bending her snout to the ground. She made several convulsive motions and, opening her tooth-filled jaws, she struggled and disgorged a huge piece of horse flesh. The larger cubs moved closer to her, but she moved toward them with a threatening air and let the little one have it all. The little cub, as if agitated, hid the flesh under himself and began to devour it. In the same way, the she-wolf disgorged more meat for the second, the third, and all the others. She then lay down across from them and rested."

"A week later, there lay by the brick barn only a large skull and two large bones: Everything else had been carried off. In the summer, a peasant who collected bones took away even these remains and put them to good use."

"Serpukhovskoy's dead body *ate, drank, and wandered the world* for many more years before it was laid into the ground. Neither his skin nor his flesh nor his bones were put to any use."

"And just as this dead body which had wandered the world and, for twenty years, had been a burden to others, so its disposal into the ground became an additional hardship for people. He had long been useless to everyone; he had long been an onus for all. But still it is the *dead who bury the dead.* They found it necessary to dress the already swollen, decaying body in a fine uniform and shoes, to put it inside a fine new coffin with new tassels on each corner, to place this new coffin into another one made of lead, to carry it off to Moscow, to dig up the bones of the people who had long been buried there, to hide this rotting, worm-eaten body in its new uniform and polished boots, and to cover everything with dirt."

This "story of a horse" is, so to speak, the story about the death of the dead.

Aldanov, in his book *The Riddle of Tolstoy*, takes stock of the number of deaths in Tolstoy's writings and asks: Why did Tolstoy, throughout his long literary life, collect so much fictional material about death? He continues: "If anyone could seriously think out a philosophy of death, it would have to be Tolstoy. But for all his usual ethical generalizations, Tolstoy did not use all the riches of his treasure chest on death. He did not say an [ethical] word about Kuragin [in *War and Peace*], who was torn to pieces by a bomb, nor about Pozdnysheva [in *The Kreutzer Sonata*], who was knifed by her husband, nor about the rich young woman who was eaten away by consumption in 'Three Deaths.' . . . [With these individuals] Tolstoy acted as 'natural scientist,' doing his job. The philosopher in him passed them by."

One reads such things and cannot believe his eyes. As Aldanov would have it, Tolstoy should have accompanied every scene of death with ethical philosophies and generalizations, but he *never* did such a thing. Aldanov and I read "Three Deaths" and "Kholstomer" quite differently.

The scenes of death in *War and Peace* begin with the paganly majestic death of old Count Bezukhov, the greatest of all of Tolstoy's "Kholstomers." Bezukhov's passing is followed by the demise of the "little princess," Liza. As regards victims of death, the episode dealing with the end of Princess Liza is the ultimate in human sadness and tenderness. Liza's death is preceded by the birth of her child. The birth begins and continues through a dark, stormy, winter night, in an old, half-dark room on the estate of old Prince Bolkonsky amid remote snow-covered fields. Golden wedding candles are lit in front of the icon case to help the suffering Liza in her labor. Everywhere there is silence and anticipation. Everyone is "ready for something." All are "anxious, their hearts tender and aware of something impending and great, but also incomprehensible. . . . Evening gives way to night. The mystery, one of the most solemn in the world, continues to unfold. And the feeling of anxiety, the tenderness of heart before the incomprehensible does not cease; it intensifies. Nobody sleeps."

Does a "natural scientist" speak like this? And if for Tolstoy, birth is a "mystery, one of the most solemn in the world," how can human death not also be a mystery, if only the individual has not already died in life, if only he is not a "walking body" like the Kuragins and Serpukhovskoys?

Having given a new human life to the world, the little princess dies.

"Prince Andrei entered his wife's room. She was lying dead in the same position as he had seen her five minutes earlier, and the same expression, despite her lifeless eyes and the paleness of her cheeks, was on this charming childish face with its small lip covered with dark down."

"'I love all of you and never harmed anyone, and what have you done to me?' her charming, pitiful, dead face was saying."

"After three days they read the burial service for the little princess, and Prince Andrei, wishing to bid farewell to her, went up the stairs to her coffin. But even in the coffin, her face was still the same, though her eyes were closed. 'Oh, what have you done to me?' it kept on saying."

Later on there is that famous "sky over the field of Austerlitz," Prince Andrei's first step toward "leaving" this world, toward his "liberation."

"Prince Andrei did not see how it ended [the struggle between the two French soldiers and the Russian gunner]. . . . 'What is this? Am I falling? My legs are giving out from under me,' he thought, falling on his back. . . . Above him there was nothing but the sky—the lofty sky, not clear yet still immeasurably lofty, with gray clouds moving softly along it. 'How quiet! How peaceful and solemn! Not at all as it was when I was running,' Prince Andrei thought. 'Not at all the way it was when we were all running and shouting and fighting . . . how different is the way that clouds are drifting now through this loftily, endless sky! How is it that I did not see this lofty sky earlier? And how happy I am to have found it at last! Yes, all is vanity, all is delusion except this endless sky. There is nothing, nothing but that. But even this sky does not exist, there is nothing but peace and stillness. Thanks be to God. . . .'

"On the Pratzen plateau,[9] the very spot where he had fallen with the flagstaff in his hand, lay Prince Andrei Bolkonsky, losing blood and, without realizing it, moaning in a soft, pitiful, and childlike whimper.

"Toward evening, he had stopped moaning and had become quite still. He did not know how long he had been unconscious. Suddenly he again felt that he was alive and suffering from a burning, lacerating pain in his head.

"'Where is it, that lofty sky that I saw today and did not know earlier?' was his first thought. 'This suffering I also did not know earlier,' he thought. 'Yes, I knew nothing, nothing until now. But where am I?'

"He began to listen carefully and heard the sounds of approaching hooves and of voices speaking French. . . . The approaching horsemen were Napoleon and two aides-de-camp. . . .

"*'Voilà une belle mort,'*[10] Napoleon said, looking at Bolkonsky.

"Prince Andrei understood that this was being said about him and that it was Napoleon who was saying it. . . . But he listened to these words as though he were hearing the buzzing of a fly. . . . There was a burning pain in his head, and he felt that he was losing blood, and far above him he saw the far-off, lofty, and endless sky. He knew that the person speaking was his hero, Napoleon, but that at that moment Napoleon seemed to him to be such a small, insignificant creature[11] compared with what was now taking place between his soul and this lofty, endless sky with clouds racing through it. . . . He was glad only that people were standing nearby, and he wanted only that these people help him and return him to life, which seemed to him to be so beautiful *because he now understood it differently.* . . .

"Looking into Napoleon's eyes, Prince Andrei thought about the insignificance of greatness, about the insignificance of life, the meaning of which no one could understand, and about the even greater insignificance of death, which no one among the living could fathom or explain."

Chapter Eighteen

HERE, FINALLY, IS the second and last "liberation" of Prince Andrei.

"Prince Andrei not only knew that he was going to die, but he also felt that he was dying, that he was already half-dead. He felt remote from everything earthly, as well as a strange and joyous lightness of being. Neither impatient nor anxious, he awaited what lay before him. *That threatening, eternal, unknown, and distant presence, that something which he had sensed throughout his life,* was now close upon him; and, together with this strange lightness of being, it was almost tangible and comprehensible. . . .

"Earlier he had feared the end. Twice he had experienced the frightful, tormenting fear of death, of the end, but now he was beyond this fear.

"The first time he encountered this fear was with the bomb shell spinning like a top before him (on the field of Austerlitz); and, looking at the stubble-field, the bushes, and sky, he knew that death lay before him. When he had regained consciousness after being wounded, he immediately felt as though he had been liberated from the oppressive bondage of life. The flower of love, a love that was eternal, free, and *not dependent on this life,* had burst into bloom in his soul, and he no longer feared or thought about death.

"The more time the wounded Andrei spent in painful solitude and half ravings, pondering the new beginnings of eternal love which had been revealed to him, *the more he unconsciously renounced earthly life. To love everyone and everything, always to sacrifice oneself for love, such a concept meant not to love anyone nor to live this earthly life.* And the more he became imbued with this principle of love, the more he came to renounce life, the more completely he came to destroy that terrible barrier which (without love) stands between life and death. . . .

"But after that night at Mytishchy,[1] when, half delirious, he had seen her [Natasha] for whom he had longed appear before him, and when, pressing her hand to his lips, he had wept quiet, joyful tears, the love for one particular woman had stolen unobserved into his heart, and had bound him again to life. And glad and anxious thoughts began to occupy his mind. . . .

132

"His illness followed its normal physical course. But what Natasha had referred to when she said—*This happened to him*[2]—had actually taken place two days before Princess Mary had arrived. 'This' was the final moral struggle between life and death, one in which death would win. This brought the unexpected realization that he still valued life, filled with his love for Natasha, and also that he faced the last overwhelming onslaught of terror before the unknown.

"It happened in the evening. He was, as was usual after dinner, slightly feverish, but his thoughts were extremely clear. Sonya had been sitting at the table. He had fallen asleep. Suddenly, a sense of happiness seized him.

"'Ah, she has come!' he thought.

"And so it was, for in Sonya's place there sat Natasha, who had just entered noiselessly.

"Ever since she had begun looking after him, he had always felt her physical closeness. She was knitting a stocking and sitting in a chair placed sideways next to him so as to block out the light from the candle shining on him. . . .

"'Can it be?' he now wondered as he looked at her and listened to the light clicking of her steel needles. 'Can it be that fate has brought us together so strangely only for me to die? Can it be that the truth of life has been revealed to me only for me to live a lie?

"'I love her more than anything else in the world,' he said to himself. 'But what am I to do if I love her?' And he suddenly gave an involuntary groan, a habit that he had fallen into during the course of his sufferings.

"Hearing this sound, Natasha put down her knitting and leaned nearer to him. Suddenly, having noticed his shining eyes, she went up to him with a light step and bent over him.

"'You're not asleep?'

"'No, I have been looking at you for a long time. I felt you coming in. . . . No one gives me such a sweet sense of peace as you . . . such radiance. I feel like crying from happiness.'

"Natasha moved closer to him. Her face shone with radiant happiness.

"'Natasha, I love you too much. More than anything else in the world.'

"'And I?' She turned away for a moment. "'Why "too" much?' she asked.

"'Why "too" much? Well, what do you think? Do you feel in your soul that I am going to live? What does it seem to you?'

"'I am sure of it, I am sure of it!' Natasha almost shouted, seizing both his hands in hers in a passionate gesture.

"He was quiet for awhile.

"'How good that would be!' he said. And taking her hand, he kissed it. . . .

"Soon after this, he closed his eyes and fell asleep. But he did not sleep for long. He woke up suddenly, anxious and in a cold sweat.

"As he was falling asleep, he kept thinking about everything that had occupied his mind for so long—about life and death. And more and more about death. He felt nearer to death.

"'Love? What is love?' he thought.

"'Love does not understand death. Love is life. Everything, everything that I understand, I understand only because I love. All is bound up in it alone. Love is God, and to die—means that I, a particle of this love, will return to the universal and eternal source.' But these were only thoughts. There was something lacking in them, and also something that was one-sidedly personal and intellectual. Everything was confused. And then there was that same uncertainty and restlessness. He fell asleep.

"He dreamed that he was lying in the actual room that he was lying in, but that he had not been wounded and was quite well. Before Prince Andrei appeared many different people, indifferent, insignificant individuals. He talked with them, arguing about trifling things. The people were intending to go off somewhere. Andrei dimly realized that all this was trivial and that he had more serious matters to attend to; but he kept on talking, surprising them with his empty witticisms. Gradually, imperceptibly, all these people began to disappear and to give way to a single impression, that of a closed door. He got up and went to the door to throw the bolt and lock it. Everything depended on whether he could lock it quickly enough. He started to rush over, but his legs did not move. He knew that he would not be in time to lock the door; nonetheless, in a frenzy, he made every effort to do so. An agonizing fear seized him. The fear was the fear of death, for *It* stood behind the door. But as he was, helplessly and clumsily, stumbling toward the door, this terrible something was pushing against it from the other side and forcing its way in. Something not human—death—was breaking through the door and had to be stopped. He struggled with the door, straining with every ounce of his strength—to lock it was no longer possible—he could seek only to stop death from coming. But his efforts were feeble and awkward, and the door, under the terrible pressure of that awful thing, opened and closed again.

"Again *It* pushed on the door from without. His last superhuman efforts to stop it were in vain, and both sides of the door opened noiselessly. *It* had entered, and it was death. And Prince Andrei died."

"But at the very moment in his dream when Prince Andrei died, he remembered that he had been sleeping; and at the very same instant when he died, he exerted himself and awoke."

"'Yes, that was death,' he thought. 'I died, and I woke up. Yes, death is an awakening.' His soul was suddenly flooded with light, and the veil, which until then had concealed the unknown, was lifted from his spiritual vision. He felt the seeming *liberation of that force that had been shackled in him earlier,* as well as that strange lightness of being which was still with him.

134

"When he, having awakened in a cold sweat, stirred on the couch, Natasha went up to him and asked if something was wrong. He did not answer, but looked at her strangely, not understanding what she had asked."

Again, this is what happened two days before the arrival of Princess Mary. . . .

"*With this awakening from his dream there began for Prince Andrei an awakening from life. . . .*"

"His last days passed in a simply and ordinary way. Both Princess Mary and Natasha, who never left his side, knew that he was dying. They did not shudder or cry; and, at the end, they felt that they were no longer attending him (for he was no longer there, but had departed them), but rather the immediate remembrance of him—his body. . . ."

"They both saw that he, slowly and quietly, was slipping away further and further from them to some other place; and they also both knew that this was the way it had to be, and that it was good."

Chapter Nineteen

TOLSTOY ONCE WROTE:
"The death of loved ones has never been very painful for me."

He wrote this in his old age, after the death of many of his family and friends. Did he write this because he had grown numb to his emotions, because he had gotten accustomed to the pain of all kinds of losses in life? But Tolstoy was always extremely thoughtful in the way he expressed himself. He would not have written the word "never" without a reason. How then can one explain that the death of loved ones did not affect him greatly? Everyone knows the great terror and bitterness he experienced when he first lost one brother, then another. Everyone also knows what Levin felt when his brother, Nikolai, lay dying. Only Kitty saved Levin during those days, only the sensation of his closeness to her young life and love and his own love for her.

Nonetheless, Tolstoy does say that the loss of close ones was for him "not very painful." Upon first glance, this "not very painful" seems strange. "I always feel people physically," he said about himself (thereby giving dull-witted people a splendid pretext to insist that he could perceive only the "flesh" of the world).[1] But did he feel everything "physically," that is, with all his being, with unusual sharpness? His feeling for death, for all its physical and spiritual workings, was especially finely honed. Tolstoy constantly lived by this law: "The intensity of the feeling for life is proportional to that of the feeling for death." Why, then, was it "not very painful" to be alongside loved ones as they lay dying? Incidentally, that is how he truly behaved in such circumstances—or, more accurately, so it seemed.

"Not very painfully" did he suffer first the death of his cherished son, little Vanechka, and then the passing of his most beloved daughter, Masha.

Alexandra L'vovna writes in her memoirs:

"Masha was passing from us. I recalled Vanechka, whom she now resembled. . . . Father would enter quietly, without a sound. He would take her hand and kiss her forehead. . . . When she was dying, everyone entered the room. Father sat down near the bed and held Masha's hand. . . .[2]

"When her coffin was carried out of the house, he followed it only up to the gates. Then he went back into the house."[3]

Ilya L'vovich describes the scene in a remarkable way:

"When people started to carry the coffin to the church, Father got dressed and went to see it off. When he reached the stone pillars [of the gate], he stopped us, said good-bye to his dead daughter, and returned home through an alleyway. He walked along the wet, melting snow with a rapid, old man's gait, pointing his feet sharply outward as always, and never looking back."

In 1903, Tolstoy wrote:

"Sufferings are always as inescapable as death. But they destroy our material illusions, the barriers that restrain our spirit. They cause us to believe again that human life is spiritual, not physical."

He wrote and said similar things many times, both earlier and later.

"People think that illness is a lost time. They say: 'When I get better, then I will. . . .' But illness is the most important time [for an individual]."

Recalling the most difficult hours of his own severe illnesses, he felt compelled to note:

"How dear to me were those minutes of dying!"

And about his daughter [Masha], he wrote:

"November 26, 1906. It is now 1:00 A.M. Masha has passed away. But, strangely, I did not feel either terror or fear or the consciousness that something out of the ordinary has happened. I did not even feel pity or grief. I felt as though I had to summon within me a special feeling of tenderness, of sorrow; and I was able to do so. But in the depths of my soul, I was calm. . . . Yes, Masha's death is a bodily happening; that is why I am indifferent to it. I kept watching how she was dying in such a remarkably peaceful way. She was now someone who was casting off her self, and who did so before my own inner release. I watched this casting off, and it gave me great joy. But what I could discern about this casting off came to an end; that is, I could not see any more of this process, though I knew that it was still going on, that such a phenomenon existed. But where? But when? These are questions that focus on the process of the casting off *here*, questions that cannot be tied to that genuine life that exists beyond time and space."[4]

Later on, he remembered his daughter:

"I relive and often recall Masha's last minutes. (But I do not want to call her 'Masha,' for such a simple name is unacceptable for the person who left me.) She was sitting, propped up by pillows. Holding her thin, dear hand, I felt how life was leaving her, how she was leaving me. Those fifteen minutes were one of the most important, remarkable moments of my life."

"'WHAT AM I ANXIOUS ABOUT? What am I afraid of?' Tolstoy asked himself. 'You are afraid of me,' the voice of death answers noiselessly. 'I am here.' A shiver ran down my spine. Yes, it was death. It will come for me. Here it is, but it should not be."

He devoted his entire life to internalizing the feeling not only that "death should not be" but that it really does not exist.

Why does death not exist? He was given the answer to the question even then, during that night at Arzamas.

"It seems that death is terrifying, but when one starts remembering and thinking about existence, it is not death but a life that is dying that is frightening."

That night he felt: "I am bored, unbearable, and tormented." But which "I" was he talking about? The "I" that lived the "dying" life, not the one that was eternally living, beyond time and space. He was in despair: "I cannot run away from myself"! But what "self" was he talking about? The one that was temporal and corporal. But he had to run away, "to liberate himself." Otherwise, he would have given way to "terror—red, white, and squarelike." Otherwise, he would have been consumed by "anger with himself and at that which has made me," that is, the Creator himself.

The temporal and bodily existence which the Creator gave to humankind invariably means anger, terror, death, and "dying life," if one does not strive for "liberation"; if one does not overcome the "subjugation" to which all living things must, to some degree, submit; if one does not yearn increasingly for return to the Creator, to intimacy and unity with Him; and if one does not know the joy at discerning His holy will to which everyone must surrender in everything without philosophizing or questioning.

There now begins Tolstoy's unending struggle with this "dying life."

"The teaching of the church about the immortality of the individual soul secures the self for all time. . . . But Christ told us not to live for this self."

He wrote this at the same time he was writing his *Confession* and *What I Believe*. Discussing this period in Tolstoy's life, Maklakov said:

"These two books contain the entire essence of Tolstoy's teaching. . . . The church denies that human life is finite, for it believes in a life beyond the grave, that is, an unending life. But Tolstoy sought meaning for that life which ends in death, for, as a nonbeliever, he saw death as the ultimate end. Tolstoy searched for this meaning and found it. 'The problem is that I have lived a bad life,' he told himself. 'A life that ends in death acquires meaning only when one follows two commandments: do not do violence to resist evil and live for your neighbor, not for yourself.'"

Maklakov claims:

"*What I Believe* is the culmination of Tolstoy's worldview."

"Culmination!" As if Maklakov has never seen Tolstoy's final notes.

"Tolstoy, as a nonbeliever, saw death as the ultimate end."

What does Maklakov base this assertion on? On the fact that "Tolstoy told me so many times," and also, I believe, because Tolstoy wrote, for example:

"Future life is nonsense."

Such things seem to confirm Maklakov's contention beyond a doubt. But how does Tolstoy's line about future life read in full?

"Future life is nonsense; life is timeless."

What else did Tolstoy write at this time?

"We truly live neither in the past nor in the future, for both of them do not exist. We live only in the present: Space and time are conventions."

"I ran into a madman on the road. When I was bidding farewell to him, I said: 'Well, good-bye, we'll see each other in the next life.' He replied: 'What other life are you talking about? Life is one.' I liked that very much!"

He "did not believe in immortality"? But what "immortality" are we talking about?

"No matter how one might wish for the immortality of the soul, it does not exist, and it cannot exist because there is no soul. There is only the awareness of the Eternal (God)."

"Death is the cessation, the alteration of that form of consciousness that has found expression in my human being. Consciousness ceases, but that which has had awareness is unchanging because it lies outside of time and space. . . . If there is immortality, it exists only in the absence of self. . . . The divine source will again appear in the self, but it will be a different kind of self. What kind of self will it be? Where will it be? How will it be? This is for God to decide."

"In order to believe in immortality, one should live an immortal life *here*."

"Death is the transference of oneself from earthly, temporal existence into eternal life *here and now*, a transference that I am (already) experiencing."

What does "death" mean in this sentence? Is it that which one usually means by death, and which Tolstoy himself also understood to mean at one

139

time in his life? No, "death" here is something quite different. It is the living and joyful return from earthly and temporal space to something that is unearthly, eternal, and boundless, to the bosom of the Lord and Father, whose being is without question.

––––––

Aldanov begins his book about Tolstoy with a well-known quotation from Kant: "Two things fill my soul with an eternally new and ever increasing reverence—the starry sky above me and the moral law within me." Aldanov says that this formula expresses the completely harmonic individual. He also says that this rubric can be divided into two parts: The first part points to the pagan Goethe, the second to the Christian Tolstoy. As Aldanov sees it, only the moral law exists for Tolstoy. *Das ewig Eine,*[1] which so "intrigued" Goethe, the "starry sky" of Kant, has no place in Tolstoy's worldview.

How does Aldanov prove his point? "Tolstoy," he says, "talks about science not as a philosopher but as a polemicist. . . . For Tolstoy, concepts such as 'cloudy spots,' the 'spectral analysis of the stars,' and the 'chemical composition of the Milky Way' were, in his own words, 'scientific science'— useless professorial nonsense. Tolstoy believed that the only science that people needed was that practical science which improved their lives."[2]

But the "starry sky" could bring Tolstoy to other thoughts and feelings which in no way were tied to his contempt for professors who studied the chemical composition of the Milky Way.

Aldanov himself affirms such an idea later on in his book. He cites one reason for Tolstoy's hostility to "scientific science" by quoting the writer himself. "People have come up with bathrooms and ways to collect taxes," Tolstoy wrote. "But the spinning wheel, the woman's loom, and the plow are exactly as they were in Ryurik's time."

But later on Aldanov himself asks: "But should one look for the real reason for Tolstoy's hostility to science in such things?" His answer: Tolstoy believed himself to be ignorant, even though [I repeat] "he was one of the most widely learned people of our time. It was only his far-reaching, anarchical frame of mind that questioned the sovereignty of science, just as it had questioned the sovereignty of the state."

Why did Tolstoy have so little respect for science?[3] Aldanov says that Tolstoy sought to overcome science with the vantage point of eternity. "You invented a vaccine for diphtheria?" Tolstoy asks. "You cured a child? All right, now what next?" Tolstoy once questioned Maupassant: "What's the point of all this?—meaning by "all this" the way the French writer understood beauty and love. Tolstoy himself answered: "How nice it would be if we could stop life. But it goes on. But what does that mean: Life goes on?

That 'life goes on' means that a person's hair turns gray and falls out, his teeth decay, his face becomes wrinkled, and his mouth exudes a foul odor."

Taking Maupassant's view of life as his own,[4] Tolstoy continued: "But where is that very thing which I have served? Where is that beauty? Beauty is everything; without it there is nothing. There is no life. But more than that, not only is there no life in what seemed to be life, but the individual himself begins to leave this very life. He becomes old, decays, and loses his mind. Before his very eyes, others snatch away from him the pleasures that had been the joy of his life."

How can one reconcile this remark with Aldanov's comment that "Tolstoy speaks about science not like a philosopher but a polemicist"? And what is his "vantage point of eternity" if not the "starry sky above me"?

Having cited Tolstoy's words to Maupassant, Aldanov adds: "What Maupassant saw as pleasure, Tolstoy regarded with the mournful contempt of an old Hellene."[5] Further on, Aldanov continues: "From the vantage point of eternity, nothing that opposes science becomes more enduring. Not at all. When the wind of eternity blows, any human edifice collapses like a house of cards, and the teachings of Tolstoy himself would be first to go. Pascal said: *'Le silence eternel de ces espaces infinis m'effraye.'*"[6]

I take issue with what Aldanov says by asserting that *"ces espaces"* are the same thing as the "starry sky." It is true that before these spaces "any human edifice will collapse." But why should only Tolstoy's teachings be the first to go? What is important here is how one understands Tolstoy. After all, Tolstoy was able to escape the terror of *"ces espaces."* How did he do so? In a way which an "old Hellene" would never be able to do, for Tolstoy was never a "Hellene."

Aldanov recalls Byron's words that "thought is the rust of life," that "reason contradicts human nature," and that "reason is a demon." He continues by saying that when Tolstoy wrote *War and Peace,* he was not far from Byron's worldview, if only because Tolstoy was, unconsciously perhaps, following an instinct for self-preservation. That is, Tolstoy foresaw where Byron's "demon" was leading him and the type of victim this "demon" would claim. Tolstoy contrasted two families: the Bolkonskys and the Rostovs (in real life, the Volkonskys and the Tolstoys). Everyone among the Bolkonskys is engaged in intense spiritual work, in "reason" and thought. But no one among the Rostovs ever thinks at all, and what of it? All the Bolkonskys are miserable, while all the Rostovs are blissfully happy. As Aldanov sees it, Tolstoy understood the differences between the two families quite well.

Aldanov also sees one of the themes in *War and Peace* as Tolstoy's struggle with Byron's demon for its minions, as well as for himself as a descendant of the Volkonskys. "Ah, dear friend," Pierre says to Prince Andrei on the eve of his fatal day at the Battle of Borodino. "As of late, I have found it very difficult to live. I see that I am beginning to understand too much. And it is not good for one to taste the fruit from the tree of knowledge of good and evil." Here Aldanov is correct. But neither Prince Andrei nor Tolstoy could resist "tasting" this fruit, for it was this "tasting" which was leading—and finally led—both of them to the "starry sky."

Chapter Twenty-one

"TWENTY THOUSAND LEAGUES in search of himself." No, not just around himself, but also around everything in the world. What did Tolstoy find in this world? Besides the fact that "people were alive," he found that everything turned out to be "not that" and "not so." But he encountered a solitude which occurs neither under the ground nor at the bottom of the sea. In the last year of his life, he would often repeat these terrible words:

> "Be silent, hide yourself
> And your feelings and your dreams."[1]

What were these feelings and dreams? Of all the feelings and dreams Tolstoy had in life, there now remained, at the end of his time here on earth, only one: "Help me, Father. I hate my loathsome flesh, I hate myself (my bodily being). . . . I have not slept all night long. My heart aches incessantly. I have prayed that You would deliver me from life. . . . Father, vanquish, expel, and destroy my loathsome flesh. Help me, Father!"

A prayer is not a request, Tolstoy liked to say. But what is prayer if not a request? How many of these requests does one find in his diaries, especially in his 1910 journal? And to whom does he address these requests? To some "abstraction" which, everyone insists, was his God? But who can pray to an abstraction? And how can one revere an abstraction with a love that was so lively, tender, filial, joyfully consoling, a love that overflowed his soul in the most intimate and horrible moments of his life?[2]

"I was lying down, trying to fall asleep. Suddenly, it was as if something had broken loose in my heart. I thought: This is how death comes during a heart attack, but I remained calm. I felt neither anger nor joy, only a blissful peacefulness. Whether I am here or there, I know that I am all right and that my situation is as it should be. I am like a baby who continues his joyful smiles when his mother tosses him into the air, for he knows that she is also taking care of him."

———

Prince Andrei asks:

"What awaits me there beyond the grave?"

Aldanov, recalling this question, says that Tolstoy answers:

"Return to Love."

Such a response leads Aldanov to reflect:

"One of Goya's most terrible fantasies depicts a frantically bent arm reaching out from under the gravestone of a barren grave and trying desperately to grab onto something—onto emptiness. Underneath there is an inscription—just one word: *Nada.* Nothing.[3] . . . Is Tolstoy's inscription—'Return to Love'—much better than *nada?* Perhaps. Perhaps, the time for Tolstoy's teachings will come, as Chekhov's Vershinin [in *Three Sisters*] says, 'in two or three hundred years.' But what then? Even then it will be all the same, for everything will be devoured by death."

I repeat, how does Aldanov understand Tolstoy's teachings? Maklakov says: "But, for Tolstoy, God was an incomprehensible, primordial power; and the immortality of the soul meant that because spiritual life had an obscure beginning, it will also have an obscure end. As regards faith, Tolstoy loved to quote Ivan Kireevsky, who said that faith was not so much a knowledge of the truth as a devotion to it. . . . Tolstoy came out against the church, having rejected its religious views; he also came out against the world, having rejected its views on earthly life."

Aldanov apparently agrees with Maklakov, but what do these two leave for Tolstoy? That Tolstoy rejected the Weltanschauung of both religions and the world? But why would he reject the Weltanschauung of the world after having rejected that of religion? "Tolstoy loved to quote Ivan Kireevsky." Let Tolstoy repeat them: Spiritually, he lived in complete opposition to these words. He lived precisely not with the "knowledge" of the truth but with "devotion" to it. As he already had said in his *Confession,* he had rejected "knowledge" in matters of faith. *Nada!* For the mind, obviously, there is *Nada.* People can find reprieve from death not with reason but feeling.

"No one should be afraid of dying, for the Savior's death liberated us."

"We celebrate the demise of death . . . and the beginning of another life in eternity."

So sings that church which Tolstoy had rejected. But he did not reject the hymns of faith (or faith in general). What liberated him? Maybe it was not "the Savior's death"; yet he "celebrated" the "demise of death" and acquired the feeling of "another life in eternity." After all, feeling was everything for him. He who does not feel this "Nothing" is saved.

"He hardly believed in future life," Aldanov writes, as he quotes Tolstoy: "I once asked myself: 'Do I believe?' And instinctively I answered that I did not believe in a definite form." He said such a thing, however, only in those moments when "he was asking himself." These were not the moments that saved him. The moments that saved him were those when he was not asking.

My old friend, Doctor I. N. Al'tshuller,[4] wrote to me:

"When I read your articles about Tolstoy, I recall a night in Crimea, at Gaspra, when I was sitting alone alongside a very ill Lev Nikolaevich. At that time, we doctors had lost almost all hope, and, in my opinion, Tolstoy himself seemed convinced of his imminent end. He was lying down, seemingly half conscious, with a high temperature. His breathing was shallow. Suddenly, in a weak but distinct voice, he uttered: 'From you I came, to you I shall return, accept me, O Lord.'" Al'tshuller adds: "He said this like any simple believer."

Paris
July 7, 1937

Prominent Individuals Mentioned
in the Text and Editors' Notes

Abdul-Hamid II (1842–1918), thirty-first sultan of Turkey
Adamovich, Georgy Viktorovich (1884–1972), writer and poet
Addams, Jane (1860–1935), American social worker
Agaf'ya Mikhailovna (1808–96), maid of Tolstoy's grandmother, Pelageya
    Gorchakova-Tolstaya
Aksakov, Konstantin Sergeevich (1817–60), Slavophile and journalist
Aksakov, Sergei Timofeevich (1791–1859), writer and memoirist
Aldanov-Landau, Mark Alexandrovich (1886–1957), writer
Alexander I (1777–1825), tsar of Russia from 1801 to 1825
Alexander II (1818–81), tsar of Russia from 1855 to 1881
Alexander III (1845–94), tsar of Russia from 1881 to 1894
Alexei Petrovich (1690–1718), son of Peter the Great
Al'tshuller, Isaak Naumovich (1870–1943), Tolstoy's doctor in Yalta
Ambrose, Father (Grenkov, Alexander Mikhailovich) (1812–91), superior of
    Optina Hermitage from 1865 to 1891
Amfiteatrov, Alexander Valentinovich (1862–1938), writer and critic
Andreev, Leonid Nikolaevich (1871–1919), writer
Annenkov, Pavel Vasilievich (1813?–87), critic and memoirist
Aristotle (382–322 B.C.), Greek philosopher
Arkhangel'sky, Alexander Andreevich (1846–1924), musician
Arnold, Matthew (1822–88), English poet, critic, and educationist
Arsenieva, Valeriya Vladimirmovna (1836–1909), consort of Leo Tolstoy
Ashvaghosa (A.D. 80?–150?), Indian poet and philosopher
Auerbach, Berthold (1812–82), German novelist
Avilova, Lidiya Alexeevna (1865–1942), writer

Bacon, Francis (1561–1626), English philosopher, essayist, and statesman
Bakhrakh, Alexander Vasilievich (1902–86), critic and journalist
Bal'mont, Konstantin Dmitrievich (1867–1942), poet
Baudelaire, Charles Pierre (1821–67), French poet

147

Bazykin, Timofei Nikonovich (1861–1934), illegitimate son of Leo Tolstoy by Aksinya Bazykina

Bazykina, Aksinya Alexandrovna (1836–1919), consort of Leo Tolstoy

Beethoven, Ludwig van (1770–1827), German composer

Beklemishev, Vladimir Alexandrovich (1861–1920), sculptor

Bely, Andrei (pseudonym of Bugaev, Boris Nikolaevich) (1880–1934), poet and writer

Berberova, Nina Nikolaevna (1901–93), poet, writer, memoirist, and second wife of Vladislav Khodasevich

Berdyaev, Nikolai Alexandrovich (1847–1948), religious philosopher

Berlioz, Hector (1803–69), French composer

Bers, Andrei Evstafievich (1808–68), doctor and father of Sofya Bers-Tolsyaya

Bers, Lyubov' Alexandrovna (1826–86), wife of Andrei Bers and mother of Sofya Bers-Tolstaya

Bers, Stepan Andreevich (1855–1910), memoirist and brother of Sofya Bers-Tolstaya

Bers-Kuzminskaya, Tatyana Andreevna (1847–1925), sister of Sofya Bers-Tolstaya

Bers-Tolstaya, Sofya Andreevna (1844–1919), wife of Leo Tolstoy

Biryukov, Pavel Ivanovich (1860–1931), friend and biographer of Leo Tolstoy

Bismarck, Prince Karl Otto Eduard Leopold von (1815–98), German statesman and founder of the German empire

Boborykin, Pyotr Dmitrievich (1836–1921), novelist and playwright

Boileau, Nicholas (1636–1711), French poet and critic

Bonch-Bruevich, Vladimir Dmitrievich (1873–1955), revolutionary, ethnographer, and party administrator

Botkin, Vasily Petrovich (1811–69), literary, art, and music critic and publicist

Boulanger, Pavel Alexandrovich (1865–1925), friend of Leo Tolstoy

Bryusov, Valery Yakovlevich (1873–1924), poet, novelist, and critic

Buddha. See Siddartha

Bulgakov, Valentin Fyodorovich (1886–1966), writer, memoirist, and Leo Tolstoy's secretary in 1910

Bunin, Alexei Nikolevich (1824–1906), father of Ivan Bunin

Bunin, Yuly Alexeevich (1857–1921), brother of Ivan Bunin

Bunina, Anna Petrovna (1774–1829), poet and translator

Butkevich, Anatoly Stepanovich (1859–1942), former student revolutionary and later Tolstoyan

Byron, Lord George Gordon Noel (1788–1824), English poet

Carlyle, Thomas (1795–1881), Scottish essayist and historian

Carus, Paul (1852–1919), American writer, philosopher, and editor

Catherine I (1684–1727), second wife of Peter the Great, empress of Russia from 1725 to 1727

Catherine II (Catherine the Great) (1726–96), empress of Russia from 1762 to 1796

Chaadaev, Pyotr Yakovlevich (1794–1856), philosopher

Chaliapin, Fyodor Ivanovich (1873–1938), bass singer

Chekhov, Anton Pavlovich (1860–1904), playwright and short-story writer

Chernyshevsky, Nikolai Gavrilovich (1828–89), radical journalist and political thinker

Chertkov, Grigory Ivanovich (1828–84), father of Vladimir Chertkov

Chertkov, Vladimir Grigorievich (1854–1936), friend and publisher of Leo Tolstoy

Chertkova, Elizaveta Ivanovna (1832–1922), mother of Vladimir Chertkov

Chesnokov, Pavel Grigorievich (1877–1944), musician

Chinelli, Delfino (1889–1942), writer and novelist

Coleridge, Samuel Taylor (1772–1834), English poet and critic

Comte, Auguste (1798–1857), French mathematician and philosopher

Confucius (551–478 B.C.), Chinese philosopher and teacher

Corneille, Pierre (1606–84), French poet and dramatist

Cromwell, Oliver (1599–1658), English soldier, statesman, and leader of the Puritan Revolution

Dickens, Charles (1812–70), English novelist

Diogenes (412–323 B.C.), Greek philosopher

Dobrolyubov, Nikolai Alexandrovich (1836–61), critic

Dosev, P. (pseudonym of Khristo Feodosovich Dosev) (1886–1919), Bulgarian Tolstoyan, scholar, and translator of Tolstoy's works

Dostoevsky, Fyodor Mikhailovich (1821–81), novelist

Druzhinin, Alexander Vasilevich (1824–64), novelist and critic

Dudchenko, Mitrofan Semyonovich (1867–1946), Tolstoyan

Dudchenko, Tikhon Semyonovich (1853–1920), Tolstoyan and brother of Mitrofan

Edison, Thomas (1847–1931), American inventor

Edward VII (1841–1910), king of Great Britain and Ireland from 1901 to 1910

Eliot, George (1819–80), English novelist

Elizaveta Petrovna (1709–62), empress of Russia from 1741 to 1762

Emerson, Ralph Waldo (1803–82), American philosopher, essayist, and poet

Epictetus (circa 50–120), Greek Stoic philosopher

Ergol'skaya, Tatyana Aleksandrovna (1792–1817), second cousin of Tolstoy's father

Esenin, Sergei Alexandrovich (1895–1925), poet

Estafy (circa 118), martyr and saint

Euripedes (480–406 B.C.), Greek dramatist

Feokritova, Varvara Mikailovna (1875–1950), companion of Alexandra Tolstaya and copier for Sofya Bers-Tolstaya

Fet, Afanasy Afanasievich (1820–92), poet

Flaubert, Gustave (1821–80), French novelist

France, Anatole (1844–1924), French novelist and critic

Francis of Assisi (1182–1226), monk, saint, and founder of the Franciscans

Franklin, Benjamin (1706–90), American patriot, writer, scientist, and diplomat

Froebel, Freidrich (1782–1852), German educator and founder of the kindergarten system

Froebel, Julius (1805–93), nephew of Friedrich Froebel

Garshin, Vsevolod Mikhailovich (1855–88), short-story writer

Ge, Nikolai Nikolaevich (1831–94), artist

George, Henry (1839–97), American economist

Gide, André (1869–1951), French writer

Gippius-Merezhkovskaya, Zinaida Nikolaevna (1867–1945), poet, critic, novelist, memoirist, and wife of Dmitri Merezhkovsky

Gluck, Christoph Willibald (1714–87), Austrian composer

Godunov, Boris (1552?–1605), tsar of Russia from 1598 to 1605

Goethe, Johann Wolfgang von (1749–1832), German poet, dramatist, novelist, and statesman

Gogol, Nikolai Vasilievich (1809–52), novelist and short-story writer

Goldenweiser, Alexander Borisovich (1875–1961), pianist, professor at the Moscow Conservatory, and friend of Leo Tolstoy

Goncharov, Ivan Alexandrovich (1812–91), writer

Gorchakov, Nikolai Ivanovich (1725–1811), prince, father of Pelageya Gorchakova-Tolstaya, and great-grandfather of Leo Tolstoy

Gorchakov, Alexander Mikhailovich (1798–1883), Russian foreign minister from 1856 to 1882

Gorchakov, Mikhail Dmitrievich (1791–1861), Russian military officer and statesman

Gorchakova-Tolstaya, Pelageya Nikolaevna (1762–1838), princess and grandmother of Leo Tolstoy

Gorky-Peshkov, Alexei Maximovich (Maxim) (1868–1936), writer and social figure

Goya y Lucientes, Franciso José de (1746–1828), Spanish painter and etcher

Gusev, Nikolai Nikolaevich (1882–1967), Tolstoy's secretary from 1907 to 1909

Hauptmann, Gerhart (1862–1946), German playwright, poet, and novelist, who received the 1912 Nobel Prize in literature

Haydn, Franz Joseph (1732–1809), Austrian composer

Herzen, Alexander Ivanovich (1812–70), writer and philosopher

Homer (ninth century B.C.), Greek epic poet

Hus, Jan (1370–1415), Bohemian religious reformer

Igor (d. 945), prince of Kiev

Ivan IV (Ivan the Terrible) (1530–84), tsar of Russia from 1547 to 1584

Ivanov, Georgy Vladimirovich (1894–1958) poet, prose writer, essayist, memoirist, and literary critic

Jefferson, Thomas (1743–1826), American statesman and third president of the United States

Kant, Immanuel (1724–1804), German philosopher

Karamzina, Maria Vladimirovna (1885–1941), writer and memoirist

Kareev, Nikolai Ivanovich (1850–1931), historian and publicist

Karonin, Nikolai (pseudonym of Nikolai Elpidiforovich Petropavlovsky) (1853–92), writer

Kataev, Valentin Petrovich (1897–1986), writer

Katkov, Mikhail Nikiforovich (1818–87), journalist, editor, and critic

Kennan, George (1845–1923), American author, journalist, lecturer, and traveler

Khodasevich, Vladislav Felitsianovich (1886–1939), poet and critic

Khilkov, Dmitri Alexandrovich (1857–1914), prince and Tolstoyan

Kingsley, Charles (1819–75), English clergyman and writer

Kireevsky, Ivan Vasilievich (1806–56), philosopher, critic, writer, and leading ideologist of Slavophilism in Russia

Kireevsky, Pyotr Vasilievich (1808–56), Slavophile, ethnographer, and brother of Ivan Kireevsky

Klopsky, Ivan Mikhailovich (1852–98), Tolstoyan

Knipper-Chekhova, Olga Leonardovna (1868–1959), actress with the Moscow Art Theater and wife of Anton Chekhov

Koltsov, Alexei Vasielevich (1809–42), poet

Konshin, Alexander Nikolaevich (1867–1919), Tolstoyan

Korolenko, Vladimir Galaktionovich (1853–1921), writer, critic, publicist, translator, and social activist

Kramskoy, Ivan Nikolaevich (1837–87), painter

Krupskaya, Nadezhda Konstantinova (1869–1939), educator, party and government figure, and wife of Vladimir Lenin

Ksyunin, Alexei Ivanovich (1880–1938), journalist and biographer of Leo Tolstoy

Kutuzov, Mikhail Illarionovich (1745–1813), army commander who repelled Napoleon's 1812 invasion of Russia

Kuzminsky, Alexander Mikhailovich (1843–1917), lawyer and husband of Tatyana Bers-Kuzminskaya

Kuznetsova, Galina Nikolaevna (1902–76), émigré poet, prose writer, and memoirist

La Bruyère, Jean de (1645–96), French writer and moralist
Lao-tzu (604?–531? B.C.), Chinese philosopher and mystic
La Rochefoucauld, Duc François de (1613–80), French writer and politician
Lazursky, Vladimir Fyodorovich (1869–1943), literary historian, professor, and tutor to the children of Leo Tolstoy
Leibniz, Gottfried Wilhelm (1646–1716), German philosopher and mathematician
Lenin, Vladimir Ilyich (pseudonym of Vladimir Ilyich Ul'yanov) (1870–1924), revolutionary leader and writer
Leontiev, Boris Nikolaevich (1866–1909), Tolstoyan
Leskov, Nikolai Semyonovich (1831–95), short-story writer, novelist, and journalist
Lessing, Gotthold Ephraim (1729–81), German dramatist and critic
Lobachevsky, Nikolai Ivanovich (1792–1856), professor and mathematician
Lombroso, Cesare (1836–1909), Italian psychiatrist and anthropologist
Lopatin, Lev Mikhailovich (1855–1920), professor of philosophy
Lopatin, Mikhail Nikolaevich (1823–1900), father of Ekaterina Lopatina
Lopatin, Vladimir Mikhailovich (1861–1935), lawyer, actor for the Moscow Art Theater, and brother of Ekaterina Lopatina
Lopatina, Ekaterina Mikhailovna (1865–1935), writer
Luther, Martin (1483–1546), German monk, theologian, and leader of the Reformation

Maklakov, Vasily Alexeevich (1870–1957), lawyer, acquaintance of Tolstoy, member of the Duma, and, in emigration, Tolstoy scholar
Makovitsky, Dushan Petrovich (1866–1921), doctor of Leo Tolstoy
Mamin-Sibiryak, Dmitri Narkisovich (pseudonym of Dmitri Narkisovich Mamin) (1852–1912), novelist, dramatist, and short-story writer
Marcus Aurelius (121–180), Russian emperor and Stoic
Maria Fyodorovna (1847–1928), wife of Alexander III
Maria Nikolaevna (1819–76), grand duchess and daughter of Nicholas I
Marx, Karl (1818–83), German economist and social philosopher
Maupassant, Guy de (1850–93), French novelist and short-story writer
Mechnikov, Ilya Ilyich (1845–1916), zoologist, microbiologist, and, in 1908, recipient of the Nobel Prize in medicine
Merezhkovsky, Dmitri Sergeevich (1865–1941), Symbolist poet, novelist, polemicist, critic, and philosopher
Michael of Chernigov (circa 1180–1245), saint and prince of Kiev
Mohammed (circa 570–632), founder of Islam
Molière (1622–73), French dramatist

Molostvova, Zinaida Modestovna (1828–97), consort of Leo Tolstoy

Montaigne, Michel de (1533–92), French moralist

Mozart, Wolfgang Amadeus (1756–91), Austrian composer

Murat, Joachim (1767–1815), French marshal and king of Naples

Muromtseva-Bunina, Vera Nikolaevna (1881–1961), third wife of Ivan Bunin

Mussorgsky, Modest (1839–81), Russian composer

Myortvago, Alexander Petrovich (1856–1917?), journalist

Nabokov, Vladimir Vladimirovich (1899–1977), novelist, short-story writer, poet, and memoirist

Napoleon I (1769–1821), French emperor

Nazariev, Valerian Nikanorovich (d. 1902), school friend of Leo Tolstoy

Nekrasov, Nikolai Alexeevich (1821–78), Russian poet, writer and publisher

Nemirovich-Danchenko, Vasily Ivanovich (1844–1936), journalist, writer, and brother of Vladimir Nemirovich-Danchenko

Nemirovich-Danchenko, Vladimir Ivanovich (1858–1943), dramatist, director, and cofounder of the Moscow Art Theater in 1898

Nicholas I (1796–1855), tsar of Russia from 1825 to 1855

Nicholas II (1868–1918), tsar of Russia from 1894 to 1917

Nietzsche, Friedrich Wilhelm (1844–1900), German philosopher

Nikitin, Ivan Savvich (1824–61), poet

Obolenskaya, Elizaveta Valerianovna (1852–1935), niece of Leo Tolstoy and daughter of his sister, Maria

Obolensky, Nikolai Leonidovich (1872–1934), husband of Maria L'vovna Tolstaya

Odoevsky, Alexander Ivanovich (1802–39), poet

Odoevsky, Vladimir Fyodorovich (1803–69), writer, educator, and public servant

Odoevtseva, Irina Vladimirovna (1901–90), poet, prose writer, and memoirist

Oleg (d. 912), prince of Kiev and Novgorod

Olsufiev, Adam Vasilievich (1833–1901), landowner and friend of Leo Tolstoy

Olsufieva, Anna Mikhailovna (1835–99), wife of Adam Vasilievich Olsufiev

Orwell, George (1903–50), British novelist and political satirist

Osten-Saken, Alexandra Ilyinichna (1797–1841), aunt of Leo Tolstoy

Panaev, Ivan Ivanovich (1812–62), writer and journalist

Panina, Sofya Vladimirovna (1871–1957), princess and owner of an estate in Gaspra in the Crimea

Pascal, Blaise (1623–62), French scientist, mathematician, philosopher, and writer

Pathé, Charles (1863–1957), French filmmaker

Paul the Apostle (d. A.D. 64 or 67), first Christian missionary to the Gentiles

Paul I (1754–1801), tsar of Russia from 1796 to 1801

Peter I (Peter the Great) (1672–1725), tsar and first emperor of Russia from 1682 to 1725

Petrovskaya, Darya Nikolaevna (1865–?), friend of Leo Tolstoy

Petrunkevich, Ivan Ilyich (1844–1928), founder of the Cadet Party

Pisarev, Dmitri Ivanovich (1840–68), journalist and critic

Pisemsky, Alexei Feofilaktovich (1821–81), writer

Plato (427?–347? B.C.), Greek philosopher

Plotinus (205?–270?), Roman philosopher, considered to be the founder of Neoplatonism

Pobedonostsev, Konstantin Petrovich (1827–1907), statesman, government official, scholar, and chief procurator of the Holy Synod

Polner, Tikhon Ivanovich (1864–1935), biographer of Leo Tolstoy

Polonsky, Yakov Petrovich (1819–98), poet

Pope, Alexander (1688–1744), English poet and satirist

Popov, Ivan Ivanovich (1862–1942), revolutionary and writer

Potyomkin, Grigory Alexandrovich (1739–91), general, administrator, and imperial favorite

Proudhon, Pierre-Joseph (1809–65), French socialist, philosophical anarchist, and political and economic writer

Proust, Marcel (1871–1922), French novelist

Prudhomme, Sully (1839–1907), French poet and, in 1901, recipient of the Nobel Prize in literature

Pusheshnikov, Nikolai Alexeevich (1882–1939), Bunin's nephew and a translator of Kipling, Galsworthy, and Jack London

Pushkin, Alexander Sergeevich (1799–1837), Russian writer, dramatist, and poet

Pythagoras of Samos (circa 580–500 B.C.), Greek mathematician and philosopher

Racine, Jean (1639–99), French dramatist

Radcliffe, Ann (1764–1823), British novelist

Radstock, Lord (1833–1913), English religious revivalist

Repin, Ilya Efimovich (1844–1930), painter

Richter, Jean Paul Friedrich (1763–1825), German author and humorist

Rolland, Romain (1866–1944), French writer

Romanov, Vladimir Alexandrovich (1847–1909), third son of Alexander II and head of the Academy of Arts in Saint Petersburg

Rousseau, Jean-Jacques (1712–78), French philosopher and author

Ruskin, John (1819–1900), English art critic and author

Ryurik (862–879), founder of the dynasty that ruled Russia from the ninth century to 1598

Saltykov-Shchedrin, Mikhail Egravovich (1826–89), writer and satirist

Schiller, Friedrich (1759–1805), German poet, playwright, historian, and critic

Schopenhauer, Arthur (1788–1860), German philosopher

Schumann, Robert (1810–56), German composer

Sedykh, Andrei (pseudonym of Yakov Mikhailovich Tsvibak) (1902–93), writer, publisher, and editor

Semyonov, Sergei Terentievich (1868–1922), writer of peasant life

Seneca, Lucius Annaeus (3? B.C.–A.D. 65), Roman philosopher, statesman, and dramatist

Shakespeare, William (1564–1616), English poet and playwright

Shakhovskaya, Zinaida Alexeevna (1906–), writer and memorist

Shatilov, Iosif Nikolaevich (1824–89), landowner and chair of the Moscow Committee on Literacy

Shaw, George Bernard (1856–1950), Irish dramatist, critic, and novelist

Shestov, Lev (pseudonym of Lev Isaakovich Shvartsman) (1866–1938), philosopher and critic

Shiskina-Tolstaya, Maria Nikolaevna (1829–1919), wife of Sergei Nikolaevich Tolstoy

Siddartha, Gautama (the Buddha) (563?–483? B.C.), the founder of Buddhism

Skabichevsky, Alexander Mikhailovich (1838–1910), critic

Socrates (469?–399 B.C.), philosopher

Sollogub, Vladimir Alexandrovich (1813–82), writer

Solomon (circa 986–circa 932 B.C.), king of the Hebrews and son of David and Bathsheba

Solovyov, Mikhail Sergeevich (1862–1903), pedagogue and brother of Vladimir Solovyov

Solovyov, Vladimir Sergeevich (1853–1900), philosopher, writer, poet, and teacher

Sophia Alekseevna (1657–1704), regent of Russia from 1682 to 1689

Sophocles (494–406 B.C.), Greek poet and dramatist

Stead, William Thomas (1849–1912), British journalist, editor, and publisher

Stolypin, Pyotr Arkadievich (1862–1911), government official and prime minister of Russia from 1906 to 1911

Strakhov, Nikolai Nikolaevich (1828–96), publicist and critic

Struve, Pyotr Bernardovich (1870–1944), economist, historian, and public figure

Sulerzhitsky, Leopol'd Antonovich (1872–1916), critic, producer, director of the Moscow Art Theater, and follower of Tolstoy

Taneev, Sergei Ivanovich (1856–1915), Russian composer and professor at the Moscow Conservatory of Music

Tatishchev, Ivan Ivanovich (1743–1802), author of *The Complete French and Russian Lexicons* (1786)

Tchaikovsky, Pyotr Ilyich (1840–93), composer

Teffi, Nadezhda Alexandrovna (1876–1952), writer, poet, playwright, and humorist

Temryuk (d. 1569), father of Ivan the Terrible's second wife

Teneremo (pseudonym of Isaak Borisovich Fainerman) (1863–1925), Tolstoyan, writer, and critic

Theophanes the Confessor, Saint (752–818), Byzantine monk, theologian, and chronicler

Thomas à Kempis (1380–1471), German mystic

Thoreau, Henry David (1817–62), American writer

Tolstaya, Alexandra Andreevna (1817–1904), Tolstoy's first cousin once removed

Tolstaya, Alexandra L'vovna (1884–1979), fourth daughter of Leo Tolstoy

Tolstaya-Obolenskaya, Maria L'vovna (1871–1906), second daughter of Leo Tolstoy

Tolstaya, Maria Nikolaevna (1830–1912), sister of Leo Tolstoy

Tolstaya-Sukhotina, Tatyana L'vovna (1864–1950), first daughter of Leo Tolstoy

Tolstaya, Varvara L'vovna (1875), third daughter of Leo Tolstoy

Tolstaya, Vera Sergeevna (1865–1923), daughter of Tolstoy's brother Sergei

Tolstoy, Alexei Konstaninovich (1817–75), poet

Tolstoy, Alexei L'vovich (1881–86), eighth son of Leo Tolstoy

Tolstoy, Andrei Ivanovich (1721–1803), great-grandfather of Leo Tolstoy

Tolstoy, Andrei L'vovich (1877–1916), sixth son of Leo Tolstoy

Tolstoy, Dmitri Nikolaevich (1827–56), brother of Leo Tolstoy

Tolstoy, Ilya Andreevich (1757–1820), grandfather of Leo Tolstoy

Tolstoy, Ilya L'vovich (1866–1933), second son of Leo Tolstoy

Tolstoy, Ivan L'vovich (1888–95), ninth son of Leo Tolstoy

Tolstoy, Lev L'vovich (1869–1945), third son of Leo Tolstoy

Tolstoy, Lev Nikolaevich (1828–1910), novelist

Tolstoy, Mikhail L'vovich (1879–1944), seventh son of Leo Tolstoy

Tolstoy, Nikolai Ilyich (1797–1837), father of Leo Tolstoy

Tolstoy, Nikolai L'vovich (1874–75), fifth son of Leo Tolstoy

Tolstoy, Nikolai Nikolaevich (1823–60), brother of Leo Tolstoy

Tolstoy, Pyotr Andreevich (1645–1729), great-great-great grandfather of Leo Tolstoy

Tolstoy, Pyotr L'vovich (1872–73), fourth son of Leo Tolstoy

Tolstoy, Sergei L'vovich (1863–1947), first son of Leo Tolstoy

Tolstoy, Sergei Nikolaevich (1826–1904), brother of Leo Tolstoy

Tolstoy, Valerian Petrovich (1813–65), husband of Tolstoy's sister, Maria

Trostsky, Leon (pseudonym of Lev Davidovich Bronstein) (1870–1940), revolutionary, Marxist, Bolshevik leader, and Soviet official

Trubetskoy, Evgeny Nikolaevich (1863–1920), religious philosopher and brother of Sergei

Trubetskoy, Nikolai Sergeevich (1890–1938), prominent linguist and son of Sergei

Trubetskoy, Sergei Nikolaevich (1862–1905), religious philosopher, editor, and publicist

Trubetskoy, Sergei Petrovich (1790–1860), prominent Decembrist

Turgenev, Ivan Sergeevich (1818–83), writer

Turgeneva, Pauline (Pelagaya) Ivanovna (1842–1919), illegitimate daughter of Ivan Turgenev

Turgeneva, Varvara Petrovna (1780–1850), mother of Ivan Turgenev

Tyutchev, Fyodor Ivanovich (1803–73), poet

Usov, Sergei Alexeevich (1827–86), professor, zoologist, and archeologist

Uspensky, Gleb Ivanovich (1843–1902), writer and journalist

Uvarov, Sergei Semyonovich (1786–1855), diplomat and minister of education

Verne, Jules (1828–1905), French science-fiction writer

Viardot, Michelle Pauline (1821–1910), French singer

Volkenshtein, Alexander Alexandrovich (1852–1925), Tolstoyan

Volkonskaya-Tolstaya, Maria Nikolaevna (1790–1830), mother of Leo Tolstoy

Volkonsky, Nikolai Sergeevich (1753–1821), maternal grandfather of Leo Tolstoy

Volkonsky, Sergei Grigorievich (1788–1865), Decembrist conspirator

Wagner, Richard (1813–83), German composer, poet, and critical writer

White, Andrew D. (1832–1918), American educator, historian, and diplomat

Yushkova, Pelageya Ilyinichna (1798–1875), paternal aunt of Leo Tolstoy

Zaitsev, Boris Konstantinovich (1881–1972), writer and dramatist

Zenzinov, Vladimir Mikhailovich (1880–1953), writer

Zhemchuzhnikov, Alexei Mikhailovich (1821–1908), poet and prose writer

Zhemchuzhnikov, Vladimir Mikhailovich (1830–84), poet and brother of Alexei Zhemchuzhnikov

Zhukovsky, Vasily Andreevich (1783–1852), poet and translator

Zola, Emile (1840–1902), French writer

Editors' Notes

PREFACE

1. D. Leon, *Tolstoy, His Life and Work* (London: Routledge, 1944), 272–73.

2. Ibid., 316.

3. I. Bunin, "Osobennosti Tolstogo," *Poslednie novosti* (April 11, 1937): 2.

EDITORS' INTRODUCTION

1. Although Bunin greatly admired all of Tolstoy's work, it was the writer's "Afterword" ("Posleslovie") to *The Kreutzer Sonata* that sparked this request to visit him. See A. Baboreko, "Iz perepiski I. A. Bunina," *Novyi mir,* no. 10 (1956): 197–98; Baboreko, "Bunin o Tolstom," in *Iasnopolianskii sbornik. Stat'i i materialy. God 1960-i* (Tula: Tul'skoe knizhnoe izdatel'stvo, 1960), 130.

2. In truth, this was not the first time that Bunin had tried to visit Tolstoy. Sometime earlier that year, he had traveled with the editor of the *Oryol Herald* (*Orlovskii vestnik*) to visit the writer at Yasnaya Polyana but did not find him at home. See Baboreko, "Bunin o Tolstom," 130.

3. See Bunin's letter to Tolstoy, dated February 7, 1893, in Baboreko, "Iz perepiski I. A. Bunina," 198.

4. See Tolstoy's letter to Bunin, written on February 20, 1893, in Tolstoy, *Polnoe sobranie sochinenii v devianosta tomakh,* 90 vols. (Moscow: Gosudarstevennoe izdatel'stvo khudozhestvennoi literatury, 1930–58), 66:297.

5. See Bunin's letter to Tolstoy, dated July 15, 1893, in Baboreko, "Iz perepiski I. A. Bunina," 198.

6. Ibid.

7. Tolstoy also did not answer Bunin's 1901 request that the writer contribute a piece to a literary anthology published by the newspaper *Odessa News* (*Odesskie novosti*) to assist the victims of a widespread famine. See Baboreko, "Bunin o Tolstom," 130.

8. See Tolstoy, *Polnoe sobranie sochinenii,* 67:49.

9. See Bunin's letter to Tolstoy, dated February 15, 1894, in Baboreko, "Iz perepiski I. A. Bunina," 199.

10. Tolstoy, *Polnoe sobranie sochinenii,* 67:48.

11. For instance, in an interview with *Odessa News* on December 28, 1902, and in a later meeting with Georgy Adamovich, Bunin confessed:

> I do not like to visit Tolstoy. . . . I find it terrifying to be with him. Tolstoy is so colossal, so demanding of the person. . . . Every word he say bears the imprint of his character. . . . [When I met Tolstoy on the Arbat,] I was as lost as a schoolboy. . . . "I am afraid to visit you," I confessed to him frankly.
>
> Insistently and assuredly, Lev Nikolaevich repeated: "People should never be afraid, never."

See G. Adamovich, "Bunin," *Odinochesto i svoboda* (New York: Izdatel'stvo imeni Chekhova, 1955), 94–95; V. Shcherbina et al., eds. *Literaturnoe nasledstvo. Ivan Bunin. Kniga pervaia* (Moscow: Nauka, 1973), 362.

12. V. Muromtseva-Bunina, *Zhizn' Bunina* (Paris: n.p, 1958), 122.

13. See Bunin's letter to a friend, dated October 10, 1896, as quoted in A. Baboreko, "Neopublikovannye pis'ma I. A. Bunina," in *Vesna prishla* (Smolensk: Smolenskoe knizhnoe izdatel'stvo, 1959), 232.

14. See Bunin's letter to Yuly Bunin, written in February 1900, as quoted in A. Baboreko, *I. A. Bunin. Materialy dlia biografii (s 1870 po 1917)* (Moscow: Khudozhestvennaia literatura, 1967), 78.

15. After the dissolution of his first marriage, Bunin was partner to two common-law arrangements, the second of which, to Vera Muromtseva, would be legitimized only in 1924 in Paris.

16. I. Bunin, "Iz zapisei," in I. Bunin, *Sobranie sochinenii v deviati tomakh,* 9 vols. (Moscow: Khudozhestvennaia literatura, 1967), 9:345.

17. Ibid., 9:352, 361.

18. B. Mikhailovskii, ed., *Gor'kovskie chteniia, 1958–1959* (Moscow: Izdatel'stvo "Akademii nauk," 1961), 71–72.

19. See Bunin's diary entry of May 29, 1919, in I. Bunin, *Okaiannye dni. Vospominaniia. Stat'i* (Moscow: Sovietskii pisatel', 1990), 144.

20. See Kuznetsova's diary excerpt of February 4, 1928, in G. Kuznetsova, *Grasskii dnevnik* (Washington, D.C.: Victor Kamkin, 1967), 49.

21. Alexander Bakhrakh, a Jew who found haven with the Bunins during the Second World War, reports that when Bunin read T. Polner's 1928 work *Lev Tolstoi i ego zhena (Leo Tolstoy and His Wife),* he could not resist writing "me, too" in the margins of the book to note the many similarities he believed he shared with the great writer. See A. Bakhrakh, *Bunin v khalate. Po pamiati, po zapisiam* (Bayville, N.J.: Tovarishchestvo zarubezhnykh pisatelei, 1979), 48–50. (Polner's study was translated into English by Nicholas Wreden as *Tolstoy and His Wife* [New York: Norton, 1945].)

22. For instance, Bunin proudly listed his family among clans who helped "ancient tsars defend the nation against the Tatars" and who gave Russia "almost all its great writers, Turgenev and Tolstoy at the head." See Bunin's "Avtobiografishceskaia zametka" and "Iz predisloviia k frantsuzskomy izdaniiu 'Gospodina iz San-Frantsisko,'" in Bunin, *Sobranie sochinenii*, 9:253, 267.

23. Bunin loved to tell the story about how Konstantin Bal'mont misinterpreted Tolstoy's laughter at his poems as approval, not ridicule. He also recalled Tolstoy's remark that Leonid Andreev's 1910 work *Anathema* was "complete nonsense" and that only folly issued forth from "the heads of all those Bryusovs and Belys." See I. Bunin, "Avtobiograficheskie zametki," *Novoe russkoe slovo* (December 18, 1948): 6; Bunin, *Okaiannye dni*, 118.

24. M. Chekhova, *Iz dalekogo proshlogo* (Moscow: Gosudarstvennoe izdatel'stvo khudozhestvennoi literatury, 1960), 235.

25. Bunin was one of few individuals to speak in the Jews' defense. For instance, on November 12, 1919, he wrote in his "Notes" ("Zapiski"):

> Pogroms against the Jews have returned. Before the Revolution they were rare, exceptional events. For the past two years, though, they have become a common, nearly everyday occurrence.
>
> This is intolerable. Always to be at the mercy of an unbridled human beast; always to be dependent upon this pig's kindness or wrath; always to live in fear for one's home, one's honor, and one's personal life, as well as for the honor and life of one's relatives and close ones; always to live in an atmosphere of fatal catastrophe, of bloody injury and theft; always to be fated to perish without any defense, and for no reason at all, on the whim of a scoundrel or a brigand—such a situation is an unspeakable horror which we all know now, too well.

Throughout his life, Bunin relished the idea that he stood alongside Tolstoy as a spokesman for goodness and truth. For instance, Adamovich recalls that, at a restaurant in Nice during World War II, Bunin responded to a question about his health by saying, "You're asking me about my health? I cannot live so long as those two lackeys intend to rule the world!" Adamovich continued:

> The two lackeys were Hitler and Mussolini. What Bunin had done was extremely risky; but, luckily, there were no consequences for his boldness. There were many informers throughout Nice, paid ones and volunteers. . . .
>
> When we left the restaurant, I reproached Bunin for his carelessness; but he replied: "I cannot keep quiet." And with a sly smile, as if laughing at himself, he added: "I'm just like Lev Nikolaevich [Tolstoy]!"

See G. Adamovich, "Bunin. Vospominaniia," *Novyi zhurnal,* no. 105 (1971): 130. Also see I. Bunin, "Zametki," in B. Lipin, "Bunin v 'Iuzhnom slove,'" *Zvezda,* no. 9 (1993): 127.

26. I. Bunin, "Ten' ptitsy," in Bunin, *Sobranie sochinenii,* 3:428, and his interview with *Vechernye izvestiia* on May 4, 1913, in Bunin, *Sobranie sochinenii,* 9:546–47.

27. See Bunin's diary excerpt written circa 1887 in S. Gol'din, "O literaturnoi deiatel'nosti I. A. Bunina kontsa vos'midesiatykh—nachala devianostykh godov," *Uchenye zapiski Orekhovo-Zuevskogo pedagogicheskogo instituta* 9, no. 3 (1958): 4. Also see his letter to Yuly Bunin, dated October 25, 1896, in Baboreko, *I. A. Bunin. Materialy,* 59.

28. For instance, in *What Is Art?* Tolstoy wrote: "No matter how terrible it may be to say, but the art of our time . . . has become a prostitute. . . . That is, it is . . . luring and pernicious . . . decked out with imitation jewels and makeup . . . and seeking to be bought and sold." See A. Nazaroff, *Tolstoy, the Inconstant Genius: A Biography* (Freeport, N.Y.: Books for Libraries Press, 1971), 216.

29. See A. Bakhrakh, "Po pamiati, po zapisiam," *Novyi zhurnal,* no. 131 (1978): 127. "I am the last," Bunin also wrote in a diary excerpt in 1919, "who feels his past, the time of our fathers and grandfathers." See Bunin, *Okaiannye dni,* 139.

30. Baboreko, *I. A. Bunin. Materialy,* 57.

31. See Bunin's letter to M. V. Karamzina, dated July 20, 1938, in Shcherbina et al., *Literaturnoe nasledstvo,* 670.

32. Compare this 1852 letter by Tolstoy, who wrote: "I am twenty-four years old and I have still done nothing. But I am sure that it is also not for nothing that, for the past eight years, I have been struggling with all my doubts and passions. But what am I destined for?" See H. Troyat, *Tolstoy* (Garden City, N.Y.: Doubleday, 1967), 93; Baboreko, *I. A. Bunin. Materialy,* 57.

33. Baboreko, *I. A. Bunin. Materialy,* 57.

34. A. Baboreko, "Pis'ma I. Bunina," in *Literaturnyi Smolensk. Al'-manakh* (Smolensk: Smolenskoe knizhnoe izdatel'tvo, 1956), 288–89.

35. Baboreko, "Bunin o Tolstom," 132.

36. See Bunin's diary excerpt, dated March 17, 1916, in M. Grin, ed., *Ustami Buninykh. Dnevniki Ivana Alekseevicha i Very Nikolaevny i drugie arkhivnye materialy,* 3 vols. (Frankfurt-Main: Posev, 1977–82), 1:149.

37. For instance, Adamovich wrote: "Bunin once said that the pages in *Anna Karenina* where . . . Vronsky is at the snow-covered station at night, and where he first tells Anna that he loves her . . . 'are the most poetic pages in all of Russian literature.'" Similarly, Irina Odoevtseva recalls Bunin's regret that he never met Anna Karenina in real life. "As far as I'm concerned, there is no more captivating image of a woman than she," Bunin confessed. "I could never—and still cannot—recall her without emotion. I am simply in love with her." G. Adamovich, "Bunin. Vospominaniia," *Znamia,* no. 4 (1988): 185; I. Odoevtseva, *Na beregakh Seny* (Paris: La Press Libre, 1983),

346. Also see Baboreko, "Bunin o Tolstom," 132; Bakhrakh, *Bunin v khalate,* 162.

38. Bunin also told Bakhrakh: "Not long ago I finished rereading *War and Peace,* undoubtedly for the fiftieth time. I read it lying down, but I often had to jump up from excitement. God, how good it is." He also remarked to Bakhrakh that *War and Peace* was the "best novel in all of world literature." See A. Bakhrakh, "Chetyre goda s Buninym," *Russkie novosti* (November 9, 1945): 5; Bakhrakh, "Po pamiati, po zapisiam," 165. Also see Bunin's 1912 interview with the journal *Footnotes and Life (Rampa i zhizn'),* in Shcherbina et al., *Literaturnoe nasledstvo,* 375, and his diary excerpt of September 17, 1933, in Grin, *Ustami Buninykh,* 2:290.

39. The admiration was not mutual, though. Tolstoy periodically expressed dissatisfaction over Bunin's early works. For instance, Tolstoy found Bunin's 1909 poem "Separation" ("Razluka") "impossible to understand." Tolstoy also had little use for Bunin's 1903 story "Happiness" ('Schast'e") (later renamed "Daybreak All Night Long" ["Zaria vsiu noch'"]).

Tolstoy told his friend Alexander Goldenweiser: "[Bunin's story] begins with a splendid description of nature. It is drizzling out, and the entire scene is written in a way that neither Turgenev or I would do. . . . But it turns out that this drizzle is necessary only so Bunin could write a story. It is usually the case that when people have nothing to say, they talk about the weather. A writer does the same thing, and it is time . . . he gave up such a practice." See S. Kryzytski, "Tolstoi i Bunin," *Zapiski russkoi akademicheskoi gruppy v SShA* 11 (1978): 131. Also see A. Baboreko, "I. A. Bunin na Kapri (Po neopublikovannym materialam)," in *V bol'shoi sem'e* (Smolensk: Smolenskoe kniznoe izdatel'stvo, 1960), 246; Baboreko, "I. A. Bunin o L. N. Tolstom," *Problemy realizma,* vol. 6 (Vologda, 1979), 168; Baboreko, "Bunin o Tolstom," 131. Also see Vera Muromsteva-Bunina's diary excerpt, dated February 26, 1919, in Grin, *Ustami Buninykh,* 1:208, and Bunin's diary entry, written on October 1, 1933, in ibid., 2:291.

40. V. Kataev, *Sviatoi kolodets. Trava zabven'a* (Moscow: Sovetskii pisatel', 1969), 166–67. Bunin was also enamored with Tolstoy's political and religious tracts. For instance, in an article he wrote in Odessa several months before he left his homeland forever, Bunin liberally quoted from such pieces as "A Letter to Alexander III" ("Pis'mo Aleksandru III," 1881), "One Thing Do We Need" ("Edinoe na potrebu," 1905), and "To the Revolutionary" ("K revoliutsioneru," 1909) to warn his countrymen about the deceptive workings of political revolutionaries in both the present and the past. See Bunin, "Zametki," 137–38.

41. Odoevtseva, *Na beregakh Seny,* 296.

42. Baboreko, "Bunin o Tolstom," 132.

43. Baboreko, "I. A. Bunin na Kapri," 246; Baboreko, "Bunin o Tolstom,"131–32. Bunin similarly told Bakhrakh: "One can hardly know how

Tolstoy draws his characters in such bold relief. Take any Tolstoyan text. Each portrait is drawn with only a few words, but the impression is that every freckle has been described. One can never confuse Natasha or Sonya or Anna with anyone else. Ivan Ilyich's portrait belongs to him alone."

Later, he continued: "How well did Tolstoy know all these 'trifles' of life. That is why his heroes and heroines are so precise. Did Tolstoy use many words to describe Natasha Rostova? Yet her actions, her gestures, and her feelings are joined together so logically that everything flows from everything else. In her there is not a single inaccuracy, a single false note, so much so that what I think of Natasha is not all that different from what you or someone else thinks of her."

Also, although Bunin did not care for the last names of characters in Gogol and Chekhov, he admired those of Tolstoy. They were for him "genuine diamonds." See Bakhrakh, "Po pamiati, po zapisiam," 176; Bakhrakh, *Bunin v khalate,* 95, 98.

44. Baboreko, "Bunin o Tolstom," 133.

45. Baboreko, "I . A. Bunin o L. N. Tolstom," 178.

46. See Bunin, "Interv'iu," in *Sobranie sochinenii,* 9:536–37.

47. I. Bunin, *Derevnia,* in *Sobranie sochinenii,* 3:68. Similarly, unin told Leonid Andreev: "I know what kind of peasants you need. Just serve you up Platon Karataev, mystical Scythians, and bearers of religious missions!"

Needless to say, Bunin rejoiced whenever Tolstoy rejected "idealist" views of the folk. For instance, in an article written in Odessa in November 25, 1919, he cited Tolstoy as saying: "If I have vaunted Russian peasants as harborers of some attractive features, I regret what I have done, and I am ready to retract my words."

Bunin also delighted in Tolstoy's hostility toward the folk fiction of Gorky and other "proletarian" writers. Such writing, he quoted his mentor as saying, was a "caricature liberally sprinkled with stupidity" and a "complete falsification of art." See I. Bunin, "Velikii durman," in Lipin, "Bunin v 'Iuzhnom slove,'" 135; Baboreko, "I. A. Bunin na Kapri," 251.

48. Kataev, *Svratoi kolodets,* 214.

49. Bunin was referring specifically to Tolstoy's celebration of Mass in the novel. Bunin had additional criticisms of Tolstoy. For instance, he objected to the "maternal" image of Natasha Rostova in the final pages of *War and Peace.* He told Odoevtseva:

> Initially, of course, Natasha is charming and fascinating. But all this charm and fascination turns into a baby-making machine; and in the end, Natasha is simply repulsive: bare-headed, slovenly, wearing a housecoat, and holding a dirty diaper in her hands. She is constantly pregnant or breast-feeding a newborn. As far as I'm concerned, Natasha's pregnancies and everything that has to do with them have always evoked repulsion in me.

Also, Bunin often had little patience for some of Tolstoy's publicism. For instance in a diary excerpt, written on March 17, 1940, he wrote: "I have just read Tolstoy's *What Is Art?* And, except for several pages, I found it boring and unconvincing. I had not read it for a long time, and I thought that it was better. Tolstoy puts forth hundreds of definitions for beauty and art . . . but they are not worth a thing." See M. Grin, "Iz dnevnikov I. A. Bunina," *Novyi zhurnal,* no. 111 (1973): 140. Also see Bakhrakh, *Bunin v khalate,* 161; Odoevtseva, *Na beregakh Seny,* 345.

50. Bakhrakh once remarked: "One could see that Bunin experienced physical pain whenever he tried to reproach or censure Tolstoy." See Bakhrakh, *Bunin v khalate,* 162.

51. Bunin, "Zapisi," 9:128.

52. For instance, Bunin told Vladimir Zenzinov:

It is not true that Tolstoy did not attach any significance to the sound of his phrases and that he did not pay any attention to his form. . . . For instance, I have seen the manuscripts for *Master and Man,* and Tolstoy made almost one hundred corrections on them! . . . No, Tolstoy attached great significance to the sounds of a phrase; he cared very much as to how words were arranged in a sentence. . . .

Indeed, I do not know of another writer whose form is so truly like a transparent piece of glass which no one knows is there. That in itself is a great accomplishment.

See V. Zenzinov, "Ivan Alekseevich Bunin," *Novyi zhurnal,* no. 3 (1942): 299–300. Also see Z. Shakovskaya, "Otrazheniia," *Nashe nasledie,* no. 1 (1990): 92.

53. Adamovich, "Bunin. Vospominaniia," *Znamia,* 181. Compare Kuznetsova's remark that, when she lived with the Bunins, "Tolstoy was invariably with us in our conversations, and in our everyday life." See Baboreko, *I. A. Bunin. Materialy,* 44.

54. Adamovich, "Bunin. Vospominaniia," *Znamia,* 180.

55. In similar fashion, Bunin countered assertions by the Symbolist poet Georgy Ivanov regarding what he saw as the "mournful kitchen-garden" of late-nineteenth-century Russian Realism by citing such works as *Master and Man, The Kreutzer Sonata,* and *The Death of Ivan Ilyich.* See Bunin's letter to Adamovich, written on December 29, 1949, in A. Zweers, "Pis'ma I. Bunina k G. Adamovicha," *Novyi zhurnal,* no. 110 (1973): 173. Also see N. Berberova, *Kursiv moi. Avtobiografiia v dvukh tomakh,* 2 vols. (New York: Russica, 1983), 1:372–73.

56. Baboreko, "I. A. Bunin o L. N. Tolstom," 169. On August 28, 1941, Gide wrote in his diary: "While in Grasse . . . I saw Bunin. It was a rather disappointing visit. Despite mutually cordial relations, we did not establish any genuine contact. One esteems too little what the other admires. His cult for Tolstoy embarrasses me as much as his scorn for Dostoevsky,

Shchedrin, and Sologub. We decidedly do not have the same saints, the same gods." (Gide, though, did like *The Death of Ivan Ilyich* and *Resurrection.*)

Two weeks later, Gide continued: "With lively interest, I am reading Bunin's book on Tolstoy. He explains Tolstoy wonderfully. That is why I feel so at ease with this writer. But Tolstoy was such a monster!"

Even émigré (and Soviet) applause for Tolstoy could evoke Bunin's scorn. For instance, on June 15, 1947, Bunin wrote to Adamovich: "Merezhkovsky's praises of Tolstoy [are like] countless kebabs on a stick, that is, his 'parallelisms, theses, and antitheses' are unparalleled in their literary vulgarity. Also, Gorky's memories and exaltations of Tolstoy are all falsehoods, the most vile lies, and nonsense worthy of battered nostrils and penal labor!" See A. Gide, *The Journals of André Gide,* 4 vols. (New York: Knopf, 1948–51), 4:83, 84; A. Zweers, "Pis'ma I. A. Bunina k G. Adamovicha," 164.

57. Baboreko, "Bunin o Tolstom," 131. Understandably, Bunin was deeply offended when Adamovich wrote in an article that the "spiritual qualities of Tolstoy's writing and, in particular, his later works . . . find little expression in Bunin's fiction." See Adamovich, "Bunin. Vospominaniia," *Znamia,* 181.

58. A. Larent'ev, "O tvorchestve I. A. Bunina," *Vrata,* no. 1 (1934): 181; Um-El'-Banin, "Poslednii poedinok Ivana Bunina," *Vremia i my,* no. 4 (1979): 10.

59. V. Sharshun, "Khvalebnoe slovo I. A. Bunina," *Chisla,* no. 10 (October 1934): 225.

60. See, for instance, P. Bitsilli, "Bunin i Tolstoy," *Sovremennye zapiski* 60 (1936): 280.

61. Z. Gippius, "Sovremennye zapiski. Kniga XXIX," *Poslednie novosti* (November 11, 1926): 3.

62. "Has Russia a New Tolstoy?" *American Review of Reviews* 54 (August 1916): 224.

63. A. Zweers, "Perepiska I. A. Bunina s M. A. Aldanovym," *Novyi zhurnal,* no. 153 (1983): 170.

64. Unlike the pre-Nobel Bunin, Tolstoy was completely unmoved when, in 1901, he learned that Sully Prudhomme had been given the Nobel Prize in literature. (In *What Is Art?* Tolstoy himself had ranked Prudhomme as one of the foremost poets in France.) To Swedish writers who expressed their anger and regret over the decision, Tolstoy replied: "I was very pleased to learn that I did not receive the Nobel Prize. [I feel this way] first because it spared me the great problem of disposing of the money from the award, since, like all money, it can lead only to evil; and second, because it has given me the honor and great pleasure of receiving such expressions of sympathy from so many highly esteemed people whom I do not know." See Troyat, *Tolstoy,* 573–74. Also see P. Bitstilli, "Sobranie sochinenii I. A.

Bunina," *Sovremennye zapiski* 48 (1935): 471; A. Bakshy, "Ivan Bunin," *American Mercury,* no. 31 (February 1934): 223.

65. Interestingly, many critics have recognized the emotional intensity of Bunin's search, ranking it second only to those of Dostoevsky and Tolstoy. See, for instance, I. Vantenkov, *Bunin—povestovatel' (rasskazy 1890–1916 gg.)* (Minsk: Belorusskii gosudarstvennyi universitet, 1974), 4; G. Struve, "Ivan Bunin," in *Russkaia literatura v izgnanii. Opyt istoricheskogo obzora zarubezhnoi literatury* (New York: Izdatel'stvo imeni Chekhova, 1956), 82.

66. Muromsteva-Bunina wrote in a diary excerpt, dated August 22, 1925: "[Bunin] said, 'Tolstoy felt the abyss no less than Dostoevsky.'" See Grin, *Ustami Buninykh,* 2:147.

67. As quoted in Leon, *Tolstoy,* 76.

68. I. Bunin, "Na khurore," in *Sobranie sochinenii,* 4:34.

69. See Bunin's diary excerpt of February 12, 1911, in Grin, *Ustami Buninykh,* 1:96.

70. See E. Simmons, *Leo Tolstoy,* 2 vols. (New York: Vintage, 1960), 1:325; E. Crankshaw, *Tolstoy: The Making of a Novelist* (New York: Viking, 1967), 58.

71. See Bunin's letter to Yuly Bunin, written on August 10, 1891, in Baboreko, "Neopublikovannye pis'ma I. A. Bunina," 221.

72. See Bunin's missive to Tolstoy of March 21, 1896, in Baboreko, *I. A. Bunin. Materialy,* 56.

73. N. Dole, *The Life of Count Tolstoi* (New York: Scribner's, 1922), 45–46.

74. Baboreko, "I. A. Bunin na Kapri," 240.

75. Bunin and Tolstoy were not alone in their adherence to Buddhistic beliefs. Indeed, they were keenly aware of the interest in Buddhism that swept much of the Western world at the fin de siècle and that enjoyed a warm reception in Russia.

For instance, Vladimir Solovyov had enthusiastically espoused such Buddhistic beliefs as *karma* and rebirth. Konstantin Bal'mont had translated *The Life of the Buddha* by the Indian philosopher and poet Ashvaghosa into Russian in 1913. And Sergei Esenin believed that with the exception of the Buddha and Christ, human beings were "sinners who had fallen into the abyss of debauchery."

Furthermore, Bunin's contemporaries F. Shcherbatskoy, S. Ol'denburg, and O. Rozenberg were among the most famous Russian Buddhologists. Russian bibliographies of the era list numerous editions and translations of Buddhist texts between 1887 and 1911. Sample titles include *Buddhism* (1887), *Buddhist Catechisis* (1902), and *The Life and Teaching of Siddartha Gotama, Called the Buddha* (1911). Many of these works were accessible to the general reading public, and some were even published as pulp fiction for as little as six kopecks and enjoyed two or three reprintings.

See G. McVay, *Esenin: A Life* (Ann Arbor: Ardis, 1976), 36; N. Rubakin, *Sredi knig* (Moscow: Nauka, 1913). For more on the reception of Eastern philosophy and religion in fin de siècle Russia, see T. Ermakova, *Buddiiskii mir glazami rossiiskikh issledovalei XIX-pervoi treti XX veka* (Saint Petersburg: Nauka, 1998); O. Slivitskaia, "Bunin i vostok (K postanovke voprosa)," *Izvestiia Voronezhskogo gosudarstvennogo pedagogicheskogog instituta,* no. 114 (1971): 87–96.

76. White had actually visited Tolstoy at Yasnaya Polyana. See Dole, *The Life of Count Tolstoi,* 419; Simmons, *Leo Tolstoy,* 2:310.

77. Interestingly, readers, critics, and biographers have sensed the Buddhistic strains in Tolstoy's writing. For instance, the 1912 literary Nobel laureate, Gerhart Hauptmann, placed Tolstoy on the same level with the Buddha as a reformer of the world. Leopold von Schroder, professor of philosophy at the University of Vienna, called him the Russian Buddha. See Dole, *The Life of Count Tolstoi,* 420; Nazaroff, *Tolstoy,* 35–36, 115, 218, 221, 297.

78. A. N. Wilson, *Tolstoy* (London: Hamish Hamilton, 1988), 351.

79. Tolstoy, *Polnoe sobranie sochinenii,* 25:887.

80. Ibid.

81. In a letter to a friend, written on October 25, 1891, Tolstoy cited Foucaux's work as having an "enormous" influence on him in his fifties and early sixties. See Tolstoy, *Polnoe sobranie sochinenii,* 66:68.

82. According to Gorky, Tolstoy placed the teaching of the Buddha over those of Christ. See N. Gusev, *L. N. Tolstoi v vospominaniiakh sovremennikov,* 2 vols. (Moscow: Gosudarstvennoe izdatel'stvo khudozhestvennoi literatruy, 1960), 2:51.

83. Tolstoy, *Polnoe sobranie sochinenii,* 25:540–43. The piece was published posthumously in 1916, both in the journal *Unity (Edinenie)* and—together with two other chapters on the Buddha written by Tolstoy—in a book by Chertkov bearing the same title as Tolstoy's work.

84. See Tolstoy, *Polnoe sobranie sochinenii,* 41:96–101. Tolstoy also published "The Buddha" as a small pamphlet that sold for one kopeck per copy and was reprinted three years later. See Rubakin, *Sredi knig,* 266.

85. Slivitskaia, "Bunin i vostok," 88.

86. See Tolstoy's diary excerpt, written on August 1, 1899, in Tolstoy, *Polnoe sobranie sochinenii,* 50:117.

87. "Karma," in Tolstoy, *Polnoe sobranie sochinenii,* 31:54.

88. Ibid.

89. Ibid.

90. Ibid., 55. In line with this denial of self, Tolstoy particularly loved to tell the legend of how Buddha fed his own flesh to a hungry tigress and her cubs. See V. Posse, "Tolstoy," in Gusev, *L. N. Tolstoi,* 2:215.

91. Leon, *Tolstoy,* 294.

92. Ibid., 295.

93. Tolstoy ended this missive: "But worldly people, priests, and the like, however much they talk about God, are unpleasant to the likes of us. Indeed, they must be a torment to someone who is dying, because they do not see what we see, namely the God who is more indeterminate and distant, but also more lofty and indubitable."

Tolstoy similarly wrote in his diary: "One should speak about Nirvana neither with jests nor with anger. To all of us, or at least to me, Nirvana is far more interesting than life." See Nazaroff, *Tolstoy,* 216. Also see Tolstoy, "Pis'ma," in *Polnoe sobranie sochinenii,* 62:271; Dole, *The Life of Count Tolstoi,* 243.

94. Tolstoy, though, did take an exception to Buddhistic teaching. He wrote: "Buddhism is wrong only in not recognizing the meaning and purpose of *this* life which leads to self-renunciation. We cannot see this purpose, but it is there; and [because of this purpose,] this life is as genuine as any other." See Tolstoy, "Pis'ma," in *Polnoe sobranie sochinenii,* 81:138–39, and his diary excerpt of November 17, 1906, in ibid., 55:274.

95. See Tolstoy, *Polnoe sobranie sochinenii,* 81:46.

96. The *Sutta-Nipata* was particularly popular among Russian readers and was often cited and debated by the intelligentsia (Bunin included) in the years immediately prior to the Revolution. It should also be noted that despite the widespread popularity of Buddhism in Russia circa 1900, not everyone approved its message. Gorky, for instance, took issue with the passivity and idleness he believed the Buddha offered as the path to salvation. "[As regards] Buddhistic teaching," he wrote to a friend on January 26, 1912, "I have read the *Sutta-Nipata* and the *Buddhistic Suttras* . . . and I do not like them. Obviously, one has to be a Hindu, live in a hot and humid climate, and sense dissolution so that this yellow tedium can be understood. Run from the East—it is time we did." See M. Gor'kii, *Sobranie sochinenii v tridtsati tomakh,* 30 vols. (Moscow: Khudozhestvennaia literatura, 1949–55), 29:221.

97. I. Odoevtseva, "Na beregakh Seny," in *Russkii almanakh* (Paris: n.p, 1981), 406. Commenting on the depth of Bunin's penetration into the Buddhistic culture of Ceylon, Kuznetsova wrote in a diary entry dated September 29, 1932:

> Bunin told me that when he was in Kandy [in Ceylon], he saw the Buddhist books in the sacred library: tablets made from palm and inscribed with circular letters. He was shown them by the religious superior, a man "with insane, deep black eyes, and in a yellow robe with his right shoulder exposed." The library was underground, with latticed windows level with the water of a ditch; and since there was so much greenery around, the room had a greenish light. The walls were very thick with drawings of dragons on them. The priest gave Bunin one of the books as a gift; on it he wrote his name with a stylus dipped in India ink and gold.

Colleagues and contemporaries attest to Bunin's enthusiastic reception of Buddhistic images and ideas. Georgy Alekseev, for instance, recalls that Bunin in 1919 professed that "this Buddhism is a remarkable thing" and that "its teachings . . . contain so much of the sun's blinding eye and soul." Boris Zaitsev summed up the case of Bunin and Buddhism by succinctly noting in 1925 that "Bunin responded to the world with an Asiatic-Buddhist sensitivity. The Buddha was quite close to him."

Kuznetsova concurred. "Bunin lived his life like a Buddhist monk . . . [like] people who embark on a spiritual journey and who gradually 'purify' themselves." Several years later, she added that whenever Bunin recalled his youth, "his eyes did not see us . . . and that he would be off somewhere else. Looking at him, I thought about hermits, mystics, and yogis—those who live in the world they summon forth." See Kuznetsova's diary excerpt of February 11, 1933, in Kuznetsova, *Grasskii dnevnik,* 279; also see 88. Also see G. Alekseev, "Zhivye vstrechi," *Vremia* (August 22, 1921): 2; B. Zaitsev, "Dni. Trinadtsat' let," *Russkaia mysl'* (November 10, 1966): 3; O. Mikhailov, *I. A. Bunin, Zhizn' i tvorchesto* (Tula: Priorskoe knizhnoe izdatel'stvo, 1987), 230–31; Baboreko, *I. A. Bunin. Materialy,* 241.

98. For instance, see such stories as "The Brothers" ("Brat'ia," 1916), "Gautami" (1919), "Night" ("Noch'," 1925), and "The Night of Renunciation" ("Noch' otrecheniia," 1921). For a more detailed treatment of Buddhistic themes in Bunin's works, see T. Marullo, *If You See the Buddha: Studies in the Fiction of Ivan Bunin* (Evanston: Northwestern University Press, 1998).

99. Again see Bunin's 1912 interview with *Footnotes and Life* in Shcherbina et al., *Literaturnoe nasledstvo,* 375.

100. Iu. Mal'tsev, *Ivan Bunin, 1870–1953* (Moscow: Posev, 1994), 8.

101. In 1938, Bunin also announced plans to write the scenario for a French film about Tolstoy, but the project never materialized. Together with Mark Aldanov, Bunin did write a film script for Tolstoy's *Cossacks;* it did not survive the war. See "Ivan Bunin v Estonii," in Iu. Shumakov, ed., *Poslednee svidanie. Materialy on poseshchenii I. A. Buninym Pribaltiiskikh gosudarstv v 1938 godu* (Estonia: "Russkaia entsiklopediia," 1992), 123. Also see Aldanov's letter to Bunin, dated February 7, 1946, in A. Zweers, "Perepiska I. A. Bunina s M. A. Aldanovym," 157.

102. Generally speaking, émigré writers and critics loudly applauded *The Liberation of Tolstoy.* For instance, Nikolai Gusev, Tolstoy's secretary in the last years of his life, wrote: "Bunin's book is an absolutely exclusive phenomenon in the colossal literature about Tolstoy. Its basic idea is profoundly just, and Bunin does the honor of being the first to such shed penetrating light on the treasured inner life of Leo Tolstoy."

Similarly, the émigré writer M. V. Karamzina, wrote to Bunin on July 2 and 16, 1938:

I gulped down *The Liberation of Tolstoy* in one day, tearing at it greedily in large bites. I will read your work many times, slowly, thinking about it and living with it. . . .

As I reflect on what you have written about Tolstoy, I hear your voice. It is as truthful as if it were a spirit; and my demanding, jealous heart wants to respond to you with instinctive trust, with nothing to disturb it.

My heart wants to do such a thing because I know your pain as well as I know the pain of Tolstoy, that is, the sharpness of your feeling for life, as well as that "sensation of being doomed" . . . [the awareness] of "decay," of the rapid passage of time, and of earthy flesh, emotions, and moments gone forever. . . . What do you and Tolstoy have in common? Is it that both of you are subject to the law of submission?

Not everyone agreed with such an assessment, though. "What horrors is Bunin writing about [Leo] Tolstoy!" Vladislav Khodasevich bemoaned to Nina Berberova on June 21, 1937. Several months later, Vladimir Nabokov sniffed: "It seems that Bunin's *Liberation of Tolstoy* has freed him from the necessity of writing his own things." See V. Alloi, "Iz arkhiva V. V. Nabokova," *Minuvshee,* no. 8 (1992): 280. Also see Baboreko, "I. A. Bunin o L. N. Tolstom," 167; Berberova, *Kursiv moi,* 2:422; Shcherbina et al., *Literaturnoe nasledstvo,* 671–72.

103. Initially, Rolland supported two joint candidacies: one that brought together Bunin and Dmitri Merezhkovsky; the other that joined Bunin and Maxim Gorky. See M. Grin, "Pis'ma M. A. Aldanova k I. A. i V. I. Buninym," *Novyi zhurnal* 80 (1965): 267, 271.

104. Less than a month later, Muromtseva-Bunina continued: "I feel as though I have the weight of the world on my shoulders." See Muromtseva-Bunina's diary excerpts of November 9 and December 12, 1934, in Grin, *Ustami Buninykh,* 3:12, 13.

105. M. Grin, "Pis'ma M. A. Aldanova k. I. A. i V. I. Buninym," *Novyi zhurnal* 81 (1965): 115.

106. Bunin, though, steadfastly resisted such a designation. For instance, two weeks later, Aldanov wrote to Muromtseva-Bunina: "I find it very painful that Ivan Alexeevich does not use his [Nobel] prize in the interest of Russian affairs or to advance his own personal goals. . . . No, he cannot be our 'ambassador,' and this is a great, great pity."

Bunin's position as a Nobel laureate only worsened with time. For instance, in the years immediately after World War II, he was the object of a bitter tug-of-war between émigrés and Soviets for his affection, allegiance, and even place of residency. See Aldanov's letters to Muromtseva-Bunina, written on January 5 and 20, 1935, in ibid., 115–16.

107. See Aldanov's letter to Bunin, dated February 14, 1935, in ibid., 116.

108. Grin, "Pis'ma M. A. Aldanova," 80 (1965): 285–86.

109. S. Kotkov, "Novoe o Bunine," *Uchenye zapiski Kabordino-Balkarskogo nauchno-issledovatel'skogo instituta* 24 (1967): 227.

110. See Muromtseva-Bunina's diary excerpt of October 3, 1934, in Grin, *Ustami Buninykh*, 2:12.

111. A. Zweers, "Pis'ma I. A. Bunina k B. K. i V. A B. Zaitsevym," *Novyi zhurnal*, no. 134 (1979): 180.

112. See Bunin's diary excerpts, of July 6, 1935, in Grin, *Ustami Buninykh*, 2:15.

113. See Bunin's letter to Pyotr Struve, written on May 29, 1934, in G. Struve, "Iz perepiski s I. A. Buninym," *Annali* 11 (1968): 26.

114. See Bunin's diary entries, written on June 7 and August 16, 1936, in Grin, *Ustami Buninykh*, 2:20.

115. See Grin, "Iz dnevnikov I. A. Bunina," 135–36; Grin, *Ustami Buninykh*, 2:7.

116. See Bunin's letter to Zaitsev, dated February 9, 1945, in A. Zweers, "Pis'ma I. A. Bunina k B. K. i V. A. B. Zaitsevym," 166.

117. In truth, Bunin was not comfortable with his research. For instance, he told Bakhrakh, "Since Tolstoy preserved his manuscripts, anyone who has half an urge can root through his dirty laundry. One should destroy all his drafts without fail. The same thing goes for his letters." See Bakhrakh, *Bunin v khalate*, 61.

118. Bunin greatly admired the most famous of the Russian *slova*, the twelfth-century *Lay of the Host of Igor* (*Slovo o polku Igoreve*). He told Bakhrakh, "In my opinion, not a single work of Western literature of that period can reach the poetic heights of *The Lay of the Host of Igor.*" See Bakhrakh, "Po pamaiti, po zapisiam," 119.

119. Generally speaking, Soviet critics overlooked *The Liberation of Tolstoy* as an important clue to Bunin's beliefs about life and art. If anything, they dismissed it as yet another example of the writer's "interminable requiems," that is, Bunin's pessimism as an émigré and his attempt to "poeticize" death. See O. Mikhailov, "Bunin i Tolstoi," in *Lev Nikolaevich Tolstoi* (Moscow: Khudozhestvennaia literatura, 1959), 215.

120. Troyat, *Tolstoy*, 565.

121. In addition to Buddhist "regression," Bunin roots his apelike portrait of Tolstoy in the theory of *l'uomo delinquente*, developed by the distinguished Italian anthropologist and psychiatrist Cesare Lombroso, who believed that one could determine "born criminals" by their anatomy, particularly their apish atavism. For instance, Bunin insisted that Leon Trotsky was "a genuine murderer à la Lombroso."

Interestingly, Lombroso visited Tolstoy at Yasnaya Polyana in 1897, but the meeting was unsuccessful. For one thing, Lombroso would have drowned in the river at the estate if the sixty-nine-year-old Tolstoy had not come to the rescue. Also, Lombroso's ideas fell on deaf ears. Lombroso recalled: "Tolstoy remained silent throughout all my arguments. Finally, knitting his brow, he glanced at me threateningly with his deeply sunken eyes and declared: 'All this is nonsense. Every punishment is criminal.'" After the visit, Tolstoy wrote in his diary: "Lombroso was here. He is a limited, naive little old man." Simmons, *Leo Tolstoy*, 2:235–36.

122. In truth, though, Bunin believed that bodily breakup attended spiritual release. For instance, the "liberated" rickshaw driver in Bunin's 1914 story "Brothers" "plunges repeatedly into nonbeing" by "breaking into parts." He dismembers self into "thought, memory, vision, hearing, pain, grief, joy, hatred—and that ultimate, all-embracing thing which is called love." See Bunin, *Sobranie sochinenii*, 4:272.

123. Bunin was not the only one to sense Buddhistic sensibilities in Tolstoy's life and art. For instance, the philosopher Nikolai Berdyaev asserted that it was Tolstoy's "eastern Buddhistic inclination" that led him to "to destroy everything that involved the personality." See N. Berdyaev, *Dukhi russkoi revoliutsii* (Riga: Obshchestvo druzei knigi Latvii, 1990), 25.

124. See Troyat, *Tolstoy*, 378.

125. Ibid., 485.

126. Bunin wrote in his diary on March 6, 1941: "Having listened . . . to a spring bird in the garden, I again thought that one cannot conceive of God in any other way than did Tolstoy (in his later years), that is, the divinity of this bird's life, its song, its mind, and its feelings." See Grin, "Iz dnevnikov I. A. Bunina," 137–38.

127. For instance, Tolstoy wrote to Sofya: "Cool grass underfoot, stars in the sky, the perfume of flowering laburnum and limp birch leaves, trills of the nightingales, buzzing of beetles, the cry of the cuckoo, the solitude . . . and the sensation of physical and moral health. As always, I thought of death. It seemed clear to me that on the other side [of this life], everything would be just as good—though in another way. I also understood why the Jews imagine paradise to be garden." See Troyat, *Tolstoy*, 553.

128. Dole, *The Life of Count Tolstoi*, 32.

CHAPTER ONE

1. The town of Astapovo, renamed Lev Tolstoy in 1927, is located approximately 200 miles southeast of Moscow.

2. Bunin is quoting from Tolstoy's *Krug chteniia. Izbrannye, sobrannye i raspolozhennye na kazhdyi den' L'vom Tolstym, mysli mnogikh pisatelei ob istine, zhizni i povedenii, 1904–1908* (*The Circle of Reading: Thoughts of Many Writers about Truth, Life, and Deportment, Gathered, Selected, and Arranged for Every Day by Leo Tolstoy, 1904–1908*).

The entire passage reads:

Know that you possess nothing other than your soul. Make it your custom to choose decisively the very best image of life so that existence will be pleasant for you. Riches are an untrustworthy anchor; glory is even more deceptive. The same thing can be said for the body, power, and recognition. All these are futile and insignificant. But what then is the reliable anchor in life? Only virtue. It is God's law that only virtue remains fast and firm; everything else is nothing.

See Tolstoy, *Polnoe sobranie sochinenii,* 41:443, 471; 86:29.

3. Tolstoy was fascinated with Marcus Aurelius. For instance, there are over two hundred references to the Roman ruler in Tolstoy's complete works. Here Bunin has paraphrased one such reference:

There is nothing more genuine than death, or that death will come for us. Death is more real than tomorrow, than the coming of night after day, than the arrival of winter after summer. So why should we prepare for tomorrow, night, and winter, and not for death? One must prepare for it. And the only way to prepare for death is by leading a good life. The better one's life, the less one's fear of death. For a saint, there is no such thing as death.

See L. Tolstoy, *Put' zhizni,* in Tolstoy, *Polnoe sobranie sochinenii,* 45:461.

4. More than a decade before Tolstoy conceptualized the character of Andrei Bolkonsky, he wrote to Fet: "With terror, I have asked this question: 'What do I love?' Nothing. Absolutely nothing. There is no possibility of happiness in life. But, because of this, it is easier to become a spiritual being, an inhabitant of earth, a stranger to the needs of men." See Leon, *Tolstoy,* 88.

5. In Buddhism, the *Dharma,* or the "Body of the Law," means the cosmic law, the "great norm" underlying our world, particularly the law of karmically determined rebirth. *Dharma* also embraces the teachings of the Buddha and the so-called factors of existence: the building blocks of the empirical personality and its world.

6. More accurately, the citation from Matthew 10:36–37 reads: "A man's foes will be those of his own household. He who loves father or mother more than me is not worthy of me."

7. Prince Gautama is more commonly known as the Buddha, the "Enlightened One."

Saint Alexis, the Man of God, is the hero of a fifth-century legend. He was said to be the only son of noble Roman parents who, either from choice or necessity, lived the life of a beggar and shared what little he had with people poorer than himself. For more on Saint Alexis, see A. Butler, *Lives of the Saints,* 4 vols. (New York: Kennedy, 1956), 1:314–16.

Saint Julian the Hospitaller is the patron saint of innkeepers, travelers, and boatmen and also the hero of a popular thirteenth-century tale.

Like many medieval heroes, he rejected earthly delights and led a "rightful" existence. Bunin knew of Julian the Hospitaller either from his time in France or from Gustave Flaubert's 1876 story "The Legend of Saint Julian." For more on Saint Julian, see ibid., 1:123–24.

8. A *starets* is an elderly monk or person whose religious life commands respect and authority from mystically minded disciples.

9. Yasnaya Polyana ("Clear" or "Ashen Glade," from *iasnyi* [clear] or *iasen'* [ash tree]) was the site of Tolstoy's family estate. It exists today and is located 130 miles south of Moscow. At age nineteen, Tolstoy inherited Yasnaya Polyana with its 4,000 acres and 330 serfs, together with an annual income of 4,000 rubles. He lived seventy out of his eight-two years at his estate.

By way of comparison, the richest families in Russia, the Sheremetevs, for example, owned 200,000 serfs and enjoyed incomes of 700,000 rubles a year. The upper ranks of the nobility, to which both of Tolstoy's parents belonged, had about a thousand "souls" to their name; members of the so-called gentry had about 500 serfs in their care. Individuals with less than a hundred estate peasants were known as "impoverished" gentrymen. Bunin's family belonged to this group. See Wilson, *Tolstoy,* 48.

CHAPTER TWO

1. Tolstoy began writing *Pervye vospominaniia* (*First Memories*) in 1878 and published it fourteen years later.

2. Pavel Biryukov was one of Tolstoy's closest friends and later his authorized biographer. A nobleman educated at the elite Institute for Pages and the Russian Naval Academy, Biryukov became disillusioned with military service and retired from the navy to follow Tolstoy's dicta on the Christian life. (He particularly liked Tolstoy's teaching of nonviolence as the essence of Christianity.) In 1897 Biryukov was banished from Russia for appealing to the public on behalf of the persecuted Dukhobors. He lived first in England and then in Switzerland, where he established a printing press in Geneva to publish Tolstoy's prohibited works.

When Biryukov first met Tolstoy, he had expected to see a "gloomy old man, absorbed in the study of the old standard works of Christian literature." Instead, he found "a sincere and good man whose simplicity could not but charm and attract." Biryukov also recalled that, during their first meeting, Tolstoy spoke to him about the incompatibility of certain professions with the Christian life. Specifically, he "serenely explained that one could be a Christian and practice any profession except two: the law and the army."

Biryukov continued: "Then, looking at my uniform, Tolstoy added: 'Excuse me for saying that in front of you.' I well recall how ashamed I was of the uniform that I was wearing."

In fact, so remorseful was Biryukov over his military attire that he never wore it in Tolstoy's presence again. See Simmons, *Leo Tolstoy,* 2:146; Leon, *Tolstoy,* 328.

3. Biryukov's work, *Biografiia L'va Nikolaevicha Tolstogo (The Biography of Lev Nikolaevich Tolstoy),* was first published in two volumes in Moscow in 1906–8. It was translated into English as *Leo Tolstoy: His Life and Work, Autobiographical Letters and Biographical Material* (New York: C. Scribner's Sons, 1911).

4. *Bunin's note:* All dates are given in Old Style. Writing *War and Peace,* Tolstoy looked to his parents as models for Princess Mary and Nikolai Rostov.

Editors' note: Dates other than Bunin's are rendered in New Style.

5. Tolstoy's mother died on August 7, 1830, five months after the birth of her only daughter, Maria, and after barely nine years of married life.

6. The individual in question is Fyodor Ivanovich Rossel, the model for Karl Ivanovich Mauer, the tutor in *Childhood (Detstvo).*

7. In truth, Nikolai Tolstoy had been in such poor health that he suffered periodic hemorrhages in his throat. On a business trip to Tula in the summer of 1837, Nikolai died of a heart attack. Rumors were rife, though, that Nikolai either had suffered an apoplectic fit or been murdered or poisoned by two of his favorite serfs.

Although the funeral for Tolstoy's father took place at Yasnaya Polyana, the nine-year-old Lev did not attend the service. As a result, he long fancied that his father was still alive. In fact, whenever Lev looked at the faces of strangers in Moscow, he dreamed that he would meet his father. See Leon, *Tolstoy,* 8–9; Nazaroff, *Tolstoy,* 21.

8. Bunin is mistaken here. Tolstoy, as a student at the University of Kazan, lived with his father's sister, Pelageya Ilyinichna Yushkova, who became his legal guardian after the deaths of his parents and of an aunt, Alexandra Ilyinichna Osten-Saken.

Tolstoy recalled that Yushkova was a "religious in the fashion of her time, that is, she assiduously performed all the rites of the church, but without realizing any special duty toward her fellow men, or any necessity of a change of character on her part."

He had ample evidence for such a view. Yushkova was a very kind but volatile social butterfly who often took bribes to finance her extravagant way of life. Also, like many people of her class, she believed that it was older women who should introduce younger men to sex.

Tolstoy, though, was greatly affected by Yushkova's passing. "It is a strange thing to say," he confided to a friend, "but the death of that eighty-year-old woman has affected me more than any other. I was very sorry to lose her; she was the last link to my parents' generation. . . . Not a day goes by that I do not think of her." See Dole, *The Life of Count Tolstoi,* 25; Wilson, *Tolstoy,* 266.

9. Kazan is an old Tatar city on the middle Volga. The University of Kazan was founded in 1804 and had four colleges: history and philology, physics and mathematics, medicine, and law. Although the school's beginnings were quite humble—it had been a grammar school given university status by a tsarist decree—the university became one of the best and most famous in imperial Russia.

Of the University of Kazan, Alexander Herzen wrote in his 1836 "Pis'mo iz provintsii" ("A Letter from the Province"): "If, as foreseen by the great Peter, Russia is to carry the West into Asia and, conversely, to acquaint Europe with the East, there can be no doubt that Kazan will be the main caravanserai [toward such goals]. . . . Such interaction was accomplished by Kazan University." See V. Shklovsky, *Lev Tolstoy,* trans. Olga Shartse (Moscow: Progress, 1978), 73–74.

10. *Bunin's note:* The social life that the young Tolstoy was leading at that time insured his lack of academic success. At first, he entered the department of Arab-Turkish literature; but because he did not apply himself, he was unable to progress from the first-year course of study to the second. He then transferred to the college of law, but such a move also did not spark in him a desire for university study.

Ironically, Tolstoy especially disliked history, seeing it as a "temple of false science" and as a "heap of myths and useless trivial details, sprinkled with names and dates." In fact, as Tolstoy saw it, the study of history made manifest the absurdity of all institutionalized learning.

He once asked a friend:

> What can we carry away from the university? What can we take from this sanctuary, once we return home, to the village? What will we be suited for? Who will need us? The death of Prince Igor, or the snake that bit Oleg—what are these events if not fairy tales? And who cares if Ioann's second marriage to the daughter of Temryuk occurred on August 21, 1562, and his fourth to Anna Koltovskaya took place in 1572? How do people write history? Beginning in 1560, Tsar Ivan the Terrible moved from a virtuous and wise ruler to a senseless and savage tyrant. But how and why did he become so? No one asks questions like these!

From this passage, one can see already see one of Tolstoy's hallmarks, that is, his defiant contempt for things that were *generally accepted,* contempt that issued from his wish for "liberation" and his struggle with "submission."

Editors' note: As regards Tolstoy's disaffection with university life, Bunin is quoting from the notes of Tolstoy's classmate Valerian Nikanorovich Nazariev, which were published in 1890 in the journal *Istoricheskii vestnik* (*Historical Herald*).

Nazariev cared little for Tolstoy, seeing him as arrogant and vain. He recalled: "I kept clear of the Count, who, from our very first meeting, repelled me by his coldness, his bristly hair, and the piercing expression of his half-closed eyes. I had never met a young man with such a strange, and to me incomprehensible, air of importance and self-satisfaction."

The feeling was mutual. For instance, on November 30, 1890, Tolstoy wrote to his son Leo: "There is no need to write or publish an article [refuting what Nazariev has written about me]. False judgments are best left unanswered."

Tolstoy, while a poor student, was justified in his disaffection for advanced schooling. In the early days of the University of Kazan, most of the teachers were hacks or holdovers from the institution's former status as a grammar school. The one bright star at the institution, the famous mathematician Nikolai Lobachevsky, spent the first part of his career there, defending himself from jealous and incompetent colleagues. In fact, having moved to Saint Petersburg, Lobachevsky was so irate at his treatment at the University of Kazan that he advised the minister of education, Sergei Uvarov, to abolish the institution.

Furthermore, if Tolstoy was disgusted with institutionalized schooling, it was partially because, at this time, university education had to conform to the doctrines and ideas of both the government and the Russian Orthodox Church. For instance, lecturers at the Oriental Faculty, where Tolstoy had studied initially, were forbidden to "enter into the details of the religious beliefs and customs of the Mohammedan peoples." Also, life at the University of Kazan was remarkably staid, the student unrest that marked Lenin's days there in the 1880s being nowhere in view. See Tolstoy, *Polnoe sobranie sochinenii*, 65:194–95; Wilson, *Tolstoy*, 39–41; Troyat, *Tolstoy*, 50.

11. Later in life, Tolstoy wrote: "The university with all its rules and regulations not only did not help me to study, but it also actually prevented me from doing so." See Crankshaw, *Tolstoy*, 58.

12. However well-intentioned, Tolstoy's early concern (1847–48) for the well-being of the several hundred peasants at Yasnaya Polyana ended in failure. Like the young Prince Nekhlyudov, the hero in his 1856 sketch "A Landowner's Morning" ("Utro pomeshchnika"), Tolstoy refused to regard the poverty of the peasants as an inevitable evil. Instead, he visited their hovels and expressed his willingness to free them and to devote his life to their happiness. As he wrote in "A Landowner's Morning," his goals were "to influence this simple, receptive, innocent class of people; to rescue them from poverty; to make them self-sufficient; to educate them to them; to reform their vices, ignorance, and superstition; and to develop their morality and make them love good."

The beneficiaries of Tolstoy's kindness were hardly enthusiastic over their master's good intentions. Suspicious peasants regarded Tolstoy's offers of assistance as only the latest in centuries-old tricks whereby "masters" extracted greater productivity from "men." The new huts that Tolstoy had built for them they regarded as "jails"; the improvements in technology and sanitation, as a nuisance. Also, the serfs at Yasnaya Polyana saw the new school that Tolstoy had established for their children only as increasing their workload, since their progeny now followed books, not plows.

Not unexpectedly, folk helplessness, deception, and trickery beset Tolstoy on all sides; the peasants remained poor, ignorant, and incorrigible.

Tolstoy's Nekhlyudov writes: "Have my peasants grown richer? Are they more educated or developed morally? Not at all! They are not better off, and every day I find it more and more difficult [to deal with them]. Oh, if only I saw my plans succeeding or met with some gratitude. . . . But no, I see nothing but wrong-headed routine, vice, suspicion, helplessness. I am wasting the best years of my life."

Revealingly, Nekhlyudov's aunt chides her nephew for wishing to reform the peasantry. Predicting failure for his experiment, she declares that Nekhlyudov's supposed "originality [with the serfs] is nothing more than morbidly developed egoism on his part." Like his hero, Tolstoy had no choice but to concur. Disillusioned and perplexed, he quickly abandoned his social experiment.

Although Tolstoy may have worshipped Russian peasants in his fiction, he was under no illusions about them in real life. Writing *War and Peace,* he remarked: "[I spent the night] in the hut of some dear Russian peasants. What swine and sluts they are!" Later, he commented: "It would be easier . . . to move mountains and forests . . . than to make a peasant see reason!" See Simmons, *Leo Tolstoy,* 1:69–70, 307; Crankshaw, *Tolstoy*, 62; Leon, *Tolstoy,* 19–21; Dole, *The Life of Count Tolstoi,* 32–33; Troyat, *Tolstoy,* 215.

13. In truth, Tolstoy had so succumbed to urban temptation that he was deeply in arrears. For instance, on March 1, 1849, he wrote to his brother Sergei:

> I know that you are saying that I am the most frivolous fellow. And, to be honest, God knows what I have been doing! I came to Petersburg without any particular reason, and have done nothing useful here. I have only spent a great deal of money and now have run into debt. How stupid! How insufferably stupid!
>
> You cannot believe how my actions torment me. Particularly the debts, which I *must* pay, and as quickly as possible, because if I do not settle them soon, I will lose more than my reputation . . . I have to pay for my freedom and philosophizing. . . . That there was no one to thrash me was my chief misfortune.

See Simmons, *Leo Tolstoy,* 1:71–73; Crankshaw, *Tolstoy,* 66; Leon, *Tolstoy,* 21.

14. In 1854 Tolstoy took part in the campaign against the mountain peoples of the Caucasus, particularly the fierce and warlike Chechens, whose continued drive for independence the Russian government was determined to destroy. Tolstoy's experience in the Caucasus was the basis for such stories as "The Raid" ("Nabeg," 1853), *The Cossacks (Kazaki,* 1856), "The Woodfelling," ("Rubka lesa," 1855), and *Hadji-Murad* (1904).

15. In the Crimean War of 1853–56, the siege of the Russian city of Sevastopol in the Crimea lasted 349 days and pitted the Russian army against the forces of France, England, Turkey, and Sardinia. The Russians finally evacuated the city, but not before losing 71,000 men together with 102,000 Allied soldiers.

16. Tolstoy wrote *Childhood (Detstvo)* in 1851–52, *Adolescence (Otrochestvo)* in 1852–54, and *Youth (Iunost')* in 1855–57. He also authored *The Sevastopol Tales (Sevastopol'skie rasskazy)* in 1855 and "The Storm" ("Metel'"), "Two Hussars" ("Dva gusara"), and "A Landowner's Morning" ("Utro pomeshchnika") in 1856. He began *The Cossacks (Kazaki)* in 1852.

17. Tolstoy's interest in popular education, coupled with his own lamentable experience as a student, caused him to travel to Europe in 1860 to learn Western methods of teaching and pedagogy. Generally speaking, he was appalled by what he found. Visiting schools in Germany, he wrote in his diary: "Have been to a school. It is terrible. Prayers for the king; blows; everything by rote; terrified, beaten children." He also objected to "impractical" theory, rigid curricula, lifeless teaching, dreary textbooks, and the ignorance of students of all ages about genuine life.

Tolstoy, though, had several high points in his travels: his meeting with Julius Froebel, a nephew of Friedrich Froebel, the celebrated educational reformer and founder of the kindergarten system; the free lectures on London's educational system at the Kensington Museum; and his readings on the educational ideas of Montaigne, Bacon, Luther, and the German novelist Berthold Auerbach, particularly his novel *Ein Neues Leben (A New Life,* 1861).

Throughout his visit to Europe, though, Tolstoy remained true to himself and his ideas. For instance, he thought that Froebelian kindergartens taught "dry doctrines, inapplicable to life." He declared to Froebel himself that it was Russia, not Germany, which stood to profit more from public education. Russia, he declared, was still "young" and "unspoiled" by civilization; its folk was a "mysterious and irrational force" which would fashion an "entirely new organization of the world."

Tolstoy was equally obstreperous to Auerbach. For instance, he surprised the famed German writer by introducing himself as Eugene Bauman, a character in *Ein Neues Leben,* who had been an imprisoned nobleman-officer, but who escapes, buys a schoolmaster's passport, and devotes himself to educating peasant children. Auerbach told Tolstoy: "All educational methods are sterile. Anybody can be a great teacher. It is the children who, together with their instructor, create the best teaching methods." Tolstoy could only agree. For more on Tolstoy's responses to Western educational theory and practice, see Simmons, *Leo Tolstoy*, 1:203–17; Leon, *Tolstoy*, 93; Dole, *The Life of Count Tolstoi*, 142, 144; Wilson, *Tolstoy*, 153–55; Nazaroff, *Tolstoy*, 145; Troyat, *Tolstoy*, 196.

18. Tolstoy's career as a teacher was a special chapter in his life. Indeed, it was a special "liberation" all its own. Tolstoy's own unhappy time as a student, coupled with the lamentable state of both education and pedagogy in Russia, convinced him not only of the need for instructional reform, but, in typical Tolstoyan fashion, also of himself as the reformer.

Regarding Tolstoy's educational activities, the Tolstoyan biographer Aylmer Maude, wrote: "There was the same characteristic selection of a task of great importance; the same readiness to sweep aside and condemn nearly all that civilized humanity had accomplished up until that time; the same assurance that he could untie the Gordian knot; and the same power of devoted genius enabling him truly to achieve more than one would have imagined possible, though he had not the slightest background and experience for what he set himself out to do."

Simply put, Tolstoy defined education as "a human activity, rooted in a desire for equality . . . and to advance in knowledge." As he wrote in the first issue of his educational review, *Yasnaya Polyana* (1862), the only criterion for learning was freedom, its only method was experience. Teachers needed only sympathy, ardor, and understanding; they had to know only how and what to teach, the sources for their information and inspiration being the folk themselves. Furthermore, Tolstoy insisted that children guide themselves and that lessons be voluntary and without charge. (The sign over the school at Yasnaya Polyana, which Tolstoy had begun in 1859 at age thirty-one, read: "Enter and Leave Freely." Similarly, a poster in the classroom said, "Do as You Like!") From their homes, students were not to bring books, notebooks, homework, or even knowledge of the preceding lesson. They were to "bring only themselves, their receptive natures, and the assurance that school would be as jolly today as it was yesterday."

Children, Tolstoy insisted, were "full of life, merry and inquisitive, eager to know everything." Their eyes "danced with fun"; their smiling lips "expressed, forcibly and distinctly, their own ideas." It was only when children were forced into routine systems of education, Tolstoy continued, that they became fatigued, bored, and frightened, and that they "timidly uttered foreign phrases in a foreign tongue, creatures whose very life, like that of a snail, were hidden inside a shell."

Regarding subject matter, Tolstoy believed that curricula should be both practical and pragmatic. Literature and art, together with reading, writing, arithmetic, took their place alongside manual labor and gymnastics. Interestingly, the Bible held a key place in Tolstoy's theory and practice of education, since he believed that children could not develop, intellectually or spiritually, without a knowledge of the Old and New Testaments.

In Tolstoy's view, it was useless, even deleterious, to teach peasant children to appreciate cultural artifacts. "Civilization perverts healthy minds," he wrote. "Even though we are all products of civilization, we must not contaminate the common people with this poison. Instead, we must purge ourselves through contact with them." Tolstoy thus reasoned that if peasant children preferred the "Song of the Volga Boatmen" to Beethoven's Ninth Symphony, it was because they were simple and pure and culture was abject and base.

Furthermore, Tolstoy did not believe that education should build character and morals in students. Such matters, he believed, were the province of the family; no teacher should engage in "criminal violence," that is, advancing his or her moral and/or social convictions into the sanctity of the home.

As for teaching methods, Tolstoy opposed the corporal abuse, rote memorization, and systems of punishment and reward that were so characteristic of Russian and European systems of education. Rather, he believed that the classroom should be a workshop for creative chaos. Schools and strategies must attend to the conditions and needs of their pupils. Kindness, humor, and simplicity banished timidity, fostered self-esteem, and won confidence from students. Tolstoy insisted that students were reasoning and reasonable beings and that collective government and censure fulfilled the need for proper conduct and motivation. Students were kept eager and competitive by answering questions in unison; individuals were to be called upon only when nothing could be discerned from the chorus of voices.

Tolstoy also affirmed that teaching was in need of constant development and perfection. "There is no such thing as the best method [of teaching]," Tolstoy wrote in 1862. "The best instructor is the one who always has ready an explanation of anything that proves to be a stumbling-block for the pupil. . . . He should know the greatest number of methods, be capable of inventing fresh ones, and refrain from a slavish adherence to any particular strategy. Rather, he should be convinced that each method has advantages all its own, and the best method is the one which successfully meets all the difficulties that a student might encounter. All this is equivalent to saying that teaching is not a method, but a talent and an art."

Finally, Tolstoy rejected the idea that education should facilitate social mobility. As he saw it, the purpose of instruction was not to have peasants rise above their rank and station but to make them better and happier beings. Education, Tolstoy insisted, must serve the individual, not society, since it was the individual's ability to foster the common good that gave meaning to life.

Not surprisingly, Tolstoy's theory and practice of education ignited a firestorm of controversy. Inflamed passions were stoked even further by Tolstoy's often perverse and dogmatic reasoning; that is, his methods were correct, all others were wrong, and public education would find salvation in his theories and ideas.

Conservatives questioned Tolstoy's sanity, derided his credentials, and charged subversion of church and state. In their view, Tolstoy was a "pedagogical nihilist"; his school a "Jewish synagogue" and "a Gypsy encampment." Liberals were of two minds. On the one hand, they were dismayed at Tolstoy's emphasis on the individual, not society. On the other hand, they saw Tolstoy's methods as original, viable, and sensitive to students' needs. One in this group noted: "[As an educator, Tolstoy seeks] to establish a simple, easy, and independent relationship between teacher and pupil; to cultivate mutual affection and trust; to free lessons from constraint and learning by rote; and to transform the school into a kind of family in which the educator is a parent. What could be more desirable and profitable for all?"

Government officials, in a rare moment of agreement with Tolstoy, sided with the liberals. One wrote: "I must state that Count Tolstoy's work as a pedagogue deserves full respect, and that the Ministry of Public Education, even though it does not share all his views, is bound to help and encourage him."

Tolstoy enjoyed his time as a teacher immensely, if only because, for the first time in his life, he indulged his instincts as an altruist. Years later, he wrote to a friend: "You know what the school meant to me from the very moment that I opened it. It was my entire life; it was my monastery and church in which I redeemed myself while being saved from all the anxieties, doubts, and temptations of life." See Simmons, *Leo Tolstoy*, 1:199–211, 218–29, 236–38; Crankshaw, *Tolstoy*, 172, 186–87; Leon, *Tolstoy*, 92, 98–104; Dole, *The Life of Count Tolstoi*, 176, 177; Wilson, *Tolstoy*, 169–70, 189; Nazaroff, *Tolstoy*, 145–46; Troyat, *Tolstoy*, 215, 220, 221.

19. Most likely, Bunin is referring to Tolstoy's short-lived term (1861–62) as the regional arbiter of the peace; that is, he served an intermediary between lords and peasants, negotiating redistribution and/or purchases of land as well as other matters in the wake of Emancipation. The experience was a disaster. Tolstoy's liberal experiments with his own peasants before and after the official "liberation," coupled with his opinionated and contemptuous demeanor, quickly earned him the fleeting admiration of the folk and the enduring opposition of the gentry.

For instance, Tolstoy demanded that landlords recompense peasants for beatings; he protested when they moved peasants from their legal homesteads to land of less value; and he uncovered swindles in which landlords sought to deny their former serfs land to which they were entitled. Outraged nobles complained to government authorities, charging that Tolstoy was fomenting rebellion, even anarchy. One went so far as to accuse Tolstoy of subversive activities, including a secret printing press, illegal manifestos, and other revolutionary paraphernalia. (The response was a government raid on Yasnaya Polyana that proved the charges false.) Other landowners wrote Tolstoy threatening letters, planned to thrash him, and even conspired to involve him in a duel.

The peasants also became disenchanted with Tolstoy. Seeing Tolstoy as their champion who would procure for them whatever they desired, they often became surly and discontented when he failed to live up to their expectations.

Although Tolstoy enjoyed the support of local authorities—many of his decisions in favor of the peasantry survived legal challenges—he soon resigned his post, citing illness as the reason. See Simmons, *Leo Tolstoy,* 1:240–41; Crankshaw, *Tolstoy,* 189–90; Leon, *Tolstoy,* 104–5.

20. Tolstoy married Sofya Andreevna Bers on October 5, 1862. He was thirty-four; his bride was eighteen. (By way of interest, Tolstoy was only two years younger than Sofya's mother, Lyubov' Alexandrovna, a childhood playmate and sweetheart, whom he had pushed off a balcony in a fit of jealousy and who, so the story goes, was lame for several years. Also, Sofya's father, Andrei Evstafievich Bers, a physician on the staff of the Imperial Palace in Moscow, was a notorious lecher who had had an affair with Turgenev's mother, Varvara Petrovna Turgeneva.) See Simmons, *Leo Tolstoy,* 1:258–59; Crankshaw, *Tolstoy,* 192; Leon, *Tolstoy,* 9.

21. Tolstoy published *The Cossacks* and began *War and Peace* in 1863.

22. Nikolai Nikolaevich Tolstoy was Tolstoy's favorite brother; he died of tuberculosis in 1860. Dmitri Nikolaevich Tolstoy was the black sheep of the family and a partial model for Levin's brother in *Anna Karenina;* he also died of consumption in 1856.

23. Sergei L'vovich (Seryozha) was born in 1863, Tatyana L'vovna (Tanya) in 1864, Ilya L'vovich in 1866, and Leo L'vovich (Lyovka) in 1869.

24. Tolstoy's educational activities, as well as his work as arbiter of the peace, affected his health, physically and spiritually. Having developed a severe cough and haunted by the specter of tuberculosis, Tolstoy heeded his doctor's (and future father-in-law's) advice for a rest. In May 1862, he headed for Samara, located approximately 500 miles southeast of Moscow. There he lived with native Bashkirs in a nomadic encampment in the Russian steppe.

Tolstoy wrote to Fet: "As is proper when one is taking a cure with mare's milk, I get drunk and sweat from morning to night, but I find pleasure in what I am doing. It is very good here, and were it not for my homesickness, I would be quite happy. . . . I could fill a hundred pages with this country and with what I am doing here."

His health restored, Tolstoy returned to Moscow two months later, though he often returned to Samara and the Bashkirs to restore his body and soul. See Simmons, *Leo Tolstoy,* 1:331–33.

25. Tolstoy wrote *Anna Karenina* in 1875–77.

26. Maria L'vovna (Masha) was born in 1871, Pyotr L'vovich in 1872, Nikolai L'vovich in 1874, Varvara L'vovna in 1875, Andrei L'vovich (Andryusha) in 1877, and Mikhail L'vovich (Misha) in 1879. Varvara died in the year of her birth; Pyotr and Nikolai died within a year of their entry into this world.

27. Tolstoy authored his *Confession (Ispoved')* in 1879–80.

28. The famed, if at times infamous, relationship between Tolstoy and Vladimir Grigorievich Chertkov began in October 1883 and continued until the writer's death in 1910. Chertkov appears to have started reading Tolstoy in 1880, being particularly impressed by the final sections of *Anna Karenina.*

When the two first met, the twenty-nine-year-old Chertkov had only recently quit a raucous life as a captain in the Imperial Guard to lead a simple, if ascetic, life among the peasants. Also, under the influence of Dostoevsky and the Gospels, he had come to denounce violence and to espouse the need for humility and productive work.

Coming into contact with Tolstoy, Chertkov believed that all his vague seekings had come to an end. Of their initial time together, he recalled: "Inevitably, the moral tie between Tolstoy and myself had a particular significance for both of us. For Tolstoy, it meant appreciation and support of all that he had recognized to be the best and highest in himself. For me it was an indispensable help in the growth of my inner life."

Tolstoy was also taken with Chertkov. Less than a year after their meeting, Tolstoy wrote to his young disciple: "I would terribly like to live with you. . . . Never cease to love me, as I love you." See Leon, *Tolstoy,* 237; Dole, *The Life of Count Tolstoi,* 354.

29. Tolstoy wrote *What People Live By (Chem liudi zhivy)* in 1881, *What I Believe (V chem moia vera)* in 1883, and *What Then Should We Do? (Tak chto nam delat'?)* in 1886.

30. Alexei L'vovich Tolstoy was born in 1881, Alexandra L'vovna Tolstaya in 1884.

31. Tolstoy understood the failure of "highbrow" literature with the folk. He wrote: "We offer the people Pushkin and Gogol. The Germans offer them Goethe and Schiller; and the French, Racine, Corneille, and Boileau. . . . But the people do not want such writers."

So, in the years 1884 and 1885, Tolstoy wrote a number of highly artistic stories that paraphrased well-liked pulp and hagiographical tales and that, published as popular literature, imparted his ideas and ideals to the folk. For instance, in 1884 and 1885, he wrote no less than fifteen "tales for the people," including such well-known pieces as "Two Brothers and Gold" ("Dva brata i zoloto")," "Where There Is Love, There Is Also God" ("Gde l'iubov, tam i bog"), "A Neglected Spark Burns the House" ("Upushtish' ogon'—ne potushish'"), and "Two Old Men" ("Dva starika"). See Shklovsky, *Lev Tolstoy*, 564.

32. *The Death of Ivan Ilyich* (*Smert' Ivana Ilycha*) and *The Power of Darkness* (*Vlast' t'my*) appeared in 1886, *The Fruits of Enlightenment* (*Plody prosveshcheniia*) and *The Kreutzer Sonata* (*Kreitserova sonata*) in 1899.

33. Tolstoy began writing *Resurrection* (*Voskresenie*) in 1898 and published it a year later.

34. Ivan L'vovich Tolstoy (Vanechka) entered the world in 1888.

35. The region about the city of Tula is 100 miles directly south of Moscow.

Throughout his life, Tolstoy campaigned against hunger in his homeland. For instance, in 1873, Tolstoy alerted Mikhail Katkov, editor of *Moscow News* (*Moskovskie vedemosti*), to a crop failure in Samara. "I hate writing jeremiads," he wrote to a cousin, "but in all my forty-five years, I have never seen such suffering." Tolstoy had ample evidence for such a view. Nine-tenths of the population in the region were destitute and starving. As a result of the writer's efforts, the empress and concerned citizens throughout Russia sent grain and over two million rubles to Samara to mitigate the suffering there.

Similarly, during the famine of 1891 to 1892, Tolstoy not only organized and presided over relief efforts in the field, but he also braved the displeasure of Alexander III by publicizing the calamity of the famine, as well as the callousness of the tsar, government officials, and the reactionary press who preferred to allow hundreds of thousands to die of starvation rather than to admit bureaucratic ineptitude and to issue appeals for help. For instance, Alexander III, fearing both outside intervention and inner revolution, announced: "In Russia there is no famine, but localities are suffering from a failure of crops." Outraged, Tolstoy wrote such pieces as "A Terrible Question" ("Strashnyi vopros") and "Help the Starving" ("Pomoshch' golodnym").

By July 1892, Tolstoy had founded 246 soup kitchens that fed over 13,000 people daily. In addition, he had organized 124 children's homes for over 3,000 youngsters. To the peasants, he also distributed desperately needed food, firewood, horses, and seed. (Despite Tolstoy's efforts, nearly half a million Russians died of hunger.)

As before, public response to Tolstoy's activities was overwhelming. "Contributions came streaming in," Sofya later recalled. "It was truly touching the way people responded to our appeal. Some of them . . . wept as they brought by their offering." (Contributions from America alone totaled over $500,000.) Regarding Tolstoy's activities to relieve hunger and suffering,

Chekhov wrote: "Tolstoy! Ah, Tolstoy! . . . He is not a man, but a superman, a Jupiter!"

As was the case with the famine of 1873, the efforts of Tolstoy to help starving peasants were regarded with suspicion by government officials, who, again attempting to conceal the true state of affairs, were particularly distressed by Tolstoy's endeavors, particularly his exposés on the hunger stalking the land. In their view, Tolstoy was a dangerous anarchist who was fomenting a peasant revolution. Government officials even circulated rumors that Tolstoy had been arrested for his "revolutionary" activity and that he had been imprisoned in the dreaded dungeons of the Suzdal monastery.

Members of the church hierarchy joined in the assault. Bishops preached sermons that Tolstoy was the Antichrist who was seducing peasant souls with gifts of money and food. "Where does Tolstoy get his power?" one cleric intoned. "He merely waves one arm and money pours down like rain! He waves the other, and a cart with bread rolls right up to him!"

Wisely, though, Alexander III stood apart from the pillaring, noting that he "had not the slightest intention of making a martyr of Tolstoy and bringing universal indignation upon [himself]."

Tolstoy, however, earnestly desired persecution for his activities. "It has been noised abroad," he wrote, "that I have been arrested. Unhappily for me . . . nothing of the sort has happened. . . . If only they would consent to imprison me! How happy I would be to suffer in my turn."

Tolstoy's willingness to suffer for his beliefs remained with him throughout his life. For instance, he wrote to a friend in 1894: "Sinner that I am, I so desire persecution [for my ideals] that I have to restrain myself not to provoke it. But it seems that I am not worthy of such a thing, and that I will have to die without having lived even approximately, or even temporarily, in the way I consider it right to live. It also seems that it will not be my lot to be a witness to the truth by any suffering."

Three years before his death, he continued: "Let me be put in prison, or better yet (so good that I dare not hope for such happiness), let me be dressed in a shroud . . . and pushed off a bench so that the weight of my body will tighten the well-soaped slipknot around my old neck." See Simmons, *Leo Tolstoy,* 1:345, 2:160, 171, 175; Crankshaw, *Tolstoy,* 268; Leon, *Tolstoy,* 260–64; Biryukov, *Leo Tolstoy,* 127; Dole, *The Life of Count Tolstoi,* 344–45, 353; Wilson, *Tolstoy,* 400–3; Shklovsky, *Lev Tolstoy,* 626–30; Troyat, *Tolstoy,* 612–13.

36. On September 16, 1891, Tolstoy wrote to major Russian newspapers: "Because of the requests which I receive for permission to publish, translate, and dramatize my works, I beg you to insert in your paper this declaration: 'I hereby give to all the rights to publish without payment, in Russia and abroad, in Russian and in translation, those of my works which were written after 1881, and which are printed in volume twelve published dur-

ing this year, 1891. I also surrender rights to all my work as yet unpublished in Russia which may appear in the future.'"

Such a stratagem, Tolstoy hoped, would disseminate his religious and sociological ideas to as large a public as possible. See Leon, *Tolstoy*, 257.

37. Tolstoy wrote *The Kingdom of God Is within You* (*Tsarstvo bozhie vnutri vas*) in 1893; *Master and Man* (*Khoziain i rabotnik*) in 1894; and *About Art* (*Ob iskusstve*) in 1882.

38. Ivan L'vovich Tolstoy (Vanechka) died on March 5, 1895.

39. In February 1901, the Most Holy Synod of the Russian Orthodox Church issued a public anathema against Tolstoy. With solemn pomp, it decreed:

> In our days, God has permitted a false teacher to appear: Count Leo Tolstoy. A writer well known to the world, Russian by birth, and Orthodox by baptism and education, Count Tolstoy has been seduced by his intellectual pride; has insolently risen both against the Lord and his Christ and against His holy heritage; and has publicly, in the sight of all humankind, repudiated the Orthodox Mother Church which reared and educated him. Also, he has devoted his literary activity and the talent given to him by God to disseminating among the people teachings repugnant to Christ and the church, and to destroying in the minds and hearts their national faith, the Orthodox faith which has been confirmed by the universe, and in which our forefathers lived and were saved, and to which, until now, Holy Russia has held, and in which she has been strong.
>
> Therefore the church does not reckon Leo Tolstoy as its member, and cannot do so until he repents and resumes his communion with her.

The document was signed by the metropolitans of Saint Petersburg, Moscow, and Kiev, all of whom prefixed the word "humble" (*smirennyi*) before their names.

Tolstoy suffered excommunication for a number of reasons, most notably for attacking the basic tenets of canonical doctrine, for example, the Trinity, the virgin birth, the crucifixion and resurrection of Christ, the existence of angels and devils, the six-day creation of the world, the Garden of Eden, and Adam's expulsion from paradise. For instance, Tolstoy wrote of the doctrine of the Trinity: "That one God equals three? . . . But no human mind can accept such nonsense!"

Additionally, Tolstoy rejected heaven, hell, the sacraments, the holy succession of bishops, and the efficacy of miracles. "To reinforce the teachings of Christ with miracles," Tolstoy wrote in his diary, "is like holding a lighted candle in front of the sun to see it better." See Crankshaw, *Tolstoy*, 218; Leon, *Tolstoy*, 196, 296–97; Dole, *The Life of Count Tolstoi*, 369; Nazaroff, *Tolstoy*, 227; Shklovsky, *Lev Tolstoy*, 446; Troyat, *Tolstoy*, 391, 392.

40. In early 1902, Tolstoy was so ill with pneumonia and later enteric (not typhoid) fever that he almost passed from this life. Still, he held fast

against the Orthodox Church. When Sofya approached her husband with a letter from Metropolitan Anthony, begging Tolstoy to make peace with the church, he replied: "Reconciliation is out of the question. I am dying without any feelings of animosity or rancor. Besides, what is the 'church' anyway? How can one make peace with such an indefinite object?"

Undeterred, members of the Holy Synod then sent a priest to Tolstoy, their hope being to announce to an astonished world that on his deathbed Tolstoy had recanted his sins, received the Eucharist, and died in the arms of Mother Church. When Tolstoy was told of this ploy by his son Seryozha, he smiled wryly and said, "Cannot these gentlemen understand that even in the presence of death, two and two still make four?"

There is also a story that family members ambushed a priest who had intended to break through to the dying Tolstoy and, no matter what the result, to proclaim that the great writer had made his peace with God and had died with his sins forgiven him. Not surprisingly, members of Tolstoy's family were so wary (and weary) of clerical shenanigans that they planned to conceal news of his passing until they could send telegrams to the press abroad with the message that Tolstoy had died true to his convictions.

Although Tolstoy recovered from his illness, his infirmity had this salvific result: It seemed to advance him into the realm of spirit that he craved so desperately. For instance, Gorky, in his memoirs, remarked that Tolstoy's "illness burnt something out of him . . . and dried him up still more. Inwardly, he seemed to become lighter and more transparent and resigned. . . . Indeed, he gave the impression of having just arrived from a different country, where people think and feel differently, and whose worldviews and language are not like those of other people. . . . Even his cheekbones beamed." See Leon, *Tolstoy*, 304–5; Shklovsky, *Lev Tolstoy*, 676; Simmons, *Leo Tolstoy*, 2:318.

41. Tolstoy's began publishing *The Circle of Reading*, along with his *Thoughts of Wise People for Each and Every Day* (*Mysli mudrykh liudei na kazhdyi den'*), in 1904. Both works were collections of extracts that testified to the writer's extraordinary knowledge and understanding of world culture and intellectual thought. Passages included selections from Hebraic, Christian, Hindu, Buddhist, and Mohammedan texts; tracts from the early church fathers, Thomas à Kempis, and Saint Francis; the teachings of Confucius and Lao-tzu; the classical philosophies of Plato, Aristotle, Seneca, Marcus Aurelius, and Epictetus; the modern thought of Schopenhauer, Kant, La Rouchefoucauld, and La Bruyère; and the fiction of Emerson, Thoreau, Ruskin, and Carlyle.

Furthermore, passages in *The Circle* were arranged according to thirty-one themes (for example, "Faith," "The Soul," "One Soul in All," "God," and "Love") to illustrate aspects of that reasoned consciousness which Tolstoy championed as the true modus vivendi in life. Although Tolstoy often showed only a modest appreciation for his fiction, he greatly admired his *Circle of Reading*. See Leon, *Tolstoy,* 310, Biryukov, *Leo Tolstoy,* 146; Simmons, *Leo Tolstoy,* 2:370.

42. Maria L'vovna Tolstaya (Masha), the second daughter of Leo Tolstoy, died of pneumonia at age twenty-five on November 27, 1906. It is easy to see why Masha was her father's favorite. When she was just two years old, Tolstoy wrote in his diary: "Masha is delicate and sickly, with a milk-white body, ash-blond hair, and strange, big blue eyes that give a serious and profound expression on her face. She is very intelligent, but plain-looking. Masha is going to be one of those perplexing people who seek and suffer; but will never find anything, because she will always search for things that are unattainable."

Years later, Masha's brother Ilya recalled of her: "Masha was the person in my family who most resembled my father . . . with her prominent cheekbones and light blue eyes. Gentle and modest, Masha gave the impression of being of a retiring disposition. In her innermost soul, she felt father's isolation, and, abandoning the society of her friends, she passed quietly, though decisively, over to his side."

To her often remote, mysterious, and emotionally undemonstrative father, Masha was the only one of Tolstoy's children who dared stroke his hand, kiss him, or, with her caresses, soothe his troubled brow. She also was singularly devoted to her father's ideas. "Do you know what Father hopes for?" she would tell visitors. "That he will bring us round to a new life, and that we will believe all that he does. . . . What a terrible task he is undertaking!"

During her lifetime, Masha achieved a singular position in the Tolstoyan household. A "Tolstoyan" in the best sense of this word, she offered a viable alternative to her father's dogmatic theorizing and spiritual self-focus by her pragmatic kindness and self-effacing style. For instance, Masha acted as Tolstoy's secretary and copied his manuscripts. She tended the sick, defended the downtrodden, and mediated misunderstandings, winning the affection and confidence of all. Most revealing, perhaps, Masha had initially refused her share of the inheritance, believing, like Tolstoy, that it was shameful to live in luxury while others were perishing from want.

Not surprisingly, Tolstoy's wife, Sofya, took a dim view of her daughter's generosity of spirit. "Masha gets to know all the terrible things that are going on in the village . . . and brings all that filth home. . . . This daughter, whom God sent me, is a curse. She has never brought me anything but worry, annoyance, pity, and unhappiness. . . . She is a stranger in the family." Having learned that Masha had relinquished her rights to the estate, Sofya continued: "I realize that the poor girl is unable to see things clearly and to imagine what it would mean . . . to be left penniless after the life she had led."

Tolstoy, though, relished Masha's allegiance and love. His daughter was both a key confidante and comforter, as well as a "fellow-traveler" in his spiritual search. "Of all my children, Masha is closest to me in spirit," Tolstoy wrote to a friend on August 22, 1889. "The others, poor things, are only oppressed by the fact that I am always around, reminding them of what their conscience demands from them." Later, he continued: "I have great tenderness only for Masha. It is as by her actions that she redeems the others."

Masha did break her father's heart, though. She enraged Tolstoy by seemingly betraying her allegiance to his teachings on the flesh; that is, in 1897, Masha married Prince Nikolai Obolensky, a distant relative and a handsome, lazy, and irresponsible individual with empty pockets and polished fingernails. Also disappointing to Tolstoy was the fact that the married Masha quickly reneged on her opposition to "property" and accepted the portion of Tolstoy's estate that Sofya was holding in trust for her.

Tolstoy wrote to Masha: "You are going to exchange your peace of mind and independence for the most agonizing and complicated sufferings. . . . You must have guessed that your decision [to marry] means failure to me. But I am glad to think that it will be easier for you to live after abandoning your ideals, or rather, after mingling your ideals with baser aspirations, by which I mean having children." See Simmons, *Leo Tolstoy*, 1:343, 381, 2:119; Crankshaw, *Tolstoy*, 253; Leon, *Tolstoy*, 168, 232–33, 259–60, 278, 311; Wilson, *Tolstoy*, 382; Troyat, *Tolstoy*, 470, 524.

43. The machinations and intrigue that surrounded the struggle over Tolstoy's literary legacy during his lifetime were almost Machiavellian in scope. Tolstoy wrote three (legitimate) versions of a last will and testament. (There also were at least two letters, claiming also to express the writer's wishes after his death.)

In his first will and testament (1895), Tolstoy wrote:

All my papers are to be given to my wife, V. G. Chertkov, N. Strakhov, and to my daughters, Tanya and Masha, for them or for such of them as survive, to sort and examine. (I have myself struck out my daughters' names. They ought not to be troubled with this.)

I exclude my sons from this bequest, not because I do not love them. (I have come of late to love them better and better, thank God, and I know that they love me.) But they do not understand my ideas or how these ideas came to be [in my life]. They also may have ideas of their own which may lead them to keep what ought not to be kept and to reject what ought to be preserved.

As I have extracted from my bachelor diaries that which is worth keeping, I wish for them to be destroyed. As regards my married diaries, I wish to be destroyed anything that might hurt anyone if they would be published. Chertkov has promised to fulfill this request even during my lifetime; and, knowing his moral sensibility as well as the great and undeserved love that he has for me, I know that he will do it in a fine and proper manner.

I wish the diaries of my bachelor life to be destroyed, not because I wish to conceal the wickedness of my life—my life was the usual vicious cycle of an unprincipled young man—but because the diaries in which I recorded only the torments arising from the consciousness of sin produce a false and tormented impression. . . . Let my other diaries remain as they are, for they show that, despite the frivolity and immorality of my early youth, I was not deserted by God, even though it was only in old age that I began, if only a little, to understand and love the Almighty.

I write this [last will and testament] not because I attribute great or even any importance to my papers, but because I know beforehand that after my death, my books will be published, talked about, and thought to be important. If that indeed will be the case, it is better that my writings should not harm other people. As for the remainder of my papers, I ask those who will have the arrangement of them not to publish everything, but only that which will be of use to people.

With regard to the publishing rights of my former works—the ten volumes and my *Primer*—I ask my heirs to give these to the public, that is, to renounce the copyrights. I only ask such a thing; in no sense do I order it. It would be a good thing to do. It would also be good for you to do it. But if you do not wish to [renounce the copyrights to my works], that is your affair. It means that you are not ready to do so. That my books for the last ten years have been sold [for money] was for me the most painful thing of my life.

In his second *Last Will and Testament*, written immediately before his death, Tolstoy requested that "all [his] works be handed over to the public . . . and that all [his] manuscripts, notes, and diaries be given to V. G. Chertkov . . . so that they may be freely accessible to all who wish to make use of them."

Because it was not possible legally to leave literary possessions to the world at large and because Chertkov envisioned a grave scandal if he were designated as Tolstoy's literary heir, he, together with Strakhov and several others, had a lawyer name Tolstoy's daughter Alexandra as the sole beneficiary of his writing.

The choice was a sound one. By this time, Alexandra had become Tolstoy's most loyal helper. She had renounced all idea of marriage to devote herself completely to her father, copying and recopying his later writings and tending to his needs in his declining years. More than anyone else in the family, it was Alexandra who understood Tolstoy's increasing loneliness and isolation and who could execute his bequest according to his directions.

Not unexpectedly, Tolstoy was greatly displeased with Chertkov's legal maneuvering. "The entire affair oppresses me," he remarked when he read this new will. "There is no need to safeguard the dissemination of one's work by various legalities." Tolstoy approved the document, though, adding that any initial profits from his unpublished works be used to buy Yasnaya Polyana from Sofya and to distribute it among the peasants.

Matters did not end here, though. Alexandra was taken with sudden illness; and although she recovered, Chertkov and company were sufficiently unnerved by the sudden threat to their plans to draft a new document. This time, the will asserted that if Alexandra died before Tolstoy, his eldest daughter, Tatyana, would be the sole legatee to his literary estate. Again Tolstoy signed the document in the presence of witnesses, but with similar qualms over what he was doing. Also as before, though, his mind was set at ease by Chertkov, who insisted that if Sofya or those of his children who opposed his views enforced their legal rights to his writings, they could threaten and even prosecute individuals who had published his works in the past or hoped to do so in the future. "Not only would your nearest and most intimate friends suffer," Chertkov warned, "but about your writings preaching harmony and love, there would flare up a scandal that would be unprecedented in literary history." See Leon, *Tolstoy*, 272, 324–26, 336, 341.

44. Tolstoy was so dissatisfied with family life that less than a year into his marriage he wanted to leave Yasnaya Polyana to help suppress the Polish insurrection of 1863. Sofya, of course, had only outrage for this Andrei Bolskonsky come to life.

> To war. What is this latest whim! Irresponsibility? No, not that, it is sheer instability! . . . With him everything is whim and passing fancy? Today he gets married, the idea appeals to him, he has children. Tomorrow he has a hankering to go off to war and to abandon us. All I can do is hope that my child will die, for I shall not live if Lyova goes. I do not believe that a man of thirty-five can have such enthusiasm and love for the fatherland. As though children were not the fatherland, as though they also were not Russian! He is ready to abandon everything because he thinks that it is fun to go galloping on a horse, admire the war, and hear the shells whistling pass him!

See Troyat, *Tolstoy*, 269.

45. Throughout the latter part of his life, Tolstoy complained bitterly of the alienation from his family. For instance, in December 1882, he recorded in his diary: "I am fairly quiet, but sad—often because of the triumphant, self-assured insanity of [my family's] life around me. I do not understand why it has been granted to me to perceive this insanity, while they are quite unable to understand their own madness and mistakes. So we stand face-to-face, not comprehending each other, and wondering at and condemning each other. But they are legion and I am alone. They are seemingly happy, and I am seemingly sad."

Several years later, he continued: "It is very painful at home, and it hurts me that I cannot sympathize with the members of my family. All their joys, examinations, successes in society, music, furniture, shopping, I consider as evils for them, but I cannot make them understand how I feel. . . . They give me the part of a peevish old man. . . . Everything I do is wrong, and I suffer horribly from this wrongness. It is as though I alone am not mad in a house of lunatics managed by lunatics."

Tolstoy's distance from his family was as much philosophical as it was personal. For instance, he wrote: "'Family' . . . I said to myself. But my family—my wife and children—are also human beings who are in the same situation as I. That is, they must either live a lie or see the terrible truth. . . . But how should they live? Why should I love them, guard them, raise them, or watch over them? So that they may come to know the despair that I myself feel or else to lead stupid lives? Loving my wife and children, I cannot hide the truth from them. Each step in knowledge leads them to that truth. And the truth is death."

Tolstoy's growing estrangement from his family, together with his near starvation for love, was one of the heaviest crosses of his later life. "I have been dull and miserable the entire day. Toward evening, though, my mood passed into tenderness—a desire for affection, for love. I longed to press up to a loving, pitying creature and to be comforted. But what creature is there to whom I could come close like that? I go over all the people I have loved; and there is not one that I can come really close to."

Not unexpectedly, Tolstoy's desire to flee Yasnaya Polyana only increased with time and drew from lifelong impulses to resolve difficult situations through flight. For instance, Sofya wrote in her diary in 1882: "[Tolstoy] loudly shouted that his most passionate desire is to get away from the family. To my dying day, I shall not forget that sincere cry of his, for it was as if he had torn my heart from me."

A decade later, he had become even firmer in his resolve. He wrote to a friend: "How many times have I said to myself how glad I would be . . . to escape this hell of dissension. . . . I am ready for everything, for every torment, humiliation—anything is better than this inferno."

A year before his actual departure from his home, Tolstoy recorded: "[Life here] is maddening. I am exhausted. I cannot stand it anymore. I feel altogether ill. I am simply unable to face [life at Yasnaya Polyana]." See Crankshaw, *Tolstoy*, 257; Leon, *Tolstoy*, 226–27, 310, 319; Troyat, *Tolstoy*, 442, 443; Simmons, *Leo Tolstoy*, 2:44, 46, 177, 204, 376.

46. For instance, Tolstoy recorded in 1885: "If I abandon my family, I would be leaving them to their fate and depriving them of my influence, which I believe to be ineffectual, but which, perhaps, makes some slight impression upon them. I would also be condemning my wife and myself to live apart and, in so doing, would be disobeying God's commandments."

Thirteen years later, he continued: "Doubts have come into my mind whether it would be better for me to go away and disappear. I refrain from doing so principally because it would be for my own sake, in order to escape from a life that is poisoned on every side. I believe that the endurance of this life is necessary for me."

Also, three days before Tolstoy left Yasnaya Polyana forever, he wrote: "It is all so unbearable. Sofya holds me suspect and spies upon me, I have this sinful longing that she will give me an excuse to leave her. But when I do decide to leave, I think of the position that she will be in; and I feel sorry for her and know that I cannot do it." See Leon, *Tolstoy*, 313; Shklovsky, *Lev Tolstoy*, 741; Troyat, *Tolstoy*, 453.

47. Tolstoy wrote his letter when he was seventy years old. He was quite taken with what he perceived as the "twilight" years of a Buddhist's life. For instance, in 1879, he wrote to Strakhov: "There exist fortunate people—our peasants or the Buddhists—who, on one foot, live the full live of the flesh until they are fifty and then suddenly shift and stand on the other foot, the spiritual." Tolstoy also told his daughter Masha: "How fine for the Buddhist when he grows old—he goes off to the desert." Additionally, Tolstoy remarked to Dushan Makovitsky: "As old Buddhists do, I want remoteness, to get far away from worldly vanity." See Tolstoy, "Pis'ma," in *Polnoe sobranie sochinenii*, 62:501; Nazaroff, *Tolstoy*, 316; Simmons, *Leo Tolstoy*, 2:432, 441.

48. In 1897, it was Sofya's morbid (but platonic) infatuation with the composer Sergei Ivanovich Taneev that had Tolstoy packing his bags. The letter that Bunin is quoting here is dated July 8 and begins:

I have long been troubled between my life and my convictions. I could not make you change your life and the habits in which I had trained you. And, until now, I have felt equally unable to go away and leave you, lest in so doing I cause you grief and also deprive the children, while they are still young, of any influence, even if slight, that I still could have upon them.

But I can no longer continue living as I have lived for the past sixteen years, sometimes struggling against and irritating you, sometimes succumbing to the familiar temptations that always surround me. So now I have decided to do what I have long wished to do—to go away.

[My reasons are twofold.] First, because this life is becoming more and more of a burden to me, and, as my years increase, I long for solitude more and more. Second, because now that the children are grown up, my influence is no longer needed in the house, and all of you have more vital interests which will make you feel my absence less.

After the passage cited in the text, Tolstoy continued:

If I were to carry out my plan openly, there would be entreaties, reproaches, arguments, and complaints. And I might weaken in my resolve and, perhaps, not carry out my intention. But it must be carried out. Therefore, please forgive me if my action hurts you. Forgive me, all of you, in your hearts, but chiefly you, Sofya. Let me go with goodwill. Do not search for me, do not complain, and do not condemn me.

The fact that I am leaving you does not mean that I am dissatisfied with you. I know that you are unable, literally unable, and are still unable, to see and feel as I do; and that you could not and cannot change your life and make sacrifices for the sake of something of which you are not conscious. I thus do not blame you. On the contrary, I remember, with love and gratitude, the thirty-five years of our life together, especially the first half of that span when, with the motherly self-sacrifice that is innate to you, you bore so energetically and resolutely what you considered to be your duty. You have given me and the world what you were able to give, that is, a great deal of motherly love and self-sacrifice, and I cannot but appreciate such a thing.

But in the last period of our life—these last fifteen years—we have grown apart. I cannot think that I am to blame for such a separation, for I know that I have changed not for my own sake or even for the sake of other people, but because I could not do otherwise. Neither can I blame you for not following me, but I think of you, and always shall think of you, with love and gratitude for what you have given me.

Sofya did not see this letter until after Tolstoy's death, and when she did, she merely muttered: "More stupidity, jealousy, and reproach." Even more spiteful, perhaps, she published the missive in the journal *Novoe vremia* (*New Time*).

As he had done so many times before, though, Tolstoy remained with his family, but only after a profound and prolonged inner struggle. For instance, he wrote to Chertkov: "Read this to no one. I teach others, but I do not know how to live myself. How many years have I asked myself the question: 'Is it fitting that I continue to live as I am living, or should I go away?' And still I cannot make up my mind. I know that everything is decided by self-renunciation, and that when I attain such a thing, the solution is clear. But such moments are rare." See Leon, *Tolstoy,* 276–77; Wilson, *Tolstoy,* 440–42; Simmons, *Leo Tolstoy,* 2:256–70.

49. The letter that Chertkov had written to Tolstoy on September 24, 1910, was one of the final salvos in the ongoing struggle between himself and Sofya over Tolstoy's literary legacy. In this missive, Chertkov berated Tolstoy for promising Sofya that he would not meet with Chertkov, give him the writer's diaries, or allow him permission to take Tolstoy's picture (an activity of which Chertkov was inordinately fond).

Only several days earlier, Chertkov had actually acquiesced to Sofya's demands. He had written to Tolstoy: "In this matter, there can be no question of my personal feelings. If [my absence] is necessary for your tranquillity, or simply because you think such a thing should be done, I am fully prepared not to see you for a day, an entire period, or even until death takes one of us."

Chertkov, though, issued this caveat: "But at the same time, I will, as always, be quite frank with you; and whether I am right or wrong, I will inform you of my fear that in your wish to pacify Sofya Andreevna, you may go too far and abandon that freedom which should always be preserved by one who wishes to accomplish not his own will, but the will of God."

To Chertkov, Tolstoy replied: "The entire matter seems to me more complicated and more difficult to solve than it can possibly appear even to a close friend such as you. I must solve it alone, in my soul, before God, and I am trying to do so, but every attempt to help me only makes my task more difficult."

Needless to say, Sofya exulted in her victory over her husband. Tolstoy was unhappy with the agreement, though, and hoped that the separation from Chertkov would be temporary. Such expectations did not come to pass, however. With each passing day, Tolstoy grew more and more despondent over the absence of his friend. "I cannot but feel joy at the approach of death," he recorded. "The separation from Chertkov grows more and more humiliating, and I am clearly to blame [for his not being here]." See Bunin, *Sobranie sochinenii,* 9:572; Tolstoy, *Polnoe sobranie sochinenii,* 88–89:217–18; Leon, *Tolstoy,* 338–39, 340–41, 343.

50. *Bunin's note:* Unless otherwise stated, all italics are mine.

Editors' note: Bunin is quoting an excerpt from Tolstoy's diary dated September 25, 1910.

51. Khisto Feodosovich Dosev was a Tolstoyan who often visited Tolstoy and who lived in a commune in Bulgaria with fellow believers. Writing extensively on Tolstoy in the years between 1907 and 1932, Dosev also translated many of the writer's works into Bulgarian. Shortly before Tolstoy's death, Dosev had written to Chertkov, denouncing Sofya as "a stupid and vulgar woman." Tactlessly, Chertkov passed the letter on to Tolstoy. See Simmons, *Leo Tolstoy,* 2:470.

52. Tolstoy was eighty-two years old when he "escaped" from Yasnaya Polyana.

53. Apparently, though, Tolstoy often did just that. Averse to using money unnecessarily, he did not use trains but walked whenever he could. Supplied only with food, a notebook, a pencil, and a change of linen, he sometimes tramped the 130 miles from Moscow to Yasnaya Polyana, either with friends or with companions whom he had met on the road. He also willingly slept in hovels along the way. See Leon, *Tolstoy,* 230.

54. In Tolstoy's 1902 play *The Light Shines in Darkness* (*I svet vo t'me svetit*), the main character, Saryntsov, is so at odds with his wife that he wishes to leave her altogether. He does not do so, though, for fear of being perverse and cruel. See Leon, *Tolstoy,* 221.

55. Optina Hermitage, more accurately, the Kozelsk Presentation Optina Independent Hermitage (Kozel'skaia Vvedenskaia Optina Zashtatnaia Pushtin'), is located in the province of Kaluga about 100 miles southwest of Moscow. The name Optina derives either from the famous fifteenth-century robber-chief Opta, who is alleged to be the monastery's founder, or from the debasement of the word *obshchii,* or "common," signifying the communal rule observed by the monks and nuns who dwelled there jointly. (Such an arrangement was later forbidden by the 1551 Stoglav Council.)

In the nineteenth century, Optina Hermitage gained renown not only as a key center of the so-called Hesychast, or "meditative-mystical" tradition of the Eastern Orthodox Church, but also as the founding place for the institution of "elders" (*startsy*), that is, individuals who espoused a life of rigorous prayer and work to teach self-sacrifice and service to their disciples.

The elders at Optina Hermitage responded to life with the inner awareness of monks, the secular concerns of laymen, and the canonical authority of priests. They regarded their disciples not only as they were seen by God but also as the possessors of a unique destiny and vocation with which to advance the world. It was the elders' own mission in life to discern the many difficulties that people faced in realizing their calling as well as to help them in their quest.

To this end, the elders at Optina Hermitage sought that their adherents escape inner fetters and bloom in divine grace. They wished to open the spiritual life of their charges, but without violating their inner freedom and will. The elders at Optina Hermitage were not content merely to know human nature; they also sought a special vision, even a divine revelation, for the individuals who asked for their counsel and help. As a result, the elders at Optina Hermitage quickly gained a reputation as perceptive mentors and dispensers of spiritual and worldly advice. They also became known as healers not only of bodies but also of souls.

The Optina Hermitage was revered throughout Russia and visited by people of all ranks and stations. It was a particular haven for Russian writers. In 1878, Dostoevsky visited the hermitage after the death of his son. Tolstoy called upon the elders at Optina Hermitage three times before his final sojourn there. For instance, in the summer of 1877, he discoursed at length with Father Ambrose, an elder famous for his holiness and wisdom. (Father Ambrose also served as a model for Father Zosima in Dostoevsky's *Brothers Karamazov* [*Brat'ia Karamazovy*, 1879–80].) The visit was fruitful, Sofya writes in her diary: "Lev made a visit to Optina Hermitage and returned highly satisfied with the wisdom, learning, and asceticism of the hermits here."

Four years later, Tolstoy again visited Optina Hermitage, this time to observe the monks there mowing, plowing, and engaged in all types of "obedience." After a second talk with Father Ambrose, Tolstoy wrote that his soul "felt light and joyous. When one speaks with such a man, one really feels the presence of God. . . . I am shaken, shaken."

Not unexpectedly, Ambrose was fatigued by Tolstoy's visits but maintained a characteristically firm but gentle hand with his charge. "I have offered you my opinion and advice," Ambrose wrote to Tolstoy after the writer had left the monastery. "But I do not force or seek or convince. You yourself must choose what you wish. The Lord Himself does not force anyone to do anything. He only proposes voluntary selection, saying in the

Gospel: 'If one desires to enter into life . . . and be perfect,' he is to do such and such. Know, though, that these commandments are so obligatory that if one does not fulfill them, one does not attain perfection or inherit the blessed life of the age to come."

At Optina Hermitage, Tolstoy was similarly impressed by another monk named Pimen, who intrigued him in different ways than Ambrose. For instance, Pimen was simple and naive. He always fell asleep whenever people discussed religion, and at the sight of women pilgrims, he would gather up his cassock and run from their sight.

One reason why Tolstoy chose to go to Optina Hermitage in the final days of his life was that he knew that he could get a room there, without presenting papers or a passport telling who he was. See Simmons, *Leo Tolstoy*, 1:369; Leon, *Tolstoy*, 230; Wilson, *Tolstoy*, 293; Nazaroff, *Tolstoy*, 224; Shklovsky, *Lev Tolstoy*, 519, 748.

For more on Optina Hermitage, see S. Chetverikov, *Optina Pustyn. Istoricheskii ocherk i lichnye vospominaniia* (Paris: YMCA Press, 1988); L. Denisov, ed., *Pravoslavnye monastyri rossiskoi imperii* (Moscow: Izdanie A. D. Stupina, 1908), 270–73; J. Dunlop, *Staretz Amvrosy. Model for Dostoevsky's Staretz Zossima* (Belmont: Norland, 1972).

56. By this time, Sofya had grown suspicious (and nervous) over the existence of a new will governing Tolstoy's literary estate. She had every reason to be distressed: Publishers were offering as much as one million rubles for a complete edition of her husband's works! As a result, Sofya regularly searched Tolstoy's quarters not only for this document but also for several of her husband's diaries and papers, which Tolstoy had promised to give to Chertkov and which, she feared, represented her in a bad light.

For instance, in 1894, she recorded: "He has no heart. He loves nobody. He is as cold as ice. . . . People will read his diaries and will say that I am a wicked woman. And what have I done?" Later, she wrote to a friend: "Biographers always distort the private life of their subjects. I am sure that they will make me out to be [Socrates' shrewlike wife] Xantippe. You must defend me!"

Tolstoy empathized with his wife's distress. For instance, in 1897, he wrote: "On my advice, Sonya has read my diary, and she was very upset at the fact that later people may think that she has been a bad wife. I tried to calm her." In another excerpt, he added: "Sofya has an idée fixe—vanity. She is afraid that people will say that she has spoiled my life, and with all her might, she wishes to prove the opposite—that she alone is good, and all the rest are scoundrels and liars." See Leon, *Tolstoy*, 330, 331; Wilson, *Tolstoy*, 509; Shklovsky, *Lev Tolstoy*, 739; Simmons, *Leo Tolstoy*, 2:299.

57. Tolstoy had long felt constrained by what he considered as Sofya's undue meddling in his literary and personal affairs. For instance, he wrote

in 1863: "Nearly all that I have written in this diary is lies—falseness. The thought that Sofya is always there to read over my shoulder restrains me and prevents me from being honest. . . . I must add some words for her, for she will read this. For her I write not what is true but what would I write if I wrote for myself alone." See Leon, *Tolstoy,* 123.

58. Tolstoy, though, did conceal his indignation from his wife. In fact, after she had left him, he attempted to continue with *The Brothers Karamazov,* which he had been reading before he had fallen asleep.

Bunin, almost neurotically hateful toward Dostoevsky, was quite distressed to learn that Tolstoy was reading *Karamazov* in the last days of his life. For instance, on November 8, 1947, he wrote to Adamovich:

> [In one of your articles] you state that Tolstoy, in his final years, turned to *The Brothers Karamazov* for his bedtime reading. Where did you get that from? I have before me a huge volume of Tolstoy's 1910 diaries . . . [in which he writes] that these 'brothers' are artificial and border on pulp fiction.
>
> Also take what Tolstoy wrote on October 12, 1910. "I have read Dostoevsky's *Brothers Karamazov.* What joking trifles he has in there: verbose, artificial, and not very funny." Also, in an entry written six days later, he continued: "I am reading Dostoevsky, and I am amazed by his slovenliness, artificiality, and fabrications."
>
> It is quite possible that *The Brothers Karamazov* was one of the last books that Tolstoy read. But what will a reader think after he reads what you wrote? Tolstoy's bedtime reading? How can you possibly say a thing like that?

Incidentally, at Sharmardino, Tolstoy asked his daughter Alexandra to send him the second volume of *The Brothers Karamazov.* See Baboreko, "I. A. Bunin o L. N. Tolstom," 165–78; A. Zweers, "Pis'ma I. Bunina k G. Adamovicha," 168. Also see Leon, *Tolstoy,* 350; Troyat, *Tolstoy,* 671.

59. *Bunin's note:* Doctor Dushan Makovitsky was a local doctor, friend, and follower of Tolstoy.

Editors' note: Dushan Makovitsky was a Slovak who, while a medical student in Prague, had read Tolstoy's moral and religious works and had become a convinced follower. Makovitsky had served as Tolstoy's doctor since the writer's illness in the Crimea. A pale, diminutive, and anemic-looking individual, Makovitsky left much to be desired as a doctor; but as someone who was also meek, humble, and self-effacing, he quickly endeared himself to Tolstoy. For instance, when Makovitsky left Tolstoy for a month's visit to his native land, the writer complained: "But how am I to live without Dushan? . . . I tell you quite frankly, I do not need his medicine, but when I do not see his hat here for a day or two, I somehow or other feel completely lost. Holy Dushan!"

Makovitsky did have his faults, though, his most glaring being that he was a vicious anti-Semite who could rattle off statistics allegedly proving the superiority of the Slavs over the Jews. He also had devised a system of notation whereby he could write down Tolstoy's every word. Because of this system, wrote Tolstoy's daughter Alexandra, "we were deprived of the great joy of having a private life, of talking nonsense, of singing and joking, of not having to be carerful of everything. Instead, we knew that every word we spoke and every gesture we made would be recorded on the spot." See Simmons, *Leo Tolstoy,* 2:203, 372–73; Troyat, *Tolstoy,* 607–8.

60. For all his distress, though, Tolstoy did manage to write a farewell letter to his wife. He wrote:

> I know that my going away will grieve you, and I am sorry for such a thing. But please believe and understand that there is nothing else for me to do. My position in the house is becoming, and has become, unbearable. And apart from everything else, I can no longer live in the luxurious conditions in which I have lived until now. I am simply doing what old men of my age often do. I am withdrawing from the world to lead the last days of my life in solitude and peace. Please try to understand my actions, and even if you should learn where I am, do not follow me.
>
> Your coming would not alter my decision and could only made my position worse for both of us. I thank you for your honorable forty-eight years of life with me, and I beg you to forgive me for everything in which I have been to blame before you, as I, from my entire soul, forgive you for everything in which you may have been of blame toward me. My advice is that you should reconcile yourself to this new situation in which my leaving places you, and that you do not harbor any unkind feelings toward me. If you wish to send me something, give it to [our daughter] Sasha. She will know where I am and forward what is necessary. But she cannot tell you where I am because she has promised not to tell anyone.

See Leon, *Tolstoy,* 351.

61. Tolstoy is referring to Varvara Mikhailovna Feokritova, a companion of Alexandra Tolstaya and a copier for Sofya Andreevna Tolstaya. Feokritova had joined Alexandra and Chertkov against Sofya and her sons in the struggle for Tolstoy's literary estate. For instance, she once wrote down Sofya's remarks as to what Sofya would do with Tolstoy's literary heritage after his death. Feokritova then passed this information to Tolstoy himself. See Simmons, *Leo Tolstoy,* 2:483.

62. The village of Shchyokino is roughly 125 miles directly south of Moscow and several miles south of Yasnaya Polyana. Initially, the plan of Tolstoy and company was to make a series of short stops in various places so that Sofya would have no idea as to their whereabouts. See Shklovsky, *Lev Tolstoy,* 748.

63. Gorbachyovo is located about 30 miles directly south of Yasnaya Polyana. When Tolstoy and company left the estate, they sought to confuse anyone who might follow them by buying tickets for each separate stage of the journey. The stratagem failed, though, since Tolstoy's flight from Yas-

naya Polyana quickly became public, with both journalists and the police in hot pursuit of the group. (Within hours of Tolstoy's escape, headlines screaming "LEO TOLSTOY LEAVES YASNAYA POLYANA" graced newspapers in Moscow and Saint Petersburg.)

Also, passengers on the train quickly learned of Tolstoy's presence and acted accordingly. One individual courteously offered him the loan of his house; others entered his carriage to steal a look at him; still others engaged him in animated discussions ranging from pacifism and nonviolence to the shortcomings of modern science and education and to the single-tax system of the American economist Henry George. At Gorbachyovo, a police detective boarded the train and kept Tolstoy and his party under constant surveillance. It was also on the train from Gorbachyovo that Tolstoy first read newspaper accounts of his flight. See Leon, *Tolstoy,* 356; Simmons, *Leo Tolstoy,* 2:499.

64. Tolstoy fails to mention that this third-class coach was so overheated, smoky, and crowded with people that he spent most of his time on the open platform outside the train car. In his memoirs, Makovitsky testified that the coach was the worst he had ever traveled on in Russia. See Leon, *Tolstoy,* 352; Shklovsky, *Lev Tolstoy,* 746.

65. All in all, the 100-mile trip from Yasnaya Polyana to Optina Hermitage took over six hours, a journey that Makovitsky found exhausting. It should also be noted that Tolstoy had only 39 rubles on his person and Makovitsky only 300 rubles. See Wilson, *Tolstoy,* 510; Shklovsky, *Lev Tolstoy,* 743, 747.

66. Novocherkassk is a city approximately 750 miles south of Moscow. Tolstoy's plan was to go to a nephew there who would obtain passports for the group to go abroad to Bulgaria or to join Tolstoyan sympathizers either on the Black Sea or in Bessarabia or the Caucasus.

67. Shamardino is located about 10 miles to the northeast of the city of Kozel'sk, about 200 miles southwest of Moscow. Father Ambrose of Optina Hermitage founded a convent there in 1884. Later, Sharmadino also featured a monastery hostel where Tolstoy stayed during his flight.

68. At the time of Tolstoy's escape, Masha was eighty years old.

69. Compare *Moravskie brat'ia* (Moravian Brothers) with *Muraveinye brat'ia* (Ant Brothers). The Moravian Brothers, or, more accurately, the Unity of Brethren (*Unitas Fratrum*), were fifteenth-century followers of the religious reformer Jan Hus.

Tolstoy later ventured that his brother Nikolai had read or heard of the Freemasons, particularly their mysterious rites of initiation and their hopes for the happiness of humankind.

70. At the time of the "Ant Brothers," Tolstoy was five years old.

71. Zakaz was a patch of thick woods on the edge of Tolstoy's estate.

72. Later, in his *Recollections,* Tolstoy wrote: "The ideal not only of Ant Brothers clinging lovingly to one another under two armchairs curtained by shawls, but of all the people of the world under the wide dome of heaven, has remained unaltered for me. As I then believed that there was a little green stick on which was written something which would destroy all evil in men and give them great blessings, so I now believe that such truth exists among people and that it will be revealed to them and will give them what it promises."

Also, two years before his death, Tolstoy dictated to his secretary, Nikolai Gusev: "Although it is a trifling matter, I wish to say something that I should like done after my death, even though it is a trifle of trifles. Let no ceremonies be performed in putting my body into the earth. A wooden coffin, and whoever wishes, carry or cart it to Zakaz, opposite the ravine at the place of the 'green stick.' At least, there's a reason for selecting that and no other place." Gusev observed that when Tolstoy mentioned the green stick, tears filled the writer's eyes. See Simmons, *Leo Tolstoy,* 1:24.

73. Bunin is quoting from the memoirs of Tolstoy's daughter Alexandra as they first appeared in the journal *Contemporary Notes* (*Sovremennye zapiski*) in 1932.

74. The struggle between Sofya and Chertkov over Tolstoy's literary legacy is one of the ugliest chapters in the writer's life. Both combatants were fanatics: practical and powerful, determined and strong willed. Both were guilty of grave breaches of ethics and decorum; both turned Tolstoy's last years into a living hell.

In truth, trouble had been brewing between Sofya and Chertkov for years. Sofya was rightfully jealous of Chertkov's influence over her husband. For instance, she wrote in 1887: "I do not like Chertkov. He is . . . clever, one-sided, and sly. Lev Nikolaevich is very partial to him because of his adulation."

Sofya was fully justified in her fears. Unlike herself, Chertkov had been a thirty-year disciple of Tolstoy's ideas and ideals. He had also been her husband's confidante and the son that Tolstoy had never had. Tolstoy's daughter Alexandra called Chertkov the "tsar of the Tolstoyans"; his son Ilya saw him as a "typical ex-calvary officer of Christiandom." The labels were valid. For instance, Chertkov ran his estate according to Tolstoyan principles. Masters and servants worked and ate together. In fact, Chertkov had his family observe such extreme simplicity of life that his obedient son, Dima, often went about unwashed and unkempt.

Even more distressing for Sofya, perhaps, Chertkov enjoyed the marital bliss that she and Tolstoy lacked. Several days after she professed her dislike for Chertkov, Sofya added: "I reread a letter by Chertkov in which he spoke of the happy spiritual communion between himself and his wife.

He also expressed his sympathy and regret that such a worthy man as Leo Nikolaevich should be ignorant of such happiness and be deprived of such a communion—an obvious allusion to me. . . . Chertkov is trying to destroy the bond which has so closely kept my husband and myself together for nearly twenty-five years! (I suppose that that is Christian!)"

In their battle over Tolstoy's literary estate, Sofya and Chertkov were victims of self-protection and self-projection. For Sofya, the issue was personal and familial. She wished to provide for her family after her husband's death. She also wanted to preserve for herself and the world the life-illusion that she had been Tolstoy's muse, the "devoted nurse of his talent," and that her time with him had been one of sacrifice, even martyrdom, at his hands. In a sense, Sofya was like a character from Dostoevsky: If she were robbed of her idée fixe, her life would have crumbled before her eyes.

For the well-to-do Chertkov, the issue was philosophical. In his view, for Tolstoy to leave his literary legacy not to the world but to his family, to be sold an exorbitant sum, would be to defame and degrade the writer's work and, more important perhaps, to legitimate the claims of hypocrisy that Tolstoy's enemies had leveled against him throughout his life. Like Sofya, Chertkov felt he had to win the struggle; as Tolstoy's most loyal disciple and disseminator of his ideas and ideals, he, too, could not face a life in ashes.

In the final years of Tolstoy's life, bitter wrangling between Sofya and Chertkov over Tolstoy's will, copyrights, diaries, and the publication of the writer's works separately and in collected editions both at home and abroad were common, even daily, events. In one ugly scene, Chertkov told Sofya that if she had been his wife, he would long ago have either shot himself or escaped to America.

Sofya's stance toward Chertkov was equally regrettable. For instance, she wanted "to kill Chertkov or to stick something into his bloated body to release the soul of Lev Nikolaevich." One time, Sofya sprinkled holy water to exorcize Chertkov's spirit from her home. Another time, she fired a pistol at a portrait of her opponent. (To her regret, she learned that the pistol was a toy.) Even more bizarre, perhaps, Sofya would often stalk Tolstoy to ensure that he was not meeting secretly with Chertkov. She even construed a 1851 diary excerpt in which Tolstoy had written that he "had been in love with men" to mean that after forty-eight years of marriage, her eighty-two-year-old husband was having sexual relations with a fifty-six-year-old man! For more on the struggle between Sofya and Chertkov, see Leon, *Tolstoy*, 254–55, 320–24, 329–30, 337; Wilson, *Tolstoy*, 508.

75. Although the marriage between Tolstoy and Sofya was often rife with bitterness and dissent, the domestic strife in the last years of the writer's life bordered on the surreal. Struggles over copyrights, property, works, diaries, and editions were flashpoints for bitterness and reproach. Long-

standing resentments and hurts, even occasional hand-to-hand combat, brought the marriage to a breaking point. "Between us there is a struggle to the death," Tolstoy once wrote to his wife.

Increasingly, the mentally distraught Sofya alternated between bouts of frenzy and raving and bizarre attempts to exert power and control over her husband and others. Daily lamentations and complaints, uncontrolled weeping and shrieking, suicide threats and attempts, violent scenes (public and private), and other shameless and sadomasochistic behavior were such common fare that members of the family threatened to remove Tolstoy from the premises. "If he leaves," Sofya commented, "I will print a death letter in the newspapers about all that he has done [to me]. Then I will poison myself and disgrace him all over Russia."

Sofya's children often became so alarmed by their mother's imbalance that they insisted that she see a psychiatrist. (The doctor diagnosed paranoia and "psychopathic nervo-psychic hysteria," but treatment proved ineffective.)

Revealingly, Sofya knew that she was not well, that she was "like Eve, despicably bad," and that she was driving Tolstoy from their home. In July 1910, she wrote to her husband:

> I am writing to you because it is difficult to speak after a sleepless night. I am too agitated. During the night I thought it over—how you caressed me with one hand and held a knife to me in the other. Even yesterday I realized obscurely that this knife has already entered my heart. This knife is the threat that you will leave me secretly if I remain what I am now, that is, a woman who is unquestionably ill. It means that every night I shall be listening to hear whether you are going away, and that at every prolonged absence I shall be tortured. . . . You know that I am really ill and must admit—as I do—that I am insane. Forgive and help me!

Perhaps even more telling, Sofya knew that she was killing her husband. Several weeks before Tolstoy left Yasnaya Polyana, Sofya told her daughter Alexandra: "I am suffering more than you. You are losing a father, but I am losing a husband for whose death I am responsible."

Tolstoy could only concur. He recorded: "If only Sofya knew and understood how she alone poisons the last hours, days, and months of my life." Later, he wrote: "It is difficult with everyone. I cannot but desire death."

Bunin concurred. For instance, in a diary excerpt written on May 2, 1943, he wrote: "I continue to read a French translation of the diaries of S. A. Tolstaya. She really is possessed!" See Grin, *Ustami Buninykh*, 3:148. Also see Leon, *Tolstoy*, 319, 335, 342, 343, 347; Nazaroff, *Tolstoy*, 230; Troyat, *Tolstoy*, 443.

76. Tolstoy was constantly tormented by the fact that he was a "have" amidst "have-nots." For instance, he wrote in 1881: "A [peasant] woman had a baby at her breast, three daughters, and no food. . . . [But] we had a

huge dinner with champagne. . . . All the children wore sashes, costing five rubles apiece. . . . Our carriage was already bound for picnic, passing peasant carts carrying toil-worn people."

A year later, Tolstoy asked: "Why do the servants cook . . . and serve, while gentlemen gorge, defecate, and eat again?" And, in mid-February 1910, he similarly noted: "[I have] tormenting pangs caused by the consciousness of my vile life, surrounded as I am by working people scarcely able to keep themselves and their families from starvation. In our dining room, fifteen people are gorging themselves on pancakes, while five or six servants who have families are running about hardly able to serve up what we devour." See Leon, *Tolstoy*, 327–28; Biryukov, *Leo Tolstoy*, 92, 264; Shklovsky, *Lev Tolstoy*, 515; Troyat, *Tolstoy*, 433; Simmons, *Leo Tolstoy*, 2:90, 374.

77. Bunin is referring to Jean Paul Friedrich Richter's first major novel, *The Invisible Lodge* (*Die Unsichtbare Loge*), written in 1793.

78. Tolstoy wrote in his diary on October 30, 1891: "I now know for certain that copulation is an abomination which, only under the influence of sexual desire, can be accomplished without revulsion. Even to have children, a man should not do such a thing to the woman he loves." Years later, he continued: "Sexual love . . . is a service of self and consequently . . . an obstacle to the service of God and man. . . . From the Christian viewpoint, it is a sin."

Tolstoy took his alleged disgust with sex into his fiction as well. For instance, he wrote in *The Kreutzer Sonata:* "The strongest passion of all, the most perfidious, the most stubborn, is sexual passion, carnal love. . . . As long as humankind shall endure, its ideal [must] not be that of rabbits and swine, who multiply as often as possible, or of Parisians or apes, who enjoy sexual pleasure with the highest possible refinement."

Sofya, of course, could only look upon her husband's demands for chastity in marriage with a bitter smile. She once remarked: "If those who read *The Kreutzer Sonata* with veneration could look for a moment at the erotic life that Lyovochka leads—the one thing that makes him happy and kind—they would cast down this little god from the pedestal on which they have placed him!"

Immediately prior to Tolstoy's escape from Yasnaya Polyana, Sofya added: "At my husband's wish, I have been pregnant sixteen times: thirteen children born and three miscarriages. In those days he suggested to me, a young woman, that he could not work, write, or be healthy if I refused to cohabit with him."

For all his protestations against sex, Tolstoy knew well its enduring power and allure. For instance, even at age seventy-two, he was so still tormented by the need for physical love that, in classical Tolstoyan manner, he sought to constrain it with a set of "rules." He wrote: "The best thing one can do with the sexual drive is (1) to destroy it utterly in oneself. The *next best* [thing] is (2) to live with one woman who has a chaste nature and shares your faith. The *next worse* [thing] is (3) to go to a brothel when you are tormented by desire; (4) to have brief relations with different women, remaining with none; (5) to have intercourse with a young girl and abandon her; (6) worse yet, to have intercourse with another man's wife; and (7) worst of all, to live with a faithless and immoral woman." See Simmons, *Leo Tolstoy,* 1:134, 157, 181, 2:481. Also see Wilson, *Tolstoy,* 391; Nazaroff, *Tolstoy,* 273, 274; Troyat, *Tolstoy,* 478, 558.

79. The book in question is V. Bulgakov, *U Tolstogo v poslednii god ego zhizni. Dnevnik sekrtaria L. N. Tolstogo V. F. Bulgakova* (Moscow: Zadruga, 1918). The work was translated into English as *The Last Year of Leo Tolstoy* by Dial Press in 1971.

80. Bunin is quoting Tolstoy out of context. On June 22, 1910, Bulgakov wrote:

Lev Nikolaevich spoke out against the obligatory nature of those Gospel texts which had been misinterpreted.
[He said:] "I do not want to say this, but I will: Earlier I used to love the Gospel, but now I do not."
We then read a splendid passage from the Gospels, but with the interpretation of Lev Nikolaevich.
"I have again grown fond of the Gospel," he said smiling.

See Bulgakov, *U Tolstogo v poslednii god ego zhizni,* 275.

81. Tolstoy's regrets over his ambition rivaled his breast-beating over his obsession with sex. For instance, in his 1855 story "Notes of a Billiard Maker" ("Zapiski markera"), Tolstoy confessed: "There is one thing I love more than goodness: fame. I am so ambitious, and this craving in me has had so little satisfaction that if I had to choose between fame and virtue, I am afraid that I would very often choose the former."

Three years later, Tolstoy continued in a letter to Fet: "For me the height of wisdom and fortitude would be to enjoy the meditations of other men and not to let my own go forth into the world in ugly garb. . . . But then, at times, one suddenly feels the ambition to be a great man, and how annoying it is that nothing as yet has brought such a thing about. One even makes haste to rise earlier and to finish dinner so as to begin."

It was toward the end of his life that the world-weary Tolstoy could see the burden of international fame; that is, it was one of those "epidemic mental diseases to which men have always been subject." See Simmons, *Leo Tolstoy,* 1:133, 314–15; Crankshaw, *Tolstoy,* 104; Dole, *The Life of Count Tolstoi,* 131; Nazaroff, *Tolstoy,* 266.

82. In matters both good and bad, Tolstoy's pride often assumed epidemic proportions. At age twenty-five (1853), he wrote:

Once and for all, I must become accustomed to the idea that I am an exception and ahead of my age, or else that I am one of those incompatible, unadaptable natures that are never satisfied. I must set a different standard (lower than my own) and measure people by that. In this way, I will less often be mistaken. I have long deceived myself imagining that I have friends who understood me. Nonsense! I have never yet met a single man who was as morally good as I.

Tolstoy, though, was clever and honest enough to see the reasons for such vanity. He wrote in 1852:

Vanity is an unintelligible passion, one of those evils like involuntarily diseases, hunger, locusts, and war, with which Providence is wont to punish humanity. The sources of vanity lie beyond discovery; but the causes which develop it are idleness, luxury, and absence of privation or cares. Vanity constitutes a kind of moral sickness which, like leprosy, destroys no definite part, but which renders monstrous the whole. It creeps in gradually and imperceptibly until it has permeated the entire organism. There is not a function that vanity does not poison. It is like syphilis—when driven out of one part, it reappears, with added force, in another. The vain man knows neither joy, nor grief, nor love, nor fear, nor hatred, nor despair. Everything in him is unnatural and forced.

Vanity is a sort of immature love and *éclat,* a sort of love of self transferred to the opinion of others. One loves oneself not for what one is, but for what one appears to be. In our age, this passion is developed to an excess; and, although men deride it, they do not condemn it because it does no harm to others. But, for the man whom such a feeling possesses, vanity is a passion worse than any other, for it poisons his entire existence.

See Leon, *Tolstoy,* 39, 44.

83. In truth, and as he later came to realize, Tolstoy's concern for society included a healthy dose of self. He wrote in 1852:

There is something in me that obliges me to believe that I was not born to be what other men are. But whence does this proceed? From a lack of agreement, an absence of harmony among my faculties, or from the fact that I really stand on a higher level than ordinary people? I am older, and the time for development is past or is passing. I am tortured with a thirst not for fame— I have no desire for fame and despite it—but for acquiring great influence for the happiness and benefit of society. But shall I die with this wish a hopeless one?

See Simmons, *Leo Tolstoy,* 1:96.

CHAPTER THREE

1. Makovitsky's notes were first published in a multivolume edition entitled *Iasnopolianskie zapiski, 1904–1910 gg. (Notes at Yasnaya Polyana, 1904–1910)* in Moscow in 1922.

2. Kursk is a city roughly 750 miles south of Moscow.

3. Oryol is a city approximately 235 miles southwest of Moscow.

4. Kozel'sk is located about 75 miles southwest of Kaluga. From Gorbachyovo, Tolstoy and company were thus heading northwest to their destination.

5. After a fairly raucous and adventuresome life, Maria Nikolaevna Tolstaya entered the convent at Shamardino in 1889. She was fifty-nine years old.

6. When he left Yasnaya Polyana, Tolstoy had asked Alexandra to remain behind until he sent for her. Tolstoy also dispatched a letter and a telegram to Chertkov, telling him of his whereabouts. The very next morning, Tolstoy received a letter from Chertkov, saying:

> I cannot put into words the joy I felt that you have gone away. With my entire being, I feel that this is what you should have done, and that it would have been wrong for you to continue living at Yasnaya Polyana with things as they were.
>
> I only think that you waited too long, fearing to act out of self-interest. But there was no selfishness in the force that compelled you to make your decision. To be sure, you will often find your new life to be simpler and more pleasant and peaceful . . . but you must not let that trouble you. I am convinced that your action will be a source of relief to all, and most of all, to Sofya Andreevna, however she may react.

In truth, Chertkov had long supported Tolstoy's plans to leave his home. "You say that you live in an atmosphere that is completely hostile to your faith," he once wrote to the writer. "Therefore it is entirely natural that, from time to time, you should have made plans to go away. . . . But this does not mean that you are weak or bad." Citing the example of Christ, Chertkov concluded that if Tolstoy had done everything in his power to correct the life of his family but had failed, he would be justified in leaving his home to live the life he desired. See Wilson, *Tolstoy*, 509, 510; Troyat, *Tolstoy*, 673; Simmons, *Leo Tolstoy*, 2:87.

7. During the last months of his life, Tolstoy kept a very detailed record of both external and internal events. "What I wish to do," he had told Biryukov some time previously, "is to try to note everything that I think and feel, every hour, every moment of my life. People will read what I have written later; and they will refuse to believe that Tolstoy thought of such trifles. [They will see that] along with serious philosophical thoughts, I often caught myself suddenly thinking: 'I hope someone will not take and eat my orange.'" See Leon, *Tolstoy*, 327.

8. The morning after Tolstoy's arrival at Sharmadino, he found a widow who was willing to rent him a hut for three rubles a month.

Tolstoy's yearning to remain at Sharmadino was not the first time that he had wished to escape to a religious sanctuary. For instance, after a government raid on Yasnaya Polyana in 1862, he wanted to shut himself away in a monastery not to pray to God—"a waste of time," he said—but simply "not to see all the nastiness of world, debauchery, and pompous self-complacency in epaulettes and crinolines." Fifteen years later, Tolstoy confided to the bishop of Tula that he wanted to be a monk.

To Sofya, too, Tolstoy confessed his love of monasteries. For instance, during their courtship, he advised her: "Don't go poking your nose into youth and poetry and beauty and love. . . . The monastery—work, there's your vocation. From its summit you can look, calmly and contentedly, down upon the love and happiness of others. I have lived in that monastery, and I shall go back to it."

Tolstoy's wish to enter religious life (and his regret that he had not done so) only increased with time. For instance, in 1908, he told a friend: "I ought to have gone into a monastery. In truth, if I had not married, I would have entered one." See Simmons, *Leo Tolstoy,* 1:252, 2:405, 432; Troyat, *Tolstoy,* 243–44, 392, 675.

9. The Dukhobors, or "Spirit Wrestlers," were an extreme, Protestant, and communal sect that originated in the second half of the eighteenth century and that included peasants from the regions around Voronezh, Tambov, Ekaterinslav, Kharkov, and Kursk.

Tolstoy was attracted to the Dukhobors because their beliefs often accorded with his own. For instance, the Dukhobors posited that the world was the site of an eternal struggle between the spirit and flesh and, in human form, between the followers of Abel and the disciples of Cain. The Dukhobors, of course, considered themselves to be the followers of Abel, that is, they were a chosen nation-race whom God had called upon to condemn violence and to build peace and brotherhood on earth. They also held that the disciples of Cain included the rich as well as secular and religious authorities, particularly corrupt judges.

As regards religious beliefs, the Dukhobors had much in common with Tolstoy. For instance, they rejected the Bible and favored direct individual revelation. They did not recognize priests, the sacraments, or any rites or rituals other than those of marriage. Their own ceremony was a meeting (*sobranie*) at which they chanted prayers around a table with bread, salt, and water. The Dukhobors also maintained a so-called Book of Life, a growing oral body of canticles and proverbs. Furthermore, the Dukhobors advocated what Tolstoy considered to be true Christian values: charity, humility, resignation, and, most important, patience and fortitude in the face of groups who were hostile to their images and ideals.

The Dukhobors were a particular thorn in the side of the Russian government. The group's proselytizing, together with their objections to military conscription and their pacificist and egalitarian beliefs, provoked sporadic persecution by the government. From 1773 onward, the Dukhobors were periodically deported to uninhabited regions in Russia.

In the late nineteenth century, though, the Dukhobors had a champion in Tolstoy. They not only endorsed Tolstoy's principles of moral and spiritual reform, but they also benefited from the writer's special patronage. The admiration was mutual. For instance, Tolstoy believed that the Dukhobors had actually realized the ideal for which he and his own followers were striving. He even declared that the group was "the germination of the seed sown by Christ himself eighteen hundred and eighty years ago."

As a result, Tolstoy defended the Dukhobors in print; he also publicly appealed to the tsar to stop the persecution of its members and to allow them to leave Russia. Also, having learned that he was being considered as a candidate for the Nobel Prize in literature, Tolstoy asked that the money for the award be given to Dukhobors, because, in his view, they had done more to advance the cause of peace than he had.

Tolstoy was successful in his quest. In 1898, the Russian government allowed Duhkobors to leave the country.

Although some 12,000 Dukhobors remained in Russia, some 7,500 other members of the sect, funded by English Quakers as well by the proceeds of Tolstoy's novel *Resurrection,* reached Canada in 1899.

Not everyone was pleased with Tolstoy's generosity. For instance, Sofya wrote: "It is more than I can grasp with my mind or my heart . . . that the money [from Leo's writing] will be given not to his grandchildren, who have no white bread to eat, and not to his starving children, but to those completely alien Dukhobors, whom I simply cannot love more than my children! The entire world will know how Tolstoy helped the Dukhobors, and the newspapers and history will praise him for what he has done! But black bread will do for his children and grandchildren."

The Russian government, along with various religious and nationalist groups, was also angry at Tolstoy for aiding the Dukhobors. In 1898, one group, bearing the name "Second Crusaders," actually threatened to murder the writer because he had offended "our Lord Jesus Christ" and was an "enemy of the tsar and the fatherland."

In part because of Tolstoy's patronage and protection, the Dukhobors found imitators in France, England, Holland, Germany and Switzerland. Agricultural community-colonies flourished, Christian publications increased, and vegetarianism become popular. Although the influence of the Dukhobors declined with time, descendants of the group exist today. See Crankshaw, *Tolstoy,* 268; Biryukov, *Leo Tolstoy,* 131–34; Dole, *The Life of Count Tolstoy,* 353–59; Shklovsky, *Lev Tolstoy,* 649; Troyat, *Tolstoy*, 538; Simmons, *Leo Tolstoy,* 2:236, 244–45.

10. In her memoirs, Maria wrote that Tolstoy committed a fatal error when he informed Alexandra of his new location, since he could have found at least temporary respite from his troubles at Optina Hermitage. See Wilson, *Tolstoy,* 511.

11. Tolstoy and company left Shamardino for fear that Sofya, once she learned of her husband's whereabouts, would pursue him there.

12. Alexei Ksyunin wrote *Ukhod Tolstogo* (*The Departure of Tolstoy*) in 1911.

13. Bunin's comments notwithstanding, evidence for Tolstoy's last-minute reconciliation with the church is slim. For instance, Tolstoy's sister, Maria, wrote to a reporter on January 16, 1911: "What was my brother looking for at Optina Hermitage? Was it a father confessor or a sage who, living with his conscience and in solitude with God, could have understood him and somehow lightened the burden of his great sorrow? No, I do not think that my brother sought such a thing. His sorrow was too complicated; he simply wanted to find peace and live for a time in quiet and spiritual surroundings. I do not think that he wanted to return to the Orthodox faith."

Tolstoy was well aware that the Russian Orthodox Church—and Sofya—would do everything in their power to reclaim him as a law-abiding "Christian." He continually resisted all attempts to being him back to the fold. For instance, although seriously ill in 1902, Tolstoy remarked: "A quiet death under the influence of the rites of the church is like death under morphine."

Also, when in 1909, a year before his actual passing, Tolstoy learned that Parfeny, the bishop of Tula, was secretly conversing with Sofya at Yasnaya Polyana, Tolstoy wrote in his diary: "I found it especially disagreeable that [the bishop] had asked Sofya to inform him when I die. It is as though the two of them are planning to convince people that I had 'repented' before my death. Therefore I declare that . . . anything that they may say about my repentance and communion before death is a lie. . . . On this occasion, I also repeat that I be buried without divine services and that my body be laid in the earth so that it will not stink." See Dole, *The Life of Count Tolstoi*, 407–8; Shklovsky, *Lev Tolstoy*, 764; Simmons, *Leo Tolstoy*, 2:319, 432–33.

14. Bunin's statements as regards Sofya's reaction to her husband's departure are true. When she reached the perilously deep pond, Sofya ran down a planked footway, slipped, and fell on her back. She then turned over and rolled into the water. Alexandra, seeing her floundering mother, jumped in after her and, together with Bulgakov, lifted her to the shore.

Tolstoy was unmoved by his wife's attempt to take her life. In his letter to Alexandra, he wrote: "If anyone would wish to drown, it is certainly not she, but I. Let her know that I desire only one thing—freedom from her . . . and the hatred which fills her entire being."

Sofya's attempts at suicide in the last days of Tolstoy's existence were not the first time that she tried to take her life. (She later admitted that such attempts were a weapon in her struggle with her husband.) In late August 1882, Sofya was so distressed by Tolstoy's wish to leave his family that she wrote in her diary: "I am begging God to let me die, for I cannot live without [my husband's] love. It is the same love which I have given him for all these twenty years. . . . If he does not return home, I will know that he loves another woman." She then plunged into a pond of ice-cold water, "hoping to catch a cold and die." Her hopes unrealized, Sofya returned home to nurse her youngest child.

Six years later, she continued: "[My husband] is killing me very systematically. . . . I want to kill myself, to fall in love with someone—anything only not to live with the man whom I have loved all my life."

Sofya's flirtations with suicide could be as dramatic as they were varied. She often threatened to poison herself (with opium, ammonia) and lay down in wet grass. At times, Sofya was Anna Karenina come to life. She wrote: "I have spasms in my throat again, and I felt like weeping all day long. I feel *so sorry for myself* . . . that I have been seriously thinking of bidding farewell to everyone and lying down on the railway line." Other times, she stumbled about in the snow, styling herself as the innkeeper in *Master and Man.* "I liked the death of Vasily Andreevich," she noted, "and I wanted to meet my end in the same way."

Tolstoy used Sofya's threats and attempts at suicide as material for his works. For instance, in his play *The Lights Shines in Darkness,* the female protagonist, Maria Ivanovna, seeks revenge for her husband's wish to leave their family by threatening throw herself under a train. See Leon, *Tolstoy,* 221, 224, 252, 253, 255, 256, 258; Wilson, *Tolstoy,* 511; Shklovsky, *Lev Tolstoy,* 719; Troyat, *Tolstoy,* 506; Simmons, *Leo Tolstoy,* 1:135.

15. Sofya also threatened to throw herself into a well. See Troyat, *Tolstoy,* 673.

16. Sofya had written to her husband: "Lyovochka, my dear one, darling, return home! Save me from a second suicide, Lyovochka, my lifelong friend. I will do everything, everything that you wish! I will give up luxury, and your friends will be my friends. I will undergo a cure, and I will be mild, tender, and kind. So come back to me. You must save me. You know that it is said in the Gospels that a man must never abandon his wife. My dear, my darling, friend of my soul, save me! Return if only to say farewell before our inevitable separation." See Leon, *Tolstoy,* 354.

17. Only a week before leaving Yasnaya Polyana, Tolstoy had entrusted a peasant-sectarian by the name of Mikhail Novikov to find him a hut in which to spend his remaining time on earth. "I shall not die in this house," Tolstoy told him. "I have decided to go away to some lonely place where I shall be quite unknown. Perhaps, I really will come to die in your hut."

Shortly afterward, Tolstoy wrote to Novikov: "Regarding what I told you before you left, I want to ask you that if I should really come to you, could you find me a separate and warm hut in your village so that I should inconvenience you and your family for only a short period of time? I also want to let you know that if I need to telegraph you, I will not so do in my own name, but in that of T. Nikolaev. I await your answer, and press our hand in friendship."

Unfortunately, Tolstoy's letter to Novikov was delayed in the post, and Tolstoy never received a reply.

In truth, it was indeed fortunate that Tolstoy never took up with Novikov, if only because the peasant dealt with his own marital difficulties in a direct and savage way. "My cross is very hard to bear," Tolstoy wrote in his diary one week before he left Yasnaya Polyana forever. "I keep remembering what Novikov told me [about his wife]: 'I took the horsewhip to her, and she got better.'" See Leon, *Tolstoy,* 349; Shklovsky, *Lev Tolstoy,* 741.

18. Tolstoy's letter to Sofya reads:

> For us to meet and, the more so, for me to return home is *now* absolutely impossible. As everyone says, it would be extremely bad for you and terrible for me, for my position would become even worse owing to your excitability and your irritable and morbid state of mind. I advise you to reconcile yourself to what has happened, to settle down in your new situation, and, above all else, to see a doctor and receive medication.
>
> If you—I do not say love me, but at least do not hate me, you should, at least to some extent, understand my position, if only a little. And if you do that, you will not only not condemn me but will also try to help me to find peace and the possibility of living some sort of human life.
>
> Help me by controlling yourself and not wishing to see me now. But your present mood, your desire and attempts at suicide, show me more than anything else your loss of self-control and, at present, make my return unthinkable. No one but you can free me or all those near to you and, above all, yourself from the sufferings that we are experiencing. . . .
>
> Do not think that I have left home because I do not love you. I love and pity you with all my heart, but I cannot do otherwise than I am doing. I know that your letter was written sincerely, but also that you are not capable of carrying out what you wish to. . . . Coming back to you, in your present state, would be tantamount for me to renouncing life. And I do not feel that I have the right to renounce it.
>
> Farewell, dear Sonya, may God help you! Life is not a joke, and we have no right to throw it away at our own whim. And to measure it by the length of days is also unreasonable. Perhaps the months which remain to us are more important than all the years we have yet lived, and they should be lived well.

See Leon, *Tolstoy,* 355; Shklovsky, *Lev Tolstoy,* 755, 756.

19. The *fortochka* is a small hinged pane in the windows of Russian houses, used for ventilation.

20. Even in the most bitter moments of their marriage, Tolstoy often expressed sympathy for his wife. He prayed to God for patience; he counseled his children to show understanding and love toward their mother. For instance, after an ugly scene with Sofya several months before his departure

from Yasnaya Polyana, Tolstoy wrote in his diary: "Things are worse than I expected. Hysteria and exasperation beyond description. I restrained myself pretty well, but was not gentle enough." He also wrote to his daughter Alexandra: "For God's sake, none of you reproach Mother, but be gentle and good to her."

Even after his flight from Yasnaya Polyana, Tolstoy expressed empathy for his wife. "I wonder how Sofya Andreevna is now?" he said to Makovitsky. "I feel sorrow for her." And as he lay dying, he told his daughter Tanya: "Much has fallen upon Sofya."

Tolstoy, though, was under no illusions about his wife's sickness. For instance, in 1884, he wrote: "Sofya is seriously, mentally ill." Years later, he noted to his secretary: "Sofya Andreevna is ill. . . . It is impossible not to feel sorry for her, and to be as hard on her as Chertkov and many others are, including myself. . . . But she has no reason for her behavior. . . . It is simply that she feels stifled here and cannot breathe. I cannot help pitying her and am glad when I feel able to do so."

Tolstoy held out little hope for Sofya's recovery and/or a change in their relationship. He was convinced that she would remain a "millstone" around his neck until he died. See Simmons, *Leo Tolstoy*, 1:80, 2:481, 495; Leon, *Tolstoy*, 329, 338, 340; Wilson, *Tolstoy*, 348, 507; Troyat, *Tolstoy*, 688.

21. The memoirs of Elizaveta Valerianovna Obolenskaya, a niece of Tolstoy's and the daughter of his sister, Maria, support Bunin's retelling of Tolstoy's visit to Optina Hermitage. She adds:

> When my mother and I heard that Lev Nikolaevich was coming to visit us, we were greatly disturbed. . . . [When I saw him] Tolstoy never seemed so wretched and old. A brown hood covered his head, but his grayish beard stuck out pitifully. The nun who brought him to us . . . later told us that he had staggered on his way to see us. . . . "It is terrible at home!" he told us and then burst out crying. . . .
>
> [The next day] he said: "You have been such a comfort to me, you have brought me such peace that I am even more resolved not to return home. . . . Such a thing would bring about my death. One more scene, one more attack—and that would be the end of me!"

See E. V. Obolenskaia, "Moia mat' i Lev Nikolaevich," in Gusev, *L. N. Tolstoi*, 175.

22. Tolstoyans were members of ethical and religious groups who, inspired by Tolstoy's writings, advocated nonviolence and moral self-improvement. (Both Chertkov and Biryukov were key propagators.)

As a popular movement, Tolstoyism first appeared in Russia in the late 1880s. Groups of men and women settled on the land, lived off manual labor, and, in theory, worked and owned everything in common. Like the Dukhobors, the Tolstoyans quickly found themselves in trouble with both the church and the state: They advocated nonviolence and refused to pay taxes, serve in the army, and swear allegiance to the emperor. Tolstoyans also criticized the doctrines and practices of the Orthodox Church. They rejected such beliefs as the Trinity, the divinity of Christ, miracles, and divine grace; they also spurned the sacraments, liturgy, icons, and fasts.

The response of the Russian government to the Tolstoyans was severe and swift. For instance, in 1897, the ministry of justice designated the Tolstoyans as an "especially harmful sect," a judicial category that made its members liable to severe penalties from the state.

Condemnation from the clergy and its representatives was similarly forthcoming. For instance, Konstantin Pobedonostsev, the vigilant procurator general of the Holy Synod of the Russian Orthodox Church, believed that Tolstoyism was more harmful to church and state that other religious sects because "it subsumed all other sectarian heresies" and "promoted atheism and nihilism in Orthodox Russia." Later, the Third All-Russian Missionary Congress denounced Tolstoyism as a well-defined and noxious movement.

After the Revolution, Tolstoyans established several societies and groups to represent a variety of religious sects in the new Soviet state and, particularly, to champion the right of conscientious objection to military service. (Chertkov appealed to Lenin directly, citing Tolstoy's rejection of any coercion between citizen and state.) Surprisingly, the Tolstoyans were initially successful in their quest. Under Lenin's personal sponsorship, the Soviet government issued a decree on January 4, 1919, allowing citizens to substitute medical service—assisting the sick in wards and hospitals—for time in the military.

With this decree, of course, Tolstoyans easily disseminated their views and gained wide support with the public. More than 40,000 men secured exemption from combat during the Civil War. The successes of Tolstoyans under the Soviet regime were short-lived, though. For instance, in 1924, the Soviet Supreme Court ruled that Tolstoyans could not appeal to the decree on exemptions from military service because they were a "free-thinking ethical group," not a religious sect.

The Tolstoyans also looked to the Revolution of 1917 to pursue their ideal of reorganizing social and economic life on cooperative, communal principles. To the Bolsheviks, they argued that because they and other sectarians were already living in groups and committed to realizing the Kingdom of God on earth, they could help implement Communism in Russia in a relatively quick and easy way. Here the Tolstoyans were only partially successful. Soviet officials, wishing to keep newly established communes under their control, supported a substantial number of collective arrangements under the aegis of Tolstoyans and other sectarians. For instance, one Tolstoyan commune was named World Brotherhood; another was called True Life Science. In fact, in the early years of the Soviet state, sectarian communes were so successful that, in 1923, Bolshevik officials gave a group of Tolstoyans the former New Jerusalem Monastery outside of Moscow; and, at the All-Union Agricultural Exposition in 1927, they awarded this group a prize for their expert production of vegetables.

Unlike the Tolstoyans' early success with exemption from military service, though, their good fortune with communes was not destined to last. For instance, Soviet officials insisted that members of sectarian communes could not restrict their memberships to adherents of a particular creed. They also demanded that such groups expel kulaks and that they embrace such cultural institutions as public schools and the League of Militant Atheists. Despite these difficulties, Tolstoyans and other sectarian groups existed in the former Soviet Union as late as the mid-1930s. (People calling themselves Tolstoyans had also formed short-lived groups in England, Holland, and the United States.)

As an identifiable movement, Tolstoyism ceased to exist mainly because of the deaths of its leaders. Several Tolstoyan-inspired sects, however, still exist in Russia to this day, for example, the Fourth International of the Holy Spirit of Yasnaya Polyana in the province of Tambov.

For more information on Tolstoyism, see A. Klibanov, *A History of Religious Sectarianism in Russia* (New York: Pergamon, 1982), and "Zametki o tolstovstakh," in *Iz mira religioznogo sektanstva: vstrechi, besedy, nabliudeniia* (Moscow: Politizdat, 1974), 114–33. Also see E. Yaroslavskii, *L. N. Tolstoi i tolstovtsy* (Moscow: Gosudarstvennoe antireligioznoe izdatel'stvo, 1938); F. Putintsev, "Tolstoi, tolstovstvo i sektantstvo," *Revoliutsiia i kul'tura,* no. 17 (1928): 17–24. .

23. *Bunin's note:* Tolstoy always talked about Tolstoyan colonies in an unpleasant way: "Saints should not live together. They will all die. But saints should not live alone."

24. Volovo is located about 50 miles to the southeast of Yasnaya Polyana. In truth, Tolstoy and his group were heading more west than south.

25. Rostov-on-the-Don is a city approximately 750 miles south of Moscow.

26. Tolstoy wished to respond to a letter that he had just received from Tanya. It read:

Dear precious Papenka,
   You have always suffered from a great deal of advice, and so I will not give you any. Like everyone else, you have to act as best as you can and as you consider necessary. I shall never condemn you. About Mother, I will only say that she is pitiable and touching. She is unable to live otherwise than she does live, and probably she will never change essentially. For her, either power or fear is necessary. We all try to calm her, and I think that our actions will be beneficial. I am tired and stupid. Forgive me.
   Good-bye, my friend.

Tanya's letter aside, it is easy to see why Tolstoy wanted to write to his daughter. About Tanya, Tolstoy wrote in 1872:

Tanya is now eight years old. . . . Everyone says that she is like her mother, and I believe such a thing, for it is quite obvious. If Tanya had been Adam's eldest child, she would have been a very unhappy girl. Her greatest delight is to look after the little ones. She displays an obvious pleasure in touching their tiny bodies, and her dearest dream is to have children. A few days ago I took Tanya to Tula. . . . . She asked me to buy a knife for Seryozha, something for this one, and something else for another. She knew how to find the exact present that would give each pleasure. As for her, I bought her nothing; and she never thought of herself for a moment. . . . Tanya is not very clever, and she does not like using her mind, though the mechanism for such a thing is good. If God gives her a husband, she will make him an admirable wife. I am ready to offer a prize to anyone who can make a "new woman" of her.

Tolstoy's affection for Tanya only increased with time. For instance, even as a child, Tanya was the only individual in the Tolstoyan household who was permitted to disturb the sanctity of her father's study while he was working on *War and Peace.* Her brother Ilya recalled: "After reading *War and Peace,* my impression was that my sister Tanya, at sixteen, resembled [the heroine] Natasha far more than my aunt [Sofya's sister, Tatyana Bers]. I was amazed to think that my father had written this book when Tanya was a child and that he had predicted her character so accurately."

Ardent, vivacious, intelligent, with brown eyes, waving chestnut hair, and a captivating turned-up nose, Tanya was devoted to and loved by both her parents. She also managed to steer her way between them with resilient ease, helping her mother with the younger children while also attending to her father's continually growing correspondence.

Although Tanya had reservations about her father's faith, she and her sister Masha were the anchors in their father's stormy life. "Tolstoy's daughters are very sympathetic," Chekhov wrote about them in 1895. "They adore their father and believe in him fanatically. [Such devotion] means that Tolstoy really is a great moral force, for if he were not sincere and beyond reproach, his daughters would be the first to be skeptical about him. They are like sparrows; they cannot be deceived with chaff."

Like Tolstoy, Tanya strove for "perfection," cared for the poor, and was a vegetarian. She did cause her father the same disappointment as her sister Masha, however: In 1897, at age thirty-three, she married a decent, but much older, widower with six children. Needless to say, Tolstoy was appalled by the union. He told his daughter:

I can understand that a depraved man may find salvation in marriage. But why a pure girl should want to get mixed up in such a business is beyond me. If I were a girl, I would not get married for anything in the world. And as far as being in love is concerned, for either men or women, I know what that means. [Love] is an ignoble, and above all an unhealthy, sentiment. It is not at all beautiful, lofty, or poetic.

I would never have opened my door to love. I would have taken as many precautions to avoid being contaminated by that disease as I would to protect myself against far less serious infections such as diphtheria, typhus, or scarlet fever.

Just now it seems to you that life is impossible without love. [Such an emotion] is also true of alcoholics and smokers. When such individuals break the habit, though, they discover life as it really is. You have not managed to avoid this intoxication, and now you feel that it is impossible to live without it. And yet it is possible!

Sofya agreed with her husband. "You cannot imagine how grief-stricken and sick at heart both Lyovochka and I were while accompanying Tanya [to the ceremony]. . . . It was all so gloomy, just like a funeral, not a wedding. When Tanya came up to say good-bye to Lyovochka, he wept so hard that it was pitiful to look at him."

Several days later, Tolstoy added in his diary: "Tanya has departed with [her husband] Sukhotin, and why? It is sad and offensive."

Years later, matters between Tolstoy and Tanya continued to be strained. After a visit to Yasnaya Polyana, Tanya wrote: "I am ashamed to have let Papa down, but I cannot feel guilty about it. [When we were together] we did not have much serious conversation. I was afraid that he would tell me that my marriage was a disappointment to him." Tolstoy concurred: "Tanya's frivolity disturbs me," he noted in his diary. "She has embarked on a purely selfish love. I hope that she will return [to me]." See Leon, *Tolstoy*, 167–68, 232–33, 354; Crankshaw, *Tolstoy*, 253; Troyat, *Tolstoy*, 467–68, 525–26, 555; Simmons, *Leo Tolstoy*, 2:298.

27. Tolstoy also wished to respond to a missive that Seryozha had sent to him. It read: "Dear Father, I write because [our sister] Sasha says that you would like to know my and Tanya's opinion [about your leaving]. I think that Mother has a nervous illness, that, in many respects, she is irresponsible, and that, however painful it is for the two of you, you had to separate yourself from her. (Perhaps you should have done it long ago.) I also think that you should not reproach yourself if anything should happen to Mother, though I do not anticipate anything happening to her. Your position was desperate, and I think that you chose the right way out of it. Forgive me for writing so frankly."

Along with his comments about the young Tanya, Tolstoy had written about Seryozha:

Seryozha is fair and quite nice-looking; there is something defenseless, patient, and very sweet in his expression. When he laughs, his laugh is not infectious, but when he weeps, I can scarcely refrain myself from weeping, too. Everyone says that Seryozha is like my eldest brother; but I am afraid to believe it, for it would be too good to be true. Seryozha is intelligent; he has a mathematical mind and is very sensitive to art. He is good at his studies and does gymnastics, but he is awkward and inattentive. He does not have a very resolute personality, since he is too easily influenced by conditions. He is two different boys, depending on whether he is well or ill. . . . Whatever his fate, Seryozha will be a fine boy and certainly the first in his class.

Seryozha was a thoughtful man and a talented musician with a streak of innate goodness and honesty. For instance, when Tolstoy once upbraided the twenty-one-year-old Seryozha for being "rude . . . bourgeois, obtuse, spiteful, and self-satisfied," the boy "suddenly burst out sobbing and started to kiss me, saying, 'Forgive me . . . I am so ashamed.'" Also, during Tolstoy's serious illness in 1902, Sergei attended to Tolstoy's every wish and carried his father in his arms like an infant. See Leon, *Tolstoy,* 167, 353–54; Wilson, *Tolstoy,* 348; Troyat, *Tolstoy,* 576.

28. As a young adult, Seryozha disappointed Tolstoy on many fronts. Socially, he was reserved, awkward, and brutally frank. Intellectually, Seryozha had turned his back on what he was saw as "all that Christian stuff" and embraced both Darwinism and agnosticism. Personally, Seryozha was the archetypical Russian aristocrat: restrained, remote, dreamy, and so fond of indolence and leisure that, Oblomov-like, he often stayed in bed until noon. Even worse, perhaps, Seryozha had little use for his father's concerns for social equality and justice. For instance, he preferred to live his life as a minor official in the very bureaucracy that Tolstoy so hated. Also to his father's horror, Seryozha once paid a sickly woman and girl only two and a half rubles for every one thousand cigarettes they had rolled for him.

Although Seryozha venerated Tolstoy, he also disliked his father's many contradictions, particularly his inability to translate his ideas into reality. "Lev Nikolaevich," Seryozha wrote, "demanded that the family simplify its way of life but failed to lay down any limits. He seldom supplied concrete details, that is, the questions of where and how the family was to live, how the property was to be disposed of, how the children were to be brought up, and so on. How were we to reconcile life according to God and the life of pilgrims and peasants with the intangible [gentry] principles that had been instilled [in us] from the cradle?"

Seryozha also took Tolstoy to task for what he perceived as his father's emotional remoteness. He wrote: "We children often felt that it was not we who did not understand our father, but he who did not understand us, because he was always busy with his 'personal affairs.'"

Tolstoy, though, tended to blame others for Seryozha's shortcomings. For instance, apropos of a conversation with his eighteen-year-old son, Tolstoy wrote:

Sergei and his ilk think that one shows wisdom and education by saying, "I do not know that," or "It cannot be proved," or "I do not need to know such a thing." On the contrary, such responses show ignorance. . . .

People have taught Sergei and others theology and church rites, knowing in advance that such things would not stand the test of maturity. They have also taught my son and others so much totally disconnected knowledge that they lack a [sense of] unity in their lives, and even think that [such a lack] is a plus in their daily existence. . . . Seryozha also admitted to me that he loves and believes in the life of the flesh. I am glad to have a clear statement of that question.

Like many Russian writers, Tolstoy was deeply suspicious of intellectuals, particularly their language and influence. "Continued association with professors," he wrote, "leads to prolixity, to a love of long words and confusion." Later, he added: "Intellectuals have brought to people's lives a hundred times more harm than good." See Dole, *The Life of Count Tolstoi*, 280; Shklovsky, *Lev Tolstoy*, 581–82; Nazaroff, *Tolstoy*, 239; Troyat, *Tolstoy*, 465–67, 591; Simmons, *Leo Tolstoy*, 2:23.

29. Tolstoy had also received letters from his sons Andrei and Ilya, but he chose not to reply to them. Both boys were at loggerheads with their father personally and philosophically; they had tried to change his mind by trying to impose varying degrees of Christian-tinged shame and guilt. For instance, Andrei had written:

[We must] keep Mother from suicide, which, I am certain, she will have the resolve to commit in the end. . . . My brothers and I are thus placed in an impossible condition, for we cannot abandon our families and duties in order to be constantly at our mother's side. . . .

As for what you said to me about the luxury that you could no longer live in, I think that you might sacrifice the last years of your life to the family and reconcile yourself to the external conditions of living, seeing that you were able to reconcile yourself to them until now.

Ilya had added:

Mother has not eaten a morsel, and has only taken a sip of water. . . . Much of her behavior is feigned; some of it is sheer sentimentality. But, at the same time, so much of her behavior is sincere that there can be no doubt that she is in grave danger. Suicide or a slow decline from grief are equally frightening. . . . I know how difficult life here was for you. Difficult in all respects. But then you looked upon this life as the cross that you had to bear, and that is how people who knew and loved you also thought of it. So I am sorry that you failed to bear this cross until the end. After all, you are 82 and Mother is 67. You have had your lives, both of you; but one should die decently.

See Shklovsky, *Lev Tolstoy*, 751, 752.

30. Tolstoy stood by Chertkov to the last days of his life. For instance, in his letter to Tanya and Sergei, he wrote: "Both of you will understand

that Chertkov, for whom I have sent, is in a unique position with regard to me. He has devoted his entire life to the service of the undertaking which I have taken up for the last forty years of my life."

In truth, Tolstoy was "addicted" to Chertkov. For instance, he once remarked: "If there were not a Chertkov, I would find it necessary to invent one—for me, at least, for my happiness." See Wilson, *Tolstoy,* 512; Simmons, 2:470.

31. That is, 104 degrees Fahrenheit. Tolstoy had apparently caught cold from an open vent in the room at Optina Hermitage where he had been sleeping as well as from exposure to a driving, icy rain on his way to Kozel'sk. See Dole, *The Life of Count Tolstoi,* 402–3.

32. Sergei L'vovich is the very Seryozha whom Tolstoy had just addressed in his letter. By accident, he had found out about his father's whereabouts from a conductor at Gorbachyovo. See Wilson, *Tolstoy,* 514; Shklovsky, *Lev Tolstoy,* 760.

33. During this time, Tolstoy suffered from repeated convulsions and fits. See Leon, *Tolstoy,* 347, 348.

34. Five doctors, including two well-known specialists from Moscow, attended Tolstoy in his final hours. See Leon, *Tolstoy,* 357.

35. At various times, the doctors also injected Tolstoy with caffeine, codeine, and morphine. See Leon, *Tolstoy,* 359.

36. Others sources say that in his final moments Tolstoy said a variety of things, for example: "I do not understand what I have to do"; "Escape, I must escape"; "The truth . . . I care a great deal . . . how they. . . ."; and "I'll go somewhere where no one will bother me. Leave me alone." See Leon, *Tolstoy,* 359; Shklovsky, *Lev Tolstoy,* 762; Troyat, *Tolstoy,* 691.

37. Father Varsonofy's visit to Tolstoy was the last attempt of the Russian Orthodox Church to return the writer to its fold. Metropolitan Anthony, having learned that Tolstoy was dying, sent a letter to the writer begging him to return to the church, and the Most Holy Synod dispatched the Optina elder to see him. Alexandra, though, mindful not only of Tolstoy's views on organized religion but also of the duplicity of the church with him at other times in his life, refused the priest access to her father.

Undeterred, Varsonofy sent a letter to Alexandra, saying: "You know that the count had told his own sister, your aunt, who is a nun, that he wished to talk to us for the peace of his soul, and that he deeply regretted that his wish could not be satisfied. I therefore respectfully beg you, Countess, not to refuse to inform the count of my presence at Astapovo. If he wishes to see me, if only for two or three minutes, I will hasten to his side. If the count's answer is negative, I will return to the Optina Hermitage and allow God's will to be done." Alexandra did not answer the letter; Varsonofy stayed at Astapovo.

Finally, when Father Varsonofy did hear of Tolstoy's passing, he said: "My mission here is at an end." When he was asked by Sofya and other members of the family if a *panikhida*, or "antiphonal service for the dead," could be performed for Tolstoy, he replied: "I know as much about such a service as I do about the inhabitants of the moon." Nonetheless, Varsonofy did conduct a liturgy over Tolstoy's remains. (The countess fainted during the service.) See Leon, *Tolstoy*, 358; Dole, *The Life of Count Tolstoi*, 407, 409; Troyat, *Tolstoy*, 691.

CHAPTER FOUR

1. Bunin tells another version of how he learned of Tolstoy's passing. In a letter to Gorky, dated November 13, 1910, he wrote: "[A friend] . . . had said [about Tolstoy]: 'The end has come.' And for several days afterward, I went about as if in a feverish dream. Taking the newspaper into my hands, I could not read anything because I was crying so hard."

Also, on December 15, 1910, Bunin told an interviewer from *Odessa News* (*Odesskie novosti*):

> The passing of Leo Nikolaevich Tolstoy has made such an unusual impression on me . . . that truly I find it difficult to express it in several words.
>
> I could not read the newspapers, because my eyes had welled up with tears. They were confused tears, though, tears of sorrow and joy. I was genuinely happy that . . . one of the greatest of the greats had taken a step that would call forth the admiration of the world. I was also happy that neither old age nor broken health could keep this genius from taking this step. . . .
>
> But I cried when I thought how great Tolstoy's sufferings must have been, as well as the contradictions that tormented him and forced him to leave his home in secret, in the dead of night, and to set out God knows where. . . .
>
> I imagined the night when the great pilgrim . . . left his home. The wind had torn off his hat; he was looking for it in the bushes; and when he found it, he ran off into the great expanse.
>
> Tolstoy's soul thirsted to embrace the whole world; but, alas, by the will of fate, this genius had to go to some obscure station to finish out his glorious days.

See B. Mikhailovskii, ed., *Gor'kovskie chteniia, 1958–59* (Moscow: Izdatel'stvo Akademii Nauk SSSR, 1961), 51; Shcherbina et al., *Literaturnoe nasledstvo*, 364–65.

2. In the first formulations of his *Last Will and Testament* (1895), Tolstoy wrote: "My death is not to be announced in the newspapers, nor obituary notices to be given.

Needless to say, everyone, including the Russian literary world, was shaken by Tolstoy's death. For instance, Dostoevsky wrote: "It was as though one of my supporting pillars had suddenly buckled from under me. I had a moment of panic; then I realized how precious Tolstoy had been to me, and I started to cry." See Crankshaw, *Tolstoy*, 214; Leon, *Tolstoy*, 272.

3. The Terek is one of the main rivers draining northward from the Caucasus. It rises in northern Georgia, flows first north and then east through Russia, and empties into the Caspian Sea.

4. The model for Eroshka was an early friend of Tolstoy's, an eighty-year-old Cossack named Epishka Sekhin, who offered a soothing solution to Tolstoy's deepening struggle between the good and bad impulses of his nature. Epishka was a larger-than-life figure: a sturdy and picturesque old reprobate with a white flowing beard, a seamed brown face, and a well-formed, muscular body. He was also a procurer of local women for the writer.

More important for Tolstoy, though, was that Sekhin appeared to have solved the mystery of life. Simply put, the old Cossack believed that God had made everything for man to enjoy. Man was like an animal, Epishka insisted. Wherever man went, there was his home; whatever God gave him to eat, that was his food.

"Look at me," he told the young Tolstoy. "I am as poor as Job. I do not have a wife or a garden or children. [I have] nothing—just a gun, a sparrow hawk, and three dogs, but I have never complained of anything and I never will. I live in the forest. I look around me—everything I see is mine. I come home and I sing a song."

It was fraudulent, Epishka also believed, to teach that man would lick red-hot plates in hell for enjoying the things of this world, for when a man died, grass would cover his grave and end his story.

"Is it a sin to look at a pretty girl?" Epishka thus reasoned to Tolstoy. "Is it wrong to have a good time with her? Is it a sin to love her? Is that how things are where you love? No, my friend, that's no sin, it's salvation. God created you, and he created the girls, too. So it is no sin to look at a pretty girl. She was created to be loved and to give pleasure. . . . People who speak of sin are fools! . . . There is no sin!" See Simmons, *Leo Tolstoy,* 1:90–91; Leon, *Tolstoy,* 34; Wilson, *Tolstoy,* 83–84; Nazaroff, *Tolstoy,* 70; Troyat, *Tolstoy,* 82.

5. Not everyone was pleased with Tolstoy's Olenin. For instance, one reviewer dismissed the character as a "petty Hamlet." Turgenev concurred, writing to Fet: "I read *The Cossacks* and went into ecstasies over it. . . . Only the personality of Olenin spoils the generally wonderful impression. There is no need to contrast civilization with fresh, primeval nature by producing that dull, unhealthy fellow who is always so preoccupied with himself. Why doesn't Tolstoy get rid of that nightmare?"

Although Tolstoy himself was also dissatisfied with the work, Bunin saw *The Cossacks* as beyond reproach. He told Bakhrakh:

> It seems that I remember every word of *The Cossacks.* . . . but I always have this wish to reread it. Although *The Cossacks* is not a mature work and takes the ideas of Rousseau for its inspiration, one can clearly feel the scope of Tolstoy's talent, his "handwriting," so to speak.

[But when *The Cossacks* was published] there were these fools who insisted . . . that the work was archaic . . . because it did not solve any problems. . . . Oh, always these 'problems'! . . . I would give half my life to be able to imitate the sweep of Tolstoy's writing. I only have to recall Olenin's first impression of the Caucasus . . . that "their beauty evoked the same feelings as the music of Bach or the love for a woman." Then Tolstoy ordered the typesetters to put the word "love" in italics! That is so Tolstoy.

See Simmons, *Leo Tolstoy,* 1:294; Leon, *Tolstoy,* 125; Dole, *The Life of Count Tolstoi,* 188; Bakhrakh, *Bunin v khalate,* 53.

6. Only three years into their marriage (1865), Sofya wrote in her diary: "I cannot understand [my husband] sufficiently. That is why I watch so jealously—his thoughts, his actions, his past and present. I should like to be able to grasp and understand him fully. . . . But I know that such a thing is impossible, and I have to accept the fact that I am too young, too silly, and not sufficiently poetic [for such a thing to happen]." See Leon, *Tolstoy,* 131.

7. In truth, the sojourns of Tolstoy's characters through nature often provoked passionate but often contradictory responses. At times, they rose to union with God and the universe; other times, though, they plunged downward into self-hatred and despair. For instance, the main character in *Youth* writes:

The more I gazed at the high, full moon . . . the nearer and nearer [I came] to Him, the source of all beauty and goodness. Tears of an unsatisfied, but agitating rapture rose in my eyes. . . .

But I also was alone . . . a worthless worm, already corrupted by petty and miserable human passions. I still possessed a boundless power for loving, though, and it seemed to me that . . . Nature and the moon and I . . . were all one.

During a visit to Switzerland, Tolstoy added: "A marvelous night. . . . What is it that I desire so ardently? I do not know. At any rate, it is not the blessings of the world. How can one fail to believe in the immortality of the soul when one feels such incomprehensible grandeur in his own? . . . It is dark, there are holes in the sky, now there is light. I could die? My God! My God! Where am I going? Where am I?" See Biryukov, *Leo Tolstoy,* 23–24; Troyat, *Tolstoy,* 175.

8. *Bunin's note:* The dying Prince Andrei, Pierre held captive by the French, and Father Sergius are all Tolstoy himself. . . . His most cherished aesthetic idea can be thought of as this: to take a person at the pinnacle of his worldly success (or to raise him there); to place him before the face of death or some other great misfortune; to show him the insignificance of all earthly things; and, finally, to divest him of his personal imaginary heights, his pride and self-assuredness. . . . Hence Tolstoy's "constant attempt to see himself and debunk all that hides in the human soul under forms that are both glittering and external."

Why did Tolstoy so admire the "folk"? Because he saw the folk's simplicity and meekness; because the millions who made up this "folk," this simple and eternally laboring people, lived and continued to live by a simple, humble faith in a Master, who sent them into the world with a purpose beyond our understanding.

9. Compare a remark by Tolstoy in 1858: "I know well . . . that I am a frozen, old, rotten potato. . . . But I often catch myself in the full blaze of a dream, that is, I am a plant that is just about to put forth its leaves with other plants, and that will go on growing simply, calmly, and happily in God's own world." See Simmons, *Leo Tolstoy,* 1:187.

10. *Bunin's note:* "The more Andrei thought of the painful isolation and raving [that he had experienced] in those hours after he had been wounded, the more he, without himself feeling it, renounced earthly life. To love everyone and everything, always to sacrifice oneself for love, [such ideals] meant not to love anyone, not to live an earthy existence."

11. Tolstoy wrote "Kholstomer" in 1863.

12. Bunin is citing John 18:36.

13. Bunin is quoting Matthew 7:13.

14. Tolstoy was, of course, familiar with all these writings. For instance, during his 1862 stay with the Bashkirs in Samara, he became interested in their Muslim beliefs, and on his way home, he bought a French translation of the Koran to read. See Simmons, *Leo Tolstoy,* 1:332.

15. Tolstoy wrote to a friend in 1865: "I know now that I have an immortal soul (at least I often believe that I know it), and I know that there is a God. . . . I admit that earlier I never believed in such things, but, of late, I have seen more and more proofs that confirm the fact. I am not a Christian—I am still far from that. But experience has taught me not to believe that my reason is infallible and that everything is possible."

Tolstoy believed that the innate suspicion of reason and knowledge was a national trait, for instance, believing that "ignorance" is indeed bliss, Tolstoy wrote in *War and Peace:*

> A Frenchman is self-assured because he regards himself personally in both mind and body as irresistibly attractive to men and women. An Englishman is self-assured, for he is a citizen of the best organized state in the world. . . . An Italian is self-assured because he is excitable and easily forgets himself and other people. A Russian is self-assured because he knows nothing and does not want to know anything, since he does not believe that anything can be known. The German's self-assurance is . . . the strangest and most repulsive because he imagines that . . . science . . . which he himself has invented . . . is the absolute truth.

See Crankshaw, *Tolstoy,* 211; Leon, *Tolstoy,* 146, 184.

16. Tolstoy's Levin similarly reflects: "I, and all other men, know only one thing firmly, clearly, and with certainty, that is, the knowledge [of God]

cannot be explained by reason, for it is outside of such a thing." See Leon, *Tolstoy*, 177.

Tolstoy's "faith" often positioned him on the horns of a dilemma. For instance, he wrote to a friend: "It is a strange and awful thing to say, but I believe in nothing that is taught by religion. But I hate and despise atheism and can see no possibility of living, and still less of dying, without faith. . . . As to the exigencies of my brain and the answers of the Christian faith, I find myself in the position of two hands wanting to clasp each other, but whose fingers resist uniting."

More interesting, perhaps, is Tolstoy's response to Gorky, who, after having admitted to the great writer that he "had no faith," was told:

> No, it is not true [that you do not believe in God]. You are a natural believer, for you cannot live without God. You will come to feel your faith soon. If you do not believe, it is because of stubbornness or hatred, that the world is not the way you want it to be. Also, people sometimes do not believe because they do not dare. Such is the case with the young. They worship some woman; but they do not want her to see it. They have no courage, for they are afraid that she will not understand. Faith, like love, demands courage and boldness. You must tell yourself, "believe," and everything will be all right.

Simply put, Tolstoy believed that "each of us must find in his faith that which is common to all faiths, and while rejecting what is exceptional in his own, support what is common to all."

Perhaps it is Tolstoy's daughter Alexandra who best sums up her father's views on religion. She recalls that when, at age fifteen, she, parroting Tolstoy's views, announced that "religion is all lies!" her father's face "softened and his eyes became gentle and loving. 'Go to to church anyway,' he said." See Simmons, *Leo Tolstoy*, 1:365, 2:432; Wilson, *Tolstoy*, 467; Troyat, *Tolstoy*, 555.

17. Briefly, the Buddhist notion of Nirvana, or "Enlightenment," describes a blissful heaven-haven state of tranquillity, freedom, and insight in which, metaphorically speaking, the individual leaves the land of "rebirth," sails over the "restless ocean of suffering," extinguishes the flames of illusion and desire, and reaches "the harbor of refuge," "the cool cave," and the "farther shore" (poetic images which Bunin used in *The Gentleman from San Francisco*).

Individuals seeking Nirvana pass from sensual desire to inner serenity to indifference to everything, and finally to the abandoning of good or bad states of mind. The rewards for such effort defy description, because those who attain enlightenment possess supreme purity and consciousness. These souls repose in a condition of spatial infinity, beyond the perception of form or plurality. So long as "Enlightened Ones" continue to focus on the infinity of consciousness and on the nonexistence of everything else, they remain in a state in which there is neither perception nor nonperception: peace.

18. Years before, Tolstoy also told the peasant students at his school: "I'll tell you what I am going to do. I will give up my estate, buy myself a peasant plot and cabin, marry a peasant girl, and live among you." He was particularly taken with the idea of a mate from the folk. "To marry a woman of society," he told one of his teachers at Yasnaya Polyana, "is to swallow all the poison of civilization."

Tolstoy held to such convictions in later life. For instance, he once confessed to Chertkov that he wanted to live "in a hut with working people, working together with them according to my strength and abilities, bartering my efforts, nourishing and clothing myself as they, and without shame, boldly speaking to all the truth of Christ that I know." See Nazaroff, *Tolstoy*, 150–51; Troyat, *Tolstoy*, 219; Simmons, *Leo Tolstoy*, 2:87.

19. Bunin is quoting Job 1:1–3, 18–19.

20. When Bunin wrote *The Liberation of Tolstoy*, six of Tolstoy's thirteen children were still alive. Of these, only Sergei remained in Russia. For the most part, Tolstoy's children-in-exile sought to disseminate their father's images and ideals. Tatyana and Mikhail were living in France. (Tatyana had been the director of the Tolstoy Museum in Moscow [1923–25] before she left Russia.) Ilya immigrated to the United States, where he worked as a writer and a journalist, but he did, in fact, die in poverty in New Haven in 1933. Leo traveled widely and lived in the United States, Italy, and France. Alexandra left Russia in 1929 and eventually settled in the United States. In 1939 she established the Tolstoy Foundation, which assisted people displaced by revolution and war.

Bunin himself was a frequent recipient of Alexandra's largesse. For instance, on March 8, 1941, he wrote to Aldanov: "We are cold and hungry; and, in our poverty, we are on the verge of a full-blown catastrophe. From America we received only 1,100 francs from Alexandra Tolstaya . . . but most of that was immediately eaten up a long time ago."

Five years later, Bunin continued: "I do not have a summer coat. Perhaps the 'Tolstoy Foundation' has one to give me?" See A. Zweers, "Perepsika I. A. Bunina s M. A. Aldanovym," *Novyi zhurnal*, no. 152 (1983): 164. Also see V. Raevskii, *Predki i potomki Pushkina i Tolstogo* ([United States]: Literary Society, 1983), 316–64; Troyat, *Tolstoy*, 699–700.

21. Bunin is citing Job 1:11, 12, and 21, but he is quoting the second citation incorrectly. In the original verse, the Lord tells Satan that the Evil One has power over Job's possessions but not his soul.

22. Bunin is quoting Matthew 4:8–11.

23. The Battle of Austerlitz, also known as the Battle of the Three Emperors, occured on December 2, 1805, and was one of Napoleon's greatest victories. In this struggle, 68,000 French troops defeated almost 90,000 Russians and Austrians, thereby forcing Austria to make peace with France.

24. *Bunin's note:* [Tolstoy wrote] "Well, it is good that you will have more than sixty thousand acres and three hundred head of horses in the Samara region. But what will come of all of this? What next? Well, it is good that you will become more famous than Gogol, Pushkin, Shakespeare, Molière, all the writers in the world—but so what? What next?" (*Confession*).

25. Bunin is quoting Job 2:8.

26. The book of Ecclesiastes, a product of the so-called Hebrew wisdom movement, is one of the most pessimistic writings in the Hebrew Bible. Traditionally associated with King Solomon, the actual author of the work identified himself as the "son of David, king in Jerusalem" to give authority to his piece.

Writing under the pseudonym Qhelet, or "Preacher," the author of Ecclesiastes expresses religious and philosophical skepticism in maxims and essays. For instance, he questions the doctrine of retributive justice, a mainstay of wisdom theology. One's fate, he contends, does not depend on conduct but on the mystery of God. He writes: "The race is not to the swift, nor the battle to the strong, more bread to the wise, nor riches to the intelligent, nor favor to the men of skill; but time and chance happen to them all" (9:11).

Crying "vanity of vanities!" the author of Ecclesiastes finds little meaning or security in wisdom, work, and wealth. Rather, he reiterates the uncertainties of life, the inscrutable ways of the Deity, and the stark and final reality of death. His only advice accords well with Bunin's (and Tolstoy's) own view; that is, people should accept and be grateful for the small, daily pleasures that God affords humankind.

27. According to Buddhistic legend, the young Gautama sought "enlightenment" in an area called "Uruvela" (near modern-day Gaya in northeastern India): "a beautiful stretch of land, a lovely woodland grove, and a clear flowing river with a pleasant ford." There, for nearly six years, he searched for the truth, practicing severe austerities and self-mortification. The result was that he seemed to "regress" to a more primitive level of being.

"Because of so little nourishment," he wrote, "all my limbs became like withered creepers with knotted joints; my buttocks, like a buffalo's hoof; my backbone, like a string of balls; and my ribs, like rafters of a dilapidated shed. The pupils of my eyes appeared sunk deep in their sockets as water appears shining at the bottom of a deep well. My scalp became shriveled and shrunk as a bitter gourd cut unripe becomes shriveled and shrunk by sun and wind. . . . When I wanted to obey the calls of nature, I immediately fell on my face; and when I stroked my limbs with my hand, my rotted hairs . . . fell off my body." (Many pictures of the Buddha portray him in this emaciated state.)

Because of such a regimen, Gautama became so weak that he once fainted and was even taken for dead. To his chagrin, also, he realized that he had not attained "enlightenment." Having resumed a proper diet and lifestyle, he remained at Uruvela to chart his own path to the truth.

28. Bunin is referring to King Solomon and paraphrasing Ecclesiastes 2:4–8.

29. Bunin is quoting Ecclesiastes 1:3.

30. In Buddhistic mythology, Mara was the Tempter and Lord of Passion who tried, unsuccessfully, to thwart the Buddha in his search for truth.

For instance, Mara, seeing the emaciated Gautama at Uruvela, sought to sway the young man from his search, saying "You are pale, emaciated, and near death. Live, sir, for life is better. What is the use of your searching?"

The Buddha replied:

> Lust is your first army; the second is dislike for the higher life; the third is hunger and thirst; the fourth is craving; the fifth is torpor and sloth; the sixth is cowardice and fear; the seventh is doubt; the eighth is hypocrisy; the ninth is gains, praise, honor, and false glory; the tenth is exalting self and despising others.
>
> Mara, these are your armies. No feeble man can conquer them, yet only by doing so can one win bliss. I challenge you! Shame on my life if defeated! Better for me to die in battle than to live defeated.

In the end, Mara, overcome with grief, vanishes from Buddha's sight, thereby enabling him to attain Enlightenment.

31. Bunin is citing a key theme of Tolstoy's confessions.

32. Bunin is paraphrasing Job 21:5–6.

33. Such sentiments were common with Tolstoy. For instance, in the early months of his marriage to Sofya, he wrote: "I am terribly dissatisfied with myself. I swing under the mountain of death, but I hardly feel strong enough to check myself. I do not wish to die; I want and love immortality. There is no need to choose, for the choice has already been made. Literature, art, pedagogy, and the family. Inconsistency, timidity, laziness, and weakness—these are my enemies." See Simmons, *Leo Tolstoy*, 1:292.

34. Tolstoy's personal messianism, together with his wild oscillations and "either/or" approach to life, periodically drove him to the brink of suicide. For instance, in 1854, as a young soldier in the Caucasus, he vowed to be of immediate service to people or to "shoot himself." Eight years later, he vowed to propose marriage to Sofya or to "blow his brains out."

Also, in 1878, the fifty-year-old Tolstoy was in such spiritual disarray that he had an almost irresistible urge to commit suicide. Indeed, he took every measure to keep from ending his life. For instance, he removed a rope from his room so as not to hang himself from a cross beam; he avoided hunting for fear that he would use a gun on himself. Similarly, before a visit to Optina Hermitage in 1881, Tolstoy confessed in his diary that he wanted to end his days.

Tolstoy's periodic flirtation with suicide was a partial impetus for his third play, *The Living Corpse* (*Zhivoi trup*), which he wrote toward the end of his life. In this work, an educated man, believing his marriage to be a failure, pretends to commit suicide so as to allow his wife to marry a devoted friend and her unconfessed lover. When the newly married (but unsuspecting) couple are later accused of bigamy and ordered to annul their union, the first husband does indeed take his own life to safeguard his wife's happiness.

Apparently, Tolstoy thought that suicide was a viable option in life. "I cannot understand why people regard suicide as a crime," he told a friend. "It seems to me to be an individual's right. It gives one the chance of dying when he no longer wishes to live. The Stoics thought like that." See Simmons, *Leo Tolstoy,* 1:116, 362; Crankshaw, *Tolstoy,* 196; Leon, *Tolstoy,* 53, 115, 252–53; Wilson, *Tolstoy,* 271, 332.

CHAPTER FIVE

1. That is, the years between 1862 and 1910.

2. Fifty years earlier, Sofya had written: "The house is so sad and empty when Lev is away." See Troyat, *Tolstoy,* 292.

3. Such emotions, though, were often short-lived. Indeed, not unlike Dostoevsky, Tolstoy often had a self-possessing attitude toward love."I love Sofya more and more," the newly married Tolstoy wrote in his diary. "But today is the fifth month [of our union], and I am experiencing what I have not experienced for a long time—a feeling of frustration before her."

A year later, Tolstoy continued: "Sofya is so impossibly pure and fine and substantial for me. At these moments, I feel that I do not possess her, despite the fact that she gives herself entirely to me. If I do not possess her, it is because I dare not do so. I do not feel myself worthy. I am nervously irritated and therefore not *completely* happy. Something torments me. Jealousy of that person who would be completely worthy of her. I am not worthy." See Simmons, *Leo Tolstoy,* 1:288.

4. Sofya often took a dim view of Tolstoy's extraliterary pursuits, since she feared that such ventures would distract him from writing. "Let the child play with whatever he likes," she once concluded in a reproachful letter to her husband, "so long as he does not cry."

Others concurred. For instance, in 1858 Turgenev wrote to Pavel Annenkov:

You have astonished me with your news of Tolstoy's various projects. What a man he is! With perfect feet, he is determined to walk on his head. Not long ago he wrote Vasily Botkin a letter in which he said: "I am very glad that I did not listen to Turgenev and become a man of letters." In answer to this, I asked: "What does Tolstoy want to be—an officer, a farmer, and the like?"

Now he tries to prove that he is a timber expert. With such capers, I fear only that he will throw the spine of his talent out of joint. In his Swiss tales, a very pronounced curvature is already noticeable.

Turgenev constantly sought to keep Tolstoy on a literary path. Even on his deathbed in 1883, he wrote to his younger colleague: "My friend, go back to literature. It is your gift, which comes from whence comes all else. Oh, how happy I would be if I could believe that my words would influence you!" See Simmons, *Leo Tolstoy*, 1:194; Leon, *Tolstoy*, 228, 242.

5. Tolstoy was alone at the time of his accident with the horse. With his arm both broken and dislocated from the fall, he fainted from the pain, but having regained consciousness, he stumbled upon some serfs, who carried him to an old peasant woman or a country doctor (accounts differ) who, after no less than eight tries, was unable to set the arm. Sofya, having heard of the misfortune, immediately dispatched to her husband a doctor from Tula, who, with the aid of two farmhands, set the broken bones and manipulated the arm back into place. (Another version of this story is that Tolstoy, fearing that his accident would send the pregnant Sofya into premature labor, somehow made his way to Tula, without informing his wife about what had happened.)

Six weeks later, Tolstoy again injured his arm by firing a gun. This time, however, surgeons in Moscow rectified the situation and brought him to full recovery. Even on the operating table, Tolstoy was the consummate teacher. Before losing consciousness from the chloroform, he bolted upright and bellowed: "My friends! We cannot go on living like this . . . I think . . . I have decided. . . ."

Furthermore, only an individual like Tolstoy would consider the metaphysical ramifications of such an event. In January 1865, several months after the accident, he wrote to Fet: "Do you know what a surprise I have in store for you? After a horse threw me to the ground and broke my arm, and just as I recovered consciousness, I said to myself: 'I am a writer. And I really am a writer, though an isolated and furtive one.' In a few days the first half of Part One [of *War and Peace*] will appear. . . . What I have published formerly, I now regard only as a trial of the pen and a kind of draft of an opus. What I now print, although I like it more than my previous work, seems weak, as introductions must be. But what comes after is tremendous!"

Such a statement has a strong basis in fact. No sooner did Tolstoy recover from surgery than he asked his sister-in-law, Tanya, to take dictation for a story. Hardly aware of Tanya's presence, Tolstoy raced up and down the room, pouring forth words as if possessed. Later, Tanya wrote: "I felt as though I was prying . . . that I had become an involuntary witness to the events in that inner world which he had hidden from us all." See Simmons,

Leo Tolstoy, 1:307; Dole, *The Life of Count Tolstoi,* 220; Shklovsky, *Lev Tolstoy,* 494; Troyat, *Tolstoy,* 277, 278.

6. Alexandra Andreevna Tolstaya was an influential figure in the Court of Saint Petersburg, being a lady-in-waiting to the Grand Duchess Maria Nikolaevna, the only daughter of Nicholas I, as well as an associate-friend of both Nicholas and his son, Alexander II.

Alexandra was also a close confidant of Tolstoy's and his first cousin once removed. Tolstoy called Alexandra "Granny," though she was only eleven years older than he and was even once the object of his strong affection. "I am so ready to fall in love that it is terrible," Tolstoy confided in his diary. "If only Alexandra were ten years younger." (At the time of this statement, she was forty, Tolstoy was twenty-nine.)

"Alexandra is a joy and a comfort," Tolstoy continued several months later. "I have never seen a woman would could hold a candle to her. . . . She is definitely the woman who charms me more than any other."

The feeling was mutual. "I saw [Tolstoy] quite clearly as a young officer who had just returned from Sevastopol," she wrote, "and I remember what a fine impression he produced on all of us. At that time he was already a public figure. Everyone was enraptured with his charming creations, and although we did not see his future renown, we were quite proud of the talent of our kinsman." Later, she added: "[Tolstoy] is simple, extremely modest, and so alive that his presence animated everyone around him. . . . He is not handsome, but his keen eyes, kind and highly expressive, make up for the favors that nature has withheld. Like a mirror broken into fragments, every facet of Tolstoy reflects a little of the brilliant light he has been given from above."

Charming, elegant, sensitive, and deeply devout, "Granny" Alexandra was friends with the most intelligent and distinguished men of her day, including Turgenev, Ivan Goncharov, and Fyodor Dostoevsky. She was also the only woman with whom Tolstoy maintained a civilized, adult relationship; she, in effect, provided her tormented "grandson" with a refuge from himself. It was "Granny" Alexandra who enabled Tolstoy to enter salons and drawing rooms which otherwise, because of his arrogance and bad manners, would have been closed to him.

More than anyone else, too, "Granny" Alexandra felt sufficiently comfortable with Tolstoy to comment upon all aspects of his life. Her criticism of her "grandson" was always affectionate, but also often penetrating and direct. For instance, she once wrote to him: "I am afraid for you, grandson. I am afraid for your ethereal, idealistic absurdities; of your vanity which often prompts you to create or re-create things that have long been soundly created and established; and even of your love of truth, which, though capriciously sophisticated and complex, often seduces you far away from it and its naturalness." On another occasion, Alexandra succinctly advised her charge: "Get married without delay, my dear Leo, before egotism has dried you up."

The affection that Tolstoy and Alexandra had for each other deepened over the years, and "Granny"'s strong intellect and love of truth inspired a trust and confidence that Tolstoy rarely accorded to other people. Despite the strong (and often stormy) feelings between Tolstoy and Alexandra, the relationship remained platonic, the two deciding to be "just friends" early in their friendship.

Not surprisingly, "Granny" Alexandra was greatly respected in the often troubled Tolstoyan household. For instance, she often acted as a mediator between Tolstoy and his children. "You have no right to desert your family or to force upon them your inclinations and convictions," she chided Tolstoy. "Until recently, you have lived happily and agreeably. They also wish to do the same, if they do not experience the slightest inclination for beggary, work in the fields, or life in a peasant hut."

"Granny" was also concerned with the effect that Tolstoy's intellectual rebelliousness was having on his offspring. She added: "Still one more word, my dear Lev. Instead of mourning over the fantastic, the impossible, and, I might even say, the useless, have you ever thought seriously over your responsibility to your children? All of them produce on me the effect of wandering between heaven and earth. What will you give them in place of the beliefs that you have probably weaned them from? For they love you too much not to attempt to follow you."

Revealingly, "Granny" continued to hold sway over her difficult "grandson." "Do you know, Granny," Sofya confessed to her, "that you are truly the only person who can talk with Lev without constraint and without concealing anything of the truth; all the others are afraid and tremble before his greatness."

In his old age, after reading their extensive correspondence, Tolstoy remarked: "When I look back on my long life, my memories of Alexandra will always be a bright gleam, a light that shines from under a door in a dark corridor." See Simmons, *Leo Tolstoy*, 1:148, 173, 2:148, 149; Crankshaw, *Tolstoy*, 78, 135–36, 168; Leon, *Tolstoy*, 80–82; Wilson, *Tolstoy*, 148–52; Nazaroff, *Tolstoy*, 119; Troyat, *Tolstoy*, 170.

7. The rest of this excerpt reads: "No, the traveling monk whom I met is right. One may have a wife, children, health, and the like; but that is not the main thing in life. . . . I have forgotten God; I must seek him again."

Even the act of writing could trigger Tolstoy's disaffection with life. "I shall write no more fiction," Tolstoy wrote in an 1859 letter to Fet. "It is shameful, when one thinks about it. People are weeping, dying, and marrying; and I should sit down and write books, saying 'how she loved him.' It's shameful." See Crankshaw, *Tolstoy*, 171; Nazaroff, *Tolstoy*, 172.

8. Bunin is citing from the memoirs of Tatyana Andreevna Bers-Kuzminskaya, entitled *Moia zhizn' doma v Iasnoi Polyane. Vospominaniia,* which were published in three volumes in Moscow in 1925–26. The work was translated into English as *Tolstoy as I Knew Him: My Life at Home and at Yasnaya Polyana* (New York: Macmillan, 1948).

9. Of this 1867 incident, Tanya continued: "I both feared and pitied him. Never had I seen him in such a state." In fact, Tolstoy himself was so alarmed by his behavior that, several days later, he consulted with a specialist in Moscow.

Tolstoy's bouts of frenzy with Sofya were frequent—and unpredictable. For instance, he was highly solicitous of his wife in childbirth. But he became outraged when he learned that Sofya, to her own grief, could not breast-feed her firstborn. He did not care that his wife's nipples had become so fissured that the doctors had ordered her to stop nursing. It was inconceivable, Tolstoy believed, that any wife of his should allow herself to have become so soft and corrupted by civilization that she could not feed her own child. In fact, when Sofya finally handed the child over to a wet nurse, Tolstoy sulked, growled, and refused to go near the nursery.

Sofya's father, Doctor Bers, scolded the new parents: "I see that you have both lost your minds. Be reasonable, dear Sofya, calm yourself, and do not make a mountain out of a molehill. . . . As for you, dear Leo Nikolaevich, rest assured that you will never be transformed into a real peasant, any more than your wife will be able to endure what [any serf] Pelageya can endure."

Bers continued to Sofya's sister, Tanya: "And you, Tanya, do not let your crazy sister out of your sight for a moment. Scold her as often as possible for her insane notions that are enough to try the patience of the Lord, and pitch the first object that comes to hand straight at Leo's head and knock some sense into it. He is a great master of speechifying and literature, but life is another matter. Let him write a story about a husband who tortures his sick wife by forcing her to nurse her baby. He will be stoned by every woman alive."

Sofya's inability to nurse found its way into Tolstoy's fiction. For instance, in *The Kreutzer Sonata,* Pozdnyshev writes: "[When my wife refused to nurse the baby] she deprived herself of her sole weapon against coquetry. A wet nurse took the child. In other words, we took advantage of a woman's poverty, ignorance, and need to tear her away from her own baby, and in return for her service, to put a cap with a ribbon on her head." See Crankshaw, *Tolstoy,* 203; Troyat, *Tolstoy,* 293–94, 477.

10. Sofya, having learned from a newspaper reporter that Tolstoy was dying at Astapovo, ordered a special train to take her, a doctor, a nurse, and three of her children—Andrei, Mikhail, and Tatyana—there. (The cost of the train was 500 rubles.) When Sofya and company arrived at the station,

the special carriage in which they had been riding was moved to a siding; the five were given permission by governmental authorities to live in it until the crisis was over. See Leon, *Tolstoy,* 357; Wilson, *Tolstoy,* 513, 514.

11. The stationmaster, Ivan Osolin, and his family had willingly vacated their house to accommodate Tolstoy and his attendants.

12. So as not to agitate Tolstoy unnecessarily, his attendants had decided to admit only his children Sergei and Tatyana to his bedside. They also ordered two nurses to prevent Sofya from seeing her husband. Such a precaution proved unnecessary, though, as Sofya had already acquiesced to the doctors' warnings that her presence in the same room with her husband would only hasten his death. (Tolstoy himself feared that a meeting with Sofya would kill him.)

As a result, Tolstoy had no idea that his wife and three other sons (Leo was still abroad) were walking about miserably outside the station. In fact, even when Tolstoy asked his daughter Tatyana about his wife's health and whereabouts, she remained noncommital and left the room.

Tolstoy was also unaware of the media circus that was taking place at the time of his dying. Relatives, friends, newspapermen, photographers, and cinematographers had quickly descended upon the area, hoping to witness a special moment in history. For instance, Charles Pathé, the pioneer of newsreel movies, sent a cable to the cameramen there, saying: "TAKE STATION. TRY TO GET CLOSEUP, STATION NAME. TAKE FAMILY. WELL-KNOWN FIGURES. CAR THEY ARE SLEEPING IN. . . ."

Tolstoy, who had desired so earnestly to spend his final hours in solitude and peace, was dying in a blaze of unprecedented publicity, with bulletins of his state continually being telegraphed to every great city in Europe and America. See Leon, *Tolstoy,* 357–58; Wilson, *Tolstoy,* 514; Simmons, *Leo Tolstoy,* 2:502.

13. Bunin fails to mention that the distraught Sofya, dressed all in black, also mingled with the crowds, justifying her actions, pouring forth lamentations to anyone who would listen to her, peering through the station windows, and even allowing herself to be photographed by cameramen. Sometimes she railed against Tolstoy and her family (with every word taken down and misreported). For instance, she claimed that her husband had left home as a publicity stunt. Other times, she wept and spoke only words of love for her husband. When Alexandra reproached her mother for her behavior, Sofya replied: "At least people will think that I have been with him."

Amidst such histrionics, Sofya managed to write a final letter to her husband. "Before we part, perhaps forever," she wrote to Tolstoy, "I do not wish to make excuses [for my behavior] but rather to *explain* the things which you have accused me of. . . . You would have left home anyway. I had a dreaded presentiment that you would." See Leon, *Tolstoy,* 358–59; Wilson, *Tolstoy,* 515–16; Shklovsky, *Lev Tolstoy,* 761; Simmons, 2:503.

14. At 3:30 A.M., two hours before Tolstoy died, Sofya was allowed to see her husband. By his bedside, she fell on her knees, kissed his hand, and whispered, "Forgive me." Tolstoy sighed deeply but remained unconscious. Sofya continued talking, often incoherently, mixing her marriage vows with words of tenderness and reproof. Since she was quickly losing control, she was led away, but she stayed for two hours on the freezing porch until her son Sergei brought her to see her husband a second time. See Nazaroff, *Tolstoy,* 341.

15. Chertkov had been reading Tolstoy extracts from *The Circle of Reading.* See Leon, *Tolstoy,* 358.

16. Tolstoy's article "I Cannot Remain Silent" ("Ne mogu molchat'"), published on July 9, 1908, was his most impassioned antigovernment tract. Its target was Prime Minister Pyotr Stolypin's system of field court martial, which had convicted and hanged dozens of suspected revolutionaries. It also bemoaned the lot of the Russian people, victimized by poverty and disease, as well as by a corrupt priesthood and an uncaring government, which had robbed them of land and conscripted them for war. "One cannot live and know that this is going on. We must cry out! Shout!"

Newspapers that printed "I Cannot Remain Silent" were fined 200 to 3,000 rubles. See Leon, *Tolstoy,* 308; Dole, *The Life of Count Tolstoi,* 388.

17. Sofya was shattered by her sudden solitude and her guilt over Tolstoy's flight and passing. For instance, on November 29, 1910, she wrote: "[I feel] unbearable depression, remorse, weakness, aching regret for my husband. How he suffered these last months! I cannot go on living." A month later, she continued: "I did not close my eyes all night. Oh, these awful nights of insomnia, with my thoughts, the tormenting of my conscience. Darkness of the winter night and darkness of my heart." She died at Yasnaya Polyana on November 4, 1919. Troyat, *Tolstoy,* 697.

18. Sofya made this remark in 1918, eight years after Tolstoy had died and only a year before she herself passed from this life. See Wilson, *Tolstoy,* 505.

19. Bunin had a similar if more Buddhist-based notion of pre-existence. For instance, he wrote in his 1924 sketch "The Book of My Life" ("Kniga moei zhizni"): "My birth lies in that (completely inscrutable) murk in which I was conceived before my birth, in my father and mother, in my grandfathers and great-grandfathers, for they are also I, only in another form, but where many things have so repeated themselves that they have become one and the same. . . . More than once, I felt that I was not only an infant, a lad, an adolescent, but also my father, grandfather, great-grandfather, and ancestor." See Mal'tsev, *Ivan Bunin,* 8; Shcherbina et al., *Literaturnoe nasledstvo,* 384–85.

20. Bunin continued in "The Book of My Life": "My concepts of time and space have been very fluid." See Shcherbina et al., *Literaturnoe nasledstvo,* 384.

21. Tolstoy first wrote these lines in 1878, incorporating them into *First Memories* twenty-five years later. Tolstoy often sought to obscure the line between his youth and old age. For instance, a year before he died, he wrote: "Today, at the age of eighty-one, I keenly experienced the consciousness of myself in exactly the same way I did when I was five or six years old. Consciousness is motionless. And it is only because of this motionlessness that we are able to see the motion of that thing we call time. If time passes, it is necessary that there should be something which remains static. And it is consciousness of self which is static."

In similar fashion, Bunin exclaimed in his 1925 story "Cicadas" ("Tsikady") (later renamed "Night" ["Noch'"]):

> Not long ago, having perchance awakened at dawn, I was suddenly staggered by the thought of my age. I had thought that a person who had lived forty or fifty years was some unique, almost awesome being. And now, I, too, have finally become such a being. "What then am I?" I said to myself. "What exactly have I now become?" And . . . looking at myself as one would a stranger—how marvelous that we can do such things—I . . . felt that I was absolutely the same person I had been at age ten or twenty. I . . . looked into the mirror; yes, my face was now gaunt, my features were rigid, there were silvery patches on my temples, and the color of my eyes was somewhat faded. . . . But so what?
>
> And with singular spriteliness, I got up and went into the other room, still largely brightening, still nocturnally serene, but always taking in the new, slowly dawning day. . . . And suddenly I again experienced that ineffable feeling that I have experienced all my life when I happened to awake at daybreak—a feeling of great happiness, the childlike, trustful, soul-touching sweetness of life, the beginning of something completely new, good, and splendid—a feeling of intimacy, brotherhood, and unity with everyone on earth.

See Bunin, *Sobranie sochinenii*, 5:304. Also see Leon, *Tolstoy,* 327.

22. Tolstoy was five years old at the time of his "descent" from the world of women to that of men.

23. Tatyana Alexandrovna Ergol'skaya was not Tolstoy's aunt but a second cousin of his father, Nikolai, who was taken in as an orphan by the Tolstoy family and for a period of time was Nikolai's childhood sweetheart. (Not surprisingly, Tatyana was the model for Sonya in *War and Peace.*)

Six years after the death of Tolstoy's mother, Nikolai asked Tatyana to marry him and be the mother to his children. She rejected the first part of his proposal but gladly accepted the second, a commitment to which she devoted the rest of her life. Tatyana was roughly in her mid-forties when she first impressed herself on the mind of the young Tolstoy. She was one of his strongest forces for goodness. For instance, it was from Tatyana that Tolstoy learned to detest corporal punishment, seek absolute chastity, understand the joy of existence, and relish the delights of a quiet, unhurried life.

For instance, Tolstoy wrote in 1859: "[Aunt Tatyana] never uttered a harsh word. She fulfilled the inner work of life and therefore never had to hurry. And these two features, love and repose, imperceptibly attracted one into her society, and gave a special delight to intimacy. . . . She never spoke about herself; never about religion, as to what one should believe, or what she herself believed and prayed for. She believed everything, though she repudiated one single dogma, that of eternal damnation, for, as she said, *'Dieu qui est la bonte meme, ne peut pas vouloir nos souffrances.'*"

As an old man, Tolstoy recalled that Aunt Tatyana had taught him "the spiritual delight of love. She did not teach me that by words; but by her whole being, she filled me with love. I saw and felt how she enjoyed loving, and I understood the joy of love. . . . She also taught me the delights of a calm, lonely life . . . the lack of material cares, [the need for] pleasant relations with others . . . and the absence of hurry or any sense of the passing of time." See Simmons, *Leo Tolstoy,* 1:17; Crankshaw, *Tolstoy,* 33–34; Leon, *Tolstoy,* 87; Dole, *The Life of Count Tolstoi,* 12, 127–28; Troyat, *Tolstoy,* 17.

24. Tolstoy is referring to the Russian practice of swaddling infants.

25. The critic Viktor Shklovsky sees these two passages from Tolstoy as the "beginning of one's perception of the world's duality." See Shklovsky, *Lev Tolstoy,* 29.

26. Bunin is mistaken here. He visited India in 1907, three years before Tolstoy's death.

27. In this and subsequent paragraphs, Bunin is quoting from "Cicadas." For a translation of this story, see I. Bunin, *The Elagin Affair and Other Stories* (New York: Funk and Wagnalls, 1935), 145–66.

28. *Bunin's note:* [Tolstoy said:] "Was it not then [in my past] that I acquired everything by which I am living now?" He acquired it then, but it was so extremely little in comparison to what he would acquire on this path!

29. A visitor to Yasnaya Polyana concurred with Tolstoy's larger-than-life image. He recalled:

> Everything in Tolstoy's character attains titanic proportions. . . . As a drinker, he absorbed fantastic quantities of liquor. As a gambler, he terrified his partners by the boldness of his play. As a soldier, he advanced gaily to Bastion Four, the bastion of death at Sevastopol, and there he made dying men laugh at his witticisms.
>
> As a country gentleman or rural cultivator, he covered the neighborhood of Yasnaya Polyana with gardens. He surpassed everyone by his prodigious activity in sport as well as in literature. Gifted with a phenomenal memory, a lively wit, and a bitter tongue, he was always ready to enter into a discussion, no matter what the subject. And in everything, he was always a *bon enfant,* loving to take part in simple games, as well as a bit of a boaster who, like children, is unable to resist the temptation to show off before a newcomer.

See Dole, *The Life of Count Tolstoi,* 123–24.

30. Friends and family frequently commented on the changes in Tolstoy brought about by the passage of time. For instance, Sofya, never one to cite the good qualities in her husband, was moved by Tolstoy's new mood to write in late 1877: "Lev Nikolaevich's character is changing more and more. Although he has always been very modest and simple in his habits and needs, he is becoming even meeker and more modest and tolerant."

Not without alarm, though, Sofya continued two years before Tolstoy's death: "My husband's spirit remains indifferent to earthly life, somewhere aloft, and more independent of the body. . . . Lev Nikolaevich is experiencing something new, strange, and far away; and I am often unbearably grieved and sorry over the loss of something in him, and in his relations to me and to everything else surrounding him."

Others agreed with the changes they saw in Tolstoy. For instance, when the poet Yakov Polonsky visited the fifty-two-year-old Tolstoy in 1880, he was struck by the writer's new gentleness and winning simplicity. He wrote: "Tolstoy appeared to me to be reborn and imbued with a different faith, a different love. . . . He did not impose his views on us, but quietly heard out [other people's] objections. In brief, he was no longer the count that I had known formerly."

A decade later, Sofya's brother, Stepan Andreevich Bers, recalled that "Tolstoy's face showed evident traces of the serious mental sufferings that he had endured. It was calm, sad, and had a quite new expression. Not only his face, but his entire personality had become completely altered. The playfulness that had been formerly present in him, and so enlivening to others, had completely vanished."

Circa 1894, a reporter for the journal *Herald of Europe* (*Vestnik Evropy*) reported that Tolstoy seemed to have shrunk in size; several years later, Gorky called him a "gnome." Tolstoy's biographers agree with such an assessment, asserting that by 1907 he was only 5 feet 4 inches; that is, since midlife, he had shrunk a full five inches! Tolstoy was now "a little old man with quick bobbing steps and slightly bowed legs." See Leon, *Tolstoy*, 186, 234; Dole, *The Life of Count Tolstoi*, 349; Wilson, *Tolstoy*, 387; Nazaroff, *Tolstoy*, 324; Shklovsky, *Lev Tolstoy*, 670; Simmons, *Leo Tolstoy*, 2:16, 20, 408.

31. The notion that Mohammed suffered from epilepsy can be traced to Saint Theophanes the Confessor in the *Chronographia* (810–14). In the late nineteenth century, doctors and scholars believed that Mohammed suffered from hysteria. Today he is thought to have suffered from acromegaly, a chronic disorder caused by the oversecretion of hormones in the pituitary gland, resulting in an enlarged face, extremities, and viscera.

Mohammed's personality and physical features were not unlike those of Tolstoy. Mohammed also had pronounced eyebrows, a large, fleshy nose, and well-developed ears. He likewise had huge fingers, hands, and feet, as well as a peculiar-sounding voice. On good days, Mohammed showed a similarly ample appetite for sex and food; on bad ones, he similarly suffered from headaches, intestinal disorders, brooding, depression, irritability, and yearnings for suicide. Unlike Tolstoy, though, Mohammed manifested psychopathological traits; that is, he periodically lost consciousness and often heard voices, bells, and revelations from supernatural beings.

32. Mount Moriah was the site for the Temple at Jerusalem, completed by King Solomon in 957 B.C. It was also believed to be the place where Abraham had built the altar to sacrifice Isaac.

33. Circa 621–22, Mohammed dreamed that he was being carried on a winged steed past Medina to a conclave of ancient prophets in Jerusalem. See W. Muir, *The Life of Mohammed from Original Sources* (Edinburgh: J. Grant, 1923), 121.

34. In early Hindu philosophy, Maya denoted the wizardry by which gods tricked mortals into seeing illusion as reality. With time, it came to mean the powerful force activating the cosmic illusion that the phenomenal world is real.

35. For instance, the author of Ecclesiastes writes:

With the help of wisdom, I have been at pains to study all that is done under heaven. Oh, what a weary task God has given humankind to labor at! I have seen everything that is done under the sun, and what vanity it all is, what chasing the wind. . . .

I thought to myself, "I have acquired a greater stock of wisdom than any of my predecessors in Jerusalem. I have great experience of wisdom and learning. Wisdom has been my careful study, stupidity, too, and folly. And now I have come to recognize that even this is chasing of the wind. [For I see] much wisdom, much grief, the more knowledge, the more sorrow."

See Ecclesiastes 1:12–14, 16–18.

36. Bunin himself often had visions of "paradise." For instance, having crossed the equator on February 15, 1911, he wrote: "We came upon a timeless summer, a completely new world which spoke to me about some long forgotten, heavenly, and blissful life." Three days later, after having journeyed with naked rowers on a river in Ceylon, he wrote to his brother, Yuly: "My feeling for that which is warm, primordial, and paradisiacal has again become alive and strong . . . A noble and awe-inspiring order." See Grin, *Ustami Buninykh*, 1:97.

37. *Bunin's note:* "Then there was neither death nor immortality" (from the *Rigveda*).

Editors' note: The *Rigveda*, or "Wisdom of the Verses," is the earliest work of the Hindu Vedas, the ancient sacred literature of India. Essentially, the *Rigveda* is a collection of more than a thousand hymns glorifying the gods and their liturgy.

38. *Bunin's note:* "Let me go, let me go!" This also means: "Let me leave the Chain!" But what is there beyond the Chain! "Would you go and look to see how it ends? One has to keep thinking about this!"

39. *Bunin's note:* Tolstoy's maternal grandfather, Count N. S. Volkonsky, also showed a pride that was legendary.

Editors' note: According to tradition, Buddha was the son of rulers of the kingdom of Sakyas (India) and thus a member of the Kshatriya, or warrior, caste.

40. Buddha named his son Rahula, or "Chain."

41. Tolstoy also suffered Buddhistic disillusionment in life. For instance, in his preface to *Christian Teaching,* he wrote:

> Until the age of fifty, I lived thinking that the life from birth to death constitutes the entire life of the individual, and that therefore his aim should be to secure his happiness in mortal life. I tried to secure that happiness, but the longer I lived, the more evident it became that such happiness does not and cannot exist. The happiness I sought did not materialize, and all that I attained ceased to be happiness as soon as I had attained it.
>
> My unhappiness became greater and greater, and the inevitability of death more and more apparent. I understood that in this meaningless and unhappy life, nothing awaited me but suffering, sickness, old age, and annihilation. And I asked myself: "Why is this so?" But I received no answer and came to despair.

See Leon, *Tolstoy,* 194.

42. Tolstoy wrote in "Notes of a Billiard Maker," "I am enmeshed in slimy nets; and I can neither free myself nor learn to bear them."

Nets are also a common image in Bunin's fiction. See, for instance, Youngbride's lace-curtain veil in *The Village;* Tonya's shawl of gold lace in *Dry Valley;* the sodden, heavy rigging that weighs down the sailors in *The Gentleman from San Francisco;* and the chainlike "nets" and leafy "lace" that envelop Mitya's home in *Mitya's Love.* See Troyat, *Tolstoy,* 103.

CHAPTER SIX

1. In another variant of Bunin's memoirs of Tolstoy, Bunin's father added: "Tolstoy was a fine bird! He could not see a deck of cards without getting excited!" See A. Kaun, "Bunin's Memories of Tolstoy," *Dial* 83 (1927): 273.

2. In the same variant, Bunin elaborated:

> Why did I have such feelings for a man of whose work I had not read a single line? The fact that Tolstoy was a writer was sufficient for me. . . . I do not recall precisely when I began to read Tolstoy and how it came about that I placed him apart from all others. . . .

For many years, I was genuinely in love with Tolstoy, in love with nearly every line of his, and with the man himself, with that image of him which I had created for myself, and which gave rise in me to the tormenting dream of actually seeing him. The dream was constant, persistent, and painful, but how to fulfill it? Go to Yasnaya Polyana? To ask Tolstoy to let me look at him at least just this once? But on what grounds, with what eyes could I present myself there, an unknown, timid boy?

See ibid., 273–74.

3. Efremov is a city near Tula, about 120 miles south of Moscow.

4. The variant continues: "[Having returned home] the peasants bantered with me, saying: 'Hey, young master, how did you manage to work up your Kirghiz so badly in twenty-four hours? Whom were you chasing? Whom did you fall in love with? Ten to one, you did not get a thing!'" See Kaun, "Bunin's Memories of Tolstoy," 274.

5. Poltava is a city approximately 175 miles southeast of Kiev and 500 miles southwest of Moscow.

6. The individual in question is the former student-revolutionary, and later Tolstoyan, Anatoly Stepanovich Butkevich. Arrested and imprisoned for his activities in 1887, Butkevich lived on a Tolstoyan commune in 1889–90 and eventually became a specialist on honeybees. He also often met and corresponded with Tolstoy.

7. Tolstoy's biographers disagree with both Sofya's and Bunin's assessments of Chertkov's physical appearance. They assert, rather, that Chertkov was a very handsome young man with the face of a gentle, religious aristocrat, graced with dark, watery eyes and a sharp, aquiline nose and ears. See Wilson, *Tolstoy*, 343; Nazaroff, *Tolstoy*, 257.

8. After a day of successful writing, Tolstoy would cast benevolent glances upon his family and announce that he had left "a little of his flesh in the inkpot." Sofya, though, puts forth a different view of her husband's literary activity. "Lyovochka is absorbed in his writing," she wrote in her diary. "He has strange, fixed eyes. He hardly ever talks, and seems not to be of this world." See Leon, *Tolstoy*, 129; Nazaroff, *Tolstoy*, 230.

9. In line with this, Tolstoy once quoted Pythagoras as saying: "Do not allow your children to kill insects, for here begins the killing of humankind." See Tolstoy, *Polnoe sobranie sochinenii*, 41:309.

10. Ivan Mikhailovich Klopsky was a former seminarian who sympathized with Tolstoy's views. A teacher at the Universities of Moscow and Petersburg, he was arrested in 1892 and later immigrated to America.

11. Nikolai Karonin published his story "The Teacher of Life" ("Uchitel' zhizni") in 1891. In this and other works, Karonin charged that the political and social troubles of the 1880s and early 1890s in Russia were rooted in the failure of intellectuals to offer an alternative to Tolstoyism.

12. Klopsky is, of course, copying Tolstoy's famed "peasant" dress.

13. Alexander Volkenshtein was a local doctor in Poltava who helped Tolstoy to buy food for the starving people there.

14. The reference is to Mitrofan and Tikhon Dudchenko, who came from the area around Kharkov but who, in 1891, lived as farmer-Tolstoyans in Poltava. A year later, local officials forced them to leave the area.

15. Bunin is referring to Boris Nikolaevich Leontiev, a former student at the Institute for Pages in Saint Petersburg, who, in 1891, was working in a carpentry workshop in Poltava. He later abandoned Tolstoyism and espoused revolutionary populism.

16. Teneremo was the pseudonym for Isaak Borisovich Fainerman, a Tolstoyan, writer, and critic. In his youth, Teneremo was a political revolutionary who had become disillusioned with socialism and wished to discover more about Tolstoy's social and religious beliefs. At the age of nineteen, he arrived unannounced at Yasnaya Polyana, saying that he wished to work for the common good and astonishing the people by suddenly giving away all his clothes to the poor. (He was immediately provided with new apparel.) Teneremo then settled in the village, converted to Russian Orthodoxy, and worked as a teacher until he was conscripted for military service. Later, he lived in an unsuccessful Tolstoyan colony and also wrote a book about Tolstoy. See Dole, *The Life of Count Tolstoi,* 236; Wilson, *Tolstoy,* 346.

17. Kharkov is both a city and a region in the northeast Ukraine.

18. Prince Dmitri Alexandrovich Khilkov is one of the more interesting Tolstoyans. Khilkov had been a member of the Imperial Hussars; but after he killed a Turk in the Russo-Turkish War of 1877–78, he became a pacifist and retired to his family estate in Kharkov. Although Khilkov never met Tolstoy personally, he read the writer's ethical tracts and put his ideas into practice. He opened a school for village children, gave away nearly all his land to the peasants, and furnished them with money and livestock. He subsisted on a plot of several acres and, for awhile, even worked for a peasant without pay. Khilkov also conducted meetings at his home, where he instructed the serfs in his understanding of Tolstoy's philosophy.

Within three years, Khilkov became the leader of some two hundred devoted followers who refused to pay taxes, serve in the army, swear allegiance to the emperor, and follow Orthodoxy. For instance, during the most solemn feast days, only five women in a parish of some six thousand souls were attending church.

Khilkov's success was brief. Government officials, alarmed at his growing influence as well as his increasing desire for outright revolutionary activity, first exiled him in 1896 to either Siberia or the Caucasus (accounts differ), where he lived with a group of Dukhobors, and then to the Baltic provinces, where, in 1898, he received permission to immigrate to England. There Khilkov lived the rest of life in a Tolstoyan colony at Purleigh.

Khilkov would know additional sorrow. For instance, in 1893, Alexander III ordered that two of Khilkov's children be taken from him and his wife and that, against the will of their parents, they be baptized and put in charge of their grandmother. Despite passionate appeals to Alexander by Tolstoy, the children were never released to their parents.

Tolstoy noted in his 1894 letter to Bunin: "The taking of Khilkov's children is an important event which calls all of us to greater moral urgencies, that is, the increasingly growing need to free ourselves from that force which perpetrates such evil." See Tolstoy, *Polnoe sobranie sochinenii*, 67:48. Also see Simmons, *Leo Tolstoy*, 1:140, 144, 187.

19. Volkenshtein is following in the footsteps of his "master," since Tolstoy always preferred to go third class so that he could chat with the common people.

As readers of *Anna Karenina* know, Tolstoy regarded the recent appearance of trains in Russia as one of the more dubious benefits of civilization. For instance, he complained of the disagreeable sensations that he experienced in railway carriages. He also had no patience with obsequious conductors and aloof travelers from the upper classes.

Regarding trains, Tolstoy once wrote to Turgenev: "Yesterday . . . I changed from the nasty railway to a stagecoach. . . . I did well to leave that Sodom. For heaven's sake . . . never go by railway. Traveling by railway is like going to a brothel for love: convenient, but unhumanly mechanical and killingly uniform." See Simmons, *Leo Tolstoy*, 2:331; Dole, *The Life of Count Tolstoi*, 212–13; Shklovsky, *Lev Tolstoy*, 250.

20. Tolstoyan colonies were often racked with rancor and dissent, victims of misplaced ideals and zeal. For instance, the community in Smolensk quickly disintegrated when its members could not decide on a course of action when one of its members stole a waistcoat but refused to return it, justifying himself by the advanced sophistries he had only recently acquired. Another Tolstoyan colony in Tver faced ruin because, having relinquished all right to property, it foolishly allowed peasants to haul away all the wood within its confines without charge. (Such a situation was common; smiling peasants routinely appropriated cows, saddles, and scythes from perplexed Tolstoyans.)

The fate of still another Tolstoyan community in Kharkov was even more bizarre. Here a cunning stranger calmly announced to people there that he was the new master of the place and that, since they had no right to resist him with violence, they would all have to leave their surroundings. Having deeded the land and buildings to the local peasants, the dispossessed members withdrew meekly.

Tolstoyan colonies outside of Russia did not fare any better. For instance, the English community at Purleigh was so fraught with quarrels, misunderstandings, and even lapses into insanity that one of its sympathizers remarked: "There is more tomfoolery to the square yard in this movement than in any other one that I have known." See Leon, *Tolstoy*, 239–40; Dole, *The Life of Count Tolstoi*, 443–45; Nazaroff, *Tolstoy*, 286–87.

21. Khamovniki was the site of a simple, wooden, twenty-room, two-story villa that Tolstoy had bought in October 1882 for 27,500 rubles; it was located on Dolgo-Khamovnichesky Street in the industrial outskirts of southwest Moscow. Close by were a stocking factory, a perfume distillery, a spinning mill, and a brewery—each with its own smells and sounds. Tolstoy's city home did have its amenities, though—for example, over two acres of walled garden, replete with thickets, fruit trees, a pavilion, and a wide, raised walk. Also, for all his alleged simplicity, Tolstoy furnished his city home with exquisite antiques, divans, and lamps. See Troyat, *Tolstoy*, 427–28; Simmons, *Leo Tolstoy*, 2:44.

22. It was during Tolstoy's move to Moscow in 1882 that he began to repudiate many of what he considered to be the idle, egotistic, predatory, and insensate accoutrements and customs of his class. For instance, he now wore peasant attire. "Tolstoy's costume," Sofya's brother recalled, "consisted of a gray flannel blouse, which in summer he exchanged for one of linen of very original cut. In fact, there was only old woman who could make it according to his prescription. It was in this blouse that he sat for his portraits by Repin and Kramskoy. Tolstoy's outer dress was composed of a caftan and a half-length sheepskin coat, or a short jacket of the simplest materials, which, like the eccentrically cut blouse, was evidently made not for show but to withstand the weather." ("What a masquerade!" "Granny" Alexandra was forced to exclaim.)

It was also at this time that Tolstoy began to adopt a simple diet, to drop the use of his title, and even to speak with a peasant accent. He also desired that the folk address him in the simple Russian manner, that is, with his name and patronymic instead of the formal *vashe siiiatel'stvo*, or "your Highness." See Dole, *The Life of Count Tolstoi*, 209, 296; Nazaroff, *Tolstoy*, 249.

23. Adamovich, in his memoirs, wrote: "Bunin constantly talked about Tolstoy. He remembered that when he first met the writer. . . . 'Tolstoy was so astute, so terrible . . . and his eyes were so frightful, gray, and deeply sunken . . . that I almost . . . ,' and he ended with words that I cannot print." See Adamovich, "Bunin. Vospominaniia," 181.

24. Although Tolstoy did, in fact, leave Sofya, he was not above reprimanding others for their attachments to married women. For instance, he once chided Chekhov for his liaison with the married writer Lidiya Avilova: "Why are you courting another man's wife? That's not proper!" See Vera Muromsteva-Bunina's diary excerpt of August 6, 1930, in Grin, *Ustami Buninykh*, 2:229.

25. The woman is Tolstoy's wife, Sofya Andreevna.

26. Throughout his life, Tolstoy believed that life in the present offered the best possibilities for happiness and success. For instance, as a soldier in the Caucasus, he wrote: "To live in the present, that is, to act in the best possible fashion, this is wisdom."

In his diary some thirty years later, Tolstoy elaborated:

Only when one lives without consideration of past or future time does one live a genuinely free life in which there are no obstacles. As soon as one remembers the past (the offenses, the contradictions, even one's own weaknesses) or thinks of the future (that something will or will not happen), one becomes dissatisfied or anxious. Only at one point, in the present alone, can one fuse with God and live in one's divine essence. When an individual uses reason to consider what will be, he is insignificant and weak; but when he uses it to do the will of He who has sent you, he is powerful and free.

Finally, in the last year of his life, Tolstoy concluded:

[One must] either live in time and space with one's actions guided by thoughts of the future and by external material conditions, and to fear, hope, and always be deceived and suffer; or [one must] live only in the present moment in one's spiritual self, in the soul, and to let oneself be guided by its activity—knowing neither fear, nor deception, nor error, nor suffering, but love, that law of the spiritual principle of the soul. Life does not permit either one or the other entirely. But life is only life when the spiritual principle triumphs over the material one, and it is in this victory alone that life consists.

See Simmons, *Leo Tolstoy*, 1:105; Leon, *Tolstoy*, 295, 328.

27. Mediator (Posrednik) was a publishing enterprise founded by Chertkov and Biryukov in 1885 to produce literature for the masses that would serve as an alternative to pulp fiction and expound the ideals and values of Tolstoy. For instance, Mediator printed translations of European classics; the moralist works of Marcus Aurelius and Epictetus; pamphlets written by Tolstoy himself; pictures by Ilya Repin; books by Charles Dickens, George Eliot, Charles Kingsley, and Matthew Arnold; and works by other writers and critics of the Russian government and the church, including Nikolai Leskov, Anton Chekhov, Vsevelod Garshin, Mamin-Sibiryak, and Gleb Uspensky. It also circulated material on agronomy, animal husbandry, hygiene, and other subjects to improve the lives of the peasantry. Interestingly, the editors of Mediator were assisted by members of the Russian populist intelligentsia, including the revolutionary Vladimir Bonch-Bruevich and Lenin's future wife, Nadezhda Krupskaya.

All of Mediator's publications were printed in large quantities and at very low cost. The success of the publishing house was phenomenal. In its first years of operation, the press printed approximately 24,000 copies of Tolstoy's books; by the fourth year, it was publishing 3,000,000 copies. Furthermore, since writers for Mediator did not copyright any of their works, their publications were often reprinted by other publishers.

With Mediator, Tolstoy and company showed that artists could serve the people in a genuine and practical way. In fact, so successful were the activities of Mediator that it served as the model for the penny Universal Classical Library, which was distributed by the noted publisher William Thomas Stead in England and which served as the seedbed for World's Classics, a key outlet for translations of Tolstoy's works in the West. See Leon, *Tolstoy*, 238–39; Biryukov, *Leo Tolstoy*, 103–5.

28. Bunin opened his ill-fated bookstore in late December 1894.

29. The *zemstvo* existed from 1864 to 1918 as an elected and self-governing institution that focused on economic concerns in Russian districts and provinces. As such, it was also a vehicle for liberalism in the country. In 1865, the *zemstvo* was introduced into nineteen provinces in Russia, including Poltava.

30. Bunin is referring to the ascendancy of Tsar Nicholas II to the throne on November 1, 1894.

31. Bunin makes clear his ambivalence about Tolstoyism in his 1895 story "In the Summerhouse" ("Na dache"). In this work, an ardent Tolstoyan named Kamensky is defeated in a debate by liberals who are ignorant and mocking. Kamensky and the liberals exchange heated views on a host of topics, for example, newspapers, railways, drunkenness, prostitution, Tolstoy's private life, and the nature of work, goodness, and love. No one, though, changes his position.

Critics were confused by Bunin's Kamensky. For instance, the Russian critic Alexander Skabichevsky wrote to Bunin: "We are sorry but we cannot print your story . . . [because] you have failed to explain the protagonist. What do you think of him? Is he a hero or a monster?" See S. Kryzytski, *The Works of Ivan Bunin* (The Hague: Mouton, 1971), 57.

32. A similar question, though, did lead Tolstoy to defend his ideas on nonviolence and passive resistance to evil. When a disciple asked Tolstoy if an individual would be justified in killing a wolf that had attacked him, Tolstoy replied: "No, he would not, for if he kills a wolf, he may also kill a dog and a man. There will be no limit to such a thing. . . . Once we admit that we may kill and resist evil, evil and falsehood will reign unchecked in the world. In fact, that is our situation now."

In line with such a response, Shklovsky notes that when people asked Tolstoy what he would do if he were attacked by a "savage Zulu," or if he saw a mother beating her son to death, they were, in fact, using Aesopic language; that is, they were posing such questions as "codes" to discuss the nature and actions of oppressive governments and autocracies. So, when Tolstoy replied that the Zulu and the mother should not be met with violence but rather should be pitied, educated, and raised to a higher level of existence, his response to his listeners was not as extreme as it may have sounded initially.

Tolstoy himself was ambivalent about Tolstoyism. On one the hand, he assisted the movement by writing articles for its press and by giving moral and financial assistance to its followers, especially those who suffered for their religious beliefs. On the other hand, Tolstoy never led or sponsored Tolstoyism in any protracted or organized way. He also did not wish to form a sect based on his ideas. "I am Tolstoy, but not a Tolstoyan," he was alleged to have said. He continued: "It is a great and gross mistake to speak about Tolstoyism or to seek my guidance or ask my decisions about problems. There is no Tolstoyism or any teaching of mine, and there never has been."

More seriously, perhaps, Tolstoy was baffled by his followers because they often seemed either to be completely alien to his way of thinking or to keep missing the point of his ideas and ideals. "I shall soon be dead," he wrote, "and people will say that Tolstoy taught men to plow and reap and make boots. But, throughout my life, the chief thing that I have been trying to say, the one thing that I believe in the most of all, they will forget."

As a result, Tolstoy believed that Tolstoyan colonies and other utopian endeavors were destined to flounder on the rocks of human imperfection. It was individuals, not sectarian or economic communities—"new monasteries," he called them—who were to realize his message in life.

"Why live in a community?" Tolstoy once asked. "Think of the numbers of people who settled in communities, and nothing came of such arrangements! All their energies first went into the external arrangements of life; and when at length they settled down, they began to quarrel and gossip, and everything went to pieces." Later, he continued: "To live in a commune . . . for a long period of time . . . is obviously foolish and sinful . . . because one is deprived of one-half of life—communion with the world, without which his life has no sense."

Still another time, Tolstoy challenged "collective" living by endorsing the "healthy egoism" of his character Platon Karataev in *War and Peace*. He wrote: "Above all, one should not look for new ways of life. . . . Let everyone first do his own work . . . and try to steadily improve his own situation. Then he will find new ways of life incidentally."

Later in life, Tolstoy pronounced succinctly: "Tolstoyans are individuals with convictions utterly opposed to mine. . . . No one is more repugnant to me than they." See Leon, *Tolstoy,* 240–41; Dole, *The Life of Count Tolstoi,* 336; Nazaroff, *Tolstoy,* 288; Shklovsky, *Lev Tolstoy,* 510–11, 584; Simmons, *Leo Tolstoy,* 2:144–45, 237, 285.

33. Tolstoy often took his children to task—unsuccessfully—for what he saw as breaches of social decorum. For instance, his daughter Tatyana recalled that whenever she said that someone was boring or stupid, Tolstoy

would reply: "More boring than you? More stupid than you?" Tatyana continued: "I understood perfectly well the lesson that Father was trying to teach me. But I refused to accept it and would reply insolently: 'Yes, more stupid and boring than me.'"

Bunin quickly forgave Tolstoy's daughters for their conduct at their initial meeting. For instance, he wrote to Tatyana on April 27, 1934: "I have been touched by your friendship so very deeply. . . . Truly, throughout my life, you Tolstoys have been like family to me."

See Baboreko, "I. A. Bunin o L. N. Tolstom," 178. Also see Wilson, *Tolstoy,* 355.

34. The first Russian Temperance Society was founded in Saint Petersburg in 1890.

35. In spite of such flippancy, Tolstoy sought to combat alcoholism and other addictions in Russia. For instance, he dealt with both smoking and drinking in an 1890 article entitled "Why Do Men Intoxicate Themselves?" ("Dlia chego liudi odurmanivaiutsia?"). He also organized a temperance society in which entrants were asked to sign a form that read: "I, the undersigned, recognize the great evil and sin of drunkenness, and I promise never to drink any alcohol, vodka, wine, or beer; or to buy or offer it to others. And, with all my strength, I will convince others, particularly young people and children, of the evils of drunkenness and of the advantages of a sober life. I also promise to attract new members to our society."

Sofya and the peasants at Yasnaya Polyana were among the first to sign this pledge. Within two years, Tolstoy managed to persuade 741 persons to take the oath, though, to his sorrow, he saw that many quickly broke their promise. Tolstoy, however, was not as severe with drunken peasants as he was with students, professors, and other cultured individuals who, he believed, were setting a bad example by drinking in the presence of waiters in restaurants. Even here, though, Tolstoy could not escape controversy. For instance, when he chided university students for their customary carousing and drunkenness on Tatyana's Day (January 12), several of them sent him a telegram in which they facetiously "drank to his health." More seriously, they even threatened to march on his house and to force him to retract his statement. (The planned demonstration never materialized.)

For the remainder of his life, Tolstoy remained committed to "temperance." For instance, when at a celebration of his seventieth birthday a guest proposed to drink a glass of wine to Tolstoy's health, Sofya immediately intervened, explaining: "One may not drink to the health of Lev Nikolaevich because he belongs to a temperance league."

Similarly, Tolstoy returned a case of cigarettes to a dull-witted manufacturer who had imprinted the writer's picture on each package. (Sofya, though, kept one package for her growing collection of Tolstoyana.) See

Biryukov, *Leo Tolstoy,* 120–21; Dole, *The Life of Count Tolstoi,* 323; Simmons, 2:110, 114, 117, 419; Troyat, *Tolstoy,* 552.

36. Tolstoy, who wrote *Master and Man* (*Khoziain i rabotnik*) in 1895, did indeed have doubts about the artistic merits of the work. "It is so long since I have written anything artistic," he wrote to Strakhov, "that I truly do not know whether my story ought to be printed. I wrote it with great satisfaction, but as to its printing—I do not know." Strakhov replied: "My God, Lev Nikolaevich! How splendid, how priceless your piece is!"

Tolstoy remained unconvinced, though. "Since I hear . . . only complements about *Master and Man,*" he continued to Strakhov, "I am reminded of the anecdote of the preacher who, surprised by the storm of applause at the end of one of his sentences, stopped short and asked: 'Have I said something wrong?'" See Troyat, *Tolstoy,* 509; Simmons, *Leo Tolstoy,* 2:207.

37. Bunin is mistaken here. It was Ivan L'vovich Tolstoy who died in 1895. Nikolai L'vovich Tolstoy (Kolya) had died twenty years earlier.

38. Maiden's Field (Devich'e pole) is located in southwest Moscow.

39. The Arbat is an old section of Moscow not far from the Kremlin.

40. Bunin's "frozen" image of Tolstoy caused him to see the writer in a dream. Years later, as an exile, he told Bakhrakh: "Lev Nikolaevich appeared to me in a dream. His face was all blue; his beard was disheveled. He was drinking gin from a bottle. 'Where did he get such a thing?' I wondered. It was clear that he did not recognize me. I approached him, introduced myself, and reminded him that we had met several times. But it was all to no avail. The old man seemed as made of stone. I was beside myself. Here I was writing in the press about my meetings with Tolstoy, but he did not recognize me."

Bakhrakh continued: "The next day Bunin and I went to Nice, and the first thing he bought there was a big bottle of gin!" See Bakhrakh, *Bunin v khalate,* 86.

41. Later in life, Bunin shamelessly concocted several details regarding his meetings with Tolstoy. For instance, when Andrei Sedykh asked Bunin how well he knew Tolstoy, Bunin replied:

> We drank some home-brewed vodka and even ate some meat together. After all, I was a Tolstoyan. . . . Now don't you laugh at me. What is there to laugh about? His lessons contained many things that were splendid, chaste, and captivating to a young heart.
> What a shame that I do not have a picture of myself at that time. I had these romantic eyes that were so blue and dreamy-like. My cheeks had such a light down on them that people sometimes took me for a young Jew.

See A. Sedykh, "Zavtrak s Buninym," *Novoe russkoe slovo* (April 26, 1942): 8.

CHAPTER SEVEN

1. Bunin met Tolstoy on the Arbat in the winter of 1901.
2. Circa 1910, Bunin gave the same advice to Valentin Kataev:

I know that there are times when you have despaired, when you think that everything has been said . . . that there are no new subjects or emotions, that all rhymes have been used up and are worn out, that one can count all the meters on the fingers of one's hand, and that, in the end, it is quite impossible to become a poet.

Thoughts like that drove me crazy when I was young. But that is nonsense, my dear fellow. Every object about you, every feeling you have is the subject for a poet. Listen carefully to your feelings, observe the world around you, and write. But write what you feel and see and not what other poets, even the most brilliant, have felt and seen before you. Be independent in art. That you can learn. And then the endless world of genuine poetry will open before you.

See Kataev, *Svratoi kolodets,* 146.

3. The day Tolstoy died was a day of public mourning in Russia. Leading newspapers were edged heavily in black; and the tsar, the Duma, and the Council of State sent letters of condolence. The writer's death also sparked widespread political protest. Students demonstrated throughout Russia, the University of Petersburg suspended lectures, and protestors rallied against the death penalty. All over the empire, hundreds of thousands of people waited at news centers and telegraph offices to hear the news that Tolstoy was dead. (Interestingly, when Lenin seized power seven years later, the Western press described the event as a Tolstoyan revolution.)

The grief of a Russian doctor aptly captured the public's darkness and despair. "What a tremendous, incomparable loss," he wrote, "and especially for us Russians. We can ill spare him, especially in our present day of almost utter reactionary demoralization, without a ray of hope for a better future. Never in my lifetime (I am forty) has the death of any great man been felt as such as personal loss as Tolstoy's passing has been felt by all of us. I only hope that this death may serve as a moral shock to awaken the dormant conscience of the Russian intelligentsia and bring it out of the stupor into which it has plunged by the events of the past few years."

Predictably, government and church officials attempted to constrain the mourning. For instance, the Most Holy Synod forbade all memorial services for the deceased writer, and the minister of the interior would not allow special trains to travel to Yasnaya Polyana. Mourning flags were banned in Moscow, inscriptions on funeral wreaths were scrutinized for "revolutionary" messages, and literary societies throughout the country were prohibited from celebrating Tolstoy's life and art. In one case, a women's school was forbidden to present Tolstoy's play *The Fruits of Enlightenment.*

In truth, though, the national mourning for Tolstoy was short-lived. For instance, in a letter dated November 26, 1910, Bunin wrote to Gorky: "Tolstoy's death was supposed to have disturbed the public, but it seems to me that no one is really upset. The indifference of everyone to everything is unbelievable." See Baboreko, *I. A. Bunin. Materialy*, 151; Leon, *Tolstoy*, 359; Dole, *The Life of Count Tolstoi*, 411; Wilson, *Tolstoy*, 516; Shklovsky, *Lev Tolstoy*, 764.

4. Kozlova Zaseka is a train station on the Tula-Oryol line several miles directly north of Yasnaya Polyana. The train carrying Tolstoy's remains arrived there from Astapovo on November 9 at 6:30 A.M.

5. Approximately four thousand people attended Tolstoy's funeral. See Wilson, *Tolstoy*, 517.

6. Just as Tolstoy, in his first *Last Will and Testament*, had declined all official announcements of his death, so, too, did he reject any large-scale observances to commemorate his passing. He had written: "Bury me where I die, in the cheapest cemetery if I die in a town, and in the cheapest coffin, as paupers are buried. Flowers and wreaths are not to be sent, speeches are not to be made. If possible, bury me without priests or burial services. But if those who bury me dislike [these requests], let them bury me in the ordinary way with a funeral service, but as cheaply and simply as possible."

Tolstoy's family acceded to his requests, with the already-noted exception that the countess had a liturgy performed over his remains at Astapovo. In truth, they had little choice, since the bishop of Tula, Parfeny, had rejected a plea from Tolstoy's son Andrei to celebrate a full-fledged Orthodox funeral for his father. As a result, Tolstoy's interment was the first public burial in Russia since the 988 conversion of Saint Vladimir to be attended without the rites of the church. See Leon, *Tolstoy*, 272; Dole, *The Life of Count Tolstoi*, 408; Wilson, *Tolstoy*, 517.

7. Tolstoy's remains were attired in the same blouse and gray trousers that people had come to associate with him in later life. Also, his corpse had seemed to have shrunk, and his face had greatly changed. His eyes were closed; his nose was sharp; his skin was like parchment. A white handkerchief bound his lower jaw, hiding the gray beard. Tolstoy's hands, shriveled and dark, lay on his breast.

Individuals were admitted ten at a time to pay their respects to the writer. Some bowed to the ground as they kissed Tolstoy's hand; others sobbed uncontrollably.

At one point, Sofya, tears streaming down her emaciated face, was seen smoothing her husband's forehead with her hand and exclaiming: "Dusha moia! Zhizn' moia!" ("My Soul! My Life!"). Before she could be induced to leave the body of her husband, she threw herself upon his remains and sobbed: "If only sufferings could expiate sins! There could be no greater agony than this!" See Dole, *The Life of Count Tolstoi,* 405, 406.

8. The local governor allowed wreaths for Tolstoy's funeral but insisted that they be without "provocative inscriptions that might incite demonstrations." See Troyat, *Tolstoy,* 694.

9. The writer Vladimir Korolenko recalled of the event:

All day long . . . by forest paths . . . and over the wide highway came the people singly and in groups, on foot and by carriage, to gather round his grave. From time to time, someone would sing "Eternal Memory." Heads were bared; the voices sounded simple and sad. Then silence would ensue, and all that could be heard was the rustle of the few dry oak leaves, mingling with the low murmur of the subdued voices of men talking solemnly. . . .

In the overall gossip about everyday affairs mingled streams of conversation about Tolstoy, who had passed away forever from this life into a world of endless mystery and eternal question. People talked about the great Russian writer and the fact that the good man had wished "to go thither" without church rites, without incense, and without the usual farewell of those whom the centuries and millions of men have recognized as the official potentates of that invisible world with its mysteries and judgments.

The talk on this subject was varied, like the murmur of a human sea. But into the elemental wide note of this sea broke a new note, into millions of yet untouched minds fell a new fact, and in millions of hearts stirred a new feeling. This thought and this feeling were those of toleration. . . .

The legendary Titans moved mountains. But in reality not legend, Tolstoy moved mountains of human feelings in a way that no king or conqueror could.

See Dole, *The Life of Count Tolstoi,* 411; Shklovsky, *Lev Tolstoy,* 764.

10. Bunin is mistaken here. Bryusov's article "At the Funeral of L. N. Tolstoy" ("Na pokhoronakh L. N. Tolstogo") was published in the journal *Russian Thought (Russkaia mysl')* in December 1912 (119–27). Bunin's error is understandable, though. *Russian News (Russkie Vedomosti),* founded in 1863, was a leading voice for moderate Russian liberals. It was closed by the Bolsheviks in 1918.

11. The coffin was also attended by Tolstoy's daughters and Sofya, who, at long last, conducted herself with dignity and restraint.

12. Tolstoy recalled that, in his youth, no one in his group believed that serfdom was wrong morally. "In our circle in the forties," he wrote, "it did not occur that one should not own serfs or that the peasants should be given their freedom. Owning the serfs that one inherited was seen as an essential condition in life; and if one were a good master, all that he could do was not simply show concern for the serfs' material condition but give them moral guidance." A decade later, Tolstoy's views had changed only slightly. In 1854 he saw serfdom as "Russian slavery" but also as a "very benevolent evil."

Still, Tolstoy's relationship with the peasants troubled him greatly. In 1856, he gathered the 309 male serfs at Yasnaya Polyana to announce that he was giving them their freedom, together with land which they could pay off after thirty years. As before, the serfs met Tolstoy's "liberation" both with an innate fear of change as well as with an equally inborn suspicion of a master bearing them "gifts."

They thus declined Tolstoy's offer, their refusal also being partly motived by a prevalent, but unfounded, rumor that the new tsar, Alexander II, at his coronation was intending to free the folk and to give them all the land. They therefore regarded Tolstoy's "emancipation" as a ruse, a pact obligating them to a prior contract before they received freedom from the government.

Also as before, Tolstoy was bitterly disappointed by the peasants' obstinacy and suspicion. On the one hand, he concluded not only that the peasants did not want freedom but that also the bond between "master" and "man" was "absurd." Lord and peasant, he believed, were like "two powerful men joined with a sharp chain that hurts both of them, and that insures when one of them moves, he involuntarily cuts the other, leaving neither room to work." On the other hand, Tolstoy believed that he, as representative of a rapacious gentry, had no one else to blame for the problem. "Despotic landowners have made for hostile peasants," he wrote to a friend. "At our meeting, the serfs told me that I should give them all the land outright. And when I replied that [if I did so] I would be left without my shirt, they simply laughed. But it was impossible to get angry at them."

With haunting prescience, Tolstoy concluded: "If, within six months, the serfs are not freed, there will be a conflagration. Everything is ripe for one. Treasonable hands are not lacking to light the fire of a revolt, and the firestorm will spread everywhere."

It should be noted here, though, that Tolstoy took a characteristically ambivalent attitude toward the actual decree of emancipation in 1861. He publicly toasted Tsar Alexander II, proclaiming that "in reality, we owe the Emancipation to the Emperor alone." Also, to the French socialist and anarchist philosopher Pierre Proudon, Tolstoy bragged—wrongly—that Russians "did not free their serfs with empty hands . . . but gave them property along with their liberty!"

Tolstoy, though, sought to dissociate himself from the national enthusiasm for the event; for, as he saw it, the proclamation was another "act of state," the province of theorists rather than of pragmatists, and as such deserving of his indifference and scorn. "Have you read the exact terms of the emancipation?" Tolstoy wrote to Herzen. "All the peasants are dissatisfied. Previously, they could hope that everything would turn out all right; but now they know for certain that everything will be all wrong . . . and that the whole thing is the work of the masters."

As he later wrote in *What Then Should We Do?* it made no sense to Tolstoy to free the serfs in name but not to allow them ownership of the land and to impose taxes upon them that they could not pay. As evidence for his view, he cited the constantly diminishing numbers of livestock (an index of folk prosperity) as well as the fact that too few peasants had purchased land and that too many of them were using their newfound freedom in taverns and inns.

Tolstoy also realized that emancipation of the folk would not forestall revolt by them. In 1865, he prophesied: "The Russian Revolution will not be directed against the tsar and despotism but against the ownership of the land." Some twenty years later, Tolstoy added:

> The revolution of workers, with its horrors of destruction and murder, not merely threatens us, but we have been living with it already for some thirty years. Only for awhile and by various temporary devices have we somehow managed to postpone its eruption. Such is the condition of Europe; such is the condition of Russia, and it is far worse for us because we have no safety valves.
>
> Except for the tsar, the classes that oppress the masses have no justification in the eyes of the people; those masses are held down in their position by violence, cunning, and opportunism. . . . Hatred among the worst representatives of the people and contempt for us among the best of them increase every hour.

Even more ominously, Tolstoy wrote in a 1901 letter to the tsar: "Again murders, again bloodshed, again punishments, again apprehension, terror, accusations and charges, threats and irritation, on the one hand; and, on the other, the desire for vengeance and the readiness for sacrifice. Again all the Russian people are divided into two hostile camps and are preparing and waiting to commit great crimes." See Simmons, *Leo Tolstoy*, 1:118, 155–56, 183, 187, 190, 213. Also see Crankshaw, *Tolstoy*, 104, 179, 187–88; Leon, *Tolstoy*, 65, 209, 213; Dole, *The Life of Count Tolstoi*, 173, 377; Shklovsky, *Lev Tolstoy*, 86; Troyat, *Tolstoy*, 204–5, 284.

13. Tolstoy's difficulties with the peasants continued almost to the end of his life. For instance, two years before his death, he had forgiven a peasant for stealing timber, but his family demanded that the offender be brought to justice. Tolstoy, bemoaning his inability to reverse the action, recorded: "The peasant overtook me with a petition and a complaint at having been sentenced to prison for stealing the trees. It was very painful. He cannot understand that I, the husband, cannot do as I like. He looks upon me as an evil-doer and a Pharisee who is hiding behind his wife."

Several months later, the artist Ilya Repin recalled how a pale and agitated Tolstoy told him of an encounter with some hostile folk:

> Tolstoy buried his face in his trembling hands. He groaned aloud and tears came to his eyes. "Ah, the things I have just seen, the words I have just heard.

. . . As I was riding along, I overtook some peasants in a cart and spoke to them. Scowling, one of them stood up and shouted at me: 'What, are you still alive, you old swine? Hasn't the devil taken you yet? You should have died a long time ago. You have lived long enough as it is. . . .'

"'What has come over you?' I asked in astonishment. 'What can you mean? I am Tolstoy from Yasnaya Polyana.'

"'Oh, we know you well enough, you old bloodsucker. You ought to be done away with.'"

See Leon, *Tolstoy*, 313.

14. Tolstoy wrote his "Afterword to *The Kreutzer Sonata*" ("Posleslovie k *Kreutserovoi Sonate*") in 1889. The piece was published in Berlin in 1890 and a year later in Russia.

15. Tolstoy had written in his "Afterword" that "it was better for the unmarried not to marry." See Dole, *The Life of Count Tolstoi*, 330.

16. Sofya could not but agree with such an assessment. "I am terribly afraid of becoming pregnant," she wrote at age forty-five on December 25, 1890. "For everyone will hear of the disgrace and jubilantly repeat the recent Moscow joke—*Voilà le veritable postscriptum de la 'Sonate de Kreutzer.'*"

Two months later, she complained: "I don't know why and how people have connected *The Kreutzer Sonata* with our married life. Yet, it is a fact that everyone, from the tsar right down to Lyova's brother . . . has felt sorry for me. But what is the good of talking to people? In my own heart, I have felt that this story was directed against me. It has wounded me and disgraced me in the eyes of the entire world. It has also destroyed the last remnant of love between my husband and me. And all this despite the fact that during the whole of my married life I have never done anything wrong." See Leon, *Tolstoy*, 247.

17. There were no universities in Novorossisk at this time, only several technical colleges.

18. Vladimir Lazursky taught Greek and Latin to Andrei and Mikhail Tolstoy. He also had been a colleague of Bunin's in Odessa in 1919.

19. Tolstoy carried his disaffection with marriage into his fiction. Prince Andrei warns Pierre in *War and Peace:*

Never, never marry, my dear fellow! That is my advice. Never marry until you can say to yourself that you have done all you are capable of, and until you have ceased to love the woman of your choice and have seen her plainly as she is. Otherwise, you will make a cruel and irrevocable mistake.

Marry when you are old and good for nothing, or else all that is good and noble in you will be lost and wasted on trifles. . . . Tie yourself down with a woman, and like a chained convict, you will lose all your freedom! All that you have of hope and strength will weigh you down and torment you with regret!

257

Later, Tolstoy wrote on the subject of marriage in fiction: "People who end their novels with marriage . . . spread terrific nonsense . . . for marriage ought to be compared with a funeral, not a happy holiday."

Tolstoy's disaffection with the institution of marriage only worsened with time. For instance, in 1899, he wrote:

> The chief cause of unhappiness in marriage lies in the fact that young people are brought up to believe in idea of married happiness. Sexual attraction, encouraged by public opinion and by literature, surrounds marriage with a charm full of promise. But marriage, far from being a happiness, is always a misery; it is the price that one pays for sexual satisfaction. Slavery, satiety, repulsion, and the physical and moral faults of one's partner—these are sufferings that must be endured. There is also malice, stupidity, lying, vanity, or drunkenness, all faults which are even more unbearable in another than in oneself, to say nothing of the physical defects such as ugliness, dirtiness, smell, sores, insanity, and the like. Of all this there is bound to be enough to make each one's burden heavy enough.
>
> We accept as a right all care, satisfaction, and help that marriage gives—things which should compensate for its bad side—and consider only its deficiencies. Thus we suffer in exact proportion to the happiness which we promised ourselves. The essential cause of this suffering is that we expect what never happens and do not expect what invariably does happen. So the only way to insure ourselves against such suffering is to expect nothing that is good and to be ready to bear that which is bad.

Tolstoy could be brutally frank in his condemnation of marriage. For instance, looking at Sofya, he intoned: "Only a husband comes to know a woman really well (and when it is too late). Only he sees his wife behind the stage. Is it for this reason that, as Lessing puts it, all husbands think: 'There is but one bad woman in the world, and it is she whom I have had the luck to marry.'" See Crankshaw, *Tolstoy*, 201–2, 254; Leon, *Tolstoy*, 251; Nazaroff, *Tolstoy*, 273, 274.

20. Sofya was often frustrated by what she saw as her husband's fickleness. "How with all our children," she wrote years later, "could I have turned like a weathercock in the direction in which my husband, constantly changing, drifted mentally. For him it was an ardent, sincere seeking; but for me, it would have been a painful imitation, and positively harmful to the family."

Tolstoy was undeterred, though. For instance, in 1859, he wrote to a friend: "A man's convictions are not those that he parades, but those that he has wrested from experience, and which others may find hard to understand." His enduring ideal was "to burn everything he had worshipped and to worship everything that he had burned." See Leon, *Tolstoy*, 90; Nazaroff, *Tolstoy*, 239; Troyat, *Tolstoy*, 339.

21. Tolstoy took quite literally Christ's commandment "Resist not him that is evil" (Matthew 5:39). For instance, in 1887, Tolstoy told the well-known traveler George Kennan:

> The revolutionaries whom you have seen in Siberia undertook to resist evil by violence. But what has been the result? Bitterness, misery, hatred, and bloodshed. The evils against which they took up arms still exist, and to them has been added a mass of previously nonexistent human suffering. It is not in this way that the Kingdom of God is to be realized on this earth. The entire history of the world is the history of violence; and, of course, one can cite violence; but surely you must see that in human society there is an endless variety of opinions as to what constitutes wrong and oppression. Furthermore, once one concedes the right of any man to resort to violence to resist what he regards as wrong, he being the judge, one authorizes every other man to enforce his opinions in the same way, and inevitably one has a universal reign of violence.

Nearly ten years later, Tolstoy elaborated: "Nonresistance to evil is important because it is a means by which an individual develops love. But nonresistance is even more important because, by absorbing evil, neutralizing it, and stopping its movement, it is the sole remedy against evil's noxious effects. Evil is like a rubber ball which is thrown against a wall. That is, it can continue only when confronted by resistance; it also requires a medium that will absorb its elasticity. Active Christianity consists of not creating something new but of absorbing evil."

Tolstoy felt so strongly about his concept of "nonresistance to evil" that when Kennan asked him if an individual could use violence to defend a woman who had been stripped naked by soldiers, he tearfully replied: "No, not even in such circumstances would [violence] be acceptable."

Later, Tolstoy concluded: "The principle of nonresistance to evil is the principle which binds all of Christ's teaching into one system . . . but only when it is understood not simply as a saying but also as a rule which must be abided by as an absolute law. Nonresistance to evil is a key which unlocks all doors, but which unlocks them only if it is pushed to the bottom of the lock." See Leon, *Tolstoy,* 265–66, 336; Nazaroff, *Tolstoy,* 235.

22. *Lapty* are bast shoes or sandals.

23. An English newspaper once wrote about Tolstoy that he was not only one of the "best abused men" in Russia but also "one of the best praised . . . critically and passionately, wisely and fanatically, for all his merits and for all his frailties." See Leon, *Tolstoy,* 314.

24. For instance, even as late as March 1909, a year before Tolstoy's death, a stranger had written to him: "I beg you to tell me, if only in a few words, why you are not poor, and what prevents you from becoming so, instead of continuing to live in conditions which not only exclude the idea of poverty but even of the least discomfort."

To this stranger, Tolstoy replied: "I have not done what you ask of me simply because of my weakness and mediocrity, and I never cease to repent for this weakness before God."

Throughout his life, Tolstoy took allegations of his hypocrisy quite seriously. For instance, he wrote to a friend:

People say to me—"If you believe that there is no reasonable life apart from the fulfillment of the Christian teaching, and if you love that reasonable life, why do you not fulfill its commands?"

I reply that I am a base creature and deserve blame and contempt for not fulfilling them. But, not so much to justify as to explain my inconsistency, I say: 'Consider my former life and present life, and you will see that I am trying to fulfill [these commands]. It is true that I do not fill a ten-thousandth part of them, and for that I am to blame. But it is not because I do not wish to fulfill them, but because I do not know how to do so. Teach me how to escape from these nets of temptation that have ensnared me. Help me, and I will fulfill [these commands]. But even with help, I desire and hope to fulfill them. Blame me—I do that myself —but blame *me*, and not the path I tread and show those who ask where the road lies! . . . With all my might, I wish to practice virtue, and at every failure I not only merely repent, but I also pray for help to enable me to perform it, and I gladly meet and listen to anyone who, like myself, is seeking the same road as I.

In fact, Tolstoy believed that acceptance of the charges of hypocrisy that people leveled at him was the catalyst for liberating his soul. "If I had heard of myself as an outsider," he recorded in his diary on July 2, 1908, "as a man living in luxury, wringing all that he could get out of the peasants, and locking them in prison, all the while preaching and professing Christianity, giving away coppers, and running from his loathsome actions by hiding behind his dear wife, I should not hesitate to call him a blackguard. . . . . But, perhaps, such an action is just what I need that I may be set free from the praise of men and live for my soul."

Immediately before his death, Tolstoy continued: "I imagine what everyone is thinking [about me]: 'That damned old fellow says one thing and does another; isn't it time for him to die before he becomes a complete Pharisee!' Such an accusation is entirely just. I often receive such letters, even from my friends, who write to me in this vein. And they are correct [in their view]. Everyday I go out on the road and there stand five battered beggars, while I ride a horse and after me is a coachman." See Simmons, *Leo Tolstoy,* 2:457; Leon, *Tolstoy,* 229–30, 312.

25. Sofya also took a dim view of her husband's "dark" disciples. "These followers of Leo Nikolaevich are such disagreeable characters!" she wrote in 1887. "There is not a single sane person among them. Most of the women are hysterical. . . . Lyova's 'dark' people . . . are a disagreeable lot of strangers, very depressing and unbearable. . . . And there are so many of

them—a heavy price to have to pay for his fame and new ideas! . . . [They are] miserable abortions of human society, aimless babblers, uneducated loafers!" Several years later, Sofya continued: "[These 'dark' ones] are the wretched spawn of human society, chatterers to no purpose, idlers with no breeding. . . . I find them to be so repulsive that I often want to use a pistol on them or feed them arsenic. Pharisees, liars, cheats, that is all they are! . . . It is very strange! Only people who are morbidly wrenched from human life—weak and stupid people—throw themselves into Lev Nikolaevich's teaching, and as such, they are doomed to perish in one way or another." (In truth, Sofya had good reason for her dislike of such "dark" people. One woman even entered her husband's room while he was still in bed!)

Gorky concurred. "It is strange to see Lev Nikolaevich among the Tolstoyans," he wrote.

> There stands a majestic belfry, and its bell resounds unceasingly throughout the world. But round about run cautious little dogs that squeal to the tune of the bell, as they look at each other, asking, stealthily and suspiciously, "Which one will squeal better?" It has always seemed to me that these people permeate the house at Yasnaya Polyana . . . with a burdensome atmosphere of hypocrisy, cowardice, petty commercialism, and the impatient expectation of an inheritance. There is something in the Tolstoyans which compares them to those Russian pilgrims . . . who sell "the Holy Virgin's tears" in a bottle and who pass dog bones as holy relics. . . . Almost all of them have false eyes and sweaty hands; they also like to sigh and kiss each other.

Not all the people who visited Tolstoy in Moscow and at Yasnaya Polyana were "dark," however. Many were genuine "seekers" in life. As one memoirist saw it, they were

> individuals oppressed by riches and boredom . . . sons of good families who had already skimmed the cream of life; women who had buried the bloom of their illusions in unwomanliness; poor half-developed students who wished to imitate the count. . . . Sons of the highest aristocracy discarded gold and lands and went into the desert to eat locusts. Ladies from Kronstadt and *dames de classe* appeared and manured the fields in galoshes and white dressing jackets. . . .
>
> [During the haymaking] counts, princes, teachers, and all sorts of blue-bloods tried to work in rivalry with the peasants. Scythes hacked awkwardly, moving the lush grass. Everyone strove to outdo the others.

See Leon, *Tolstoy*, 231, 255; Nazaroff, *Tolstoy*, 287; Simmons, *Leo Tolstoy*, 2:114, 146, 202–3, 208; Troyat, *Tolstoy*, 470–71.

26. Sofya also had little patience with her husband's water-carrying activities. "He pumps water for the entire house," she complained to her sister, "and lugs it in an enormous tub." See Wilson, *Tolstoy*, 346.

27. Because Tolstoy believed that the spiritual censor would prohibit *What I Believe* from being published, he printed only a small edition of the

work for friends. The authorities seized all copies of the work, but they did not destroy them. Rather, they sent the printed versions of *What I Believe* to Saint Petersburg, where they enjoyed considerable popularity among influential governmental officials. Tolstoy's *Confession,* published earlier, had a similar fate. The work was not allowed to be published, but it circulated freely in manuscript form. See Leon, *Tolstoy,* 204.

28. Briefly, the critic and idealist philosopher Nikolai Strakhov saw the works of Tolstoy and Dostoevsky as a pinnacle of Russian national and religious spirit, as well as a catalyst in the political and philosophical search for the folk as an ideal.

"A spirit of light radiates from you as from everything you write," Strakhov wrote to Tolstoy. "My only wish is to know that you are well and writing happily." Another time, he continued: "Rest assured that even if you never write another word, you will still be one of the most original and profound authors in all of Russian literature. When the Russian empire is no more, new nations will learn what the Russians were by reading *War and Peace.*"

Although Strakhov was a faithful fellow traveler in Tolstoy's spiritual quest, this tender but firm individual could drive the writer to distraction. For instance, Tolstoy once remarked that Strakhov tore into things not with his teeth but with strong, soft paws. Also, Tolstoy took issue with Strakhov's idea that human beings were the center of creation as well as the most highly developed product of nature. He wrote to Strakhov: "The zoological perfection of the individual, upon which you lay so much stress, is extremely relative, for the very reason that man himself is the judge of it. The household is just as much the center and pinnacle of creation." See Troyat, *Tolstoy,* 222, 330; Simmons, *Leo Tolstoy,* 2:18.

29. The many disagreements between Tolstoy and Solovyov often came dangerously close to full-blown quarrels. At the end of each visit, though, Tolstoy would always extend his hand and, with a guilty smile, ask forgiveness for his outbursts of temper. Tolstoy regarded Solovyov with the same dismissive air with which he regarded most intellectuals; that is, Solovyov was an intelligent individual but knew life only from books.

Tolstoy did support a request by Solovyov to oppose new official restrictions against Jews in 1890. "With all my soul, I am glad to take part in this matter," Tolstoy wrote to Solovyov, "for I know in advance that if you, Vladimir Sergeevich, express what you think about outrage, you will also express my own thoughts and feelings on the matter. The basis of our abhorrence of oppressing the Hebrew nationality is one and the same—a recognition of the brotherly union of all people and more so with the Hebrews, among whom Christ was born, and who have suffered so much and still suffer from the heathen ignorance of so-called Christians."

In truth, though, Solovyov was more a fan of Dostoevsky than Tolstoy. For instance, Solovyov was so irked by the abundance of the colors, smells, and sounds in Tolstoy's fiction that he made an astonishing (if absurd) prediction: that the humorous poems of Alexei K. Tolstoy would survive in readers' memories longer than *Anna Karenina* and *War and Peace*. See Kryzytski, *The Works of Ivan Bunin*, 199. Also see Simmons, *Leo Tolstoy*, 2:42, 137.

30. As a child, Ilya Tolstoy, Tolstoy's second son, was peevish, lazy, and always ready to cross forbidden lines. Of the six-year-old Ilya, Tolstoy wrote in 1872:

> Ilya . . . well-built, strong, radiant, and pink and white. He is, though, a poor scholar, and is always thinking about things that he shouldn't. He invents his games by himself and is concerned with his own personality. He is passionate, violent, and apt to hit out suddenly; but at the same time, he is very sensitive and gentle. He is a sensual fellow: fond of eating and of lying in a comfortable bed. His lips moisten whenever he eats raspberry jelly or buckwheat. He is individualistic in everything he does. When he weeps, he is furious and perverse; when he laughs, his laughter wins all hearts. Forbidden things attract him irresistibly, and he has a particular gift for discovering them. . . . If I were to die . . . Ilya would be lost without a stern and loving guide.

Although Tolstoy's sons were generally unsympathetic to their father's ideas, the warm-hearted Ilya came to see the lasting importance of Tolstoy's thoughts on Russia and life. Indeed, even as a young child, Ilya tended toward his father's irony. For instance, he once wrote a story in which a young boy asks: "Does God go to the lavatory?" God is so outraged by such a question that he punishes the boy by making him go to the lavatory every day for the rest of his life.

Tolstoy apparently felt close enough to Ilya to ask him if he was a virgin. (At the time of this incident, Tolstoy was sixty, Ilya was twenty-two.) Ilya recalls:

> My father's delicacy in his relations with his children amounted almost to shyness. There were certain matters that he could never touch on for fearing of causing us pain. I will never forget how, one day in Moscow, I happened to run into my room to change my clothes, and found him . . . writing at the table there. My bed stood behind a screen so I could not see him from there. . . . Hearing my footsteps he spoke without looking round,
> "Is that Ilya?"
> "Yes."
> "Are you alone? Shut the door. . . . Now no one can hear us; nor will we see each other so we will not have to be ashamed. Tell me, have you ever had anything to do with women?"
> When I said "No," I suddenly heard him begin to weep, sobbing like a child. I also cried; and, for some time, with the screen between us, we continued to shed tears of joy. We were not ashamed, but both so happy that I con-

sider that moment to be one of the happiest in my life. No discussion, no reasoning could have done for me what that moment did. The tears of a father of sixty can never be forgotten, even in the moments of greatest temptation.

The Tolstoyan biographer A. N. Wilson, relating this incident, could not refrain from asking: "What would have happened if Ilya has said 'Yes'?"

Tolstoy, though, was never one to leave well enough alone. For instance, he counseled Ilya on the eve of his son's marriage in 1888: "Your purpose in life must not be to enjoy the delight of wedlock but . . . to bring more love and truth into the world. The object of marriage is to help one another to attain that purpose."

The innocence that Tolstoy ascribed to Ilya was short-lived. For instance, Tolstoy was shocked by what he judged to be the luxury of his son's wedding. He also had little use for Ilya's innate lazy, erratic, and often dissolute nature, his concerns for money, his fondness for the bottle, his exclusive passion for hunting, and, most damning, his paying of "slave" wages to the workers at his estate. See Simmons, *Leo Tolstoy,* 1:343, 2:109, 114, 115. Also see Leon, *Tolstoy,* 167; Wilson, *Tolstoy,* 258, 356, 357.

31. The woman in question had been a serf-maid of Tolstoy's grandmother, Pelageya Nikolaevna Gorchakova-Tolstaya. After her mistress's death, she lived with the Tolstoy family until her own passing in 1896.

32. Ilya's remarks are plausible. For instance, when war broke out between Russia and Turkey in April 1877, Tolstoy was deeply conflicted over the struggle. He soon fell sway, though, to the patriotic enthusiasm sweeping the country. He followed events with anxious expectancy, his inner agony over the morality of war quickly ceding to external anger over the lack of success of Russian arms. In fact, Tolstoy became so distressed at the both the size and number of Russian defeats by Turkish forces that he begin to write an article on the reasons for these military failures.

Tolstoy was even more distressed with the outcome of the Russo-Japanese War, but here he was careful to rein in his patriotism. For instance, he told an interviewer: "I am neither for Russia nor for Japan," he wrote, "but for the working people of both countries who have been deceived by their governments and forced to go to war against their own good, their conscience, and their religion." Later, he continued: "The surrender of Port Arthur grieves me. My emotions are from patriotism. I have been reared in it, and am I not yet freed from it, just as I am not free from a personal egoism, a family egoism, and even an aristocratic egoism and patriotism. All these egoisms live in me. I also, though, have a consciousness of the divine law, and this consciousness holds in check all these egoisms, so that I manage to live without serving them. And little by little, these egoisms become transformed."

A year later, though, Tolstoy was again a son of Russia. He wrote: "My daughter Masha pounced on me when I said that it would have been better to blow up Port Arthur than to surrender it to the Japanese." And to his sister-in-law, Tanya, he said: "I was in the army myself once. In my day, we would have never surrendered Port Arthur. We would have all stood to the death; we would have died, but not have surrendered it."

Publicly, though, Tolstoy was more pronounced in his opposition to patriotism. For instance, in his 1894 article "Christianity and Patriotism" ("Khristianstvo i patriotizm"), he lampooned what he considered to be the absurdity of political alliances. See Simmons, *Leo Tolstoy*, 1:368, 2:356; Leon, *Tolstoy*, 310–11, 350; Shklovsky, *Lev Tolstoy*, 694.

33. More tantalizingly, Turgenev said: "Certainly you must have been a horse in one of your previous incarnations!" See Nazaroff, *Tolstoy*, 179.

34. Leopol'd Antonovich Sulerzhitsky was an artist, critic, and singer; he was also a producer, a director of the Moscow Art Theater, and a follower of Tolstoy. Sulerzhitsky was a welcome guest at Yasnaya Polyana if only because of his humor, high spirits, facility with Gypsy songs, and easygoing relationship with Tolstoy. Of Sulerzhitsky, Gorky once wrote: "What might Sulerzhitsky do tomorrow? He might drop a bomb or join a chorus of tavern singers. There's enough energy in him to last three centuries. He is so fired with life that, like an overheated iron, he even sweats in sparks."

Sulerzhitsky, though, soon ran afoul of Cherktov and other Tolstoyans. Having been banished to Central Asia as a conscientious objector in 1896, Sulerzhitsky quickly retracted his opposition to military service to assuage his parents' grief. Such surrender to the "enemy," Chertkov and company insisted, deserved neither understanding nor forgiveness from true believers like themselves. See Shklovsky, *Lev Tolstoy*, 650–51; Simmons, *Leo Tolstoy*, 2:217–18.

35. Tolstoy loved men in uniform. Once, seeing two guardsmen in the distance, he suddenly began to inveigh against military service, exclaiming caustically, "What pompous idiocy! Like animals trained by a whip!" Just as quickly, though, Tolstoy countered with a smile: "But, oh, how splendid! Like Old Romans! What strength and beauty! O Lord, how charming it is when a man is handsome, how very charming!" See Leon, *Tolstoy*, 234–35.

CHAPTER EIGHT

1. *Russian Herald* (*Russkii vestnik*) was a reactionary, Slavophile journal published by Mikhail Katkov in Moscow from 1856 to 1906.

2. At least five tutors and governesses—English, French, Swiss, and German—were resident in the house, while as many more visited the estate to give lessons in music, drawing, theology, mathematics, and anything else that Tolstoy happened to consider necessary for the education of his children. See Leon, *Tolstoy*, 190.

3. Tolstoy's children loved their English governess, and Sofya was an Anglophile who spoke English well. In fact, in the fall of 1872, Tolstoy was so disgusted with his situation in Russia that he actually considering moving his family to the southern coast of England, near good schools and aristocratic families. "Only in England," he kept repeating, "is the freedom of the individual guaranteed. . . . It is indispensable that my children be brought up there."

He also recorded in his diary: "With my gray beard and six children, with my consciousness of living an industrious and useful life, with my firm conviction that I am not guilty [of treason], with a contempt that I cannot hide for the modern form of justice, and with my sole desire to be left in peace as I leave others in peace, I consider it impossible for me to remain in Russia. . . . If I do not die of rage and grief in the prison into which my enemies are going to throw me . . . I have decided to immigrate to England for the rest of my days, or at least for as long as personal liberty and honor are not safe here. My wife approves of my plan. . . . I shall have enough money. If I sell everything, I will have nearly two hundred thousand rubles." See Simmons, *Leo Tolstoy,* 1:341; Leon, *Tolstoy,* 160–61; Wilson, *Tolstoy,* 257–58; Troyat, *Tolstoy,* 334.

4. Positivism, a system of philosophy rooted in the ideas of Auguste Comte, espouses a worldview that is worldly, secular, antitheological, and antimetaphysical. That is, positivism rejects all speculation concerning ultimate origins and causes and asserts that all knowledge derives from actual (positive) phenomena, experience, and facts.

5. Myortvyi Lane is located in southwest Moscow.

6. Others had an even dimmer view of Tolstoy's physical "regression." For instance, Turgenev wrote to the critic Pavel Annenkov: "You cannot picture to yourself what a dear and remarkable man Tolstoy is, though I have nicknamed him the 'troglodyte,' because of his savage ardor and buffalolike obstinacy." See Simmons, *Leo Tolstoy,* 1:140; Troyat, *Tolstoy,* 128.

7. The Battle of Borodino took place on September 7, 1812, about seventy miles west of Moscow. Here Napoleon's 130,000 troops defeated General Kutuzov's 120,000 Russians, thereby allowing the French leader to occupy the ancient Russian capital a week later. In the struggle, the Russians lost 45,000 men, the French, 30,000.

8. Podsolnechnaya Station is located about 70 miles northwest of Moscow.

9. Tolstoy had raised Bul'ka from a puppy. He wrote of his pet:

When I went to the Caucasus, I did not wish to take Bul'ka with me; so I went away quietly, ordering that the animal be chained. At the first post station, though . . . I suddenly saw something black and bright dashing along the road. It was Bul'ka in his brass collar. He was flying with all his might toward the station. He leaped up at me and licked my hand; then he stretched himself out in the shadow of the cart. . . . Afterward I learned that he had broken his chain, jumped out of the window, dashed over the road on my trail, and run twenty miles [to meet me] in the heat of day.

Moved by such devotion, Tolstoy took Bul'ka to the Caucasus, where, after many exciting hunting adventures with pheasants, wolves, bears, and wild boars, Bul'ka went mad from a wolf bite and, in classic Tolstoyan style, went off by himself to die. See Dole, *The Life of Count Tolstoi*, 40–41, 49.

10. Tanya entered society at the Shcherbatovs' home in December 1882 and remained with her mother at the affair until 6 A.M. the following day. "It now seems that we are fully launched in society," Sofya informed her sister, Tatyana, "but the money vanishes terribly!" Sofya's own dress cost 250 rubles. See Simmons, *Leo Tolstoy*, 2:46.

11. Tanya is parroting her father's views. In fact, Sofya once confessed to her own sister, Tanya, that she could not go to a ball dressed in a gown with an open neck for fear of incurring her husband's wrath. She said: "How often he condemns married women who, in his words, go about 'naked.'"

Tolstoy particularly opposed women who wore décolleté gowns in wintertime, his concern being for their coachmen who almost froze to death outside waiting to take these ladies home. See Simmons, *Leo Tolstoy*, 1:299; Dole, *The Life of Count Tolstoi*, 296.

12. Pokrovskoe-Glebovo is an area located just east of the Moscow River.

13. Lopatina is referring to Sviatoi Nikolai Ugodnik, or the Saint Nicholas who is today's Santa Claus. Tolstoy was well aware of Saint Nicholas's alleged prowess. For instance, as an officer in Sevastopol, he severely criticized his superiors, who, instead of planning strategy against the enemy, "have taken leave of their senses, common sense, and initiative . . . and are relying on Saint Nicholas to send storms and foul weather to drive away the intruder." See Troyat, *Tolstoy*, 116.

14. Tolstoy is referring to Vasily Ivanovich Nemirovich-Danchenko, the brother of the famous dramatist and director, who wrote novels of "manners" as well as historical fiction on Russia's wars with Turkey and in the Caucasus.

Tolstoy constantly shook off the reproaches of friends and acquaintances as regards his lack of writing. He would shake his head and reply with a smile: "You know, when [people chide me for not writing], such rebukes are simply like the responses of former admirers of some elderly French whore, who tell her: 'How enchantingly you used to pick up your petticoats and sing chansonnettes!'" See Leon, *Tolstoy*, 229.

15. Tolstoy's biographers unanimously attribute difficulties with the physical aspect of marriage to Sofya. For instance, two weeks after her union to Tolstoy, she wrote in her diary: "All physical manifestations [of marriage]

are repugnant." Her first pregnancy, with son Sergei, only increased her protest. "Lyova deserts me more and more," she wrote in her journal. "The role of the physical side of love plays a great part with him. And that is awful. For me, it means nothing." Her desire was for "spiritual closeness to Lyova, not just that disgusting bodily intimacy." She continued: "In my heart of hearts, I have never wanted my husband's passion. I have always dreamed of a platonic relationship, a perfect spiritual communion."

Sofya's disgust with marital intimacy deeply affected her daughter Tanya. Before her marriage, she wrote: "I am very happy to think that I am a virgin and have not had to undergo that fearful humiliation all married women suffer. Mother told me that on the morning after her wedding, she was so ashamed that she did not want to leave the room. She hid her face in the pillow and cried. I am proud not to have known such [physical closeness], and I hope that I may never know it." See Leon, *Tolstoy,* 278, 286; Troyat, *Tolstoy,* 469, 491.

16. Throughout her life with her husband, Sofya was constantly beset by periods of inner rage, depression, and inferiority before her husband. For instance, only two years after her marriage (1864), Sofya wrote in her diary: "I often feel that the feminine world must bore him and that I am incapable of making him happy. I am beginning to believe that I am a good nurse and nothing else. No brains, no education, no talent, nothing. . . . For all I know, he may be hating me secretly."

Four years later, and pregnant with her fourth child, Sofya continued: "I want nothing but [Leo's] love and sympathy, but he will not give them to me. All my pride is trampled in the mud. I am nothing but a miserable crushed thing whom no one wants, a useless creature with morning sickness and a big belly, two rotten teeth, a bad temper, a battered sense of dignity, and a love which nobody requires and which nearly drives me insane."

Sofya's inner turmoil only deepened with age. As her sister, Tanya, saw it, she always seemed to be "suspicious of happiness; she never could grasp or enjoy it fully." Unbalanced, querulous, self-pitying, and completely humorless, Sofya became increasing frustrated and dissatisfied with both the passing of years and with her growing alienation from her family. Circa 1875, she wrote: "This excessively isolated county existence has become insufferable," she confided in her diary. "[I feel only] a sad apathy, an indifference to everything; today the months, the years are all the same to me."

Several years later, she added: "It was sad for me to come home, for no one seemed to pay the slightest attention to the fact that I had returned. I often wonder why [my family] does not love me and why I love them so much. It must be because of my outbursts of temper, when I become disagreeable and say unpleasant things." As usual, Tolstoy was the focus of her disharmony. Sofya pronounced succinctly: "[My husband] is a man ahead of his age who points the way for others to follow. But I, I am one of the crowd.

I live with him, and I see the light which is carried by every advanced man like him. . . . but I cannot keep up with him—the crows and my hands and environment all hold me back."

Sofya was also distressed that her husband was giving his writings to his daughters and others to copy. "I used to copy everything Leo wrote, and I loved doing so," she wrote in her diary. "But now he carefully conceals everything from me and gives it to his daughters instead. In so doing, he is systematically destroying me by driving me out of his life, and such a state of affairs is unbearably painful."

Not surprisingly, Sonya became increasingly obsessed about her physical appearance, the one thing she believed that she had left to keep her husband in toe. (She bore thirteen children in the first twenty-six years of her marriage.) "I hate people who tell me that I am beautiful," she continued to write. "I never thought such a thing, and now it is too late anyway. What good would beauty do me? What do I need it for? . . . Lyovochka would grow accustomed to the most hideous wife, if only she were quiet, worshipful, and live the kind of life that he selected for her. . . . I am beginning to dream about a life other than what I am leading. I want to read much, to be educated, to be intellectual. I want to be beautiful and to think about clothes and other stupid things. . . . I feel like curling my hair. . . . I like ribbons and bows. I should like a new leather belt; but, after writing that, I feel like crying."

By 1876, fourteen years into their marriage, Sofya was the victim of repeated illnesses, even though the doctors could find nothing wrong with her health. Sofya, however, continued her downward trend. In her view, everyone was against her. In 1886, she recorded: "Everyone, Leo Nikolaevich as well as the children, who follow him like a flock of sheep, has come to think of me as a scourge."

Tolstoy intuitively understood the reasons for his wife's inner distress, and, in a good-natured lampoon, entitled *Bulletin of the Patients at the Yasnaya Polyana Lunatic Asylum,* he came up with this revealing diagnosis of his wife. "Countess S. A. Tolstoy is harmless but sometimes has to be suppressed. The patient is subject to *petulanta hurryupica maxima*. . . . She thinks that everyone demands everything of her and that she cannot manage to get everything done. Symptoms: solving problems that have not been proposed; answering questions before they have been put forth; repelling accusations that have never been made; and satisfying demands which have not yet been put forward. . . . . Treatment: hard work, diet, and segregation from frivolous and worldly people." See Simmons, *Leo Tolstoy,* 1:357–58; Leon, *Tolstoy,* 129, 131–32, 225, 226, 254, 256; Wilson, *Tolstoy,* 382; Troyat, *Tolstoy,* 233, 336.

17. In her later years, Sofya had undertaken to write an immense work, entitled *The Story of My Life (Istoriia moei zhizni),* which she com-

piled from her voluminous and not always accurate diaries. At other times in her life, Sofya had tried her hand at fiction. For instance, under the pseudonym of "The Weary One," she once wrote a poem entitled "Moans." Sofya also penned a novel, entitled *Who Is to Blame?* (*Kto vinovat?*), a disastrously feeble attack on *The Kreutzer Sonata.* In this work, a thirty-five-year-old lecher-prince named Prozorovsky makes life miserable for his wife, Anna, a poor, innocent girl of eighteen. For instance, reeking of tobacco, he literally rapes his wife on their wedding night, an event that Sofya wanted readers to see as autobiographical. Furthermore, when Anna has a platonic relationship with a painter, the jealous Prozorovsky kills her. Mercifully, Sofya's friends prevailed upon her not to publish the piece. See Leon, *Tolstoy,* 311; Wilson, *Tolstoy,* 386; Simmons, *Leo Tolstoy,* 2:134, 352.

18. Neither Tanya, Masha, nor Alexandra Tolstaya enjoyed a peaceful or healthy relationship with her mother, and for several reasons. The first was that Sofya's increasing anger and instability made for constant friction and distress. The second was that Tolstoy's daughters identified with their father's spiritual teachings, which the more pragmatic Sofya often dismissed as quixotic ravings. "[Masha and Tanya] are utterly lacking in moderation or judgment," Sofya complained. "They take after their father there. At least he has struggled to improve his life, whereas they have simply let themselves go." See Troyat, *Tolstoy,* 504.

19. Tanya was not the only one who cast aspersions on her mother's work. For instance, in a long and naively critical article published in 1903, Sofya countered what she saw as the filth and immorality of Andreev's writing with the beauties "of that great production, *War and Peace.*"

Needless to say, reaction to the piece was swift and cruel. Irate readers sent letters to Sofya, indicting not Andreev but Tolstoy himself for bringing "filth" to Russian literature. Chekhov wrote to his wife, the actress Olga Knipper: "Have you read S. A. Tolstoy's article on Andreev? I have, and it has thrown me into a fever. It is positively incredible; the absurdity of it is so glaring. If you had written anything like that I would have kept you on bread and water and beaten you every day for a week." See Leon, *Tolstoy,* 311; Simmons, *Leo Tolstoy,* 2:344.

20. Tolstoy's contempt for examinations may have been rooted not only in his own lamentable educational experiences but also in the awe with which the ever practical Sofya looked upon government and university testing for prospective employees and students. See Shklovsky, *Lev Tolstoy,* 466.

21. Lopatina's memoirs aside, education was a key value in the Tolstoyan household. With his own children, Tolstoy did not employ the democratic pedagogy that he had fashioned for peasant youth, and for a straightforward reason: He was well aware of the prevailing views of education and upbringing in the social circles in which his children would have

to move. In particular, he knew that his sons had to prepare for entrance into the university.

From the very beginning, Tolstoy believed that education was a serious undertaking. For instance, he forbade toys and playthings in the nursery. At first, the foreign governesses and tutors gave the Tolstoy children lessons in English, German, and French. Later, Tolstoy taught them arithmetic; Sofya taught them reading, grammar, writing, and music.

Furthermore, unlike the peasant pupils in Tolstoy's school, who could pursue what they liked, Tolstoy's own children were not allowed to study only subjects that caught their interest. But like their serf contemporaries, they were rewarded for success and not punished for failure. With his own children, though, Tolstoy was exacting, irritable, and unfair. What he saw as endearing in his peasant charges he often found intolerable in his own progeny.

The moral formation of Tolstoy's children was equally rigorous. They were taught to love nature and all of God's creatures, especially individuals of humbler birth. For instance, when they needed assistance from a servant, they were expected to request it as a favor, not to demand it as a right. Also, whenever Tolstoy's sons or daughters told falsehoods or engaged in other wrongdoing, they were not physically punished or humiliated but confined to their rooms until they expressed sorrow or regret for what they had done.

The upbringing of Tolstoy's children, though, was not without its contradictions and flaws. Years later, Ilya Tolstoy recalled: "The world was divided into two parts: one composed of ourselves and the other, of everyone else. We were special people, and the others were not our equals. . . . It was mostly *maman*, of course, who was guilty of entertaining such notions, but *papa*, too, jealously guarded us from associating with the village children. To a considerable degree, he was the one responsible for the groundless arrogance and self-esteem that such an upbringing inculcated into us, and from which I found it so hard to free myself."

Later in life, though, Tolstoy's preoccupation with religious and moral questions caused him to lose all interest in his children's education. In fact, he believed that formal or conventional instruction was harmful, since it allowed one group of people to subjugate another. The only kind of education that Tolstoy came to see as worthwhile was that which taught service to the masses as well as love and compassion for humankind. See Crankshaw, *Tolstoy*, 253; Dole, *The Life of Count Tolstoi*, 210–11; Simmons, *Leo Tolstoy*, 2:110.

22. Sofya had her supporters. Many people saw her, accurately, as a woman of extraordinary qualities: tenacious, energetic, intelligent, loving, and, of course, long-suffering. (She is alleged to have copied *War and Peace* seven times.) For instance, one visitor to Yasnaya Polyana remarked: "If there are two kinds of halos in heaven, Sofya's may be larger than that of

her husband. To be a genius of this type is no small thing, but to be the wife of such a man requires particular greatness."

Gorky also admired Sofya. For instance, recalling his visit to the seriously ill Tolstoy in the Crimea, he wrote:

> I could see very well that in the whirling, pestilential trivia of life, Sofya had to keep her feet and head in an effort to guard her ailing husband's peace and his manuscripts, to accommodate the children as comfortably as possible, to keep at bay the noisy pestering of the "sincerely sympathizing" visitors, professional spectators for the most part, and to provide food and drink for everyone. . . .
>
> From morning until night, Sofya Andreevna lived in the whirl of this blinding everyday dust with her teeth bared in a nervous grin and her clever eyes narrowed for keenness, amazing everyone with her tirelessness, her ability to be everywhere at the right time, to tranquilize everyone, and to put a stop to the petty whining of people who were forever mutually displeased with one another.

The marital difficulties of Tolstoy and Sofya were often the subject of raging debates among Bunin, his wife, and colleagues and friends. For instance, Kuznetsova wrote in a letter to the Bunin scholar Alexander Baboreko: "[When I lived with the Bunins in Grasse] we argued about the drama between Tolstoy and his wife until we were hoarse. Bunin would take Tolstoy's side, Vera Nikolaevna was for Sofya, and I wavered between the two. The argument came to a halt, though, when Nadezhda Teffi, whom Ivan Alexeevich respected and loved, wrote a large newspaper article in defense of Sofya Andreevna." See Baboreko, "I. A. Bunin o L. N. Tolstoy," 176; Dole, *The Life of Count Tolstoi,* 338; Shklovsky, *Lev Tolstoy,* 673.

23. In truth, Sofya visited Empress Maria Fyodorovna only after she had gone to Tsar Alexander III himself to ask that the ban on *The Kreutzer Sonata* be lifted. She did so not because she believed in the innocence or quality of the work, but to deflect public opinion that it was an exposé of their married life. "If *The Kreutzer Sonata* had been written about me and my life with Tolstoy," she reasoned, "I would not have asked the tsar to release it [for publication]. Everyone will look at it in this light."

If the empress was shocked by *The Kreutzer Sonata,* Alexander III liked the work; but he soon rejected it, courtesy of Pobedonostev and other reactionaries who were determined to clip Tolstoy's wings. For instance, the archbishop of Kherson denounced Tolstoy as a wolf in sheep's clothing and clamored for his destruction; other religious saw it as "an incoherent, dirty, and immoral tale." Even more noteworthy, perhaps, Tsar Alexander accepted Sofya's specious claim that her husband needed official encouragement in his writing; he allowed the story to be published, but only as part of his *Complete Works.* (Alexander's idea here was that since few people could afford to buy a multivolume edition of Tolstoy, *The Kreutzer Sonata* would not be widely read.)

Needless to say, Sofya reveled in her personal triumph. "I wanted to show myself in public so people could see how little I resemble a victim. I wanted people to talk about me. I did it instinctively!" She continued: "There is no doubt that my personality did the job. I told everybody that if only I could feel sufficiently inspired, even for a moment, to influence the emperor as a man, I should be successful. And indeed, the inspiration came, and I persuaded him. It was not an impossible task, though, for he is a kind-hearted man and quite capable of yielding to a good influence. Whoever reads this will think me boastful, but such an individual will be wrong and unfair [in his assessment]."

Later, Sofya added: "I am told on all sides that the emperor has spoken of me highly. He told [one person] that . . . he would have liked to continue such a pleasant and interesting conversation. [Another] wrote that I had created an *excellent* impression. [Still another] said . . . that the emperor had found me pleasant, natural, and sincere, and that he had been surprised to see how young and handsome I was. All of this tickles my feminine vanity; and I feel revenged for the way my husband has always treated me; for not only did he never try to raise me socially, but, on the contrary, he always did his best to lower me [in other people's eyes]."

Initially, Tolstoy was less than happy with his wife's actions. "Leo is displeased with my adventures," Sofya wrote, "and particularly with my interview with the emperor. He said that it looked as though he had undertaken obligations that we might be unable to fulfill. [He also said] that previously he and the emperor had always ignored each other, but now that this business might harm us and lead to complications."

Tolstoy himself wrote to a friend: "Yesterday my wife arrived from Petersburg, where she had seen the tsar and had spoken to him about my writings—quite unnecessarily. He promised to allow the publication of *The Kreutzer Sonata*—a thing that does not please me at all. . . . I disliked her groveling before the tsar. . . . I almost lost control and spoke sharply, but the storm blew over."

It should be noted here that after Tolstoy had repudiated all rights to his post-1881 works, publishers immediately came out with special editions of *The Kreutzer Sonata,* thereby violating Alexander's stipulations concerning the printing of the work. "*The Kreutzer Sonata* is now in the hands of young girls and high-school students," Pobedonostev wrote to Alexander. "On the road from Sevastopol, I saw it on sale in the station and people reading it on trains. The book market is full of the things."

However unjustly, Alexander blamed Sofya for the state of affairs, exclaiming, "If that woman has deceived me, I know not whom I can trust."

Not unexpectedly, Tolstoy himself turned against the work. "There is something nasty in *The Kreutzer Sonata*," Tolstoy wrote to Chertkov. "Every remembrance of it has become terribly revolting to me. There was something bad in my motives for writing the piece, for it has evoked such wickedness." See Leon, *Tolstoy*, 249–50; Dole, *The Life of Count Tolstoi*, 330–31; Shklovsky, *Lev Tolstoy*, 610; Troyat, *Tolstoy*, 484; Simmons, *Leo Tolstoy*, 2:138, 139.

24. Ivan L'vovich Tolstoy, dead at age seven from scarlet fever, was reputed to be a boy of great promise. Of all of Tolstoy's children, he was the one who looked most like his father; he had the same bright, pensive eyes and the same earnest spirit. Understandably, Ivan was both his mother's and father's favorite, so much so that Leo hoped that Ivan would carry on his work. For instance, Tolstoy's daughter Alexandra wrote: "Vanya was more just and wise than grown people. With some deep intuition, he sensed the truth and reached out for it as a plant reaches toward the sun. How many times did he unconsciously teach the older ones around him."

Others concurred. For instance, the famous scientist Ilya Mechnikov wrote: "The first time I met Vanechka, I knew that he would either die an early death or become an even greater genius than his father."

Apparently, Vanya sensed a tie to Tolstoy. "Mummy, I feel that I really *am* like Papa!" he once told a startled Sofya. He also seemed to have an instinctual affinity for this father's ideas. "No, Mummy," he went on to tell Sofya. "Don't say that Yasnaya Polyana will be mine! Everything belongs to everyone!" Also, several weeks before he died, Vanya labeled his few possessions and attempted to give them away.

Alexandra continues that at the passing of Ivan, Leo and his wife were "nearly unconscious with sorrow." She had ample evidence for such a view. For instance, Sofya wrote to her sister, Tanya: "Lyova has grown quite old. He wanders about stooping and has a sad look in his bright eyes. I feel that the last day of sunshine of his old age has vanished. Two days after Vanechka's death, he sat down and wept, saying: 'I have lost heart for the first time in my life.' It is painful to look at him, simply terrible! The sorrow has crushed him."

Three days later, though, Tolstoy rallied. "We have buried Vanechka," he wrote in his diary. "It is a terrible loss. No, not terrible, but a great spiritual event. I thank Thee, Heavenly Father." He continued to "Granny" Alexandra: "Vanya was one of those children whom God sends prematurely into a world that is not quite ready for them. . . . [He is] like a swallow who arrives home too early and freezes to death." See Leon, *Tolstoy*, 271; Dole, *The Life of Count Tolstoi*, 352; Wilson, *Tolstoy*, 428–29; Nazaroff, *Tolstoy*, 314; Simmons, *Leo Tolstoy*, 2:211.

25. Sergei Nikolaevich Tolstoy was seen by his famous writer-brother as an inscrutable, mysterious, and endlessly fascinating personality. For instance, as a child, Sergei had dazzled his younger sibling with his talent, spontaneity, and egotism. As a young adult, Sergei was a model of such self-contained and self-assured elegance that he became Leo's long-standing idol, confidante, and guide.

"I adored, imitated, loved, and wanted to be so much like Sergei," Tolstoy wrote about his brother. "I worshiped his handsome exterior, his singing (he was always singing), his drawing, his gaiety, but, strange to say, especially his frank egoism. . . . I worshiped Sergei as something strange and foreign to my nature. Such a human life appeared to me to be beautiful, but also quite incomprehensible and mysterious, and therefore especially attractive."

The feeling was mutual. Sergei was very fond of "Leon" and admired his brother's talents. Not unexpectedly, though, he cared little for Tolstoy's asceticism. "Our dear Leon has licked the caviar off the sandwich," he once remarked, "and now offers us the dry crust which remains." See Biryukov, *Leo Tolstoy*, 16; Nazaroff, *Tolstoy*, 239.

26. In 1865 Sergei Nikolaevich was briefly engaged to Sofya's sister, Tanya. More than twice her age (he was twenty-two years older), he ended the relationship to marry Maria Shishkina, a Gypsy singer and his mistress of sixteen years' standing, and to legitimize their offspring. (Some say that it was Tanya who, though desperately in love with Sergei, broke the engagement; others add that earlier Sergei had sought to marry off the young Tolstoy to another Gypsy singer.)

Needless to say, both Tolstoy and Sofya were distressed over Sergei's behavior. "Sergei is completely and inexcusably wrong," Tolstoy wrote to Tanya's parents. "It would be less painful for me if he were not my brother. . . . [He] has hurt Tanya terribly . . . but with her honest, passionate nature . . . she has the greatest consolation in life, that of knowing that she has acted well. . . . From being a child, she has turned into a woman, a splendid woman."

To Sergei himself, Tolstoy wrote: "I cannot help sharing at least a tiny part of the hell to which you have subjected not just Tanya but the entire family, myself included."

Sofya added in her diary: "[The engagement] has fallen through: Seryozha has deceived Tanya. He has behaved like a perfect cad. An entire month has now passed by [since the rupture], and it breaks my heart to look at Tanya. To think that such a charming, poetic girl should be wasted like this. . . . Tanya's attitude toward the entire affair was very noble. She loved Seryozha very much, while he only pretended to do so, for his Gypsy woman was dearer to him. Masha, though, is a good woman. I feel sorry for her, and really have nothing against her."

Additionally, both husband and wife were concerned over the declining state of Tanya's health. The unfortunate girl had tried to poison herself in the aftermath of the affair. Though unsuccessful in her attempt, Tanya grew pale and thin; she even developed a cough and brought up blood. The doctors diagnosed consumption, but it was Tanya's mental condition that most worried family and friends. "Tanya is kind, gentle, and submissive," Tolstoy wrote to her father. "And, for this reason, one pities here all the more and would do anything to help her, but to no avail. Tanya seldom, hardly ever, takes up the guitar. And if one does ask her to sing, she will do so, but in a subdued voice that will soon break off."

Tanya, though, took communion and grew calmer. Within a year, she married, gave birth, and became absorbed in family life. Sadly, though, Tanya's marriage to Alexander Kuzminsky, a good-natured but dull magistrate, was not a happy one, if only because during their courtship she decided to follow Tolstoy's example and to have her husband read her diary, rife with her misfortunes with Sergei. More important, perhaps, Tanya entered into Tolstoy's *War and Peace* as the heroine, Natasha, involved in an "affair" with Anatoly Kuragin. Doctor Bers was hardly pleased with such an outcome to events. "Father is most annoyed," Sofya recorded in her diary. See Simmons, *Leo Tolstoy,* 1:299, 302, 306; Leon, *Tolstoy,* 133–34; Wilson, *Tolstoy,* 214–15; Shklovsky, *Lev Tolstoy,* 101, 388; Troyat, *Tolstoy,* 295.

27. Tolstoy's father had received the estate of Pirogovo for taking into their household a girl by the name of Dunyasha, the illegitimate daughter of a wealthy bachelor and distant relative of the family. After his death, Pirogovo was jointly owned by Tolstoy's sister and brother, Maria and Sergei.

28. Portochki means "underpants" in Russian.

29. "Who Are the Cherubim?" ("Izhe kherumimy?") is a popular chorale piece rendered by such musicians as Pavel Chesnokov and Alexander Arkhangel'sky.

30. Although it was the birth of Maria that had cost his mother's life, Tolstoy enjoyed an impassioned, if at times stormy, relationship with his sister. For instance, Tolstoy often doubted his sister's love for him. He was also dismayed that Masha was briefly attracted to Turgenev, whose morality Tolstoy did not value highly.

Tolstoy, though, was greatly fond of his sister. "Masha is so naively sweet," he wrote in his diary in 1853, "that she remains fine even in wretched society. One involuntarily regrets that there is no one here to appreciate her charm." Also, Tolstoy assumed periodic responsibility for his sister, for several reasons. Ten years into her marriage (1857), Maria discovered that her husband (and distant cousin), Valerian Petrovich Tolstoy, had been consistently unfaithful to her. ("A very nasty sort of rustic Henry VIII," Turgenev noted of the man to Pauline Viadot.) "Not wishing to be the chief mistress in her husband's harem," Maria left Valerian and took her three children with her.

Animated, passionate, attractive, and always in need of money, Maria engaged in several romantic adventures (including a brief flirtation with Turgenev) before she entered the convent. For instance, she became pregnant by a Swedish viscount, whom she later married, but without the benefit of legal divorce. (Valerian Tolstoy died in 1865.) Also, Maria cared little for motherhood and the domestic life; during frequent trips abroad, she would leave her daughters at Yasnaya Polyana for extended periods of time.

Tolstoy closed his eye to Maria's shenanigans, though. "Your brother, Leo, who loves you more the older he grows," Tolstoy signed off in a letter to Maria in 1909. Such affection, however, did not keep Tolstoy from teasing his sister about taking the vow of obedience as a nun. After visiting her at the convent at Sharmardino, he told her: "There are six hundred fools here, all living according to someone's judgment."

Maria returned her brother's love. In fact, after Tolstoy's death, she prayed for her brother's soul, even though elders and monks had forbidden her to do so, believing that Leo was in hell. "God grant that everyone might believe as strongly as he did," she said. Maria eventually received permission to intercede with God on her brothers behalf. See Simmons, *Leo Tolstoy,* 1:108, 162, 183, 306, 316; Leon, *Tolstoy,* 37, 85; Dole, *The Life of Count Tolstoi,* 188; Wilson, *Tolstoy,* 270, 506; Shklovsky, *Lev Tolstoy,* 268.

31. The Academy of Arts was founded in 1757 in Saint Petersburg by Empress Tsaritsa Elizaveta Petrovna. It focused on "classical" painting, sculpture, and architecture; by the end of the prerevolutionary period, it had become the largest and most important school for artists in Russia.

32. In contrast to Alexander III's judicious handling of *The Kreutzer Sonata,* the excommunication of Tolstoy from the church by Pobedonostsev and the members of the Most Holy Synod touched off a furor that made a martyr of the writer. Attempts by religious leaders to justify their action and to turn public opinion against the writer failed miserably. Although Tolstoy was periodically accosted by fanatics who, believing he was the devil incarnate, threatened to kill kim, the writer's excommunication increased his popularity to unprecedented levels.

In Kiev, more than a thousand students from the technical school there signed a telegram announcing their support for Tolstoy. In Moscow, masses of enthusiastic students voluntarily separated themselves from the church and congregated before Tolstoy's house. A deputation of women came to express their sympathy; excited crowds paraded down main streets and squares; and admirers and sympathizers sent him letters, telegrams, and even gifts. (At one point, Tolstoy was almost crushed to death by an enthusiastic mob in Theater Square.)

In Petersburg, some people decorated Repin's famous 1887 portrait of Tolstoy with masses of flowers. Others, including Tolstoy's daughter Alexandra, secretly circulated two fables, entitled *The Lions and the Asses* and *The Victorious Pigeons,* mocking both the government and Pobedonostev. In fact, two months after Pobedonotsev issued the edict of excommunication, a public attempt was made on his life.

Some groups touched Tolstoy in a highly personal way. For instance, an assembly of factory workers sought to assure Tolstoy by asking: "For the same reason, did not our great Teacher suffer on the cross?" Also, workers at a glassworks sent him a block of glass inscribed with gold letters, which read: "You have shared the fate of many great men who walked ahead of their age. In olden times they were burnt at the stake or left to rot in prison or exile. Let the Pharisees, the pontiffs, excommunicate you from whatever they like. The Russian people will always be proud of you. For them you will always be great, dear, and beloved."

Not surprisingly, civil authorities sought to restore calm and to deflate Tolstoy's sudden celebrity. Repin's flower-bedecked portrait was removed from the gallery where it had been on display; many of Tolstoy's books were removed from public libraries; and the press was forbidden to report on demonstration in his honor or to publish his photograph or telegrams of condolence and support. Also, postmasters were instructed to return all congratulatory messages to their senders; the secret police kept track of the correspondence entering and leaving Tolstoy's home.

Leo and Sofya responded to the edict and its aftermath differently. Sofya felt deeply humiliated and affronted by the events. She wrote a vigorous latter of protest to the metropolitan, which later she had lithographed and distributed both in Russia and abroad. She even brushed aside the most serious threat arising from her husband's excommunication, that is, that he would be denied a Christian burial. "Is it conceivable," she wrote, "that I will not find a priest so honest that he will be unafraid of people before the true and merciful God and perform a funeral service for my husband; or else a dishonest one whom I will generously bribe for that purpose?"

Leo was initially amused by the edict, but he refused to accept the congratulations of his friends. A month later, he replied to the Most Holy Synod:

Whether or not these beliefs of mine offend, grieve, or prove a stumbling block to anyone, I can as little change these as I can change my body. I myself must live my own life; I myself must meet death (and that very soon). Therefore, preparing to go to that God from whom I came, I cannot believe otherwise than I do now.

I do not believe that my faith is the one indubitable belief of all time. But I see no other that is plainer, clearer, or answers better all the demands of my reason and heart. Should I find such a one, I will accept it at once because God requires nothing but the truth. But I can no more return to that from which, with such suffering, I have escaped than a flying bird can reenter the eggshell from which it has emerged.

It was Coleridge who said: "He who begins by loving Christianity better than the truth will proceed by loving his own sect or church better than Christianity; he will end in loving himself (his own peace) better than all." I have traveled in just the opposite way. First I loved the Orthodox faith more than my peace; then I loved Christianity more than my church. Now I love truth better than anything else in the world. Until now, truth for me corresponds with Christianity as I understand it. And I cling to this Christianity, and, to the degree in which I cling to it, I live peacefully happily. Peacefully and happily, also, I approach death.

See Leon, *Tolstoy,* 298–99; Dole, *The Life of Count Tolstoi,* 369–73; Shklovsky, *Lev Tolstoy,* 664; Troyat, *Tolstoy,* 560–64; Simmons, *Leo Tolstoy,* 2:303–9.

33. Bunin is referring to Tolstoy's celebration of Mass as a monstrous farce, a scene which served as the impetus for Pobedonostsev to issue the edict of excommunication against the writer. For instance, portraying communion, Tolstoy wrote:

> The priest lifted the napkin covering the plate, cut the central piece of bread into four parts, dipped it in wine, and put it in his mouth. He was supposed to be eating a piece of the body of God and drinking a mouthful of his blood. . . . [Later] he carried the goblet behind the partition where he proceeded to eat up all the little pieces of God's body and drink the remaining blood. Then he carefully sucked on his mustache, wiped his mouth, cleaned the cup, and, feeling very chipper, strode resolutely forth, the thin soles of his calfskin boots creaking smartly.

Bunin also rejected this scene. For instance, when Zinaida Shakovskaya asked Bunin if he, with his own enmity toward religious mysteries and ritual, could ever use the "same blasphemous words that Tolstoy had used," Bunin replied: "No, I would not." See Shakovskaya, "Otrazheniia," 93. Also see Leon, *Tolstoy,* 297; Troyat, *Tolstoy,* 544.

34. More accurately, Sergei died a hideous death of cancer of the face and tongue. Although in life Sergei was quite practical, he was quite hopeless in business matters. In fact, Sergei enjoyed his hunting and Gypsies with such lordly ease that merchants did not demand payment for overdue bills, since they believed that Sergei was not poor but only in temporary financial difficulty. See Wilson, *Tolstoy,* 470; Shklovsky, *Lev Tolstoy,* 163.

35. When Tolstoy visited Sergei almost twenty years before his brother's death, he noted that he had received "a most joyful impression"; that is, Seryozha had become a kindred spirit. "My brother has undoubtedly undergone a spiritual transformation," Tolstoy wrote. "He himself has formulated the essence of my belief (and he evidently recognizes it as being true for himself) to subject the animal self and to raise one's spiritual essence."

After Sergei died, though, Tolstoy retreated from his earlier statement, if only because by the end of his life Sergei had become a hard-drinking and cynical miser-recluse who approached his end without a belief in the Almighty or even an awareness that he was passing from this life. Tolstoy's affection for Sergei remained unchanged with time, however. "Just the same, all is well with Sergei," Tolstoy recorded. "He valued my attachment to him; he was proud of me, and wished to agree with me, but could not. He remained what he had always been: himself, quite singular, handsome, thoroughbred, proud, and above all, such a truthful and sincere man, the likes of which I have never met anywhere else." See Leon, *Tolstoy*, 293, 309; Wilson, *Tolstoy*, 470.

36. Such a statement is not true.

CHAPTER NINE

1. If Tolstoy mentioned Chertkov in "either a restrained or negative way," it was because Tolstoy did not wish to inflame Sofya's undisguised hatred of Chertkov or because he was angry with his disciple for struggling with Sofya over the writer's literary heritage.

2. Like Tolstoy, Chertkov hailed from a position of power and privilege, as his parents belonged to the highest circle of Saint Peterburg society. Chertkov's father had been a very rich general and aide-de-camp to the tsar; his mother was a confidante of the empress who compensated for her unhappy marriage by spending a good deal of time abroad and by becoming a strict follower of Lord Radstock's Evangelist movement, which sought to renew Russia on moral and ethical ideals. (Sofya later recalled Chertkov's mother as a "very handsome, but not quite normal," individual who believed that Christ dwelled in her entrails. Also, rumors were rife that Chertkov was the illegitimate son of Alexander II.)

The Chertkovs owned many estates and serfs, one of whom was the grandfather of Anton Chekhov. See Wilson, *Tolstoy*, 343; Shklovsky, *Lev Tolstoy*, 558; Troyat, *Tolstoy*, 644.

3. Just as Tolstoy's daughters disliked their mother, so the three youngest of Tolstoy's sons—Leo, Andrei, and Mikhail—were deeply antagonistic toward their father's views. From motives of self-interest (only Sergei L'vovich made a living) as well as from dislike of the "simple" life and discomfort with their father's fame, they sided with their mother in the struggle between Leo and Sofya over the writer's property and literary heritage.

For instance, Leo L'vovich, who lived abroad and dabbled in sculpture and painting, remarked: "Nothing can be worse than being the son of a great man. Whatever you do, people compare you with your father." Leo was particularly incensed by what he saw as his father's hypocritical indifference to his mother's suffering. "It is revolting," he wrote during one conflict between Tolstoy and his wife. "He, with his forgiveness and nonresistance, sits quietly in his armchair, while Mother lies on the ground, ready to kill herself." Also, Leo defied his father's views on "nonviolence" and "passive resistance to evil" by writing a series of articles in which he both supported the Russo-Japanese War (he demanded a struggle to the death) and indicted his father as the source of revolutionary fervor in Russia. In fact, it was Leo's mounting anger with Tolstoy that led him to smash a bust of his father when Tolstoy was late for a sitting.

Leo also penned a story, entitled "Chopin's Nocturne," as a foil to *The Kreutzer Sonata*. In this piece, the heroine escapes her husband's wrath by entering a convent and having a likeness buried in her place. Although Tolstoy was angered by the work—"stupid, untalented, and tactless," he said—he tried several reconciliations with Leo, but to no avail. Also, feuilletonists, angered by Leo's public disrespect for his father, lampooned him as "Tiger Tigerovich Toddlekins," even though Leo was only thirty years old. About his son, Tolstoy wrote in 1907: "It is an amazing and pitiful business, but Leo's envy of me is developing into hatred."

Andrei L'vovich was hardly better. Having a led a dissipated life replete with gambling, a broken marriage, and numerous love affairs—a broken engagement to a Georgian woman ended in her suicide—Andrei joined the notorious Chernosotentsy, or Black Hundreds, a reactionary, anti-Semitic group that opposed revolution in Russia. Also, despite his father's pacifist beliefs, Andrei shot village dogs for sport; he also volunteered to serve in the Russo-Japanese War, but on his own terms—that is, he went as an aide-de-camp, not a private, and he was soon allowed to return home for "reasons of health" (he had been thrown by a horse). Andrei Tolstoy may not have been needed in the war, but his name certainly was. About Andrei, Tolstoy remarked in 1910: "Andrei is simply one of those men of whom it is hard to believe that they have a Christian soul. (They do, though, I must not forget.)"

The hostility that Tolstoy's sons had for their father was mutual. "Among my children there will be no one to carry on my work," Tolstoy wrote to Strakhov. "If I were a carpenter, my sons would be beside me at my bench. . . . But, alas, it is exactly the opposite." Later, he continued: "My sons swamp Sofya with requests for money. It will still get worse. Would it not be better if she would reject at least the income that she gets from my writing. How it would leave her in peace, her sons morally healthful, and me joyous."

Despite the alliance of Sofya and her male offspring, the woman often disliked her sons as much as he she did her daughters. She once wrote in her diary: "Andryusha has again wasted all his money at the Gypsies and has had to borrow 300 rubles. . . . He has no morals and drinks heavily. . . . I find him and his disgraceful way of living most unpleasant and distressing." Ilya, too, earned Sofya's censure. "Ilya starts drinking bouts with the neighbors," she continued, "and [things get so out of hand] that his wife has to leave the house with the children."

As regards her family, Sofya was distressed that on her husband's money she had to feed no less than thirty-eight mouths: Tolstoy's sons and their (first and often second) wives, their grandchildren and great-grandchildren, as well as distant relatives and other dependents. All had grown accustomed to servants and other amenities, thereby adding additional pressures to the already beleaguered Leo and Sofya. See Leon, *Tolstoy,* 278, 304, 312, 332, 339; Shklovsky, *Lev Tolstoy,* 601, 673, 694, 719, 724, 734; Troyat, *Tolstoy,* 466; Simmons, *Leo Tolstoy,* 2:153, 275, 326, 436.

4. Starokonyushennyi Lane is off the Arbat and located in central Moscow.

5. The Sumskoy Regiment was a military outfit founded by Russian authorities in 1658, initially to protect Russia's southern flank from attacks by Crimean and Nogay Tatars. Ilya, in fact, did serve time with this group.

6. Tolstoy engaged in such activities not from incipient insanity, but because he wished to live the "simple" life and to identify with the folk.

7. Tolstoy had long been disenchanted with the Gospels. For instance, he wrote in 1859: "I found that immortality exists, that there is love, and that one has to live for others to be eternally happy. I was surprised to see how these discoveries corresponded to [the tenets of] the Christian religion, and from that time onward, I began to search for them in the Gospels instead of in myself. But I found little there. I did not find God, or the Redeemer, or the Sacraments—nothing. I searched with all the vigor of my soul. I wept and tormented myself, craving for only one thing—the truth."

By "truth," of course, Tolstoy meant his own ideas of God and Christ. So, in 1880, with typical energy and aplomb, he wrote *An Examination and Harmony of the Four Gospels* (*Soedinenie, perevod i issledovanie chetyrekh Evangelii*). (The work was not published until later, though an abridged form, entitled *The Gospel in Brief* [*Kratkoe izlozhenie Evangeliia*] circulated freely by hand.) In *An Examination,* Tolstoy sought to rescue the essential truth of the Christian Testament from what he saw as the unnecessary ceremony and dogma of the Orthodox Church. He also sought to free the Gospels from what he considered to be the church's arbitrary designation of canonical and apocryphal works, as well as from its highly selective interpretation and interpolation of words and phrases in various translations and texts.

Tolstoy scrutinized every line of the original Greek in the New Testament to assert that the Gospels contained the highest truth. From his study of the Gospels, he also came to realize that Christianity was not an "exclusive divine revelation," a historical phenomenon, or a strange doctrine that tormented believers with ideas that were contradictory, obscure, and even absurd. Rather, Tolstoy saw Christianity as offering a practical and positive system of belief that was realizable in the here and now, that offered a profound and clear explanation of life, that filled the highest needs of the human soul, and that promised salvation not in some future heaven but on this very earth. For Tolstoy, "the Gospels expressed not the ideas of one superman, but the sum of the wisdom of all the best moral teaching expressed by many people at various times in history."

Not surprisingly, Tolstoy was rather subjective in his editing. For instance, in *An Examination,* he shocked scholars and commentators alike by simply omitting those biblical passages that he did not understand or that seemed incompatible with the truth as he saw it. The Old Testament, Tolstoy believed, was an anthology of Hebrew literature and contained much that was crude, primitive, useless, and immoral. The New Testament included the writings of Saint Paul, who, he insisted, was responsible for the alliance of church and state.

Sister Maria was not the only one who took a dim view of Tolstoy's study of the Gospels. Sofya wrote to her sister with a similar hope that Tolstoy's interest in the New Testament would "pass like an illness." Sofya elaborated: "[Tolstoy] is writing some kind of religious dissertation to prove that the church disagrees with the teaching of the Gospels. There will be barely ten people in Russia who will be interested in it."

Tolstoy disagreed. For instance, he persisted in his belief that *An Examination* was the turning point of his life, that it was thousand times more important than anything he had written previously, and that it would serve as a seedbed for future works.

In his rethinking of the Gospels, Tolstoy had an ally in Strakhov, who thought that the writer's analysis of the New Testament was strikingly simple and acute and that his *Examination* was a truly magnificent work. He wrote to Tolstoy: "Not only do you continue to amaze me, inestimable Lev Nikolaevich, but this time, you have given me peace and warmed my heart. . . . My God, [your Gospels] are good. When I think of your tastes, your habits, your work, and when I remember the horror of every form of deceit that is expressed in all your books and permeates your life, I can understand at how you arrived at where you are now. . . . Please do not chide me for these words of praise. I need to believe in you, for that belief is my sole support. . . . I shall cling to you, and, I hope, be saved."

Even more enthusiastic in praise for Tolstoy's rewriting of the Gospels was an American writer who, reporting for the Sandusky *Times,* audaciously proclaimed Tolstoy to be the thirteenth apostle. See Simmons, *Leo Tolstoy,* 1:193, 2:296; Leon, *Tolstoy,* 91, 197–98, 222; Dole, *The Life of Count Tolstoi,* 265, 269, 272–73, 324; Wilson, *Tolstoy,* 309; Troyat, *Tolstoy,* 398.

8. Tolstoy himself loved dressing up in costumes and deceiving family and friends. For instance, one Christmas, the Tolstoy children were delighted to see an old man leading a bear on a rope. At their command, the bear alternately growled, crawled, danced, and rolled over. It was only when the children realized that their father was no longer with them did they realize that he was the bear in a fur coat turned inside out. See Simmons, *Leo Tolstoy,* 1:345.

9. Lopatin recalls his amazement at hearing how Tolstoy had erupted into hearty peasantlike laughter, slapping his sides and nodding his head in

approval at Lopatin's performance. He also recalled that at a rehearsal for the play, Tolstoy had thrown a lavish banquet for the attendants, but that he had purposely omitted vodka from the table. A member of the group, though, had prepared for such a possibility and, and unbeknownst to the host, offered swigs from a bottle to people in a corner under the stairs.

In time, though, Tolstoy turned against such home productions. "To see such a lot of money spent on staging plays while the peasants wallow in misery!" he grumbled. See Dole, *The Life of Count Tolstoi*, 327; Nazaroff, *Tolstoy*, 283.

10. The Moscow Art Theater was founded in 1898 by Konstantin Stanislavsky and Vladimir Nemirovich-Danchenko; it championed theatrical naturalism in Russia. Both men, recognizing Bunin's talent for public speaking, once invited him to join the troupe. See A. Baboreko, "Chekhov i Bunin," in *Literaturnoe nasledstvo*, vol. 68 (Moscow: Izdatel'stvo Akademii nauk SSSR, 1960), 401.

11. Tolstoy's dislike of Shakespeare led him, at the age of seventy-five, to write an essay entitled "Shakespeare and the Drama" ("O Shekspire i o drame"), in which he summed up a lifetime of animosity toward the writer. Tolstoy asserted that Shakespeare's plays were tedious and repulsive; his subjects represented the lowest and most vulgar view of life; his characters did and said things that were unnatural, unnecessary, and overblown.

Tolstoy was particularly harsh in his judgments of *King Lear*. He charged that no monarch, suddenly and without warning, would abdicate and divide his kingdom based on his daughters' professions of love for him. Also, Tolstoy found it incomprehensible that a father would disinherit a favorite daughter because she professes to love her future husband as much as she does him.

Tolstoy's attacks on Shakespeare distressed critics both in the writer's time and later. For instance, in 1852, the writer Ivan Panaev told a friend: "What marvels you would have learned [from Tolstoy had you been with us]! You would have learned that Shakespeare is an ordinary writer, and that our astonishment and delight over Shakespeare are rooted in nothing more than a desire to keep up with others as well as in the habit of repeating foreign opinions. . . . How curious! Tolstoy simply does not wish to know any traditions, either theoretical or historical."

Tolstoy's criticism of Shakespeare, though, found strong support from George Bernard Shaw. "After the criticism of Tolstoy," Shaw wrote, "Shakespeare as a *thinker* must be discarded, for under the scrutiny of such a gigantic, bold critic and realist as Tolstoy, he will in no sense pass the test. . . . In no small degree has Tolstoy endeavored to open the eyes of Englishmen to the emptiness of Shakespeare's philosophy, the superficiality and unoriginality of his moral views, his weakness and confusion as a thinker, to his snobbery, vulgar prejudices, and his ignorance, to every aspect of his undeserved reputations as a great philosopher."

Others had more discriminating views. For instance, George Orwell, in a famous 1947 essay, suggested that Tolstoy himself was King Lear; that is, he was not only blind to the folly of giving away all his possessions but also seeking, unconsciously, to run, white-bearded and half mad, into the storm. Orwell's remarks are plausible, given the fact that the very things Tolstoy rejected in Shakespeare—the writer's sunny wisdom, together with his grand and humanistic view of life—also defined the writer in earlier periods of his life.

Chekhov was similarly exasperated by Tolstoy's lack of respect for cultural tradition and intellectual thought. "All these great sages are as despotic, ignorant, and indelicate as generals," he wrote to a friend, "because they feel that no one can touch them. Diogenes spat in people's faces, knowing that he would not suffer for it. Tolstoy . . . also displays his ignorance of great questions just because he, too, is a Diogenes who will not be locked up or abused in the newspapers. And so to the devil with the philosophy of all the great ones on this earth!" See Simmons, *Leo Tolstoy,* 1:143, 2:342; Crankshaw, *Tolstoy,* 220–21; Leon, *Tolstoy,* 250, 358–59; Wilson, *Tolstoy,* 478–80; Troyat, *Tolstoy,* 577.

12. Like everything else in Tolstoy's life, religion was alternately a matter of deep fervor or profound indifference. For instance, Tolstoy wrote in 1859: "Without question, I love and reverence religion. Without it, I believe that a man can be neither good nor happy. . . . Above all, with me, it is life that awakens religion and not religion that molds life. When I live a good life, I feel very near to it and ready to step into its blissful realm at any moment. But when I live badly, it even seems that I do not need it. At present . . . I feel such self-disgust, such coldness of heart, that it fills me with horror and repulsion, and the need for religion is very clear. With God's help, it will come."

Tolstoy also liked the fact that religion invalidated all notions of earthly power. He wrote: "Religion, as long as it is religion, cannot, by its very essence, be subject to authority. . . . Religion negates temporal authority (war, torture, plunder, theft, and everything bound up with government). That is why a government must make certain of its control over religion; for if it does not lock up this bird, this bird will fly away."

In truth, though, Tolstoy's disaffection with religion often overrode his affection for it. For instance, he recalled: "As a child, I believed passionately, sentimentally, and unthinkingly. Then, at age fourteen, I began thinking about life in general and came up against religion because it did not fit into my theories; and, of course, I considered that I was doing the world a service by destroying it."

As Tolstoy saw it, religion only complicated the process of salvation. "The religious problem," he wrote to a friend in 1876, "is exactly like the problem of a shipwrecked man. He looks out for something to seize in order to save himself from the imminent danger that he feels with all his be-ing. . . . Religion has held out to me this possibility of salvation. . . . But the fact of the matter is that every time I seize this plank of salvation, I drown with it. Somehow I seem able float along so long as I do not catch hold of this plank."

On the other hand, Tolstoy dismissed much of traditional Christian doctrine. For instance, as a boy learning his faith, he wrote: "I saw clearly that the entire catechism was false." In his *Confession,* he recalled:

> I shall never forget the painful feeling that I had when I took communion for the first time after many years. The service, the confession, the prayers, all these I understood, and they produced in me the joyful conviction that the meaning of life lay open to me. . . . It was such happiness for me to humble myself with a quiet heart before the priest, a simple and mild old man, and, repenting of my sins, to lay bare all the past troubles of my soul. I also found it joyful to be united with the meek Fathers of the church who composed these prayers; such happiness to be one with all those who have believed and who do believe. . . .
>
> But when I drew near to the altar, and the priest called upon me to repeat what I believed, that what I was about to swallow was genuine body and blood [of Christ], I felt a sharp pain in my heart. It was no unconsidered word; it was the hard demand of someone who could never have known what faith is. . . . I humbled myself again, and, in the wish to believe, I swallowed the blood and the body without any mocking thoughts. But the shock was still there, and knowing what awaited me another time, I could never go again.

See Simmons, *Leo Tolstoy,* 1:194, 365–66; Leon, *Tolstoy,* 91, 185–87; Wilson, *Tolstoy,* 36, 315; Nazaroff, *Tolstoy,* 228; Shklovsky, *Lev Tolstoy,* 469; Troyat, *Tolstoy,* 186, 394.

13. Although Tolstoy desperately wanted to be awarded the Cross of Saint George, he missed at least four occasions to receive the little silver testimony of courageous conduct under fire. For instance, in 1852, he was cited twice to receive the Cross of Saint George for bravery in the Russian campaign in the Caucasus, but bureaucratic delays prevented him from be-ing accorded this distinction.

A year later, Tolstoy was again recommended for the Cross of Saint George, but having stayed up late over a game of chess on the night before he was to receive the honor, the following morning he failed to appear on duty, and he spent the rest of the day in the guardhouse. From his prison cell, Tolstoy listened in abject despair as drums beat and bands played while others received the coveted award.

Somewhat later, Tolstoy was again scheduled to receive the one Cross of Saint George that had been allotted to his battery, but, upon a hint from his colonel, he stepped aside in favor of an old soldier for whom the award meant a pension for life.

As regards receiving miliary honors and awards, Tolstoy was his own worst enemy. He was hardly a soldierly ideal. A colonel wrote: "Count Tolstoy, as sublieutenant of artillery, is in command of two mountain batteries, but he himself roams wherever he pleases. . . . He is eager to smell powder, but only fitfully . . . avoiding the hardships and difficulties of war. He travels about to different places like a tourist, but as soon as he hears firing, he immediately appears on the field of battle. When it is over, he is off again at his own discretion. wherever his fancy takes him. Not everyone is able to make war in so agreeable a manner."

Needless to say, Tolstoy was bitterly disappointed that he did not receive the Cross of Saint George, since, as he wrote in his diary, he could not "impress the people of Tula" when he returned home for the war. In fact, Tolstoy so wanted the Cross of Saint George that he actually preferred receiving the little silver pendant over seeing his work *Childhood* in print. Mercifully, though, such priorities were short-lived. For instance, in his later opposition to secular governments and institutions, Tolstoy rejected the military honors and awards that had meant so much to him in his youth. See Simmons, *Leo Tolstoy,* 1:95, 106; Crankshaw, *Tolstoy,* 101; Leon, *Tolstoy,* 50; Nazaroff, *Tolstoy,* 67; Troyat, *Tolstoy,* 99.

14. In truth, Tolstoy was insanely jealous of any prospective suitor who entered the home.

15. As was the case with Sofya, family and friends often expressed exasperation at Tolstoy's intellectual and spiritual fickleness. For instance, in a letter, dated December 7, 1857, Vasily Botkin chided him, saying:

No matter how I cudgel my brains, I cannot make out exactly what you are, if not an author. Philosopher? Founder of a new religion? Civil servant? Businessman? Do be kind enough to help me out of my predicament by informing me which of the alternatives that I propose best suits you.
I am joking of course, but joking aside, I would like to see you sail out into the open at last, full speed ahead.

Three years later, Botkin was even more distressed by what he perceived as Tolstoy's instability. He continued to a friend: "Unfortunately, Tolstoy's mind is in chaos. By this, I mean that he has not reached any definite point of view in life and the business of the world. That is why he changes his convictions so often, and also why is he is so inclined to go to extremes. . . . Without some firm ground under him, it is impossible to write. And that is why Tolstoy *cannot* write, and will not be able to do so until his soul finds something upon which it can rest. . . . When will Tolstoy turn his last somersault and stand on his feet?"

Konstantin Aksakov concurred. "[Tolstoy is] a strange person," he wrote. "Why does he behave so immaturely. Why is he so unsettled? . . . It seems as though there is still no center to him."

Some, though, saw Tolstoy's intellectual fickleness as a strength. For instance, Turgenev once wrote to him: "You are too solidly planted on your own feet to become a disciple of anyone!" See Simmons, *Leo Tolstoy,* 1:256; Crankshaw, *Tolstoy,* 127, 154; Dole, *The Life of Count Tolstoi,* 138; Troyat, *Tolstoy,* 180.

CHAPTER TEN

1. People often commented on Tolstoy's "magnetic" personality. Some found the writer mesmerizing. For instance, a teacher at Tolstoy's school in Yasnaya Polyana commented: "I have never met a man so capable of firing another mind to such white heat. In the course of my spiritual relationship with Tolstoy, I felt as though electric sparks were striking into the very depths of my soul and setting in motion all kinds of thoughts and plans and decisions."

Others were less than charitable with Tolstoy's facial features. Lev Shestov commented that Tolstoy would fix his friends with a belittling, unanswerable gaze and dare them to question his sincerity. Turgenev wrote to Vsevelod Garshin that he "had never experienced anything so disagreeable as that piercing look [of Tolstoy's], which, coupled with two or three venomous remarks, was enough to drive a man insane unless he had considerable control." See Crankshaw, *Tolstoy,* 126, 132, 54; Leon, *Tolstoy,* 62.

2. The lines are from Pushkin's poem "Angel," published in 1827.

3. Bunin is quoting a piece from Tolstoy's 1857 diary, entitled "Travel Notes through Switzerland" ("Putevye zametki po Shveitsariiu"). See Tolstoy, *Polnoe sobranie sochinenii,* 5:193–94.

4. Tolstoy was a student at the University of Kazan from 1844 to 1847. In this picture, therefore, he was about seventeen years old.

5. A biographer of Tolstoy, commenting on an 1849 picture of the writer, similarly picked up on the "regressive features" of his subject. He wrote: "[The photograph] shows a lean, extremely youthful twenty-two-year-old. . . . His face is sharp, wary, and looks at though it could have developed into the bony visage of an Alexander Pope or a Voltaire. The very short hair emphasizes large, protuberant ears. The full lips are not merely sensuous, but satirical. But the most interesting feature [of Tolstoy's face] is the preternaturally straight brown hair, which overhangs very dark, deep-set eyes. It is a face of extreme liveliness and alertness. But it stares at us, as though a complete stranger to its cravat, frock coat, and sofa. It seems to be asking, 'What in the world am I doing here?'" See Wilson, *Tolstoy,* 61–62.

6. Tolstoy was appointed a Junker in 1852; so here he is in approximately his twenty-fourth year.

7. In December 1855, the twenty-seven-year-old Tolstoy made the acquaintance of such literary progressives as Ivan Turgenev, Nikolai Nekrasov, and other writer-contributors of the journal *The Contemporary (Sovre-*

mennik). Initially, Tolstoy greatly impressed his new colleagues. "What a fine, intelligent fellow Tolstoy is!" Nekrasov wrote to Vasily Botkin. "He is a dear, energetic, generous young hawk! Perhaps, an eagle!"

Tolstoy was flattered with the attention of his new colleagues, but he quickly became disenchanted with their vanity, posturing, and "base literary intriguing," as well as with their fear and envy of his talent. For instance, Alexei Pisemsky remarked gruffly to a friend: "We all just might as well give up writing; this young eagle will one day eclipse us all." Tolstoy was also dismayed by what he perceived as his colleagues' coldness and desire to isolate him. He wrote in his diary: "Goncharov, Annenkov—they all disgust me, especially Druzhinin. . . . I want friendship and affection, but they are not capable of giving them to me."

Tolstoy also objected to the lifestyle of his colleagues; that is, they professed their love for democracy and progress amidst cardplaying, luxurious dinners, hunting expeditions, and the like. Such individuals, Tolstoy believed, were worthless and immoral; so long as they received money and prestige for their writing, they were parasites, not prophets.

Additionally, Tolstoy so disliked being caught in the tug-of-war that existed between such aristocratic liberals as Turgenev, Ivan Goncharov, and Alexander Druzhinin and such déclassé radicals as Nikolai Chernyshevsky and Nikolai Dobrolyubov that he sought to dissociate himself from both camps. As he saw it, both liberals and radicals were tilting at windmills, their grandiloquence and "civic" views on literature and art being empty, hypocritical, and self-aggrandizing.

For instance, in a speech given to the Moscow Society of the Lovers of Russian Literature on February 4, 1859, Tolstoy opposed social tendentiousness in art. He declared: "The majority of the public has begun to think that the problem of all literature consists only in denouncing evil, in debating and correcting wrong, in short, in nurturing a civic feeling in society." Russian writers, Tolstoy insisted, needed more ideal and diverse approaches to art. "A literature of the people . . . should reflect a popular love of goodness and truth, as well as the popular contemplation of beauty."

In all fairness, Tolstoy's arrogance, posturing, and independence did little to endear him to his new literary colleagues. His cantankerous "self" was a thorn in every literary id and ego. "What nonsense Tolstoy poured out yesterday at dinner," Nekrasov wrote to Botkin. "The devil knows what is in his head. He said much that is stupid and nasty. . . . God alone knows what putrid and backward ideas fill his head." Turgenev agreed. "Not one word, not one movement of Tolstoy's is natural," he remarked. "He is eternally posing before us, and I find it difficult to explain. . . . this impoverished count's arrogance."

The writer Dmitri Grigorovich added: "The greater the authority of the speaker on a subject, the more Tolstoy insisted on maintaining an opposite judgment and making a sharp retort." See Simmons, *Leo Tolstoy,* 1:139–46, 197; Crankshaw, *Tolstoy,* 130; Leon, *Tolstoy,* 59, 62, 64; Dole, *The Life of Count Tolstoi,* 94; Nazaroff, *Tolstoy,* 90; Troyat, *Tolstoy,* 179.

8. A colleague of Tolstoy's in the Caucasus recalled: "Tolstoy was far superior to the average man, and from the first, I could not resist the giant's influence. At that time, Tolstoy's love of gaiety was very striking, and when I saw him going out for a walk in his new coat, with its gray beaver collar, his dark curly hair worn long under his fashionable hat, set jauntily on one side, and his smart cane, I would cite this expression from a popular song: 'He leans on his stick and boasts that it is made of hazelwood.'" See Dole, *The Life of Count Tolstoi,* 123.

9. Tolstoy left army life in 1856.

10. As a youth in Kazan and with characteristic snobbery and aplomb, Tolstoy had classified society into two broad classes: *comme il faut* and *comme il ne faut pas.* Of course, he wished to belong to the former group. "My way of being *comme il faut,*" he wrote, "consisted first of all in the perfect mastery of French and, in particular, the proper accent. A man who pronounced French badly aroused in me a feeling of contempt. . . . The second requirement for being *comme il faut* was to have fingernails that were long, well-shaped, and clean; the third was to be able to bow, dance, and converse; and the fourth (very important) was to appear indifferent and to wear a certain air of distinguished and disdainful boredom at all times." People who were not *comme il faut,* Tolstoy believed, were commoners and boors who wore untidy boots, a fault he could not abide.

Although Tolstoy saw *comme il faut* as the height of human perfection, his ungainly frame and boorish behavior precluded any genuine entry into the elitist group he so esteemed. For instance, he was an extremely poor dancer. "My dear Leo, you are nothing but a sack of flour!" one partner exclaimed (in French).

As he matured, though, Tolstoy gave up all pretensions to *comme il faut.* Writing to a friend on his first tour of Europe, he noted: "There is nothing more stupid that a Frenchman who is *comme il faut.*" See Simmons, *Leo Tolstoy,* 1:52–53; Leon, *Tolstoy,* 83; Wilson, *Tolstoy,* 41–42, 45.

11. Tolstoy first visited Paris in 1857. Although he initially enjoyed the society, culture, and sights of the city, a public execution shocked the young man's sensibilities and shook his faith in all forms of political organization. Tolstoy wrote to Botkin:

The spectacle of the guillotine made such an impression on me that I shall not recover from it for a long time. I saw many horrors of war in the Caucasus and elsewhere, but if a man were torn to pieces before my eyes, it would not be so repulsive as this dexterous and elegant machine which, in a flash, kills a powerful, fresh, and healthy person. In the first instance, there would be no intelligent will, but the human feeling of passion; in the other, there is a refined quiet and convenience in killing and nothing at all that is majestic. The insolent, audacious desire to fulfill justice, the law of God. . . . The repulsive crowd, the father who explains to his little daughter the clear, convenient mechanism that does this and that. . . . Human law—nonsense! . . . I understand the laws of custom, of morality and religion . . . and I feel the laws of art that give happiness always. But for me, political laws are such a horrible lie that I do not see in them anything that is either better or worse. . . . I will never again look at such a thing, and I will never anywhere serve *any* government. . . . The only ideal is anarchy.

Twenty years later, Tolstoy was still haunted by his memories of the guillotine. He wrote in *Confession:* "When I saw the head divided from the body, and heard the sound with which they fell separately into the box, I understood, not with my reason, but with my entire being, that no theory of the reasonableness of progress could justify such a deed, and that although, no matter what theory, everyone since the creation of the world believed such a process to be necessary, I knew it to be both unnecessary and bad."

Tolstoy's encounter with the guillotine turned an otherwise pleasant visit to Paris into a nightmare. "Paris made me so sick that I almost lost my mind," he told "Granny" Alexandra. "The things I saw there! First, in the lodging house, I lived with twenty-six couples, nineteen of them unmarried. I was horrified beyond belief. Then, to test myself, I went to see a criminal being executed by the guillotine. After that, I could not sleep, nor could I stay there any longer."

After witnessing a Parisian-style execution, Tolstoy also turned his back on the French nation. "There is no poetry in this people," he wrote, "their only poetry is politics. . . . Generally speaking, I like the French way of life and the French people, but I have yet to meet one man of real value, either in society or among the folk." See Simmons, *Leo Tolstoy,* 1:170; Leon, *Tolstoy,* 79–80; Troyat, *Tolstoy,* 167, 169.

12. Lake Geneva is situated in the southwest corner of Switzerland.

13. Fribourg is a French-speaking, mainly Catholic canton in western Switzerland, about 60 miles northeast of Lake Geneva.

14. Lake Leman is the old Latin name for Lake Geneva.

15. The Savoy mountains are located just south of Lake Geneva.

16. The village of Montreux is a resort town on the easternmost shore of Lake Geneva.

17. The city of Villeneuve is several miles south of Montreux.

18. The Valais Alps are just north of the border between Switzerland and Italy and include the Matterhorn.

19. The village of Chillon lies between Villeneuve and Montreux.

20. Bunin's own impressions of his first visit to Switzerland echo those of Tolstoy. "Dear sweet one!" he wrote his brother, Yuly, on November 18, 1900.

I left Paris on the tenth and arrived in Geneva that evening. . . . We went out early the next day; we marveled at the quiet warm morning. In the delicate fog . . . mountains and a lake, soft and azure green, appeared in the distance. . . . One could hear the pure ringing of bells, and the silence, the eternal silence of the lake and mountains.

I have thought about the quiet that reigns in the Alpine kingdom, where only the muffled sounds of waterfalls and eagles greet the afternoon. . . .

A Swiss man came out with a long wooden horn. . . . He soaked it in water, stood it like a giant pipe on the ground, blew into it, and made a sound. Hardly had the sound of the horn begun to die when it echoed into a thousand harmonies . . . as if someone with a mighty hand had struck a crystal harp . . . and created a heavenly harmony . . . that rose to the sky. It was marvelous!

See Baboreko, "Iz perepsiki I. A. Bunina," 207–9.

21. Clarens is also located between Villeneueve and Montreaux. Tolstoy was enchanted with Clarens not only because its physical beauty, but also because of its sentimental association with Rousseau's *Nouvelle Heloise.* "I will not attempt to describe the beauty of the country," Tolstoy wrote to Aunt Tatyana, "especially at the present time when everything is in leaf and flower. I will say only that it is literally impossible to tear oneself away from the lake and its shores, and that I spend most of my time gazing in ecstasy. . . . I am very happy."

Tolstoy was also enchanted with his surroundings in Switzerland because they allowed him to forget not only his self but also all sense of time and space. To "Granny" Alexandra, Tolstoy continued: "Nature gives one the supreme delight of forgetting everything about one's precious self. One no longer sees how one lives; the past and the future vanish; the present alone, like a thread, unrolls itself and disappears." See Leon, *Tolstoy,* 82, 83; Nazaroff, *Tolstoy,* 117.

22. For all his love of Switzerland, though, Tolstoy did not care for vast panoramas of mountains and the like, since they seemed to defy his wish to merge with the universe. "I do not like what are called glorious and magnificent views," he wrote at this time, "for they are somehow cold. . . . I like nature when I seem to be a part of it, when it surrounds me on all sides and stretches out into infinite distances. I like nature . . . when blades of tender grass . . . melt into the green of boundless meadows; when the leaves that flutter in the wind run their shadows across my face and form the line of the distant forest; when the air that I breathe creates the deep azure of the illimitable heavens. I do not exult and rejoice in nature alone, but with myriads of buzzing and whirling insects. All around me, beetles cling together and creep about, and birds pour forth in song." See Simmons, *Leo Tolstoy,* 1:174; Dole, *The Life of Count Tolstoi,* 119–20.

23. *Bunin's note:* One of the defining traits of Tolstoy's personality was that he was very shy.

Editors' note: Especially as a youth, Tolstoy often became paralyzed by an almost morbid shyness. See Troyat, *Tolstoy,* 45.

24. Tolstoy is referring to the cultivated Russian travelers whom he met in Switzerland and who accompanied him on excursions there. Interestingly, Tolstoy had little use for the English and French tourists whom he met in the region. He wrote in his diary: "When middle-class Frenchmen converse, they never fail to mention *ma pauvre mere.*" Their counterparts across the Channel fared even worse. Tolstoy continued: "The English are a morally naked people who live without shame." Several days later, he added: "I have listened to more than five hundred conversations with the English. I have talked to them myself, but if I have ever heard a single living word from them . . . may I be struck dead from lightning." Zeroing in on his attack, he continued: "[I met] an Englishwoman whose sole interest in life lies in restaurants, and who thinks that the essential thing is to speak French, but that what she says is immaterial."

Even the Swiss raised Tolstoy's hackles. "Absence of poetry," he wrote, "along with prevailing mediocrity . . . amiable, jovial, stupid people—grown-up children." See Simmons, *Leo Tolstoy,* 1:172; Crankshaw, *Tolstoy,* 162; Leon, *Tolstoy,* 83; Nazaroff, *Tolstoy,* 121.

25. Tolstoy's later pictures, though, show the effect of his triumphs and tragedies. For instance, Romain Rolland commented upon a 1882 photograph of the writer at age fifty-four: "He looks overwhelmed. A double furrow traces symmetrical lines in the large, comely face. There is so much goodness, such tenderness in the great, doglike muzzle, in the eyes that regard one with so frank, so clear, and so sorrowful a look. They read one's mind so surely. They pity and implore." See Nazaroff, *Tolstoy,* 247.

26. Pokrovskoe was an estate that belonged to Tolstoy's sister, Maria.

27. Tolstoy is quoting from *Childhood.* The entire passage is:

To be accepted as one of my chosen readers, I ask very little, only that you be sensitive, that is, able sometimes to pity with your entire soul and even to shed a few tears when recalling a character that you have loved deeply, that you should rejoice in him without being ashamed of it, that you should love your memories and be devout so that, when reading my works, you will look for places that will touch your heart and not make you laugh. . . .

Above all, you should be an understanding person—one who, when I get to know him, need not have any feelings and inclinations explained but who I see understands me and in whom every note of my soul finds a response. It is difficult, and I think even impossible, to divide people into intelligent and stupid groups, or good and bad ones. But between people who understand and those who do not, there is for me such a sharp line that I cannot help drawing it between all I know.

Tolstoy, though, did know the way to his reader's hearts. He wrote in his diary in 1856: "The first condition of a writer's popularity, that is, the way to make himself loved, is the way he treats all his characters. That is why Dickens's characters are the friends of all humankind; they serve as a bond between humanity in America and in Petersburg. But Thackeray and Gogol, though artistic and faithful to life, are pitiless and not at all loving." See Simmons, *Leo Tolstoy,* 1:150; Leon, *Tolstoy,* 42.

28. Right before beginning *War and Peace,* Tolstoy wrote: "I am reading Goethe, and many thoughts swarms within me." Although Tolstoy did not care for Goethe, he was sufficiently drawn to the writer to read all forty-four volumes of Goethe's works in 1894. See Simmons, *Leo Tolstoy,* 1:295, 2:199.

29. Bunin is quoting from Tolstoy's 1856 "Sevastopol in May" ("Sevastopol' v mae"). Twelve years later, he similarly wrote to a friend: "I have my weaknesses, habits of vanity, and warm ties, but up to now—I shall soon be forty—I have loved truth more than anything. I do not despair of finding it, and I am still searching and searching."

About the workings of truth, Tolstoy later wrote: "I went for a moment to the water closet. I pulled the chain. But I really didn't pull it hard enough and the water kept running. Then I suspected that I had not pulled it hard enough; and when I did, the water stopped. That's the way it is with these questions [of life]: You've either got to tell the whole truth or nothing at all." See Simmons, *Leo Tolstoy,* 1:325, 2:446.

30. Although Tolstoy's mother died when he was only two years old, stories about her told by aunts and servants, together with his mother's letters and diaries, led him to make a near cult of the woman he never knew. Specifically, Tolstoy came to see his mother as embodying the ideals of love, chastity, and even sainthood. He also believed that his mother was like himself: a restless individual who constantly strove for things that were infinite and eternal.

For instance, in his memoirs, Tolstoy wrote:

By a strange coincidence, not a single portrait of my mother exists. Thus I cannot represent her to myself as a real and physical being. I am partly pleased by this fact, because in my imagination there exists only her moral personality. All that I know about her was beautiful, and that is not because the people who told me about her wished to say something kind, but because there really was great goodness in her. . . .

My mother appeared to me to be such a pure and moral being that when I, as a middle-aged man, was often seized by doubts, I prayed to her soul for assistance, and that prayer always helped me.

Even as an old man, Tolstoy wrote in his diary: "I walk in the garden, and I think of my mother, of *maman.* I do not remember her, but she has always been an ideal of saintliness for me. . . . As when I was a child, I want to nestle against some tender and compassionate being and weep with love and be consoled . . . to become a little boy, close to my mother, the way I imagined her. . . . [My mother] is my highest conception of a love that is not cold or divine, but pure, warm, earthly, and maternal This is what attracts my bitter, weary soul. Mummy dear, caress me!"

See Simmons, *Leo Tolstoy,* 1:13; Crankshaw, *Tolstoy,* 32; Biryukov, *Leo Tolstoy,* 9–10; Wilson, *Tolstoy,* 52; Troyat, *Tolstoy,* 14.

31. Bunin is quoting from part 1, scene 4, of Goethe's *Faust,* which was written in 1808. Tolstoy read the work in the years between 1857 and 1859. See Simmons, *Leo Tolstoy,* 1:186.

32. Tolstoy first read the works of Schopenhauer in the late 1860s; some twenty years later, he asked Strakhov for the thinker's 1850 *Parega and Paralipomena.* Tolstoy was greatly impressed by Schopenhauer, if only because Schopenhauer's "systematized" sense of pessimism helped to explain his own "chaotic" sense of the futility and terribleness of life. "Life should not be," Tolstoy read in Schopenhauer, "and the sole good is the passage from being to nothingness."

In August 1869, Tolstoy wrote to Fet: "Do you know what this summer has been for me? An endless ecstasy over Schopenhauer and a series of mental pleasures such as I have never experienced before. I have brought all his works and have read them over and over. . . . Assuredly, no student in Schopenhauer's course has learned and discovered so much as I have during the summer. I do not know if I shall ever change my opinion, but at present I am convinced that Schopenhauer is the greatest genius among men. . . . Indeed, I cannot understand how his name can be unknown. The only explanation [for such ignorance] is the one that he so often repeats, that is, there is scarcely anyone but idiots in the world."

Tolstoy's admiration for Schopenhauer was so strong that, at one point, he thought of translating the philosopher's works into Russian. Also, a portrait of Schopenhauer hung in Tolstoy's study.

It should be noted that not everyone in Russia was taken with Schopenhauer and his ideas. "That Buddhist, that corpse," Alexander Herzen pronounced summarily. See Simmons, *Leo Tolstoy,* 1:317, 328; Crankshaw, *Tolstoy,* 237; Dole, *The Life of Count Tolstoi,* 222; Wilson, *Tolstoy,* 127, 388; Troyat, *Tolstoy,* 316, 377.

33. As a beginning writer, Tolstoy remarked about his method of composition: "To look over work that has been completed in rough draft, striking all that is superfluous and adding nothing—that is the first process." Upon further reflection, he continued: "When I write, I am frequently frustrated by hackneyed expressions that are not exact, poetic, or true. . . . To tolerate these expressions means to drift with one's age; to correct them, to be in advance of it."

Apparently, Tolstoy heeded the words of Druzhinin, who, having read *Childhood,* felt compelled to remark:

You are unliterary to a marked degree. Sometimes your illiteracy is that of a word-coiner or of a great poet who is forever reforming the language in his own way, or even that of a military officer who sits in a bunker and writes to a friend. It may be said with assurance that all that you have written with love . . . is admirable, but that as soon as you grow cold, your word entangle themselves and fiendish forms of language make their appearance. . . . Above all, avoid long sentences. Chop them into two or three. . . . Do not be afraid of periods. . . . Be unceremonious with particles and cut out by dozens the relatives "which," "who," and "that." . . . When in difficulty, take a sentence and imagine that you want to say it to someone in a fluent, conversational way.

Druzhinin and others particularly objected to what seemed to be Tolstoy's obsession with analysis and detail. For instance, Druzhinin told the writer: "One occasionally feels that you are about to write: 'X's thighs showed that he wanted to take a trip to India.'" Also, apropos of the first part of *War and Peace*, Turgenev remarked to a friend: "The thing is positively bad, boring, and a failure. . . . All those little details so cleverly noted and presented in a baroque style, those psychological remarks which the author digs out of his heroes' armpits and other dark places in the name of verisimilitude. Such things, cast against the broad historical background of the novel, are so paltry and trivial. . . . One feels so strongly Tolstoy's lack of imagination and naïveté!" See Leon, *Tolstoy*, 44; Dole, *The Life of Count Tolstoi*, 111; Troyat, *Tolstoy*, 156, 281.

34. Alexander Goldenweiser was a pianist and friend of Leo Tolstoy. Bunin is paraphrasing Goldenweiser's memoirs, entitled *Vblizi Tolstogo* (*Inside Tolstoy*), first published in Moscow in 1922–23.

35. Bunin also used to speak with the folk in their own language.

36. Bunin was extremely proud of his literary roots. In a 1926 article, he wrote: "All of our [Russian] literary language comes from a comparatively small area . . . [a region bordered by] Kursk, Oryol, Tula, Ryazan, and Voronezh. Almost all of our major Russian writers . . . are from this region. . . . Zhukovsky and Tolstoy are from Tula; Tyutchev, Leskov, Turgenev, Fet, and the brothers Kireevsky and Zhemchuzhnikov are from Oryol; Anna Bunina and Polonsky are from Ryazan; Koltsov, Nikitin, Garshin, and Pisarev are from Voronezh. . . . Even Pushkin and Lermontov are partially ours, for their ancestors came from there and 'drank our type of *kvas*,' as people from our area say."

Fifteen years earlier, Bunin similarly had told an interviewer: "I am fond of genuine folk language . . . but examples of the folk speech of central Russia, I find only in the works of Gleb Uspensky and Leo Tolstoy. As regards the contrivances and stylization that the Modernists pass off as folk language, these I consider the utmost vulgarity."

See A. Ninov, "K avtobiografii I. Bunina," *Novyi mir*, no. 10 (1965): 225; I. Bunin, "K vospominaniiam o Tolstom," *Vozrozhdenie* (June 20, 1926): 3.

37. Bunin is referring to N. Gusev, *Zhizn' L'va Nikolaevicha Tolstogo* (*The Life of Lev Nikolaevich Tolstoy*), published in Moscow in 1927. Nikolai Gusev was Tolstoy's friend and secretary who had come to Yasnaya Polyana in 1904. Earlier, when Gusev had been arrested by the government for disseminating revolutionary books and ideas, Tolstoy wrote to him: "How I wish they would put me in jail, into a real, stinking one—cold and hungry. Evidently, though, I have not yet deserved this honor." Tolstoy also wrote to the prime minister, requesting that he be imprisoned in Gusev's place. Needless to say, the writer's request was ignored.

In 1909, Gusev was again arrested and this time exiled for distributing works of Tolstoy that had been banned by the censor. See Leon, *Tolstoy,* 309; Wilson, *Tolstoy,* 491.

38. Language aside, Tolstoy could not punish his serfs without remorse. On November 27, 1859, he wrote: "Today [one of my serfs] lied. I put myself into a rage and, in accordance with a deplorable habit, ordered him to be flogged. . . . Later I sent someone to stop it, but the man arrived too late. I am going to ask his forgiveness. Never again shall I have people punished without reflecting beforehand for two hours. . . . I asked forgiveness [from the serf] and gave him two rubles. But my actions still torment me."

Such remorse, though, did not keep the hot-tempered Tolstoy from beating the soldiers in his battalion during the Caucasian campaign. See Simmons, *Leo Tolstoy,* 1:130; Leon, *Tolstoy,* 88.

39. Although during the Caucasian campaign Tolstoy was so disgusted at the way officers swore at their troops that he invented a meaningless "cuss word" to replace the most obscene oaths, his own troops told Tolstoy's successor that they had never known such a swearer as he. See Simmons, *Leo Tolstoy,* 1:130.

40. On a visit to the ill Tolstoy in the Crimea, Gorky asked Chekhov if he "fucked a lot of whores in his youth." Chekhov, embarrassed by the question, mumbled something in reply; but Tolstoy filled in the silence by replying: "I could fuck for days on end." Gorky continued: "Tolstoy said such a thing penitently. . . . And for the first time, I noticed how simply he used such words, as though he knew no more fitting ones to use. Coming from his shaggy lips, they sounded simple and natural, for they had lost their soldierly filth."

Tolstoy's sexual prowess aside, Gorky was so overawed by his older colleague that he once remarked that there was no room for God and the greater writer in the same universe. "They would be like two bears in one den." Reconsidering, Gorky added: "Tolstoy is like a God, not a Sabaoth or an Olympian, but the kind of Russian god who sits on a maple throne under a golden lime tree, not majestic, but, perhaps, more cunning than all the other gods."

Tolstoy, though, cared little for his young colleague. He wrote: "Gorky is an unkind man. . . . He has the soul of a spy. He has come into the land of Canaan where he feels himself to be a stranger. So he watches everything that goes on around him; he notices everybody and reports to a god of his own. And his god is a monster."

Tolstoy also disliked much of Gorky's fiction."I started reading *Foma Gordeyev,*" Tolstoy told Gorky, "but I could not finish it. What you have written is much too dull." Tolstoy also took issue with the innocence of Gorky's heroines in such works as *Varenka Olesova* (1896) and *Twenty-Six Men and a Girl* (*Dvadtsat' shest' i odna,* 1899). Gorky recalled:

> I was crushed by Tolstoy's tone, and thrown into confusion by his frank language and his brusqueness as he tried to prove to me that modesty was not natural to a healthy young girl.
>
> He said: "If a girl is over fifteen and is healthy, she likes to be embraced and touched. . . ." [Later he added:] "There is nothing worse than when a man marries a physically chaste but immoral woman and spends the rest of his life with her."
>
> I never liked the way Tolstoy spoke about women. It was much too vulgar. Also, his words sounded not quite sincere, but rather affected and not very personal.

Parenthetically, Bunin cared little for Gorky's memoirs of Tolstoy, if only because, in his view, they said more about Gorky than they did about the greater writer. Bunin told Bakhrakh: "What we have here is not Lev Nikolaevich, but Lev 'Alexeimaximovich!'" See Bakhrakh, *Bunin v khalate,* 142. Also see Crankshaw, *Tolstoy,* 107–11, 203, 262; Dole, *The Life of Count Tolstoi,* 332; Wilson, *Tolstoy,* 466; Simmons, *Leo Tolstoy,* 2:322.

41. Even as a child, Tolstoy was so sensitive about his ungainly face and torso that he prayed to God for a transformation in physical appearance. He detested his large ears, his full, thick lips, and his coarse, wide nostrils. He also disliked his dark, stubbornly tufted hair; his deep-set, narrow steel-gray eyes; and his ridged,"cabbagelike" nose. The young Tolstoy plucked his eyebrows (they grew in more thickly) and, trying to be a pensive Byron or Werther, brushed his hair with elaborate art, but in vain.

Many of Tolstoy's child characters are similarly unhappy with their faces and torsos. For instance, the adolescent in Tolstoy's *Youth* writes:

> I was not only convinced that my appearance was plain, but also that I was unable to take comfort with the usual reflections: I could not say that my face was expressive, intellectual, and noble. . . . The features were of the coarsest, homeliest, and most ordinary description. My small gray eyes were stupid rather than intelligent, particularly when I looked into the mirror.
>
> There was still less of manliness about me. Although I was not so very diminutive in stature and strong for my age, all my features were soft, flabby, and unformed. There was nothing aristocratic about them. On the contrary,

my face was like that of a common peasant; and I had such big hands and feet. At that time, everything about me seemed particularly disgraceful.

Even when Tolstoy was a dashing young officer in the Caucasus, he remained unhappy with his appearance. "I stand for hours before the mirror," he wrote, "and suffer because my left mustache is not as thick and healthy as the right one!" See Leon, *Tolstoy*, 7, 11–12; Dole, *The Life of Count Tolstoi*, 22, 26; Nazaroff, *Tolstoy*, 58; Troyat, *Tolstoy*, 47, 234.

42. In a 1926 article, Bunin rejected Goldenweiser's statements as to the cause of Tolstoy's alleged lisp. Rather, Bunin insisted that the linguistic "peculiarities" of the writer's speech were common to the region in which both Bunin and Tolstoy lived. "*We all always* used to say things like that!" Bunin wrote. See I. Bunin, "K vospominaniiam o Tolstom," *Vozrozhdenie* (June 20, 1926): 2–3.

43. As a university student, Tolstoy practiced gymnastics daily in the hope of becoming the strongest man in the world; and, as an officer in the Crimea, Tolstoy would often amaze his fellow officers by lying down and lifting two heavy men from the ground, standing each of them on his outstretched hands. (He even wrote a treatise in French on the subject.) One army colleague wrote: "Tolstoy left behind . . . the memory of a good horseman, a high liver, and a Hercules."

Tolstoy's love for gymnastics often took a humorous turn. For instance, Fet recalled: "It was worth the trip [to the gym] to see Tolstoy's fierce concentration, trying to leap over a vaulting horse in his gymsuit." His brother Nikolai added:

Leo desires to take up everything, but not to miss gymnastics in the process. Now he has erected a bar outside his window. Of course, if we put aside the prejudice against which he is always fighting, Leo is quite right: Gymnastics do not interfere with the management of the estate. But the bailiff looks somewhat differently on the matter. "I go to the master," he says, "to get orders. But the master, in a short red jacket, swings with one leg over the bar head down, his face red, hair hanging down and flying about. I wonder: Must I wait for orders or look at him?"

Even more outrageous, perhaps, is the retort of a servant girl who refused to work inside Tolstoy's house because, as she told Tolstoy's sister, Maria, "[the master] runs about the place naked, turning somersaults." See Simmons, *Leo Tolstoy*, 1:52, 130–31; Biryukov, *Leo Tolstoy*, 47; Troyat, *Tolstoy*, 63, 117, 183, 188.

44. Tolstoy's lapses into gluttony caused him considerable distress throughout his life. For instance, as a soldier, he would gorge on ices one day, on melon the next, and on "Turkish delight and other trash" the next. Later, as a married man, Tolstoy would eat such inordinate quantities of watermelon or peas that Sofya became "quite frightened." See Leon, *Tolstoy*, 35, 232.

45. Tolstoy gave up eating meat not only because "such food excited the passions . . . as well as the greediness and desire for appetizing food," but also because "it involved killing, the performance of an act contrary to moral feeling." Perversely, though, Tolstoy demanded meat on fast days. "Pass the meat!" he growled at onlookers one Ash Wednesday. See Leon, *Tolstoy*, 232; Troyat, *Tolstoy*, 393.

46. "I am not afraid of death but pain," Tolstoy wrote in his diary on February 5, 1852. "What I am afraid of is not being able to bear [such a thing] with dignity." See Troyat, *Tolstoy*, 89.

47. Rats—swift, restless, and cruel—horrified Tolstoy because, in his view, they personified sin itself. Tolstoy, though, could also show pity for rats. For instance, when Yasnaya Polyana was once infested with these rodents, he did not kill them but set them free in a remote part of the estate. See Leon, *Tolstoy*, 301; Dole, *The Life of Count Tolstoi*, 336.

48. *Bunin's note:* One time he almost died when he was out hunting bears. The rules of such an activity require that the hunter stamp the snow around his feet so that he can move about freely. But he paid no attention to such things.

"Nonsense," he said, "one should shoot the bear straight off, not engage in hand-to-hand combat with it."

So he stood in the snow up to his waist. A huge she-bear ran out of the forest straight toward him. He fired at the animal and missed. He fired again, point-blank, but the bullet only struck the bear in the teeth, and she jumped on him. The deep snow did not allow him to jump to the side, and the bear began gnawing at him. He was saved only because another hunter came running up and shot the animal.

Editors' note: Tolstoy's encounter with the bear took place on December 22, 1858. Bunin's remarks on the event are only partially correct. The hunter frightened the bear not with a gun but by brandishing a stick. Also, the skin both above and below Tolstoy's eye was so badly torn that he was taken to a nearby town for treatment. He suffered no ill effects from his injury, though; and, to family and friends, he even flaunted the marks of the bear's teeth above his eye. (For instance, immediately after the incident, the badly bleeding Tolstoy said: "What will Fet say? But I am proud of what happened.") Tolstoy was equally laconic when he described the event in his diary. "Went bear hunting . . . [on the second day] an animal took a piece out of me. Spent a lot of money."

Tolstoy, though, described his encounter with the bear in greater detail in his tales for children, for example, in "The Bear Hunt" ("Kak medved' poimali") and "The Wish Is Stronger than Bondage" ("Okhota pusche nevoli"). More important, he used his encounter with near-death as the seedbed for the reflections of the wounded Prince Andrei in *War and*

Peace. Indeed, when telling people of the event, he was Andrei come to life. He told friends:

[With the bear] I felt no pain. I lay beneath him and looked into his warm, large mouth with its wet, white teeth. He breathed above me, and I saw how he turned his head to get into position to bite into both my temples at once. In his hurry, or from an excited appetite, he made a trial snap in the air just above my head. He again opened his mouth—that red, wet, hungry mouth dripping with saliva. I felt that I was about to die, and I looked into the depths of that mouth as one condemned to execution looks into the grave that is dug for him. I looked, and remember that I felt neither fear nor dread. I saw with one eye, beyond the outline of that mouth, a patch of blue sky gleaming between purple clouds roughly piled together, and I thought how lovely it was up there.

Tolstoy's bear was eventually killed, and its skin is still on display at Yasnaya Polyana. See Simmons, *Leo Tolstoy,* 1:191, 230; Leon, *Tolstoy,* 88–89, 232; Biryukov, *Leo Tolstoy,* 47; and Dole, *The Life of Count Tolstoi,* 132–33.

49. Tolstoy's brother-in-law, Stepan Andreevich Bers, recalled of the writer: "With all Tolstoy's zeal for sport, I never saw him whip a dog or beat his horse." In fact, the one time young Tolstoy whipped his horse to make him go, he was so reproached by a peasant that he slid off the horse's back, kissed the animal on the neck, and begged his pardon for mistreating him." See Leon, *Tolstoy,* 130; Troyat, *Tolstoy,* 22.

50. Immediately after Tolstoy gave up hunting, he wrote to Sofya: "Today I busied myself with the affairs of the estate. Then I went off for a ride on my horse . . . [because] I wanted to test my feeling for hunting. For forty years, riding and pursuing game has been for me a very agreeable habit. But when a hare jumped out, I wished him luck. Above all, I felt ashamed [for my previous life as a hunter]."

Like all of his obsessions, though, Tolstoy's late-life rejection of hunting assumed absurd proportions. For instance, a visitor to Yasnaya Polyana actually convinced him that one "slaughtered" plant life by reaping grain and that, as evidenced by man's cousin, the monkey, it was humane and judicious to pick nuts and fruits off trees. See Dole, *The Life of Count Tolstoi,* 306; Simmons, *Leo Tolstoy,* 2:67.

51. In 1876, Tolstoy owned as many as four hundred horses at his estate in Samara, though, like so many of his projects, his plan to develop a large stud farm ended in failure. See Simmons, *Leo Tolstoy,* 2:355.

52. The critic Nikolai Strakhov had such respect for Tolstoy's *War and Peace* that he even saw the dogs in the work as individualized. See Simmons, *Leo Tolstoy,* 1:314.

53. The Zaseka was a long ribbon of imperial forest domain located not far from Yasnaya Polyana.

54. As a child, Tolstoy could cry so easily that his brothers nicknamed him "Lyova-ryova," or "Leo Crybaby." Bunin showed a similar propensity to tears. See Leon, *Tolstoy,* 5.

55. In the summer of 1850, the twenty-two-year-old Tolstoy threw himself zealously into the study of music; but, like everything else in his life, his passions soon overruled his purpose. At first, he practiced the piano faithfully and had dreams of becoming a virtuoso and a composer. He even began to write a treatise, entitled "The Fundamental Principles of Music and Rules for Its Study" ("Osnovnye nachala muziki i pravila k izucheniiu onoi"). In fact, the subject so absorbed Tolstoy that he experienced the "happiness of the artist, although in a very incomplete way."

Clouds soon darkened Tolstoy's musical horizon, though. A noisy, drunken German composer named Rudolph Kisewetter, whom Tolstoy had met in a cabaret in Saint Petersburg and had taken back with him to Yasnaya Polyana, was hardly a source of inspiration. After impregnating several peasant girls, Kisewetter was dispatched from the estate. (He was to become the model for the protagonist of Tolstoy's story "Albert"; he also was the inspiration for the musician Efemov in Dostoevsky's *Netovchka Nezvanova* [1849].) Whatever theories the restless Tolstoy had about music soon gave way to (also unrealized) plans for a second treatise: new rules for cardplaying. See Simmons, *Leo Tolstoy,* 1:75; Crankshaw, *Tolstoy,* 71; Shklovsky, *Lev Tolstoy,* 275.

56. In 1896, Tolstoy walked out of a performance of Wagner's *Siegfried,* muttering, "Fit for a circus, idiotic, pretentious! . . . One cannot tell whether the orchestra has already started to play or is still tuning up." See Troyat, *Tolstoy,* 513.

57. As a youth, Tolstoy liked the music of Bach, Haydn, Gluck, and Mozart. He also admired Beethoven, though he believed that his Ninth Symphony "brought about disunion among men." See Dole, *The Life of Count Tolstoi,* 35; Nazaroff, *Tolstoy,* 264, 266. For more on Tolstoy's stance toward Beethoven, see R. Rischin, "Allegro Tumultuosissimamente: Beethoven in Tolstoy's Fiction," in *In the Shade of the Giant: Essays on Tolstoy,* ed. H. McLean (Berkeley: University of California Press, 1989), 12–60.

58. Tolstoy once boldly declared that Pushkin's poems and Beethoven's Ninth Symphony were not as "universally good" as certain Russian folk songs and melodies. "Pushkin and Beethoven please us," he said, "not because they are absolutely beautiful, but because . . . they flatter our perverted and abnormal sensitivities and weaknesses." Inherent here was Tolstoy's belief that what society vaunted as "poetry" and "music" was the product of minds that had been falsely educated. Such "culture," he insisted, not only lacked importance and a future but also paled in comparison to what the folk spontaneously did in art.

He continued: "Why, without any special training, is the beauty of the sun . . . the human face . . . a folk song . . . or an act of love or self-denial intelligible to all?" See Dole, *The Life of Count Tolstoi*, 179; Troyat, *Tolstoy*, 218.

59. Tchaikovsky, much to his chagrin, evoked similar disapproval from Tolstoy. As a youth, Tchaikovsky had greatly admired Tolstoy and his works; at first, the feeling was mutual. When Tolstoy heard Tchaikovsky's Andante in D Major, he was so moved that he burst into tears, greatly flattering its composer.

"Never in my life," Tchaikovsky wrote in his diary, "have I felt so flattered and proud of my creative ability as when Leo Tolstoy, sitting next to me, listened to my *andante* with tears coursing down his cheeks." In a letter to his sister, Tchaikovsky added that while he was "perfectly fascinated by Tolstoy's ideal personality," he was also terrified that this "great searcher of human hearts" could read the inner workings of his soul.

Disillusionment quickly set in, though. Tolstoy had sent Tchaikovsky a collection of local folk songs, along with a strange request: for Tchaikovsky to develop these songs "in the manner of Mozart and Haydn, not in the artificial style of Beethoven, Schumann, and Berlioz."

Tchaikovsky thought little of both Tolstoy's request and the collection. The songs, he believed, had been transcribed by an unskilled hand and showed only traces of beauty. "The chief defect," Tchaikovsky wrote to Tolstoy, was that they had been "artificially squeezed and forced into a regular measured form. Only Russian dance music has a rhythm and a regular and evenly accentuated beat. Folk songs, of course, have nothing in common with dance melodies. Furthermore, it seems to me that most of the songs that you sent to me are written arbitrarily, in a solemn D minor, which again does not suit a genuine Russian folk song."

Furthermore, Tchaikovsky resented the fact that Tolstoy did not wish to probe his inner being but merely to chat with him about music. "Not a demigod, but garrulous old man," Tchaikovsky concluded. (At the time, Tolstoy was forty-nine, Tchaikovsky, thirty-seven.) As time went on, Tchaikovsky avoided meeting with Tolstoy, though he still delighted in the writer's novels.

Tchaikovsky later mitigated his harsh views of Tolstoy, though the writer, particularly his moralist bent, would always irk him. "I often feel so angry with Tolstoy that I almost hate him," Tchaikovsky continued in his diary.

Why, I ask myself, should this man . . . have the power to depict the human soul, . . . fathom our poor intellect, and follow the most tortuous windings of our human nature . . . with such wonderful harmony? Why must he have to be a preacher and set himself up to be our teacher and monitor? Hitherto Tolstoy has succeeded in making a deep impression with simple, everyday events. We might have read between the lines about his noble love for humankind, his compassion for our helplessness, our mortality, our pettiness. How often have I wept over his words without knowing why. . . . Perhaps it was because for a moment and with him as a medium, I was brought into contact with the ideal, with absolute happiness, and with humanity.

Also, Tchaikovsky deeply admired Tolstoy's writing. "I have read *The Death of Ivan Ilyich*," Tchaikovsky wrote on August 12, 1886. "More than ever, I am convinced that Lev Tolstoy is the greatest author-painter who has ever lived. He alone can keep Russians from bowing their heads in shame when all the great things of Europe are lined up before them."

In time, Tolstoy recanted his views on Schumann, though he continued to castigate Beethoven for the "obscure, almost morbid excitement" of his works. In passing, it is also of interest to note that Tolstoy cared little for the music of Fyodor Chaliapin, especially what he saw as the singer's "profusion, lack of restraint, and vaunting of his energy and talent." See I. Bunin, *Vospominaniia* (Paris: Vozrozhdenie, 1950), 111. Also see Simmons, *Leo Tolstoy*, 1:356–57, 2:462; Crankshaw, *Tolstoy*, 166; Dole, *The Life of Count Tolstoi*, 249–51; Troyat, *Tolstoy*, 462.

60. *Bunin's note:* "Tolstoy went to Bashkiria to drink fermented mare's milk not only to cure his lungs and to rest from all his labors, but also to free himself temporarily from the tormenting burden which urban life always had been for him. 'From time to time, he experienced a special longing for nature and for *primitive existence.*' And in Bashkiria he rose from the dead both physically and spiritually, with unusual speed."

Editors' note: Bunin does not identify the source of the above quotation.

61. Zola disagreed with Tolstoy on the nature of progress, civilization, and work as well as on Tolstoy's ideas of "nonaction" and "love" to solve the world's ills. "To love one another," Zola wrote, "is a rather vague idea." (Interestingly, Sofya once chided her husband for the same thing. "We ordinary mortals," she wrote, "do not wish to turn into freaks and justify our lack for *anyone* by a vague sort of love *for the entire world.*")

He also took offense at Tolstoy's low opinion not only of his writings but also those of his countrymen. For instance, Tolstoy had accused Zola of "what [he] believed to be a key defect in French writers in general, that is, [Zola's] total failure to understand the lives and hopes of the workers, while at the same time depicting them as repulsive animals moved only by lust, anger, and greed." (For this reason, Tolstoy asked that Sofya not read Zola—a request that she honored until late in their marriage.)

Despite the disagreement between the two writers, it was because of Zola's assistance that Tolstoy's play *The Power of Darkness* enjoyed such a rousing success in Paris. See G. King, *Garden of Zola: Emile Zola and His Novels for English Readers* (London: Barrie and Jenkins, 1978), 224; M. Josephson, *Zola and His Time* (New York: Book League of America,

1928), 380. Also see Shklovsky, *Lev Tolstoy,* 533–34; Nazaroff, *Tolstoy,* 280; Simmons, *Leo Tolstoy,* 2:105, 196.

62. Bunin is quoting from Bulgakov's memoirs of Tolstoy.

63. Bunin is referring to the memoirs of Stepan Andreevich Bers, entitled "Vospominaniia o grafe L. N. Tolstom" ("Recollections of Count L. N. Tolstoy"), published in Smolensk in 1893.

CHAPTER ELEVEN

1. Ovsyannikovo was a family estate that had been given to Tolstoy's daughter Tanya.

2. Tolstoy is referring to the wooded area around Spasskoe, Turgenev's family estate, located about one hour from Yasnaya Polyana and 14 miles from Pokrovskoe, the estate of Tolstoy's sister, Maria.

3. In truth, Europeans were often harsh in their view of Tolstoy. For instance, in a letter to a friend, written circa September 1946, Bunin took issue with the French critic Leon Dode for calling Tolstoy a "savage barbarian." See Um-El'Banin, "Poslednii poedinok Ivana Bunina," 34.

4. *Bunin's note:* Incidentally, Tolstoy himself was also guilty of the absolutely absurd view that people asserted about his ideas on art. "He thought Shakespeare to be worthless," they say, "but he lauded Semyonov, a talentless writer from the people." Indeed, such a view insured Semyonov's fame.

But as a memoirist later recalled:

Lev Nikolaevich suddenly entered a room where one of Semyonov's stories was being read aloud.

"How artificial!" he said frowning. "Oh, how artificial!"

But having heard Semyonov's story to the end, especially the part where Semyonov talked about how the city corrupted innocent village souls, Tolstoy suddenly and with particular fervor began to praise the story. But he had to force himself to do so.

5. Tolstoy truly loved being his own confessor. A fellow officer at Sevastopol recalled: "Whenever Tolstoy returned [from his merrymaking], he was the very picture of the prodigal son. . . . He would take me aside, quite apart, and begin his confessions. He would tell me how he had caroused and gambled, and where he had spent his days and nights. . . . He would condemn himself and suffer as though he were a genuine criminal. He would become so distressed that it was pitiful to look at him."

During his time in Sevastopol, Tolstoy recorded:

I am ugly, awkward, slovenly, and uneducated in the worldly sense. I am also irritable, a bore to others, rude, intolerant, and bashful as a child. I am almost completely ignorant. Anything I know I have learned in any old way, independently, in snatches, incoherently, and in such a disorderly way that it all comes to so little. As are all people with a weak character, I am self-indulgent, irresolute, inconstant, and stupidly vain and hotheaded. I am cowardly, disorganized, and so lazy that for me idleness has almost become a necessary habit.

I am intelligent, but my intelligence has not as yet been thoroughly tried on anything. I have neither a practical nor a worldly or business acumen.

Bunin himself relished lurid confessions. For instance, the Englishman in his story "Brothers" ("Brat'ia," 1914) says: "In Africa I slaughtered men by the hundreds; . . . in Japan I bought little girls to be my wives; in China I beat . . . old men with sticks; in Java and Ceylon, I drove rickshaw men until I heard the death rattle in their throats." See Bunin, *Sobranie sochinenii*, 4:277. Also see Crankshaw, *Tolstoy*, 93; Dole, *The Life of Count Tolstoi*, 77; Nazaroff, *Tolstoy*, 43.

6. Not enough, according to Tolstoy. For instance, in his "secret" 1908 diary, he wrote: "Everyone is writing my biography . . . [but] there will be none of all the terrible filth of my masturbation and worse, [the sins] from my thirteenth to sixteenth years (I do not remember when I began my debauchery in brothels)." See Simmons, *Leo Tolstoy*, 2:429.

7. Tolstoy is referring to the matriarch of the family, Pelageya Nikolaevna Gorchakova, a very silly and spoiled spendthrift who, though superficially educated, was fond of the novels of Ann Radcliffe and spoke French better than Russian. She was also very decidedly of the ancien régime: narrow-minded, capricious, and despotic. One of Tolstoy's earliest childhood memories of his grandmother was Gorchakova sitting in her carriage while footmen lowered branches to her so that she could pluck nuts without having to rise from her seat. See Biryukov, *Leo Tolstoy*, 5; Wilson, *Tolstoy*, 23; Shklovsky, *Lev Tolstoy*, 65.

8. Despite the grief he caused his family, Ilya Andreevich refused to change his ways. For instance, as governor of Kazan, he ordered sturgeon from Astrakhan, had his linen washed in Holland, and kept a domestic theater and orchestra. Although he won a reputation of not accepting bribes, his wife was not above taking gifts on the sly. Eventually, Ilya became so imperiled by his inept management of his office that the Russian Senate appointed a committee to investigate his activities. Ilya was acquitted of any serious wrongdoing; but, in 1820, he was relieved of his post. Within a month after his dismissal, Ilya fell ill and died; some said he had committed suicide.

Tolstoy himself characterized Ilya as "a man of limited intelligence, very gentle, merry, and generous, but senselessly prodigal." Not surprisingly, Ilya was a model for Count Ilya Rostov in *War and Peace*. See Simmons, *Leo Tolstoy*, 1:6; Troyat, *Tolstoy*, 9.

9. Bunin's comment is incorrect. After the death of Tolstoy's parents, the family property was placed in trust and expenses had to be cut. Aunt

Alexandra Osten-Saken, now the legal guardian of the Tolstoy children, moved them into a small five-room apartment, a marked contrast from the huge rambling houses that the brood had lived in earlier. Also, with the famine of 1840, a small property had to be sold to buy wheat to feed the family's serfs. For Christmas, the Tolstoy children may have received presents that were not as lavish as those of their cousins—a situation that outraged the young Leo—but they never knew hunger or want.

Furthermore, after the death of Alexandra, Aunt Pelageya Yushkova assumed guardianship of the children, moving them to Kazan where they took up residence in the spacious Yushkov house.

Additionally, if and when Tolstoy found himself in dire financial straits, he had only himself and his gambling to blame. As a young man, he had entered military service in the Caucasus to escape his debts. Also to settle liabilities from cardplaying and other games of chance, he ordered his agent in 1855 to sell the gracious timbered house which his eccentric and fastidious grandfather had built at Yasnaya Polyana. (In his later dislike of possessions, Tolstoy never repurchased the building.) See Simmons, *Leo Tolstoy,* 1:34, 43; Crankshaw, *Tolstoy,* 104; Leon, *Tolstoy,* 25, 26, 52, 56; Shklovsky, *Lev Tolstoy,* 24, 33.

10. Countess Sofya Vladimirovna Panina owned an estate at Gaspra on the southern shore of Crimea, about twelve miles from Yalta. Her house was a huge stone affair, built in the style of a Scottish castle. Tolstoy wrote to his brother Sergei: "Gaspra, the estate of Countess Panina, and the house in which we are living are the epitome of luxury and comfort—far superior to anything that I have lived in in my entire life. So much for the simple living that I wanted to find." See Shklovsky, *Lev Tolstoy,* 667.

11. Pavel Alexandrovich Boulanger was an office worker for the Moscow-Kursk railway who, having known Tolstoy since 1886, wrote a series of articles on the writer. Bunin is quoting from Boulanger's memories of Tolstoy.

The Tolstoy home at Yasnaya Polyana was a fine wooden house, built in the classical style and consisting of more than forty rooms; but it was far from luxurious. The dwelling itself was a plain two-story structure of stuccoed brick, simple and unpretentious, without vines, piazzas, towers, or striking architectural features. The driveway to the house was rough and neglected; the entranceway was like a back door that one reached by climbing a flight of steps onto a small, square platform that featured gray, uncut stones with grass growing in the chinks.

The rooms of Tolstoy's house were similarly simple and spartan. The floors were bare; the windows were shaded with simple muslin curtains; the walls were whitewashed and hung with old portraits. Most of the lighting was from stinking tallow candles; and a good deal of the furniture was homemade: hard, plain, and old-fashioned. The bedrooms at Yasnaya Polyana were especially icy and bleak. For instance, there were almost no carpets and little in the way of bed linen for the comfort of the occupants. In fact, the only note of luxury in the house was the gilt of the frames around mirrors and paintings.

Visitors to Yasnaya Polyana were often awestruck—and discomforted—by the simplicity of Tolstoy's daily life. For instance, a rabbi recalled:

> The simplicity of Tolstoy's attire, the plainness of his manner, and, notwithstanding his hard work in the fields, the frugality of his evening meals . . . imparted to his presence a grandeur that made my fashionable clothes seem the coarser of the two, and that made me ashamed of ever having indulged in luxuries at my table at home. Despite the friendliness of Tolstoy and his family, I felt so uncomfortable in their presence that, by some magical wand, I sincerely wished to exchange my fashionable suit for a homespun blouse . . . my immaculate linen for a coarse woolen shirt . . . and my polished gaiters for a pair of common bast shoes.

See Dole, *The Life of Count Tolstoi,* 337–38; Wilson, *Tolstoy,* 204.

12. Panina's house was indeed luxurious, but oppressive. See Leon, *Tolstoy,* 300.

13. Merezhkovsky wrote *Tolstoy and Dostoevsky* in 1901–2. "*Tolstoy and Dostoevsky* is really bad and good for nothing. Merezhkovsky understood nothing about either writer," Bunin remarked to Odoevtseva.

According to Shestov, Tolstoy was not even aware that Merezhkovsky had written *Tolstoy and Dostoevsky,* a fact that Shestov gleefully told its author as soon as he could!

Not unexpectedly, Tolstoy and Dostoevsky approached each other with admiration and respect, but also with caution, awkwardness, and jealousy. For instance, Tolstoy wrote to Strakhov in summer 1880 that "in the whole of modern literature, not excepting Pushkin . . . [he knew] of no finer work than Dostoevsky's *House of the Dead.* . . . Its attitude is so wonderfully sincere, natural and Christian. . . . If you see Dostoevsky, tell him that I love him." (Strakhov did as Tolstoy had requested.)

Similarly, with Dostoevsky's death a year later, Tolstoy continued to Strakhov:

> I only wish I could express all that I feel about Dostoevsky. Although I neither met him or had any personal communication with him, now that he is dead I realize that he was nearer, dearer, and more important to me than anyone else. . . . Not once did it ever occur to me to compete with him. Everything he did was so good and sincere that the more he did, the happier he was. . . . I always thought of Dostoevsky as a friend, and I hoped that one day I would know him. But it was not meant to be. . . .
>
> When I read of Dostoevsky's death . . . I felt as though a supporting pillar had buckled under me. I first panicked; then realizing how precious he was to me, I burst out crying. I am still crying.

Later, though, Tolstoy expressed only animosity for the corpus of Dostoevsky's writing. For instance, he told a friend: *"The House of the Dead* is a fine thing, but I do not set great store by his other books. People cite passages to me. And indeed there are some very fine parts here and there; but, on the whole, it is dreadful stuff. Dostoevsky's style is turgid. He tries so hard to make his characters original, but in fact they hardly have outlines. Dostoevsky talks and talks; but in the end, all that one is left with is a sort of fog floating above what he is trying to prove. He melds the most lofty Christian concepts with panegyrics on war and submission to the emperor, the government, and the popes."

Dostoevsky was more gracious than his colleague. For instance, apropos of Tolstoy's *Childhood,* he wrote: "I like Tolstoy enormously, but in my view, he will not write much of anything else. (But, after all, I can be wrong!)"

Later, he continued: "After the 'new word' of Pushkin, Tolstoy, with *War and Peace,* arrives too late [in Russian literature]. And, no matter how high he may go, he cannot change the fact that that new word was uttered before him, and for the first time, by a genius."

Dostoevsky, though, had the graciousness to admit his "mistake." For instance, about *Anna Karenina* he wrote: "The novel is unprecedented, incomparable. Who among our writers can compare with Tolstoy? And in Europe, whoever wrote anything that can approach this work?"

Still, relations between the writers continued to be strained, Tolstoy's dislike of Panslavism being a particular thorn in Dostoevsky's side. See Baboreko, "I. A. Bunin o L. N. Tolstom," 167. Also see Odoevtseva, *Na beregakh Seny,* 373; Leon, *Tolstoy,* 193; Wilson, *Tolstoy,* 97; Nazaroff, *Tolstoy,* 210; Troyat, *Tolstoy,* 98, 299, 356, 400; Simmons, *Leo Tolstoy,* 2:17.

14. Bunin never wavered in his dislike of Merezhkovsky, both as a person and a philosopher.

15. The animals responded in kind. When Emperor Adrian ordered Saint Estafy to be torn apart by wild animals, he emerged from the pit unharmed.

16. In his reflections on absolute chastity, though, Tolstoy had little use for the Skoptsy and other groups who practiced castration. He wrote: "Judging by what I have heard about the Skoptsy, they lead a moral and laborious life. But whether they correctly understand the Gospels upon whose authority they mutilate themselves, I answer with the fullest assurance that they understand the Gospels wrongly, and that by mutilating themselves and especially others, they act in direct opposition to true Christianity. Christ preaches chastity, but chastity, like every other virtue, has worth only when it is attained by an exertion of the will, supported by faith, not when it is attained by the impossibility of sinning." See Leon, *Leo Tolstoy,* 250–51.

17. "How Love Will Die" ("Kak gibnet liubov'") was an early title for an 1853 piece entitled "Evening at Christmastide" ("Sviatochnaia noch'").

18. Tolstoy's loss of his own virginity at age fourteen or sixteen (accounts differ) with a liquor-sodden girl brought to him similar shame. For instance, when he was writing *Resurrection*, he confessed to a friend: "When my brothers took me to a brothel for the first time and I accomplished the act, I stood by the woman's bed and wept." (Another version is that Tolstoy first had sexual relations in a room in a monastery in Kazan which had been set apart specifically for his initiation into physical love.) Also, Tolstoy drew upon his first sexual experience to detail the moral disintegration of the hero in his short story "Notes of a Billiard Maker." To his friends who have forced him to sleep with a prostitute, the unhappy man says: "You think it is funny, but I am sad. Why did I do it? I won't forgive you or myself for as long as I live."

Despite his reverence for family values, Tolstoy once endorsed prostitution as a necessary, even crucial, evil in life. In an 1862 letter, he wrote to Strakhov:

> You perhaps will be astonished when I say that, in the list of honorable callings, I include that of the "Magdalen." For when I consider the present state of society, I am obliged to do so. These unfortunates have always existed and will continue to do so. As I see it, it would be monstrous to suppose that God made a mistake . . . when He created this order of being; and was our Savior in error when He pardoned the woman who was the sinner? . . .
>
> Should we permit promiscuous sexual intercourse, as many "liberals" think we should? Impossible! [Such license] would be the ruin of family life. To meet the difficulty, the law of development has evolved a "golden mean" in the form of the prostitute. Just think of London without its 70,000 prostitutes! What would become of decency and morality, how would family life survive without them? How many wives and daughters would remain chaste? No, I believe that the prostitute is necessary for the maintenance of the family.

It was only after many years that Tolstoy repudiated such a view. See Simmons, *Leo Tolstoy,* 1:54, 110, 333–34; Wilson, *Tolstoy,* 43; Troyat, *Tolstoy,* 47.

19. It was Nekrasov who "discovered" Tolstoy. On July 2, 1852, Tolstoy sent him a copy of *Childhood,* together with this missive:

> Look through this manuscript, and if it is not suitable to you for publication, return it to me. If you appraise it otherwise, tell me what it is worth . . . and print it in your journal. . . .
>
> I am convinced that an experienced and well-intentioned editor, especially in Russia, by virtue of his position as a constant intermediary between author and reader, can always indicate in advance the success of a work and the public opinion. Therefore I await your answer with impatience. It will either encourage me to continue a favorite occupation or oblige me to cease at the very beginning.

In fact, Tolstoy was so uncertain about the quality of *Childhood* that he had signed the manuscript only with "L.N.," the initials of his first name and patronymic. Only Aunt Tatyana and his brother Nikolai were aware of his efforts to publish.

Tolstoy's confidence in Nekrasov was not misplaced. The famous editor agreed to print *Childhood* in *The Contemporary,* adding "Not knowing the continuation, I cannot say definitely, but it seems to me that the author has talent. In any case, the author's bent, together with the simplicity and realism of his work, constitutes the unquestionable worth of this piece." Nekrasov concluded his letter with a request for the continuation of the piece as well as a a plea that Tolstoy reveal his name.

Having read Nekrasov's missive, Tolstoy noted in his diary that it "drove him mad with joy."

For several years, Nekrasov served as Tolstoy's mentor and guide. He was particularly supportive during the novice writer's first run-in with the censor. For instance, Tolstoy's bitterness over the censor's distortion of his sketch "Sevastopol in May"—the piece had been transmuted from a diatribe against war to propaganda for the government—was somewhat assuaged by Nekrasov's indignation and praise. He wrote the novice writer:

> The shocking disfiguring of your piece has upset me greatly. Even now I cannot think of it without regret and rage. Your work, of course, will not be lost. . . . It will always remain as proof of a strength that has been able to speak such profound and sober truth amidst circumstances which few men would have endured. Your truth is exactly what Russian society now needs: the truth . . . so little of which has remained since Gogol's death.
>
> You are right to value greatly that side of your gifts. Truth—in the form that you have introduced into our literature—is something entirely new among us. I do not know another writer of today who so compels the reader to love him and to sympathize heartily with him as to whom I now write. And I only fear that time, the nastiness of life, and the deafness and dumbness which surround us, should do to you what they have done to most of us, and kill the energy without which there can be no writer—none at least such as Russia needs.
>
> You are young. Changes are happening [in Russia], and we hope that they will result in some good. Then a wide field may be opened before you. You have begun in such a way as to compel the most cautious to cherish high expectations.

See Simmons, *Leo Tolstoy,* 1:97–98, 133; Dole, *The Life of Count Tolstoi,* 85.

20. Boborykin, though, was sufficiently honest to realize that Tolstoy periodically repudiated his sins and shortcomings. See Dole, *The Life of Count Tolstoi,* 296.

21. According to tradition, the Buddha died from eating a tainted meal.

22. Like other aspects of Tolstoy's personality, rumors about his "very stormy youth" and "voluptuousness" have been greatly exaggerated. More revealing, perhaps, is that Tolstoy's fervid repentance for his sexual sins typically ceded to equally impassioned remembrances of wrongdoing. He wrote in 1856: "We went to Pavlovsk. Disgusting! Girls, stupid music, girls, heat, cigarette smoke, girls, vodka, cheese, wild shrieks, girls, girls, girls! Everyone trying to pretend to be jolly, but without success. . . . I promise myself never to enter a cabaret or a brothel again." See Leon, *Tolstoy*, 66.

23. It is a well-accepted fact that Tolstoy's ongoing trenchant formulas and Franklin-like "rules of conduct" far outstripped his observance of them. He himself wrote in his diary: "It is easier to write ten volumes of philosophy than to put a single precept into practice."

Such frustration is understandable when one considers the unrealizable demands that Tolstoy placed on himself. For instance, as a student in Kazan, he wrote: "Have a goal for your entire life, a goal for a section of your life, and a goal for a shorter period. [Have] a goal for every year, a goal for every month, a goal for every week, a goal for every day, a goal for every hour, a goal for every minute. Also, always sacrifice the lesser goal to the greater one."

At times Tolstoy wished to abandon his "rule-governed" behavior. For instance, as a young man in Saint Petersburg, he wrote: "A powerful means of securing happiness in life is to spin out in all directions, without any rules, and, like a spider, to weave a complete web of love and catch in it all that one can—old women, young children, policemen."

Furthermore, Tolstoy believed that he had little support for the law and order that he had imposed on his life. For instance, in 1847, he wrote: "I honestly desired to be a good and virtuous man; but young and passionate, I stood alone in my search for virtue. Every time I tried to express the longings of my heart for a truly virtuous life, I was met with contempt and derisive laughter. But as soon as I gave way to the lowest of my passions, I was praised and encouraged. I found that ambition, acquisitiveness, love of power, lechery, pride, anger, and vengeance were all held in high esteem."

Tolstoy, though, never abandoned his precepts for self-improvement. He again wrote in his diary: "It is ridiculous that, having started to write rules at fifteen, I am still writing them when I am almost thirty, and that I have never trusted or followed any one of them. Nonetheless, I still need and believe in rules."

Tolstoy harshly berated himself for his failure to observe his prescriptions. For instance, as a young man at Yasnaya Polyana, he chalked up his lack of virtue to "irresolution, want of energy, self-deception, haste, *fausse-honte*, a bad frame of mind, instability, a lack of originality, fickleness, and thoughtlessness." Also, only days before he left Yasnaya Polyana forever, he recorded: "No, I am not a saint. I am a man who often gets carried away and sometimes, no, rather always, cannot say exactly what I think and feel . . . because I often exaggerate or simply blunder. . . . In deeds, the case is even worse, for I am only a weak man of evil habits who desires to serve the God of Truth but continually goes astray."

Needless to say, it was Tolstoy's love of the ladies that most often led him astray. "I could hold out no longer," he wrote in his diary on April 18, 1851. "I beckoned to something in pink that seemed to me to be very attractive in the distance. I opened the door; and in she came. Now I cannot bear to look at her, for she is repulsive, hateful, and vile, and has caused me to break my rules." See Simmons, *Leo Tolstoy,* 1:64; Crankshaw, *Tolstoy,* 71; Leon, *Tolstoy,* 20, 52, 350; Dole, *The Life of Count Tolstoi,* 30, 36, 109; Troyat, *Tolstoy,* 58.

24. As a young man in Kazan, Tolstoy had the courage to admire Zinaida Modestovna Molostvova only from across the room. The relationship did not improve with time because mutual timidity cooled any attraction. Although Zinaida was charming and intelligent as well as a close friend of Tolstoy's sister, Masha, she was not a great beauty. Worse, perhaps, Tolstoy's boorish behavior probably bewildered and even frightened the poor girl.

On a weeklong visit to Kazan five years later (1851), Tolstoy was no less shy, but Zinaida's intelligence, wit, humor, and kindness rekindled his interest. This time, Zinaida reciprocated his affection, but their love for each other was more unspoken than acknowledged. As Tolstoy later wrote, silence preserved the "pure yearning of two souls for one another."

Tolstoy left Kazan with his love for Zinaida buried in his heart. His feelings for her, though, stirred a poetic urge. "I am so intoxicated with Zinaida," Tolstoy wrote to his sister, "that I have had the courage to write some verses:

> Toward Syzran' I lingered,
> As my own wound I fingered. . . ."

Such poetry notwithstanding, Tolstoy never acted on his love; but as a soldier in the Caucasus, he pined for Molostvova from afar and feared that she would marry another. A year later, Zinaida did, in fact, declare for someone else, but the sudden termination of the romance did not disturb Tolstoy. "The fact vexes me," he wrote, "the more so because I feel so little perturbed." See Simmons, *Leo Tolstoy,* 1:83, 97; Crankshaw, *Tolstoy,* 73.

25. Upon his return from the Crimea, the twenty-six-year-old Tolstoy decided to get married and was advised by a friend to wed Valeriya Vladimirovna Arsenieva, a twenty-year-old neighbor. His initial impressions of the girl were hardly flattering. Tolstoy wrote in his diary: "A pity that she is without backbone and fire—like spaghetti. Sweet, though. Her smile is painfully submissive."

The relationship so worsened that it bordered on the Dostoevskian. Tolstoy was attracted to Valeriya, but without genuine reason or cause. He was repelled by her physically, her thin, angular arms and elbows being a particular bone of contention. He also saw Valeriya as stupid, provincial, frivolous, poorly educated, and "completely empty, without principle, and cold as ice." Even worse, perhaps, he strove to be Valeriya's teacher, guide, and salvation—a stance that doomed any shared future for them.

In fact, with Valeriya, Tolstoy became insufferable. Mixing sugary endearments with harsh hectoring, he regularly lectured the unfortunate girl on behavior and dress; chided her for her love of society, balls, and aides-de-camp; and pontificated on the meaning of love and the need for study, exercise, and self-improvement. He even demanded that Valeriya review the activities of the past day and plan new ones for the next.

"Please go for a walk every day," Tolstoy once advised Valeriya. "And wear a corset when you do. . . . Christ be with you." On a second occasion, he recommended: "Alas, you are deluding yourself into thinking that you have taste. . . . The elegance of bright colors and the like is excusable, though ridiculous, in an ugly young lady, but for you with your pretty little face, it is intolerable to make such a mistake. . . . Christ be with you." And on a third, he wrote to his "love": "Religion is a great thing, especially for women"; "How is it that you say nothing of Dickens and Thackeray?"; and "What is this nonsense that you have been reading?"

Perpetually dissatisfied with his Valeriya, he continued: "How are you spending your time? Do you work? Do not laugh at this word! To work wisely, sensibly, for goodness and self-improvement is the greatest thing that one can do. But it is good also to work on some trifle, to carve a piece of wood or something like that. A good moral life, and consequently happiness, are impossible without work."

At times, Tolstoy showed a sadistic rancor to his love. "I spent the entire day with Valeriya," he wrote in his diary. "Her unattractive arms so angered me . . . that I began to pinch and prick her morally . . . and with such cruelty that she became embarrassed and smiled. In her smile were tears." Even Valeriya's language revolted him. "Valeriya is hopelessly uneducated, ignorant, not to say stupid. She used the verb 'to prostitute,' which pained me greatly . . . and coming on top of my toothache, plunged me into gloom."

After six months of such "tutelage" qua abuse, Valeriya revolted, thereby ending the relationship. Tolstoy's last letter to Valeriya shows how strained the association had become; in it he tells his "love" of a dream in which he envisions a murdered body lying on the floor and a whispering, naked brown woman astride his chest.

Tolstoy's association with Valeriya Arsenieva was the inspiration for his short novel *Family Happiness* and more specifically for the disastrous scene in *War and Peace* in which Mademoiselle Bourienne prepares Maria Bolkonskaya to meet Anatoly Kuragin. See Simmons, *Leo Tolstoy,* 1:158–66, 196; Crankshaw, *Tolstoy,* 145–52; Leon, *Tolstoy,* 67–78; Wilson, *Tolstoy,* 140–41; Nazaroff, *Tolstoy,* 108, 110; Troyat, *Tolstoy,* 145.

26. Into the hands of his eighteen-year-old bride Tolstoy passed the complete diary of his life since his student days at Kazan. Such a practice was far more common in nineteenth-century Russia than is sometimes realized. For instance, Nicholas II gave his diaries to his bride to read. Furthermore, Tolstoy had the permission of Sofya's father to surrender his personal accounts to his beloved.

Nonetheless, Sofya was so shocked at Tolstoy's intimate confession of youthful irregularities that she almost broke her engagement to her intended. For her reading pleasure (disgust?) were twenty years of whoring and wenching, affairs with peasant women, repeated bouts of venereal disease (and their cures of mercury through the penis), and even homoerotic attractions to schoolboy friends. She was also privy to his wild ambitions, his intellectual acrobatics, even his bouts with diarrhea.

Years later, Sofya wrote: "I remember how terribly shocked I was by the reading of these diaries that Tolstoy, from a sense of personal duty, gave to me before my marriage. Upon glancing into his past, I wept a great deal, but to no purpose."

Later, she recorded:

I don't think that I have ever gotten over all the horror that I experienced when I read Lyova's diary before our marriage, and I doubt that the sharp sting of jealousy and my bewilderment at the thought of such filth and debauchery has ever quite disappeared.

[My husband's] self-adoration comes out in every one of his diaries. It is amazing how people existed for him only insofar as they affected him personally. And the women! . . . I copy his diaries in a state of jealousy over the women he describes. . . . In fact, it is beginning to worry him that I do so. . . . He would like to destroy them and to appear before his children and the public only in his patriarchal robes. His vanity is immense!

Sofya, though, was not the only one to know of Leo's indiscretions. For instance, in 1852, he wrote to his brother Nikolai: "My illness has cost me dearly. Twenty rubles to the druggist; twenty visits to the doctor; and now cotton wadding and daily trips by cab are costing me another one hundred and twenty. . . . The venereal infection has been cured, but the aftereffects of the mercury are painful beyond belief."

Interestingly, Bunin thought little of Tolstoy's sexual honesty with his wife. "I am reading Zhdanov's *Love in the Life of Leo Tolstoy.* It is repulsive— to what lengths will a husband and wife go to reveal themselves for the sake of extreme intimacy." (V. Zhdanov published *Liubov' z zhini L'va Tolstogo* in Moscow in 1928.) See M. Grin, "Iz dnevnikov I. A. Bunina," *Novyi zhurnal*, no. 116 (1974), 162. Also see Simmons, *Leo Tolstoy*, 1:272; Leon, *Tolstoy*, 256; Wilson, *Tolstoy*, 196–97; Troyat, *Tolstoy*, 86.

CHAPTER TWELVE

1. Valentin Bulgakov served as Tolstoy's secretary after the arrest of his first one, Nikolai Gusev.

2. "If one is married," Tolstoy wrote to Chertkov on November 6, 1889, "let him live with his wife as brother and sister. . . . You will object that [such a state of affairs] would mean the end of the human race? . . . What a great misfortune that would be! The antediluvian animals are gone from the earth, the human animals will also disappear. . . . I have no more pity for these two-footed beasts than for the ichthyosaurus."

Tolstoy, though, knew the near impossibility of such a demand, particularly for himself. That same year, he continued: "I shall not overcome [this desire for absolute chastity] in a hurry, because I am a dirty, libidinous old man!" See Troyat, *Tolstoy*, 476.

3. In truth, though, Bunin took a dim view of Tolstoy's siring prowess. He told Odoevtseva: "Despite my admiration for Tolstoy, I could never understand his passion for childbearing. Such a thing has always evoked squeamishness in me. I am sure that most men also feel this way, even some women, too." See Odoevtseva, *Na beregakh Seny*, 346.

4. Aksinya Bazykina was a pretty twenty-three-year-old married peasant woman who lived in a hamlet seven miles from Tolstoy's house and who, apparently, became a willing object of his affection. Upon an initial tryst, Tolstoy wrote in his diary in 1857: "Today in the big old wood. I am a fool, a brute. Her bronze flesh and her eyes. . . . I am in love as never before in my life. Have no other thought."

Unusual for Tolstoy's liaisons was that the fleeting attachment between master and serf soon developed into a firm, enduring, quasi-marital bond that culminated in the birth of a son, Timofei (not Ermil). Although Aksinya accepted the relationship philosophically, she became an obsession with Tolstoy. At the same time, though, Tolstoy so worried about his tie to Aksinya that it hastened his search for a mate. In a diary excerpt in 1860, he continued: "I am afraid when I see how attached I am to her. The feeling is no longer that of a stag, but of a husband for his wife." (The liaison lasted three years.)

In fact, Tolstoy was so tormented over his affair with Aksinya that three months before his death, he confessed to Biryukov that his liaison with her was one of the two moral lapses in his youth that most tormented him in his life. Revealingly, though, Tolstoy never expressed any remorse that he had refused to acknowledge Timofei publicly or to take care of him in any substantial way. "People say that Timofei is my son," Tolstoy wrote. "But I have never asked his pardon. I have not repented. I am not repenting every hour of the day, and I set myself up to criticize others!"

Timofei, who resembled his father more closely than Tolstoy's legitimate children, later became a coachman for one of Tolstoy's sons. Although his half-brothers and half-sisters treated him with dignity and respect, Sofya was both angry and embarrassed by his presence. See Simmons, *Leo Tolstoy,* 1:189, 191; Crankshaw, *Tolstoy,* 168–69, 174, 185; Troyat, *Tolstoy,* 492, 623.

5. Bunin is referring to the love between Eugene and Stepanida in *The Devil.* (Not surprisingly, Tolstoy concealed the manuscript from his wife.) Tolstoy's attachment for Aksinya also appears in such works as *Polikushka,* "An Idyll" ("Idilliia"), and "Tikhon and Malanya." See Simmons, *Leo Tolstoy,* 1:189, 282.

6. Tolstoy wrote "Who Are the Murderers?" ("Kto ubiistsy?") in 1908–9.

7. Sofya is quoting from an excerpt from Tolstoy's diary, dated May 13, 1858. See Tolstoy, *Polnoe sobranine sochinenii,* 48:15.

8. Aksinya would always be a thorn in Sofya's side. Although Sofya knew that Tolstoy had severed all relations with Aksinya shortly before their marriage, she could not contain her jealousy and rage at the former object of her husband's passion and love. For instance, she prefaced the above remarks by writing: "Sometimes I think that I will put an end to myself from jealousy." Having noted the dagger and rifles, she continued: "[I could kill Aksinya] with one blow—it would be easy, while there is still no child." (Aksinya was, in fact, pregnant by Tolstoy at this time.) Exasperated, Sofya concluded: "Aksinya is right here, several steps away. I am simply like an insane woman. I am going for a drive. . . . How he loved her! If only one could burn his diary and all his past."

Three years later, Sofya still suspected that Tolstoy was in love with Aksinya. Distressed that her husband went out frequently for long walks, she wrote in her diary: "I begin to think—does he not go to Aksinya? Such a thought tortured me all day."

Even years after Tolstoy's death, Aksinsya stalked Sofya's thoughts. For instance, most likely with Aksinya in mind, she confessed to Biryukov that in her first year of marriage she dressed as a peasant girl and roamed about the forest, hoping that Tolstoy would hail her by Aksinya's name.

Sofya also wrote of a terrible dream in which peasant women from the village appeared as ladies of fashion in her garden. "The last one to enter was Aksinya," Sofya wrote.

> She was wearing a black silk dress. I talked with her for awhile, but such a vicious feeling came over me that I seized her child . . . and began tearing it to pieces. In my fearful rage, I ripped off its feet, head, everything.

Lyovochka came up to me, and I told him that I would be sent to Siberia for what I had done. But he gathered up the legs, arms, all the bits and pieces, and told me that I had done nothing wrong, that what I had thought was a child was only a doll. I took a second look, and, in fact, instead of a genuine body, there was only leather, cotton, and wool. [Such a development] greatly vexed me.

In truth, any woman close to Tolstoy aroused Sofya's jealousy. For instance, in 1895, she took to reading the letters that Tolstoy had written to Valeriya Arsenieva more than forty years earlier. Sofya was particularly unnerved by "Granny" Alexandra. For instance, opening a letter from Alexandra to Tolstoy in Tolstoy's absence, she wrote to her husband: "Alexandra writes you many tender things, and it annoys me. I think that it would have been better if you had married her." The insecure Sofya was even uneasy with her sister, Tanya. She wrote in her diary: "I am angry with Tanya for poking her nose too much into Lyova's life. . . . My jealousy burst out yesterday . . . and now it makes me sad to think of it." See Simmons, *Leo Tolstoy,* 1:282–83, 321, 2:209; Crankshaw, *Tolstoy,* 185; Leon, *Tolstoy,* 130–31; Troyat, *Tolstoy,* 258, 285.

9. Tolstoy was so seized by desire for Domna that he implored his sons' tutor to accompany him on walks so as to avoid meeting her alone and succumbing to temptation. Eventually, Tolstoy had the seductive Domna removed from the estate. See Leon, *Tolstoy,* 161; Simmons, *Leo Tolstoy,* 2:20.

10. Abreks were young rebels and adventurers who waged war against the Russians for control of the Caucasus. Their bravery was recognized even by their enemies, and their exploits were sung by such Russian poets as Pushkin and Lermontov.

11. Compare Tolstoy's remark: "The Venus of Melos can evoke in people only disgust before nakedness, before the impudence of debauchery."

Tolstoy often commented on various aspects of the human body. "For me," he wrote in 1885, "the back is an important mark of physiognomy, especially the place where the neck joins the back. No other part of the body so clearly reveals lack of self-confidence and false sentiment. . . . A straight back is a sign of passionate temperament. . . . The physiology of wrinkles can be very telling and accurate."

As regards the back, Tolstoy often put theory into practice; for example, "Sofya Ivanovna had the singular, florid complexion one encounters in very short and stout old maids who wear corsets." See Nazaroff, *Tolstoy,* 148; Troyat, *Tolstoy,* 157.

12. Smolensk is an administrative and cultural center, 350 miles south of Saint Petersburg.

13. That is, cannon fodder. As an officer in Sevastopol, Tolstoy also objected to being regarded as *chair à canon.* See Nazaroff, *Tolstoy,* 83.

14. Bunin told Bakhrakh: "I do not know if you have read the unpublished excerpts from *Hadji-Murad* which were printed several years ago; but among them is a scene in which a junior officer is shown the head of Hadji-Murad. I do not know of a more terrifying scene in all of world literature. I have reread it over and over again; and, each time, I am seized by such a mystical horror that my hair stands on end." See Bakhrakh, *Bunin v khalate*, 94.

CHAPTER THIRTEEN

1. Bunin is quoting from Psalms 90:10. The passage reads:

> Seventy is the sum of our years,
> Or eighty, if we are strong;
> And most of them are fruitless toil;
> For they pass quickly and we drift away.

2. Despite his powerful physique, the youthful Tolstoy suffered from a variety of illnesses, which he tended to regard as a moral good for which he should thank God. Gluttony, exacerbated by his contradictory and high-strung nature, resulted in chronic stomach and bowel disorders. Inflammation of the lungs, liver complaints, rheumatism, feverish colds, angina pectoris, enteritis, headaches, toothaches, nosebleeds, sore throats, and mysterious spells of weakness were all frequent ailments.

Tolstoy, though, had little use for doctors or medicine; and, in his personal and fictional writings, he often satirized physicians who, he claimed, were quite ignorant of the causes and treatments of maladies. Tolstoy agreed with Rousseau that the practice of medicine should not be confined to any one profession. He also preferred the time-honored remedies that the folk had used against illness. See Simmons, *Leo Tolstoy*, 1:102; Leon, *Tolstoy*, 35; Dole, *The Life of Count Tolstoi*, 213; Troyat, *Tolstoy*, 91.

3. The professor was wrong in his view.

4. Although both of Tolstoy's brothers died of consumption, and although the writer himself often thought himself to be a victim of the disease, Bunin's allegation has no basis in fact. See Leon, *Tolstoy*, 70, 108.

5. Briefly, Tolstoy's father, Nikolai Ilyich Tolstoy, was a well-built, handsome, debonair, and kind individual with a pleasant face but eyes that always seemed sad. Raised in a pleasure-loving household, Nikolai had a mind and tastes that conformed to the lax social patterns and sexual license characteristic of landowning gentry. For instance, his parents sought to promote his physical well-being by arranging a liaison between the sixteen-year-old Nikolai and a pretty serf girl. Tolstoy writes:

> That union resulted in the birth of a son, Mishenka, who became a postilion and who, while my father was alive, lived a stable life, but afterward went to pieces.

After we brothers had grown up, Mishenka used to come to us begging for help. I remember this strange feeling of perplexity I experienced when this brother of mine, who, more so than any of us, was very much like my father and who, now destitute, was grateful for the ten or fifteen rubles we would give him.

Returning to Nikolai, Tolstoy's father defied his parents and served in the Russian army during the war with Napoleon. He saw action in most of the important engagements of the conflict; in October 1813, he was captured by the French and sent under guard to Paris. It was not until March 1814, when the Russians entered the French capital, that Nikolai was released. With the return of peace, Nikolai entered the civil service; but the death of his father in the 1820s left him with an estate that was so encumbered with debt that Nikolai refused to accept his inheritance. Virtually penniless, he sought escape in an advantageous marriage to the wealthy Princess Maria Volkonskaya in 1822 and settled down at Yasnaya Polyana to enjoy a large income from the efforts of some eight hundred serfs.

Although Tolstoy greatly loved and admired Nikolai, he actually saw little of his father in real life, since Nikolai divided his time among hunting, farming, reading, and attending to the numerous lawsuits that had been filed against his estate.

Interestingly, Bunin's own father, Alexei Nikolaevich Bunin, resembled Nikolai Tolstoy in that he, too, was an "old-world landowner" who had married a relatively wealthy woman. Unlike Nikolai, though, Alexei lost most of his wife's estate through gambling and negligence. See Simmons, *Leo Tolstoy,* 1:6–7, 33; Leon, 8–9.

6. Bunin is inaccurate here. It was Tolstoy's brother Dmitri, not his father, who had a facial tic.

7. Maria Volkonskaya was a plain, bushy-browed, and awkward woman who was six years older than her husband and whose large, luminous eyes were her only saving grace. By nature and temperament, Maria was dreamy and sentimental, meek and reserved. Under the tutelage of her strict father, though, she became an accomplished and highly educated individual who spoke five languages, played the piano well, managed the estate, and was the epitome of charm and kindness, simplicity and taste. Maria was particularly adept at storytelling. In fact, at parties and balls, her friends preferred to listen to Maria's tales than to dance and make merry.

Maria's *mariage de convenance* to Nikolai lasted nine years. Because her husband was often gone from the estate, she did not see much of her him during that time, but devoted herself to her children and domestic affairs. See Simmons, *Leo Tolstoy,* 1:9–10; Crankshaw, *Tolstoy,* 20–21; Leon, *Tolstoy,* 3.

8. God's fools (*iurodovyi*) were "madman-idiots" who possessed gifts of prophecy and other spiritual powers. Wealthy Russians often kept one or

more God's fools in their households to serve as "spiritual guardians" to ward off evil and other calamities. Because of the attraction of his mother and aunts to God's fools, the young Tolstoy had greater contact with such individuals than other boys of his class. In fact, he was so taken with God's fools that he depicted one—the wild-eyed, misshapen, and incoherent boy named Grisha—in his *Childhood*.

Of God's fools, Tolstoy recalled:

We had many of these half-crazy saints at our house. I was taught to treat them with deep respect; and for this, I am truly grateful to those who raised me. If there were some among them who were insincere, or who experienced periods of insincerity and weakness, but whose aim in life, however absurd and impractical, was so lofty, I am nonetheless glad that I, as a child, learned unconsciously to comprehend the loftiness of their achievements. They accomplished what Marcus Aurelius speaks of when he says, "There is nothing higher than to endure contempt for a good life." So harmful and spontaneous is the desire for the human glory which always contaminates good deeds that one cannot help sympathizing with the efforts not merely to avoid praise, but even to evoke contempt.

See Dole, *The Life of Count Tolstoi*, 15.

9. Tolstoy's mother, herself deeply spiritual, was so fond of these religious pilgrims that she chose one, Maria Gerasimova, to be the godmother for her daughter, even though the woman masqueraded as a monk and assumed the name Ivanushka.

In fact, before her marriage to Nikolai and not unlike her famous son, Maria had also wished to be a pilgrim. "I shall go to some town to pray," she wrote, "and then, before I have time to settle down and become attached to it, I shall move on. I will walk until my feet give way beneath me. Then I will lie down and die somewhere, and at last reach that eternal, peaceful haven where there are no more sorrows and sighs." See Simmons, *Leo Tolstoy*, 1:17; Troyat, *Tolstoy*, 6–7.

10. Bunin is referring to Alexandra Ilyinichna Osten-Saken, a kind, devout, and handsome woman who suffered greatly in life. For instance, Alexandra had married a wealthy but extremely paranoid Baltic count, who attempted first to shoot her and then to cut out her tongue. In fact, the count so frightened his pregnant wife that she gave birth to a stillborn child. Alexandra, though, was not told of her child's death but was given a peasant infant to raise in its stead. Her husband eventually being confined to an asylum, Alexandra lived in her brother's house and voluntarily did without comfort and service.

After the death of Tolstoy's parents, Alexandra became the legal guardian of the children. She died at Optina Hermitage in 1841. See Simmons, *Leo Tolstoy*, 1:17, 43; Crankshaw, *Tolstoy*, 34–35; Shklovsky, *Lev Tolstoy*, 69; Troyat, *Tolstoy*, 20.

11. The "recollections" that Bunin cites here and later are taken from Biryukov's biography of Tolstoy.

12. Lyubov' Sergeevna was actually a distant relative of Tolstoy's family. About the relationship between Dmitri and Lyubov', Tolstoy continued: "Dmitri began to talk and read to her. My other brothers and I were so dense morally that we only laughed at what he was doing. Dmitri, though, was so superior spiritually, so free from caring about what others thought of him. By word or hint, he never showed any belief that what he was doing [with Lyubov'] was good. He simply did it. Furthermore, his kindness to her was not a momentary impulse, but one continued all that time that we were in Kazan." In fact, Dmitri was so fond of Lyubov' that family and friends feared that he would marry the girl. Wilson, *Tolstoy*, 34–35; Troyat, *Tolstoy*, 42.

13. Dmitri was fired with the romance of Christ's poor. For instance, he prepared for his first Holy Communion not at the fashionable church at the university but the more somber one in the town prison. (On holy days, he would also drag the entire family there for services.) Furthermore, during Holy Week, Dmitri used to stand at strict attention, while a very ascetic and pious priest read all the Gospels aloud. See Wilson, *Tolstoy*, 35.

14. Dmitri Tolstoy was his mother's favorite child and the constant object of her abundant affection. Dmitri was closest to Leo in age (he was only a year and a half older), but he was a capricious, difficult individual— features that, later in life, would liken him to a character from Dostoevsky. Well built and graced with "large, dark, serious eyes," Dmitri was thoughtful, pure, kind, and resolute. Prone to religious mania, he was also strange, morbid, and cruel.

For instance, as a student at the University of Kazan, Dmitri lived in a bare room, cared nothing for society or rank, and was stoop-shouldered and slovenly, diffident and hot-tempered. As would his famous brother, Dmitri also believed that he was duty-bound to undertake the moral guidance of hundreds of serf families. Not surprisingly, Dmitri could not find his place in life. People ridiculed him for his ascetic ways; they were even more astonished when he, entering the civil service, merely asked for a place where he could be useful. Unsuccessful in finding work, Dmitri returned to his estate, continuing his asceticism among pilgrims, hermits, and monks.

Although Tolstoy idolized Dmitri in his memory, he often poked fun at his sanctimonious brother in life. For instance, he doubted Dmitri's sanity, called him Noah in public, and choked with delight when a university official attempted to persuade Dmitri to learn to dance.

It was a trip to Moscow that introduced Dmitri to sin. He began to drink, smoke, play cards, and frequent brothels. His face was often puffy and marked by a bristling beard, bleary eyes, and looks of profound sadness and dissatisfaction. Tolstoy, in his memoirs, explained his brother's sudden change in behavior as rooted in the influence of a very seductive and immoral man; but he did not specify either the individual or the nature of the relationship.

Even in his debauchery, though, Dmitri still clung to the high road. Opposing his entire family, including Leo, the future author of *Resurrection,* he resolved to keep Masha, the prostitute who had initiated him into the pleasures of the flesh. The couple roamed Russia until Dmitri's sickness forced them to stay in Oryol.

Tolstoy hardly saw Dmitri between the time the writer left Kazan in 1847 and his brother's death in 1856. In fact, as Dmitri lay dying, Tolstoy confessed that he could not rouse any emotions for his brother, other than horror at his brother's final agony and disgust at the smells of the sickroom and his awkwardness with the good and kind women—his sister Maria, Aunt Tatyana, and Dmitri's Masha—who attended the patient.

Later, Tolstoy recalled: "Dmitri's enormous wrist was as if soldered to the bones of his forearm. His face was devoured by eyes that were as beautiful and serious as ever, but now with an expression that was inquisitorial. He coughed and spat constantly. He did not want to die; he did not want to believe he was about to die."

Tolstoy did not remain for his brother's passing. He also did not attend Dmitri's funeral, a breach of conduct that tormented him in later years. He wrote in his diary: "I was particularly loathsome at that time. I had just come from Saint Petersburg . . . and was bursting with conceit. I pitied Dmitri, but not very much. . . . His death troubled me primarily because it prevented me from taking part in a party at the court . . . to which I had been invited."

Elements of Dmitri's character can be found in the portraits of Prince Neklyudov in *Childhood* and Nikolai Levin in *Anna Karenina.* Masha also appears as Levin's faithful, pockmarked Maria Nikolaevna. See Simmons, *Leo Tolstoy,* 1:112, 141–42; Leon, *Tolstoy,* 67–68; Dole, *The Life of Count Tolstoi,* 29; Troyat, *Tolstoy,* 42–43, 106, 134–36.

15. According to medieval (and often historically inaccurate) annals, Indris came to Russia from the West in 1353, together with his two sons and three thousand retainers. He was well received by the ruler of Chernigov in the Ukraine, where he adopted the Russian Orthodox faith. His great-grandson settled in Moscow and was honored by Grand Duke Basil the Blind, who bestowed upon him the surname Tolstoy.

Leo Tolstoy seems to have been of the opinion that his family was of German origin and that his name was a translation of the German family name Dick, or "fat" (compare *tolstyi* in Russian). More likely, though, Indris, for whom Tolstoy represented the twentieth generation, was of Lithuanian descent. See Simmons, *Leo Tolstoy,* 1:3.

16. The history of Tolstoy's family occupies a prominent, if colorful, page in the development of imperial Russia. For instance, Tolstoy's great-

great-great-grandfather, Pyotr Andreevich Tolstoy, was a cowardly, cruel, and treacherous individual who was well versed in the politics of court intrigue. For instance, he had supported Peter's half-sister, Sophia, in her struggle with her brother for the throne, but he quickly deserted the woman when Peter emerged triumphant in the contest.

In 1701 Pyotr Tolstoy was chosen by Tsar Peter to be the first Russian ambassador to Constantinople and in 1714 as his minister of state. (At several points during his stay in Turkey, Pyotr spent time in the dungeon of the Seven Towers, an experience that is commemorated in the family coat of arms.) Pyotr also won special favor from the tsar because of his growing reputation for learning. He accompanied Peter abroad in 1716 and tricked Peter's mutinous son, Alexei, into returning to Russia from Italy in 1717. In fact, Tolstoy's great-great-grandfather not only was a member of the tribunal that tried, tortured, and executed Alexei but was alleged even to have helped suffocate the condemned man with pillows in his prison cell. For his loyalty to the throne, Pyotr was again rewarded with estates and promoted to head of the secret chancellery. (Leo, who once considering writing a novel on Peter the Great, was revolted by the murder of Alexei.)

It should be noted here that for all of Pyotr Tolstoy's service to the state, Peter the Great did not entirely trust his charge. For instance, whenever the tsar had too much to drink, he would often pat Tolstoy's head and say: "Head, head, if you were not so quick, I should have ordered you cut off long ago."

Indeed, Pyotr Tolstoy was too clever for his own good. Having been implicated in Alexei's death, as well as in a plot to have Elizabeth, not Alexei's son, succeed to the throne, the reigning monarch, Catherine I, who had bestowed on Pyotr the title of *graf,* or "count," now deprived him of his rank, orders, and estates. She also sentenced the hapless man to the Solovetsky Monastery, a prison on the White Sea to which Pyotr Tolstoy himself had condemned victims of Peter the Great's wrath. He died there in 1729 at the age of eighty-four.

The family fortunes were repaired by Pyotr Tolstoy's grandson, Andrei Ivanovich Tolstoy. Having served in both the army and the government, Andrei regained his title of "count" as well as several of the estates that had been confiscated from his grandfather. Andrei sired twenty-three children in twenty-five years, his household earning the nickname "the great nest." See Simmons, *Leo Tolstoy,* 1:5.

17. Like many Russian families in the restricted circle of the nobility, both the paternal and material branches of Tolstoy's family were related by intermarriage to nearly every homeland family of consequence in the nineteenth century. In literature alone, Tolstoy could claim kinship with such writers as Alexander Pushkin, Pyotr Chaadaev, Alexei Konstaninovich Tolstoy, Alexander Odoevsky, and Fyodor Tyutchev. See ibid., 1:10.

18. The Ryurikovichians (Ryurikovichi) were members of the dynasty of Russian princes and Muscovite tsars who ruled Russia from the ninth century to 1598. They were the descendants of Prince Igor, who, legend has it, was the son of Ryurik, the founder of the dynasty.

19. Throughout the course of the early Russian state, the Volkonskys served as generals, administrators, and courtiers. They were also the social and political equals of the Romanovs at the time when Michael Romanov was chosen to begin a new dynasty in 1613.

The Volkonskys claimed several colorful pages in their family history. For instance, Fyodor Ivanovich Volkonsky died a hero at the Battle of Kulikovo; Sergei Fyorodovich Volkonsky was a general in the Seven Years' War. A family member played a leading role in the murder of Catherine the Great's son, the mad Emperor Paul; another, the Decembrist conspirator Prince Sergei Grigorievich Volkonsky, was exiled to Siberia for thirty years, accompanied by his wife, who later became the heroine of a famous epic poem by Nikolai Nekrasov, entitled "Russian Women" ("Russkie zhenshchiny," 1871–72).

Tolstoy's maternal grandfather, Count Nikolai Sergeevich Volkonsky, had been commander-in-chief of the Russian armed forces and an ambassador to Berlin also under the Catherine the Great, but he lost his position when he refused to marry Varvara Engelhardt, the niece and mistress of Catherine's paramour, Potyomkin. "What made him think that I should marry his whore?" Nikolai asked in indignation.

After the death of his young wife, Maria Trubetskaya, Nikolai served as governor of Arkhangelsk, before he retired in 1800 to one of his estates at Yasnaya Polyana, vowing never to leave it again. A true son of the Enlightenment, Nikolai conducted himself as a model landlord, treating his serfs with stern but kindly paternalism. For instance, he protected his charges from provincial authorities, advised them on cultivating the land, and saw that they were decently housed, fed, and clothed. Unlike his famous grandson, though, Nikolai believed both in the education of women and the superiority of European culture over Russian. His sole companion was his daughter (and later Leo's mother), Maria Nikolaevna, whom he raised and educated more along masculine lines than conventional feminine ones. Prince Volkonsky was also the model for Prince Bolkonsky in *War and Peace*. See Crankshaw, *Tolstoy*, 16–17; Wilson, *Tolstoy*, 11; Troyat, *Tolstoy*, 4.

20. More accurately, a certain Prince Ivan, a thirteenth-generation descendant of Ryurik, received the fiefdom of Volkonsky, situated on the Volkonka River in the Kaluga province in the early fourteenth century. It was from Ivan that the Volkonsky family is said to have descended. Also, in a picture of Tolstoy's family tree, Michael of Chernigov is seen as holding the trunk See Biryukov, *Leo Tolstoy*, 5; Troyat, *Tolstoy*, 4.

21. Bunin was quite solicitous of such folk types. For instance, in his *Cursed Days*, he wrote: "A giant soldier looms over others. . . . He is a full

head taller than anyone else, in a magnificent gray overcoat drawn in tightly with a handsome belt at the waist, and wearing a gray round hat like Alexander III used to wear. Everything about him is massive. He is a genuine thoroughbred with a full triangular beard and a Bible in his gloved hand. He is so unlike anyone else, the last of the Mohicans." See Bunin, *Okaiannye dni,* 77.

22. In his metaphysics, Leibniz popularized the notion of monads to espouse pluralism in the world as well as to challenge both the dualism of Descartes ("thought and extension") and monism of Spinoza ("the single substance that is God").

Essentially, Leibniz saw monads (from the Greek *monus,* or "unit") as infinitesimal, psychophysical entities which made up and reflected the order of the universe, and which formed the basis for the physical properties of the world. Every monad, Leibniz believed, was unique, indestructible, dynamic, self-sufficient, and soul-like. It also lacked a spatial dimension but existed with other monads in a preestablished harmony created by God. As Leibniz saw it, therefore, objects of the material world did not exist per se, but merely appeared as collections of monads.

23. Goethe saw "entelechy" as the nonmaterial beginning of life which supposedly directs the development of organisms.

24. In fact, Tolstoy's family and friends thought that he was at death's door. The writer, though, later gave thanks for his malady. "My illness was of great help to me," Tolstoy wrote to Biryukov. "When I placed myself sincerely and face-to-face with God, with the All of which I am but a transient particle, much of that which was foolish left me. I also saw a great deal of evil in myself, something I did not observe previously. I also felt much relieved afterward. Generally speaking, one should say to one's beloved: 'I do not wish you health, but illness.'"

Later, he continued: "One must suffer a severe illness in order to convince himself of what life consists, that is, the weaker the body, the stronger one's chance for spiritual development." See Leon, *Tolstoy,* 304; Biryukov, *Leo Tolstoy,* 139; Simmons, *Leo Tolstoy,* 2:317.

25. Visitors frequently marveled at the aging Tolstoy's energy and verve. For instance, circa 1890, one guest at Yasnaya Polyana noted how the writer "could dance a waltz with as much lightness and agility . . . as those of his former days. . . . Quite unconsciously, he sometimes shook twenty years off his shoulders." Six years later, Tolstoy could still outperform his son Mikhail in difficult gymnastic exercises; at age seventy-four, Tolstoy was challenging his guests to do knee bends. See Leon, *Tolstoy,* 234; Shklovsky, *Lev Tolstoy,* 678; Simmons, *Leo Tolstoy,* 2:220.

26. The speed and thoroughness with which the forty-year-old Tolstoy mastered Greek shows both his intellectual toughness and his formidable powers of concentration. For instance, he wrote to Fet that, after several

months of study, he could read Herodotus and Xenophon at sight and Homer with a dictionary. (Fet had so doubted Tolstoy's success with Greek that he offered his own skin as parchment for a diploma if the writer attained proficiency in the language. To such a challenge, Tolstoy replied: "Then your skin is in danger.") In fact, Tolstoy's rapid knowledge of Greek became so far-reaching that, in his view, Russian translators of Homer from German renderings had spoiled both the form and content of the poet's writing. As he saw it, such translations were like "boiled, distilled water." Tolstoy even taught Greek to his fourteen-year-old son, Sergei, the two translating Xenophon's *Anabais*.

Indeed, Tolstoy's enthusiasm for Greek knew no bounds. "How glad I am that God has sent this folly upon me!" Tolstoy continued to Fet. "In the first place, I enjoy it, and second . . . without a knowledge of Greek, there is no education."

More interestingly, perhaps, critics posit that Tolstoy's sudden interest in Greek sprang from his desire to write in a simpler and more compact manner. They also assert that his full-scale immersion in the language not only influenced the language and form of *Anna Karenina* but also his attitude toward fate and human tragedy. "Knowing Greek," he told Fet, "I now believe that I will write no more gossipy twaddle of the *War and Peace* type." Sofya added: "Lev wants to write something pure and elegant, from which not one word could be removed, something like the works of ancient Greek literature or art."

In truth, though, Tolstoy learned Greek partially because he needed a respite from writing, and eventually he lost his zeal for the language. For instance, after resuming his study of Greek during his 1862 visit to the Bashkirs in Samara, he quicky tired of the subject and even allowed his nephew to press leaves between the pages of his huge Greek lexicon.

Sofya saw her husband's study of Greek as both impairing his health and distracting him from his writing, so she implored him to abandon his study of language. For instance, she complained that Tolstoy muttered Greek in his sleep; in a letter to him, she wrote: "If you keep slaving away at your Greek, you will never get well. That is the cause of your anxiety and indifference to life here and now. Not for nothing is Greek a dead language; it puts the mind in a coma." See Simmons, *Leo Tolstoy*, 1:329–33; Crankshaw, *Tolstoy*, 237, 239; Dole, *The Life of Count Tolstoi*, 223; Wilson, *Tolstoy*, 353; Shklovsky, *Lev Tolstoy*, 406; Troyat, *Tolstoy*, 327–29.

27. Tolstoy first read Homer between the years 1860 and 1862, initially seeing the writer as a worthless phrasemaker. Later on, though, he confessed: "The *Iliad* has forced me to revise my whole concept of the story." See Simmons, *Leo Tolstoy*, 1:255; Crankshaw, *Tolstoy*, 132; Troyat, *Tolstoy*, 183.

CHAPTER FOURTEEN

1. Bunin is quoting from Sergei Aksakov's "Istoriia moego znakom-stva s Gogolem" ("The History of My Acquaintance with Gogol"), published in 1890.

2. The writer in question is Gleb Uspensky.

3. Jules Verne published *Twenty Thousand Leagues under the Sea* in 1870. Interestingly, Tolstoy delighted in doing sketches of Verne's novels. See Leon, *Tolstoy,* 164.

4. Tolstoy, of course, was also not above attempting to fly physically. For instance, as a young boy in Moscow, he convinced himself that he could accomplish such a feat if he sat down on his heels, clasped his arms firmly around his knees, and jumped off into space. Testing his theory, he hurled himself from a third-floor window, falling some eighteen feet below. Mercifully uninjured (he suffered only a slight concussion), Tolstoy regained consciousness only after eighteen hours of unbroken sleep.

Later, Tolstoy confessed that he had jumped out the window more to "impress others" than to attempt to fly. "I remember," he wrote, "that I was continually preoccupied with myself. Rightly or wrongly, I was always conscious of what people thought of me . . . and [such consciousness] always spoiled my pleasure."

Tolstoy, though, did not give up his ideas on "wings" in life. For instance, he wrote in 1879:

> There exist heavy people without wings who manifest themselves here below. Among them are powerful men—Napoleon. They sow discord on earth and leave terrible traces among humankind.
>
> There also exist light men who grow wings for themselves and who slowly learn to fly—monks. Additionally, there exists a third group of men with strong wings, but whose carnal desires drag them down among the crowd, where they break the wings they have. Of such am I. I flap my broken wings, hurl myself powerfully into the air, and fall again. But my wings will be healed. I shall fly high. May God help me.
>
> Finally, there are men with heavenly wings who, for the love of humankind, descend upon earth by folding their wings and teach men to fly. Then, when they have done their work, they ascend once more. Christ.

See Simmons, *Leo Tolstoy,* 2:43, 373; Crankshaw, *Tolstoy,* 44; Leon, *Tolstoy,* 12; Troyat, *Tolstoy,* 31.

5. Metaphysical issues greatly entranced the young Tolstoy. He recalled: "I used to love the moment when ideas, flowing faster and faster and growing more and more abstract, finally became so nebulous that I could no longer find any words to express them, or that I was saying something quite different from what I meant. I loved the instant when, after rising higher and higher into the realms of thought, I suddenly sensed the immensity

beyond and recognized the impossibility of going any further." See Troyat, *Tolstoy,* 46.

6. Tolstoy was similarly fascinated by how the sun illumined patterns of frost on the windows. See Shklovsky, *Lev Tolstoy,* 488.

7. Bunin is quoting from Tolstoy's *Adolescence.* In real life, though, Tolstoy was about twelve years old when he adopted this "reasoned" stance toward reality as well as derived a theory of incarnation from what he understood to be the laws of symmetry in life. Although Tolstoy never forfeited his egoism, he soon relinquished his demands for teleological geometry in life.

For one thing, he felt unworthy of the mob that he felt destined to teach. He wrote in *Childhood:* "My vanity was immensely flattered by my [early] philosophical discoveries. I often imagined myself as a great man discovering new truths for the benefit of humankind, and I contemplated other mortals with a proud awareness of my own worth. But the strange thing was that the moment that I encountered these same mortals, I lost all my confidence before the lowliest of them; and the higher I held myself in my own esteem, the less capable I was, not only of imposing my own sense of worth upon them, but even of teaching myself not to blush for my simplest remark or most ordinary action."

Also, life itself brought home to Tolstoy the fallacy of his early ideas. Shortly after his return from Europe in 1856, he wrote in his diary: "My youth is past! I mention this as something good. I am calm and want nothing. I even write calmly. It is only now that I understand that . . . it is not the life surrounding one which must be arranged symmetrically, but that one must break oneself up and become pliable so as to adapt oneself to life."

Tolstoy's disaffection with philosophical abstraction proved to be his salvation. For instance, as a young man on a fishing trip, Tolstoy had gotten so carried away by his rational quandaries that he absentmindedly bypassed a load of bread and stuffed a handful of worms into his mouth. See Crankshaw, *Tolstoy,* 48–49; Leon, *Tolstoy,* 13, 85.

8. Bunin is quoting from an 1881 letter from Sofya to her husband. The entire text of the missive reads: "I am very sad. I see that you have remained at Yasnaya Polyana not for mental work, which I value above all in the world, but to play Robinson Crusoe. . . . From morning to night, you do senseless physical work which, even in peasant households, only young folks do. . . . Such mental faculties are being wasted in cutting wood, lighting samovars, and making boots!"

Sofya did not voice her anger over her husband's nonliterary pursuits to her husband alone. For instance, to a Tolstoyan disciple she wrote: "I will tell you quite frankly, [my husband] is not at all what you imagine him to be . . . or even what he himself tries to be. What if he does stitch boots and split wood? He was and still is a count, and all this simplicity . . . is only affectation, simply a pretense, a kind of amusement. [My husband] has always loved originality. Even in his youth, he played various tricks to shock people and make them speak about him."

Tolstoy was hardly deterred by his wife's distress. For instance, for the readers of *What Then Should We Do?* he prescribed a full round of physical and mental activity. For instance, in the hours before breakfast, individuals should plow, build, dig wells, tend cattle and the like; in the time before the midday meal, they should employ their fingers and wrists in making clothes, boots, utensils, and other articles of craftsmanship. Further, between noon and the evening repast, people should use the intellect and the imagination to work at science and art; and in the evening, they should take up social intercourse.

Tolstoy was particularly proud of his boot-making. "My boots cost only two rubles, whereas at a store they would cost seven!" he would exclaim proudly. Understandably, people vied to acquire Tolstoy's domestic wear. For instance, one friend proudly stood a pair of Tolstoy's boots next to the first twelve volumes of the writer's works, labeling them as "Volume XIII." Tolstoy's prowess as a boot-maker, though, cost him his close friendship with Fet. Fet, wanting to showcase a pair of boots that Tolstoy had fashioned for him, asked the writer to sign a paper certifying that he had indeed made them. Tolstoy did so, but with a sadness that eventually ended their ties. See Shklovsky, *Lev Tolstoy,* 551; Dole, *The Life of Count Tolstoi,* 310; Nazaroff, *Tolstoy,* 249–50; Troyat, *Tolstoy,* 440; Simmons, *Leo Tolstoy,* 2:95.

9. Bunin is paraphrasing from an 1881 letter of Sofya to Tolstoy. The missive reads in full: "I am more and more convinced that if a happy man suddenly sees only the evil side of life and closes his eyes to the good, he must be ill. You must get well. I say such a thing with no ulterior motive. It seems to me to be true. I grieve much for you, and if you will reflect without taking umbrage at my words, perhaps you will find some remedy for your state. You began to suffer long ago. You used to say: 'I want to hang myself because I cannot believe.' But why are you so miserable now that you have faith? Did you not know earlier that there are ill, unhappy, and wicked people in the world? But there are also good, joyful, charitable, and happy ones. May God help you! But what can I do?" See Leon, *Tolstoy,* 223.

10. In 1873, Tolstoy reopened his school at Yasnaya Polyana, returning to his interest in pedagogy with even greater zeal than previously. He wrote: "As was the case fourteen years ago. I am filled with love for these thousands of children with whom I am dealing. . . . When I enter a school and see . . . dirty, tattered, thin lads with light eyes and—how often!—angelic faces, I am seized with fear and anxiety. I feel as though I am beholding drowning people. Lord, how to save them, and whom to save first! And what is drowning is the most valuable—that spiritual element which children express so strongly."

Appearing before a group of Muscovite pedagogues, Tolstoy insisted that his sole aim was to teach children to read, write, and cipher only that which they needed for life. His methods, he continued, he had learned from the peasants themselves, not from theory-ridden pedants. Again, though, his ideas fell on deaf and hostile ears, particularly Sofya's.

At one point, Tolstoy seriously considered founding a secondary school for peasant children who wished to continue their education without changing their way of life. Specifically, he wished for a *lapty,* or "bark-shoe," university in which every farmhand would learn higher mathematics and foreign languages.

Again as earlier, though, Tolstoy's interest in education was short-lived. By 1878, he had lost all interest in pedagogy, since he believed that formal learning only increased social inequality and injustice; that is, educated individuals surpassed and subjugated uneducated ones. Tolstoy also ceased to be involved with the education of his children and became quite displeased when Sofya continued to employ governesses and tutors and to send their children to school. When his oldest son, Sergei, graduated from the University of Petersburg and asked his father about choice of career, Tolstoy advised him to seek the work of a peasant.

Tolstoy tried teaching for a final time in his twilight years, in 1908. This time, though, he was interested solely in the religious and moral education of his students. He derived deep satisfaction from such activity, but it continued to irk Sofya. "Lev drills some Christian truths into youngsters' heads. The children repeat them by heart, and he feels assured that something will remain in their heads. . . . But it will not make any difference, for when they grow up, they will still be thieves and drunkards." See Simmons, *Leo Tolstoy,* 1:347–50; Dole, *The Life of Count Tolstoi,* 237–39, 318; Nazaroff, *Tolstoy,* 203; Troyat, *Tolstoy,* 332–33.

11. Tolstoy's study of Hebrew in 1882 was as rapid and successful as his venture into Greek. Rabbis and others were amazed to see how quickly Tolstoy caught not only the spirit of the language but also the textual meanings that had escaped their attention.

Of course, the ever practical Sofya had as little use for her husband's interest in Hebrew as she did for his enthusiasm for Greek and all the other nonliterary activities of Tolstoy's life. "A useless imbecility" she remarked. See Leon, *Tolstoy,* 222; Dole, *The Life of Count Tolstoi,* 296.

12. Bashkiria is in the southern Urals about 600 miles directly west of Moscow.

13. In early 1871, Tolstoy suffered a physical and spiritual breakdown. The deadening "lull" after the prolonged "storm" of *War and Peace* left him without an all-absorbing task and induced a host of ills: fever, insomnia, rheumatic pain, nervous exhaustion, and depression. "Never have I experienced such misery," Tolstoy wrote to a friend. "I do not wish to live."

To Fet, he complained of failing powers, expectations of death, and an absence of spiritual peace. As he had done in 1862, Tolstoy headed to Samara and the Bashkirs for a cure. See Simmons, *Leo Tolstoy,* 1:330–31.

14. Tolstoy's enduring interest in education led him, in 1872, to read through a series of American elementary readers and to publish what came to be a nine-volume *Novaya azbuka,* or *Primer,* which was published both in Russian and in Old Church Slavonic. Tolstoy's *Primer* embraced a complete curriculum for beginning students, including sections on arithmetic and the natural sciences as well as units on reading and writing with drawings, exercises, and various typographical exercises to aid in spelling and pronunciation. The work included adaptations of Chinese and Persian tales, translations of Aesop's *Fables,* sample pages from Plutarch, and episodes based on Hugo's *Les Miserables.* (Leaving nothing to chance, Tolstoy included a detailed manual of instruction for teachers.)

His method of selecting appropriate materials was characteristically Tolstoyan: Fascination with knowledge superseded any and all facts connected with it. Tolstoy eschewed knowledge that he believed was useless, erudite, and beyond the comprehension of his students. In his view, a pupil who thought that the world stood in water had a healthier awareness of reality than one who believed that the earth spun on its axis but who could not explain the process.

For his *Primer,* Tolstoy strained life through his own filter. "From the natural sciences," he wrote to Strakhov, "I chose . . . only that which was clear and beautiful; and when things seemed to me insufficiently clear and beautiful, I tried to express them in my own way." Literature also did not escape Tolstoy's scrutiny. For instance, for his *Primer,* he wrote a number of moralistic stories, later regarding such pieces as "A Prisoner in the Caucasus" ("Kavkazskii plennik") and "God Sees the Truth, but Waits" ("Bog vidit pravdu no ne skazhet") as being among his best works. He also simplified and clarified both the content and form of Russian, Oriental, and Western folktales, legends, saints' lives, and historical narratives. (Some of the stories in Tolstoy's *Primer* so fulfilled the needs of beginning readers that they were used in primary schools throughout the former Soviet Union.)

Having worked on his *Primer* for almost three years, Tolstoy was so satisfied with his project that he wrote to "Granny" Alexandra to say that he had "the right to die in peace." In truth, though, Tolstoy had little hopes for its success. He wrote to Strakhov:

> I do not expect much money for the book. I am certain that, despite its merit, my *Primer* will earn but little. The first edition will sell out immediately. But schoolmasters will begin to criticize the book's peculiarities; everything will be stolen by the anthologies; and it will not sell. *Habent sua fata libelli;* and authors sense this fate. . . .

When I published *War and Peace,* I was aware of its many faults, but I was certain of the success that it eventually attained. On the other hand, in my *Primer,* I see but few faults, and I am quite certain that it is better than every other book of its kind. I do not expect any success from it, though, particularly the kind of success that a schoolbook should have.

Tolstoy's misgivings were correct. The *Primer* was a failure, selling only four hundred copies in the first few months of its publication. Pedagogues advised "our great novelist" to write *only* novels. Some attacked the *Primer* viciously, seeing it as challenge to conventional methods of learning, which stressed reason, logic, and science over faith, instinct, and imagination. Others berated the work for its lack of style, false simplicity, and moralizing pretentiousness. The censure of the work was as scrupulous as it was silly. For instance, in 1891, Sofya complained: "The Academic Council has not passed the *Primer* because it contains such words as 'lice,' 'fleas,' 'devil,' and 'bedbug.'" In fact, if a cousin of Tolstoy's had not been the minister of education, anxious government officials would have suppressed the *Primer* altogether.

Colleagues and friends also objected to Tolstoy's *Primer.* For instance, Turgenev had little use for the work, complaining to Fet that "A Prisoner in the Caucasus" was the only worthwhile item in the publication. He also objected to what he considered as the absurdly high price of two rubles for four paper-covered books. (Because the *Primer* sold so poorly, the price for the work was quickly and greatly reduced.)

If Tolstoy gave up on the "reality" of his *Primer,* he clung to the "idea" of it. For instance, he wrote: "The future artist will understand that to compose a fairy tale, a song, a joke, a maxim, which can teach or amuse a child, is infinitely more important than to compose novels, symphonies, and dramas, which, after having amused a few people of the rich class, will be forgotten by all."

In time, families and tutors took an interest in Tolstoy's *Primer.* New printings followed in rapid succession, and by the end of his life Tolstoy was pleased to learn that nearly a million copies of his much-maligned book had been sold. See Simmons, *Leo Tolstoy,* 1:336–38; Leon, *Tolstoy,* 164; Dole, *The Life of Count Tolstoi,* 229–30; Wilson, *Tolstoy,* 254; Shklovsky, *Lev Tolstoy,* 399; Nazaroff, *Tolstoy,* 203–4, 267; Troyat, *Tolstoy,* 331–32.

15. Sofya, among others, was appalled at Tolstoy's renewed interest in pedagogy. In 1873, Sofya wrote to her sister, Tanya: "He has completely forgotten [*Anna Karenina*]; and [such forgetfulness] vexes me." She continued to her brother: "I look with perplexity on all [of Leo's efforts with education]. And I regret the efforts that he expends on such occupations, instead of composing a novel. I do not understand how such activities are useful, since they are restricted to such a tiny corner of Russia."

Several weeks later, Sofya added to Tanya: "It is not the money I regret. The chief thing is that I love [my husband's] literary work. I appreciate it and it affects me. This primer, this arithmetic, this grammar—I despise it all, and I cannot even pretend to be interested in it. Now there is something lacking in my life, something that I loved . . . [It is] Leo's work . . . an activity which has always given me so much pleasure and inspired me with so much respect. You see, Tanya, I am a true writer's wife; so greatly do I take his work to heart."

Needless to say, Sofya was ecstatic whenever Tolstoy turned his back on educational and publicistic writing to focus on works of art. "What a joyous feeling suddenly seized me," she wrote to her husband, "when I learned that you want to write again in a *poetic* vein. In that is salvation and happiness; in that which gives you solace and brightens our life, we will again be united. This is the real kind of work for which you were created, for outside of this sphere there is no peace in your soul." See Simmons, *Leo Tolstoy,* 1:347, 351; 2:56–57, 398. Also see Leon, *Tolstoy,* 165.

16. Tolstoy's excerpt continues:

The girl looked like my thirteen-year-old Masha. She was wearing nothing but a torn, dirty dress. Her voice was drunken, hoarse. She refused to go and was trying to light a cigarette. "Get up, you slut, or I'll break your neck!" the policeman shouted. I looked into her face—snub-nosed, gray, old, savage. I asked her how old she was; she answered, "Fifteen." Then they led her away. . . .

They led her away. I did not take her with me; I did not make her sit at my dinner table; I did not bid her stay and live with my family; I did not fall in love with her. . . . I went home to lie down in a clean, comfortable bed and to read books. . . . In the morning, I decided to go to the police station; but when I arrived, she was no longer there. . . .

I am praying. Lord, teach me how I must live so that my entire life should not be abominable to me.

In truth, though, Tolstoy should not have been surprised by a fifteen-year-old prostitute. As a census-taker three years earlier, in the winter of 1882, he had sought to penetrate the worst slums of Moscow, his hope being somehow to alleviate the suffering of the urban poor. Of one lodging, he wrote:

All the places were full, all the bunks occupied . . . often by two people . . . a horrible spectacle in which men and women mingled together. Women who were not dead drunk slept with men. Many women with children were sleeping with strange men in narrow bunks. Terrible was the sight of the destitution, filth, raggedness, and fear of these people. And especially horrible was the immense number of individuals in this condition—first one tenement, then another, then a third, a tenth, a twentieth, without end. Everywhere was the same stench, the same overcrowding, the same mingling of the sexes, the same spectacle of men and women drunk to stupefaction; [everywhere was] the same fear, submissiveness, and culpability on all faces.

Appalled by what he had found, Tolstoy publicly beseeched Moscow society for assistance; but his request went unheeded. (The three thousand or so rubles that people promised him never materialized.)

Yet, Tolstoy had himself to blame for his failure, since, in his appeal to citizens, he not only castigated money as the root of all evil but also judged potential donors as doing more harm than good. The goals of Tolstoy's appeal were also impractical. In his view, Moscow should not harbor a single soul who needed clothing or food or who could be bought and sold for money. He also insisted that unfortunates needed individual time and care, and that they needed to improve their lives by changing internally, not externally.

In response to the failure of his appeal, Tolstoy wrote *What Then Should We Do?* indicting both himself and his class for their cruel indifference to the down-and-out. He wrote:

> At the sight of the hunger, cold, and degradation of thousands of people, I understood, not with my mind or heart, but with my entire being, that despite everything that learned people . . . say about the necessity of poverty, and also despite the fact that I and thousands of others stuff ourselves with beefsteaks and sturgeon . . . the existence of such individuals is a crime that is committed not once but constantly; and that I, with my luxury, not only tolerate it, but also share in it.

> I sit on a man's back, choking him and forcing him to carry me. But, at the same time, I assure myself and others that I feel very sorry for him and wish to ease his lot by every possible means except by getting off his back.

See Leon, *Tolstoy,* 206, 208; Nazaroff, *Tolstoy,* 251; Simmons, *Leo Tolstoy,* 2:35, 68.

17. Tolstoy began this letter to Fet: "Lately I have been satisfied with my personal affairs, but . . . the impending misery of famine torments me more and more every day. . . . All the peasants murmur and scold . . . against us, who, under our shady lime trees and in our muslin dresses, can have creamy butter on a painted dish."

For all of Tolstoy's anger at public indifference to the poor, though, he had little use for what he saw as the pandering and the superficial attempts of many individuals to help those in need. For instance, that Turgenev's (illegitimate) daughter once mended the torn clothes of a serf girl was for him "a false and theatrical farce." Tolstoy's comment almost led to a duel between the two writers; but he was later vindicated when Turgenev gave the girl a fortune, married her off to a French aristocrat, and watched in horror as the two squandered the money.

Tolstoy similarly took on Jane Addams of Hull House, who visited Yasnaya Polyana in 1898. Touching the loose sleeve of Addams's silk gown, Tolstoy remarked that there was enough material in it to make a frock for a little girl. He also asked Addams if such a dress posed a barrier between herself and the people and advised that she should don clothes like those of the unfortunates she served. Addams laughingly replied that she would find it difficult to wear the various apparel of the thirty-six different nationalities that resided at Hull House. Undeterred, Tolstoy retorted: "Well, that is all the more reason why you should choose some cheap and simple dress that any of these people might adopt and by your costume not cut yourself off from those you wish to serve."

Addams was deeply moved by Tolstoy's remark, as well as by what she perceived as the gentleness and Christian spirit of the writer. When Addams returned to Hull House, she resolved to follow Tolstoy's advice by working in the bakery there for several hours each day; but she soon abandoned such an activity, realizing that her energies could be put to better use elsewhere.

Tolstoy's concern for the poor was often not with without self-interest. For instance, during his first trip to Switzerland, Tolstoy came across a ragged and deformed Tyrolean singer-wanderer who, despite a spirited performance, evoked only rebuke and scorn from his listeners. Outraged, Tolstoy forced the unfortunate man back to his hotel for a bottle of champagne. The gathering was a disaster. The Tyrolean was mortified; the guests were wrathful; and the waiters were variously insolent, amused, and annoyed. Tolstoy, though, was content, having—in his own mind at least—demonstrated to the world his moral superiority and nobility of soul.

Tolstoy also used this incident with the waiter to sing a hymn to both God and the "little man." He wrote in "Lucerne":

> Who has weighed the internal happiness which lives in the souls of each of these men? There he sits now, somewhere on a dirty threshold, gazing on the bright, moonlit sky and joyfully singing to the quiet, fragrant night. There is no reproach, no anger or regret in his soul. And who knows what is passing in the hearts of those people behind these rich and lofty walls? Who knows whether they possess as careless and serene a joy of life and harmony with the world as lie in the heart of this little man?
>
> Unlimited are the mercy and wisdom of the Almighty who permitted and ordered the existence of these contradictions. Only to thee, worthless worm, impudently, lawlessly trying to penetrate the Deity's laws, the Divine's intentions, only to thee do they appear as contradictions. God looks down from His bright, immeasurable heights with tenderness; and, he enjoys the endless harmony in which you all in your contradictions are eternally moving. In your pride, you thought to evade the universal law. Nay, you, little man, with your petty, vulgar contempt for the waiters, you also respond to the harmonious necessity of the eternal and the endless.

See Simmons, *Leo Tolstoy,* 1:323; Crankshaw, *Tolstoy,* 162; Leon, *Tolstoy,* 83–84, 97; Biryukov, *Leo Tolstoy,* 45–46; Dole, *The Life of Count Tolstoi,* 361; Shklovsky, *Lev Tolstoy,* 295.

18. Bunin is wrong here. His citation from Merezhkovsky appeared in an article entitled "The Day-Worker of Christ" ("Podenshchik Khristov"), published in the newspaper *Resurrection* (*Vosrozhdenie*) in Paris on November 20, 1935. The article begins: "To talk about the Christianity of Lev Tolstoy in today's 'Christian Europe' is like talking about the rope in the home of a hanged man."

19. The Roman philosopher Plotinus used the metaphysics of Plato, particularly his dialectic of love, to fashion a mystical religion in which union with the One was achieved through contemplation and ecstatic vision.

20. Lev Shestov was a idealist philosopher and a representative of Russian existentialism. His insistence on the primacy of discovery over reason echoed Bunin's own beliefs.

21. Both the Gorchakov and Trubetskoy families were particularly influential in nineteenth-century Russia. For instance, Mikhail Dmitrievich Gorchakov was a military officer and statesman who played a major role in the Crimean War (1853–56). Alexander Mikhailovich Gorchakov was Russia's foreign minister for the quarter century that followed that conflict. Sergei Petrovich Trubetskoy was a prominent Decembrist. Sergei Nikolaevich Trubetskoy was a religious philosopher, editor, and publicist. Sergei's brother, Evgeny Nikolaevich, was also a philosopher and a follower of Vladimir Solovyov; and Sergei's son, Nikolai Sergeevich, was a distinguished linguist.

22. The young Buddha's palace was located in Kapilavastu, the capital of the Shakya Kingom, thought to have been located somewhere in the Tarai region of Nepal.

CHAPTER FIFTEEN

1. It was the French writer Romain Rolland who saw Tolstoy as the "conscience of the world." See Nazaroff, *Tolstoy*, 285.

2. Bunin is citing John 18:36.

3. Telegraphs did not excite Tolstoy because he believed that they served only the educated classes. It was only with difficulty that Tolstoy came to see the value of labor-saving devices. For instance, his first encounter with a typewriter was a disaster. After typing his first letter, he told his daughter Alexandra: "Oh, I am so tired. I do not see how people can use such a thing! Perhaps, it is suitable for well-balanced Americans, but for us Russians, it is no good." With time, though, Tolstoy appreciated the invention.

Tolstoy was more amenable to Edison's dictaphone, however. To his great satisfaction, he used the machine to record selections from *The Kingdom of God Is within You*. (He was equally delighted to learn that Edison had been a thirty-year vegetarian.)

Tolstoy was even more delighted with emerging cinema and film. "Just imagine," he told a friend, "one could reach masses of people, all the people of the earth! . . . One could write four, five, ten, fifteen films!" See Shklovsky, *Lev Tolstoy,* 284; Troyat, *Tolstoy,* 636; Simmons, *Leo Tolstoy,* 2:410–11.

4. Regarding his hatred of machines, Tolstoy was so horrified that nearly every month a worker was killed on the railway at Ryazhsk that he consigned all technology to the devil. He also believed that since railways and telegraphs were little used by the folk, they brought no advantage to people in general.

Throughout his life, Tolstoy asked, "What for?" For instance, on August 16, 1857, at age twenty-nine, he wrote in his diary: "Everything seems useless. The ideal is unattainable, and I have already ruined myself. Work, a small reputation, money. What for? Means of enjoyment. Again, what for? Soon an eternal night." Later, as his family grew older, he continued: "Beginning to think of how I would educate my children, I asked myself: 'What for?'"

Years later, he similarly wrote of shoppers in Moscow: "Why are they bustling about? Where are they hurrying to? Always business, but they do not see the principal thing. As a result, all their life passes before them, and they do not notice that death approaches." Goldenweiser added: "Tolstoy was amazed at the tall houses, the trolleys, and the traffic. He was frightened by the immense human anthill. Every step brought fresh confirmation of his long-standing hatred of so-called civilization." See Simmons, *Leo Tolstoy,* 1:183–84; 2:28. Also see Dole, *The Life of Count Tolstoi,* 213, 283; Nazaroff, *Tolstoy,* 219; Troyat, *Tolstoy,* 628.

5. Vasily Maklakov delivered his lecture "Tolstoy as a World Phenomenon" ("Tolstoi kak mirovoe iavlenie") in Prague on November 15, 1928, and published it in the journal *Contemporary Notes* (*Sovremennye zapiski*) in 1929 (vol. 38, 224–45).

6. That is, the hundredth anniversary of Tolstoy's birth.

7. Tolstoy wrote "For Shame" ("Stydno") in 1895.

8. Henry George was an American economist who, in his *Progress and Poverty* (1879) and *Social Problems* (1883), advocated both the nationalization of land and a single tax based on unearned income. Having read George's work, Tolstoy wrote in his diary: "Once again, I have become keenly conscious of the sin of possessing land. George has laid a durable foundation for the building of a future economic structure. . . . Humanity will always remember [him] with gratefulness and esteem." In fact, Tolstoy so valued George's ideas that he wrote an introduction to a Russian edition of *Social Problems.*

Tolstoy believed that if George's ideas were brought to Russia, the land would fall into the hands of those who worked it. Tolstoy also worked George's theories into his fiction. For instance, in *Resurrection,* Nekhlyudov seeks to cure social evil in part by allowing peasants access to his land according to the economist's principles.

It is also of interest to note that when Tolstoy and daughter Tanya tried to implement George's single tax on one of their estates, the experiment was a failure. Peasants ceased to pay any money for the land and even began speculating with their holdings. Tolstoy, though, still believed in the efficacy of George's theories. In fact, when he stopped at a train station during his flight from Yasnaya Polyana, he engaged a crowd on George's ideas. See Leon, *Tolstoy*, 289, 352; Dole, *The Life of Count Tolstoi*, 348; Simmons, *Leo Tolstoy*, 2:200–2, 392.

9. Tolstoy wrote *Christian Teaching* (*Khristrianskoe uchenie*) between 1894 and 1896. The work was published in 1898, first in England, then in Russia.

10. Although Tolstoy was always in a state of crisis, he experienced a particularly severe struggle with questions of God and life in the late 1870s and early 1880s.

11. Not unexpectedly, Tolstoy did not see socialism as a cure for human ills. In 1898, he wrote: "Socialists will never destroy property and the injustice of unequal capabilities. The strongest and more intelligent will always make use of the weaker and more stupid." He also had little use for Western constitutional democracy. For instance, he wrote: "The subjects of a constitutional state . . . are like prisoners who are free because they have been allowed to choose their warden." In 1906, he wrote to his daughter Masha:

> To my great regret, I observe that we are continually borrowing bits of [things from Europe]: political parties, electoral campaigns, blocs, etc. Abysmal! . . . The only possible result of all these constitutions is to allow a different set of people to exploit the majority. The faces will change, as they do in England, France, America, and everywhere else. And men, in their eagerness to make greater and greater profits from each other, will come more and more to abandon the soil, which is the only basis for a rational and honest existence. . . . Materially, the European way of life is very clean, but morally, very dirty. . . .
>
> Everything that the Western people do can and ought to be an example for the peoples of the East, not as an example of what should be done, but of what ought not to be done under any circumstances. To pursue the path of the Western nations [o democracy] means to pursue a direct path of destruction. . . .
>
> If the Russian people are truly uncivilized and barbarian, then we have a future. Westerners are civilized barbarians; so they have nothing more to live for. It would be as aberrant for Russians to imitate Westerners as for a stalwart, hardworking, healthy young man to envy a rich Parisian who is bald before thirty and who sits in his townhouse, moaning, "Ah, how tedious it all is!" Such an individual should be pitied, not envied.
>
> One wants a constitution, another wants a monarchy, and the revolutionaries want socialism. . . . Well, I can tell you that the lives of men in general will not improve until every man strives to live well himself and not interfere in the lives of others.

See Simmons, *Leo Tolstoy*, 2:253, 389; Troyat, *Tolstoy*, 591–93.

12. Tolstoy wrote "[An Appeal] to the Government, Revolutionaries, and the People" ("Obraschenie k pravitel'stvu, revoliiutsioneram i narodu") in 1907.

13. Tolstoy is paraphrasing the ideas of Count Eugene Falkenberg, the hero in Berthold Auerbach's first major novel, *A New Life*. See Simmons, *Leo Tolstoy*, 1:216.

14. Tolstoy did not accept orthodox notions of Christ. For instance, he wrote in 1878: "[People say] that Christ offered us salvation. But who is this Christ: a God or a man? He is what he says he is. He says that he is the Son of God; he says that he is the Son of Man. He says: 'I am what I tell you I am. I am the truth and the life.' . . . But from the moment that [the church] began to mix it all up together and say that he was God and the second person of the Trinity, the result was sacrilege, falsehood, and nonsense. If he were that, he would have been capable of saying so." See Troyat, *Tolstoy*, 395.

15. In March 1855, Tolstoy wrote in his diary: "Yesterday, a conversation about divinity and faith suggested to me a great and tremendous idea, the realization of which I feel capable of dedicating my entire life—the founding of a new religion corresponding to the development of humankind. [This idea] is the religion of Christ, but purged of mystery and faith, a practical religion, not promising future bliss, but realizing bliss on earth. . . . *Consciously* to contribute to the union of religion and humankind is the basic idea which I hope will dominate me."

Such religious pragmatism remained with Tolstoy throughout his life. Indeed, his vision of Christ and Christianity owed more to such individuals as Rousseau, Thomas Jefferson, and Benjamin Franklin and to such groups as the American Quakers and the French rationalists than it did to Russian Orthodox spirituality. For instance, in the aftermath of the Crimean War, Tolstoy believed that what people needed was not "the Red Cross, but the simple cross of Christ to destroy falsehood and deception." Several years later, he continued, saying that "Christ did not impose but revealed a moral law that will always remain as a standard of good and evil." After the 1860 death of his brother Nikolai, Tolstoy asserted that wished to write a "materialist" Gospel, a life of Christ as a "materialist."

Tolstoy, though, understood that the Christian ideal was an unrealizable goal in life. He wrote: "Man's striving after Christ's ideal is like one holding a lantern on a long stick before him." Also, the one portrait of Christ that had Tolstoy's unqualified approval was Nikolai Ge's 1890 controversial painting *What Is Truth?* (*Chto est' istina?*), which depicted Christ before Pontius Pilate. See Simmons, *Leo Tolstoy*, 1:186, 208; 2:140. Also see Crankshaw, *Tolstoy*, 112; Dole, *The Life of Count Tolstoi*, 92; Wilson, *Tolstoy*, 7; Nazaroff, *Tolstoy*, 279.

16. It would be fair to say that although Tolstoy did not deny the existence of God, he wrestled with the precise nature of the Deity.

Simply put, Tolstoy was more comfortable with the "idea" of God than the "reality" of a Divine Being. That is, he saw the Almighty as a law, a force, and an entity that sprang from "man's recognition of his own failings" and that served as a purpose, a direction, a goal, and a focus of faith. For Tolstoy, God was also a goal and an endpoint which humankind should know, love, and serve so as to transcend death and to give meaning to life. He wrote in 1852: "The man whose purpose is his own happiness is bad; he whose purpose is the opinion of others is weak; he whose purpose is the happiness of others is virtuous, he whose purpose is God is great."

About God, Tolstoy continued in 1877: "At the thought of God, happy waves of life welled up inside of me. Everything became alive and took on meaning. The moment I thought I knew God, I lived. But the moment I forgot him, the moment I stopped believing, I also stopped living. . . . In fact, would I not have killed myself long ago if I did not have a dim hope of finding Him? And I live, truly live, when I feel Him and seek Him. 'What else do I need then?' an inner voice exclaimed in me. 'There is He. He is that without which one cannot live. To know God and to live is the same thing. God is life. Live, seek God, for there will be no life without God.'"

Even more emphatically in *War and Peace,* Tolstoy wrote of Pierre's quest for God: "Pierre [attained] not faith in any kind of rule, or words, or ideas, but faith in an ever-living, ever-manifest God. Formerly he had sought the Almighty in aims that he had set for himself. But that search for aims had been simply a search for God. Suddenly in his captivity [by the French] Pierre had learned that . . . God was greater and more infinite and unfathomable than the Architect of the Universe that the Freemasons had acknowledged. He felt like a man who, after straining his eyes into the far distance, finds what he sought at his very feet."

Not surprisingly, though, Tolstoy had a clearer idea on the nature of devils. For instance, in his most devastating assault on institutional Christianity—a 1903 piece entitled "The Restoration of Hell" ("Vosstanovlenie ada")—devils are beings who created the church as well as art, culture, education, medicine, social, science, and drunkenness. See Simmons, *Leo Tolstoy,* 1:104–5; Leon, *Tolstoy,* 33, 142; Wilson, *Tolstoy,* 469; Nazaroff, *Tolstoy,* 223; Troyat, *Tolstoy,* 378.

17. Maklakov is citing from Luke 2:13–31.

18. Tolstoy's problems with the Russian church of his day were longstanding. For instance, in a 1861 meeting with the French socialist and anarchist philosopher Pierre-Joseph Proudhon, he said: "You are very much read in Russia, but the people there do not understand the importance that you attach to your Catholicism. Only after I had visited England and France did I understand how right you were, since, in Russia, the church amounts to zero!"

In truth, Tolstoy took issue with the institutional church almost from its early days. For instance, he wrote in the fall of 1879: "From the third century until today, the church has been nothing but lies, cruelty, and deceit."

Tolstoy saw the institutional church (and its Russian Orthodox variant) not only as an insult to his reason but, more seriously, as a monstrous obstacle to human moral progress. In his view, the church promoted a corrupt and hypocritical Christianity which, together with the state, blasphemed against the Holy Spirit and thwarted the kingdom of God on earth. For instance, in his 1902 *Appeal to the Clergy* (*Obrashchenie k dukhovenstvu*), Tolstoy protested that "the Christianity preached by you is an inoculation of false Christianity, resembling the inoculation for smallpox or diphtheria, and making the inoculated immune to the true faith. [Because of you], people have built centuries-old lives on principles irreconcilable with true Christianity, but they feel fully persuaded that they are living Christian lives, and thus are unable to return to true Christianity."

As a key criticism of institutionalized Christianity, Tolstoy objected to the fact that the so-called Universal Church was split into various factions who condemned each other as heretics. Moreover, he was dismayed that the Russian variant prayed for the success of armed might against enemies at home and abroad. For instance during the Russo-Turkish War of 1877–78, Tolstoy wrote: "Went to Mass on Sunday. I can find a satisfactory explanation for everything that happens during the service. But wishing 'long life' to the tsar and praying for victory over our enemies are a sacrilege. A Christian should pray for his enemies, not against them." (Even more galling to Tolstoy were military manuals which coupled texts from the Gospels with cold-blooded instructions on how to kill opponents.)

Tolstoy also cared little for theologians: "Go to your father, the Devil," he told them. "You have taken the keys of the Kingdom of Heaven and since you will not enter it yourselves, you are closing it to others."

In truth, the Russian Orthodox Church that Tolstoy censured had much to be sanctioned for. True, it harbored monks who were intelligent, simple, and sincere and who lived arduous and deeply religious lives according to the principles of the early church fathers. The Russian Orthodox Church, though, was also a decadent and corrupt institution that sought to shore up its waning temporal and spiritual authority by espousing the unholy alliance of "miracle, mystery, and authority" that Dostoevsky had so condemned in *The Brothers Karamazov*. For instance, church officials wielded their power to support autocracy and the throne, not to challenge persecution and injustice. Even worse, perhaps, they encouraged the most flagrant superstition among believers. For instance, catacombs in Kievan monasteries featured lifelike torsos that monks had stuffed with straw but proclaimed as the "incorruptible" bodies of saints. Icons were periodically taken about in carriages, allegedly to cure the sick, but, more practically, to raise money for the church. Not for nothing, therefore, did the outraged Tolstoy demand that monks stop begging for crusts and kopecks and earn their own keep.

Tolstoy himself was privy to clerical abuse. For instance, on a visit to Optina Hermitage, he encountered a woman who had wished to buy a copy of the Gospels for her son but who had been persuaded by a monk to buy more suitable reading, that is, a book dealing with the history of the monastery and the miracles of the saints. In response, Tolstoy bought an edition of the Gospels and gave it to the woman, with the advice that both she and her son read the work.

The story does not end there, though. The monk hastened to inform the archimandrite that a man "dressed like a pauper" was spending money like water in the monastery bookstore. Another monk was sent to investigate and, himself being from Yasnaya Polyana, immediately recognized Tolstoy. The writer was immediately given the best room in the place.

If Tolstoy hated the "reality" of the church, he loudly vaunted the "ideal" of it. He wrote:

> The church that sought to detach people from error and to weld them together again by the solemn affirmation that it alone was the truth has long since fallen into decay. But the church composed of individuals united not by promises or sacraments, but by deeds of truth and love, has always lived and will live forever. Now, as eighteen hundred years ago, this church is made up not of those who say "Lord, Lord" and bring forth iniquity, but of those who hear the words of truth and reveal them in their lives.
>
> The members of this church . . . practice the commandments of Jesus and thereby teach them to others. Whether this church be in numbers great or small, it is, nevertheless, the church that will never perish and that will finally unite the hearts of all humankind within its bonds.

See Simmons, *Leo Tolstoy,* 1:213; 2:310. Also see Leon, *Tolstoy,* 188, 196, 308; Dole, *The Life of Count Tolstoi,* 262, 279–80; Wilson, *Tolstoy,* 339; Shklovsky, *Lev Tolstoy,* 507–8; Troyat, *Tolstoy,* 391.

19. Maklakov is citing Luke 10:27.

CHAPTER SIXTEEN

1. Bunin is citing from Shestov's article "Overcoming Self-Evident Things" ("Preodolenie samoochevidnostei"), published in 1921 in the journal *Contemporary Notes* (*Sovremennye zapiski*), nos. 8–10.

2. Dostoevsky wrote *Notes from the Underground* (*Zapiski iz podpol'ia*) in 1864.

3. Tolstoy was not the only one who thought he was insane. For instance, Sofya wrote circa 1870: "Sometimes Lev thinks that he is losing his mind; and his fear of insanity is often so intense that I am terrified when he tells me about it afterward." Turgenev reacted to Tolstoy's spiritual crisis of

the late 1870s by telling Dmitri Grigorovich that the writer was deranged and had even gone mad. Dostoevsky, too, had written to his wife: "As for Leo Tolstoy, Katkov also confirmed that he has gone mad. [A friend] urged me to visit him at Yasnaya Polyana . . . but, although it would be interesting, I will not go." See Leon, *Tolstoy,* 192; Troyat, *Tolstoy,* 327.

4. Penza is both a region and a city about 300 miles southwest of Moscow.

5. Arzamas is a city located about 200 miles south of Moscow.

6. Tolstoy wrote his "Notes of a Madman" ("Zapiski sumasshed-shego") in 1884–86.

7. Tolstoy wrote that in Arzamas he was given a small room, "a freshly whitewashed little square chamber." He continued: "I remember how distressed I was that this room should have been a square. There was also a window with a curtain, a red one." (The floors and woodwork were also dark red.) See Shklovsky, *Lev Tolstoy,* 394; Troyat, *Tolstoy,* 318.

8. Needless to say, after the ominous revelations of Arzamas, Tolstoy did not buy the property. See Troyat, *Tolstoy,* 320.

9. The "Book of Wisdom of Jesus, Son of Sirach," also known as "Ecclesiasticus," was written circa A.D. 190. Resounding themes from both Ecclesiastes and the Book of Proverbs, it is one of the foremost representatives of wisdom literature of the Apocrypha.

10. Specifically, Ecclesiastes 1:12–13.

11. Aldanov's *Zagadka Tolstogo* (*The Riddle of Tolstoy*) was published in Berlin in 1923.

12. Chekhov visited Tolstoy at Panina's estate at Gaspra in September 1901. The meeting was apparently a successful one, although Chekhov was distressed by what he saw as the precipitous decline in Tolstoy's health. He wrote to Gorky: "Before leaving Yalta, I went to see Lev Nikolaevich. He likes the Crimea very much; it excites a purely childish joy in him. His health worries me, though. He has aged very noticeably, and the worst thing is that his illness—senility, that's what it really is—has taken hold of him completely." See Shklovsky, *Lev Tolstoy,* 669.

13. About the seriously ill Tolstoy, Chekhov wrote to a friend:

I am afraid of Tolstoy's death. If he were to die, there would be a huge vacuum in my life. First, because I have never loved anyone as much as I love him, and because, although I am not a believing man, I consider his faith to be the nearest and most akin to me. Second, because while Tolstoy is in literature, it is easy and pleasant to be a writer. Even to be aware that one has done nothing and is doing nothing is not so terrible because Tolstoy does enough for all. His work serves as a justification for all the hopes and anticipations that are arise from literature.

Third, Tolstoy stands firmly and his authority is immense. So long as he lives, bad taste in literature, banalities of every kind, be they impudent or lachrymose, and all the bristling, exasperated vanities will remain far away and deep in the shade. Tolstoy's moral authority alone is capable of maintaining the so-called literary moods and currents at a certain height. Without him, writers would be a flock without a shepherd, or give way to a hotchpotch in which it would be difficult to make out anything.

See Leon, *Tolstoy,* 301–2.

14. In this and subsequent citations from Chekhov, Bunin is quoting from his own recollections of the writer. See I. Bunin. "Chekhov," in *Sobranie sochinenii,* 5:265–81.

15. In his memoirs, Bunin reported that Chekhov so feared Tolstoy that he once changed his dress repeatedly before he called upon the writer. He wrote:

Chekhov spent almost an hour trying to decide which pants to wear to visit Tolstoy. He . . . kept coming out of his bedroom first with one, then with another pair.

"No, these are indecently narrow!" he said. "Tolstoy will think I'm a hack!"

Then he went to put an another pair and came out laughing. "These are as wide as the Black Sea! Tolstoy will think I'm a smart aleck."

Tolstoy was particularly fond of Chekhov. For instance, Gorky recalled: "Tolstoy loved Chekhov; and every time he turned his eyes on the young writer, he seemed to caress his face with a truly tender look. Once when Anton Pavlovich was walking in the garden with Alexandra L'vovna, Tolstoy . . . said under his breath: 'What a good man Chekhov is, so modest and quiet like a well-bred girl. He really walks like a well-bred girl, too, A charming, really charming man.'"

Tolstoy particularly admired Chekhov's literary style. "His language is extraordinary,"

Tolstoy told a friend. "I am utterly captivated by it. . . . With no false modesty, I maintain that, technically, Chekhov is far superior to me."

Parenthetically, Bunin discounted Tolstoy's remark as to the maidenlike features of Chekhov's personality and walk. Also, it was Chekhov who encouraged Bunin to record his encounters with Tolstoy. "Mark my word, with Tolstoy's death, everything will go to the devil," Chekhov told Bunin. "You know Tolstoy better than I. So be sure your write down your impressions [of him]. Just think how we envy those who saw Pushkin in person." See Kaun, "Bunin's Memories of Tolstoy," 272. Also see I. Bunin, "O Chekhove," *Opyty,* no. 6 (1956): 25, and "Chekhov," 5:274; Shklovsky, *Lev Tolstoy,* 672; Troyat, *Tolstoy,* 569.

16. Tolstoy thought that Chekhov was a better writer than Maupassant. See Troyat, *Tolstoy,* 71.

17. Tolstoy was quite harsh with Chekhov's plays. "Tolstoy does not like my dramas," Chekhov told a friend. "He swears that I am not a play-

wright. . . . He told me: 'You know, I cannot abide Shakespeare, but your plays are even worse. Shakespeare, however, grabs the reader by the scruff of the neck and leads him to a definite objective. But where are you going with your heroines? From the divan where they lie to the closet and back. . . . No, your plays are altogether vile.'"

Another time, Tolstoy remarked to a friend: "Chekhov has a heart of gold but an atheist's head. . . . He has so much talent, but in the name if what does he write? It is not so much that he has no overall view of the world but that he has a wrong one: base, materialistic, and self-satisfied. . . . Chekhov would write better if he were not a doctor." See Simmons, *Leo Tolstoy,* 2:289–90; Troyat, *Tolstoy,* 569, 571.

18. Tolstoy wrote "How Much Land Does a Person Need?" ("Mnogo li cheloveku zemli nuzhno?") in 1886.

19. Ivan Tatishchev first published his *French and Russian Lexicon* (*Leksikon rossisskoi i frantsuzskoi*) in two volumes in 1762.

20. Beethoven wrote *Pathetique* in 1798 and published it a year later.

21. Bunin is quoting Romans 7:15.

22. In truth, Tolstoy so hated pig farming that he actually starved the animals to death. "I weakened my pigs by giving them as little food as possible," he recalled. "My strategy worked! If they were still squeaking the next time I saw them, I gave them even less to eat. Whenever they became quiet, I knew their end had come." See Wilson, *Tolstoy,* 219.

23. In August 1871, Tolstoy purchased 6,750 acres in Samara for 20,000 rubles. See Simmons, *Leo Tolstoy,* 1:336, 2:20.

CHAPTER SEVENTEEN

1. In truth, Leo was only eighteen months old when his mother died. See Biryukov, *Leo Tolstoy,* 8.

2. A *venchik* is a paper or silk band that is placed on the forehead of a dead person to symbolize the "crown of righteousness" noted by Saint Paul in Timothy 4:8.

3. Tolstoy wrote "Three Deaths" ("Tri smerti") in 1859. Unfortunately, the piece only fortified the growing feeling among critics that together with such literary "failures" as "Lucerne" and "Albert," Tolstoy was losing his literary gifts.

4. Bunin is citing Isaiah 55:9.

5. Tolstoy is paraphrasing Psalms 104:29–31.

6. Tolstoy was profoundly affected by Nikolai's death, if only because, as some said, Nikolai practiced the humility that Leo preached. As he wrote to friends, Tolstoy loved and admired Nikolai more than anyone in the world. It had been Nikolai who had held the secret to happiness with the

"green stick" and the "Ant Brotherhood." Tolstoy's regard for his brother only increased with age. For instance, having joined Nikolai in the Caucasus in 1852, he wrote to his other brother, Seryozha: "Nikolenka is on excellent footing here. All the commanders and fellow-officers like and respect him; and, he enjoys the reputation of being a brave officer. I love him more than ever. When we are together, I am completely happy, and without him, I feel dull."

Tolstoy even included Nikolai in his vision of "family happiness." "Nikolai will often be with us," Tolstoy wrote of his fantasy to Aunt Tatyana. "[I see him as] an elderly bachelor, bald, retired from the army, still as fine and noble as ever. I picture to myself how he will tell stories to my children . . . how they will kiss his hands (they deserve to be covered with kisses), how he will play with them, how my wife will cook his favorite dishes for him, and how we will all talk over our memories together."

Although Nikolai had his faults—he was often lazy, slovenly, and too fond of drink—he was for Tolstoy an ideal: modest and kind, sensitive and charming, poised and self-assured, good-natured and intelligent. He practiced "neither egotism nor self-renunciation but a strict mean between the two." He "never sacrificed himself for anyone else and always avoided not only injuring others but also interfering with them."

Others concurred. For instance, Turgenev wrote: "The attitude that Leo Tolstoy cultivated in theory was actually applied by his brother Nikolai. Nikolai always lived in some impossible slum in a remote part of town and was ready to share whatever he had with the poor."

Nikolai was also a very well-read and artistic individual who, like his mother, possessed an inexhaustible imagination and a gift for storytelling. For hours on end, he could tell humorous tales and Radcliffe-style ghost stories with such earnestness and verve that his listeners often forgot that his tales were fiction. In fact, memoirists assert that Nikolai also could have become a great writer, but he did not have his brother's discipline, energy, and desire for fame. In his final days, though, Nikolai lost his lust for life. "Nikolai is terribly clever and clear-headed," Tolstoy wrote in his diary, "but he has no energy for living."

Needless to say, Nikolai's passing only intensified Tolstoy's questions about life, death, and immortality. The letter that Bunin is citing is from Tolstoy to Fet, and reads in full:

> On September 20, Nikolai passed away, literally in my arms. Never in my life has anything made such an impression on me. Nikolai spoke the truth when he said that there is nothing worse than death. And when one clearly realizes that death is the end, there is nothing worse than life either. Why should one worry or strive if nothing remains of what was Nikolai Nikolaevich Tolstoy?

My brother did not say that he felt the coming of death, but I know that he watched every step of its approach and that he knew with certainty how much of [his] life remained. Some moments before his death he dozed off, but suddenly he awoke and whispered with horror: "What is that?" That was when he saw "it"—the absorption of himself into nothingness. And if Nikolai found nothing to cling to [at the time of his passing], what will I find then? Still less.

But it is most unlikely than I or anyone else will be like Nikolai and struggle with his end up until the last minute. A couple of days before his passing, I said to him, "We will have to put a chamber pot in our room." But he replied: "No, I am weak but not as weak as that. We will struggle on a bit longer." Up to the last minute, also, Nikolai did not give into death. He did everything himself; he continually tried to occupy himself; he wrote, asked me about my writing, and gave me advice. But I felt that he was no longer doing all these things from any inner desire, but on principle.

One thing remained for Nikolai to the end: nature. The night before he died he went into his bedroom . . . and fell exhausted on the bed by the open window. I entered; and, with tears in his eyes, he said: "How I have enjoyed the entire last hour." From the earth one comes, to the earth one will return. The one thing that remains is the vague hope that there, in nature, of which one will become a part in the earth, something will remain and be discovered. All who knew Nikolai and attended to him during his last moments said: "How calmly and peacefully he died." But I know the terrible pain he endured, for not one feeling of my brother escaped me. . . .

Of what use is anything when the agonies of death, with all the abomination of falsehood and self-deception, . . . will end in nothing, in absolute oblivion? An amusing situation indeed! A thousand times, I have told myself: "Let the dead bury the dead." Somehow one must use whatever strength one has. . . . People say to each other: "Be useful, virtuous, and happy while you are alive"; but happiness and virtue and usefulness consist only in this truth which I have learned after thirty-two years of life, that is, the position that we are placed in life is terrible. "Take life as it is," these same people continue, "for it is you who have put yourself in this position." Quite right. I do take life at it is. As soon as someone reaches the highest degree of development, he sees clearly that everything is nonsense and deceit, and that the truth—which he still loves better than all else—is terrible to behold.

And when one looks long and hard at death and sees it clearly for what it is, he awakes with a start and, as did my brother, cries out in terror and says: "What is that?"

Tolstoy conveyed his grief over his brother's passing to members of his family. Indeed, his missives to them expressed a variety of conflicting emotions: happiness that Nikolai was at peace, doubt in the existence of the afterlife, and sorrow at the futility of existence. For instance, he wrote to his brother Sergei: "Nikolai was a genuine man to both of us, one whom we loved and respected more than anyone else on earth. The day after his death, I went over to him, fearing to uncover his face. . . . You cannot imagine how beautiful his face was, with the best and most merry expression on it." To "Granny" Alexandra, Tolstoy continued: "Nikolai was my best friend; and [with his death] half of my life has been destroyed, and all my energy has been buried with him. Why live if he is dead? . . . You are able to deal with death. Your dead live in a world beyond; you believe that you will see them again. But as I see it, such a view is too beautiful, no one can believe in it sincerely, and my dead have disappeared like burning smoke."

A month after Nikolai's passing, Tolstoy was still grieving both for his brother and for himself. "Nikolai's death has severed me terribly from life," he wrote. "Again the same questions: Why? Whither? . . . I try to write, to force myself, but I do not succeed. I cannot give to my work the importance—the energy and patience—that it needs. . . . Nikolenka's death is the most powerful impression that I have ever known."

Tolstoy's distress over Nikolai's passing also affected Bunin. For instance, Bakhrakh reports: "I will never be able to forget these words—'the absorption of the self into nothing.' I think about them all the time. What could be more terrible?"

Also, Bunin continued to Bakhrakh that when he wrote *Liberation*, he wanted to devote several more pages to Nikolai but lacked sufficient materials to do so. See Simmons, *Leo Tolstoy*, 1:207–8; Crankshaw, *Tolstoy*, 176; Leon, *Tolstoy*, 37, 93–95; Biryukov, *Leo Tolstoy*, 13–14; Wilson, *Tolstoy*, 155–56; Troyat, *Tolstoy*, 88, 197; Bakhrakh, *Bunin v khalate*, 53, 54.

7. Tolstoy began writing "Kholstomer" in 1863; but, dissatisfied with the work, he finished it only in 1886. The idea for the piece, though, had been with him for a long time. Once, on a walk, Tolstoy and Turgenev had stopped before an old broken-down horse, and Tolstoy delighted his companion with an imaginary account of the animal's thoughts and feelings.

In citing "Kholstomer," Bunin unwittingly bypassed yet additional evidence for Tolstoy's "regression." Turgenev, amazed at the insightfulness of his friend, commented that, most likely, Tolstoy had once been a horse. See Simmons, *Leo Tolstoy*, 1:294.

8. It is of interest to note that the writer Count Sollogub and others objected to Tolstoy's use of the word "gelding" in the story. "The word 'gelding' is unpleasant . . . like 'eunuch' or 'castrate.' It is a direct hint at sexual organs." See Shklovsky, *Lev Tolstoy*, 354.

9. The Platzen plateau, located west of the city of Austerlitz in the Czech Republic, was the focal point for the famous Battle of Austerlitz.

10. "What a splendid death."

11. Tolstoy had long seen Napoleon as his enemy. For instance, standing before Napoleon's tomb in Paris on his trip to Europe, he recorded: "The deification of this criminal is awful." See Leon, *Tolstoy*, 79.

349

CHAPTER EIGHTEEN

1. Mytishchy is a town located 14 miles north of Moscow.
2. *Bunin's note:* The italics are Tolstoy's.

CHAPTER NINETEEN

1. In a diary excerpt written on January 22, 1922, Bunin wrote: "Tolstoy said, 'I feel people physically.' But I feel *everything* physically . . . and all so sharply that, good God, it even hurts!" See Grin, *Ustami Buninykh,* 2:75.

2. At Masha's bedside, Tolstoy read the epistles of John. "There is no fear in love," he intoned. "Beloved, now are we the children of God, and it does not yet appear what we shall be. But we know that when He shall appear, we shall be like Him."

On her deathbed, Masha was calm, courageous, and resigned. (She had apparently contacted a fatal disease from one of the peasants whom she was attending.) Conscious to the end, she took her father's hand, laid it on her breast, and whispered, "I am dying." She then passed from this life.

Tolstoy immediately went into his study and wrote: "Masha is dead. Strange, I feel neither horror, nor fear, nor consciousness that something out of the ordinary has occurred. I do not even feel any pity or pain. . . . I watched Masha all the time when she was dying. Her death was so amazingly calm. For me she was in a state of revelation, one which preceded my own." See Wilson, *Tolstoy,* 488; Shklovsky, *Lev Tolstoy,* 709.

3. Although Tolstoy found the telegrams and letters of condolence regarding Masha's death to be "falsely sympathetic," he was greatly moved by the genuine response of the peasants to his daughter's passing. In fact, it took an extremely long time for Masha's coffin to be carried from the main house to the cemetery, since it had to stop at the door of every peasant's hut on the way there.

4. Regarding Masha's passing, Sofya wrote to her sister: "Of all the children, Masha loved him [Tolstoy] more than all; and in her, we lose that zealous supporter who was always ready to help and sympathize with everyone, and more so with things that concerned her father." See Simmons, *Leo Tolstoy,* 2:383.

Tolstoy had exhibited similar indifference to death some thirty years earlier, with the earthly departure of his sister-in-law's five-year-old daughter and a general favorite with the Tolstoy family. Only religion, he declared to the grieving mother, could comfort her. "Why does a child live and die?" he wrote. "This is a terrible problem. But for me, there is only one explanation: *It is better off.*" He then advised the child's mother to read and recite the 130th Psalm daily. See ibid., 1:347.

CHAPTER TWENTY

1. The Eternal One.

2. In *War and Peace,* an old Freemason tells Pierre: "The highest wisdom is not founded on reason alone, nor on those worldly sciences of physics, history, chemistry, and the like, into which intellectual knowledge is divided. The highest wisdom has but one science—the science of the whole, the science explaining the whole and one's place in it. To receive this science, it is necessary to purify and renew one's inner self . . . and to have the light called conscience that God has implanted in our souls."

Tolstoy carried his quarrel with science into his personal life. For instance, he told his doctors: "I have always spoken ill of medical people, but now that I have come to know you better, I see that I have done you a great injustice. You are really good and know all that your science teaches. The only pity, though, is that your science knows nothing."

Later, he told Mechnikov: "I highly value true science, that which interests itself in humankind, in its happiness and fate. But I am the enemy of that false science which imagines that it has done something unusually important and useful when it has determined the weight of Saturn's satellites or something of this sort. True science is entirely in harmony with true religion."

The only valid science, Tolstoy wrote in his article "On Science" ("O Nauke"), is "the knowledge of what every individual must do in order that he may live out as well as possible . . . the brief span of life which God or the laws of nature have allotted to him in this world." See Simmons, *Leo Tolstoy,* 2:434–35. Also see Leon, *Tolstoy,* 140; Dole, *The Life of Count Tolstoi,* 383.

3. Tolstoy had little use for progress in general. For instance, he wrote: "Strange is the religion of our day, the religion of progress. Who said that progress was good? Progress is only an absence of faith and a need for conscious activity clothed as a creed."

At another time, he continued: "When the life of people is immoral and their relations are based on egoism, not love, then all technical improvements, the increase of man's power over nature, steam, electricity, the telegraph, every machine, gunpowder, and dynamite, produce the impression of dangerous toys placed in the hands of children." See Simmons, *Leo Tolstoy,* 2:343; Shklovsky, *Lev Tolstoy,* 269.

4. One of Tolstoy's best critical articles was his 1894 introduction to a translated collection of Maupassant's tales. Tolstoy believed that Maupassant was one of the best writers of the age, in part because of the writer's talent for portraying the difficulties between the sexes. See Simmons, *Leo Tolstoy,* 1:297.

5. Tolstoy often tempered his esteem of Maupassant by protesting what he saw as the "moral filth" of the writer's fiction. See ibid., 1:195.

6. "The eternal silence of endless spaces frightens me."

CHAPTER TWENTY-ONE

1. Bunin is citing from Tyutchev's poem "Silentium," written in 1833, the last line of which—"An uttered thought is a line"—was one of Bunin's favorite quotations.

2. Regarding prayer, Tolstoy wrote in 1851:

> It is impossible to convey the blissful feeling that I experience in prayer. . . . But if prayer is defined as a petition or thanksgiving, I was not praying. Rather, I was yearning for something lofty and good. What that something was, I cannot explain, although I clearly recognized what I desired. I wanted to become fused with the All-Embracing Being. And I besought [this Being] to pardon my sins. . . . I could not separate the feelings of faith, hope, and love from my general feeling. No, the feeling that I experienced last night was love for God, uniting in itself all that is good and renouncing all that is bad.

In fact, Tolstoy's conception of prayer was not unlike that of Buddhistic Nirvana. "This alone is the state of prayer," he wrote. "It is not imagination but a state of consciousness in which one clearly feels the passing from confusion and suffering to clarity and calm."

At times, Tolstoy's prayers were, like himself, simple and direct. For instance, circa 1853, he chose the Lord's Prayer as the most efficient way of addressing the Almighty. "All my supplications to God," he wrote, "are in words most dignified and worthy of the Almighty—'Thy will be done on earth as it is in heaven.'" Later on, Tolstoy reaffirmed his belief in the efficacy of unadorned prayer. "The language of God is different than mine," he wrote. "But the Deity will understand and translate in His own way when I say: 'Help me. Come to me. Do not abandon me.'"

At other times, though, Tolstoy lifted his voice to heaven with elaborate entreaties. "I pray Thee," Tolstoy addressed the Deity, "for good thoughts and actions, and grant me happiness and success in them. Help me to correct my faults, spare me from sickness, sufferings, quarrels, humiliations, and debts. Grant me to live and die in firm faith and hope in Thee, with love for others and from others, and to be of use to my neighbor. Grant me to do good and to shun evil; but whether good or evil befall me, may Thy holy will be mine. Grant me what is truly good. Lord have mercy . . . upon me."

Whatever his prayer life, however, Tolstoy had little use for liturgy, Masses, or communal prayer. For instance, in 1856, he wrote to "Granny" Alexandra: "[In church] one seems to be watching a Punch-and-Judy show:

numerous people kissing icons and one prostrate old woman braying for joy." Three years later, he wrote to her regarding Easter services: "Church-going, hearing unintelligible and incomprehensible prayers and watching the priest and that incongruous crowd around him—I find it all utterly impossible. That is why my Easter prayers have gone all wrong for the last two years."

Tolstoy's belief in the efficacy of prayer, though, failed to end, or at least to mitigate, his earthly cravings. No sooner did he express his wish to merge with God than he wrote: "But, no, the petty, vicious side [of my na-ture pulled me down again. Within an hour [of my praying] I again head the voices of vanity and vice. I feel asleep, dreaming of glory and women." See Simmons, *Leo Tolstoy,* 1:88, 192; Leon, *Tolstoy,* 55, 89, 293, 295; Dole, *The Life of Count Tolstoi,* 72–73, 88; Nazaroff, *Tolstoy,* 66; Troyat, *Tolstoy,* 137.

3. Goya painted *Nothing. The Event Will Tell* (*Nada. Ello dira*) be-tween 1812 and 1820. The original title was *Nothing. Those Were His Very Words.* The painting shows a putrefying corpse rising from a ditch and holding a sheet of paper on which the word *nada* is written. The right hand of the corpse is still clutching the pen.

For a reproduction of Goya's *Nothing,* see Oto Bihalji-Merin, *Goya Then and Now: Paintings, Portraits, and Frescoes* (New York: Harcourt Brace Jovanovich, 1981), 86.

4. Isaak Al'tshuller was Tolstoy's doctor in Yalta.

Index

Abreks, 94, 318n.10
Addams, Jane, Tolstoy's disagreement with, 335–36n.17
alcoholism in Russia, Tolstoy's view of, 49, 250–51n.35
Aldanov, Mark: letters of, 171n.106–7; Tolstoy's beliefs described by, 140–45; Tolstoy's wide range of knowledge described by, 120
Alexander III: ban on *Kreutzer Sonata* by, 65, 272–73n.23; denial of famine and starvation by, 186–87n.35; persecution of Dmitri Alexandrovich Khilkov's family by, 245n.18
Amfiteatrov, Alexander Valentinovich, criticism of Tolstoy by, 89
Ant Brothers, 9, 202n.69–70
Arsenieva, Valeriya Vladimirovna, Tolstoy's attraction to, 91, 313–16n.25, 318n.8
Astapovo: death of Tolstoy at railroad station on November 7, 1910 at, *xv, xxxiii–xxxiv*, 3, 23, 26, 53, 252n.3; final days of Tolstoy at railroad station at, 11, 18–22; visit of Sofya Andreevna with Tolstoy at, 33–34

Bakhrakh, Alexander Vasilievich, Bunin's dream about Tolstoy told to, 251n.40
Bazykina, Aksinya Alexandrovna, as mistress of Tolstoy bearing son, Timofei, 92–94, 316–17n.4–5, 317n.8
Bers-Kuzminskaya, Tatyana Andreevna (Tanya) (Sofya's sister): broken engagement to Tolstoy's brother Sergei of, 275n.26; as intermediary between Tolstoy and Sofya, 235n.9; jealousy of Sofya for, 318n.8; letters of Sofya to, 333–34n.15; marriage of, 276n.26;

memoirs of, 235n.8; as model for Natasha in *War and Peace,* 276n.26
Biryukov, Pavel: biography of Tolstoy by, 175n.2, 176n.3; relationship with Tolstoy of, 175–76n.2; as Tolstoyan, 215n.22
Brahma-Atman as essence of human spirit, 40
Brahmans for Tolstoy, 104–5
Buddha (Siddartha Gautama): appearance of, 38; caste of, 242n.39; consciousness of, 37–39; death of, 311n.21; denunciation of wrongs by, 108; first exposure of Tolstoy in 1884 to, *xxiv;* importance for Bunin of, *xxviii;* insight into Unity of Life of, 107; Mara's temptation of, 230n.30; marriage and fatherhood of, 39–40, 90; palace of, 337n.22; references in Tolstoy's writings to, *xxiv–xxvi,* 168n.77; search for salvation by, 39–40; search for truth and enlightenment by, 229–30n.27; son named Rahula (Chain) by, 242n.40; ten sins addressed by, *xxv;* understanding of Bunin and Tolstoy of meaning of, *xxiv*
Bulgakov, Valentin Fyodorovich: remembrances of Tolstoy of, 70, 92, 207n.80; as Tolstoy's secretary, 316n.1
Bul'ka (Tolstoy's dog), 62, 266–67n.9
Bunin, Alexei Nikolaevich (Bunin's father), marriage of, 320n.5
Bunin, Ivan: aborted meeting with Tolstoy of, *xiii,* 41; arguments about Tolstoy and Sofya between his wife and, 272n.22; as bookseller and librarian, 47–48, 248n.28; contrast between Tolstoy and, *xv–xvii;* correspondence with Tolstoy of *xiii–xv, xviii,* 47, 167n.72; criticisms of shortcomings in Tolstoy's writings, *xx–xxi,*

Index

diaries read by, 315n.25; Tolstoy's distractions from writing as annoying, 231n.4, 261n.26, 331n.10–11, 333–34n.15; view of Tolstoy's health and personality of, 98, 104–5, 243n.8, 329–30n.8, 330n.9, 343n.3; visit to Alexander III to remove ban on Kreutzer Sonata by, 65, 272–74n.23; writings of, 64, 269–70n.17

Tolstaya, Varvara L'vovna (Tolstoy's daughter), birth and death of, 185n.26

Tolstaya-Sukhotina, Tatyana L'vovna (Tanya) (Tolstoy's daughter): beliefs of, as mirroring Tolstoy's, 72, 218n.26; birth of, 184n.23; charm for Lopatina of, 64; entry into society of, 62–63, 267n.10–11; family estate given to, 305n.1; letter of Bunin to, 250n.33; letter to Tolstoy about Sofya from, 217n.26; life in France of, 228n.20; marriage of, 218–19n.26, 268n.15; meeting of Bunin and, 49; recollection of Tolstoy correcting her manners of, 249–50n.33; relationship with her mother of, 64, 270n.18–19; Tolstoy's closeness to, 218–19n.26; Tolstoy's final letter to, 19; in Tolstoy's will, 193n.43; village life of, 27

Tolstoy, Alexei L'vovich (Tolstoy's son), birth of, 185n.30

Tolstoy, Andrei Ivanovich (Tolstoy's ancestor), 324n.16

Tolstoy, Andrei L'vovich (Andryusha) (Tolstoy's son): birth of, 185n.26; disagreements between Tolstoy and, 221n.29; dissipated life of, 281n.3; request for Orthodox funeral for Tolstoy by, 253n.6; as siding with Sofya in struggle over Tolstoy's writings, 280n.3; as traveling with Sofya to Astapovo, 235n.10

Tolstoy, Dmitri (Miten'ka) (Tolstoy's brother): appearance of, 320n.6; death of, 6, 99, 184n.22, 319n.4, 323n.14; decadent lifestyle of, 100, 184n.22, 322–23n.14; personality of, 99, 322n.14; relationship with Lyubov' Sergeevna of, 99–100, 322n.12; relationship with prostitute Masha of, 100, 323n.14; religious life of, 322n.12, 322n.14; treatment of servant Vanyusha of, 99

Tolstoy Foundation, 228n.20

Tolstoy, Ilya Andreevich (Tolstoy's grandfather), wastefulness of, 87, 306n.8

Tolstoy, Ilya L'vovich (Tolstoy's son): birth of, 184n.23; Bunin's view of, 57–58; death in poverty of, 28, 228n.20; death of sister Masha described by, 137; disagreements between Tolstoy and, 221n.29; marriage of, 264n.30; Masha described by, 190n.42; relationship with Tolstoy of, 58, 263–64n.30; Sofya's displeasure with lifestyle of, 281n.3; view of his father's reaction to war of, 58, 264–65n.32

Tolstoy, Ivan L'vovich (Vanechka) (Tolstoy's son): birth of, 6, 186n.34; death of, 6, 65, 136, 188n.38, 251n.37, 274n.24; as parents' favorite, 274n.24; Sofya as mourning deeply for, 65

Tolstoy, Leo (Lev): appearance of, 38, 46, 61, 74–75, 77, 79–82, 88, 172–73n.121, 246n.22–23, 266n.6, 288n.5, 293n.25, 298–99n.41; arrogance about *comme il faut* of, 290n.10; births of children of, 6, 184n.23, 185n.26, 185n.30; changes with age of, 240n.30; childhood and education of, xv, 5, 36–38, 87, 119–20, 177–78n.10, 178n.11, 180n.17, 181–82n.18, 288n.4, 294–95n.30; consciousness of, 36–38, 106–9, 192n.43, 238n.21, 328–29n.4–5, 337n.1; contrast between Bunin and, xv–xvii; critics of, xxi, 85–86; death in 1910 at Astapovo of, xv, xxxiii–xxxiv, 3, 7, 23, 26, 29, 98, 252n.3; denial of Nobel Prize to, 166–67n.64; diary of, 7, 74–75, 104, 143, 169n.93, 191–92n.43, 197n.50, 199n.56, 199–200n.57, 204n.74, 212n.13, 215n.20, 219n.26, 231n.3, 266n.3, 288n.3, 293–94n.27, 294–95n.30, 306n.6, 315n.25, 329n.7, 338n.4, 340n.15; dichotomy of beliefs of, xvii, xxxi–xxxiii, xxxvi, 3–4, 38–39, 55–59, 70–79, 89–91, 119, 224n.4, 230n.34, 259–60n.24, 287–88n.15; distinctiveness of, 24–25, 225n.8; education of children of, interest in, 61, 64–65, 263n.3, 265n.2, 270–71n.21, 331n.20; escape from Yasnaya Polyana of, xi, xxxiii, 14–18, 52–53, 197n.52, 201n.62–202n.68, 223n.1; estrangement from and reported reconciliation with church of, 15–16, 22, 212n.13, 222n.37, 341–42n.18; excommunication by Russian Orthodox Church of, xi, 6, 68,